THE NEW

FOOD LOVER'S

TIPTIONARY

—Expanded, Revised and Updated

THE NEW

FOOD LOVER'S

TIPTIONARY

—Expanded, Revised and Updated

More Than 6,000 Food and Drink Tips,

Secrets, Shortcuts, and Other Things

Cookbooks Never Tell You

SHARON·TYLER·HERBST

WILLIAM MORROW

An Imprint of HarperCollins*Publishers*

THE NEW FOOD LOVER'S TIPTIONARY — EXPANDED, REVISED AND UPDATED. MORE THAN 6,000
FOOD AND DRINK TIPS, SECRETS, SHORTCUTS, AND OTHER THINGS COOKBOOKS NEVER TELL YOU.
Copyright © 2002 by Sharon Tyler Herbst. All rights reserved.
Printed in the United States of America. No part of this book may be used or
reproduced in any manner whatsoever without written permission except in the
case of brief quotations embodied in critical articles and reviews. For information,
address HarperCollins Publishers Inc., 10 East 53rd Street, New York, NY 10022.

HarperCollins books may be purchased for educational, business, or sales
promotional use. For information please write: Special Markets Department,
HarperCollins Publishers Inc., 10 East 53rd Street, New York, NY 10022.

FIRST EDITION

Designed by Leah Carlson-Stanisic

Printed on acid-free paper

Library of Congress Cataloging-in-Publication Data has been applied for.
ISBN: 0-06-093570-7

02   03   04   05   06   WBC/RRD   10 9 8 7 6 5 4 3 2 1

*Dedicated to Tia, my beautiful, talented sister,
who's not only a wonderful cook in her own right
but an inspiration to all who know her.*

CONTENTS

ACKNOWLEDGMENTS

Working on a book is always a group effort—there are myriad people who support such a project in countless ways big and small, personally and professionally. A warm and loving thanks to:

Close friends and family, who enthusiastically support me no matter what I do: Kay and Wayne Tyler (Mom and Dad), Tia and Jim McCurdy (my sister and her hubby), Tyler and Anderen Leslie, Jeanette "Sis" Kinney, Lee and Susan Janvrin, Beth Casey, Sue and Gene Bain, Leslie Bloom, Lisa Ekus, Daniel Maye, Phillip Cooke, Irena Chalmers and Walt and Carol Boice.

The William Morrow Cookbooks family: editorial director and good friend Harriet Bell, with whom I've done five books, each one pure pleasure; editorial assistants Tara Donne and Karen Ferries, who always had smiles in their voices and an answer for everything; copy editor Sonia Greenbaum, for her amazing talent and expertise and without whom I'd be lost; production editor Ann Cahn, the "shepherd" who molded this book into shape; Jayne Lathrop, for her amazing proofreading skills; cookbook art manager Leah Carlson-Stanisic, whose genius creates the book's "look"; publicity wizard Carrie Weinberg, who gets the word out; and the dozens of behind-the-scenes people who labor tirelessly and without fanfare to make William Morrow books the best they can be.

THE NEW

FOOD LOVER'S

TIPTIONARY

—Expanded, Revised and Updated

INTRODUCTION

All good cooks learn something new every day.
—Julia Child

The world of food and drink is endlessly intriguing in great part because it's in a constant state of evolution. Old "truths" are dispelled, innovative techniques are tried and become true, and "new" foods and drinks from around the world are continually making their way to the table. That being said, I was delighted when my editor Harriet Bell called and asked if I'd like to update *The Food Lover's Tiptionary*. "Update it?" I said. "I want to completely rewrite it!"

The culinary world's continual expansion isn't the only reason I wanted to revise this book. I've longed to do so ever since I began using it frequently on a radio show and realized, much to my chagrin, that it wasn't as user-friendly as it could be. Several times while on live radio, I found myself madly searching through dozens of tips to find the one I wanted. Accessing information just wasn't fast enough for me, and I figured I wasn't the only one having that problem.

This *New Food Lover's Tiptionary* is still organized in an easy A-to-Z format, but now each listing is broken down into boldface categories (such as "purchasing," "storing" and "cooking") for easy access to just the information you're looking for. And not only does this edition have a different format, but it's greatly expanded. There are over 6,000 practical culinary tips, shortcuts and techniques on these pages. Plus quick and easy reference charts, a handy system of cross-referencing and well over a hundred shorthand-style recipes.

In short, this *New Food Lover's Tiptionary* is bigger and better than ever, all for the love of food and drink. On the following pages you'll find everything from answers to simple culinary questions to rescues for cooking disasters. And let's face it—anyone who's cooked has had some sort of kitchen catastrophe (or two, or three), whether it's a cake that won't come out of the pan, rice burned onto the bottom of a pot or an egg-based sauce that's separated. But savvy cooks know that such culinary quandaries needn't spoil the day. The trick is in learning to cook smarter, not harder.

The New Food Lover's Tiptionary has something for everyone—from the accomplished cook, to the occasional cook, to the novice cook . . . even for someone whose idea of cooking is serving take-out, but who wants to know how to open champagne, make a cocktail or simply how to properly set the table. There are hundreds of subjects, including foods, beverages, cooking techniques, preparations, kitchen equipment and appliances, table settings and cleaning up. You'll find tips and techniques for deglazing a pan, making high-altitude adjustments, testing eggs for freshness, cooking with wine, reducing calories, fat and salt, measuring accurately, using chopsticks, understanding label terms and opening coconuts, just to name a few.

Bottom line? Life's too short and cooking's way too much fun to get upset over. To that end, my hope is that this book makes your cooking adventures easier and, in the best of all worlds, filled with confidence and joy. May *The New Food Lover's Tiptionary* become your trusted kitchen companion, there when you need it to inform, inspire or simply help you out of a jam.

Bon Appe*Tip*!

It is said that abalone also makes good chowder, but I cringe at the thought.
It would be too much like making an ordinary beef stew of filet mignon.
—Euell Gibbons, American naturalist, author

ABALONE *see also* FISH, GENERAL; SHELLFISH

TIDBIT Abalone is a mollusk found clinging to rocks along the coast-lines of California, Mexico and Japan. It attaches to the rocks with a broad foot (the adductor muscle), which is actually the edible portion. Abalone can be purchased fresh, canned, dried or frozen. It's also known as *ormer, awabi, muttonfish* and *paua*.

PURCHASING Like all fresh shellfish, abalone should be alive when purchased (the exposed muscle should move when touched) and smell sweet, not fishy. Choose those that are relatively small.

STORING

* Fresh abalone: Refrigerate immediately and cook within 1 day.
* Canned abalone: Once opened, cover with water, then refrigerate in a sealed container for up to 5 days.
* Dried abalone: Wrap tightly and store in a cool, dry place indefinitely.
* Frozen abalone: Freeze for up to 3 months.

PREPARING

* Abalone is a muscle, so it must be pounded to make it tender. Use a mallet to flatten the meat to a ⅛- to ¼-inch thickness.
* Slash the meat at ½-inch intervals with a sharp knife to prevent it from curling during cooking.

COOKING

* Sauté abalone briefly for no more than 20 to 30 seconds per side—over-cooking makes it as tough as shoe leather.
* Mince and add leftovers to soup or chowder.

ACIDULATED WATER

TIDBIT This is water to which a small amount of acid (such as lemon juice or vinegar) has been added. It's used to prevent the cut surfaces of some fruits and vegetables (such as pears, apples, avocados and artichokes) from darkening when exposed to air.

STORING Refrigerate, covered airtight, for up to 2 weeks.

PREPARING For each quart of cold water, add 1½ tablespoons vinegar, or 3 tablespoons lemon juice, or ½ cup white wine. One tablespoon salt will also produce the same results, but does not actually "acidulate" the water.

USING

* Fill a small spray bottle of acidulated water and keep it in the refrigerator to have ready to spritz cut fruits or vegetables.
* Use as a soak or dip for foods like artichokes and avocados, or in the preparation of some variety meats, like sweetbreads.

ALCOHOL *see* BEER; CHAMPAGNE; COCKTAILS; FLAMBÉING; LIQUOR AND LIQUEURS; WINE; WINE IN FOOD

ALMOND PASTE; MARZIPAN

TIDBIT **Almond paste** is a combination of blanched ground almonds, sugar, glycerin or other liquid, and sometimes almond extract. **Marzipan** is a similar mixture that contains more sugar, and sometimes egg whites. Though almond paste is the basis of marzipan, the two cannot successfully be interchanged in most baking recipes.

PURCHASING Supermarkets carry almond paste and marzipan in cans and plastic tubes.

STORING Unopened, almond paste and marzipan can be stored at room temperature for at least a year. Once opened, wrap airtight and refrigerate for up to 3 months.

USING

* Soften hardened almond paste or marzipan by microwaving on high for 2 to 3 seconds.
* Combine chopped almond paste or marzipan, chopped dried apricots and chopped nuts; use as a filling for baked apples.
* Scatter chopped almond paste or marzipan over the top of fruit tarts before baking.
* Make cinnamon-almond toast by spreading butter on one side of a piece of toast, then sprinkling with cinnamon, then chopped almond paste or marzipan. Broil until bubbly.

ALMONDS *For general purchase, storage, toasting and usage information,* *see* NUTS, GENERAL

TIDBIT Almonds aren't really nuts, but the kernels of the almond-tree fruit. These kernels contain the trace mineral boron, thought to be instrumental in preventing osteoporosis. Almonds also carry a healthy dose of oleic acid, an antioxidant. In a nutshell, almonds are a nutritional powerhouse packed with calcium, fiber, folic acid, magnesium, potassium, riboflavin and vitamin E. Blanched unsalted almonds contain about 170 calories per ounce, dry-roasted unsalted, about 150 calories. The good news is that most of an almond's fat is monounsaturated—as it is in olive oil.

EQUIVALENTS
* In shell: 1 pound = 1½ to 2 cups
* Shelled: 1 pound = 3 to 3½ cups whole, 4 cups slivered

PREPARING
* Taste almonds before blanching them. The skin adds flavor to many dishes and baked goods, so if it isn't bitter, leave it on.
* To blanch whole almonds, cover with boiling water; set aside for 3 minutes. Strain, then slip off the skins by squeezing the almonds between your fingers and thumb. Blot with paper towels; spread the almonds in a single layer on a baking sheet and bake at 325°F for about 10 minutes.
* Adding pure almond extract (just a little—it's potent) to baked goods containing almonds will intensify the flavor.
* Almond extract also makes cherries taste cherrier—add just a drop or two to cherry pies and other baked goods.

ALUMINUM FOIL *see also* PARCHMENT PAPER; PLASTIC WRAP; WAXED PAPER
* Foods containing acidic ingredients (such as tomatoes, lemons or onions) should not come in direct contact with foil. Natural acids create a chemical reaction that can eat through the foil and/or affect the food's flavor.
* Don't reuse aluminum foil to wrap foods for the freezer because tiny holes, created when the foil is crinkled, increase permeability.
* When baking food in foil, keep it from overbrowning by wrapping it shiny side out.
* To easily line a square or oblong baking pan for brownies or other bar cookies, turn the pan upside down, form the foil to fit and tightly crease the corners. Lift off the foil, flip the pan over, and insert the formed foil into it.
* Line a bread basket with foil, then a napkin to keep breadstuffs warm longer.

A

* Use foil to cook food *en papillote* (*see* PARCHMENT PAPER) for a delicious, moist result and pain-free cleanup.

ANCHOVIES *see also* FISH, GENERAL

TIDBIT The true anchovy is found only along the Mediterranean and southern European coastlines, although many species of tiny, silvery fish are known as "anchovies" in their country of origin. The flavor of fresh anchovies is mild and their texture is tender.

PURCHASING **Fresh anchovies** are sometimes available in specialty fish markets and in Italian and Portuguese markets. **Canned anchovies** are most often filleted, salt-cured, then packed in oil (olive oil is best) and sold in cans or jars. They're sold flat and rolled. **Anchovy paste,** a pounded mixture of anchovies, vinegar, spices and water, is sold in tubes.

EQUIVALENTS

* Anchovies: 2-ounce can = 10 to 12; 1 anchovy fillet = ½ teaspoon anchovy paste
* Anchovy paste: 2-ounce tube = 4 tablespoons; ½ teaspoon = 1 anchovy fillet

STORING

* Fresh anchovies: *See* Fish, Storing, page 195.
* Canned anchovies and anchovy paste: Store at room temperature for at least 1 year. Once opened, cover with oil, seal tightly and refrigerate for up to 2 months. Reseal and refrigerate anchovy paste for at least 3 months.

PREPARING

* To reduce the saltiness of processed anchovies, soak them in cold water for about 10 minutes. Change the water and soak for 20 minutes more. Drain, then blot with paper towels before using.
* Use a garlic press to instantly PURÉE anchovy fillets.
* Make your own anchovy paste by using a mortar and pestle (or a small plate and fork) to mash anchovy fillets with a little vinegar, water and seasonings to taste.
* To prepare fresh anchovies for cooking: Scrape with a knife to remove any scales. Working under running water, cut or twist off the head and slit the belly, slipping your finger into the cavity to remove internal matter. Grasp the tail and remove the skeleton, cutting it away from the flesh in places if necessary. Rinse well and pat dry. The skin is edible and most people don't bother removing the minuscule feathery bones, which are essentially indiscernible on the palate. To cook, open the fish flat like a book.

USING
* A dab of anchovy paste can enliven flat-flavored soups or stews.
* Anchovies can add a rich background to many sauces, such as a marinara sauce for pasta. But start slowly, adding one fillet (or ½ teaspoon paste) at a time, tasting after each addition.
* Anchovies are high in sodium, so whenever adding them or their oil to a dish, taste the food before salting.
* Use the oil from canned anchovies to flavor sauces, salad dressings or marinades.

GRILLED FRESH ANCHOVIES
Marinate cleaned, filleted anchovies for at least an hour (in the refrigerator) in a combination of extra virgin olive oil, minced garlic, lemon zest, salt and pepper. Oil a fish rack. Place the anchovies on it, skin side down, and brush with the marinade. Grill over a hot fire until the flesh turns white and the skin crisps. Serve immediately.

Adam was but human—this explains it all. He did not want the apple for the apple's sake, he wanted it only because it was forbidden.
—Mark Twain, American author, humorist

APPLES   *see also* APPLESAUCE; FRUIT, GENERAL
TIDBIT   Most archaeologists don't agree with the legend that the apple was the forbidden fruit with which Eve tempted Adam. You see, apples didn't grow in the Middle East when Genesis is thought to have been written. Indeed the Bible's words describing the tree of knowledge are not at all specific: ". . . good for food and pleasant to the eyes, and a tree to be desired to make one wise." For all we know, the provocative fruit in question might, as many think, more likely have been a luscious apricot.
PURCHASING
* Buy firm, well-colored apples with a fresh, not musty, fragrance. The skins should be tight, smooth and free of bruises and punctures. A dry, tan- or brown-colored area (called "scald") on the skin may be slightly tough, but doesn't usually affect flavor.
* Choose the variety by how it'll be used—fresh (for eating out-of-hand, in salads, and so on), or cooked (as for applesauce and pies), or for baking whole. **All-purpose apples,** good for both cooking or eating raw, include Baldwin, Braeburn, Cortland, Criterion, Fuji, Gala, Golden Delicious, Granny Smith, Gravenstein, Jonagold, Jonathan, Lady Apple, Macoun, McIntosh, Newtown Pippin (also simply Pippin), Northern Spy, Pink

A

Lady, Red Delicious, Rhode Island Greening, Stayman Winesap, Wine-sap and York Imperial. **Apples good for cooking:** Gravenstein, Rhode Island Greening and York Imperial; firmer varieties that are particularly good for baking whole include Braeburn, Cortland, Gala, Northern Spy, Rome Beauty, Winesap and York Imperial.

EQUIVALENTS

* Fresh: 1 pound = 2 large, 3 medium or 4 small; about 2¾ cups chopped or sliced; 1⅓ cups applesauce
* Dried: 1 pound = 4⅓ cups, 8 cups cooked

STORING

* Fresh apples: Store in a cool, dark place, or refrigerate in a plastic bag. They'll keep longer if they don't touch each other during storage.
* Dried apples: Refrigerate indefinitely sealed tightly in a plastic bag.

PREPARING

* Keep cut apples from browning in one of several ways: (1) Toss or brush with lemon, orange or grapefruit juice; (2) dip in ACIDULATED WATER; (3) use a "color keeper" product (based on ascorbic acid), available in super-markets.
* Apples in a salad dressed with a vinaigrette won't brown because of the acid in the dressing.
* Coring apples: Peel, if desired, then quarter apples from the stem end. Using a paring knife and cutting from the blossom end to the stem end, core each quarter. Or use an apple corer (available in supermar-kets) to core and wedge the apple in one motion. **For baked apples,** use a corer or melon baller to carve out the core, making sure not to cut through to the blossom end (leave a ½-inch base to be safe). The more core you cut out, the more room you'll have to stuff the apples with goodies.
* Apples past their prime lose moisture and flavor. To revive them, chop coarsely, cover with cold apple juice and refrigerate for 30 minutes.
* Apples produce a natural ethylene gas that speeds the ripening of other fruits such as avocados and pears. Put a ripe apple in a paper bag with the fruit to be ripened, pierce the bag in a few places with the tip of a knife, then seal and let stand at room temperature for 2 to 3 days.

COOKING

* Cooked apples pair nicely with meats like chicken, pork or veal and with vegetables like cabbage, onions or potatoes. They also complement many soups and stews.
* To help cooked apples hold their shape, add any sugar called for in the recipe at the beginning of the cooking time. *See also* APPLESAUCE.

* The skins of baked apples won't crack or burst if you cut several shallow slits around the sides of the fruit from which the steam can escape during baking.
* Reduce baked apple shrinkage by removing a ½-inch horizontal strip of peel from around the middle.
* Provide support for baked apples by setting them in lightly greased muffin tins before baking.

SAUSAGE-STUFFED BAKED APPLES

A sweet and savory combination that's wonderful for breakfast or brunch. Core the apples and scoop out all but about a ¾-inch thick shell. For each apple, chop the scooped-out apple and combine with 2 tablespoons crumbled, crisply cooked sausage, 2 teaspoons raisins and a dash of nutmeg. Return the mixture to the apple shells and bake for about 45 minutes at 350°F.

APPLESAUCE   *see also* APPLES

TIDBIT   Applesauce is often called "apple sass" in New England.

COOKING

* Any tart apple (cooking or all-purpose–*see* page 8) can be used to make applesauce.
* Combining two or more apple varieties adds flavor interest to applesauce.
* Leaving the apple peel on adds color to homemade applesauce.
* Sugar added at the beginning of the cooking time helps retain the apple's shape. So, for chunky applesauce, add the sugar before beginning to cook. For a softer applesauce, cook the apples first, then stir in the sugar.
* A teaspoon or two of lemon juice will enliven an oversweet applesauce.
* Try honey or maple syrup instead of sugar for sweetening.
* Cranberry or cranapple juice adds both color and flavor.
* For kids, young and old, stir in a few tiny cinnamon candies.
* Add your own personal touch to store-bought applesauce by stirring in raisins, spices (such as nutmeg and cinnamon) or toasted nuts.

SPICY FRESH APPLESAUCE

This uncooked version is quick and easy and full of flavor. Combine chunks of apple (peeled or not) with a little orange juice, cinnamon and nutmeg in a blender or food processor; process (using quick on/off pulses) to desired texture.

APRICOTS   *see also* DRIED FRUIT; FRUIT, GENERAL

TIDBIT   Is there an ape in apricot? Put another way: Do you say APE-rih-kaht or AP-rih-kaht? Well, according to Charles Harrington Elster, in his fascinating tome *There Is No Zoo in Zoology,* the second (short-A) version has been preferred since about 1970, when dictionaries gradually began to shift to this more common pronunciation. But longtime "ape"ricot articulators needn't worry—the variant pronunciation is also acceptable.

PURCHASING Buy plump, reasonably firm apricots with a uniform-colored skin. The color, depending on the variety, can range anywhere from pale yellow to deep burned orange. Avoid fruit that's hard, green-tinged or noticeably bruised.

STORING Store unripe apricots at room temperature until ripe. Put ripe apricots in a plastic bag and refrigerate for up to 3 days. Apricots are very perishable and rapidly lose their flavor.

EQUIVALENTS
* Fresh: 1 pound = 8 to 14 whole, 2½ cups sliced or halved
* Dried: 1 pound = 2¾ cups, 5½ cups cooked

USING
* Apricots can be eaten raw or cooked in pies. They can be poached, or even quickly sautéed in butter and sugar.
* Wash apricots just before using. Handle them gently—they bruise easily and bruised flesh turns soft and flavorless.
* To peel apricots, blanch (*see* BLANCHING) them by dropping them into a pot of boiling water for about 10 seconds. Use a slotted spoon to remove the apricots from the hot water and immediately place in a bowl of ice water to stop the cooking process. Use a paring knife to peel the skin away.
* Save the summer bounty of apricots by halving and pitting them, then cover with SUGAR SYRUP to which you've added 1 tablespoon lemon juice per cup of syrup. Cover and freeze for up to 6 months.

ARROWROOT   *see also* CORNSTARCH; FLOUR; THICKENERS

TIDBIT Arrowroot, a fine powder used for thickening, comes from the dried rootstalks of a tropical tuber.

PURCHASING Arrowroot is available in all supermarkets.

STORING Store airtight at room temperature.

SUBSTITUTIONS For 1 rounded teaspoon arrowroot use: 1 rounded teaspoon potato starch, 1½ teaspoons cornstarch, or 1 tablespoon all-purpose flour or quick-cooking tapioca.

COOKING
* Arrowroot's thickening power is about 1½ times that of all-purpose flour.

* Like cornstarch, arrowroot should be mixed with enough cold liquid to make a paste before being stirred into hot mixtures.
* Unlike cornstarch, arrowroot doesn't impart a chalky taste when under-cooked.
* Arrowroot thickens mixtures at a lower temperature than either cornstarch or flour.
* Overstirring an arrowroot-thickened mixture can cause it to become thin again.
* Some British and early American recipes call for arrowroot flour, which is the same thing as arrowroot.

After all the trouble you go to, you get about as much actual "food" out of eating an artichoke as you would from licking 30 or 40 postage stamps.
—Miss Piggy

ARTICHOKES   *see also* JERUSALEM ARTICHOKES; VEGETABLES, GENERAL

PURCHASING Choose deep green artichokes that are heavy for their size and have a compact leaf formation. The leaves should "squeak" when pressed together. Avoid shriveled, lightweight, mottled or loose-leaved specimens. A slight browning of the leaf edges (called "winter's kiss"), which is caused by frost damage, doesn't usually affect the artichoke's quality. An artichoke with generous browning, however, is usually beyond its prime. In general, the smaller the artichoke, the more tender it will be; the rounder it is, the larger a heart it will have. Baby artichokes (about the size of a small egg and typically available only in the spring) are so tender when cooked that they can be eaten whole.

STORING Refrigerate unwashed artichokes in a plastic bag for up to 5 days. They're best, however, if used within a day or two of purchase.

PREPARING
* Wash artichokes just before using. To flush out all the dirt hiding between the leaves, plunge the artichokes up and down in cold water.
* Wear rubber gloves to protect your hands from pricks while working with artichokes.
* Use stainless-steel knives and kitchen shears to cut artichokes—carbon blades will darken and discolor the flesh.
* To prepare whole artichokes for cooking: Slice off the stem to form a flat base. Snap off the tough outer leaves closest to the stem. If desired, trim about ½ inch off the pointed top. Use kitchen shears to snip off the prickly tips of the outer leaves. Rub all cut edges with lemon to prevent

discoloration. If you're removing the choke, a grapefruit spoon or melon baller works perfectly.

* An artichoke's color and tenderness will be enhanced by soaking it in ACIDULATED WATER for an hour before cooking.

COOKING

* Cook artichokes in a stainless-steel, Teflon-lined or enamel-coated pan. Aluminum or iron pans will turn artichokes an unattractive gray green color. For microwaving, use a microwave-safe ceramic or glass dish.

* Add 1 teaspoon lemon juice per artichoke to the cooking water to retain the vegetable's color.

* Flavor the cooking water with seasonings such as minced garlic, chopped shallots or peppercorns.

* To give artichokes a slight sheen, add 1 tablespoon olive or vegetable oil to the cooking water.

* Enhance the color and flavor of over-the-hill artichokes by adding 1 teaspoon each sugar and salt for each quart of cooking water.

* There are several methods by which you can cook whole artichokes, the timing depending on the size of the artichoke: (1) steaming or boiling for 25 to 40 minutes; (2) baking (a method usually reserved for stuffed artichokes) for at least 45 minutes; (3) pressure cooking for 8 to 10 minutes; (4) microwaving (also good for stuffed artichokes) 12 to 14 minutes on high plus 5 minutes standing time. Cook artichokes positioned upright, stem side down.

* A microwaving tip from the California Artichoke Advisory Board: Pour ¼ cup water and ½ teaspoon each lemon juice and vegetable oil in a 2-cup glass measuring cup or small glass bowl. Place a medium prepared artichoke upside down in the cup or bowl; cover with plastic wrap. Cook on high for 6 to 7 minutes. Let stand, covered, for 5 minutes.

* Don't throw out those stems! Cut off about ½ inch of the end, then peel off the fibrous outer layer to reach the tender insides. Cook the stems with the artichokes. Either eat the artichoke as is, or chill and slice into rounds or JULIENNE for use in stir-fries, salads or pasta.

* **Testing for doneness:** Artichokes are done when the leaves pull off easily and the base can be readily pierced with a knife tip.

* Use tongs to remove artichokes from their cooking water. Turn upside down on a rack or colander to drain for a minute or two before serving.

SERVING

* **How to eat an artichoke:** No need to feel intimidated when this globelike vegetable is set before you. The first thing to remember is that the base of each leaf is the edible portion—the rest of the leaf is too tough to eat.

Begin by pulling the leaves off one at a time with your fingers. If there's a sauce, dip the leaf's base into it, then draw the leaf through your teeth, scraping off the tender portion at the base. Discard the leaf (it's nice to have a "discard" plate) and pull off another one. When all the leaves have been removed, use a spoon to scoop out and discard the small, pale, purple-tinged leaves at the bottom and the fuzzy portion called the "choke." The remaining piece is the succulent, meaty artichoke bottom, which should be eaten with a fork.

* Dipping sauces for artichokes don't have to be the usual caloric lemon or herb butters, flavored mayonnaise-based dips or oil-rich vinaigrettes. Cut calories by dipping the leaves in various salsas, or yogurt-based sauces, or even your favorite commercial low-calorie salad dressing.

* Most experts agree that artichokes ruin the flavor of wine. Certainly, wine shouldn't accompany artichokes served with any kind of vinaigrette sauce because the acid would kill the wine's flavor. If you do serve wine with artichokes, choose one with high acidity, such as a Chenin Blanc.

EASY ARTICHOKE SOUP
Combine artichoke leftovers with 1 garlic clove, 2 teaspoons lemon juice, ½ cup chopped parsley and enough chicken broth (or artichoke cooking water) to cover in a saucepan; bring to a boil. Reduce the heat; cover and simmer for 20 minutes. Pour the mixture into a blender; cover and process (starting at low speed and gradually increasing to high) until puréed (*see* PURÉEING). Pour the mixture through a fine strainer back into pan, add milk or cream and season to taste. Serve hot or cold.

ARTIFICIAL SWEETENERS *see* SUGAR SUBSTITUTES

You needn't tell me that a man who doesn't love asparagus and oysters and good wines has got a soul, or a stomach either.
—Saki (H. H. Munro), Scottish author

ASPARAGUS *see also* VEGETABLES, GENERAL
TIDBIT This venerable vegetable has long been considered an aphrodisiac, and ancient Egyptians so revered asparagus that they offered it to the gods. This cultivated member of the lily family comes in a range of colors, from lush green to deep purple (a variety called *viola*) to creamy white (grown underground and harvested just as the tips break through the soil). Although prime asparagus season is February through June, hothouse ver-

A sions are generally available year-round. Dieters have long enjoyed this high-fiber, low-calorie vegetable and why not?—94 percent of its weight is water.

PURCHASING Choose firm stalks with tight tips and no sign of shriveling. The color should be strong for the variety—green, deep purple or ivory (for white asparagus). In general, the thinner the spear, the more tender it will be. Choose asparagus stalks that are all approximately the same size and thickness—they'll cook more evenly.

EQUIVALENTS 1 pound = 12 to 20 spears, 3½ cups chopped

STORING As soon as you get home from the market, cut ½ inch off the base of the stalks. Stand the asparagus upright in about an inch of water; cover the container with a plastic bag and refrigerate. Or wrap the stem ends in a wet paper towel, then seal the asparagus in a plastic bag. Asparagus is always best cooked the day it's purchased but it will keep for up to 3 days.

PREPARING

* Wash asparagus just before using.
* To revive limp asparagus, cut off ¼ inch of the ends, stand the spears vertically in 2 inches of ice water and refrigerate, covered with a plastic bag, for 2 hours.
* Asparagus spears will snap off naturally where they become tough. With one hand, hold the stem end about 1 inch from the bottom. With your other hand, hold the spear about halfway down the stalk and bend the spear until it snaps.
* The skin on older or larger asparagus spears can be tough. Remedy the problem by peeling them with a vegetable peeler.

COOKING

* Ideally, asparagus should be cooked standing up in water with the tender tips above the water level. Use kitchen string to tie the stalks together so they'll stand up easily.
* If your asparagus cooking pot isn't tall enough so that the asparagus can stand up and still be covered, invert a deep saucepan over the spears to use as a cover.
* A clean glass or ceramic coffeepot makes a good asparagus cooking pot.
* Cook asparagus only until the stalks are crisp-tender. Residual heat will continue to cook the spears for 30 to 60 seconds after they're removed from the heat.
* Thoroughly drain cooked asparagus to remove excess moisture in the spear tips that could dilute a sauce.

Microwaving asparagus: For 1 pound asparagus, arrange the spears spoke-fashion, tips toward the center, in a round baking dish. Add 2 table-spoons water; cover and cook on high for 7 to 10 minutes until crisp-tender. Rotate the dish a half turn after 4 minutes.

USING

* Thin, fresh asparagus is wonderful thinly sliced and served raw in salads.
* Serve fresh (or briefly blanched, *see* BLANCHING) spears as crudités, with a dip.
* Chop and use leftover cooked asparagus in omelets, soups or stir-fries, adding it at the last minute just so it warms through but doesn't over-cook.
* Overcooked leftover asparagus can be puréed (*see* PURÉEING) and used for soups or sauces.
* Save the fibrous base that snaps off the spears, cover with water or broth and cook until very tender. Purée, strain and use in sauces and soups. The purée can be frozen for up to 3 months.

AVOCADOS

TIDBIT The avocado is a fruit, not—as some believe—a vegetable. The two most widely marketed avocado varieties are the pebbly textured, almost black Hass and the green, smooth- and thin-skinned Fuerte. The Hass has a smaller pit and a more buttery texture than the Fuerte. Although avocados are high in unsaturated fat, the good news is that, according to the California Avocado Advisory Board, half an 8-ounce avocado contains only 138 calories.

PURCHASING

* Fresh avocados: Choose those that are heavy for their size and yield slightly to gentle palm pressure (prodding with your finger can bruise the flesh). They should be unblemished, free of dark or sunken spots. With your fingernail, gently pry the stem—if it pops off easily and the cavity is green, the fruit is ripe. For use in guacamole or other dips, choose slightly overripe avocados, which will mash more easily.
* Frozen avocado pulp and guacamole: Both are available in supermar-kets. They're not great, but will do in a pinch.

EQUIVALENTS 1 pound = 2 medium; about 2½ cups sliced, diced or chopped; 1½ cups puréed

STORING Store unripe avocados at room temperature, ripe ones in the refrigerator for up to a week. Speed the ripening of hard avocados by plac-ing them in a paper bag with an apple. Pierce the bag in several places, then set aside at room temperature for 1 to 3 days.

A

PREPARING

* To soften an underripe, hard avocado: Microwave at medium (50% power) for 30 to 45 seconds, rotating halfway through; let stand for 3 minutes. The avocado won't be or taste ripe, but it will be softer.
* **Seeding**: Cut the avocado lengthwise all the way around, then gently twist the halves in opposite directions to separate them. Firmly whack the seed with the blade of a sharp, heavy knife; twist the knife slightly and lift out the seed, still attached to the blade.
* **Peeling**: Perfectly ripe avocados are the easiest to peel. The skin of underripe fruit is hard to remove, the flesh of overripe avocados easily mashes during peeling. Peel an avocado half by using the point of a very sharp paring knife to make a lengthwise cut down the middle of the skin. If you want unblemished halves, cut only through the skin and not into the flesh. At the stem end, grasp one piece of the skin between your thumb and the knife edge; pull the skin down and off the fruit. Repeat with the other strip of skin.
* Retard the browning of avocados by brushing cut surfaces with lemon juice or an ascorbic-acid "color keeper" available in supermarkets.
* If the cut surface of an avocado turns brown, simply scrape off the discoloration to expose the brightly colored flesh underneath.
* You can hold peeled chunks of avocado (to be used in salad, for instance) by placing them in a bowl of iced ACIDULATED WATER; cover and refrigerate for up to 4 hours.
* Always add lemon or lime juice to guacamole—the acid not only helps keep the avocado from browning, it also brightens the flavor of this ultra-rich fruit.
* Keep guacamole from browning by placing a piece of plastic wrap directly on the surface of the dip. It's oxygen that browns avocado, so the less air that gets to the surface, the better.

USING

* Fill avocado halves (brush the flesh with a little lemon juice to prevent browning) with seafood, chicken or pasta salad.
* Create mini-bowls for salads or dips by scooping out all the avocado flesh, then filling the shell. The Hass avocado is best for this type of container because it's thicker and firmer.
* For almost-instant avocado dressing: Combine half an avocado with ½ cup of your favorite vinaigrette dressing in a blender; process until smooth.

AVOCADO TREE

Want to try your hand at growing an avocado tree? Start by using a sharp knife to trim a scant ⅛-inch sliver off both ends of an avocado pit. Plant the pit, large end down, in damp potting soil so that the dirt covers about two-thirds of the pit. Water well, then invert a drinking glass over the pit to retain moisture. Once the pit splits (be patient), cover it with soil. When the plant is about 6 inches tall, cut off the top 2 inches. This will force lower growth and prevent the plant from becoming spindly.

I've long said that if I were about to be executed and were given a choice of my last meal, it would be bacon and eggs. . . . Nothing is quite as intoxicating as the smell of bacon frying in the morning, save perhaps the smell of coffee brewing.
—James Beard, American cookbook author

BACON *see also* HAM; MEAT, GENERAL; PORK

TIDBIT In the United States, bacon is cured, smoked side pork (the pig's side). The ideal ratio of fat to lean is one-half to two-thirds.

PURCHASING

* Choose firm, well-colored bacon with no sign of sliminess. Check the date stamp (reflecting the last date of sale) on packages of vacuum-packed bacon to make sure it's fresh.
* Slab bacon, generally cheaper than presliced bacon, is typically sold with the rind, which should be removed before slicing.
* Bacon bits are preserved, dried, precooked pieces of real bacon that must be refrigerated. Bacon-flavored bits are an imitation-flavored, vegetable-based product that can be stored at room temperature. Be particularly careful when using the imitation bits in recipes—their strong, ersatz flavor can ruin a dish.

EQUIVALENTS

* Raw: 1 pound = 18 to 22 regular slices, 20 thin, 10 to 14 thick
* Cooked: 1 pound = 1½ cups crumbled; 1 slice = 1 tablespoon crumbled

STORING

* Sliced bacon: Refrigerate an unopened package for no longer than a week past the date stamp. Once opened, tightly wrap and refrigerate for up to a week. Freeze for up to 3 months.
* Slab bacon: Tightly wrap and refrigerate for up to 3 weeks; freeze for 3 months.

* Cooked bacon: Wrap airtight and refrigerate for up to 5 days; freeze for up to 6 weeks. Cushion layers of bacon strips with paper towels.

PREPARING

* To facilitate separating the bacon slices, roll the package into a tube and secure it with a rubber band before refrigerating.
* Or separate a pound of bacon into individual portions, wrapping each serving in plastic wrap. Freeze the single-serving packets in a plastic bag; defrost and use as you need them.
* Slices are easier to separate if you remove the bacon from the refrigerator at least 30 minutes before cooking.
* Microwaving a package of bacon on high for 30 seconds will also loosen the slices.
* Separate cold bacon by using the dull edge of a dinner knife.
* Semifrozen bacon is easier to dice than refrigerated bacon.
* To reduce excess curling, prick the bacon with a fork before cooking.

COOKING

* The thinner the bacon, the crisper it becomes when cooked.
* Defrost frozen bacon in the refrigerator overnight to prevent excessive spattering and shrinkage during cooking.
* Or defrost in the microwave oven, according to the manufacturer's instructions. Or simply unwrap the bacon and cook on high for 15 to 30 seconds, depending on the amount.
* To minimize shrinkage, start the bacon in a cold skillet and cook over medium heat.
* To reduce spatters and produce crisper fried bacon, pour off the fat as the bacon cooks.
* To bake: This easy method creates flat strips. Place bacon rashers in a single layer on a baking sheet with sides. Bake in a preheated 400°F oven for 10 to 15 minutes until done to your preference. There's no need to turn baked bacon. Thoroughly blot the bacon on paper towels before serving.
* To microwave: Line a microwave-safe rack or paper plate with a double layer of microwavable paper towel. Place bacon strips side by side on the rack or plate and cover with another sheet of paper towel. Six slices cooked on high will take 5 to 6 minutes. You can add a second and third layer of bacon strips crosswise to each other and the first layer. Put a double thickness of paper towels between the bacon layers. Cover the top layer with a paper towel to keep your oven from getting spattered.
* Make cracklings by dicing and frying the rind of slab bacon.

* Use a bulb baster to remove excess fat from the pan while bacon cooks.
* To recrisp bacon: In a skillet over medium-high heat, or in a 350°F oven for 5 to 10 minutes, or in a microwave oven on high for 60 to 90 seconds.

USING

* Use crisp, crumbled bacon to garnish salads, deviled eggs, baked potatoes or other vegetables.
* Add crumbled bacon to casseroles and stir-fry dishes, and to muffin, drop-biscuit or cornbread batter.
* Bacon grease adds wonderful flavor to myriad foods. Many cooks—particularly in the South—use it in cornbreads, to fry foods like hush puppies and catfish, as a flavoring for vegetables, and so on.
* To reuse bacon drippings, pour through a fine sieve into a container with a tight lid. Refrigerate or freeze to be used as desired.
* Never pour bacon grease down the drain (unless you want a visit from your plumber). If you don't plan to use it, pour the grease into a can, refrigerate until solid, then toss into the trash.

PEPPERED CARAMEL BACON

Sugar-and-spice makes everything nice—even this ultracrispy bacon, which is perfect for special-occasion brunches. Fry 1 pound lean, thick-sliced bacon in a large skillet over medium heat until very crisp. Cook in batches, pouring off excess fat as necessary. Drain the cooked bacon on two layers of paper towel. Combine 3 tablespoons sugar, 1 teaspoon ground allspice, 1 teaspoon coarsely ground pepper and 2 tablespoons water in a small bowl. Drain the skillet of all fat; return the bacon to the pan. Drizzle the sugar-spice mixture over the bacon, tossing to coat. Cook over medium-high heat for 3 minutes, tossing often. Turn out onto a waxed paper–lined baking sheet, separating the pieces with two forks. Keep warm in a 250°F oven until ready to serve.

The bagel, an unsweetened doughnut with rigor mortis . . .
—Beatrice and Ira Freeman, American authors

BAGELS *see also* BREAD, GENERAL
TIDBIT In seventeenth-century Poland, bagels were believed to have powers to ward off evil spirits and were therefore reserved for women in childbirth, their midwives and any women present during birthing. Today bagels are for everyone, and bagel aficionados know that the only true bagel is the water (eggless) bagel, with its classic, chewy texture.
STORING Store in a plastic bag at room temperature for up to 3 days,

depending on how fresh the bagels were when you bought them. Refrigerating bagels hastens staleness. If you're not going to consume them quickly, slice the bagels in half, then double wrap and freeze them for up to 6 months.

USING

* Slicing bagels can be dangerous, which is why there are several styles of bagel slicers available in supermarkets and kitchenware stores.
* To cut bagels by hand, place the bagel on a flat surface, place your hand on top of it and use a serrated knife to cut the bagel crosswise halfway through. Turn the bagel cut side up and, holding the top half, slice downward to complete the process.
* To refresh whole bagels, lightly brush the exterior with water, then bake at 350°F for 5 to 8 minutes.
* Frozen, halved bagels need not be thawed before toasting.
* For bagel pizzas, cut bagels in half. Spread tomato sauce on the cut surfaces, sprinkle with cheese and other toppings, and bake in a preheated 400°F oven until the cheese is melted and bubbly.
* Make a bagel bruschetta by splitting and toasting a sesame or garlic bagel, then topping it with a mixture of chopped, seeded tomatoes, minced garlic, a little olive oil, and salt and pepper to taste. Broil just until hot and enjoy.
* To make croutons, cut bagels into ½-inch chunks, brush or spray with a little olive oil and toast in a 300°F oven until golden brown. Use for salads or in stuffings.
* Don't throw out over-the-hill bagels. Cut them into chunks, then process to crumbs in a food processor. Freeze until the next time you need bread crumbs.

BAGEL CHIPS

Cut bagels crosswise into ⅛-inch slices and arrange in a single layer on a baking sheet. Toast in a preheated 350°F oven for 5 minutes a side, or until golden brown. If desired, the bagel slices can be brushed lightly with extra virgin olive oil and sprinkled with salt, herbs, sesame seeds or other topping of your choice before baking.

BUBBA'S BAGELS

Halve bagels and scoop out the insides (freeze and use for bread crumbs or soup thickener), leaving a ⅓-inch shell. Toast the shells until golden brown, then fill each shell with a sautéed mixture of ground beef, onions, garlic, green peppers and barbecue sauce. If you like, sprinkle with grated Cheddar or Jack and broil until the cheese melts. Serve open-faced.

B

BAKED GOODS, GENERAL *see also* BREAD; CAKES; COOKIES; GREASING PANS; HIGH–ALTITUDE ADJUSTMENTS; OVENS; PAN SIZES; THERMOMETERS; PIE

* Every baker's *batterie de cuisine* should include an oven thermometer, ruler and thermometer for reading liquid temperatures.
* Position the oven rack(s) before heating the oven.
* Unless a recipe indicates otherwise, always preheat an oven for 10 to 15 minutes before beginning to bake.
* Have your utensils and ingredients ready, your pans greased (*see* GREASING PANS) and the oven turned on before beginning to mix a cake, quickbread batter or cookie dough.
* Glass conducts and retains heat better than metal, so reduce oven temperatures by 25°F whenever using glass bakeware.
* Room-temperature ingredients produce baked goods with better volume than cold ingredients. Quickly take the chill off milk, nuts, flour and so on by warming briefly in the microwave oven.
* Whipped butter contains 30 to 45 percent air, so it should never be used in baked goods.
* Shortcut to sifting: Put the dry ingredients to be sifted in a bowl, and stir well with a whisk.
* When baking more than one item at a time (two pies or two loaves of bread) on the same oven shelf, leave at least 2 inches of space between the pans, as well as between the pans and the oven walls.
* If using both oven racks, position baking pans so that one is not directly above the other.
* For more even baking, rotate baking sheets or pans front to back and top to bottom halfway through the baking time. When using two shelves at once, position them at least 6 inches apart.

BAKEWARE *see* COOKWARE AND BAKEWARE

BAKING *see also* COOKWARE AND BAKEWARE; BAKED GOODS; ROASTING
TIDBIT The terms "bake" and "roast" are often thought of as the same method because they're both done in an oven, with hot air being the cooking medium. In truth, ROASTING (*see* page 403) is a dry-heat method of baking, whereas "baking" itself has many guises. Some foods (like coq au vin, pot roast and baked beans) are baked in a moderately deep pan or dish with added liquid (such as sauce, broth or wine) and a lid to retain moisture. Breads and potatoes, on the other hand, use neither added liquid or lids, yet they're "baked," not "roasted." Potatoes are "baked" with dry heat

unless, of course, you cut them into pieces and cook them in a shallow pan with oil, in which case they're "roasted." And therein lies the conundrum.

BAKING POWDER *see also* CAKES; COOKIES; BAKING SODA; BREAD, QUICK; HIGH-ALTITUDE ADJUSTMENTS

TIDBIT This leavener is a combination of baking soda, an acid (such as cream of tartar) and a moisture-absorber (like cornstarch). The most common type of baking powder is double-acting, which releases some of its gas when it becomes wet and the rest when exposed to heat.

PURCHASING Check the date on the bottom of the can to be sure it's fresh. Baking powder is very perishable so, unless you use it often, buy it in small cans.

STORING Store in a cool, dry place. Tightly reseal opened baking powder, which should be effective for at least 6 months.

SUBSTITUTIONS For 1 teaspoon baking powder, use: ¼ teaspoon baking soda plus ⅝ teaspoon cream of tartar; or ¼ teaspoon baking soda plus ½ cup buttermilk or sour milk (as a substitute for ½ cup other liquid in the recipe).

PREPARING

* To test the effectiveness of baking powder: Combine 1 teaspoon baking powder with ½ cup hot water. If it bubbles energetically, it's good to go.
* Never dip a wet measuring spoon into a baking powder can—moisture causes deterioration.

USING

* For baked goods, the general rule of thumb is 1 teaspoon baking powder per 1 cup flour.
* Since some of baking powder's gas (leavening power) begins releasing the minute it's moistened, combine the wet ingredients in one container, the dry ingredients in another, then mix them together just before baking.
* For lighter batter-fried foods, add ½ teaspoon baking powder per ½ cup flour.

BAKING SODA *see also* CAKES; COOKIES; BAKING POWDER; BREAD, QUICK; HIGH-ALTITUDE ADJUSTMENTS

TIDBIT Baking soda, also known as bicarbonate of soda and sodium bicarbonate, produces carbon dioxide gas when combined with a liquid acid ingredient such as buttermilk, yogurt or molasses.

PURCHASING   Check the date on the bottom of the box to be sure it's fresh.

STORING   Store baking soda in a cool, dry place for up to 6 months. It's extremely perishable and will keep better if transferred to an airtight container.

USING

* Check baking soda's integrity by combining ¼ teaspoon soda with 2 teaspoons vinegar. If the mixture bubbles, the soda's still active.
* Never dip a wet measuring spoon into a baking soda container—contact with moisture will begin to activate the soda.
* As a general rule, use ½ teaspoon baking soda for every cup of liquid, such as buttermilk or sour milk.
* Baked goods that contain molasses (which is naturally acidic) will be more tender if you add ¼ teaspoon baking soda for each ⅓ cup molasses.
* The immediate rising action of baked goods containing baking soda and baking powder makes it important to have the oven preheated and the pans greased (see GREASING PANS) before combining ingredients.
* Because baking soda begins releasing its gas the instant it's moistened, it should always be mixed with the other dry ingredients before any liquid is added. Once the wet and dry ingredients are combined, the batter should be placed in the oven immediately.
* A pinch of baking soda in the cooking water will help preserve the color of green vegetables, but will also destroy their vitamin C.
* To keep your refrigerator smelling fresh, place an opened box of baking soda on a center shelf. Replace with a new box every 3 months.
* Sweeten the garbage disposal and kitchen drain by pouring in ½ cup baking soda and letting it stand for an hour before flushing with water.
* Sprinkle pans with baked-on food with baking soda, add a little hot water and allow to sit overnight. The next day, cleaning should be a breeze.

BANANAS   see also FRUIT, GENERAL

TIDBIT   Bananas grow in 50-pound bunches, comprising several "hands" of around a dozen bananas each. They're picked green because, contrary to nature's norm, bananas are one fruit that develops better flavor when ripened off the plant.

PURCHASING   Choose plump, evenly colored, yellow bananas. A faint flecking of tiny brown spots indicates ripeness. Bananas with greening at the tips are slightly underripe.

EQUIVALENTS

✳ Fresh: 1 pound = 3 to 4 medium, 2 cups sliced, 1¾ cups mashed; 1 medium = ½ cup puréed
✳ Dried: 1 pound = 4½ cups slices

STORING Store, uncovered, at room temperature (about 70°F). Refrigerate overripe bananas for up to 3 days. The peel will turn brown, but the flesh will remain relatively firm.

USING

✳ To ripen bananas: Place in a perforated brown paper bag with a ripe apple; let sit at room temperature for a day or two.
✳ To keep sliced bananas from browning, toss with lemon, lime or orange juice.
✳ Add banana slices or chunks to fruit salads and desserts just before serving to retain their color and texture.
✳ Slightly underripe bananas hold their shape better when cooked than ripe fruit.
✳ Don't toss out overripe bananas. Peel and mash them (speedy in the blender) with 1 teaspoon lemon juice for each banana. Freeze in an airtight container (indicating the amount it contains) for up to 6 months. Defrost the purée overnight in the refrigerator; use in quick breads, cakes, puddings, daiquiris (see COCKTAILS) and other drinks (see BEVERAGES), and so on.
✳ Bananas can also be frozen whole (in their peels), wrapped airtight, for up to 6 months. If the banana wasn't overripe when you froze it, it can be peeled and sliced into a salad while still slightly frozen. Add it at the last minute so it won't have time to discolor. Or eat the whole banana frozen, like a popsicle. Or mash and use it in baked goods or drinks.
✳ Freeze banana slices (dipped in orange juice to preserve their color) on a baking sheet until hard, then store in a freezer-proof plastic bag to have on hand for snacks. For an extra treat, dip the banana slices in melted chocolate after freezing and let harden before transferring them to the plastic bag.
✳ Grilled bananas make a delicious accompaniment for grilled meats. Place slightly underripe bananas (in their peels) right alongside the meat. Cook 6 to 8 minutes, turning the bananas once during that time. Cut lengthwise and eat directly out of the peel.

SPICED BROILED BANANAS

For a quick low-fat dessert, cut a peeled banana lengthwise and place it, cut side up, on a baking sheet that's been coated with cooking spray. Sprinkle

B banana halves with brown sugar, cinnamon and nutmeg; broil 4 inches from the heat until the sugar is bubbly. Serves 1.

NUTTY 'NANAS

Makes a great breakfast, lunch, snack or dessert. Halve a banana lengthwise, spread each half with ½ to 1 tablespoon peanut butter, then sprinkle (lightly or liberally) with chocolate chips. Serves 1.

BARBECUE SAUCE *see also* GRILLING

* Barbecue sauce is great on baked potatoes, burgers, hot dogs, grilled cheese and fried-egg sandwiches, and so forth. Add it to hearty soups and stews, baked beans, scrambled eggs, and burger or meat loaf mixtures. Bake chicken or pork in it or brush it over grilled or broiled meats 5 to 10 minutes before they're done (barbecue sauce is high in sugar and will burn if cooked too long).
* Customize bottled barbecue sauce in minutes with any of the following: sautéed minced garlic, green pepper and onion; lemon, orange or lime juice and/or zest; a dash of bourbon, port, sherry or full-bodied beer; chopped fresh chile peppers, dried red pepper flakes, cayenne or Tabasco sauce; Worcestershire or soy sauce; maple syrup, honey, molasses or brown sugar; chopped fresh herbs such as basil, cilantro, oregano or parsley; toasted sesame seeds; ground roasted peanuts or sunflower seeds; sesame or extra virgin olive oil; minced fresh ginger; horseradish or spicy brown mustard; cracked black pepper; minced, fresh, seeded red or green tomatoes.

BARBECUING *see* GRILLING

BARDING *see also* LARDING

TIDBIT Barding refers to covering meat or fowl with a layer of fat to keep the flesh from drying out during roasting. This technique is used for lean cuts where natural fat is absent. The layer of fat bastes the meat while it cooks, keeping it moist and adding flavor.

PREPARING

* Fat used for barding can be either that which has been cut off the meat or fat from another source, such as pork fat.
* When using a salted fat like bacon, first boil it for 5 minutes to remove some of the salt.
* To bard meat, simply lay strips of fat over the surface, or use kitchen string to tie on the fat.
* Remove the barding fat about 15 minutes before the meat is done to let the meat brown.

BARLEY

PURCHASING **Pearl barley,** the style most commonly available in supermarkets, comes in three sizes—coarse, medium and fine. Natural food stores also carry **hulled** (or **whole-grain**) **barley,** which has only the outer husk removed, as well as **barley grits** (coarsely cracked hulled barley grains) and **Scotch barley** (coarsely ground grains), which are used primarily for cereal.

EQUIVALENTS
* Medium barley: 1 cup = 3½ to 4 cups cooked
* Quick-cooking barley: 1 cup = 3 cups cooked

STORING   Store at room temperature, tightly wrapped, for up to a year.

COOKING
* Cooked barley has a distinctively chewy texture that pairs well with hearty-flavors, such as those of garlic, spinach, beef, and so on.
* Toasting barley first gives it a light, nutty flavor. Place the barley in a nonstick skillet over medium heat. Cook, stirring or shaking constantly, for 5 minutes, or until grain is golden.
* To cook barley: Bring 6 cups water, 1 teaspoon salt and 1 garlic clove, crushed (optional), to a boil in a medium saucepan. Stir in 1 cup pearl barley. Reduce the heat to a simmer and cook, uncovered, for 45 minutes. Drain thoroughly and, if desired, toss with fresh herbs, 1 tablespoon butter or oil, and salt and pepper to taste.
* Give soups and stews a hearty touch by adding barley. Adjust the amount of liquid to allow for the barley to expand.

BASIL   *see also* HERBS

TIDBIT   The word "basil" comes from the Greek *basilikon* ("royal") and, indeed, basil was called the "royal herb" by ancient Greeks. Basil, a mint-family member, is plentiful during the summer months and is an essential ingredient in many Mediterranean dishes, such as the popular pesto.

PURCHASING   Fresh basil is typically sold in small bunches. Look for evenly colored, bright green leaves with no sign of wilting or dark spots. **Opal basil,** a purple-leaved variety, should have a deep color with no browning edges. **Lemon** and **cinnamon basil** have green leaves and a fragrance that matches their respective names.

STORING   Refrigerate unwashed fresh basil, loosely wrapped in barely damp paper towels and then in a plastic bag, for up to a week. Or cut off ½ inch of the stems and refrigerate a basil bouquet, stem ends down, in a tall glass filled halfway with cold water and a pinch of sugar. Loosely cover with a plastic bag secured to the glass with a rubber band. Change the water every 2 days.

PREPARING

* Wash basil just before using; thoroughly blot dry on paper towels.
* Basil discolors rapidly when chopped. Slow the process by rubbing the chopping surface, blade and basil leaves with a little extra virgin olive oil before cutting.
* Basil chiffonade makes a showy, flavorful garnish for everything from meats to vegetables. To create, stack 4 to 5 large basil leaves and roll them into a tight tube (roll them lengthwise for long strips, crosswise for shorter strips). Cut crosswise into ⅛-inch sections.
* To freeze basil in the summer for use all year long: PURÉE cleaned and blotted dry basil leaves with enough water or extra virgin olive oil to make a paste. Spoon tablespoonsful of the paste into ice cube trays or onto a plastic wrap–lined baking sheet and freeze until solid. Transfer to a plastic bag and use as needed to flavor sauces, soups, salad dressings, and so on.
* To dry-preserve fresh basil, wash the leaves and blot dry with paper towels. Air-dry the leaves for about 15 minutes. Place alternate layers of basil and a light layer of coarse salt in a container that can be tightly sealed. Store at room temperature for up to 6 months.

USING

* Use fresh basil in salads, omelets and scrambled eggs, stir-fry dishes, in the inimitable pesto (a purée of basil, extra virgin olive oil, pine nuts and Parmesan) or minced or JULIENNED as a garnish.
* Because basil loses much of its flavor in long-cooking dishes, add a lively, fresh flavor by stirring in 1 or 2 tablespoons minced fresh basil just before serving.

BAY LEAVES   *see also* HERBS

TIDBIT Bay leaves are used to add pungent, woodsy flavor to long-cooking dishes like soups, stews and meats. Leaving them in food too long can turn a dish bitter.

PURCHASING **Dried bay leaves** are available in any supermarket. Buy them from a store with rapid turnover to ensure the freshest product. Don't use leaves that are mottled with brown spots. **Fresh bay leaves** are occasionally available in produce markets, primarily in California, where bays grow rampantly. The short, oval Turkish bay leaves have a more subtle flavor than the long, narrow California variety.

USING

* Remove bay leaves from food before serving—they never soften and make an unpleasant mouthful.
* For easy retrieval, spear the bay leaf with a toothpick before adding it to the dish, or put it in a tea infuser.
* Never crumble a bay leaf before adding it to a dish—retrieving the pieces will be impossible.

BEAN CURD   *see* TOFU

BEANS, CANNED   *see also* BEANS, DRIED
EQUIVALENT   15½-ounce can = about 1¾ cups drained
PREPARING   Drain and rinse unflavored canned beans to remove excess salt.
USING   For almost-instant soup, PURÉE a can of your favorite beans, add a drained can of whole beans, plus enough broth to thin it to the desired texture. Season with herbs, preferably fresh.

> *Beans, beans, the musical fruit*
> *The more you eat, the more you toot*
> *The more you toot, the better you feel*
> *So eat some beans at every meal!*
> —Anonymous

BEANS, DRIED   *see also* BEANS, CANNED; LENTILS; LIMA BEANS; PEAS, DRIED
TIDBIT   Sad but true—beans can cause a problem for some people. The gas-producing troublemakers in beans are oligosaccharides—complex sugars that, because they're indigestible by normal stomach enzymes, proceed into the lower intestine, where they're fermented by friendly bacteria, a process that produces that lyrical *gas*.
PURCHASING   Choose plump dried beans; discard any that are discolored or shriveled. Tiny holes in dried beans signal bug invaders. The label term "quick-cooking" describes beans that have been soaked and dried. They don't require presoaking and take considerably less time to cook. However, their cooked texture isn't as firm to the bite as regular dried beans.
EQUIVALENTS   1 pound = about 2½ cups uncooked (depending on the size), 5½ to 6½ cups cooked; 1 cup = about 2½ cups cooked

STORING

* Dried beans: Store in an airtight container for up to a year in a cool, dry place. They can be frozen indefinitely.
* Cooked beans: Refrigerate and use within 5 days.

PREPARING

* Check beans thoroughly for tiny pebbles or other debris.
* Most beans require being soaked in water for several hours or overnight to rehydrate them before cooking. Use a large bowl or pot (to allow the beans to increase in size as they soak) and cover the beans with at least 3 inches of cold water.
* To stave off flatulence, change the water at least twice during the soaking process.
* **Quick-soak method:** If time is short, put beans in a large pan, cover with water and bring to a boil. Remove from the heat, cover and let stand for 1 to 2 hours before cooking.

COOKING

* Before cooking beans, drain off the soaking water and start with fresh water in which to cook the beans.
* When making a dish that contains two different types of beans (black beans and Great Northern beans, for example), cook them separately, then combine them when they're done. Every variety requires a slightly different cooking time and if they are cooked together, one is bound to be overdone or underdone.
* Reduce foaming and boilovers by adding 2 to 3 teaspoons vegetable oil to the cooking water.
* Salting the cooking liquid for dried beans tends to slow the cooking and toughen the beans. Salt the beans after they're cooked.
* Acidic ingredients, such as tomatoes or wine, also slow down the cooking time, so either make allowances for this or add the acidic food when the beans are almost done.
* Cook beans over low heat. Boiling can cause the cooking liquid to overflow, the beans to break apart and the skins to separate.
* For firm-textured beans, cook them uncovered; for softer beans, cover the pot.
* Fear of flatulence? Start the beans in water, simmer them for 30 minutes then drain off the water. Replace with fresh boiling water or other liquid. Continue cooking the beans until they are done.
* Since the cooking time for dried beans varies greatly, always test for doneness by tasting the beans. They should be smooth yet firm and not

mushy. Or gently squeeze a bean between your thumb and index finger—if the core is still hard, cook the beans longer.

* When the beans are done, immediately drain off the hot cooking liquid
  or they'll continue to cook.

BEANS, FRESH GREEN OR WAX *see also* BEANS, DRIED; LIMA BEANS; VEGETABLES, GENERAL

TIDBIT   Green beans are also called *string beans* and *snap beans*; a pale yellow variety is known as *wax bean.*

PURCHASING   Select fresh beans that have firm, smooth, brightly colored pods. They should be crisp enough to snap when bent in half. Avoid
those that are discolored, spotted or leathery-looking.

EQUIVALENT   1 pound = 2¾ cups trimmed and cut

STORING   Refrigerate unwashed fresh green beans in an airtight plastic
bag for up to 4 days.

PREPARING

* Wash beans just before using; remove the strings and ends, if necessary.
* Most fresh beans available today don't require stringing, as the fibrous
  string has been bred out of the species. If the beans do need stringing,
  simply snap off the stem end and use it to pull the string down and off
  the pod.

COOKING

* Use a pot large enough for the beans to move around in freely—don't
  overcrowd the pot.
* Don't add baking soda to the cooking water. It may keep beans green,
  but it'll also leach out valuable nutrients and adversely affect their flavor.
* A pinch of sugar in the cooking water brings out the flavor of fresh beans
  and reenergizes that of over-the-hill beans.
* Acidic ingredients like lemon juice or tomatoes cause green beans to lose
  some of their bright green color.
* Covering the pot will also reduce a green bean's bright color.
* Perfectly cooked fresh beans are crisp-tender when done. The only test
  for doneness is tasting them.
* Young, thin green beans are wonderful raw in salads. Accentuate their
  bright green color by BLANCHING them in boiling water for 10 seconds,
  then plunging them into ice water to stop the cooking process. Thoroughly blot dry with paper towels before using.
* Toasted slivered or sliced almonds are a flavorful garnish for cooked
  beans.

B

BEAN SPROUTS *see* SPROUTS

BEAN THREADS *see* CELLOPHANE NOODLES

> *"Roast Beef, Medium" is not only a food. It is a*
> *philosophy . . . safe and sane, and sure.*
> —Edna Ferber, American Pulitzer Prize-winning author

BEEF *see also* GROUND MEAT; MEAT, GENERAL; ROASTS; STEAKS; VEAL

TIDBIT The United States Department of Agriculture (USDA) grades beef on three factors: (1) conformation (proportion of meat to bone); (2) finish (proportion of fat to lean); and (3) overall quality. The three top grades—Prime, Choice and Select—are those commonly available to consumers. Prime cuts are usually found only in upscale meat shops and fine restaurants. The meat's grade is stamped within a purple shield at regular intervals on the outside of each carcass, so consumers rarely see the imprint.

PURCHASING

* **Cuts:** Look for brightly colored, red to deep red cuts and moderate marbling (flecks or streaks of fat in the meat). The most tender cuts (rib, short loin and sirloin) come from the animal's most lightly exercised muscles, namely along the upper back. Heavily used muscles produce less tender cuts such as chuck (near the animal's front end) and round (from the rear).
* **Ground beef** comes in several forms: ground sirloin, ground round, ground chuck and plain ground beef (sometimes simply labeled "hamburger"). The name indicates the cut from which the meat was ground; ground beef (or hamburger) is customarily a combination of several cuts. The leanest of these is **ground sirloin** (sometimes labeled "extra lean"), which contains about 15 percent fat. **Ground round** (labeled "lean") has between 20 and 23 percent fat; **ground chuck**, depending on the market (some markets label regular ground beef as "chuck"), can range between 23 and 30 percent. **Regular ground beef** touts a hefty 30 percent fat (as much as most sausage). The label typically indicates the percentage of fat or, conversely, that of lean. Fat contributes both flavor and texture to meat.

STORING Refrigerate in the coldest part of the refrigerator—ground beef for up to 2 days; other cuts for up to 3 days. If a meat cut is to be cooked within 6 to 8 hours of purchase, leave it in its plastic-wrapped package. Otherwise, remove the packaging and wrap loosely with waxed paper. The object is to let the air circulate and keep the meat's surface somewhat dry, thereby inhibiting rapid bacterial growth. Leave ground beef in its shrink-wrap packaging. **To freeze:** Wrap airtight and store ground beef for up to 3 months, solid cuts for up to 6 months.

COOKING

* As a general rule, the cheaper the cut, the less tender it is and the longer it takes to cook. Choose moist-heat cooking methods (such as BRAISING or STEWING) for inexpensive cuts.
* Instead of using water as the liquid for pot roast, substitute something more flavorful, such as beer, wine, stock or tomato or vegetable juice.
* Tender cuts of meat should be prepared with a dry-heat cooking method like BROILING, GRILLING, SAUTÉING or ROASTING.
* For specific cooking tips, *see* GROUND MEAT; ROASTING; ROASTS; STEAKS; VEAL
* Beef cooking temperatures: rare—120° to 130°F; medium—140° to 150°F; well-done—165° to 175°F.

> *Teetotalers seem to die the same as others, so what's*
> *the use of knocking off the beer?*
> —A. P. Herbert, British author, politician

BEER *see also* CHAMPAGNE; COCKTAILS; LIQUORS AND LIQUEURS; WINE

TIDBIT Beer is a generic term for a variety of mash-based, yeast-fermented brewed beverages whose alcohol content ranges from 3 to 13 percent.

PURCHASING The most popular beers available in liquor stores and supermarkets:

* **Lager**—pale-colored and light-bodied with a mellow flavor; **ale**—light to dark amber in color, with a flavor slightly more bitter and stronger than lager; **bock**—a dark brown German brew that's full-bodied, slightly sweet and almost twice as strong as lager; **malt liquor**—robust and dark, with a bitter flavor and relatively high alcohol content; **porter**—strong and full-bodied, with a slightly bittersweet flavor and dark brown color; **stout**—dark-roasted barley gives this brew an intensely dark color, bitter flavor and extremely dense body; **wheat beer**—made with malted wheat, this beer has a pale color and subtle, lagerlike flavor; **fruit beer**—mild brews flavored with fruit concentrates.
* **Light beer** in the United States refers to beer with reduced calories and, usually, less alcohol. In Europe the term distinguishes between pale and dark lagers.

* **Nonalcoholic brews** (which can't by law be called "beer") are generally light in flavor and body and have negligible alcohol levels ranging between 0.2 and 0.5 percent.

STORING Store beer standing upright—laying it on its side exposes more of the liquid to the air in the bottle, which diminishes flavor. Either store in a cool, dark place or refrigerate. Refrigerate unpasteurized beer; consume within 1 or 2 weeks.

SERVING

* Unlike wine, beer should not be aged. It's best when consumed as fresh as possible.
* For maximum aroma and flavor, the ideal serving temperature for light (lager-style) beers is 45° to 50°F; ales, porters and stouts are best in the 50° to 60°F range.
* Temperature fluctuations can cause beer to lose flavor, so don't move it in and out of the refrigerator excessively.
* The thinnest film of soap or oil on a beer mug will cause beer to lose its sparkle and collapse the foam. After washing beer glasses, thoroughly rinse and, if possible, air-dry them. To completely avoid any soap residue, wash the glasses in hot, salted water.
* Keep beer mugs in the freezer; there's nothing like a cold beer served in a frosty mug on a sweltering summer day.
* For a full head of foam, pour beer straight down into the center of the glass. This method also releases more of the beer's aroma.
* To create less of a head, slowly pour the beer onto the side of the glass.
* The amount of foam that beer produces also depends on its temperature. Ice-cold beer will produce light foam, whereas room-temperature beer promotes a thicker froth.
* Beer is a particularly compatible beverage with spicy cuisines such as Chinese, Indian, Mexican and Thai. Spicy or smoked sausages are great paired with dark beer. As a general rule, the more highly seasoned the food, the more full-bodied the beer should be.

COOKING WITH BEER

* Beer makes a great addition to many dishes, including soups, sauces, stews and breads. Substitute beer for an equal amount of the liquid called for in the recipe.
* Beer's also great for steaming clams and mussels. Or use it as the cooking liquid when boiling shrimp.
* A full-flavored brew like ale or bock beer will contribute more flavor to a dish than a light lager.

The beet is the most intense of vegetables. . . . Beets are deadly serious.
—Tom Robbins, American novelist

BEETS   *see also* GREENS; VEGETABLES, GENERAL

TIDBIT   Beets range in color from the classic garnet red, to bright gold, to white, to the intriguing **Chiogga beet** (also called "candy cane") with its concentric red and white rings.

PURCHASING   Choose firm beets with smooth, unblemished skins. In general, small or medium beets are more tender than large ones. If the beet greens are attached they should be crisp and brightly colored.

EQUIVALENT   1 pound, trimmed = 2 cups cooked and chopped

STORING   Refrigerate in a plastic bag for up to 3 weeks.
Beet greens leach moisture from the bulb and should be removed before being refrigerated. Leave 1 to 2 inches of the stem attached to prevent loss of nutrients during cooking.

PREPARING

* Just before cooking, wash beets gently, being careful not to pierce the thin skin.
* To avoid the loss of nutrients and color, don't peel beets or trim their stems until after cooking, at which point the skin slips off easily.
* The exception to this rule is beet soup, for which beets are peeled before being cooked.
* Wear disposable latex gloves (available at drugstores and hardware stores) to keep your fingers from becoming stained.
* No gloves? Get rid of stains by sprinkling your hands with salt, and rubbing them together vigorously. Wash with soap and water.
* Beet stains are almost impossible to remove from plastic or wood. Generously rubbing a storage container or chopping block with oil helps, but isn't fail-safe.

COOKING

* Boiled beets will retain more color if you add 2 tablespoons lemon juice or vinegar to the cooking water.
* The flavor of older beets can be improved by adding ½ teaspoon each sugar and salt to the cooking water.
* To peel cooked beets, cut off both ends, then hold the beets under cold, running water and slip off the skins.
* When combining beets with other vegetables, add them last so they don't discolor the other food.
* Use raw, finely grated beets in salads.

B

* Don't toss out flavorful beet greens—wash them, blot dry with paper towels, and refrigerate in a plastic bag for up to 3 days. Cook the greens as you would spinach. *See also* GREENS.
* Young, tender beet greens can be washed, shredded and used raw in salad.

BELL PEPPERS; SWEET BELL PEPPERS; SWEET PEPPERS *see also*
CHILES; VEGETABLES, GENERAL

TIDBIT Red bell peppers are simply vine-ripened green bell peppers; because they've ripened longer, they're very sweet. There are also yellow, orange, purple and brown bell peppers.

PURCHASING Choose sweet bell peppers that have a richly colored, shiny skin and are firm and heavy for their size. Avoid those that are limp and shriveled, or that have soft or bruised spots.

EQUIVALENTS 1 pound = 2 large, 2½ cups chopped; 1 medium = 1 cup chopped

STORING Refrigerate in a plastic bag for up to a week. Freeze seeded, chopped peppers for up to 6 months.

PREPARING

* Wash bell peppers thoroughly before seeding. Cut the peppers in half by slicing vertically from one side of the stem all the way around to the other side of the stem. Break the halves apart and the seed core should pop right out. Cut away the membranes, which can be bitter.
* Another way to seed a bell pepper is to hold it firmly in your palm and smack the stem end firmly against the countertop or other flat surface. The jolt should loosen the seed core, which can then be pulled right out.
* If bell peppers "repeat" on you, eliminate the offending agent by removing the skin with a vegetable peeler.
* Peppers are much easier to cut if you cut them from the flesh (not the skin) side. Place halved, seeded peppers, skin side down, on the cutting board and slice or chop as desired.
* Freeze whole bell peppers, then core, seed and chop while frozen for use in soups, stir-fries and so on.

COOKING

* Place roasted, peeled peppers (*see recipe*, page 37) in a large screw-top jar, cover with extra virgin olive oil and refrigerate for up to 1 week. The peppers can be used in salads, stir-fried dishes, as a garnish, and so on.
* Rubbing vegetable oil over the skins of peppers before stuffing them will keep them supple.

* To give stuffed peppers added support during baking, cut them cross-wise (rather than lengthwise), stuff them, then place them in lightly greased muffin tins and bake as usual.
* Contribute flavor and texture to a stuffed-pepper filling by adding a few of the pepper's seeds.
* Leftover mashed potatoes make an excellent bell-pepper stuffing. Mix them with diced, seeded tomatoes, fresh corn, some grated Cheddar and crumbled crisp bacon and you'll have your guests asking for seconds.

USING
* Make an edible container for salads or dips by cutting off the top inch of large bell peppers, then removing the core and seeds. If the peppers are huge, cut them in half crosswise.
* Substitute roasted red peppers or pimientos (both commonly available in jars) when fresh red bell peppers aren't available.

ROASTED PEPPERS

Use tongs to hold a whole pepper over a gas flame, turning as the skin blackens. To roast more than one at a time, place halved, seeded peppers on a baking sheet, skin side up. Position the peppers 3 to 4 inches from a broiling unit and char until the skins are black. Put the charred peppers in a plastic bag; seal and let stand for at least 15 minutes to allow the steam to loosen the skin (or invert a bowl over the peppers and let steam). Alternatively, you can broil the peppers on a large piece of aluminum foil, then tightly wrap the foil around the peppers and steam. When the peppers are cool enough to handle, use your fingers or a knife to peel off the skin. Tiny bits of char remaining on the peppers are perfectly acceptable.

ROASTED RED PEPPER SAUCE

This uncooked fusion is a perfect complement for grilled fish and meats. Roast, peel and seed 1 large red bell pepper as in the preceding recipe, "Roasted Peppers." Cut the pepper into 4 pieces and put into a blender jar or food processor. Add 3 tablespoons extra virgin olive oil, 1 quartered medium garlic clove, 2 teaspoons fresh lemon juice and a pinch of cayenne. Process until smooth and creamy. Salt and pepper to taste. Makes about ¾ cup.

BERRIES, GENERAL *see also* BLACKBERRIES; BLUEBERRIES; CRANBERRIES; DRIED FRUIT; RASPBERRIES; STRAWBERRIES

TIDBIT For berryations on a theme, consider the berry. For instance, the surface of a strawberry is coated with an average of 200 tiny seeds. On the other hand, a raspberry is composed of many connecting drupelets (individual fruit sections), each one containing a single seed. Cranberries and blueberries have many tiny seeds in the center of the fruit.

B PURCHASING   Check the bottom of a berry container; see-through baskets should show no unripe, bruised or moldy berries, cardboard baskets should have no sign of berry-juice stains, indicating that at least some berries are crushed. *For pointers on choosing ripe berries follow purchasing suggestions for individual berry listings*.

STORING

* Retard bruising and spoilage by storing berries in a single layer on a paper towel–lined jelly-roll pan or other large pan with shallow sides. Discard any bruised or moldy berries. Cover the berries lightly with paper towels and refrigerate (*see information on individual berries for storage time*).

* **To freeze berries:** Wash and blot dry, arrange in a single layer on a jelly-roll pan (or other baking sheet with sides), freeze until hard, then transfer to a freezer-proof plastic bag. Or place a large plastic bag on a baking sheet and place a single layer of berries in the bag. When the berries are frozen solid, seal the bag and return to the freezer. Berries may be frozen for up to 9 months.

PREPARING

* Wash berries just before using. Some berries (like strawberries) easily become waterlogged, so wash them quickly and gently. Refrigerated berries aren't as likely to bruise during washing as room-temperature berries. Thoroughly blot dry berries on paper towels.

* To defrost frozen berries, place the sealed plastic bag containing them in a large bowl of cold water for about 10 minutes. After defrosting, the berries will be flavorful but not as firm as when fresh.

* If the berries aren't sweet enough, toss them with 1 tablespoon granulated sugar per cup of berries; let stand at room temperature for 30 to 60 minutes, stirring once or twice. Sugar softens berries—particularly those that are usually cut, such as strawberries—so don't add it too far in advance of serving.

* Remove berry stains from your hands by rubbing them well with lemon wedges.

USING

* Berries—particularly the larger, heavier ones like blackberries—sink in thin cake batters. To use such berries in cakes, make sure the batter is thick enough to hold the fruit in suspension. Add the berries at the last minute to avoid bruising that might be caused by excessive stirring.

* Frozen berries exude much more juice than the fresh berries, so always reduce the liquid and increase the thickener when using them in pies or cobblers.

* Add a sophisticated touch to berries by drizzling them with a little liqueur. Frangelico (hazelnut-flavored), Grand Marnier (orange) or Amaretto (almond) all complement berries nicely.

* Pour heavy cream over berries a few minutes before serving. Their natural acid will begin to slightly coagulate the cream, making it extra thick and luscious.

* For an elegant and extraordinarily easy dessert, pour champagne over strawberries or raspberries in a stemmed glass. Or add a tablespoon or two of liqueur, like Grand Marnier, to berries, then top with a healthy dollop of softly whipped cream. Or whip the cream to soft peaks, then beat in 1 or 2 tablespoons liqueur; spoon over the berries.

BERRY CRUSH

Crush ½ cup berries (strain out the seeds, if necessary) and fold into 1 cup whipping cream that's been beaten until stiff (sweetening is optional). Either spoon over or fold into whole or sliced berries.

BERRY SYRUP

A topper for everything from pancakes and waffles to ice cream. Combine 1½ cups water, 3 cups sugar and ½ teaspoon salt in a medium saucepan. Cook, without stirring, over high heat until syrup reaches 200°F on a candy THERMOMETER. Stir in 2 cups berries (chopped, if large); cook for 2 more minutes. Cool, then refrigerate in an airtight container for up to 2 months.

BEURRE MANIÉ see THICKENERS

BEVERAGES see BEER; BUTTERMILK; CHAMPAGNE; COCKTAILS; COFFEE; CONDENSED MILK; CREAM; EGGNOG; EVAPORATED MILK; HOT DRINKS; LIQUORS AND LIQUEURS; MILK; PUNCH; SWEETENED CONDENSED MILK; TEA; WINE

BISCUITS see also BAKED GOODS, GENERAL; BAKING POWDER; BAKING SODA; BREAD, GENERAL; BREAD, QUICK; GREASING PANS; HIGH-ALTITUDE ADJUSTMENTS; MUFFINS; POPOVERS

MIXING

* For the tenderest, flakiest biscuits, the fat (butter, margarine, and so on) should be cold, even frozen.

* Cut fat into the dry ingredients only until the mixture resembles coarse (about ¼-inch) crumbs. The distribution of tiny lumps of fat creates flaky, tender biscuits; overmixing produces crumbly biscuits.

* For yeastlike biscuits, substitute 1 teaspoon each baking soda and ascor-

bic acid (vitamin C) powder for the baking powder (or for the yeast, if it's a yeast-biscuit recipe). Mix and bake as usual; no rising time is necessary.

* Overworking a biscuit dough creates tough biscuits. Press the dough together gently only until it holds together.
* Cheese biscuits: Add ⅔ to 1 cup grated cheese to the dry ingredients.
* Herb biscuits: Add 1 teaspoon dried herbs (such as oregano or tarragon) or 1 to 2 tablespoons minced fresh herbs to the dry ingredients.
* Whole-wheat biscuits: Substitute 1 cup whole-wheat flour for 1 cup all-purpose flour; add 2 tablespoons wheat germ.
* Shortcake: Add ¼ to ⅓ cup sugar and ½ teaspoon ground allspice to the dry ingredients. Split baked biscuits; fill and top with your favorite berries.

SHAPING

* Lightly sprinkle flour over the work surface before rolling out biscuit dough. Too much flour will produce heavier biscuits.
* Once you roll out the dough, cut as many biscuits as possible from that first rolling. Biscuits made from subsequent rollings won't be as tender.
* If you don't have a rolling pin, lightly flour your fingers and quickly pat the dough into the desired thickness.
* Biscuit cutters come in all sizes and shapes but if you don't have one, use a thin-lipped glass or an empty, clean 14- to 16-ounce can.
* Dip the biscuit cutter (or other cutting implement) in flour so the dough won't stick.
* Biscuits don't have to be round. Form the dough into a large square, then cut into smaller squares, rectangles or triangles with a sharp knife. Or use the divided insert from an old-fashioned metal ice cube tray to make tiny biscuit squares.
* Another way to shape biscuits is to form the dough into a circle ½ inch thick, then cut the dough into 6 or 8 wedges (farls), as with scones.
* A bonus from making square biscuits: no leftover scraps to roll out and cut.
* A rolling cookie cutter can be used to cut out several biscuits in one motion.
* For biscuits that split open easily, roll out the dough to about ¼ inch thick, then fold it over before cutting. Make butter biscuits by brushing melted butter over the dough before folding and cutting.
* Jam biscuits: After placing unbaked biscuits on a baking sheet, place ½ to 1 teaspoon jam in the center of each biscuit, slightly pressing it into the dough with the tip of the spoon.
* If you don't like the way drop biscuits spread, drop the batter into greased muffin tins and bake as usual.

TOPPING

* For biscuits that are crisp on the outside, brush the surface with water; arrange the biscuits 1½ inches apart on the baking sheet.
* For soft biscuits, brush the surface with milk or melted butter; arrange them on the baking sheet so they're touching.
* For a sweet touch, add 1 tablespoon sugar to the liquid used to glaze the biscuit dough.
* Add flavor by mixing 2 tablespoons maple syrup or honey with 1 tablespoon water; brush the glaze over the biscuits before baking.
* Sprinkle the tops of biscuits with cinnamon sugar before baking.

GENERAL

* Burned bottoms on your biscuits? Lightly rub the burned part over a grater to remove the scorched area.
* Leftover biscuits: Wrap in foil and store at room temperature for up to 3 days. Freeze, wrapped airtight in heavy-duty foil, for up to 3 months.
* To reheat: Put foil-wrapped biscuits in a 300°F oven for about 10 minutes. Thaw frozen biscuits at room temperature before heating, or heat frozen biscuits at 300°F for about 25 minutes. Thawed biscuits may be microwaved on high for 10 to 30 seconds.

BISCUIT CRUMBLE

A crispy topping for pot pies and other casserole dishes. Crumble leftover biscuits and toss with a little melted butter or extra virgin olive oil. Spread the mixture evenly over a baking sheet and bake in a preheated 350°F oven for 10 to 15 minutes until golden brown. Sprinkle over the dish just before serving.

EASY CREAM BISCUITS

Easy because there's no cutting in of butter, no rolling out the dough! Preheat the oven to 450°F. Combine 2 cups all-purpose flour, 1 tablespoon plus 1 teaspoon baking powder, 1½ tablespoons sugar and ½ teaspoon salt in a medium bowl. Have standing by 1 to 1½ cups heavy whipping cream—stir in enough cream to make a soft dough. Turn the dough out onto a lightly floured surface; *gently* knead 5 to 10 strokes, just until the dough holds together. Pat out the dough into a ½-inch thick square about 8 × 8 inches. Cut the dough into 9 squares, making three cuts each way. If desired, dip the squares in ⅓ cup melted butter. Arrange the biscuits 2 inches apart on ungreased baking sheets. Bake about 12 minutes, or until golden brown. Serve hot. Makes 9 biscuits.

FRUIT SHORTCAKE

Split large leftover biscuits and use them as shortbread, layering them with berries and whipped cream. Moisten dry biscuits by sprinkling lightly with almond- or orange-flavored liqueur.

BLACKBERRIES *For storage and cleaning information,* see BERRIES, GENERAL

TIDBIT Blackberries are shaped like long raspberries, but are firmer in texture and have a black to purplish black color (the darker the color, the riper and sweeter the berry). Their flavor can range from tart to relatively sweet. In some parts of the United States, blackberries are called *bramble-berries* because they grow on thorny (bramble) bushes.

PURCHASING Choose plump, glossy, deep-colored berries without hulls. If the hulls are still attached, the berries were picked too early, which means the flavor will be tart.

EQUIVALENTS
* Fresh: 1 pint = 2 cups
* Frozen: 10-ounce package = 2 cups

USING Blackberries are great for breakfast, snacks or dessert. They can be baked in muffins, pies and cobblers; served over cakes, puddings, and so on; and are a wonderful addition to fruit compotes. Puréed fresh blackberries become a sweet-tart sauce for everything from pancakes to ice cream. Blackberries have lots of seeds, which you may want to strain out of sauces.

BLANCHING *see also* COOKING, GENERAL

TIDBIT Blanching is the technique of partially cooking food in boiling water, then plunging it into ice-cold water to stop the cooking process. This method is used to firm the flesh, to loosen skin (as with peaches or tomatoes), and to heighten and set both color and flavor (as with vegetables before freezing). Blanching and parboiling are basically the same technique, with the primary difference being that parboiled food is cooked slightly longer. This is particularly useful for dense foods like carrots, which if partially cooked can be combined with quick-cooking ingredients like celery in sautés and stir-fries, so that all the ingredients reach doneness at the same time.

* To blanch on the stoveop: Bring a pot of water to a full rolling boil. Plunge the food into the boiling water; begin timing the second the food hits the water (the timing depends on the food being blanched). If necessary, test the food for degree of doneness by piercing it with a fork. Use a slotted spoon to remove the food from the water and immerse it immediately in a bowl filled with ice water to stop the cooking process.

* When blanching small ingredients (like peas or pearl onions) that would be difficult to scoop out of the hot water quickly, put them in a metal sieve. Submerge the vegetables in the boiling water, then in the ice water to stop the cooking.

* Microwave "blanching": Cover and cook the vegetables (with enough water to cover the bottom of the dish) on high for 2 to 3 minutes per pound. Immediately transfer the vegetables to ice water.
* After cooling, blanched or parboiled food can be covered and refrigerated for 24 hours before being used as desired. The food should be at the same temperature as the other foods with which it will be cooked.

BLENDERS *see also* FOOD PROCESSORS; IMMERSION BLENDERS

TIDBIT Nothing beats the blender for making silky-smooth PURÉES, soups and sauces, or for whipping up frothy drinks from breakfast shakes to frozen daiquiris. It makes quick work of chopping small amounts of food that would get lost in a food processor workbowl (such as nuts, bread crumbs and whole spices). The blender's tall, narrow, leakproof container is preferable to the food processor for liquid mixtures. The container's shape, however, means that not much air can get to the ingredients, making it impossible to whip air into foods like egg whites and whipping cream. Some manufacturers offer 1-cup blender jars that can be attached to the blade housing. They're perfect for chopping small amounts of food and blending salad dressings. These small containers usually have screw-on tops so the food can be stored in the same jar in which it's blended.

GENERAL

* Fill a blender jar no more than two-thirds full to allow for expansion as the ingredients blend. If necessary, blend in batches.
* Before turning on the motor, always put the lid on; place your hand on it to keep it from popping off in case it's not firmly seated.
* Put liquid ingredients in first, then dry or solid ingredients.
* Rule of thumb: Start blending on low and gradually increase the speed. This is particularly important when blending hot mixtures where starting at high speed could cause the hot mixture to explode up and out of the blender, scalding hands or face.
* Never leave a blender unattended while the motor is running.
* If a mixture is so thick that it won't move, add a little more liquid.
* Don't tax your blender motor with heavy ingredients or too much volume. If the machine begins to labor, increase the speed. If that doesn't help, stop the machine and remove half the ingredients, then process in two batches.
* Stop blending occasionally and scrape down the sides of the blender jar.
* If the motor stalls, immediately turn off the machine.
* Cut food into 1-inch pieces before chopping.
* If pieces of food become lodged in the blades, stop the machine (make

sure the blades have come to a complete stop) and use a narrow rubber spatula or the handle of a long wooden spoon to dislodge the food.

* Make sure the blades have stopped completely before removing the blender jar from the base.
* Wash and dry the jar and blades thoroughly after each use. Most are dishwasher-safe.

USING

* Liquefy frozen juice concentrate for a few seconds, then add the required water and process until the juice is frothy.
* Turn any oil-based salad dressing into a creamy-style dressing by blending it until slightly thick and smooth.
* Lumpy gravy? Whirl it in the blender for a few seconds until smooth.
* The same technique rescues an egg-based sauce that has separated.
* Use a chopstick to loosen ingredients stuck in the bottom of a blender.
* Don't let a used blender stand so long that food dries on the blades. If you can't clean the blender right away, pour some hot water in it to soak.
* Quickly clean a blender jar by filling it halfway with hot water, adding a couple of drops of dishwashing detergent, and whirling the mixture for 30 seconds. Rinse thoroughly.

BLUEBERRIES *For storage and cleaning information*, see BERRIES, GENERAL

TIDBIT The first written record of the native North American blueberry was made by Captain James Cook in the late eighteenth century. Native Americans sun-dried blueberries, and also used them in savory dishes like stews, as well as in curing meat.

PURCHASING Choose berries that are plump, firm, uniform in size and have a silver-frosted indigo blue color.

EQUIVALENTS

* Fresh: 1 pint = 2 cups
* Frozen: 10-ounce package = 1½ cups

USING

* Blueberries in baked goods: Frozen blueberries will "bleed" in baked goods if they're defrosted before being added to a batter. Always add frozen berries to a batter in their solid state, stirring them in at the last minute. Fresh blueberries won't expel their juice unless the skins are broken.
* Canned blueberries must be well drained, then blotted thoroughly on several layers of paper towels.
* Have you ever made a blueberry cake, muffins or other baked goods

only to find that the berries have turned an ugly greenish brown color? The culprit is likely baking soda, which creates an alkaline condition that affects the color of blueberries. (Baking soda is generally used in baking to counteract an acid ingredient, such as buttermilk or yogurt.) The solution? Substitute milk for buttermilk or yogurt, measure for measure, and 1 teaspoon baking powder for every ½ teaspoon baking soda.

BLUEBERRY HEAVEN

Toss 1 pint blueberries with 2 to 3 tablespoons pure maple syrup and 2 teaspoons freshly grated orange zest. Crown the maple-kissed berries with a drizzle of heavy cream. Or fold ½ cup vanilla-flavored yogurt into the berries.

BOK CHOY *see also* VEGETABLES, GENERAL

TIDBIT Also called *pak choy* and *Chinese white cabbage*, bok choy is a mild, versatile vegetable that resembles a bunch of wide-stalked celery with long, full leaves. Baby bok choy is the tiny young version of this vegetable.
PURCHASING Choose bok choy that has firm, white stalks topped with crisp, green leaves. Avoid any bunches with wilted leaves or soft stalks.
STORING Refrigerate in an airtight plastic bag for up to 4 days.
PREPARING Wash and trim off the base just before using.
COOKING Use a light touch when cooking bok choy. Sauté or stir-fry the chopped stalks for just a minute or two before adding the chopped or shredded leaves, which only take about 30 seconds to cook.
USING Raw bok choy is great in salads. Chop the crunchy stalks as you would celery; shred the leaves.

BOTTLES *see* JARS AND BOTTLES

BOUQUET GARNI

TIDBIT A bouquet garni is a bundle of herbs (classically enclosed in a cheesecloth bag) used to flavor liquid mixtures such as soups or sauces. The bouquet garni is removed at the end of the cooking time.
GENERAL
* The classic herbs for bouquet garni are parsley, thyme and bay leaf (4 sprigs parsley, 3 sprigs thyme and 1 bay leaf). Any combination of herbs may be used, however, depending on the food to be flavored.
* Lightly bruise the herbs first with a mallet or pestle to release their fragrance and flavor.
* Besides herbs like tarragon, rosemary and dill, other bouquet garni addi-

tions include peppercorns, lemon or orange zest, allspice berries, garlic cloves and celery.

* Cheesecloth is the traditional wrapping for bouquet garni. Cut a square of cheesecloth, place the herbs in the center, then pull up the edges, tying the bundle at the top with string.
* A paper coffee filter may also be used to wrap the herbs. Put the herbs in the filter, stem end up; tie at the top with string.
* An easier way to enclose the herbs is to put them in a tea infuser.
* Make a substitute tea infuser by encasing the herbs loosely in a packet of foil, sealing the seams, then piercing the foil all over with the tines of a fork.
* Another trick is to place the herbs on a long leek leaf, folding the leaf from tip to tip to encase the herbs; tie the leaf in several places with twine to secure it. Of course the leek will also add its flavor to the mixture.
* If you've used string to tie the bouquet garni, tie one end of it to the pot handle so the bundle can be retrieved easily.
* At the end of the cooking period, retrieve the bouquet garni with a fork or a slotted spoon.

All good cooks learn something new every day.
—Julia Child, American author, teacher, TV cooking icon

BRAISING *see also* COOKING, GENERAL

TIDBIT Braising is a slow, moist cooking method used for less tender cuts of meat and other foods. Typically, the food is browned, then covered airtight and slowly cooked in a small amount of liquid. STEWING is a similar method, the primary difference being that the food is typically covered with liquid. The term "pot roasting" really refers to braising a large cut of meat.

* Choose a heavy pot just *slightly* larger than the ingredients plus the liquid. This allows the food (rather than the space around it) to absorb the heat.
* Cut vegetables for braising in large chunks.
* Brown the meat or vegetables. Foods brown better if blotted dry with a paper towel. Dust the meat with flour for better browning. The pan and fat should be hot (not smoking) before the food is added.
* Once the meat or other food is browned, add the liquid called for in the recipe, but not too much or the food will end up poaching. In general, the liquid shouldn't come more than halfway up the food being braised.

* After adding the liquid, bring it quickly to a boil. Immediately reduce the heat to low and cover vegetables with a piece of buttered waxed paper, meat with a piece of foil. Then cover the entire pot with a sheet of foil, topped by the lid. Double sealing the pot keeps as much steam in the pot as possible.
* At this point, you can either simmer the food on the stovetop or transfer the pot to a 250°F oven. Oven braising cooks more evenly because the heat completely surrounds the pot. Cook according to recipe directions, or until fork-tender.

BRAZIL NUTS *For general purchase, storage, toasting and usage information, see* NUTS, GENERAL

TIDBIT   Brazil nuts are actually the seed of a giant tree that grows in the Amazon. They come in clusters of 8 to 24 inside a hard pod that resembles a small coconut.

EQUIVALENT   1 pound shelled = 3 cups

* Brazil nut shells are extraordinarily hard and must be tempered so they're easier to crack. To do so, you can freeze the nuts for 6 hours or bake them at 400°F for 15 minutes (cool for 15 minutes). Or put the nuts in a pan and cover with water. Bring to a boil, then boil for 3 minutes. Drain off the hot water, then cover with ice water and let stand for 3 minutes before draining and cracking.
* If you don't have a heavy-duty nutcracker, use a hammer or mallet to crack the brazil nut's armorlike shell.

The smell of good bread baking, like the sound of lightly flowing water, is indescribable in its evocation of innocence and delight.
—M.F.K. Fisher, American author

BREAD, GENERAL   *see also* BAGELS; BAKING POWDER; BAKING SODA; BIS-CUITS; BREAD, QUICK; BREAD, YEAST; BREAD CRUMBS; FLOUR; FRENCH TOAST; GREASING PANS; HIGH-ALTITUDE ADJUSTMENTS; MEASURING; MUFFINS; PAN SIZES; PITA BREAD; PIZZA; POPOVERS; YEAST

TIDBIT   Bread can be divided into one of four basic categories: **yeast breads,** which are leavened with yeast and require kneading to stretch the flour's gluten; **batter breads,** which are yeast-leavened breads that are beaten instead of kneaded; **quick breads,** which use baking powder, baking soda or eggs for leaveners, and require gentle mixing; and **unleavened breads,** like matzo, which are quite flat because they contain no leavening at all.

STORING

* Most breads stay fresh for 5 to 7 days at room temperature if wrapped airtight. The exception is a bread made without fat, such as French or Italian, which will stay fresh for only a day or two. Either store bread at room temperature or freeze it. Bread turns stale fastest when stored in the refrigerator. Moldy bread should be immediately discarded.
* To freeze, double wrap bread airtight—yeast breads for up to 3 months; quick breads for up to 6 months. With most frozen unsliced bread, simply slice off what you want and return the loaf to the freezer. Exceptions to this rule are very dense loaves, such as rye bread, and some quick breads like banana bread.

PANS *see also* PAN SIZES

* When using a glass baking pan, reduce the oven heat by 25°F.
* Loaf pan substitutions: A round, 1½-quart casserole or soufflé dish can be substituted for an 8 × 4-inch loaf pan; a 2-quart dish can replace a 9 × 5-inch loaf pan.

INGREDIENTS

* A flour's protein content has a definite effect on bread—the more protein, the more gluten (desirable in yeast breads). Check the Nutritional Information on the flour package label to help you select one that has a protein level appropriate for what you're baking. Flours with 12 to 14 grams protein per cup are best for yeast breads; those with 9 to 11 grams are better for quick breads.
* Room-temperature ingredients speed rising and baking times. Bring milk, juice, beer, and so on, to room temperature before adding them to the other ingredients (zap them in the microwave oven until tepid). Dry ingredients that have been refrigerated should also be brought to room temperature.
* The liquids used bring their own characteristics to bread. **Water** creates a crisp crust and brings out the flour's wheat flavor. **Potato water** (water in which peeled potatoes have been boiled) adds flavor and gives bread a smooth crumb; the additional starch makes the dough rise slightly faster. **Milk products** (milk, buttermilk, yogurt and sour cream) give bread a creamy beige color and produce a fine texture and a soft, brown crust. **Eggs** give bread a rich, moist crumb, a creamy yellow color and a brown crust. **Fruit and vegetable juices** add flavor and body. Baking soda is added to quick breads made with fruit juice to neutralize its natural acid. **Liquid sweeteners** such as molasses, honey and maple syrup give bread a moist crumb and a dark crust. **Vegetable and meat broths** add flavor and create a lightly crisp crust. If the broth is salted, reduce the salt

in the recipe. **Beer, wine, cider** and **liquors** give bread a smooth grain and a distinctive flavor. **Coffee** and **tea** provide a rich color and a dark, crisp crust.

* Scalding milk is unnecessary unless you're using raw, unpasteurized milk, which contains an organism that breaks down the gluten structure of flour.

* One beaten large egg has a leavening power equal to ½ teaspoon baking powder.

* For extra leavening in loaves that contain a lot of heavy ingredients, substitute 1 beaten large egg for ¼ cup of the liquid called for in the recipe.

* Add nutrition to any bread with the Cornell Enrichment Formula: Before measuring the flour into a measuring cup, add to it 1 tablespoon each soy flour and nonfat milk powder, and 1 teaspoon wheat germ. Spoon in the flour and level it off. Repeat for each cup of flour used in the recipe.

* Breads made without fat—like French bread—have a shorter shelf life than those with fat because fat holds moisture in baked goods.

* Breads that contain moist ingredients such as carrots, dried fruit or potatoes will stay soft longer than plain breads.

BAKING AND COOLING *see also* BREAD, QUICK; BREAD, YEAST

* Baking breads at lower temperatures creates thicker, chewier crusts; higher temperatures produce thinner, crisper crusts.

* To allow for oven discrepancies, check the bread 10 to 15 minutes before the end of the recipe's designated baking time.

* If the bread is browning too fast, cover it lightly with a "tent" of aluminum foil. Make sure the bread is on the middle rack of the oven.

* Completely cool the bread (sitting upright on a rack) before cutting or wrapping for storage. Any residual warmth will cause moisture to condense on the inside of the wrapping, and make the bread soggy.

* Burned spots on the crust? Gently rub them off with the fine side of a grater.

SLICING AND SERVING

* Don't ruin a loaf of freshly baked bread by using the wrong knife. A good serrated bread knife is worth its weight in gold. A serrated electric knife also works well.

* Round loaves require a slightly different slicing technique than the standard loaf shape. Cut the bread vertically in half, then place the cut side down and cut vertical slices. Or if you're not using the bread for sandwiches, simply cut a round loaf into wedges.

* It's much easier to cut bread into very thin slices if it's frozen.

* A pizza cutter makes quick work of trimming bread crusts.
* Line a bread basket with foil, then a napkin, to keep breadstuffs warm. Cut the foil off at the rim of the basket so it doesn't show.
* Or heat a ceramic tile in the oven, then put it in the bottom of a bread basket. Cover it with a napkin and add the bread or rolls.
* Thaw frozen bread slices for 10 to 15 minutes at room temperature. Or microwave them on high for 5 to 10 seconds. Bread that's been frozen dries out quickly.

LEFTOVERS

* Revive a loaf of less-than-fresh bread by slicing it thickly, and spreading it with softened butter mixed with grated Parmesan or other cheese, minced herbs or crushed garlic. Wrap in foil and heat in a 325°F oven for about 15 minutes, or until warmed through.
* Another way to restore dried-out bread or rolls is to sprinkle lightly with water, wrap loosely in foil or place in a sealed paper bag, and heat until warm in a 300°F oven. For crusty rolls, brush with water and heat, uncovered, at 350°F.
* To moisten and warm dried-out bread, place it in a colander set over a pot of simmering water. Cover and steam just until the bread is warmed through.
* Freeze leftover bread slices and trimmings (adding to the bag as you have them) and use them to make bread crumbs, stuffing, croutons, bread pudding, and so on
* Cut leftover croissants crosswise into ¼-inch thick slices and toast them on both sides under the broiler until golden brown. These crispy treats make great partners with soups and salads.
* Use leftover bread crumbs in pork or poultry stuffings.

CROSTINI

Italian for "little crusts," crostini can easily be made with day-old French or Italian bread. Cut the bread into ¼-inch thick slices, brush one side with extra virgin olive oil, and broil for 30 to 60 seconds on each side until crisp and golden brown. The olive oil can be seasoned with herbs, garlic or other flavorings. Crostini makes great soup or salad accompaniments. Or top with pâté or cheese, or olive or other spread to serve as hors d'oeuvres.

Bread cast upon the water comes back éclairs.
—Bert Greene, American author, journalist, wit

BREAD, QUICK *see also* BAKING POWDER; BAKING SODA; BISCUITS; BREAD, GENERAL; BREAD, YEAST; BREAD CRUMBS; FLOUR; GREASING PANS; HIGH-ALTITUDE ADJUSTMENTS; MUFFINS; POPOVERS; YEAST

TIDBIT   Quick breads are those leavened by baking soda, baking powder or eggs. Biscuits, cornbread, muffins and banana (or other fruit/nut) bread are among the most popular quick breads.

PREPARING

* Before beginning to mix a quick-bread batter, prepare the pans (*see* GREASING PANS) and preheat the oven. The immediate rising speed of baking soda and baking powder breads makes it important to have everything ready before combining ingredients.
* As a general rule of thumb, place all the dry ingredients in one bowl, and all the wet ingredients in another. Mix them together quickly and gently; immediately turn the batter into the prepared pan and put the pan in the oven.
* Use a light touch when combining the dry and wet ingredients, stirring just until the dry ingredients are moistened. Don't worry about small lumps, they'll disappear during baking. Beating or overmixing a quick-bread batter will produce dense, tough bread.
* Baking soda and baking powder begin producing gas the instant they're moistened, so they should always be mixed with the other dry ingredients before any liquid is added.
* Too much baking powder or baking soda gives bread a crumbly, dry texture and bitter undertaste. It can also make the batter overrise, causing the bread to fall.
* Too little baking powder or baking soda produces a bread with a heavy, gummy texture.
* Self-rising flour produces slightly lighter quick breads because it contains less gluten. It can be substituted for all-purpose flour in quick breads by omitting both salt and baking powder.
* For a decorative touch, sprinkle the top of the batter with seeds, coconut, chopped nuts, and so on. The topping should be an ingredient integral to the bread.

BAKING

* Check a quick bread for doneness by inserting a toothpick or wooden skewer near the loaf's center. It should come out clean.
* It's natural for quick breads to have a cracked top, a result of leavening gases expanding during baking.
* Cool quick breads in the pan for 10 minutes before transferring them to a rack to cool. This allows the bread to "set," making it easier to handle.

LEFTOVERS

* Muffins and loaf breads dried out? Rehydrate by poking holes in them with a skewer, then drizzle with fruit juice, rum, brandy or liqueur, or other complementary flavored liquid. Seal the bread tightly in foil or a plastic bag and refrigerate for at least 3 hours.
* Quick breads past their prime can be thinly sliced, placed on a baking sheet and toasted on both sides under the oven broiler. If desired, the slices can be brushed lightly with melted butter before toasting.
* Or place the slices in a toaster oven and toast until golden brown.
* For a delicious, triflelike dessert, cut overly dry, sweet quick bread into 1-inch chunks, drizzle with liqueur or fruit juice, and layer with fresh berries or other fruit and pudding and/or whipped cream. Cover and refrigerate for 4 to 6 hours.
* Make an instant bread pudding by coarsely crumbling leftover sweet quick bread and folding it into custard or pudding. Cover and refrigerate for 4 hours before serving.
* To make crumbs from leftover quick bread, arrange thin slices in a single layer on a baking sheet, and bake at 350°F until crisp and golden brown. When cool, crumble and use as a topping for cobbler, ice cream or pudding.

Bread that must be sliced with an axe is bread that is too nourishing.
—Fran Lebowitz, American writer

BREAD, YEAST *see also* BREAD, GENERAL; BREAD, QUICK; BREAD CRUMBS; FLOUR; GREASING PANS; HIGH-ALTITUDE ADJUSTMENTS; YEAST

TIDBIT There are two basic kinds of yeast bread—those that are kneaded and those that are beaten, called *batter breads*. Batter breads require extra yeast and vigorous beating but no kneading. Because the gluten isn't completely developed by a long kneading process, the texture of a batter bread is more open and coarse, the flavor slightly more yeasty due to additional leavening.

BATTER BREADS: The batter should be thick enough for a wooden spoon to stand up in. The batter rises once in the bowl in which it was mixed. It's then stirred down and turned into the baking pan, where it rises a second time before being baked. In theory, almost any yeast-bread recipe can be converted to a batter bread by simply adding less flour and doubling the yeast.

INGEDIENTS *(for detailed information, see* BREAD, GENERAL; FLOUR; YEAST)

* The most commonly used flour in breadmaking is derived from wheat, which contains a protein called "gluten." When dough is kneaded or beaten, gluten forms the elastic network that holds in the carbon dioxide gas created by the leavener. The gas bubbles cause the gluten to stretch and expand, forming the bread's framework. The less gluten (protein) in the flour, the weaker the elasticity. And without a strong elastic network, the gas bubbles escape into the air rather than leavening the bread.

* Dense, low-gluten doughs like those made with rye flour will rise better and faster if you double the amount of yeast. The bread will taste slightly yeastier, but not to its detriment.

* Flour absorbs less liquid during hot, humid months than in dry weather because it will already have absorbed some of the moisture from the atmosphere. That's why many yeast-bread recipes give a range of flour amounts. Your best guideline is to start with the lower amount, adding only enough flour to keep the dough from being too sticky to work with.

* Too much flour creates bread that's dry and dense. A dough that is slightly tacky to the touch will yield a lighter loaf.

* Yeast needs "food" in order to grow and expand, and that nourishment usually comes from some type of sugar. If you want to make a sugar-free loaf, omit the sweeteners and add 1 teaspoon malt (available in natural food stores) for each package of yeast used.

* In general, sweet yeast doughs take longer to rise than those that are savory. This is because, though sugar is "food" for yeast and encourages its growth, a lot of sugar overpowers the leavening action and slows rising.

* On the plus side, sugar adds flavor and tenderness to bread, helps brown the crust and creates a nicely textured loaf.

KNEADING

* Kneading mixes and works a dough into a cohesive, pliable mass. During kneading the gluten in the flour forms a network of strands that stretches and expands. This gluten framework enables the dough to hold in the gas bubbles formed by a leavener, thereby making the bread rise. Kneading can be done either manually or by machine.

* Kneading by hand is done with a pressing-folding-turning action: Press down into the dough with the heels of both hands (throw your weight into it), then push the dough away from your body. Fold the dough in half, give it a quarter turn and repeat the process. Depending on the

dough and the method used, kneading time can range anywhere from 5 to 20 minutes. Well-kneaded dough is smooth and elastic.

* Mechanical kneading can be done in a large mixer equipped with a dough hook (some machines have two hooks) or a food processor with a plastic or metal blade (consult the manufacturer's guide for specific directions). There are also special breadmaking machines that mix, knead, rise and bake bread all in a single container.

* Spraying an electric mixer's dough hook(s) or a food processor's blade with cooking spray (or coating it with a thin layer of vegetable oil) keeps the dough from climbing up the hook or blade during kneading. It also speeds cleanup.

* A damp kitchen towel placed under the pastry board on which you knead bread will keep the board from sliding around on the countertop.

* Keep your work surface lightly dusted with flour to keep the dough from sticking.

* Sticky dough, such as one made with rye flour, is easier to handle if you lightly oil your hands. Wetting them with cold water also helps.

* Keep hands clean while kneading by wearing thin latex gloves (found in drugstores), or slip plastic bags over your hands. Of course, feeling the dough is half the fun of kneading.

* If you mistakenly knead too much flour into the dough, lightly sprinkle it with warm water. Gradually knead in enough water to make the dough pliable.

* If layers of flour and dough build up on your palms, rub your hands together over a sink or wastebasket. Don't knead these dry dough particles back into the dough.

RISING

* No need to dirty another bowl for the dough's first rising. Use the bowl in which the ingredients were mixed, wiping it out with a paper towel, then oiling it lightly. Or oil the baking pan you'll be using and let the bread do its first rise in that. A spritz of cooking spray makes oiling easy.

* Using a clear glass container with straight sides for rising dough makes it easy to see when it's doubled. Use a marking pen or a piece of masking tape to indicate where the dough started.

* Give the dough a boost during rising by filling a heatproof bowl with boiling water; let it stand while you're kneading the dough. Discard the water, dry the bowl and put the dough in the warm bowl.

* During rising cover the dough's container with a slightly damp towel to retain natural moisture.

* Yeast doughs must have warmth in which to rise. The ideal temperature

is an 80°F environment, but dough can rise at temperatures up to 100°F without killing the yeast.

* Warm places where dough can rise: inside a gas oven warmed only by the pilot light (tape a note to the oven door to remind yourself that bread is rising inside); in an electric oven heated at 200°F for 1 minute, then turned off; set over a pan of hot water placed on the bottom shelf of a closed oven; if you're doing laundry, put the dough (in its bowl or pan) near (not on top, because of vibrations) the washer or dryer; or run the clothes dryer on the heat cycle for 1 minute, then turn off the machine and put the dough inside; bring 2 cups water to a boil in your microwave oven to create a warm, moist atmosphere, then turn off the power, set the dough inside and close the door. You'll find all kinds of creative places in your house where your bread dough can incubate.

* **Microwave-rising bread dough:** Dough can rise in a microwave oven in about half the regular time of conventional methods. However, any form of quick rising means that the dough won't have as much time to develop its full flavor. You must have a microwave oven with 10 percent power. Any higher than that and your dough could turn into a half-baked lump. Don't try to rise butter-laden doughs (such as for brioche) in the microwave—much of the butter will melt and drain from the dough. To microwave-rise enough dough for 2 standard-size loaves, set 1 cup hot water at the back corner of your microwave oven. Place the dough in a large, greased, microwave-proof bowl. Cover with plastic wrap, then a damp towel. Set the power level at 10 percent; cook for 8 minutes. Let the dough rest for 5 minutes. Repeat at 10 percent power for 5 to 8 minutes longer until the dough has doubled in bulk. The second rising—after the dough is shaped into loaves—will take about 10 minutes, but the loaves must be in glass baking dishes.

* Wherever you choose to let bread dough rise, be sure the location is draft free. Drafts cause dough to rise unevenly and slowly.

* If your dough just isn't rising (and you've proofed the yeast to make sure it's alive), it could be because the environment is too cold. If that's not the case, dissolve another package of yeast (*see* YEAST) in ¼ cup warm water and ½ teaspoon sugar. Add this mixture to the dough slowly, kneading it in well. Cover the dough, set it in a warm place and it should rise.

* Yeast dough should rise to double its original bulk. To test it after the first rise, poke two fingers into the dough; don't be timid—jab them in a good ½ inch. If the indentations stay, the dough's ready. The finger-poke method is good only for the first rise.

* If the rising time is disrupted, simply put the dough in the refrigerator to

rise more slowly. If you're gone too long and the dough overrises, give it a couple of kneads and start the rising over at room temperature.

* Once the dough has doubled, give it a good sock in the middle with your fist. This is called "punching down" the dough. Knead it for about 30 seconds to remove any air bubbles before shaping it into loaves.

* Though two risings are traditional, bread will be lighter and finer textured if you give it three risings (twice in the bowl, the last in the pan).

* Or after punching down the dough after the first rising, you can return it to the bowl, cover tightly and refrigerate for up to 2 days. It will continue to rise in the refrigerator and should be punched down once a day. Remove the dough from the refrigerator at least 3 hours before shaping it into loaves.

* It's not necessary for the dough to rise to the top of the pan for the final rising. On the contrary, if you allow the shaped loaves to increase by more than double, you run the risk of the bread collapsing during baking because it's overrisen.

* Yeast dough can be easily frozen before baking. Let the dough rise once, then punch it down and form into a loaf. Lightly oil a large piece of plastic wrap (with enough overlap to cover the bread). Place the plastic wrap, oiled side up, in a loaf pan. Add the shaped dough and seal the plastic wrap; freeze until the dough is solid. Remove the frozen dough from the pan and double wrap it in freezer-weight foil or a plastic bag; return to the freezer for up to 2 months. Before thawing, remove the plastic wrap and put the frozen dough into a greased pan. Cover and thaw overnight in the refrigerator. The next day, cover the dough lightly with a kitchen towel and let the bread rise in a warm, draft-free place until doubled in size. Bake as usual.

* To cut rolled dough (as for cinnamon rolls), wrap a long piece of strong thread or unflavored dental floss around the area to be cut, cross the ends and pull the ends together slowly. The thread (or floss) will "slice" cleanly through the dough.

GLAZING AND FINISHING

* The tops of many yeast breads are slashed just before baking; some are slashed before the second rising. Slashing not only gives bread a professional look, but allows excess gas to escape during baking, preventing ragged splitting of the loaf's top. Use a very sharp knife or a serrated knife (a tomato knife works well), razor blade or metal food-processor blade to do the slashing. Pointed kitchen shears can also be used to snip the top of the dough. Make slashes ¼ to ½ inch deep.

* Glazes add shine, color and flavor to the top crust. Use a pastry brush to coat the dough with glaze before it goes into the oven. You can slash the

tops of unbaked loaves before or after brushing them with a glaze and sprinkling with seeds or nuts.

* Egg glazes add color and shine, and hold seeds in place. Egg yolks give a dark brown crust; egg whites a shiny crust; whole eggs give shine and color. *Whole egg glaze*: Mix 1 whole egg with 1 tablespoon water. *Egg white or egg yolk glaze*: Mix 1 egg yolk or white with 2 teaspoons water. For the deepest sheen, brush with glaze and let dry 5 minutes before brushing again.

* Milk or melted butter creates a soft, tender crust.

* Syrupy sweeteners like honey, molasses or maple syrup create a soft, shiny, slightly sweet crust. Mix 1 teaspoon syrup with 2 teaspoons water or melted butter.

* Water produces a crisp crust. Brush the dough with water before it goes into the oven, then again 10 minutes before baking time is complete. Placing a pan of hot water on the oven shelf below the bread will also create steam for a crisper crust. Remove the water from the oven 10 minutes before the bread is done to let the crust dry out.

DUTCH-CRUNCH TOPPING

This crackly, flour-crunchy topping is one of my favorites. Dissolve three ¼-ounce packages active dry yeast and 1 teaspoon sugar in ¾ cup warm (110°F) water. Let stand until foamy, about 5 minutes. Add 1 tablespoon sugar, 1 teaspoon salt, 1 tablespoon vegetable oil and 1 cup rice flour (not oriental sweet rice flour). Beat until smooth, then cover and let rise until doubled, about 30 minutes. Spread over the tops of dough just before the second rising. Makes enough for 2 loaves.

BAKING

* Have the oven preheated and ready to go so the bread can begin baking as soon as it's doubled.

* For a crisper crust, place a shallow pan (9 × 13 inches is perfect), filled halfway with hot water, on the oven's bottom shelf. The water creates steam, which in turn promotes a crisp crust.

* A baking tile (found in gourmet stores) or an unglazed terra-cotta tile (available in a tile store or masonry supply store) produces a wonderfully crisp bottom crust.

* Place bread baking pans about 4 inches apart near the center of the middle shelf.

* Resist opening the oven door to peek during the important first 15 to 20 minutes of baking time. It's not unusual for a loaf to increase in size by one-third during the first 15 minutes of baking. This dramatic rise—known as "oven-spring"—could be diminished by a sudden draft.

* Bread can also be started in a cold oven if you're in a hurry and trying to speed the last few minutes of rising time. When a dough has almost doubled, place the loaves in a cold oven and set the temperature 25°F higher than called for in the recipe. Bake 5 minutes less than the time called for in the recipe before checking for doneness.
* For even, golden brown side and bottom crusts, remove the bread from its pan 5 or 10 minutes before it's due to be done and place it directly on the oven rack.
* Doneness test for yeast breads: Remove from the pan (use oven mitts) and lightly tap the bottom of the loaf. If it sounds hollow, it's done. If it's not done, place the loaf directly on the oven rack and bake for 5 minutes longer.
* Another way to test a yeast bread for doneness is with a quick-read THERMOMETER. Insert it into the bottom middle of the loaf; a reading of 180° to 185°F means the bread is done.
* For quick, oven-fresh bread at the last minute: Bake the bread for 10 minutes less than the recipe suggests. Remove from the oven, let it cool in the pan for 10 minutes, then transfer to a rack to cool completely. Freeze for up to 3 months. When ready to use, remove the bread from the freezer and thaw in the wrapping at room temperature. Remove the wrapping and bake on the middle shelf at 350°F for about 20 minutes, or until golden brown.
* Cool the bread right side up on a rack. For the best texture, cool for 2 to 3 hours before slicing.
* Disappointed with a dense, dry loaf of bread? Simply slice it thinly (cut large slices in halves or thirds) and toast until dry in a 275°F oven. Serve these crisp "crackers" with spreads, with soups or salads, or with cheese as a tidbit with cocktails.

BREADSTICKS

Almost any kneaded yeast dough can be made into breadsticks. Pinch off walnut-sized pieces of dough and use your palm to roll them into pencil-thin ropes. Place, ½ inch apart, on a lightly greased baking sheet; cover and let rise in a warm place for 20 minutes. Brush with a glaze and sprinkle with sesame or other seeds, salt, cracked pepper, grated Parmesan, chili powder—whatever you like. Bake at 350°F for 20 to 30 minutes, until crisp and golden brown.

BREAD CRUMBS see also BREAD, GENERAL; BREADING; CRUMBS, GENERAL

TIDBIT There are two types of bread crumbs—fresh (or soft) and dried, and they should not be used interchangeably. By the way, I don't recommend using stale bread—it usually tastes like what it is, *old.*

EQUIVALENTS

* Bread: 1 untrimmed slice = about ½ cup fresh bread crumbs
* Toast: 1 slice = about ⅓ cup crumbs
* 8-ounce package dried crumbs = 2⅓ cups

STORING   Bread crumbs can be refrigerated, tightly sealed, for 1 week; frozen for at least 6 months.

PREPARING

* **Fresh (soft) bread crumbs:** Tear or cut bread slices (trimmed of crusts or not) into quarters and turn into a food processor. Process, using quick on/off pulses, until crumbs reach the desired texture. The blender can also be used but, because of the narrow blender jar, process only 2 slices of bread at a time.

* **Dried bread crumbs:** Place a single layer of bread slices on a baking sheet; bake at 300°F until completely dry and lightly browned. Cool completely before breaking into pieces and processing until fine in a blender or a food processor. If using a blender, process only 1½ to 2 slices at a time. If you don't have either of these appliances, put the dry bread slices in a heavyweight plastic bag, seal, then crush the slices with a rolling pin.

* Seasoning bread crumbs (at a fraction of the cost of store-bought crumbs) is easy to do: Simply add salt, pepper, crumbled dried herbs and, if desired, finely grated cheese.

* Leftover cornbread? Crumble it finely, spread evenly over a baking sheet, and bake at 300°F until completely dry and lightly browned.

USING

* Sautéed bread crumbs make a delicious topping for vegetables, casseroles and even some salads. In a large skillet, over medium-high heat, heat 1 tablespoon butter or extra virgin olive oil for each cup of soft crumbs (2 tablespoons for dried crumbs). When the butter or oil is hot, add the bread crumbs, tossing until evenly coated. Sauté, stirring often, until crumbs are golden brown. Cool at least partway before using. The longer the crumbs cool, the crisper they'll become.

* Bread crumbs are a quick and nutritious thickener for soups, sauces, sauced dishes and casseroles. Use whole-wheat or rye crumbs for hearty meat soups or stews.

* Bread crumb substitute: Many cereals can be crushed and used as a substitute—try corn, wheat or rice flakes, but stay away from those that are sweetened. Three cups flakes yield about 1 cup crumbs.

* Cracker crumbs may also be substituted for bread crumbs—use ¾ cup cracker crumbs for each cup of bread crumbs called for in a recipe.

BREADING

TIDBIT Food is breaded before being cooked to give it a crispy coating. Most breaded food is fried or deep-fried, although it may also be baked.

* For fail-safe breading, first dry the food by blotting it with paper towels. Have three shallow bowls or pie plates ready for the process—one to hold seasoned flour, one for the beaten eggs (which can be lightened with a tablespoon of water) and a third for the bread or cracker crumbs. Place a piece of waxed paper on the third plate, then add crumbs (you'll see why shortly). Use one hand to dip the food in the flour, shaking off any excess. Use your other hand to dunk the floured food in the egg mixture, coating both sides and letting the excess drain (you can also use tongs for the "wet dip"). Then lay the food on the crumbs and, with your dry hand, lift the waxed paper slightly to toss the crumbs onto the egg-dipped food (that way, your hand won't get messy). Coat both sides of the food with crumbs, using your fingers if necessary to pat the crumbs over any bare spots.

* Milk can be used instead of egg for a dipping mixture, but doesn't provide as much "glue."

* Save on cleanup by tossing egg- or milk-dipped food in a plastic or paper bag filled with crumbs and shaking until it's well coated.

* Breading will stick better if you refrigerate the breaded food for 30 to 60 minutes before cooking.

* Besides bread and cracker crumbs, many unsweetened cereals (like corn, wheat or rice flakes) can be crushed and used for breading. Three cups flakes yield about 1 cup crumbs.

* When frying breaded foods, use a pancake turner to flip them so the crust doesn't break.

BREAD MACHINES *see also* BREAD, GENERAL; BREAD, YEAST

TIDBIT: These microcomputer-driven machines mix, knead, rise, punch down, bake and sometimes cool bread—all in a single compartment. You simply measure and add the ingredients, press a button to specify the cycle and let the machine do its thing while you're doing something else. Three to four hours later, you have fresh-baked bread. The machine's nonstick canister serves as both mixing bowl and baking pan, which reduces cleanup time. A motor-driven blade at the bottom of the canister mixes and kneads the dough, a heating coil handles the baking. If you're new at baking bread, you'll undoubtedly love these machines, which produce a loaf of bread with a fair, though somewhat cakelike texture. However, if you're used to good bakery bread, or have ever baked your own, you'll undoubtedly be unhappy with the results obtained from bread machines. Bottom line? They do fine at kneading and rising dough, but you'll be better off letting the bread rise the second time in a regular pan and baking it in the oven.

GENERAL

* The more popular bread-machine manufacturers include: American Harvest, Black & Decker, Breadman (Salton), Hitachi, Panasonic, Regal, Sunbean/Oster, Toastmaster, Welbilt, West Bend and Zojirushi. Prices range from $140 to $350. For information on and links to bread machine models, see www.breadmachinedigest.com.

* The loaf shape depends on the machine brand and model. It can be square, vertical rectangle, horizontal rectangle or cylindrical. Depending on the brand, bread machines produce loaves weighing from 1 to 2 pounds, with the average being 1½ pounds. At this writing, at least one maker (American Harvest) has a two-loaf machine.

* Besides their unconventional shapes, bread-machine loaves are character-ized by a bottom hole, created by the mixing blade. Some machines also have a removable kneading pin, which creates a small hole in the loaf's side.

* Timing for the various cycles differs from machine to machine. For instance, the basic bread setting takes 4¼ hours on one machine and only 3 hours and 10 minutes on another—with almost identical results. Some machines have a rapid-bake setting, which produces a loaf of bread in about 2¾ hours. Check the owner's manual to see how long each cycle will take.

* A programmable timer on most machines allows you to delay the machine's starting time for up to 12 hours. Calculate the time according to how long your machine takes to produce a finished loaf. Set the timer so the bread finishes baking about an hour before you want to serve it so it has time to cool and set, making it easier to slice.

* Some bread machines have a raisin-bread setting that sounds an alarm indicating that the kneading will end in 5 minutes. This allows raisins, nuts, chopped dried fruit, and so forth to be added with just enough time to be kneaded into the dough without being pulverized. If your machine doesn't have such a feature, check the user's manual to see how long kneading takes, then set a timer to go off 5 minutes before kneading is to be finished and add the ingredients.

* Some machines have settings specific to the type of bread—a whole-wheat setting, for example, is engineered for heavy, whole-grain doughs, a sweet-bread mode is specifically for breads with a high proportion of sugar, and a French-bread setting allows for less kneading and more ris-ing time.

* If your machine doesn't have a viewing window in order to see how the bread's developing, it won't hurt to lift the lid and check the dough's progress during the kneading cycle. Don't lift the lid of a machine with a yeast dispenser until the yeast has been added. However, never open the lid during the rising or baking cycles.
* Many bread machines have a cooling feature whereby a fan cools the bread and crisps the crust while it's still in the machine. This is necessary if the bread bakes while you're at work or before you get up in the morning. No such cooling means the hot bread would sit in the machine and steam in its own heat, creating a soggy crust and an overly moist interior. If your machine doesn't have a cooling cycle, immediately remove the bread from the machine when it's finished baking.

INGREDIENTS

* Follow the manufacturer's instructions for how to add and layer ingredients. Some machines say to put the yeast in first, whereas others start with the liquid, followed by the dry ingredients and topped with the yeast. Some machines have a separate yeast dispenser, which automatically adds the leavener.
* One-pound loaf recipes typically take 2 to 2½ cups flour, 1½-pound loaves take 3-plus cups. If you're converting a recipe, start with the amount of flour your machine can hold and adjust the liquid accordingly.
* Ingredients should be at room temperature (between 70° and 80°F).
* The timing for most bread machines is programmed for the use of active dry yeast. Some machine manuals give directions for using quick-rising yeast. Compressed fresh yeast shouldn't be used for machine-baked breads.
* Use bread flour, a high-protein flour formulated expressly for making yeast breads.
* Substituting ¼ cup gluten flour for whole-wheat flour in whole-grain loaves will give them a better texture.
* Unless the recipe calls for melted butter, always cut butter into pieces and soften it before adding to the mixture. This makes it easier for the butter to combine with the other ingredients.
* Substituting honey or other liquid sweeteners for sugar can cause over-browning, so make allowances when choosing the crust selection.
* When using the timer for delayed starting, don't let the yeast touch the liquid, and don't use ingredients that might spoil, like eggs or fresh milk products.

"MAKING" THE BREAD

B

* Bread machines with containers shaped like a horizontal rectangle sometimes have trouble blending in ingredients in the corners. If that's the case, simply use a rubber spatula to move the ingredients from the corners toward the center during the mixing process.

* All machines have a dough setting, which mixes the ingredients, kneads the dough and takes it through its first rising. The dough can then be removed from the machine, shaped into loaves, rolls, coffee cakes, breadsticks or whatever, and set to rise the second time outside the bread machine. Some machines have a timer that can be used with the dough setting, which means that when you get home from work the dough will be ready and waiting to be shaped into pizza, rolls, and so forth.

* The dough has reached the proper consistency when it forms a soft, pliable mass around the blade. If the dough is lumpy or in chunks, it's too dry. Add a tablespoon of liquid and let it mix into the dough. Check after a minute or so and add a little more liquid if necessary. Conversely, an overly moist dough can be brought to the right consistency by adding flour, a tablespoon at a time, until the dough is soft but not sticky.

* Dough that's too dry won't rise properly, and the resulting bread will be dense and heavy with a cracked top.

* An overly soft dough can mushroom out of the pan, causing the baked loaf to fall. Such dough can also create bread that is dense, moist or with an uneven crumb.

* If a cooled bread is hard to remove from the container, gently rap the pan on the side of the counter. Or use a rubber mallet to tap lightly on the sides of the pan.

* If the mixing blade comes loose and gets stuck in the bottom of the baked loaf, simply wait for the loaf to cool, then pull the blade out with your fingers, being careful not to scratch the blade's nonstick finish.

* Bread-machine success will come with experience, so don't give up if you have a few failures. Whenever a loaf doesn't turn out right, make a note to adjust the recipe the next time you use it. Before long, your bread machine will be turning out a successful loaf every time you use it.

Only dull people are brilliant at breakfast.
—Oscar Wilde, Anglo-Irish playwright, critic

BREAKFAST/BRUNCH   *see also* BACON; BISCUITS; EGGS; MUFFINS; PAN-CAKES; WAFFLES

* For a speedily assembled company breakfast or brunch without having to get up at the crack of dawn, gather recipe ingredients the night before. For instance, for biscuits or muffins, combine the dry ingredients in one bowl and the liquid ingredients in another (refrigerating the latter); grease (*see* GREASING PANS) the muffin tins so they'll be ready to go. Or chop and refrigerate the vegetables for an omelet or scramble, and mix and refrigerate the egg mixture.

* Set the table the night before, put out the serving dishes and utensils that will be used, and line a roll basket with a napkin. Put condiments like syrups, honey and jam in small pitchers or dishes, cover with plastic wrap, and leave at room temperature (unless the room's very hot). Do the same with butter, cream cheese, crème fraîche, and so on, and refrigerate.

* Must-have cookware for making life easier for morning cooks is a good, heavy nonstick skillet—makes cooking eggs a breeze.

BRINING

TIDBIT   Brining is a technique whereby meat is soaked in salt water, which tenderizes, moisturizes and flavors it, and thereby reduces cooking time. Brining is an age-old process that has recently enjoyed a resurgence in popularity. The trick to brining is the right amount of salt—too little and it won't do any good, too much and the food will taste salty.

* Poultry benefits most from brining; large roasts and less tender cuts do as well.

* Choose a noncorrosive container that's just large enough to hold the food and brine to cover. Too large a container will require more brine.

* You'll need enough brine to cover the food completely. Figure out how much by putting the meat in the container to be used, then covering it with water. Remove the meat; measure the water and figure out how much salt is needed, using a ratio of 1 cup kosher salt (don't use salt with additives, like iodine) per gallon of water (or ¼ cup per quart). Other liquids can replace or be substituted for part of the water in the brining mixture. Apple juice, full-flavored beer or wine are all options. Keep in mind, however, that the salty brine can't be used in cooking so will be discarded at the end of the process.

* Pour the salt into a large saucepan and add 2 cups of liquid for each cup

of salt; refrigerate the remaining liquid. Add any seasonings (herbs, peppercorns, fresh ginger, garlic) to the mixture in the pan. Sweet additions like brown sugar or maple syrup are particularly complementary to pork or poultry. Bring the mixture to a boil, stirring to dissolve salt. Remove from the heat and cool to room temperature.

* Pour the cooled brine and remaining refrigerated liquid into the container to be used for brining. It's important that this mixture is cold, or at least cool, to prevent any chance of bacterial growth.
* Place the meat in the brine. If it doesn't stay submerged, weight it with a plate topped with a can. For food safety, no part of the meat can be exposed to the air. Refrigerate brined meat, counting on about 2 hours per pound.
* Don't leave the meat in the brine longer just "to make it more tender." Overbrining can make the meat mushy and exceedingly salty.
* After brining is complete, remove the meat (don't rinse it unless you've used a particularly strong solution) and discard the brine. The meat may now be cooked as desired. The brining mixture turns beef and pork gray, so such meats should be seared to brown them before they're braised, roasted, and so on.

BROCCOFLOWER   see also VEGETABLES, GENERAL

TIDBIT Broccoflower is a cross between BROCCOLI and CAULIFLOWER. It looks like a light green-colored cauliflower, and its flavor is milder than that of either of its parents.

PURCHASING Choose a firm broccoflower with compact florets; the leaves should be crisp and green. The size of the head doesn't affect the quality, but avoid any specimens with brown spots.

EQUIVALENT 1 pound = about 1½ cups chopped or sliced

STORING Refrigerate unwashed broccoflower, tightly wrapped, for up to 5 days.

PREPARING Wash thoroughly, remove the leaves at the base and trim the stem.

COOKING Broccoflower can be cooked in any way suitable for CAULIFLOWER.

> *Broccoli is one of the most amazing pharmaceutical*
> *packages in nature's food pharmacy.*
> —Jean Carper, American nutritional author

BROCCOLI   see also BROCCOFLOWER; BROCCOLINI; VEGETABLES, GENERAL

TIDBIT The Roman emperor Tiberius' son, Drusus Caesar, so loved broccoli that he ate little else for more than a month and stopped only when his urine turned green.

PURCHASING Choose broccoli with a deep, strong color—green or green tinged with purple. The buds should be tightly closed and the leaves crisp.

EQUIVALENTS
* Fresh: 1 pound = 2 cups chopped
* Frozen: 10-ounce package = 1½ cups chopped

STORING Refrigerate, unwashed, in an airtight plastic bag for up to 4 days. Or trim ½ inch off the end and stand up in about ½ inch of water; cover the container with a plastic bag and refrigerate for up to 1 week.

PREPARING Wash and trim broccoli before using. If the stalks are tough, peel before cooking.

COOKING
* The quicker you cook broccoli, the greener it'll remain.
* Adding an acid like lemon juice or vinegar to the cooking water will cause broccoli to turn an unappetizing gray green.
* Broccoli heads cook more quickly than the stems. To ensure even cooking, cut the stems in 2 or 3 places, slicing all the way through the florets. Or remove the florets and cut the stalks into 1-inch lengths. Cook the stalks for a minute or two before adding the florets.
* The heads will cook more quickly if you cut them into 3 or 4 pieces.
* When a recipe calls for broccoli heads and you don't plan to use the stems within a few days, blanch (see BLANCHING) the stems in boiling water for 2 minutes. Cool, then freeze in an airtight plastic bag for up to 3 months. The stems are great for stir-fries, soups, and so on.
* When using broccoli in stir-fries, casseroles or other dishes with mixed foods, blanch it for a few minutes, cooling it immediately in ice water to stop the cooking.
* When serving broccoli as crudités, brighten its color by blanching it for 1 minute in boiling water. Plunge it into a bowl of ice water to stop the cooking.
* Don't like the smell of cooking broccoli? Try throwing a couple of thick chunks of bread into the cooking water. Bread slices work, too, though they sometimes dissolve and are hard to remove. Or toss a couple of red bell pepper pieces into the pot. Use a slotted spoon to retrieve the pot sweeteners before serving the broccoli.

BROCCOLI BISQUE

Turn leftover or overcooked broccoli into a delicious soup. Put the cooked broccoli and a small clove of garlic into a blender (you may have to do this in batches if there's a lot of broccoli), add milk, cream, sour cream or broth and a dash of sherry; cover and process until smooth. Strain, if desired, and season with salt and pepper. Heat gently or serve cold.

BROCCOLINI   *see also* BROCCOLI; VEGETABLES, GENERAL

TIDBIT   Also called *baby broccoli*, Broccolini is a trademarked name for a hybrid of broccoli and Chinese kale. It has long, slender stalks tipped with tiny buds evocative of miniature broccoli florets. Broccolini's texture is crunchy, its flavor subtly sweet, with a peppery edge.

PURCHASING   Choose firm, brilliant green Broccolini with no sign of yellowing.

STORING   Refrigerate in a plastic bag for up to 5 days.

PREPARING   Wash just before using; trim ¼ inch off stem ends. Broccolini stems are less fibrous than broccoli or asparagus and therefore require no peeling.

COOKING

* Broccolini is extremely versatile and can be steamed, blanched (*see* BLANCHING), sautéed, grilled or microwaved.
* Brief cooking only until the stems are crisp-tender is the key.
* When grilling Broccolini, protect the florets by wrapping them in foil.
* Dip Broccolini into a light batter and deep-fry for a great appetizer or accompaniment to grilled meats.
* BLANCH this vegetable and serve as crudités.

BROILING   *see also* COOKING, GENERAL

PREPARING

* Spray the broiler pan and grill with cooking spray (or coat lightly with vegetable oil) before beginning to cook and cleanup will be easy.
* Or line the broiler pan with foil, discarding the foil after it cools.
* Always preheat the broiler and broiling pan.
* A piece or two of bread in the bottom of the broiler pan soaks up grease and forestalls a potential fire.
* Reduce fire risk by pouring a little water in the bottom of a broiler pan. The drawback with this method is that it creates steam, which isn't desirable for most broiled foods.
* If excess fat does cause a fire, smother it by covering with a large pan lid or sheet of heavy-duty foil.

COOKING

* Broiled meat, fish or poultry will brown more evenly if brought to room temperature before cooking.

* Blot excess moisture from the surface of food to be broiled.
* Reduce the risk of flare-ups by trimming excess fat from meats, and removing poultry skin.
* Instructions to "broil 4 inches from the heating element" refers to the food's surface, not to the bottom of the pan. If you measure from the rack on which the pan sits, the food will be too close to the heat and could burn before it's done. Use a ruler to accurately measure the distance between the food's surface and the heat source.
* In general, the thinner the food you're broiling (thin pork chops, chicken breasts or fish fillets), the closer to the heat source it should be. Rare-cooked steaks and other such foods should also be close to the heat. Food that is thick or that should be cooked through (such as chicken halves) should be positioned farther from the heat source.
* Most broiled food requires basting. Warm the basting liquid so it doesn't slow down the cooking process.
* Watching calories? Baste broiled foods with low-calorie salad dressing.
* Drain off rendered fat as it accumulates to avoid fire potential.
* If you forgot to oil the broiler pan or line it with foil before using, liberally sprinkle the dirty pan with powdered soap or salt and cover with wet newspaper or paper towels as soon as you're done cooking. Let stand for an hour, then wash as usual.

BROTH, CANNED

TIDBIT There are two basic styles of canned broth: ready-to-serve (which is already diluted) and condensed (which requires added liquid). Check the label carefully—using undiluted condensed broth in a recipe could produce an unpalatably salty dish.

USING

* Boost the flavor of a can of chicken or beef broth by simmering it, covered, for 30 minutes with 2 chopped medium celery stalks, 1 chopped small onion, 1 chopped medium carrot, 3 parsley sprigs, 1 bay leaf and ½ cup water. Strain before using.
* Dried mushrooms enrich canned broth. Bring the broth to a boil, then remove it from the heat and add 1 to 3 dried mushrooms. Cover and let stand for 1 hour. PURÉE in a blender and strain, if desired. Water or red wine can be added to dilute the mixture. This fortified broth makes a great base for soups, stews and sauces.
* Refrigerate canned broth overnight to congeal the fat, which can then be easily lifted off the broth's surface.
* Use a muffin tin to freeze ½-cup portions of leftover broth, then turn the

broth "cubes" out into a freezer-proof plastic bag, seal tightly and freeze for up to a year.

BROWN SUGAR   *see* SUGAR

Remember when you were a child, and your mom wouldn't let you leave the dinner table until you ate all your Brussels sprouts, and so you took your fork and mashed them into smaller and smaller pieces in hopes of eventually reducing them to individual Brussels-sprout molecules that would be absorbed into the atmosphere and disappear?
—Dave Barry, American humorist

BRUSSELS SPROUTS   *see also* VEGETABLES, GENERAL
TIDBIT   This member of the cabbage family grows in rows of sprouts on a long, thick stalk. The sprouts range in size from ½ to 1½ inches—the smaller the sprout, the more tender it will be.
PURCHASING   Choose small, bright green Brussels sprouts with compact heads. Loose-leaved, dull sprouts are over the hill. Try to buy sprouts that are the same size so they'll all cook in the same amount of time.
EQUIVALENTS
* Fresh: 1 pound = 3 cups, 20 to 24 sprouts
* Frozen: 10-ounce package = 18 to 24 sprouts
STORING   Refrigerate unwashed sprouts in a plastic bag for up to 3 days. The longer they're stored, the stronger their flavor.
PREPARING   Wash and blot dry just before cooking. Pull off any loose or pale leaves and trim the stem end.
COOKING
* Cut an X in the base of the stem end. The X-cut allows the heat to penetrate the sprout's center more easily, thereby cooking it more quickly and evenly.
* Don't add an acid like lemon juice to the cooking water or you'll end up with gray green sprouts.
* Cook sprouts only until crisp-tender, usually about 10 minutes. Their color should be a bright, intense green. Overcooking turns them an ugly olive drab.
* Check for doneness by piercing the stem end with a fork, which should penetrate easily.
* If you don't like the smell of Brussels sprouts cooking, toss a couple of thick chunks of bread into the cooking water (slices may dissolve and be hard to remove). Or throw a couple of red bell pepper pieces into the pot.

Use a slotted spoon to retrieve the pot sweeteners before serving the sprouts.

* Brussels sprouts' nutty flavor is enhanced by a lightly toasted almonds.
* Cooked and cooled Brussels sprouts can be halved or quartered and added to tossed salads. Or toss them with diced tomatoes and a vinaigrette to be served on a bed of greens.

GINGER-GARLIC BRUSSELS SPROUTS

Cut cooked, cooled sprouts into quarters or into ¼-inch slices and sauté briefly with finely chopped scallions, minced garlic and minced fresh ginger.

Many of us hope wanly for the day when butter, cream, and cheese will be discovered to be better for us than their pale and ascetic low-fat equivalents.
—Francine Prose, American author

BUTTER *see also* FATS AND OILS; MARGARINE

PURCHASING The two most common types of butter are **salted butter** and **unsalted butter**. Products labeled "sweet cream butter" (a term for any butter made with fresh cream) actually contain salt. Unsalted butter is labeled as such. **Whipped butter** has air (30 to 45 percent) beaten into it, thereby increasing its volume and creating a softer, more spreadable consistency when cold. It comes in salted and unsalted forms. **Light** (or **reduced-calorie**) **butter** contains water, nonfat milk and gelatin, and has about half the calories of real butter. Neither whipped butter or light butter should be substituted for real butter in baked goods.

EQUIVALENTS

* Regular (salted or unsalted): 1 pound = 4 sticks (2 cups); 1 stick = ½ cup (8 tablespoons)
* Whipped: 1 pound = 3 cups regular

STORING Refrigerate regular butter for up to 1 month. Butter absorbs flavors like a sponge, so wrap it airtight. Since salt acts as a preservative, unsalted butter is more perishable than salted butter and should be refrigerated for no more than 2 weeks. Both salted and unsalted butter can be frozen in freezer-proof wrapping for up to 6 months.

SUBSTITUTIONS For 1 cup butter (for cooking or baking), use: 1 cup margarine; or ⅞ cup vegetable oil, lard or shortening; or ⅕ cup strained bacon fat; or ¾ cup strained chicken fat.

USING

* Salted and unsalted butter can be used interchangeably in cooking or baking. However, if a recipe calls for unsalted butter and you use salted butter, reduce the salt called for in the recipe. There's about ⅜ teaspoon of salt in every stick of butter.

* Unsalted butter gives the cook more control over the final flavor of a dish.
* Unsalted butter is better for GREASING PANS than salted butter because the latter can make baked goods stick to pans.
* Use a butter wrapper to grease a pan with remnants of the butter.
* To cleanly cut cold butter, cover the knife blade with plastic wrap.
* Soften a stick of butter (for spreading) by microwaving it at medium (50 percent power) for about 30 seconds. Let stand for 1 minute; repeat the process if necessary.
* To quickly soften a stick of hard butter to use in a recipe, cut it into ½-inch slices and place on a microwave-safe plate. Microwave at medium-low (30 percent power) until soft, about 30 seconds. Let stand for 1 minute.
* No microwave oven? No worries. Quickly soften butter by grating or thinly slicing it, using either a grater or vegetable peeler, or a food processor fitted with a slicing disk. Let it stand for about 10 minutes. Speed things up by setting it over (not in) a bowl of hot water.
* Create company-pretty butter in several ways: Make butter curls with a butter curler, or butter balls with a melon baller; press butter into decorative butter or candy molds; or use a PASTRY BAG with a large star tip to pipe softened butter into small glass bowls. Butter curlers and molds, pastry bags and melon ballers can all be found in cookware shops and often in supermarkets.
* Make your own whipped butter by using electric beaters to whip softened butter until very light and fluffy.

COOKING WITH BUTTER

* Butter scorches easily when used in high-heat cooking techniques like sautéing. Remedy the problem by substituting olive oil for one-quarter of the butter.
* If butter burns, throw it out—its bitter flavor will affect the food being cooked.
* Melting butter in the microwave oven is quick and easy. In a 600- to 700-watt oven on high, 2 tablespoons cold butter will melt in about 45 seconds, ¼ cup in about 50 seconds and ½ cup in about 1½ minutes. Residual heat will continue to melt the butter even after it's removed from the oven. Cover the container in which the butter is melting with a piece of waxed paper to protect the oven walls from spatters.

BROWNED BUTTER

Cut 1 stick of butter into 8 pieces and put in a 2-cup measuring cup. Cover with a paper towel and cook on high for about 7 minutes, or until browned as desired. Before using, strain through a paper towel–lined sieve.

CLARIFIED BUTTER

Melt a stick of butter over low heat in a small saucepan. Or place in a 2-cup measure, cover with waxed paper and microwave on high for 1½ minutes, or until melted. Skim off and discard any foam. Let stand until the solids settle, about 5 minutes, then pour off the clear, golden liquid. Or refrigerate until solid, then lift off the butter and discard the milky remains at the bottom. Makes about ⅓ cup clarified butter.

HOMEMADE BUTTER

Put the processor bowl and metal blade in the freezer for 15 minutes. Pour 2 cups cold, heavy whipping cream (not ultrapasteurized) into the work-bowl fitted with the metal blade. Process for 2 minutes; scrape down the sides of the bowl. Continue to process until the solids separate from the liquid, about 4 minutes. Pour off the liquid (whey), cover and refrigerate, and use for sauces and soups within 3 days. Turn the butter out onto a square of cheesecloth or heavy-duty paper towel; twist to extract as much liquid as possible. Cover the butter and refrigerate for up to 2 weeks. Let stand at room temperature for 30 minutes before serving. Makes about 6 ounces butter and 1 cup liquid.

COMPOUND BUTTER

Jazz up plain butter with flavorful ingredients and serve with everything from grilled meats to vegetables to morning treats like biscuits and pancakes. Use an electric mixer or food processor to process softened unsalted butter until smooth, then add the flavor enhancers (*see* following tip) and blend until incorporated. When adding a liquid ingredient such as juice or honey, have the mixer or food processor running and slowly drizzle in the liquid. Adding a liquid too fast can cause the mixture to separate. Spoon compound butter into a small bowl to serve and refrigerate until 30 minutes before serving. Or form the butter into a log about 1½ inches in diameter. Wrap in plastic wrap, then in a freezer-proof plastic bag; freeze for up to 3 months. When needed, cut off disks of the flavored butter and place atop hot vegetables, rice or meats just before serving.

Flavor Enhancers for Compound Butters: For each stick (½ cup) of softened butter use: 2 to 3 tablespoons minced fresh herbs or 2 to 3 teaspoons dried, crumbled herbs; ½ to ¾ cup grated cheese (such as Cheddar, Parmesan or Swiss); ½ cup blue cheese; 4 softened roasted garlic cloves; ⅓ cup toasted sesame seeds (ground or whole), ½ to ¾ teaspoon ground spice (like allspice, cinnamon or a mixture of spices); 2 to 3 tablespoons prepared mustard; 3 tablespoons honey or maple syrup; ⅓ cup chopped chutney; 1 teaspoon minced fresh ginger; ¼ cup orange juice; 2 to 3 tablespoons jam or jelly; or 1 tablespoon orange or lemon zest.

BUTTERMILK *see also* MILK

TIDBIT In the old days, buttermilk was the liquid left after butter was churned. Modern-day buttermilk is nonfat or low-fat milk that has been treated with special bacteria, which causes the texture to thicken and the flavor to become tangy.

STORING

* Fresh buttermilk: Refrigerate for up to a week after the carton date. Keep tightly sealed so it doesn't absorb refrigerator odors.
* Buttermilk powder: Store, unopened, in a cool, dry place for up to 3 years. Once opened, refrigerate for up to 1 year. The powder will stay fresher if you cover the open can first with foil, then the lid.

SUBSTITUTIONS For 1 cup buttermilk (for baking), use: 1 cup plain yogurt; or 1 tablespoon vinegar or lemon juice mixed with enough whole milk to equal 1 cup (let stand for 5 minutes); or 1¾ teaspoons cream of tartar plus 1 cup milk.

USING

* To substitute buttermilk for regular milk in baked-good recipes: For each cup of buttermilk, reduce the baking powder in the original recipe by 2 teaspoons and add ½ teaspoon baking soda.
* Buttermilk can be substituted for yogurt or sour milk in most recipes.
* Buttermilk adds its delicious tang to baked goods, salad dressing, soups and sauces.
* Buttermilk powder is a boon for those who don't keep a carton of buttermilk in the fridge. **To use in baking recipes that call for buttermilk or sour milk:** Substitute ¼ cup buttermilk powder plus 1 cup water for each cup of fresh buttermilk needed. Mix the buttermilk powder in with the dry ingredients, the water with the other moist ingredients.

Cabbage as a food has problems. . . . It can smell foul in the pot, linger through the house with pertinacity, and ruin a meal with its wet flab. Cabbage also has a nasty history of being good for you.
—Jane Grigson, British food writer

CABBAGE   *see also* VEGETABLES, GENERAL

TIDBIT   The word "cabbage" is a derivation of the French word *caboche*, a colloquial term for "head." The denigrating term "cabbagehead" refers to someone who's not too bright. Those in the know question this slur. The American Cancer Society tells us that cabbage is definitely smart eating because it (along with other cabbage-family relatives) protects against colon, lung, rectal and stomach cancers. So, go ahead—be a cabbagehead— you'll most likely live longer than "fatheads"!

PURCHASING   Choose a cabbage with crisp-looking, firmly packed leaves; the head should be heavy for its size. Avoid heads with dull, withering leaves or brown spots.

EQUIVALENTS   1 pound = about 3½ to 4 cups shredded, 2 cups cooked

STORING   Refrigerate, tightly wrapped in a plastic bag, for up to 2 weeks.

PREPARING

* Wash and blot dry; cut out the core.
* To remove whole cabbage leaves and soften for stuffing: Immerse cored cabbage in a pot of boiling water. Reduce the heat to low and simmer for 1 minute. Remove the cabbage from the water, drain well and blot dry with paper towels. Carefully remove the softened outer leaves and, when they'll no longer peel off with ease, return the cabbage head to the simmering water. Repeat as necessary.
* Or soften the leaves by popping the whole head of cabbage in the freezer overnight. The next day, let the cabbage head sit out on the countertop for about 30 minutes, then begin peeling off the leaves.

* To shred cabbage, quarter the head and cut away the core. Stack the leaves and cut crosswise into thin strips.
* For ultracrisp slaw, cover shredded cabbage with ice water for an hour. Drain well and blot dry before combining with remaining ingredients.

COOKING

* It's a well-known fact that the smell of boiled cabbage can stink up a kitchen, sometimes an entire house. Science tells us that that distinctive odor (hydrogen sulfide) doubles during the fifth through seventh minutes of cooking time. So cook cabbage in 5 minutes or less if possible. Key: The smaller the cabbage is cut, the less cooking time it needs.
* Adding ½ tablespoon lemon juice or vinegar for each cup of cooking water for red cabbage preserves its color and keeps it from turning dark purple.
* Boil just until tender, about 5 minutes for coarsely shredded cabbage, longer for cabbage chunks. Overcooking will turn it limp and produce an awful odor.
* To reduce cabbage-induced flatulence: Boil the vegetable for 5 minutes, drain off the water, cover with fresh boiling water and continue cooking. This technique works only with whole or large chunks of cabbage—preparing shredded cabbage this way would overcook it.
* Steamed cabbage wedges will hold together better than boiled.
* Shredded cabbage can be cooked ahead of time, refrigerated, then added at the last minute to stir-fries and other quickly cooked dishes. Just cook the cabbage as usual, then plunge it into a bowl of cold water to stop the cooking. Drain well and blot dry, then wrap it in a plastic bag and refrigerate for use within 3 days.
* Reduce the odor of cooking cabbage by tossing a couple of thick chunks of bread into the cooking water. (Bread slices can dissolve and are hard to remove.) Use a slotted spoon to retrieve the pot sweeteners before serving the cabbage.

For me, the cinema is not a slice of life, but a piece of cake.
—Alfred Hitchcock, Anglo-American filmmaker

CAKES *see also* BAKED GOODS, GENERAL; FLOUR; FROSTING; FRUITCAKE; GREASING PANS; MEASURING; PAN SIZES; PARCHMENT PAPER; PASTRY BAGS

PANS

* Shiny pans are best for cakemaking because they reflect the heat, thereby producing cakes with tender crusts.
* Whenever using a glass baking pan instead of a metal one, reduce the oven heat by 25°F.

* Be generous when GREASING PANS (about 1 tablespoon per layer-cake pan) and your cakes won't stick.
* Lining the bottom of a greased pan with PARCHMENT PAPER will make it easy to turn the cake out of the pan. Simply invert the cake onto a rack and gently peel off the paper.
* Tube pans (used for chiffon, sponge or angel-food cakes) are never greased. The ungreased sides of the pan allow enough traction for the delicate batter to rise and cling to them as it bakes and cools.
* For something different in layer cakes, use square instead of round pans. Substitute an 8-inch square baking pan, or two to three 8 × 4-inch loaf pans. Reduce the baking time slightly, checking for doneness about 15 minutes before the time suggested.

INGREDIENTS

* For cakes with better volume, use room-temperature ingredients. Take the chill off cold milk and other liquids by heating on high in a microwave oven for 30 seconds or so, or just until body temperature. Refrigerated dry ingredients like flour or nuts can either sit at room temperature for 30 minutes or be heated in the microwave oven for a minute or two.
* Quickly warm refrigerated eggs by placing them in a bowl of very warm (but not hot!) water for 5 to 10 minutes. If you are separating eggs, place the yolks in one bowl, the whites in another, and then place the separate bowls in a pan of warm water, making sure the water doesn't get into the eggs.
* Add richness to cakes by substituting 2 egg yolks for 1 whole egg.
* To soften cold butter in preparation for beating: Cut a stick into ½-inch thick slices, place on a microwave-safe plate and heat at medium-low (30 percent power) for about 30 seconds; or grate or thinly slice butter using a grater, vegetable peeler or a food processor fitted with a 2mm slicing blade. Let the butter stand for about 10 minutes (set it over— not in—a bowl of hot water to speed things up).
* Cake flour produces lighter cakes because it contains less gluten than all-purpose flour.
* To substitute all-purpose flour for cake flour: Use 1 cup stirred all-purpose flour, minus 2 tablespoons, for each cup of cake flour.
* In general, count on using about 1½ teaspoons baking powder for every cup of flour in layer, Bundt or pound-cake batters.
* Before measuring syrupy sweeteners such as honey and corn syrup, lightly coat the measuring cup or spoon with vegetable oil. Every drop of the syrup will easily slip out. The same result can be obtained if you mea-

sure the fat called for in a recipe and then use the same (unwashed) utensil as the measure for the sweetener. Or dip the measuring implement in very hot water before measuring the sweetener.

❋ Buttermilk produces a light, tender cake, and can be substituted for regular milk in most layer-cake recipes. Add ½ teaspoon baking soda to the dry ingredients for each cup of buttermilk.

PREPARING

❋ When greasing and flouring pans for a chocolate cake, try using unsweetened cocoa (or carob) powder instead of flour.

❋ When creaming butter and sugar together, add salt and any spices called for. This technique better disperses them throughout the batter.

❋ Be sure to beat the butter (or other fat) with the sugar for as long as the recipe directs. Not beating thoroughly can create a coarse-textured or heavy, compact cake.

❋ Don't worry if a whipped butter–sugar mixture looks "curdled" after the eggs are beaten in. The problem will correct itself once the flour is added.

❋ For lighter cakes, separate the eggs and add the yolks to the butter mixture. Beat the whites until almost stiff; fold them into the batter just before baking.

❋ Word to the wise: Many factors can prevent a foam-type cake (chiffon, sponge or angel food) from rising properly: The egg whites were overbeaten until stiff and dry, rather than firm yet moist and glossy; the whites were underbeaten—too soft to hold in the air; the batter was overmixed, rather than gently folded, as the flour was added (which can also cause such cake to be tough); or the cake was cooled right side up.

❋ Use an electric mixer for heavy batters (such as for pound cakes) in order to incorporate as much air as possible.

❋ Raisins, chocolate chips and large nut pieces will settle to the bottom unless the cake batter is thick enough to suspend them. If the batter is thin and you're determined to add these ingredients, finely chop them (they still might sink).

❋ Tossing nuts, raisins and other chopped dried fruit in flour helps to suspend them in cake batters.

❋ To allow room for the cake to rise during baking, fill the pan only half to three-quarters full with batter.

❋ When pouring a batter into a tube pan, cover the tube with a small paper cup.

❋ After pouring a layer-cake batter into a pan, rap the pan's bottom against the countertop several times to release any large air bubbles. Don't do this with batters laden with ingredients like chopped nuts or chocolate chips or they might sink to the bottom.

* Dispel large pockets of air from delicate chiffon, sponge or angel-food-cake batters by gently running a knife in a zigzag pattern through the batter.

BAKING

* Ovens are often temperamental and can be off by 75°F or more, which could spell disaster for a cake. Buying a good oven THERMOMETER is one of the best investments you can make.
* Always preheat the oven for 10 to 15 minutes.
* For oven heat to circulate freely and evenly, arrange cake pans so they have at least 2 inches between each other and the sides of the oven. If cakes are baked on two shelves, position them so that one doesn't sit directly beneath the other. Don't bake more than three cake layers at a time in one oven.
* Don't open the oven door during the first 15 minutes of baking time, and then only open it gently. Sudden movement or temperature changes can cause a cake to fall.
* To compensate for oven hot spots, reverse the position of a cake pan or pans from side to side after 20 minutes of baking time. Don't move the cake during the first 20 minutes or it could fall.
* If a cake "domes" slightly in the middle, next time cover it lightly with foil. Remove the foil during the final 15 minutes of baking.
* Cake that's browning too fast should be covered lightly with a "tent" of aluminum foil.
* To allow for oven variances, test a cake for doneness 5 to 10 minutes before the end of the baking time.
* Test deep cakes (like Bundt or pound cakes) for doneness with a long wooden skewer, commonly found in supermarkets (an uncooked spaghetti strand can be substituted). If the skewer comes out clean, the cake's done. Some recipes say the skewer should be "almost clean," meaning a few crumbs clinging to the pick are fine.
* A chiffon, sponge or angel-food cake is done when it springs back when lightly touched in the center with your finger. Layer cakes can also be tested this way.

COOLING

* Spray the cooling rack with cooking spray to keep a cake from sticking to it.
* Cool layer cakes in the pan for 10 minutes before turning out onto a rack to cool completely.

* For cakes that have a tendency to stick (like Bundt cakes), set the pan on a wet towel during that waiting time, before inverting the cake.
* Run a dinner knife around the edge of a layer cake to loosen it from the pan. Press the knife against the pan so as not to dig into the cake.
* If a cake cools in a waxed paper–lined pan so long that the paper sticks, use a hair dryer to blow hot air over the pan's bottom until the cake releases. Or return the cake to a 350°F oven for 3 to 5 minutes; invert the pan and remove the cake.
* If parchment or waxed paper sticks to the bottom of a cake, lightly brush the paper with warm water. Let stand 1 minute, then remove the paper.
* To speed the cooling of layer cakes, place them in the freezer for 10 to 15 minutes while you make the frosting. Keep in mind that the warm cake will lower the freezer's temperature slightly.
* If cake isn't thoroughly cooled before being transferred to a serving plate, it may stick to the plate.
* Cool a jelly-roll cake by immediately inverting it onto a kitchen towel that's been dusted with confectioners' sugar. Or reverse the process and heavily dust the cake in the pan with sugar, then turn it out onto the towel. Roll the warm cake up in the towel, let stand until cool, then unroll and fill as desired.
* Chiffon, sponge and angel-food cakes are cooled by inverting the pan, which keeps the cake from falling. Many tube pans have legs on which the pan can stand so air can circulate underneath. If yours doesn't have built-in legs, invert the pan and position the tube over a narrow-necked bottle.
* You can leave a cooled angel-food cake in the pan, covered tightly with foil, for up to a day.
* To loosen an angel-food cake from its pan, use a long knife with a thin blade or a metal spatula. Press the instrument firmly against the side of the pan and slowly rotate the pan until you're back to where you started. It's important to keep the knife or spatula pressed against the pan so it doesn't tear the cake. Angel-food cakes must be completely cool before being removed from the pan or they could collapse.

FINISHING

* To split cake layers, loop a long piece of unflavored dental floss tightly around the center of the cake horizontally. Cross the ends, then slowly but firmly pull on each end. The floss will cut cleanly through the cake.
* Another splitting method is to stick toothpicks at 1½-inch intervals at the level you want to cut the cake. Let the toothpicks guide you as you use a long, thin (preferably serrated) knife to cut the cake.

* For a quick and pretty cake decoration, place a paper doily on top of an unfrosted cake and sprinkle it liberally with sifted confectioners' sugar or cocoa powder (or sift the sugar and cocoa together for a third color). Carefully remove the doily from the cake to reveal the lacy design. To reserve the sugar or cocoa, place the used doily over a piece of waxed paper, shake the sugar or cocoa powder off, then transfer it back into its container. For special designs, make your own stencil or choose one from a crafts or fabric store. You can stencil a name, or numbers, or even a decorative border. Or use several stencils together with contrasting colors.

* *For cake frosting techniques, see* FROSTING (Frosting the Cake, page 213).

* Instead of frosting your next summertime cake, make an easy ice cream cake by removing the cake from the pan and splitting it horizontally. Return the bottom half to the pan; spread with softened ice cream. Replace the top half of the cake and finish with more ice cream. Place the cake in the freezer for about 2 hours, or until the ice cream is firm. If an ice cream cake has been frozen so long that it's hard, remove it from the freezer 20 to 30 minutes before serving. Cut into squares or wedges in the pan and top with fresh berries or a chocolate or caramel sauce.

* Make any cake company-pretty by serving it on a doily-lined plate.

* If a cake is too dry to be served as is, make a triflelike dessert by cutting it into chunks and placing it in a large bowl. Sprinkle with liqueur or fruit juice, cover with plastic wrap and let sit at room temperature for an hour or so. Then combine the cake chunks with custard or whipped cream (or a mixture of the two) and maybe some chopped fresh fruit. Spoon into stemmed glasses, cover and refrigerate for at least 3 hours before serving.

* Another remedy for cake that's too dry (or too moist) is to make crumbs out of it. Put the cake in a food processor; process until the crumbs reach the desired texture. Work in batches for more control. If the crumbs are too moist, spread them in a single layer on a baking sheet and bake at 300°F until dry. Freeze dried cake crumbs, tightly wrapped, for up to 6 months. Use as a topping for desserts like fresh fruit, ice cream or puddings. Or fold the cake crumbs into a custard or pudding, then cover and refrigerate for at least 3 hours before serving.

CUTTING

* Use a serrated knife or one with a long, thin blade. Knives will cut more easily if you soak the blade first in very hot water for a couple of minutes; dry thoroughly before using.

* If you serve a lot of cakes, invest in a cake cutter, which has long, thin metal tines attached to a handle.

* Angel-food cakes "set" and are easier to slice if you freeze them, wrapped airtight, for 24 hours. Bring to room temperature before frosting.

STORING

* Keep cakes fresh by investing in a cake cover or a covered cake carrier. Or invert a large pot or salad spinner over the cake. The more airtight the container, the longer the cake will stay moist and fresh. A couple of apple wedges placed in the container will help retain moisture.
* If you need to cover a cake with a soft frosting and don't have a cake cover, stick toothpicks to 1 inch deep at 4-inch intervals in the top and sides of the cake; lightly drape a large sheet of plastic wrap over the picks, tucking the edges under the plate.
* Unfrosted layer cakes and sponge-type cakes like chiffon and angel food can be frozen in a freezer-proof plastic bag for up to 6 months. Thaw at room temperature for 1 to 2 hours.

UPSIDE-DOWN CAKE

Almost any single-layer (8- to 9-inch) cake can be turned into an upside-down cake. Generously grease the pan, then drizzle the bottom with ⅓ cup melted butter, sprinkle evenly with ½ cup packed brown sugar and ½ teaspoon each ground cinnamon and nutmeg. Top with ½ to 1 cup chopped nuts, then add sliced fruit such as apples, peaches, plums, canned pineapple, and so on. Pour the cake batter over the fruit and bake as usual. When the cake tests done, invert it onto a serving plate. Let stand for 5 minutes before lifting off the cake pan.

CAKE 'N' ICE CREAM CONES

Fill flat-bottomed ice cream cones halfway with cake batter, set them on a baking sheet and bake until done. Reduce the baking time to about the same as for cupcakes; test doneness with a toothpick. Cool the cake cones on a rack. When ready to serve, top with a scoop of ice cream; add sprinkles, if desired.

CANDLES

* Candles will burn slower and drip less if stored in the refrigerator or freezer.
* Beeswax candles that have been stored in the refrigerator or freezer will get a dull film. Let them come to room temperature; then run them over your palm and the film will disappear.
* Soaking candles in a concentrated solution of salt water will make them almost drip-proof. Mix 2 tablespoons salt per candle with just enough water to cover. Let the candles soak for 2 to 3 hours; rinse well and dry. Wait at least a day before using so the wicks can dry.

* Use a long wooden skewer or a piece of dry spaghetti to light several candles at a time without burning your fingers.
* Lighted candles help dispel the odor of cigarette smoke.
* Clean soot marks off candles by wiping them with rubbing alcohol.
* If candles have burned unevenly, heat a sharp knife blade (use an old knife) for 2 minutes in boiling hot water. The hot blade will slice cleanly through the candle, making it like new. Carve a little hollow around the wick with the tip of the knife. Remove the wax residue from the blade by dipping the knife back into the hot water, then wash with hot, soapy water.

> *The great thing about candy is that it has no redeeming social characteristics. Its only purpose is to please.*
> —Irena Chalmers, Anglo-American wit, author, teacher

CANDY *see also* CANDYMAKING TEMPERATURES; CARAMELIZING SUGAR; SUGAR SYRUPS; THERMOMETERS

TIDBIT Candy's been around for eons, which is attested to by hieroglyphics in the Egyptian pyramids. Of course, the ancients were eating confections made of honey-sweetened dried fruits and nuts, not jellybeans and gumdrops. Today Americans consume an annual average of 23 pounds of candy per person, and candy manufacturers are racing to produce treats with less sugar and fat so we'll buy even more. Talk about the sweet life!

STORING Store in an airtight container in a cool, dry place for up to 3 weeks. Keep hard and soft candies separate to prevent sticky hard candy. Place a sheet of waxed paper or plastic wrap between candy layers to prevent them from sticking. Freeze candies like fudge and caramels, wrapped airtight, for up to a year. Thaw unopened at room temperature for about 3 hours.

EQUIPMENT
* The right candymaking equipment can spell the difference between success and failure.
* A candy THERMOMETER (*see* page 465) is indispensable for candymaking. It is an inexpensive investment for what it delivers: taking the guesswork out of candy temperatures.
* If you don't have a candy thermometer, test candy syrups using the cold-water method (*see* page 84).
* Use heavy saucepans (preferably aluminum because of their superior heat conductivity) that are the size called for in the recipe. Too small a

pan, and the candy mixture could boil over; too large a pan, and the mixture may not cover the candy thermometer's tip.

PREPARING

* Before beginning the candymaking process, gather and measure out all the ingredients and assemble the necessary equipment.

* Candy recipes are based on an exacting balance between ingredients, so follow them precisely and measure everything accurately. Only experienced candymakers should substitute ingredients.

* Doubling a candy recipe will affect the cooking time and possibly alter the candy's final quality.

* High humidity (over 60 percent) in the room in which you're cooking will affect the finished candy. On rainy days, cook the candy mixture a degree or two higher than called for in the recipe. Candies like divinity become grainy when made on a humid day. Either wait until it's dry or make something else.

COOKING

* Sugar crystallization is one of the most common candymaking problems. This can happen by stirring a mixture during boiling or, more commonly, when even a single sugar grain clinging to the side of the pan is stirred back down into the syrup. To prevent this, stir the ingredients together, then heat the mixture over low heat, without stirring, until the sugar's completely dissolved. To dissolve any sugar crystals on the side of the pan, tightly cover the pan and let the mixture cook for about 3 minutes. The steam that forms will melt the sugar crystals, which trickle down into the syrup. Or dip a natural-bristle pastry brush in hot water and wash down the sides of the pan to dissolve any clinging sugar crystals.

* To discourage crystallization in candy mixtures, many recipes call for cream of tartar, lemon juice or corn syrup.

* The microwave oven has a major advantage in candymaking, and that's the indirect heating, which minimizes overcooking or scorching. To avoid boilovers when microwaving, use a container that holds at least twice as much as the volume being cooked. Check your oven's cooking guide for full directions.

* The final temperature of a candy syrup affects how moist the finished candy will be; the lower the temperature, the softer the candy.

* If you overcook a candy syrup (such as to the hard-ball instead of the soft-ball stage), remove it from the heat and stir in ¼ cup hot water for each cup of syrup. Begin cooking the syrup again, watching the temperature carefully on a candy thermometer.

* Before beginning to make fudge, line the pan with buttered foil or plastic wrap, letting enough excess foil or wrap hang over the edges to use as "handles." Pour the fudge into the pan and cool. Use the "handles" to lift out the block of cooled fudge and cut it on a cutting board, rather than scratching the pan with the knife. It also eliminates washing the pan.
* The secret to successful fudge is in the beating. Use a wooden spoon to beat fudge from the thin, glossy stage to the stage where it becomes slightly thick. At that point, add nuts or other ingredients, then continue to beat just until the fudge begins to lose its gloss. Immediately turn the fudge into the pan and cool until firm enough to cut.
* If you've overbeaten fudge so that it's too thick to pour into the pan, use your hands to shape it into logs. Wrap the logs in plastic wrap, cool until firm, then unwrap and slice as desired.

CANDYMAKING TEMPERATURES AND COLD-WATER TESTS

If you don't have a candy thermometer, here are the tests for telling the temperature of a candy syrup. A cold-water test is performed by letting a drop or two of candy syrup fall into a glass measuring cup of very cold water.

Stage of hardness	Temperature	When a small amount of sugar syrup is dropped into very cold water it:
Thread	230° to 234°F (110° to 112°C)	Forms a soft 2-inch thread
Soft ball	234° to 240°F (112° to 116°C)	Forms a soft ball that flattens of its own accord when removed
Firm ball	244° to 248°F (118° to 120°C)	Forms a firm but pliable ball
Hard ball	250° to 265°F (121° to 129°C)	Forms a rigid ball that is still somewhat pliable
Soft crack	270° to 290°F (132° to 143°C)	Separates into hard, though pliable, threads
Hard crack	300° to 310°F (149° to 154°C)	Separates into hard, brittle threads

CANDY THERMOMETERS see THERMOMETERS

CANTALOUPE see MELONS

CAPERS

C

TIDBIT Capers are the sun-dried flower buds of a native Mediterranean bush. Commonly pickled in a vinegar brine, capers can also be found bottled in oil as well as salted and sold in bulk. Capers range in size from the tiny nonpareil variety from southern France, to the giant buds from Italy and Spain, which can be as large as the tip of your finger. There are also huge, stemmed caperberries, which are about the size of an olive.

STORING Refrigerate brine- or oil-packed capers, tightly sealed, for up to 9 months (the buds must be covered with liquid). Salt-packed capers, sealed airtight, will keep at room temperature for about 6 months.

PREPARING Oil-packed capers may be used as is. Brine- or salt-packed capers should be turned into a sieve and flushed well with cold, running water to remove excess salt. Blot well with paper towels before using.

USING

* Capers add piquancy to all manner of foods, including eggs, fish, meat, pasta, pizza, poultry, salads, sauces and vegetables. They may be sprinkled over the top of the food, used as a garnish, or chopped (if they're large) and incorporated into the dish.

* Combine capers with a little olive oil and lemon juice and spoon atop grilled, baked or broiled fish.

* Make your next tuna- or egg-salad sandwich something special by adding capers.

CARAMELIZING SUGAR *see also* CANDY; SUGAR (GRANULATED)

TIDBIT Caramelized sugar is simply a mixture of sugar and water cooked until it becomes syrupy and darkens. It's used for both sweet and savory purposes—from coating a custard mold (as for crème caramel) to enriching soups, stews and sauces. Caramelizing sugar can be done on the stovetop or in the microwave oven.

* **Caramelizing sugar on the stovetop**: You'll need a medium, heavy-bottomed pan. Choose a pan that's light-colored (such as one that's enamel-coated) or shiny so you can see the caramel turn color (impossible to do in dark pans). Combine 1⅓ cups granulated sugar and ⅛ teaspoon cream of tartar in the pan. Add ⅓ cup water, stirring well. Cook over medium-low heat, without stirring, until the mixture comes to a boil. Cover and continue cooking for 3 minutes so steam can melt any sugar crystals on the pan's sides (stirring even a speck of sugar crystal back into the cooking syrup can cause the entire mixture to crystallize). Remove the cover and continue boiling until the syrup turns a deep

golden brown color. Remove from the heat and set the pan in a larger pot or bowl of cold water to stop the cooking process.

* **Microwave caramelizing**: Combine 1 cup sugar with ⅓ cup water in a 4-cup glass measure. Cover tightly with plastic wrap, pierce the top of the wrap once with a pin. Cook on high, without stirring, as follows: soft-ball stage—5 minutes; hard-ball—6 minutes; hard-crack—7½ minutes.

* If caramelized sugar has hardened before you want it to, pop it into the microwave oven on high for 5 to 10 seconds.

> *Some guy invented Vitamin A out of a carrot.*
> *I'll bet he can't invent a good meal out of one.*
> —Will Rogers, American humorist

CARROTS   *see also* VEGETABLES, GENERAL

TIDBIT Will Rogers was right—carrots are extremely high in vitamin A. And scientists have now discovered that they also contain calcium pectate, an extraordinary pectin fiber that's been found to have cholesterol-lowering properties.

PURCHASING The best carrots are young and slender. Choose those that are firm and smooth; avoid any with cracks or signs of softening or withering. Carrot greenery should be moist and bright green. But carrot greens rob the roots of moisture and vitamins, so remove them as soon as you get home.

EQUIVALENTS

* Fresh: 1 pound, trimmed = 3 cups chopped or sliced, 2½ cups shredded, 2 cups cooked
* Frozen: 14-ounce package = 2½ cups sliced

STORING Refrigerate in a plastic bag for up to 2 weeks. As they age, carrots lose flavor and firmness. Don't store carrots near apples, which can give them a bitter taste.

PREPARING

* Some of a carrot's flavor and nutrients go down the drain when it's peeled. Unless they're very old or the peel is discolored, simply scrub carrots well and leave the peel on. A light rinsing is all that's necessary for young carrots.
* Use a vegetable peeler to remove the bitter skin from older carrots. Trim the ends before using.
* Another peeling technique is to drop carrots into boiling hot water. Let stand for 2 to 3 minutes, then plunge into a bowl of ice water. When the

carrots are cool, use your fingers to rub off the skin. This technique is particularly useful when you find yourself with lots of carrots to peel.

* The core of older carrots can be woody and bitter. To remove it, cut the carrot lengthwise in quarters, then slice out the slightly darker midsection.
* Recrisp limp carrots by soaking them in ice water for 30 minutes.

USING

* When using carrots in stir-fries and other dishes containing several foods mixed together, blanch them first (*see* BLANCHING) for a few minutes, then cool them immediately in cold water to stop the cooking. They can be dried and stored in a plastic bag in the refrigerator until you're ready to toss them in with the other foods to finish cooking.
* Shredded carrots can be added raw to myriad dishes, including stir-fries, soups, salads, and so on.
* Substitute an equal amount of cooked, puréed (*see* PURÉEING) carrots for mashed pumpkin.
* Make carrot curls (see page 225) for a fun garnish.

CASSEROLE DISHES; CASSEROLES   *see also* PAN SIZES

* Casserole dishes are measured by volume. If you're unsure of how large a dish is, fill it with water, then measure the liquid. Casserole dishes are most commonly found in the following sizes: 1, 1½, 2 and 3 quarts.
* For a crisp topping, don't cover a casserole dish during baking.
* Freeze a cooked or an uncooked casserole by lining a casserole dish with heavy-duty aluminum foil, leaving enough overhang on all sides to cover and seal the food. Add the casserole ingredients and either freeze until solid, or bake, cool to room temperature and then freeze (it's not necessary to seal the dish during the relatively short time it takes to freeze). Once the food is frozen, use the foil overhang to lift it from the dish; cover the food with the foil overhang, sealing airtight. Double wrap in a freezer-proof plastic bag, label and freeze until ready to use. Meanwhile, your casserole dish can be used for other purposes.
* To thaw a frozen casserole, remove the wrapping and place the frozen food back in the dish in which it was baked or formed.
* When reheating frozen casseroles, it's best to defrost them in the refrigerator overnight. If that isn't possible, cover and reheat in a 350°F oven, allowing almost double the baking time. To test for doneness, insert a dinner knife into the center of the food, leave for 10 seconds, then check the knife with your fingertips for heat.
* Turn any casserole into an au gratin dish by sprinkling the contents with a

topping of bread crumbs and grated cheese; butter may also be dotted over the top. After the dish is baked, the topping will be crisp and golden brown.

CATSUP   *see* KETCHUP

> *Cauliflower is nothing but cabbage with a college education.*
> —Mark Twain, American author, humorist

CAULIFLOWER   *see also* VEGETABLES, GENERAL

TIDBIT The word "cauliflower" comes from the Latin *caulis* ("stalk") and *floris* ("flower"). Though the cauliflower most commonly found in markets today is white or ivory-colored, there are also pale purple and green varieties, all equally flavorful.

PURCHASING Choose a firm cauliflower with compact florets; the leaves should be crisp with no sign of discoloration or withering. Avoid specimens with signs of yellowing or brown spots. The size of the head doesn't affect the quality.

EQUIVALENTS
* Fresh: 1 pound = 2½ to 3 cups florets, 1½ cups chopped or sliced
* Frozen: 10-ounce package = 2 cups chopped or sliced

STORING Refrigerate unwashed cauliflower, tightly wrapped, for up to a week.

PREPARING
* Wash the cauliflower thoroughly, remove the leaves at the base and trim the stem.
* Separate the cauliflower into florets, and cut the florets into several pieces to shorten cooking time.
* Once the florets are cut off, the cauliflower stems can be chopped or sliced and cooked or used raw in salads.

COOKING
* The green leaves at the base of a cauliflower head are edible. They take longer to cook and have a stronger flavor than the florets.
* Cauliflower can be cooked whole. Since the stem is denser than the florets, either remove it by cutting into and removing some of the core, or trim it and slash a ½-inch deep X in the base. Cook a whole head in 3 quarts boiling water for 20 to 30 minutes.
* Adding 2 tablespoons lemon juice, 1 tablespoon vinegar or 1 cup milk to the cooking water will keep cauliflower white. Do this whether completely cooking the cauliflower, or simply BLANCHING the vegetable for use as crudités.

* Cooking cauliflower florets in milk will not only turn them as white as possible, but will also sweeten their flavor. The flavored milk can be used for soups or sauces.

* Cook cauliflower only until crisp-tender. Overcooking will turn the texture mushy and the flavor strong; it'll also stink up the house.

* If you mistakenly overcook cauliflower, use a blender or food processor to turn it into a PURÉE. Add butter and plenty of freshly ground pepper, and you've created a delicious side dish.

* Dispel cauliflower's smell during cooking by tossing a couple of thick chunks of bread into the cooking water. Bread slices work, too, though they sometimes dissolve and are hard to remove. Or toss a couple of red bell pepper pieces into the pot. Use a slotted spoon to retrieve the pot sweeteners before serving the cauliflower.

> *There is more simplicity in the man who eats caviar on impulse than in the man who eats Grapenuts on principle.*
> —G. K. Chesterton, English poet, essayist

CAVIAR

TIDBIT For many people, caviar is the ultimate indulgence, while for others it's nothing but a mouthful of fish eggs. If you're a neophyte at the caviar game and haven't made up your mind yet, the following terms should help you out. The most prized (and costliest) caviar is **beluga**, from the beluga sturgeon that swims in the Caspian Sea. Its soft, extremely large (pea-sized) eggs can range in color from pale silver-gray to black. **Osetra** caviar (medium-sized, gray to brownish gray) and the smaller gray **sevruga** are next in quality. Other popular (and much less expensive) types of caviar include **whitefish, lumpfish** and **salmon** (also called *red caviar*). **Pressed caviar** is fresh caviar comprised of damaged or fragile eggs and can be a combination of several different roes. **Pasteurized caviar** is roe that's been partially cooked.

PURCHASING Fresh caviar is extremely perishable. Buy only as much as you need and keep it cool in an insulated bag on the way home from the market. Fish eggs should have a fresh, briny smell and be firm, shiny and separate. The label term **malossol** (Russian for "little salt") indicates that minimum salt was used in processing, which means the caviar is more perishable.

STORING

* Fresh caviar: Refrigerate, unopened, for up to a month. The ideal storage temperature is about 28°F, which is much cooler than a home refrig-

erator. To achieve this: Pack the caviar container in a plastic bag filled with ice. Place the bag in a large bowl (in case it leaks); store in the coldest part of the refrigerator. Drain the melted water and replenish the ice as necessary. Once opened, cover and refrigerate the caviar for no more than 3 days.

* Pasteurized caviar: Store at room temperature until opened. After opening, refrigerate and consume within 3 days.

SERVING

* Serve caviar very cold, preferably in a bowl surrounded by ice. Present it with toast points and lemon wedges. Minced onion, sour cream and hard-cooked egg whites and yolks are customary, but purists think unnecessary, garnishes.

* Champagne and iced vodka are the traditional potables served with caviar.

* Caviar has long been touted as a hangover cure due to its inherent acetylcholine content, which is linked to increased alcohol tolerance.

COOKING Caviar's flavor and texture are greatly diminished by cooking, so add it to a hot dish just before serving, stirring gently to keep the eggs from breaking and turning mushy.

CAYENNE *see* PEPPER

CELERIAC *see* CELERY ROOT

CELERY *see also* VEGETABLES, GENERAL
TIDBIT Did you know that chewing celery burns up more calories than it contains? Plus it's a good source of vitamins A, C and E, and is loaded with fiber. No wonder it's so popular with dieters.
PURCHASING Choose a firm bunch of celery that is tightly formed. The leaves should be green and crisp, not yellowing or wilted.
EQUIVALENT 2 medium ribs, trimmed = about ½ cup chopped
STORING Refrigerate in a plastic bag for up to 10 days.
PREPARING

* Leave the ribs attached to the base until ready to use. Wash the celery and trim the base and leaves just before using.

* Celery leaves are wonderful in soups, salads and stuffings, and also make an attractive garnish.

* To "string" tough ribs, snap a ½-inch length at the top so it's still hanging on, then pull the piece down the length of the rib. The strings will pull right off.

* Revive limp celery by soaking trimmed ribs in a bowl of ice water for at least 1 hour. Add 2 tablespoons fresh lemon juice to perk up the flavor.
* Make celery brushes (page 224) for a showy garnish.

COOKING
* Celery can be braised, steamed or boiled, and none of these methods takes long. Cook the celery just until crisp-tender or it will become unappealingly limp.
* Add chopped celery to soup in the last 10 minutes of cooking so it retains some of its crunchy texture.

CELERY ROOT *see also* VEGETABLES, GENERAL

TIDBIT Also called *celeriac*, celery root is a knobby, brown root vegetable with an ivory-white interior. It tastes like a cross between parsley and strong celery.

PURCHASING Choose a relatively small, firm celery root with a minimum of knobs and rootlets. Avoid those with soft spots, which signal decay. Any green leaves still attached to the root are inedible.

EQUIVALENT 1 pound, trimmed and peeled = about 2½ cups chopped

STORING Refrigerate in a plastic bag for up to a week.

PREPARING Wash, trim and peel just before using. To prevent darkening, soak celery root for 15 minutes in ACIDULATED WATER.

USING
* Raw celery root is wonderful grated or shredded and used in salads.
* This vegetable can be boiled, braised, sautéed, baked or cooked in soups. It's also great cooked and puréed (*see* PURÉEING).

CELLOPHANE NOODLES *see also* PASTA

TIDBIT Also called *bean threads, Chinese vermicelli* and *glass noodles*, these translucent threads are made from the starch of green mung beans.

PURCHASING Available in Asian markets and the ethnic section of many supermarkets.

STORING Dried noodles should be stored airtight in a cool, dry place for up to 6 months. Leftover deep-fried noodles can be stored in an airtight plastic bag at room temperature for up to 3 days.

COOKING
* Cellophane noodles are an almost-instant food. To use them in stir-fries or other cooked dishes, simply soak them in very hot water for about 30 seconds, then drain thoroughly.
* No presoaking's necessary when these noodles are used in soups. Just add them at the last minute and cook only until soft, about 30 seconds.

C

* When dried cellophane noodles are deep-fried, they explode into puffy, gossamer strands in a mere 2 or 3 seconds. These crispy threads are used in many Chinese chicken salad recipes.

CELSIUS *see* TEMPERATURES—FAHRENHEIT AND CELSIUS

CENTIGRADE *see* TEMPERATURES—FAHRENHEIT AND CELSIUS

Champagne, if you are seeking the truth, is better than a lie detector.
—Graham Greene, English novelist

CHAMPAGNE *see also* BEER; COCKTAILS; LIQUORS AND LIQUEURS; WINE
TIDBIT Although the term "champagne" is commonly used by consumers for a variety of sparkling wines, true Champagne comes only from the Champagne region in northeast France (other French regions call their sparklers *vins mousseux*). Most countries bow to this tradition by calling their bubblies by other names, including *spumante* in Italy, *Sekt* in Germany, or simply "sparkling wine." Although it's legal to use the term "champagne" in the United States, most top-quality producers of sparkling wines label them *méthode champenoise*, indicating that the wine was made by the French method. Seventeenth-century Abbey of Hautvillers cellarmaster Dom Perignon is credited both with developing the art of blending wines to create superior champagnes and with using thicker bottles and tie-down corks to help retain their explosive pressure.
PURCHASING Champagne label terms: In wine parlance, the term "dry" (*sec* in French) describes a wine that isn't sweet. The levels of sweetness are: **brut**—bone-dry to almost dry, less than 1.5 percent sugar; **extra sec** or **extra dry**—slightly sweeter, 1.2 to 2 percent sugar; **sec**—medium sweet, 1.7 to 3.5 percent sugar; **demi-sec**—sweet, 3.3 to 5 percent sugar; **doux**—very sweet, over 5 percent sugar. *Méthode champenoise* on the label tells you that the wine has undergone a second fermentation in the bottle, typically signaling a superior sparkling wine.
EQUIVALENTS
* 750-milliliter bottle = 25.4 ounces
* magnum = 50.7 ounces
* double magnum = 101.5 ounces
CHILLING
* Champagne and other sparkling wines should be served quite chilled, from 40° to 50°F, depending on the quality. Since cold mutes flavors, the

cheaper the sparkler, the colder you want it. On the other hand, the complexity and subtle flavors of vintage champagnes are showcased at about 50°F.

* Refrigerate champagne for only about 2 hours before serving. Extensive chilling can dull both flavor and bouquet.

* Speed-chill champagne in about 20 minutes by completely submerging the bottle in a bucket filled with half ice and half water, which chills the wine much faster than ice alone. If the bucket is shallow, invert the bottle for the last 5 minutes to make sure all the wine is chilled.

OPENING

* If champagne is properly chilled and handled, the cork should release from the bottle with a muted "poof," rather than a loud "pop." The wine should never explode out of the bottle when the cork's removed. It's a good idea, however, to have a glass standing by just in case.

* To open champagne, begin by removing the foil, which often has a "zipper," or perforation, to facilitate detachment. Untwist and remove the wire cage that encloses the cork. Hold the bottle at a 45-degree angle, making sure the cork isn't pointed at anyone. With your fingers over the cork to keep it from ejecting prematurely, gently rotate the bottle (not the cork) with your other hand. As you feel the cork begin to loosen and lift, use your thumb to gently ease it from the bottle.

SERVING

* Serve sparkling wines in slender champagne glasses called "flutes," which provide less surface from which the bubbles can escape. You'll also get more of the wine's bouquet from a flute. The old-fashioned shallow, wide-brimmed champagne glass allows both bubbles and bouquet to disperse twice as fast.

* Soap film or dust on a glass will destroy champagne's effervescence.

* It's cheating, but if you want maximum bubbles in your champagne, use a sharp, pointed knife to etch an X in the bottom of the flute.

* To keep the sparkle in leftover champagne, invest in a metal champagne stopper, available at wine stores, kitchenware shops and many supermarkets.

If you're given champagne at lunch, there's a catch somewhere.
—Lord Lyons, British aristocrat

CHAMBORD ROYALE
Chambord is a liqueur with an intense black raspberry flavor. Pour ¼ to ½ teaspoon Chambord into a champagne flute. Slowly add about 4 ounces cold

Champagne or other sparkling wine; don't stir. Drop a fresh raspberry into the glass. Serves 1.

CHARD *see* GREENS

> *It is a bit of a mystery why so many aspiring American hosts—gourmet and otherwise—came to think of mass quantities of cheese before dinner as an appropriate hors d'oeuvre; but cheese for dessert was strictly for the sophisticated set.*
> —Jane and Michael Stern, American authors

CHEESE

TIDBIT There are two broad categories of natural cheese—fresh (such as cottage cheese and cream cheese) and ripened (such as Cheddar, Swiss and Brie). **Fresh (unripened) cheeses** are made by allowing milk to thicken (sometimes with the aid of rennin or bacteria) until it separates into curds and whey (semisolids and liquid). The whey is drained off, leaving the curds which, depending on the variety of cheese, may be pressed into shapes. **Ripened cheeses** are cured by various processes, including heat or friendly bacteria. Some are flavored and others, like many Cheddars, are colored with natural dyes. After curing, natural cheese begins a ripening process at a controlled temperature and humidity until the desired result is obtained. **Processed cheeses** have been pasteurized for added storage life, combined with emulsifiers for smoothness, and mixed with colorings and preservatives. The reason processed cheese lacks the distinctive flavor and texture of natural cheese is that United States government standards require that only 51 percent of a processed cheese's final weight actually be *cheese*. Products labeled "cheese spread" or "cheese food" contain added liquid for a softer, more spreadable mixture. Processed cheese should definitely not be paired with fine food and drink.

RIPENED CHEESES (*see also* Fresh Cheeses, page 97)

TIDBIT Ripened cheeses are classified according to texture: firm (also called "hard")—like Parmesan and pecorino; semifirm—like Cheddar, Edam and Swiss; semisoft—like Gouda, Monterey Jack and Tilsit; and soft-ripened—like blue cheese, Brie and Roquefort.

PURCHASING

* Semifirm or semisoft packaged cheese (like Cheddar and Monterey Jack): Check the wrapping to be sure it's not torn. Inspect the cheese for signs of mold or cracked or dry edges. Check the package for a "sell by"

date to make sure you're not getting a product that should have been pulled from the shelf.

* Firm or hard cheeses (like Parmesan and Romano): The color should be even from the outer edge to the center. Uneven coloration and cracking are signs that the cheese is beginning to dry out.
* Soft-ripened cheeses (such as Brie and Camembert): When ripe, the texture throughout will be soft and creamy. Look for rounds no more than 1 inch thick; thicker than that and they can get overripe on the edges before ripening in the center.

EQUIVALENTS

* Firm, semifirm or semisoft cheese: 4 ounces (¼ pound) = about 1 cup grated
* Soft-ripened cheese: 4 ounces = about 1 cup crumbled

STORING

* Firm, semifirm or semisoft cheeses: Wrap airtight in a plastic bag or foil; store in the refrigerator's cheese compartment (or the warmest location). Most will keep for several weeks. For longer storage, dampen a sheet of paper towel with cider vinegar and wrap it around the cheese, then put inside a plastic bag and seal. Check the paper towel every couple of days and remoisten, if necessary. The vinegar will inhibit the growth of mold. Rubbing cheese with vegetable oil before wrapping and refrigerating helps keep it from drying out. Cover cheeses like feta and chèvre with oil and refrigerate.
* Soft-ripened cheeses: Bring to perfect, creamy-thick ripeness by storing, tightly wrapped, at a cool room temperature for a day or two. Once the cheese has ripened, tightly wrap and refrigerate; bring to room temperature before serving.
* Freezing causes most cheese to undergo a textural change. Harder cheeses will turn crumbly, while softer ones might separate slightly. Such changes won't be noticeable if you use the cheese in cooked dishes. To freeze, double wrap and place firm and semifirm cheeses in the freezer for up to 6 months, soft and semisoft for up to 4 months. Thaw in the refrigerator and use within a few days of defrosting.

PREPARING

* To remove the white rind of soft-ripened cheese (like Camembert), chill the cheese and use a sharp knife to cut away the rind. Or soften the cheese at room temperature, then use a spoon to scoop it out of the rind.
* The natural, downy-white rind of soft-ripened cheeses is edible—leave it on when serving such cheeses as an appetizer or for dessert. The excep-

tion is when serving the cheeses with wine—the salt concentration and slight ammonia compound in the rind will kill the flavor of most wines.

* Use a fork to crumble blue cheeses like Roquefort into large or small chunks.

* Leave rinds on hard cheeses during storage. When ready to use, cut away the rind and slice cheese as desired. Hard cheeses are easier to slice at room temperature.

* Quickly bring a chunk of cheese to room temperature by heating it in the microwave oven at medium (50 percent power) for about 1 minute.

* If a little mold appears on the surface of a hard or semifirm cheese, simply use a sharp knife to carve away the bad spots, plus a little extra for insurance.

* Use a vegetable peeler to shave off thin shavings or slivers of cheese for salads and garnishes.

* Soft cheeses like Muenster and fresh mozzarella are hard to slice. An easy method is to place a chunk in an egg slicer, then slowly bring the cutting wires down and through the cheese.

* Cut a log of goat cheese into slices with a thin-bladed knife that has been heated in a glass of hot water. Wipe off the knife and reheat as necessary. Or wrap a long piece of strong thread or unflavored dental floss around the goat-cheese log, cross the ends and slowly pull the ends together.

* For maximum flavor, let cheese sit out at room temperature for 30 to 60 minutes (depending on how warm the room is) before serving.

* Cheeses like Cheddar, Swiss and Monterey Jack are easier to grate—either by hand or in the food processor—when cold. On the other hand, hard cheeses like Parmesan and Romano are easier to handle if they're at room temperature.

* For food-processor grating, use the steel blade for hard cheeses like Parmesan, the shredding disk for cheeses like Cheddar and Jack. Cut the cheese to be chopped into 1-inch chunks—larger pieces can jam the blade. Spray the metal blade or grating disk with cooking spray and cleanup will be a breeze. When working with softer cheeses like Muenster, spray the inside of the workbowl and lid as well.

* A box grater with large holes does a good job of grating semisoft cheeses like Monterey Jack. Spray the grater with cooking spray to keep the cheese from sticking and to facilitate cleanup.

* Grate a large chunk of hard cheese like Parmesan, then refrigerate it in an airtight container to have on hand when needed.

* Use a citrus zester to shred small amounts of hard cheeses.

* Firm and semifirm cheeses can be grated ahead of time and refrigerated in a plastic bag until ready to use.

* If grated cheese sticks together, simply break up the pieces with your fingers.

* Use the red wax rind of Edam cheese as a decorative container for dips or spreads. Simply cut off the top inch, then use a spoon to scoop out most of the cheese, leaving a ¼-inch shell. Room-temperature cheese is easier to remove from the shell; it will also blend more readily with other ingredients for a dip or spread.

COOKING WITH CHEESE

* Chunks of room-temperature Brie or Camembert (rind removed) are wonderful tossed with pasta. The cheese melts quickly and deliciously coats the pasta.

* Cheese can turn stringy, rubbery or grainy when exposed to high heat. Avoid this problem by shredding or cutting the cheese into small pieces; add it to a sauce or other mixture toward the end of the cooking process. Cook over low heat, stirring constantly, only until the cheese melts.

* To avoid overheating a cheese sauce and turning it grainy, cook it in the top of a double boiler over simmering water. Make sure that the bottom of the top pan doesn't touch the water.

* To rescue overcooked cheese that has become a rubbery mass, cut it into medium pieces and process in a blender until smooth, adding a little cream, if necessary. If the rubbery cheese is part of a sauce, include some of the sauce liquid in the blender. Return the cheese to the pan and cook, stirring constantly, over very low heat until it's melted and smooth.

* Low-calorie cheeses contain less fat and therefore don't melt as well as regular cheese.

* Though not nearly as flavorful as natural cheeses, processed cheeses melt more easily and with fewer problems because they contain emulsifiers.

Age is not important unless you are a cheese.
—Helen Hayes, American actor (in the play *New Woman*)

FRESH CHEESES   (cottage cheese, cream cheese, pot cheese and ricotta)
PURCHASING

* Fresh cheese is highly perishable, so buy it at a market with a rapid turnover. Check the date on the container to make sure you're buying the freshest cheese available.

* Cottage cheese: There are several forms, including **creamed** (4 to 8 percent milk fat), **low-fat** (1 to 2 percent fat) and **nonfat**. The curd size can be small, medium or large.

* Cream cheese: The styles include **regular**—about 33 percent milk fat, **Neufchâtel**—about 23 percent milk fat, **light or low-fat cream cheese**—about half the calories as the regular version, **whipped cream cheese**—regular cream cheese made soft and spreadable by whipping, and **nonfat cream cheese**—with zero fat grams.

EQUIVALENTS

* Cottage, pot or ricotta cheese: 16 ounces = 2 cups
* Cream cheese: 8 ounces = 1 cup; 3 ounces = 6 tablespoons

STORING

* Cottage cheese: Store in its container in the coldest part of the refrigerator for up to a week. Turn the tightly sealed container upside down and it'll stay fresh longer.
* Cream cheese: Store in its original wrapping in the coldest part of the refrigerator. After opening, rewrap airtight and use within a week.

PREPARING

* To speed-soften cream cheese in the microwave oven, remove it from the foil package and place, uncovered, on a microwave-safe plate. For 8 ounces, cook at medium (50 percent power) for about 1 minute; 3 ounces for about 30 seconds. Let stand for 1 minute before using.
* If mold shows up on soft cheeses like cream cheese or cottage cheese, throw them out! There's no way they can be salvaged.

USING

* It's true that cream cheese has about half the calories of an equal amount of butter or margarine. Just don't forget to spread the cream cheese almost as thinly as you do butter or you'll wind up with more calories than you want.
* Low-fat cottage cheese makes a tasty topping for baked potatoes. Slit a baked potato, spoon in the cottage cheese and microwave on high for about 1 minute.

Sesame Schmear

Great on everything from bagels to pancakes. Combine one 8-ounce package softened cream cheese, ½ cup coarsely ground toasted sesame seeds, 1 to 2 tablespoons honey and a pinch of salt in a medium bowl.

> *A cheese may disappoint. It may be dull, it may be naive, it may be over-sophisticated. Yet it remains cheese, milk's leap toward immortality.*
> —Clifton Fadiman, American author

CHEESECAKE see also CHEESE; CRUMBS, GENERAL; PIE CRUSTS

TIDBIT Cheesecakes require a delicate balance of ingredients, particularly eggs, cheese and liquid. Don't make any major substitutions or the finished product may be drastically altered.

CRUST

* **To keep a pastry crust from becoming soggy,** brush it lightly with well-beaten egg white to seal the surface. Refrigerate for 15 minutes before filling and baking.
* When making a crumb crust, form a "skirt" of aluminum foil around the outside bottom of the springform pan to prevent any fat in the crust from leaking out.
* Prebaking a crumb crust for 10 minutes at 350°F helps keep it crisp. Completely cool a prebaked crust before filling.
* Seal a prebaked crumb or pastry crust by using the back of a dinner teaspoon to spread 2 to 3 ounces of melted, semisweet chocolate over the crust, to within ¼ inch of the outside edge. Put the coated crust in the refrigerator for about 10 minutes to set the chocolate before filling with the cheesecake mixture.

FILLING

* Before mixing the filling, position the oven rack in the middle of the oven; preheat the oven 15 minutes. Use an oven THERMOMETER for accurate temperature.
* It's essential to use the size pan specified in the recipe.
* Add and blend cheesecake ingredients in the precise order given.
* The cheese must be at room temperature in order for it to blend smoothly with other ingredients.
* Beat cream cheese until light and fluffy before blending in the other ingredients.
* Ricotta and cottage cheese should be beaten or processed in a blender until completely smooth before the remaining ingredients are added. Otherwise, your cheesecake could have a grainy texture.
* Once the cheese is beaten until smooth, add the other ingredients slowly, beating or stirring gently. Beating too much air into the filling at this stage could cause the cheesecake to puff up beautifully during baking, then fall drastically while cooling. This creates cracking and a dense cheesecake.
* Egg whites must be at room temperature in order to reach full volume when beaten.
* Beat all ingredients together until very smooth before gently folding in stiffly beaten egg whites (in baked cheesecakes) or whipped cream (in unbaked cheesecakes).

* Convert a plain dessert cheesecake to a savory cheesecake by omitting the sugar and adding various herbs or spices like ground cumin, chili powder or minced fresh herbs. For the crust, use cracker instead of cookie crumbs.

BAKING

* Cheesecakes require even heat in order to rise properly. For this reason, it's important not to open the oven door during the first 30 minutes of baking time.
* Cracks are a common problem for which there are several reasons. Drafts caused by opening the oven during the first half hour, and cooling a cheesecake too fast are two causes. Another is moisture evaporation—if too much is lost, or if it dissipates too quickly, surface cracking will occur. To alleviate this problem, increase the oven's humidity by placing a shallow pan of hot water on the bottom shelf before beginning to preheat.
* Partially cooling a cheesecake in the oven, with the oven door ajar, helps prevent cracks in the top of the cheesecake.
* Some delicate, custard-style cheesecakes are baked in a "water bath," which simply means that the cheesecake pan is immersed halfway in another pan filled with hot water. The water acts as insulation and diffuses the oven heat so the mixture will set without separating. Although solid pans are suggested for use with water baths, springform pans may be used if heavy-duty foil is firmly pressed over the outside of the pan to prevent leakage.
* Cheesecakes baked in a very slow oven for a longer period of time will shrink less when cooled.
* To allow for variations in ovens, test cheesecake 5 to 10 minutes before the minimum time indicated in a recipe.
* Don't worry if your cheesecake's center is slightly jiggly or soft—it will firm up as the cheesecake cools.
* Concentric cracking and/or an overbrowned top indicate either the oven heat was too high or the cheesecake was baked too long.

COOLING AND FINISHING

* Set a baked cheesecake on a rack to cool. After 30 minutes, run a thin-bladed knife between cheesecake and pan to loosen. Continue cooling until room temperature.
* Leave the cooled cheesecake in its pan, cover tightly and refrigerate overnight or at least 6 hours before serving. This allows the cheesecake to set and will make it easier to cut; it also makes the texture creamier.
* Cracks do not ruin a cheesecake! Disguise any scars with a topping such

as slightly sweetened sour cream or whipped cream, fresh berries, your favorite jam (stir until easily spreadable, or stir in 1 tablespoon liqueur). Let any filling sink into the cracks for a few minutes, then add more if necessary so the surface is even.

CHEESECLOTH

PURCHASING Cheesecloth is a lightweight natural cotton cloth that won't fall apart when wet or flavor the food it touches. It comes in both fine and coarse weaves, the latter commonly available in supermarkets. There are also cheesecloth bags, which are perfect for poaching large foods like whole fish. The bags and fine-weave cheesecloth will more likely be found in kitchenware stores.

USING

* Cheesecloth has many uses, including bundling herbs and spices (*see* BOUQUET GARNI) to season soups and stews; forming a self-basting cover for chicken and poultry (*see* POULTRY); wrapping baked goods like fruit-cakes and soaking with alcohol; wrapping whole fish so they don't fall apart during poaching; lining molds (such as for coeur à la crème); wrapping around a lemon half to squeeze out seedless juice; and straining soups or sauces.

* Out of cheesecloth? Use a clean piece of nylon stocking as a strainer for soups and other liquid mixtures.

> *If Life Is a Bowl of Cherries, What Am I Doing in the Pits?*
> —Erma Bombeck, American humorist, author (book title)

CHERRIES   *see also* FRUIT, GENERAL

TIDBIT Cherries, which date back at least to 300 B.C., were named after the Turkish town of Cerasus. There are two main groups of cherries—sweet and tart. The larger of the two are firm, heart-shaped sweet cherries, which range from the dark red to purplish black Bing, Lambert and Tartarian to the golden, red-blushed Royal Ann cherries. The smaller, softer sour cherry varieties include Early Richmond, Montmorency and English Morello. Sour cherries are usually too tart to be eaten fresh, but make excellent pies and other baked goods. They're seldom found fresh in markets, but are widely available canned.

PURCHASING Choose brightly colored, shiny, plump fruit. Sweet cherries should be quite firm, but not hard. Sour varieties should be medium-firm. Stemmed cherries are a better buy, but those with stems last longer.

EQUIVALENTS

* Fresh: 1 pound = 2½ to 3 cups pitted
* Frozen: 10-ounce package = 1½ cups
* Canned: 16-ounce can = 1½ cups drained

STORING Refrigerate unwashed cherries in a plastic bag for up to 5 days. Freeze cherries—pitted or not—for up to a year. Rinse and dry them before storing in freezer bags. Seal all but about ½ inch of the bag, then insert a straw into the opening and suck out as much air as possible; remove the straw and quickly zip up the opening. The less air in the bag, the better the cherries will keep. Thaw overnight in the fridge or for 30 minutes at room temperature.

PREPARING

* Wash and stem the cherries just before using. Pit them from the stem end with a cherry pitter, clean needle-nose pliers, the tip of a vegetable peeler or a pointed knife. Or poke a plastic drinking straw through the cherry from the bottom to the stem end.
* Dried sour or sweet cherries—available in most supermarkets—can be used as you would raisins in cookies, cakes, breads, sauces, desserts, and so on. If desired, rehydrate the cherries by covering them with boiling hot water or liqueur and letting them stand for about 30 minutes.
* Canned pie cherries are usually not as red as nature intended, due to their processing. Add a drop or two of red food coloring to a cherry pie or cobbler mixture to help bring back nature's blush.
* Pure almond extract makes magic in baked cherry desserts. Just a little bit—⅛ to ¼ teaspoon—makes cherries taste more like cherries.

CHOCOLATE-COVERED CHERRIES

Wash and thoroughly dry big, sweet cherries with stems. Make sure they're thoroughly dry—the slightest bit of moisture will cause the chocolate to seize up. Dip the cherries in melted chocolate; set them 1 inch apart on a waxed paper–lined baking sheet. Refrigerate until the chocolate is set.

BRANDIED CHERRIES

Combine 2 cups pitted, whole sweet cherries with ½ cup each brandy and sugar in a medium saucepan. Cook over low heat, stirring often, for about 5 minutes, or until the cherries begin to soften. Cool until slightly warm; spoon cherries and sauce over vanilla ice cream. Makes about 2 cups.

CHESTNUTS *For general purchase, storage, toasting and usage information, see* NUTS, GENERAL

TIDBIT Chestnut trees were said to be copious on the summit of Mount Olympus, which legend tells us was the home of the Greek gods.

PURCHASING Fresh, unshelled chestnuts are in season from September through February. Choose firm, plump nuts without shell blemishes. Chestnuts can also be found canned—whole, in pieces, or as a purée. Prepared chestnuts are sold unsweetened or sweetened, as in marrons glacés. Dried chestnuts can be found in ethnic markets.

EQUIVALENTS
* In shell: 1 pound = 2½ cups shelled
* Shelled, peeled and cooked: 1 pound = about 1 cup purée
* Dried chestnuts: 3 ounces = 1 cup fresh

STORING Refrigerate fresh chestnuts in a plastic bag for up to 2 weeks; freeze for up to 4 months.

PREPARING
* Chestnuts have a dark, leathery shell and a brown skin, both of which must be removed before eating (the skin usually comes off with the shell).
* Heating chestnuts facilitates shelling and peeling. The nuts can either be heated, then peeled and cooked as directed in a recipe, or they can be cooked until tender and then peeled. Before doing either, use the point of a paring knife to slash an X on the flat side of each nut, being sure to cut through the skin.
* **Stovetop peeling method:** Place the nuts in a saucepan, cover with cold water and bring to a boil. If you just want to peel the nuts, cook for 4 minutes, then remove them from the heat and peel. To cook chestnuts until tender, cover and simmer for 20 to 30 minutes (depending on the size of the nuts). Chestnuts are done if they're tender when pierced with the tip of a knife.
* **Oven peeling method:** Bake in a single layer at 425°F for 10 to 15 minutes.
* To oven-*roast* chestnuts until tender: Bake in a single layer at 425°F for 15 to 25 minutes, stirring occasionally.
* Peel chestnuts while they're still warm. If they cool so much that the shell won't come off easily, reheat them briefly.
* Rehydrate dried chestnuts by covering them with boiling water, bringing the water to a boil again, then simmering for about 1½ hours, or until tender.

*. . . like bread, potatoes and rice, chicken may be eaten
constantly without becoming nauseating.*
—André Simon, French gastronome

CHICKEN *For general information on buying, storing and testing for doneness, see* POULTRY. *See also* CORNISH GAME HENS; ROASTING

TIDBIT Three ounces of cooked, skinless white meat contains, 147 calories, 4 grams fat and 72 milligrams cholesterol; the same amount of dark meat has 174 calories, 8 grams fat and 79 milligrams cholesterol.

EQUIVALENTS

* Whole chicken = about 1 cup cooked meat per pound
* ¾ pound skinned, boned chicken breast = about 2 cups cooked

PREPARING

* How much per serving: Bone-in—about ½ pound; boneless—¼ to ⅓ pound.
* Reduce shrinkage in boneless chicken breasts by removing the clearly visible white tendon.
* To form chicken cutlets, cut halved breasts in half horizontally. To pound that cutlet into an even thickness, place the chicken between two layers of plastic wrap and use a meat pounder or a small, heavy pan to flatten it.
* If you're watching calories, fat and/or cholesterol, remove the skin and pockets of fat.
* Help tenderize an older chicken by marinating it overnight in the refrigerator.
* Add flavor by rubbing chicken all over with a paste of minced, fresh herbs (tarragon is a classic), garlic and extra virgin olive oil. If you don't have fresh herbs, soak 1 to 2 teaspoons dried herbs in twice as much wine or water for 30 minutes. Add a little oil, then rub the mixture all over the chicken.
* When stuffing a chicken, count on about ¾ cup stuffing per pound (see STUFFING).
* For broiled chicken, blot the surface with a paper towel to remove excess moisture. Trim all excess fat and remove the skin to reduce flare-ups.
* Rubbing mayonnaise all over the skin produces a crisp, deep golden brown roasted chicken. One caveat: It won't work with low- or nonfat mayo.
* To help fried-chicken coating stick, dip the meat into a mixture of egg and a little milk beaten together.
* Toss the egg- and milk-coated chicken pieces in a plastic or paper bag filled with crumbs or seasoned flour and shake until they're well coated.
* The coating will stick better if you refrigerate the coated chicken, uncovered, for 30 to 60 minutes before cooking.

* For supercrispy fried chicken, use half flour and half cornstarch instead of flour only. Add ½ teaspoon baking powder to the flour/cornstarch mixture and season as desired.
* Sneak a little fiber into the coating of fried or oven-fried chicken by using oat bran mixed with your favorite seasonings.
* Cracker or unsweetened cereal (like bran, corn or wheat flakes) crumbs also make a nice coating for fried chicken.

COOKING

* As with any poultry, the younger the chicken, the more tender it is. Older birds, however, have more flavor. Younger chickens (broilers, capons, fryers, roasters and Cornish game hens) can be cooked with dry-heat methods such as BAKING, FRYING, GRILLING, ROASTING and SAUTÉING. For older birds—like hens and baking and stewing chickens—use moist-heat methods such as braising and stewing.
* For a dry, crispy fried-chicken coating, fry chicken pieces only until nicely browned, then finish cooking in a 350°F oven.
* Brown chicken over medium heat. High heat can cause the outside meat to turn stringy.
* Get a head start on grilling whole chickens by partially cooking them in the microwave while the coals preheat. *Immediately* transfer the partially cooked chicken to the grill.
* Chicken halves should be placed farther away from the broiler's heat source to prevent burning the top before the insides are done.
* **To roast a 3- to 4-pound chicken,** brush with oil or melted butter, then salt and pepper to taste. Don't bother trussing the bird. Roast on a rack in a preheated roasting pan, breast side down, in a 375°F oven for 25 minutes. Flip the bird, roast another 25 to 35 minutes until a meat THERMOMETER inserted in the thigh registers 165° to 170°F. Let the chicken stand 15 minutes for the juices to redistribute.
* If boiling chicken specifically to use in a casserole, salad or other dish, cook it three-quarters through, then turn off the heat and cover the pan. Let the chicken rest in its cooking liquid for 1 hour before cooling and cutting into pieces. This rest period produces a juicier bird with a tender texture.
* **Doneness test:** Both under- and overcooking produce a tough chicken. Test for doneness by inserting a THERMOMETER into the thickest (innermost) part of the thigh—it should register 175°F, the breast (at the thickest part) should be 160° to 165°F. If the bird is stuffed, the center of the stuffing should read 165°F.
* When the thermometer registers about three degrees below the desired

temperature, remove the chicken from the oven. Residual heat will continue to cook it.

* No thermometer? Pierce the chicken with a fork—the juices should run clear, not pink. The meat should be fork-tender, the leg move easily in the joint.

* To render chicken fat for use in cooking, place the pieces of fat in the top of a double boiler over simmering water. Cook until the fat liquefies; strain into an airtight jar and refrigerate.

CHIFFONADE see GARNISHING AND GARNISHES

So I popped [a jalapeño] into my mouth and chomped down. As my teeth met I had a spiritual experience. Every cell in my body flipped over, tucked in, and said "Yaaah!" Tears gushed from my eyes, sweat exploded all over me tip to toe, I couldn't speak. . . . I think I was with the angels.
—Richard Atcheson, American writer

CHILES; CHILE PEPPERS see also BELL PEPPERS; CHILI

TIDBIT A chile's seeds and membranes can contain up to 80 percent of its capsaicin, the potent compound that gives some chiles their fiery nature. Since neither cooking nor freezing diminishes capsaicin's intensity, removing a chile's seeds and veins is the only way to reduce its heat.

PURCHASING

* As a general rule, the larger the chile, the milder it is. Small chiles are much hotter because, proportionally, they contain more seeds and veins than larger varieties.

* **Fresh chiles** should be firm, have a shiny, smooth skin and be heavy for their size. Avoid shriveled examples with soft spots. Popular dried chiles include: **Mild to medium**—Anaheim, chawa, chilaca, Hungarian cherry, New Mexico and poblano; **medium to hot**—habanero, jalapeño, Jamaican hot, Scotch bonnet, serrano, Tabasco and Thai.

* **Dried chiles** should have a rich (not dusty), uniform color, unbroken skins and a slight flexibility. Don't buy those with skin blemishes. Popular dried chiles include: **Mild to medium**—ancho, guajillo, mulatto, New Mexico and pasilla; **medium to hot**—cayenne, chipotle, de árbol, habanero and pequín.

* **Canned chiles**. The two most popular are jalapeño (whole, sliced and chopped) and chipotle chiles (typically packed in adobo sauce).

STORING

* Fresh chiles: Refrigerate in a plastic bag for up to 2 weeks.

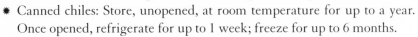

* Dried chiles: Store airtight in a cool, dark place for up to 6 months.
* Canned chiles: Store, unopened, at room temperature for up to a year. Once opened, refrigerate for up to 1 week; freeze for up to 6 months.

PREPARING FRESH CHILES

* Wash chiles thoroughly before cutting. Caution is the byword when working with chiles because the seeds and membranes contain oils that can severely irritate skin and eyes. Once the chile is cut open, don't touch your mouth, nose or eyes.
* The surest way to keep the irritating oil off your hands is to wear rubber or disposable latex gloves; the latter are commonly found in most drugstores and many supermarkets. Otherwise, cover your hands with thin plastic bags.
* Wash your hands with soap and water as soon as you're finished handling the chiles—and still *don't touch your eyes*. Most soaps just don't remove all the oil from your hands.
* To seed fresh chiles, lay the chile on its side and cut a lengthwise strip of flesh off one side. Roll the pepper onto its flat side and cut another strip of flesh, repeating four to five times, or until the flesh is removed and the seed-embedded core is exposed. Discard the core and chop the flesh as desired.
* To freeze fresh chiles, blanch (*see* BLANCHING) the whole chiles, immersing them in ice water to cool. Place the chiles on a plastic wrap–lined baking sheet and freeze until solid. Transfer to a freezer-proof plastic bag and freeze for up to 6 months. Freeze canned chiles the same way, skipping the blanching process. For adobo-packed chipotles, place a spoonful of the adobo sauce atop each chile before freezing.
* When cooking chiles over high heat on the stovetop, avoid breathing in the harsh fumes, which can irritate your throat, nose and eyes.
* Technique for roasting fresh chiles: *see* ROASTED PEPPERS, page 37.
* Chile-pepper flowers make a showy garnish (*see* page 224).
* Is your mouth on fire with chile heat? Beat the heat with milk, yogurt, bread, rice, potatoes, ice cream or a banana. Don't expect a cold beer or margarita to help—alcohol increases the absorption of capsaicin.

PREPARING DRIED CHILES

* To remove the seeds from a dried chile, pull or cut off the stem, split the chile lengthwise, then scrape out the seeds with a spoon.
* Dried chiles are typically roasted and rehydrated before being used. Place stemmed and seeded chiles in a dry skillet over medium-low heat. Cook for about 10 minutes, shaking the pan several times to toss the chiles. Or roast them in a single layer in a 250°F oven for 20 minutes.
* Rehydrate roasted dried chiles by covering with very hot (not boiling)

water. Place a plate or other weight on top of the chiles to completely submerge them; let stand for 30 minutes.

* Combine rehydrated dried chiles with a little of the soaking water in a blender and PURÉE. Taste the soaking water before adding it to the chiles—if it's bitter, use regular water instead. Add the purée to sauces, dips, soups and stews—anything to which you want to add a rich flavor.

HOMEMADE CHILE POWDER

Using a combination of chiles gives complexity to the blend. Add chile powder to everything from sauces to soups, and rub on meats to be grilled. Roast a mixture of stemmed, seeded dried chiles (such as mild anchos, midrange chipotles and fiery habaneros) in a 250°F oven for 20 minutes. Cool, then put the chiles in a blender; cover and process to a powder (don't inhale the fumes!). Transfer to a freezer-weight plastic bag; freeze for up to 6 months.

CHILI   see also BEANS, DRIED; CHILES; SOUPS AND STEWS

* A touch of unsweetened cocoa powder or instant-coffee powder gives chili a rich, husky flavor.
* Make a double batch and freeze half for future meals.
* Reduce calories by using ground turkey or chicken instead of beef. Enhance the flavor of beef with beef broth or bouillon.
* Freeze leftover chili in individual servings for a quick heat-up in the microwave.
* Serve chili with bowls of accompaniments such as sour cream, chopped cilantro, crushed tortilla chips, grated Cheddar or Monterey Jack, and let everyone garnish their portion as they please.
* Leftover chili is great spooned over spaghetti, in tacos and burritos, as an omelet filling, as a topping for burgers or frankfurters, or spooned into a split baked potato and topped with cheese.

> *He who bears chives on his breath*
> *Is safe from being kissed to death.*
> —Martial, Roman epigrammatic poet

CHIVES   see also SCALLIONS

TIDBIT   Although chives are related to both onions and garlic, they are, in fact, an herb. Keep a pot of chives on a well-lit windowsill and have fresh chives on hand whenever you want. Snip off whole chives close to the base, rather than lopping off the tops of the entire bunch.

PURCHASING   Choose chives with a uniform green color and no signs of wilting or browning.

STORING

* Fresh chives: Refrigerate, wrapped in a paper towel, then in a plastic bag, for up to 1 week. To freeze whole or snipped chives, wash and blot dry, then seal airtight in a freezer-proof container for up to 6 months.
* Frozen chives: Keep in their container, then put in a freezer-weight plastic bag; freeze for up to 6 months.
* Dried chives: Store in a cool, dark place and use within 3 months.

PREPARING

* Wash chives just before using. Blot thoroughly with paper towels.
* Use kitchen shears to easily snip fresh chives into the length desired. Snip the tops of the entire bunch, rather than snipping each chive individually.
* Substitute finely chopped scallions instead of dried chives for fresh chives. If your only alternative is dried chives, add them directly to a hot dish without reconstituting them.
* Chives lose almost all their flavor when dried. Because of their appearance (even when reconstituted), dried chives don't work well as a garnish.
* The frozen, snipped chives found in supermarkets aren't as flavorful as the fresh form, but they're better than the dried. Simply remove what you need and quickly return the chives to the freezer.
* Add frozen chives directly to a dish without thawing.

USING

* Stir chives into cooked or cold preparations at the last minute to preserve their delicate, fresh flavor. If chives are added to a dish too soon, their flavor becomes harsh and slightly sour.
* Use long, uncut chives to create a variety of interesting garnishes. Tie them into bows; form them into circles or triangles—securing the shape by sticking the tip into the cut end; fan out 3 to 5 chives atop a dish, use chives to tie bundles of julienned vegetables; and so on. If the chives are too stiff to manipulate, BLANCH them for 5 seconds in boiling water.

I have always been quite clear on the fact that I am one of those individuals for whom chocolate is more than a casual acquaintance but is, instead, a passionate, sensuous connection to all my hedonistic yearnings.
—The author of this book (and dedicated chocoholic)

CHOCOLATE   *see also* COCOA POWDER

TIDBIT   The word "chocolate" comes from the Aztec *xocolatl* (transliter-

C ated to *chocolatl*), meaning "bitter water," an apt name for the unsweetened drink the Aztecs made with pounded cacao beans, vanilla and spices. Aztec emperor Montezuma was said to have been exceedingly fond of this bitter potion, his daily consumption up to fifty goblets. But *chocolatl* was reputed to be an aphrodisiac (the cacao beans came from a tree Aztecs held divine), so who knows if Montezuma really liked the flavor, or if he was just trying to maintain his royal reputation with the ladies.

PURCHASING There are many chocolate products on the market today, all classified according to percentages of key ingredients that conform with the U.S. Food and Drug Administration's Standards of Identity.

* Unsweetened chocolate (also called *bitter* or *baking chocolate*): Unadulterated, hardened **chocolate liquor** (the dark brown paste made from the cocoa bean's ground nibs). It must contain between 50 and 58 percent **cocoa butter** (a natural vegetable fat extracted from cocoa beans).

* Semisweet (and bittersweet) chocolate: "Semisweet chocolate" is primarily an American term, "bittersweet chocolate," the European idiom. Both must, by weight, be at least 35 percent chocolate liquor. They also contain sugar, added cocoa butter, lecithin (an emulsifier) and vanilla or other flavorings. These two chocolates can vary slightly in sweetness, but are generally interchangeable. Semisweet chocolate is the most popular choice for cooking and is available in chips (regular, giant and miniature), squares and bars.

* Sweet chocolate: This is dark chocolate that contains at least 15 percent chocolate liquor; it also has flavorings and more sugar than semisweet chocolate.

* Cocoa powder: dried, powdered chocolate liquor with some of the fat extracted. This unsweetened powder contains 10 to 22 percent cocoa butter. **Dutch-process** cocoa powder (also called *European-style*) has been treated with an alkali, which helps neutralize cocoa's natural acidity and make it more soluble. Its flavor is slightly more mellow, its color darker. When substituting Dutch-process cocoa for regular cocoa, omit any baking soda (which acts as an alkalizer) in the recipe.

* Liquid chocolate (also called *premelted*): a mixture of cocoa powder and vegetable oil. It doesn't have the same flavor or texture of melted unsweetened chocolate, primarily because it doesn't contain as much cocoa butter.

* Milk chocolate: This version must contain at least 12 percent milk solids and a minimum of 10 percent chocolate liquor. It also contains sugar, cocoa butter and vanilla or other flavorings. Because of the heat sensitiv-

ity of the milk protein, this chocolate is not recommended as a dark-chocolate substitute.

* Couverture: a specially formulated professional-quality dark coating chocolate that is extremely glossy. It contains a minimum of 32 percent cocoa butter. Couverture is generally available only in specialty candy-making shops or baker's supply houses.

* White chocolate: Not truly chocolate, because it doesn't contain chocolate liquor, white chocolate is typically a mixture of sugar, cocoa butter, milk solids, lecithin and vanilla. Read the label carefully—if it doesn't contain cocoa butter, it's *not* white chocolate. It should not be substituted for other chocolates.

* **Note**: Beware of products labeled "artificial chocolate" or "chocolate-flavored." These in no way resemble the real thing, which is obvious in both flavor and texture.

EQUIVALENT   6-ounce package chocolate chips = 1 cup

STORING   Dark chocolate, when stored tightly wrapped in a cool (60° to 70°F), dry place, will last for years. Because milk chocolate and white chocolate contain milk solids, they can only be stored for about 9 months. Never store chocolate near odoriferous foods like onions. Warm temperatures can cause chocolate to develop a pale gray "bloom" (surface streaks and blotches), caused when the cocoa butter rises to the surface. Damp or cold conditions sometimes produce minuscule gray sugar crystals on the surface of chocolate. Even if improperly stored, chocolate can still be used, its flavor and texture only slightly affected.

SUBSTITUTIONS   (*for use in cooking or baking*)

* For 1 ounce unsweetened chocolate, use: 3 tablespoons unsweetened cocoa plus 1 tablespoon butter; or 3 tablespoons carob powder plus 2 tablespoons water.

* For 1 ounce semisweet chocolate, use: ½ ounce unsweetened chocolate plus 1 tablespoon granulated sugar.

* For 6 ounces semisweet chocolate chips, use: ½ cup plus 1 tablespoon unsweetened cocoa, plus ¼ cup plus 3 tablespoons granulated sugar, plus 3 tablespoons butter.

MELTING

* Spray the container you melt the chocolate in with cooking spray, and the chocolate will slip right out.

* Because all chocolate scorches easily—which completely ruins its flavor—it should be melted slowly over low heat. Chocolate chips melt faster than squares.

* Various chocolates have different consistencies when melted. Unsweetened chocolate becomes runny. Semisweet, sweet and white chocolate can melt yet hold their shape until stirred. If you wait until they "look" melted you're liable to singe the chocolate.

* Double-boiler melting: Place coarsely chopped chocolate in the top of a double boiler over simmering water. Remove the top of the pan from the heat when the chocolate is a little more than halfway melted and stir until it's completely smooth.

* Microwave melting: Put the chocolate in a microwave-safe bowl and heat at medium (50 percent power). Four ounces of chocolate will take about 3 minutes in a 600- to 700-watt microwave oven, but the timing will vary depending on the oven and the type and amount of chocolate. White chocolate has a tendency to scorch easily, so it should be handled with extra care.

* One-ounce, paper-wrapped squares of chocolate can be melted right in the paper in the microwave oven at medium (50 percent power)—it saves on cleanup. One 1-ounce square takes 1½ to 2 minutes, 2 squares about 3 minutes and 3 squares about 4 minutes.

* To melt chocolate for decorating: Put finely chopped chocolate or chocolate chips in a small, heavy-duty plastic bag (a lighter-weight bag could melt). Set the unsealed bag upright in a small bowl and microwave at medium (50 percent power) until almost melted; let stand for 5 minutes until completely melted. Another method is to seal the bag and set it in a bowl of very hot water until the chocolate is melted (make sure that no water gets into the bag, or the chocolate could stiffen). Thoroughly dry the bag with a paper towel before snipping a tiny hole in a corner of the bag. Pipe a decorative design directly onto the dessert, or onto a sheet of waxed paper for later transfer.

* Though chocolate can be melted with liquids (at least ¼ cup liquid per 6 ounces chocolate), a single drop of moisture in *melted* chocolate will cause it to seize (clump and harden).

* Seizing can sometimes be corrected if vegetable oil is immediately stirred into the chocolate at a ratio of about 1 tablespoon oil per 6 ounces chocolate. Slowly remelt the mixture and stir until smooth.

* Cool melted chocolate to room temperature before adding it to cookie doughs or cake batters or you risk melting the fat in the mixture and creating a textural change in the baked product.

TEMPERING

* This melting-and-cooling technique is used for stabilizing the cocoa butter crystals in chocolate to make it more malleable and glossy. Commer-

cially available chocolate is tempered, but goes out of temper when it is melted or improperly stored. When that happens, the surface of the chocolate can form the dull gray streaks or blotches called "bloom." Tempering chocolate isn't necessary for most recipes, but is often done when chocolate will be used for candymaking or decorations.

* **Classic tempering method:** Melt chopped chocolate until it reaches a temperature of 115°F. Stir and check often, and don't worry about tiny lumps—they'll melt from the residual heat. Pour two-thirds of the melted chocolate onto a marble slab or other cool, nonporous surface; work the chocolate back and forth with a metal spatula until it becomes thick and reaches a temperature of about 80°F. Turn the thickened chocolate back into the remaining melted chocolate and reheat to about 89°F for semisweet chocolate, about 85°F for milk or white chocolate.

* **Easier tempering method:** Set a heatproof bowl of chopped chocolate over a pan of boiling water, making sure the bowl doesn't touch the water. Let stand for about 5 minutes, then stir until the chocolate is smooth and at a temperature of 115°F. Set the bowl of chocolate in a larger bowl of ice cubes with a little cold water (make sure *no* water gets into the chocolate!). Stir the chocolate until the temperature drops to 80°F. Place the bowl of chocolate over a pan of hot water again, stirring until it reaches 89°F for semisweet chocolate, about 85°F for milk or white chocolate.

* **Quick tempering method:** Melt two-thirds of the chocolate to a temperature of 115°F, then add the remaining one-third (finely chopped) chocolate to the melted mixture; stir until the mixture is smooth and has reached 89°F.

* **Microwave tempering:** Put the chopped chocolate in a glass container (a 2- or 4-cup measuring cup works well). Microwave for 30 seconds on high; remove and stir. Repeat until the chocolate reaches 115°F. Be careful not to overheat, and remember that residual heat will continue to melt tiny lumps. Remove from the microwave oven and let stand at room temperature. As the chocolate cools and begins to set around the edges, stir the set chocolate back into the melted portion.

* **Tempering test:** Swipe a bit of tempered chocolate evenly onto a piece of waxed paper; let stand for 5 minutes. Properly tempered chocolate will be glossy and hard.

GRATING

* Grated or flaked chocolate can be used to decorate or garnish myriad desserts from cakes to ice cream.

* Room-temperature chocolate is easier to grate than chocolate that's too warm or too cold.

* To grate chocolate by hand, start with a large, thick piece—it's easier to handle. Place a box grater over a piece of waxed paper. Hold one end of the chocolate in a piece of paper towel to prevent the heat of your hands from melting it. Firmly rub the chocolate over the coarse side of the grater. Or use a Mouli rotary grater for fast and easy results.
* Food-processor grating can be done in several ways. Using either the thin slicing blade or the grating disk, gently press the chocolate into the blade with the plunger. Or break the chocolate into small chunks and chop with the chopping blade, using on/off pulses.
* Run a vegetable peeler across a chilled bar of chocolate to create chocolate flakes.
* Once grated, chocolate should be refrigerated until ready to use.

QUICK CHOCOLATE SAUCE

In a 2-cup measure or bowl, combine 6 ounces semisweet chocolate chips with ⅓ cup Kahlúa, Cointreau or other liqueur (or use 2 tablespoons liqueur and 3 tablespoons heavy cream). Microwave on high for 1 minute. Let stand for 2 minutes; stir until smooth. If the chocolate isn't melted completely, cook for 30 more seconds. Stir in ¼ teaspoon pure vanilla extract. Makes about 1 cup.

INSTANT CHOCOLATE FONDUE

In a small saucepan over low heat, melt 8 ounces chopped semisweet chocolate and 1 cup whipping cream together, stirring until smooth. Remove from the heat; stir in 1 teaspoon pure vanilla extract and 1 to 2 tablespoons brandy or liqueur. Serve warm with whole strawberries or chunks of fruit or cake to dip into the chocolate. Serves about 6.

CHOCOLATE DECORATIONS

* **Chocolate Leaves:** This extraordinary garnish is surprisingly easy to make. Begin by choosing 6 to 8 nonpoisonous, firm leaves (such as camellia or citrus) with stems attached; wash and thoroughly dry the leaves. Melt about 2 ounces chocolate. Using a small metal spatula or the back of a dinner teaspoon, thickly spread melted chocolate over the underside of the leaves. Be careful not to let chocolate run over the edges of the leaves; use your fingertip to remove any excess chocolate from the edges. Place the leaves, chocolate side up, on a waxed paper–lined baking sheet; chill until the chocolate is set. Hold the leaves up to the light to look for bare spots. Patch with additional chocolate, then chill again to set. Remove the leaf from the chocolate by grasping the stem and pulling the leaf gently away from the chocolate. Refrigerate the chocolate leaves until ready to use.
* **Chocolate Curls:** To make these, use a large, long bar of chocolate. If the chocolate is too cold, the shavings will be brittle and break. Hold the

chocolate firmly to warm it slightly, or place it in a warm location (90°F) for about 15 minutes. Place a piece of waxed paper on the work surface. Holding the chocolate in one hand, and using a swivel-blade vegetable peeler in the other, firmly draw the blade toward you along the edge of the bar. The pressure you apply will determine the thickness of the curl. Let the curls drop onto the waxed paper. Refrigerate in an airtight container until ready to use. Use a spoon to gently transfer the chocolate curls to the desired dessert.

* **Chocolate Scrolls:** Line a large baking sheet with waxed paper. Melt 6 ounces chocolate. Pour onto a smooth work surface, such as marble, the countertop or the back of a baking sheet. Use a narrow, metal spreading spatula to spread the chocolate about ⅛ inch thick over the work surface. Let the chocolate cool until firm but not hard. Starting at one end of the chocolate and at the side closest to you, with a flexible pastry scraper or wide metal spatula tilted at a 45-degree angle, slowly and firmly move the scraper or spatula forward. The spatula's edge will lift the chocolate and cause it to roll around itself. Use the spatula to gently transfer the chocolate scrolls to the prepared baking sheet; refrigerate until firm, then place in an airtight container and refrigerate until ready to use.

* **Chocolate Triangles:** Line a large baking sheet with waxed paper. Draw an 8- or 9-inch circle on the waxed paper. Spread 3 ounces melted chocolate evenly within the circle. Refrigerate until almost set. Using a large, sharp knife, cut the chocolate circle into 10 to 12 pie-shaped pieces. Refrigerate until completely set. Gently break the triangles apart; peel away the waxed paper, handling the chocolate as little as possible. Refrigerate in an airtight container until ready to use.

* **Chocolate Cutouts:** Line a large baking sheet with waxed paper. Spread 2 ounces melted chocolate 1/16 to ⅛ inch thick on the prepared baking sheet. Refrigerate until almost set. Using canapé cutters, small cookie cutters or a pointed knife, cut out desired shapes in the chocolate. Refrigerate until completely set. Gently break the shapes apart; peel away the waxed paper, handling the chocolate as little as possible. Refrigerate in airtight container until ready to use.

CHOPSTICKS

* Chopsticks are typically the thickness of a pencil. Their length can range from 10 to 12 inches; shorter, kid-sized chopsticks are also available. Japanese chopsticks are pointed at the eating end, and Chinese chopsticks are blunt.

* To use chopsticks: Position one chopstick, narrow end down and about

two-thirds from the pointed end, in the crook of your thumb. Let the other end of the stick rest on your ring finger, with your middle finger on top of it. Slightly squeeze the stick with the base of your thumb to hold it in place. This bottom chopstick will remain stationary while you're eating. Hold the other chopstick between your index finger and the tip of your thumb, much as you would a pencil. Move this stick in an up-and-down, pincerlike motion to pick up food between it and the bottom chopstick, always keeping the tips of the chopsticks even. Practice at home with two long wooden skewers and you'll look like a pro the next time you eat at an Asian restaurant.

* When eating rice with chopsticks, it's traditional to lift up a small bowl of rice to just below your mouth.
* If there's no ceramic piece on which to rest your chopsticks between bites and at the end of a meal, simply rest them across your plate.

CHUTNEY
TIDBIT Chutney enhances myriad dishes. Just be sure to finely chop any large pieces of fruit in the chutney before using it in other preparations.

* Create an instant glaze for grilled or broiled meat, poultry or fish. PURÉE chutney, then thin with a little vegetable oil and brush over the food about 10 minutes before cooking is finished.
* For an exotic salad dressing, combine 2 to 3 tablespoons puréed chutney with extra virgin olive oil, mayonnaise or sour cream.
* Purée chutney with a little cream, chicken or vegetable broth, oil or melted butter, and drizzle over hot vegetables or meats.
* Whip finely chopped chutney with softened butter or cream cheese for a delicious spread for bread.
* Serve chutney as an accompaniment to a variety of cheeses from Cheddar to chèvre.

CINNAMON   *For storage and purchasing information, see* SPICES
TIDBIT Cinnamon is the inner bark of a tropical evergreen tree. Ceylon (or true) cinnamon has a tan color and mildly sweet flavor. Cassia—a close relative of true cinnamon—is what's commonly sold in the United States as ground cinnamon. It has a darker, reddish-brown color and a more pungent, slightly bittersweet flavor.
USING

* As with any whole spice, the flavor of stick cinnamon is more intense than that of commercially ground cinnamon. It can also be stored longer.

* Cinnamon sticks make great swizzle sticks for all kinds of hot drinks, including cider, cocoa, coffee, hot buttered rum, mulled wine, and so on.
* Cinnamon sugar can be found in bottles in your supermarket's spice section. But you can make your own for a third the cost (*see following recipe*).
* Use cinnamon sugar to sweeten coffee, as an ingredient in desserts, for decorating cookies, cakes and other baked goods, or for sweetening fruit and other desserts.
* A pinch of cinnamon makes magic in many savory dishes like soups, stews, casseroles and meat marinades.
* Fill your house with that "something's in the oven" fragrance by combining 1 teaspoon ground cinnamon or 1 cinnamon stick (broken into several pieces) with 6 cups water and bring to a boil. Reduce to a simmer and let the scent waft deliciously through the house.

CINNAMON SUGAR

Store this mixture in a clean, used herb or spice jar with a shaker top. Combine ½ cup granulated sugar with 1 to 1½ tablespoons ground cinnamon. Store airtight at room temperature.

CINNAMON-FLAVORED SUGAR

This style of cinnamon sugar differs from the preceding one because it stays white. Bury 3 cinnamon sticks in a pound of granulated or confectioners' sugar. Store at room temperature in an airtight container for 2 weeks, stirring once a week.

CHOCOLATE-CINNAMON TOAST

This fragrant comforter starts the day off right and makes blue days better. The recipe can easily be doubled to have on hand any time you want. In a small bowl, combine 1 tablespoon unsweetened cocoa powder, 3 tablespoons sugar and ½ teaspoon ground cinnamon. Store, tightly sealed, at room temperature. Makes enough topping for about 8 slices of toast, depending on the size. Spread 1 slice of toasted bread with butter; sprinkle evenly with a rounded teaspoon of chocolate mixture. Broil 3 inches from the heat source until the top is bubbly. Watch carefully; it only takes a few seconds.

CITRUS FRUITS
For specific purchasing information, see individual listings for GRAPEFRUIT; LEMONS; LIMES; ORANGES. *See also* CITRUS STRIPPER; FRUIT, GENERAL

PURCHASING Fruit that's heavy for its size will be juicier than its lightweight counterparts.

JUICING
* Room-temperature fruit yields more juice than refrigerated fruit.

C

* Using the palm of your hand, roll citrus fruit around on the countertop a few times before squeezing to maximize juice yield.

* Get more juice from citrus fruits by pricking the skin in several places with a fork, being careful not to go all the way to the flesh. Microwave on high, uncovered, for 10 to 20 seconds, depending on the size of the fruit. Let stand for 2 minutes before rolling the fruit between your palm and the countertop. Cut open and squeeze out the juice.

* If you don't have a microwave oven to encourage the juice, place citrus fruit in a preheated 300°F oven for 3 minutes. Cool before juicing.

* To juice without seeds, put the halved lemon, lime or orange in a kitchen towel; squeeze the juice directly into the preparation.

* Squeeze an entire lemon (or other citrus), use what you need, then refrigerate the rest of the juice in an airtight screw-top jar for up to 5 days.

* Remove the seeds but leave the pulp in the juice whenever possible—it delivers a nice flavor bonus.

* Freeze whole citrus fruit for at least 24 hours. Thaw overnight in the fridge, and they'll juice with ease.

ZESTING

* The word "zest" refers to the outer colored portion of the citrus peel. The white pith directly under the colored part is bitter. Freshly grated citrus zest packs a flavor wallop no bottled dried zest can match.

* Thoroughly wash citrus fruit before using the peel (zest).

* It's easier to grate or zest a whole citrus fruit, then juice it afterward. Run the fruit diagonally across a grater, rather than up and down.

* Cover the grater with plastic wrap and the zest will cling to the wrap when removed.

* By far the easiest way to remove the zest from a citrus fruit is to use a citrus zester or stripper (*see next listing*). A vegetable peeler also works.

* Even if you aren't planning on using the zest immediately, remove it, either in grated or strip form. Freeze for up to 6 months and use as needed to flavor everything from baked goods to beverages.

GENERAL

* Pith-free citrus sections are great for salads and desserts. Immerse the whole fruit in a pot of boiling hot water and let stand for 4 minutes. Remove the fruit from the water and cool until it's easy to handle. When you peel away the skin, the pith should come right off with it. Any remnants can be pulled off with a grapefruit knife.

* Scoop the flesh from orange or small grapefruit halves and use the shells as "bowls" for fruit salad or a dessert fruit compote.

❋ Hollowed-out orange or lemon halves make great sherbet cups.

CITRUS-FLAVORED VODKA

Combine the zest of 1 large lemon or 1 medium orange with 2 cups vodka in a screw-top jar. Refrigerate for 1 week before using. Use the zest in recipes and add the vodka to beverages (it's great in martinis), sauces, and so on.

CITRUS STRIPPER; CITRUS ZESTER

❋ **Citrus strippers** have a notched, stainless-steel edge that cuts ¼-inch wide strips of citrus peel.

❋ **Citrus zesters** have five tiny cutting holes that create threadlike strips of peel. A good-quality citrus zester (available in gourmet specialty shops and many supermarkets) is an easy way to get long, thin strands of zest. Press firmly as you draw the zester down along the skin of the fruit.

❋ For long, continuous strips of zest, use a citrus stripper to begin at one end, spiraling around and down the fruit. Don't press so hard that you cut into the bitter white part (pith) of the skin.

Recently I sat across from a person who was deliberately eating clams; she'd open up a shell, and there, in plain view, would be this stark naked clam, brazenly showing its organs . . . if a restaurant is going to serve these things it should put little loincloths on them.
—Dave Barry, American humorist

CLAMS *see also* SHELLFISH

TIDBIT Native Americans once used clam shells to make wampum— different colored beads that served many purposes, including ornamental (belts with pictographic designs), ceremonial and spiritual (white beads), and as a currency for barter. The word "wampum" is Algonquian for "white string of beads."

PURCHASING

❋ Hard-shelled clams (like littleneck, cherrystone, chowder, pismo or butter clams): Choose those with tightly closed shells that are whole, not broken or cracked. Lightly tap a shell that's slightly open—if it doesn't snap shut, the clam is dead and should be discarded.

❋ Soft-shelled clams (like razor or geoduck clams): Lightly touch the clam's neck—if it moves, it's alive.

❋ Shucked clams: They should be plump, the liquor (liquid) surrounding them clear.

❋ How much per serving: In the shell = 2 to 3 pounds

EQUIVALENTS

* Live: 2 dozen medium in shell = 3 cups shucked
* Shucked: 1 pint = about 18 clams
* Canned: 7½-ounce can minced clams = about 9 shucked clams

STORING

* Store live clams in an open container, covered with a moist cloth, for up to 2 days in a 40°F refrigerator.
* Refrigerate shucked clams in their liquor for up to 3 days, in the freezer for up to 3 months.
* If there's not enough liquor to cover the shucked clams, make your own by dissolving ½ teaspoon salt in 1 cup water.

CLEANING

* Rid live clams of sand by soaking them in cold, salted water (⅓ cup salt per gallon water) for an hour.
* Sand can also be removed by covering the clams with cold water, then sprinkling liberally with cornmeal. Let stand for about 3 hours.
* Clams found floating after either of these procedures should be discarded.
* Scrub live clams well under cold, running water.

SHUCKING

* Clams will be easier to open if you freeze them (in a single layer) for 20 to 30 minutes.
* A quicker method for relaxing clams so they're easier to open is to drop a few at a time into boiling water. Retrieve with a slotted spoon after 15 seconds and open.
* If you don't have a clam knife for opening clams, use a short screwdriver or beer-can opener.
* Hold the clam firmly in the palm of your towel- or glove-covered hand. Insert the clam knife into the broad side opposite the hinge, sliding it between the two shells until you can pry them apart. Slide the knife along the inside of the top shell to separate the clam from the muscle attaching it to the shell. Open the shells, then slip the knife under the clam to detach it from the bottom shell.

COOKING

* All clams should be cooked at low heat to prevent toughening.
* Clams cooked in their shells are done just when their shells open.
* Use only fresh or frozen clams for soups and stews. The texture of canned clams is too soft for long-cooking dishes.
* Add minced clams to soups and stews at the last minute so they retain their texture.

CLAY-POT COOKING; CLAY COOKERS

* Immerse both the top and bottom of a clay cooker in tepid water for 15 minutes before using.
* Clay-pot cooking should always begin in a cold oven; set the heat after the dish is in position. Adjust cooking times for recipes not specifically designed to start in a cold oven.
* Sudden changes in temperature can crack clay cookers. When removing the dish from a hot oven, always set it on a rack or triple-folded towel or wooden chopping block—never directly on a cold countertop.
* Clay cookers are not designed for stovetop cooking and will most likely crack if exposed to direct heat.

Cooking is a lot like making love. It just takes a little longer to clean up.
—Michael Tucker, American actor, author

CLEANUP, KITCHEN   *see also* OVENS, CONVENTIONAL

* Cleaning up as you cook makes life a lot simpler. While a dish is cooking on the stovetop or in the oven, wash the utensils, cutting boards or other cookware you used to prepare the food. Pop whatever dirty dishes there are into the dishwasher and set the pans to soak just before sitting down to eat. The only things that shouldn't be soaked are items made of wood or those that are glued.
* Reduce cleanup time by using cookware designed to go from freezer to microwave or thermal oven.
* Keep the stovetop clean by resting spoons and spatulas on a saucer adjacent to the cooking area.
* Store leftovers that will be used within a few days in the pot or casserole dish in which the food was cooked; reheat them in that same container.
* Use foil to line your stove's burner pans, or buy the foil liners found in supermarkets.
* Lining baking pans with foil or PARCHMENT PAPER makes cleanup quick and easy.
* Line the bottom of an electric oven with foil to catch spillovers. Don't cover oven racks with foil—it prevents air from circulating and causes uneven heat distribution.
* To help diminish lingering, unpleasant cooking odors: Fill a large pot halfway with water. Add 2 lemon halves (squeeze the juice into the water before dropping in the halves) and 8 whole cloves. Bring to a boil; cook for 10 minutes. Turn off heat and let pot stand.

* A paste of baking soda and water makes a good odor-eater for hands. Lemon juice also works well.

* Make scrubbing pans easier and prevent grease and debris from going down the drain by wiping out greasy pots with used paper napkins or paper towels before washing.

* Never scour iron pots and pans—simply wash them with soap and hot water. Dry thoroughly to prevent rusting.

* Pans with burned residue on the bottom will be easier to clean if you fill them with 2 inches of water, add 1 tablespoon baking soda, and bring to a boil. Cover and boil for 5 minutes, then remove from the heat and let stand for 30 minutes before scrubbing.

* Or remove burned-on food by scraping the pan well, then filling it three-quarters full with water and adding ½ to 1 cup salt (depending on the pan's size). Bring to a boil, then boil for 20 minutes. Remove the pan from the heat, cover and let stand overnight. Use a metal spatula the next morning to loosen as much of the burned area as possible and finish the job with a scouring pad.

* Remove stains from aluminum pans by filling them with water and adding 2 tablespoons vinegar, lemon juice or cream of tartar per quart of water. Bring to a boil, then continue to boil gently for 15 minutes. Let the water cool in the pan. Scour lightly, then wash well.

* If you can't get stains out of Corningware or Pyrex, spray them with oven cleaner, following manufacturer's directions.

* Clean copper pots or bowls with a paste of salt and lemon juice or vinegar; rub it on with a crumpled wad of paper towel.

* Use a paste of water and baking soda to remove coffee or tea stains on chinaware.

* Deodorize an off-smelling plastic container by filling it with hot water to which you've added 1 tablespoon baking soda. Let stand overnight.

* Kitchen sponge getting smelly? Soak it overnight in a mixture of 2 cups warm water and 2 tablespoons baking soda. Rinse thoroughly before using.

* Toss your kitchen sponge on the top rack of the dishwasher when it needs cleaning. Rinse out by hand after the cycle is finished.

* Or wash the kitchen sponge with a load of clothes. Dry at room temperature.

* An old toothbrush is great for cleaning small places in garlic presses, electric can openers, strainers, grinder parts, or along the edges of a sink molding—you name it. Clean the toothbrush first by running it through a dishwasher cycle in the silverware holder.

* Protect your good china and crystal during washing by lining the sink with a dishtowel.
* Silver serving pieces can be returned to their original glory by using a soft cloth and rubbing with a paste of baking soda and water.
* Remove stubborn waterlines on vases by rubbing them with a vinegar-soaked cloth or paper towel.
* To remove soap film from countertops, rinse with a mixture of 1 quart water and 1 teaspoon white vinegar.
* Use a generously salted lemon half to clean stainless steel kitchen sinks. A plain lemon half will work on smooth aluminum pans.
* Clean an electric can opener by running a damp piece of heavyweight paper towel through the cutting mechanism.
* To clear a grease-clogged sink, pour in 1 cup each baking soda and salt, followed by 1½ to 2 quarts boiling water.
* Use nail polish or paint remover to get rid of sticky label residue from bottles or jars you want to keep. Keep in mind that these removers can mar the surface of some plastic containers.

CLOVES   *For storage and purchasing information, see* SPICES
TIDBIT   The reddish brown, nail-shaped clove is the dried, unopened flower bud of the tropical evergreen clove tree.

* Cloves are sold whole and ground. Both forms are very pungent, so use in moderation.
* Make your own pomander balls by inserting whole cloves into apples, lemons or oranges. To prevent snapping off the end of the cloves as you insert them, use a skewer or toothpick to pierce a small hole in the fruit, then position the clove. A bowlful of these fragrant pomanders can be used as a centerpiece, or use one at each place setting for a favor.

If you were to ask me if I'd ever had the bad luck to miss my daily cocktail, I'd have to say that I doubt it; where certain things are concerned, I plan ahead.
—Luis Buñuel, Spanish filmmaker

COCKTAILS   *see also* BEER; BEVERAGES; CHAMPAGNE; FLAMBÉING; GLASS-
WARE; HOT DRINKS; ICE; LIQUOR AND LIQUEURS; WINE
TIDBIT   You don't have to be a bartender to create professional-looking cocktails. A few tricks of the trade and you're in business.

* **Stocking the bar:** The basic rule of stocking a home bar is to buy what you'll use most. If none of your friends drink Scotch, don't buy it. Bottom line whether buying liquor or mixers: Your drinks will only taste as

good as the ingredients that go into them, so buy the best you can afford. Spirits you might want to have on hand include Scotch, bourbon, gin, vodka, rum and tequila. Wine (red and white), Cognac, brandy, and sweet and dry vermouth are also options. Basic liqueurs (crème de cassis, plus coffee- and orange-flavored liqueurs) are a good bet for the home bar and can flavor desserts as well.

* **Mixers** comprise two-thirds or more of many drinks, which means that a bargain-priced mixer with an mediocre flavor can ruin the blend. Mixers include sparklers (club soda, seltzer water and tonic water), fruit juices (orange, lemon or tomato juice) or rich additions like cream and coconut milk. Refrigerate mixers—cold liquids won't melt ice and dilute drinks as fast as those at room temperature.

* **Additional flavorings** for cocktails include bitters, orange flower water, grenadine, Tabasco sauce and Worcestershire sauce.

* **Chilled or frosted glasses** look great and keep drinks cold. Freeze glasses for 10 minutes, or refrigerate for 30 minutes. For last-minute chilling, pack glasses with crushed or cracked ice and let stand for about 5 minutes. For a frosted look, put glasses in the freezer for about an hour. For an ultrafrosty look, dip glasses in cold water, shake off any excess and place in the freezer. Hold frosted glasses by their stems or handles so as not to ruin the frosted effect.

* **Sugar- or salt-rimmed glasses** for drinks like Cosmopolitans or Margaritas can be prepared in advance and stored in the refrigerator or freezer. Dip the glass rim in water, liquor or fruit juice (such as lime juice for Margaritas). Shake off the excess liquid, then dip the glass into a saucer of granulated sugar or salt (preferably coarse). The rim can also be dampened by simply dipping your fingertip into a liquid, then running it around the glass rim. Or run a lemon, lime or orange wedge around the rim of a glass before dipping.

* **Ice** used for either mixing or chilling drinks is extremely important. If the ice doesn't taste good, neither will your drinks. *See* ICE for complete information on everything from cracking ice to making flavored ice cubes.

* **Shaking or stirring** a cocktail both chills a drink and mixes the ingredients. Each technique creates the smooth texture you want for drinks like Manhattans and Martinis as the melting ice emulsifies into the other ingredients. When shaking a drink, start by filling a cocktail shaker half to two-thirds full with ice. Most shakers will only accommodate ingredients for two drinks. Add the ingredients (the order doesn't matter) and shake or stir vigorously. The longer you shake or stir, the more diluted the drink will become as the ice melts into the mixture. Immediately

pour the drink into a chilled glass—letting it sit on the ice will dilute it.
Don't add a sparkler like club soda until after a drink is poured from the
shaker; then stir it gently to retain its effervescence.

* **Serving** drinks should be done as soon as they're mixed. If you've filled
the glasses and have some left over, strain it into a small pitcher or other
container and refrigerate until you're ready for seconds. When making
several drinks at once (like blender Margaritas) be sure that everyone
gets the same amount by lining the glasses up, filling each one halfway,
then going back and filling each glass to the same level. Remember to
leave room to add any garnishes.

* **Garnishing** adds a finishing touch that gives cocktails a professional
look. You won't go wrong if you choose a garnish integral to the drink.
For example, a Piña Colada (a mixture of pineapple juice and cream of
coconut) could be garnished with a pineapple spear. Some classic garnishes are: an olive or lemon twist for a Martini, a mint sprig for a Mint
Julep and a maraschino cherry for a Manhattan. Other garnishes include
celery sticks, mint sprigs, whole strawberries and wedges or slices of
lemon, lime or orange. Edible flowers (*see* FLOWERS) make particularly
showy garnishes for myriad tropical drinks. *See also* GARNISHING.

COCOA POWDER, UNSWEETENED   *see also* CHOCOLATE

TIDBIT   After cocoa beans are processed, about 75 percent of the cocoa
butter is extracted, leaving a dark brown paste (chocolate liquor), which is
subsequently dried, then ground into a powder known as unsweetened
cocoa.

PURCHASING   There are two styles of unsweetened cocoa powder—
regular and Dutch. **Dutch-process cocoa powder** has been treated with an
alkaline solution, which helps neutralize cocoa's natural acidity. This process creates a darker, richer-flavored powder.

STORING   Store cocoa, sealed airtight, in a cool, dark place for up to 2
years.

USING

* Increase chocolate flavor by adding cocoa powder to a brownie or cake
recipe. For every 2 tablespoons cocoa you add, decrease the flour by 1
tablespoon. To compensate for the cocoa's added bitterness, add 2 to 3
teaspoons sugar for each tablespoon cocoa used.

* Add 1 or 2 tablespoons unsweetened cocoa powder to chili or meat stews
to give them a rich, husky flavor.

* Cocoa mixes (which have added milk powder and sugar) should not be
substituted for unsweetened cocoa powder in recipes.

COCONUTS; COCONUT MILK

PURCHASING

* Fresh coconuts: Choose one that's heavy for its size and that sounds full of liquid when shaken; avoid those with damp "eyes." Fresh coconuts are available year-round, with a peak season from October through December.
* Packaged coconut: This is available in cans or plastic bags, sweetened or unsweetened, shredded or flaked, and dried, moist or frozen. *Unsweetened, dried coconut* is most often available at natural food stores and Asian markets.
* Unsweetened coconut milk: This canned product can be found in regular and reduced-fat forms and is available in Asian markets and some supermarkets.
* Cream of coconut: A thick, sweet mélange of coconut paste, sugar and water, which is typically used in desserts and drinks like Piña Colada.

EQUIVALENTS

* Fresh: 1 medium = 4 to 5 cups shredded coconut
* Bag: 7-ounce shredded or flaked = 3 cups
* Canned: 3½-ounce can = 1½ cups

STORING

* Fresh coconut: Store whole, unopened coconuts at room temperature for up to 6 months, depending on the degree of ripeness. Chunks of coconut meat should be submerged in the juice drained from the coconut (or water) in a tightly sealed container and refrigerated for up to 5 days. Seal grated fresh coconut in an airtight plastic bag and refrigerate for up to 1 week; freeze for up to 6 months.
* Packaged coconut: Unopened cans of coconut may be stored at room temperature for up to 18 months; coconut packaged in plastic bags for up to 6 months. Refrigerate both after opening.
* Coconut milk: Store, unopened, at room temperature for up to 18 months. After opening, refrigerate for up to 1 week.

PREPARING

* **To open a coconut:** First, pierce the shiny black dots ("eyes") with an ice pick or screwdriver and hammer. Make sure you've gone all the way to the coconut's center. Drain out the juice (which can be used as a beverage, though it shouldn't be confused with coconut "milk"). Put the drained coconut in a preheated 375°F oven; bake for 15 minutes. Tap the shell with a hammer to split it. Use a butter knife or screwdriver to separate the meat from the shell. Use a paring knife or vegetable peeler to remove any brown skin that's stuck to the meat.

* **Microwave opening method:** Pierce and drain the coconut as in the previous tip. Place the coconut in a microwave-safe bag. Seal the bag tightly, then pierce it once with the tip of a knife. Put the coconut in the oven with the bag pointing pierced side up. Cook on high for 6 minutes; let stand for 4 minutes. Remove from oven and open the bag—be careful, it's hot. If the shell hasn't opened by itself, give it a whack along one of the cracks. Cool until you can easily handle it, then remove the meat and skin as in previous tip.
* Chunks of coconut meat can be grated or chopped either by hand or in a food processor.
* If packaged coconut has become dry, soak it in hot milk for 30 minutes before using. Drain well, then blot dry on paper towels. Refrigerate the coconut-flavored milk; use for baking or sauces within 5 days. Or combine the milk with chunks of fresh fruit in the blender for an exotically flavored beverage.
* Coconut milk, store-bought or homemade, adds a subtle flavor and silky texture to many soups, sauces and desserts. It can also be used to cook rice and pasta.
* Toasted unsweetened coconut makes a wonderful garnish for many Asian dishes, fruit salads and some vegetables. Toasted sweetened coconut is great on desserts. **To oven-toast:** Spread coconut in a single layer on a baking sheet with shallow sides. Bake at 325°F, tossing occasionally, for about 10 minutes, or until golden brown. **Microwave toasting:** Spread coconut on a paper plate and cook on high for 2 to 3 minutes, stirring twice during that time.
* Colored coconut: Combine 1 cup shredded coconut with 3 to 5 drops food coloring in a bowl; toss until evenly colored.

HOMEMADE COCONUT MILK

Combine equal parts water and shredded fresh or dried unsweetened coconut; simmer until foamy. Cover and remove from the heat; let stand for 15 minutes. Pour the mixture into a blender; process for 1 minute. Strain the liquid through a very fine sieve or a sieve lined with a double thickness of cheesecloth. Cover and refrigerate for up to 5 days. Repeat the process for a second, diluted batch of coconut milk, discarding the coconut meat afterward.

COCONUT "CREAM"

Make in the same manner as coconut milk, but use 1 part water to 4 parts coconut. For an even richer result, substitute milk for water.

I think if I were a woman I'd wear coffee as a perfume.
—John Van Druten, American playwright

COFFEE

TIDBIT Ever wonder what all those coffees on some restaurant menus are? Here's a brief summary: **espresso**—a very strong brew made under pressure with dark-roasted coffee, served in a tiny espresso cup; **café macchiato**—espresso with a dollop of steamed-milk foam, served in an espresso cup; **cappuccino**—espresso topped with foamy steamed milk, served in a regular-sized cup or glass mug; **caffé latte**—espresso plus a liberal amount of foamy steamed milk, usually served in a tall glass mug; **café mocha**—caffé latte with chocolate added; **café au lait**—equal portions of hot milk and coffee; **café brûlot**—coffee blended with spices, orange and lemon peel and brandy, then flamed; **Irish coffee**—strong coffee, Irish whiskey and sugar, usually served in a glass mug with a dollop of whipped cream; **Thai coffee**—coffee mixed with sweetened condensed milk; **Turkish coffee**—very strong coffee made by boiling water, finely ground coffee, and sugar together; **Viennese coffee**—strong, usually sweetened coffee served in a tall glass and topped with whipped cream.

PURCHASING If possible, purchase coffee (whole bean or freshly ground) from specialty coffee stores or markets with rapid turnover. The flavor of both regular and decaffeinated beans is greatly superior to the canned preground supermarket coffee. A blend of two or more types of coffee beans typically produces a richer, more complex brew than a single-bean coffee. Decrease caffeine by buying a half-and-half mixture of regular and decaffeinated coffee.

STORING Air is one of coffee's worst enemies, so make sure there's minimal airspace between the lid of the storage container and the surface of the beans or ground coffee.

* Whole beans: Store, in an airtight container in a cool, dry place for up to 2 weeks. Beans may be wrapped airtight and frozen for up to 3 months.
* Ground coffee: Refrigerate in an airtight container for up to 2 weeks. Or double wrap and freeze for up to 2 months.

GRINDING

* For maximum flavor, grind only as many beans as needed to brew each pot of coffee.
* Generally, the finer the grind, the fuller the flavor.
* Whether you grind coffee beans in a coffee grinder or in a special unit of your coffeemaker, it's important to remove all of the ground residue after each use. Otherwise, the natural oils in the coffee-bean particles

will turn rancid, giving an off flavor to subsequent batches. A narrow rubber spatula does a great job of removing ground-coffee residue, as does a small brush or a slightly dampened piece of paper towel.

BREWING

* There are several ways to brew coffee. **Drip** coffee is made by manually pouring hot water slowly through a filter holding the grounds into a heatproof carafe. **Autodrip** coffeemakers work the same way automatically. A reservoir holds cold water that is passed through a heating unit, then slowly sprays over the grounds in a filter basket. The coffee drips into the pot below, which typically sits on a warming plate. The **French press** method employs infusion. Coffee grounds are placed in a carafe, hot water is added and the coffee's allowed to steep for several minutes. A stainless-steel mesh plunger is then pressed down through the mixture, trapping the grounds at the bottom. A **percolator** shoots heated water up through a central tube and down through a basket of coffee grounds, repeating the process until the coffee obtains the desired strength.

* Make sure your equipment is scrupulously clean. Residual oils are left inside the pot each and every time you brew coffee. If that residue is not removed completely, it will affect each fresh pot of coffee, giving it a bitter, rancid flavor.

* Use freshly drawn cold water, and be sure that the water tastes good. If your tap water's highly chlorinated or has a distinctive mineral taste, your coffee won't taste good. If that's the case, use bottled water.

* Make sure you're using the correct amount, grind and brewing time for your coffeemaker.

* For a full-flavored cup of coffee, use 2 level tablespoons (1 coffee measure or ⅛ cup) for each 6 ounces (¾ cup) water. (Remember that a standard coffee cup holds 6 ounces, whereas a mug often holds 10 to 12 ounces.) For stronger coffee, use 2 level tablespoons for each 4 ounces (½ cup) water.

* For an emergency coffee-filter replacement, cut a piece of paper towel to fit your coffeemaker basket.

* To save a pot of weak coffee at the last minute, stir in a teaspoon or two of good-quality instant coffee. Let stand 3 minutes before serving.

* If you find coffee too acid, add a pinch of salt to the grounds before brewing begins.

* Spice up your coffee by sprinkling a dash or two of cinnamon, allspice or nutmeg over the grounds before brewing. Orange or lemon zest can also be added in this way. Just before serving, a drop (not too much) of pure vanilla extract can be stirred into the brew.

* Coffee's flavor begins to deteriorate within 15 minutes after it's brewed. Leaving coffee on a heating element accelerates this problem, which is caused by the evaporation of the aromatic oils, leaving the flavor bitter and flat.
* To retain first-cup freshness, transfer the coffee to a vacuum-insulated carafe that's been preheated with hot water. These thermos carafes are available in a wide variety of attractive colors and styles.
* Reheating coffee just makes it bitter.
* Instant coffee is more palatable if you combine the water and coffee granules in a pan over medium heat, bring barely to a boil, then remove from the heat, cover and let stand for 3 minutes.
* Make your own "instant" coffee by putting 2 tablespoons ground coffee in a tiny strainer (or tea infuser) lined with paper towel. Place the strainer or infuser in a coffee cup, then pour 6 ounces boiling water over the grounds. Cover and steep for 3 minutes, or until the coffee reaches the desired strength. Remove the strainer and drink. For larger mugs, increase the coffee and water ratio accordingly.

SERVING

* Pass sticks of cinnamon to use as coffee stirrers.
* A dollop of whipped cream makes any coffee a special occasion. Flavor the whipped cream with liqueur, or try the Chocolate Whipped Cream, page 159.
* Whenever pouring hot coffee into a glass cup or mug (as for Irish coffee), put a spoon in the cup first, then pour the coffee onto the spoon. This diffuses the heat and keeps the glass from cracking.
* Having a dinner party and don't want to bother with making coffee afterward? Brew it beforehand and pour it into a thermal carafe (preheat the carafe with boiling water). The coffee can be served while you're still clearing the table.
* **Iced coffee:** If you have the time, start by making coffee ice cubes: Pour cooled coffee into ice cube trays, and freeze until solid. Fill a glass with coffee ice cubes, and top with chilled coffee and, if desired, milk and sweetener. If you don't have time to make coffee ice cubes, brew the coffee stronger than you normally would so the flavor will still be rich even after being diluted by melting regular ice.

CLEANING

* Dish soap and detergent can leave an infinitesimal soap film on a coffeepot that will distort coffee's flavor. Clean the pot with a little baking soda and hot water. Be sure to rinse thoroughly!
* Never use anything abrasive to clean a coffeepot. Brushes, cleansers and

the like will scratch the container's interior—every scratch captures coffee oils (which quickly turn rancid) and mineral deposits. Metal coffeepots are more susceptible to scratches than those made of glass or porcelain.

* Clean an automatic coffeemaker by putting 2 teaspoons baking soda in the water reservoir, adding a full pot of cold water, then brewing as usual. Run plain water through the machine before making coffee.
* Freshen a stale-smelling coffeepot by filling it with a mixture of boiling water and 2 teaspoons baking soda. Cover and let stand until cool. Rinse thoroughly.
* A paste of salt and vinegar will remove coffee or tea stains from china cups.

MALLOCCINO

A perfect warmer-upper for cold winter days. In a medium saucepan, combine 2 cups milk, 12 to 16 large marshmallows (depending on your sweet tooth) and ⅛ teaspoon ground cinnamon (optional). Cook over low heat, stirring often, until marshmallows are almost melted (leave a few small lumps). Add 1½ tablespoons instant espresso powder (or 2 tablespoons instant-coffee granules); stir to dissolve. Pour into warm 12-ounce mugs. Serves 2

COLANDERS *see* SIEVES

COLLARD GREENS *see* GREENS

CONDENSED MILK *see* SWEETENED CONDENSED MILK

CONDIMENTS *see* CHUTNEY; HORSERADISH; KETCHUP; MAYONNAISE; MUSTARD; SALSA

CONFECTIONERS' SUGAR *see* SUGAR

CONVECTION OVEN COOKING *see also* COOKING, GENERAL; MICROWAVE COOKING; OVENS, CONVENTIONAL

TIDBIT Convection ovens have a fan that provides continuous circulation of hot air, which cooks food more evenly and up to a third faster (even when the oven's crowded). The hot-air circulation makes convection ovens particularly suited for baked goods and roasted and broiled meats and fish.

* When converting a recipe from a conventional to a convection oven, reduce the temperature by 25° to 75°F (follow manufacturer's instructions).
* Because they heat up so fast, convection ovens usually require little or no preheating.

* Unlike microwave ovens, convection ovens require no special cookware or major adjustments in cooking time or technique.
* For meats and fish, the convection oven temperature can be lowered 25°F, and the roasting time decreased by 25 to 30 percent.
* Convection ovens can easily overbrown baked goods, so be on the safe side and lower the oven temperature by 50°F to 75°F, but keep the baking time about the same.

Shortbread has beneficial effects on the soul. The warm glow it gives is better than alcohol, and more readily available than sex.
—Lucy Ellman, American author

COOKIES

TIDBIT There are six basic cookie styles. **Drop cookies** are made by dropping spoonfuls of dough onto baking sheets; **bar cookies** are created when a batter or soft dough is spooned into a shallow pan, then cut into bars after baking; **hand-formed (or molded) cookies** are made by shaping dough by hand into balls, logs, crescents and other shapes; **pressed cookies** are formed by pressing dough through a cookie press (or a PASTRY BAG with a decorative tip) to form fancy shapes and designs; **refrigerator cookies** are made by shaping the dough into logs that are refrigerated until firm, then sliced and baked; **rolled cookies** are made by rolling out dough out into a thin layer, then cutting it out with cookie cutters.

MIXING COOKIE DOUGH
* Never substitute diet or whipped margarine, or anything labeled "spread," for butter. Such ingredients have a low fat and high water content and could produce disastrous results.
* Sifting flour is usually unnecessary, unless the recipe so directs. Measure by stirring the flour, then spooning it lightly into the measuring cup and leveling off the top with the back of a dinner knife.
* Once the flour has been added, you'll get better results by mixing the dough by hand with a wooden spoon than with an electric mixer. Too much mixing will overdevelop the flour's gluten and produce tough cookies.
* Most unbaked cookie doughs can be refrigerated for at least a week, frozen for up to 6 months. To freeze, form the dough into a log and double wrap it. You can also simply drop the dough onto a plastic wrap–line baking sheet (or roll the dough into balls and place on the baking sheet), freeze until solid, then wrap in a freezer-proof plastic bag.

FORMING THE DOUGH

* When ready to bake a frozen dough log, remove it from the freezer, slice and bake. If the dough is too hard to slice immediately, let stand at room temperature for 15 to 30 minutes.

* Whether a dough log's frozen or simply chilled, give the log a quarter turn every 4 to 6 slices to keep it round.

* Form cookies the same size and shape for even baking and browning. Keep a ruler at hand when forming balls of dough to make sure all the cookies will be the same size.

* When rolling out cookie dough, work with a small amount at a time, covering the rest with plastic wrap to keep moist.

* For easy cleanup, roll out dough on a waxed paper–covered countertop, anchoring the waxed paper by sprinkling a few drops of water on the countertop before arranging the paper.

* Or spray a countertop with cooking spray, then roll out dough without sticking. Clean the countertop with a soapy sponge or cloth.

* When rolling out dough, always start at the center and roll outward.

* A pizza cutter works well for cutting rolled-out dough.

* Cookie dough won't stick to cookie cutters if you spritz them first with cooking spray. Or dip them in flour or confectioners' sugar whenever the dough begins to stick.

* Drop-cookie recipes call for scooping up cookie dough with a spoon, then dropping it onto a baking sheet. The "teaspoon" or "tablespoon" called for in most recipes generally refers to regular tableware, not measuring spoons. Keep your hands clean by using a small ice cream scoop to drop the dough.

* To freeze drop-cookie dough, drop it onto a greased baking sheet and freeze until solid. Transfer dough drops to freezer-proof wrapping.

BAKING SHEETS AND PANS

* Shiny heavy-gauge aluminum baking sheets are good heat conductors and will produce the most evenly baked and browned cookies.

* Dark sheets absorb more oven heat and can cause cookies to overbrown or burn. Lining dark sheets with heavy-duty aluminum foil alleviates the problem.

* Insulated baking sheets are made of two sheets of aluminum with an air pocket sealed between them. Cookies may take 1 to 2 minutes longer to bake on insulated sheets.

* If all you have are thin, lightweight baking sheets, place one on top of the other to prevent cookies from burning.

C

* Use this double-panning technique if you're baking cookies in the lower third of your oven. The same goes for bar cookies—place one pan inside another to protect cookies from that bottom heat.
* In a pinch, invert a jelly-roll pan and use the bottom as a cookie sheet.
* Always use the pan size called for in a bar-cookie recipe. A smaller pan and the cookies will be too thick and gummy in the middle. A larger pan will produce thin, dry cookies.
* If using a glass pan instead of one made of metal for bar cookies, reduce the oven temperature by 25°F.

PREPARING THE PANS

* Speed cleanup by lining baking sheets with PARCHMENT PAPER, which you don't have to grease. Cookie bottoms won't burn on parchment-lined sheets and you can slip the baked cookies on the parchment right off the baking sheet, onto a rack to cool. You can use greased foil the same way.
* Grease (see GREASING PANS) baking sheets and pans with shortening, cooking spray or unsalted butter or margarine. Salted butter or margarine can cause cookies to stick and overbrown on the bottom. Too much grease of any kind can cause cookies to spread and their bottoms to burn.
* Greasing baking sheets is typically unnecessary for high-fat cookies like shortbread.
* To flour greased baking sheets or pans, sprinkle the surface with about ½ tablespoon flour; tap and rotate the sheet until the entire surface is coated with flour. Invert sheet over the sink and shake it gently to remove excess flour.
* Grease and flour cookie sheets or pans in one step with Pan Magic, page 426.
* For bar cookies: Line the pan (usually 8 × 8 inch or 9 × 13 inches) with foil or parchment paper, leaving at least 3 inches of overhang on each end. For easy foil lining, turn the pan upside down and form the foil to fit, tightly creasing the corners. Lift off the foil, flip the pan over and insert the formed foil into it. If the recipe calls for a greased pan, grease the foil (parchment doesn't require greasing). Once the cookies are baked and cooled, use the overhang to lift the cookie slab out of the pan, then cut into bars or squares.

BAKING, COOLING AND FINISHING COOKIES

* Preheat the oven for about 10 minutes before beginning to bake. When using glass baking pans (as for bar cookies), reduce the oven temperature by 25°F.

✳ Use an oven THERMOMETER for accurate temperatures. Invest in a good mercury thermometer, available in gourmet or kitchen-supply shops. The all-metal, spring-style thermometers found in supermarkets can become unreliable after a small jolt or fall.

✳ The best place to bake cookies is the upper third of the oven. When baking more than one sheet at a time, switch positions as in the following tip.

✳ All ovens have hot spots, so if you're baking more than one sheet of cookies at a time, ensure even browning by rotating the sheets from top to bottom and front to back halfway through the baking time.

✳ To allow for oven variances, prevent overbaking by checking the cookies a couple of minutes before the minimum baking time.

✳ If you're baking successive batches of cookies and using the same baking sheet, always let it cool to room temperature before putting more dough on it (quick-cool by running cold water over it). Otherwise, the cookie dough can begin to melt and spread, which will affect the cookies' final shape and texture. It can also cause the cookie bottoms to brown before the inside is done.

✳ When baking several batches of cookies, speed your turnaround time by dropping cookie dough (or placing cookie-dough cutouts) onto sheets of parchment paper or foil, then carefully slide the loaded sheet onto the cooled baking pan.

✳ To bake frozen dough drops: Place the drops on baking sheets, cover lightly with waxed paper, and let thaw for 30 to 45 minutes at room temperature before baking.

✳ In general, bar cookies are done when a toothpick inserted in the center comes out clean.

✳ Cool individual cookies by transferring from the pan to a rack.

✳ If cookies start to fall apart as you're removing them from the baking sheet with a spatula, wait a minute or so until they "set," then transfer to a cooling rack.

✳ Bar cookies are usually cooled and stored right in the baking pan. Most are cut after they've cooled. The exception are crisp-style bars, which must be cut while warm—before they become crisp—to prevent unsightly crumbling.

✳ **Chocolate-glazed bar cookies:** Make an almost-instant glaze for bar cookies by sprinkling the surface with chocolate chips as soon as you remove the cookies from the oven. Cover with foil or a baking sheet and let stand for 3 to 5 minutes until the chocolate melts (chocolate chips look whole, even when they're melted). Use a rubber spatula or the back of a spoon to gently and evenly spread the chocolate over the surface of the cookies. Cool completely before cutting into squares or bars.

* **Frosting plain or store-bought cookies:** Dip half of each cookie into melted chocolate and then, if desired, into toasted coconut, chopped nuts, chocolate jimmies or colored sprinkles. Place on a waxed-paper–lined baking sheet and refrigerate until the chocolate sets.
* **Cookie sandwiches:** Spread the bottom of one cookie with 1 to 2 teaspoons (the amount depends on the size of the cookie) of jam, frosting or a mixture of peanut butter and honey or jelly. Place a second cookie, bottom side down, on top of the filling. If desired, dip the cookie sandwich halfway into melted chocolate.

STORING COOKIES

* Make sure cookies are completely cool before storing or they'll "sweat" and get soggy.
* Store cookies in airtight containers such as screw-top jars or sealed plastic bags. This prevents humidity from softening crisp cookies and air from drying soft cookies.
* Don't store crisp and soft cookies in the same container or the crisp ones will soon soften.
* Recrisp cookies that have become too soft by reheating them for about 5 minutes in a 300°F oven.
* Keep soft cookies moist by adding 1 or 2 apple quarters to the storage container. Cover tightly and let stand for 1 to 2 days before removing the fruit. This same technique works with soft cookies that are dry because of overbaking or age.
* Separate layers of decorated, moist or sticky cookies with waxed paper or plastic wrap to prevent their sticking together.
* Bar cookies may be stored, tightly covered, in the pan in which they were baked.
* Cookies that require refrigeration should be covered tightly so they don't absorb other food odors.
* Cookies in the freezer are culinary security! Make sure cookies to be frozen are wrapped airtight, either in freezer-weight plastic bags or foil; expel as much air as possible. Rigid, plastic freezer containers may also be used and are especially good for delicate cookies.
* Cookies can be frozen from 4 to 6 months, depending on the temperature and conditions in the freezer. Place a sheet of waxed paper or plastic wrap between cookie layers.
* If planning to freeze cookies, it's safer to frost them after freezing and thawing.

* Frosted cookies can be frozen for up to 6 months if you first freeze them individually. To do so, place a tray of uncovered cookies in the freezer; freeze until hard. Immediately transfer frozen cookies to an airtight storage container and return to freezer as quickly as possible.

* Label your storage containers with a piece of tape indicating name of cookie, quantity and date stored.

* Most baked cookies defrost at room temperature in 10 to 15 minutes.

* Don't throw out those cookie crumbs! Sprinkle them over ice cream and puddings, or freeze them until you have enough to make a cookie-crumb crust for a pie or cheesecake.

GIVING AND MAILING COOKIES

* Bar cookies or other soft cookies are best for mailing. Choose those that won't dry out or crumble during the journey. Fragile, thin cookies run the risk of becoming cookie crumbs by the time they reach their destination. Avoid cookies with frostings or pointed edges.

* Use foil to wrap cookies in pairs (flat sides together) or in small stacks.

* Pack cookies close together so they won't have room to jiggle around and break during transit.

* Separate layers of cookies with waxed paper or plastic wrap.

* When packing a variety of cookies in one container, place several of one kind of cookie in separate paper or foil cupcake liners.

* **Shrink-wrapping** large individual cookies or small stacks of cookies preserves their freshness, makes them sturdy for mailing, and adds a professional look for gift-giving. Here's how to shrink-wrap: Preheat the oven to 325°F, then line a baking sheet with two layers of heavy-duty paper towels; set aside. Wrap cookie stacks or large single cookies firmly in a good-quality plastic wrap (bargain brands will melt!), overlapping the edges at the bottom middle of the cookie. Cut away any excess plastic wrap that bunches up at the overlap. Place the paper towel–lined baking sheet in the oven for 5 minutes. Remove from the oven and arrange the wrapped cookies, 1 inch apart, on the hot baking sheet. Return the sheet to the oven, leaving the door ajar so you can watch the cookies closely. The plastic wrap will shrink tightly around the cookie packages in just a few seconds. Cool the wrapped cookies on racks.

* Rigid containers such as cookie tins, plastic or cardboard boxes, coffee or shortening cans with plastic lids or clean cardboard half-gallon milk cartons make good mailing containers.

* Before mailing cookies, pack the container in a sturdy, corrugated box with plenty of room for a cushion of filler (crumpled newspaper or other

paper, Styrofoam pellets, popcorn or plastic bubble-wrap). Pad the bottom of the box with several inches of filler, add the container of cookies, then more filler around the sides and on top.

❋ Don't skimp on postage when mailing cookies. You don't want all your hard work to become tasteless and dry by mailing cookie packages third class.

The only real stumbling block is fear of failure.
In cooking you've got to have a what-the-hell attitude.
—Julia Child, American author, teacher, TV cooking icon

COOKING, GENERAL   *see also* BAKING; BARDING; BLANCHING; BLENDERS; BRAISING; BREADING; BRINING; BROILING; CLAY-POT COOKING; CLEAN UP; CONVECTION OVEN COOKING; COOKING AND EATING LIGHT; COOKWARE AND BAKEWARE; DEEP-FRYING; EN PAPILLOTE; FOOD PROCESSORS; FOOD SAFETY; FREEZING FOOD; GRILLING; HIGH-ALTITUDE ADJUSTMENTS; JULIENNE; LARDING; MEASURING; MICROWAVE COOKING; POACHING; PRESSURE COOKING; PURÉEING; REDUCING; ROASTING; SAUTÉING; SIMMERING; SLOW COOKERS; STEAMING; STIR-FRYING; TEMPERATURES

TIDBIT Kitchen panache is sometimes just as important as the food. When things go wrong, don't tell anyone—flops can be handled with style and flair. So what if the corn soufflé collapses into a dense puddle? Smile jauntily, call it "corn pudding" and act like that's just how it's *supposed* to look. It will still taste great and no one will be the wiser.

GETTING ORGANIZED

❋ Secure a notepad to the inside of one of your kitchen cabinet doors and create a running grocery list by jotting down items as you think of them or run out.

❋ Turn on the oven the minute you walk through the door so it can be preheating while you start meal preparations.

❋ Room-temperature foods cook and bake faster than chilled food, so take ingredients out of the refrigerator as soon as you know you'll need them.

❋ Read a recipe all the way through to be sure you have the necessary ingredients and cooking utensils.

❋ Have several kitchen timers on hand, setting them for each dish that's cooking. It's easy for busy cooks to forget timing and wind up with a ruined dish.

❋ It's a good idea to chop, measure and otherwise prepare all the ingredients for a recipe before beginning to cook.

PREPARING

* Start preparing each meal by beginning with the dish that takes longest—it can be cooking while you prepare the other items.
* When preparing several dishes, scan the recipes to see if there are any of the same ingredients called for. If so, chopping them at the same time saves on time and cleanup. In other words, if one recipe calls for ¼ cup onions and another for ¾ cup, chop 1 cup to begin with.
* Wear disposable latex gloves (available at drugstores and supermarkets) to protect your hands from stains (as with beets) or volatile oils (as with chiles).
* No gloves? Generously coat your hands with vegetable oil, then wash off when you're through.
* When beating or whisking a mixture in a bowl on the countertop, keep the bowl from moving around by setting it on a slightly dampened kitchen towel.
* Before stirring a sticky or staining mixture, spray the utensil with cooking spray or coat it lightly with vegetable oil. Be sure to spray the utensil over the sink so you don't get an oily film on your kitchen floor.
* Instead of using a pastry brush to coat foods (like meat or bread) with oil, fill a small, clean spray bottle (from hairspray, glass cleaner, and so on) with oil and lightly spritz it over the food. Less oil = fewer calories.
* If you put raw meat, poultry or fish on a dish during preparation, or use it to transfer the food from kitchen to grill, don't put the cooked food on that same dish without first washing it thoroughly or you will transfer the raw food's bacteria to the cooked food.

SEASONING

* Taste as you cook, and sample all the components of the dish—filling, sauce, and so on. How else will you know what the finished product will taste like?
* Remember that chilling food mutes its flavor, so when serving cold salads, soups, and so on, be sure to taste them just before serving and adjust the seasoning if necessary.
* Add pizzazz to a dish that tastes "flat" by stirring in 1 to 2 teaspoons full-flavored vinegar, such as balsamic.
* A little vinegar will balance the flavor of an oversweetened savory dish (such as vegetables, dressings or salad dressings).
* Add flavor and flair with ethnic ingredients that are intrinsic to various cuisines: **Caribbean**—hot chiles, cilantro, cinnamon, cloves, coconut, ginger, lime juice, nutmeg and turmeric; **Chinese**—black bean sauce, garlic, fresh ginger, oyster sauce, sesame oil (dark) and soy sauce;

Greek—allspice, cinnamon, cloves, dill, fennel, garlic, mint, nutmeg and oregano; **Italian**—basil, fennel, garlic, onion, oregano and tomato; **Japanese**—garlic, ginger, miso, scallions, soy sauce, plum or rice vinegar and wasabi; **Mexican**—cayenne, chile pepper, cilantro, onion, oregano and unsweetened cocoa powder; **Thai**—basil, bean sauce, chili paste, curry, fish sauce, lemongrass and mint.

COOKING

* Cook once, eat twice—grill or broil extra meat, fish or vegetables. Refrigerate and serve the next day in a different guise. The grilled food can be used in a salad or sandwich, tossed with pasta, added to a stir-fry, and so on.

* Packet cooking: Place an individual serving of chicken or fish on a piece of foil large enough to enclose it. Top with minced vegetables, herbs, sauce or whatever; seal the packet and bake or grill. Do the same thing with PARCHMENT PAPER.

* To keep a pot from boiling over, give steam a tiny outlet by placing a toothpick between the pot and the cover. The toothpick trick also works well with a covered casserole dish in the oven.

* Rubbing vegetable oil around the inside of the top of the pot prevents boilovers in custards, milk, pasta, and so on.

* When using a double boiler, put a few marbles or a jar lid in the bottom pan to warn you by rattling when the water gets too low. It'll save the pan from scorching.

* When cooking particularly odoriferous foods like broccoli, Brussels sprouts or cauliflower, toss a couple of thick chunks of bread into the cooking water (rye bread works best). Bread slices work, too, though sometimes they dissolve and are hard to remove. Or toss a couple of red bell pepper pieces into the pot. Use a slotted spoon to retrieve the pot sweeteners before serving the food.

* Keep odors at bay by draping a cloth (dampened with a half-and-half solution of water and vinegar, then wrung out) over the cooking pot, making sure the edges are well away from the heat source.

* Reheat frozen foods (such as sauces, soups and stews) over low heat. Add just enough water to cover the bottom of the pan, cover and cook, stirring often to break up the food as it defrosts. Once defrosted, increase the heat to medium and cook until heated through.

* Before removing a pan from the stove, turn off the burner.

* Make sure oven mitts or pads are dry before handling a hot pan or dish. Wet material lets the heat through and could result in a burn.

If you want to look young and thin, hang around old fat people.
—Jim Eason, American radio talkshow host

COOKING AND EATING LIGHT *(reducing calories, fat and salt)* see *also* COOKING, GENERAL; LABEL TERMS

TIDBIT With all the talk about reducing dietary fat (definitely a good idea), many people seem to think that calories simply don't count anymore—or at least that they're not as important as once thought. Fat, they decry, is the culprit that offends our hearts and hips. In fact, calories *do* count and, to confuse matters further, all calories are not alike. To begin with, calories come from four sources—alcohol, carbohydrates, fats and proteins—and they don't all count the same. Here's how it breaks down: Fat packs a hefty 9 calories per gram, over twice as much as the 4 calories per gram carried by both carbohydrates and proteins. And those who enjoy a cocktail before or wine with dinner should know that alcohol contains 7 calories per gram, almost as many as fat! All of which is good food for thought. But you might also consider the words of Julia Child, who said: "Those food labels that say 'no fat, no cholesterol' might as well say 'no taste, no fun.'" A statement she appended with "moderation is the key."

GENERAL

* Most experts, including the American Heart Association, recommend that no more (and preferably less) than 30 percent of daily calories come from fat. To calculate the percentage of fat calories a food contains, find the "fat grams per serving" on the label and multiply by 9. This gives you the total calories from fat. Now divide that number by the total calories per serving. The result is the percentage of calories that come from fat.
* Keep portion sizes small to medium.
* Eating more slowly is one way to eat less. It takes about 20 minutes for the "I'm satisfied" signal to go from stomach to brain. Cut food into tiny pieces and chew each piece 20 times.
* Make it a habit to put your fork down between bites.
* Slow down by eating with your nondominant hand.
* Using chopsticks (unless you're skillful with them) will also slow your eating pace.
* The plethora of food label terms can be confusing. To make sure you know what's in the food you buy, as well as the difference between phrases like "reduced calorie" and "low calorie," *see* LABEL TERMS, page 264.

PORTION SIZES Few of us have time to measure everything we eat. Knowing what portions are supposed to look like makes life easier. The following visuals are adapted from those suggested by the American Dietetic Association (www.eatright.org):

* One cup = an average-sized woman's fist.
* 1½ cups = an average-sized man's fist.
* A 3-ounce portion of meat, fish or poultry = the size of a deck of cards or a cassette tape.
* One ounce of cheese = the size of an average thumb.
* One teaspoon peanut butter = the size of a small grape.
* An average bagel = the size of a hockey puck.
* An average muffin = the size of a medium fist.
* A medium potato = the size of a computer mouse.

SUGAR

* Fructose, a natural by-product of fruits and honey, is sweeter than sugar with fewer calories. It comes in granulated and syrup forms. It can be used in many preparations, including jams, condiments, desserts and baked goods.
* Both vanilla and cinnamon raise the level of perceived sweetness. Add one or both to salad dressings, desserts and baked goods.
* Choose fresh fruit for dessert, knowing that many fruits (like bananas) intensify in sweetness when cooked.
* PURÉE cooked or raw fresh fruit, flavor with vanilla and cinnamon or allspice, and use as a sauce for angel-food cake, fruit compotes, and so on.

SALT

* The daily recommended sodium intake is 2,400 milligrams, about 1 teaspoon salt. Most Americans use five times that much.
* Look for foods with "reduced sodium" on the label.
* Use herbs and spices instead of salt to enhance flavor.
* Garlic, onions and peppers add loads of flavor with just a trace of sodium.
* Flavored vinegars and oils brighten foods without salt.
* Lemon juice enhances flavors with barely a trace of sodium.
* Add flavor by replacing water in recipes with juice, wine or fat-free vegetable or meat broth.
* Avoid smoked or pickled foods and high-sodium condiments such as ketchup and barbecue sauce.
* Substitute high-sodium tomato sauce with ⅜ cup salt-free tomato paste mixed with ½ cup water.

FAT

* Avoid saturated fats, including butter, lard, coconut or palm oil, suet and hydrogenated oils such as margarine or shortening.

* Use cooking sprays instead of oils or fats to grease pans.
* Nonstick cookware cuts way down on the necessity for oil when sautéing foods.
* Sautéing doesn't require oodles of oil. Get into the habit of measuring it, starting with 1 or 2 teaspoons, adding more only if necessary.
* Substitute wine, fat-free broth, citrus juice, tomato juice or vegetable juice for the oil in marinades.
* Substitute juices or nonfat sour cream, yogurt or half-and-half for oil in salad dressing.
* Refrigerate canned broth overnight to congeal the fat, which can then be easily lifted off the surface.
* Make soups a day in advance and refrigerate. The next day, lift off any solidified fat on the surface before reheating.
* Thicken sauces the low-fat way with cooked vegetable PURÉES.
* Substitute ROUX (a fat-flour mixture used for thickening) with corn-starch, arrowroot or puréed vegetable.
* Many commercial foods like refritos (refried beans) and tortillas contain lard, a saturated fat. Look for products made with vegetable oils, or those that are fat free.
* Low-fat dairy products can make a big caloric difference. For example, a cup of regular sour cream contains about 493 calories, compared with about 280 calories for the low-fat version; plain low-fat yogurt is only about 143 calories. An 8-ounce glass of whole milk contains about 157 calories, while 2 percent low-fat milk equals 121, 1 percent equals 102; and nonfat, a scant 86 calories.
* Nonfat or low-fat evaporated milk adds texture to sauces and other dishes without excess calories. Freeze leftover evaporated milk in ice cube trays, then pop out the milk cubes and put in a freezer-weight plastic bag for future use.
* Choose cheeses that are made from low- or nonfat milk. If salt is a concern, select low-sodium cheeses.
* Fat adds texture and body to dishes so, when substituting reduced-calorie dairy products, it's best not to go down more than one step. If a recipe calls for whipping cream, you can use half-and-half or rich milk and the dish won't suffer as much as if nonfat milk were substituted.
* Quark—a soft, unripened cheese with the texture and flavor of sour cream—is a good low-calorie sour cream substitute. It comes in low-fat and nonfat versions, isn't as tart as yogurt and has a richer texture than either low-fat sour cream or yogurt. Do not use Quark as a substitute when baking.

MEAT

* Reduce your meat-portion size to 3 ounces (about what you get in airline meals). Rather than making meat the focus, or "star," of your meal, make it a "supporting player."
* Choose lean cuts of meat and trim all excess fat before cooking. The younger the animal, the lower the fat content—veal has less fat than beef. Lean cuts include pork and lamb loin, and flank and round steak. Veal is low fat, but has a higher cholesterol content than beef.
* Organ meats (like liver) are typically low in fat but high in cholesterol.
* Turkey is even lower in fat than chicken, and ground turkey and turkey cutlets are commonly found in supermarkets. The cutlets cook in minutes, and ground turkey can substitute for part or all of the beef called for in burgers, chili, stuffed peppers, and meat loaf.
* Substitute turkey pastrami and sausage for the high-fat versions.
* Remove the skin from chicken when using moist-heat cooking methods like BRAISING or STEWING. For dry-heat methods like GRILLING and BROILING, leave the skin on to keep the meat moist, then remove it after cooking.
* For moist, low-fat meat and fish, cook EN PAPILLOTE. Place an individual serving of chicken or fish on a piece of parchment (the classic way) or foil large enough to enclose it. Top with minced vegetables, herbs, tomato sauce or whatever; seal the packet and bake.
* For a juicy, flavorful hamburger with fewer calories, substitute shredded carrots for a third to half the meat. Other substitutions include tofu or cooked and mashed pinto beans or potatoes.
* Substitute the meat in casseroles with cooked, fiber- and protein-rich dried legumes like beans or lentils.
* Thoroughly drain cooked ground meat of as much grease as possible by placing it in a colander over a plate and pressing down firmly with the back of a large spoon. Take it one step further by blotting the meat with a paper towel.
* Make a small portion of cooked meat seem larger by thinly slicing it, then fanning the slices over one side of the plate.
* For a quick and delicious, low-calorie sauce for meat or fish, combine puréed roasted peppers (fresh or those from a jar) with a little stock, wine or evaporated skim milk, and heat until warmed through.

WHIPPED DESSERT TOPPING

Pour low- or nonfat evaporated milk into a shallow metal cake or pie pan; freeze until ice crystals form around the edges. Put a mixing bowl and beaters in the freezer at the same time. Turn the icy-cold milk and ½ to 1 teaspoon pure vanilla extract into a mixing bowl and whip until fluffy. To sweeten, gently beat 1 to 2 tablespoons confectioners' sugar into the whipped milk.

SOUR CREAM SUBSTITUTE

Combine ½ cup low-fat cottage cheese, ¼ cup nonfat milk and 2 teaspoons lemon juice in a blender; cover and process until smooth and creamy. Cover and refrigerate for up to 4 days. Blend with fresh herbs and seasonings for an easy low-calorie dip. Makes about ¾ cup.

CREAMY LOW-CALORIE SALAD DRESSING

Combine ½ cup nonfat yogurt, 1 cup fresh herbs and 1 to 2 tablespoons fresh lemon, lime or orange juice in a blender jar. PURÉE until smooth; add salt and pepper to taste. If the dressing is too thick, thin it with a little non- or low-fat milk. Make about 1 cup.

COOKING SPRAYS

TIDBIT Cooking sprays (primarily a combination of vegetable oil and lecithin or other emulsifier) are a boon to health-conscious cooks who want to control fat intake. They not only prevent food from sticking, but make cleanup easy. Cooking sprays are also called *vegetable cooking sprays* and *nonstick sprays*.

PURCHASING Available in a supermarket's cooking oil section, in both aerosol and nonaerosol versions, plain or flavored.

STORING Store in a cool place for up to a year.

USING

* Coat baking pans, muffin tins, casseroles, skillets, broiling pans, waffle irons and griddles for nonstick cooking and baking. Keep the surrounding area clean by placing the item to be sprayed in the sink or on the open door of the dishwasher, both of which will be cleaned in the normal course of the day.
* Coat the grid of an outdoor grill, but never spray the grill over the fire or you could have a flare-up. Do the same for a grill fish basket.
* Never heat a skillet coated with cooking spray for longer than 2 to 3 minutes or the spray will scorch.
* Before cutting ingredients that stick together (like dried fruit or gumdrops), give the kitchen shears or knife a spritz.
* Spray box or other hand graters before grating foods like chocolate and cheese.
* Coat the inside of a food processor (including the lid), as well as the cutting implement, when processing sticky mixtures or grating cheese.
* Lubricate the inside edge of a food processor lid that sticks.

- Spray the beaters or dough hook(s) of an electric mixer to prevent sticky mixtures like doughs from climbing the hooks.
- Spray the dish or pan used for melting chocolate and the chocolate will slip right out.
- Bake pies that tend to boil over on a baking sheet coated with cooking spray.
- Spray a cake-cooling rack to keep a cake from sticking.
- When rolling out cookie or pie dough on a countertop or other smooth surface, spritz it first with cooking spray.
- Use on cookie cutters to keep the dough from sticking.
- Before stirring a sticky or staining mixture, spray the utensil (spoon or rubber spatula) with cooking spray.
- Use it on one side of plastic wrap to keep it from sticking to delicate surfaces like frosting.
- Coat the molds for gelatin-based dishes.
- Spray a thin coating on ice cream scoops and the ice cream will slip right off the scoop.
- Coat your hands with it when working with food (like beets) that could stain them.
- Lightly spritz air-popped popcorn before seasoning and the flavorings will stick to the corn.
- Liberally spray plastic utensils and storage containers to reduce staining by tomato-based mixtures.

COOKWARE AND BAKEWARE see also PAN SIZES; SEASONING PANS; CLAY-POT COOKING

TIDBIT The materials that make up pots, pans and bakeware can make a huge difference in how your food turns out. The properties of each substance (whether metal, glass or ceramic) make it suitable for some culinary tasks but not for others. Choose your cookware and bakeware not only for its size, shape and function, but for the material from which it's made. Following are some basics on materials used for cook- and bakeware that should help you choose the right pan for the job at hand.

- **Nonreactive** is a term used for pans made of metals that don't react negatively to foods, particularly those with acidic ingredients like tomatoes and lemon juice. Cooking such foods in reactive-metal pans (like aluminum, copper and unseasoned cast iron) can cause discoloration and a metallic taste. Stainless steel is a nonreactive metal, which is why most copper and aluminum pans are lined with it (or other nonreactive metal).

* **Nonstick** cookware and bakeware has a fused coating on interior surfaces that permits fat-free, stick-free cooking and minimal cleanup. Higher-priced nonstick pans have a coating that's bonded right to the metal, making for a stronger, more durable finish. Prolong the life of nonstick cook- and bakeware by using low to medium heat and non-abrasive implements for both cooking and cleaning. Don't worry about a nonstick coating that becomes scratched and scarred (which means bits of it have transferred to food). The pan's surface may not be completely "nonstick" anymore, but at least the coating is nontoxic and will simply pass through the body.

* **Aluminum** is an excellent heat conductor and moderately priced. The heavier the gauge, the more evenly food will cook. *Anodized aluminum* (available in matte, polished or dark gray finishes) has a surface that's been electrochemically treated. This gives the surface a remarkably hard (chip-, stain- and scratch-resistant), low-stick finish that's *almost* nonreactive to acids (just don't store acidic foods in it). Stay away from *untreated aluminum cookware*, which can flavor and discolor foods containing acidic ingredients.

* **Cast iron** is very efficient at absorbing, conducting and retaining heat, and it is relatively inexpensive. There's enameled cast iron (*see following entry on* Enamelware) and regular cast iron. The latter requires seasoning (*see* SEASONING PANS), which produces a surface that's nonreactive and nonstick. Care must be taken in cleaning regular cast iron, which should be gently washed and wiped dry with a soft cloth.

* **Copper,** the cookware of choice for many professionals, is heavy-duty and has excellent heat conductivity. It's also very expensive. Copper is typically lined with stainless steel or tin to make it nonreactive (unlined copper not only reacts to acids but is potentially toxic). Copper pots need to be relined every few years.

* **Earthenware** comes in two basic styles—glazed and unglazed. Neither is a good heat conductor, but both retain heat well and release it slowly, making earthenware particularly suitable for long-cooking dishes like casseroles and baked beans. *Glazed earthenware* has a hard, nonporous coating. It must be cooled slowly and completely before washing to prevent the glaze from cracking. *Unglazed earthenware* is porous and must be thoroughly soaked in water before use.

* **Enamelware** is made of either cast iron (a good heat conductor) or steel (a poor heat conductor) that's been coated with a hard layer of porcelain enamel. Enamelware is nonreactive and easy to clean; however, over-heating it can cause the surface to crack.

- **Glass, glass-ceramic** and **porcelain** are nonreactive and easy to clean, but are relatively poor heat conductors, though they retain heat efficiently. Glass-ceramic dishes can go from freezer to oven without a problem; glass-porcelain combinations may crack with sudden temperature changes.
- **Stainless steel** by itself has poor heat conductivity, but it's strong, nonreactive, corrosion-resistant and easy to clean. *Clad metal stainless cookware* has a core of either copper or aluminum (both excellent heat conductors) sandwiched between two sheets of stainless steel, offering consumers the best of both worlds.
- **Stoneware** is made of strong pottery that's typically fully glazed, then fired at very high temperatures. This creates a nonporous, chip-resistant container that's safe to use in both microwave and standard ovens. Stoneware is ideal for baking and slow cooking.

People have tried and they have tried, but sex is not better than sweet corn.
—Garrison Keillor, American author and radio personality

CORN *see also* VEGETABLES, GENERAL

TIDBIT According to an old New England adage, *"You may stroll to the garden to cut the corn but you had darn well better run back to the kitchen to cook it!"* So true! As soon as an ear of corn is picked, its sugar begins its gradual conversion to starch. This natural process lessens the corn's natural sweetness and eventually turns the juicy, sweet kernels into starchy, mealy bites. That's why it's important to buy corn as soon after it's picked as possible, preferably from a farmer's market or specialty produce market where you know the turnover is brisk.

PURCHASING Choose ears with bright green, snugly fitting husks. The silk should be fresh looking and dry (not soggy), and pale golden to golden brown in color. The kernels should be plump and milky, and come all the way to the ear's tip, the rows tightly packed. Don't buy husked corn—the market most likely removed the husk because it was discolored or wilted, a sign of old corn. Even if the husks were removed with the greengrocer's best intentions, husked corn deteriorates faster.

EQUIVALENTS
- Fresh: 2 medium ears = 1 to 1¼ cups kernels
- Frozen: 10-ounce package = 1¾ cup kernels
- Canned: 12-ounce can = 1½ cups

STORING Refrigerate fresh corn in a plastic bag for no more than a day after purchase. It's best used the day you buy it. There's always an exception to every rule: University of Maryland professor of food science Don

Schlimme says he's discovered a way to keep corn tasting fresher longer. Put a cooler with ice in your car and, as soon as you leave the market, place the fresh corn inside. At home, prepare a solution of 1 drop lemon juice and 2 drops Clorox for each gallon of ice water, a mixture that curbs starch conversion and significantly reduces the possibility of bacteria and mold. Remove the husks and silk, and plunge the corn into the water. Remove the corn from the water, shaking off excess moisture; place 5 ears into a 1-gallon plastic freezer bag that's at least 0.8 mil thick. Remove as much air as possible, sealing tightly and refrigerating immediately. According to Schlimme, processing and storing corn this way will keep it fresh tasting for 2 weeks. As for me, I'd rather eat it *fresh*.

PREPARING

* Strip off the husks and silk, and rinse off the corn just before cooking. Don't put the husks and silk in the garbage disposal.
* Remove silk remnants by rubbing a damp paper towel over husked corn from tip to stem. A rubber glove or clean, damp, soft-bristled toothbrush also works well.
* To remove corn kernels from the cob, begin by cutting a small piece off the tip so that it stands flat. Holding the stem end, stand the cob upright on its flat end. Set it on a plate and use a firm-bladed, very sharp knife to cut downward, removing three or four rows of corn at a time. To get the "milk," use the back of the blade to scrape what's left of the juice from the cobs.
* For whole kernels of corn, blanch (*see* BLANCHING) the ears for 1 to 2 minutes (depending on the size), then immediately transfer to a bowl of ice water. Remove the kernels as in the previous tip.
* Scrape the cobs clean and save the juices to use in sauces, soups, and so on.

COOKING

* For sweeter corn, add 1 teaspoon sugar for each quart of water.
* Adding salt to the cooking water toughens corn.
* Cooking corn in equal amounts of milk and water tenderizes and sweetens corn.
* Unlike many vegetables, corn becomes tougher, rather than softer, when overcooked. Depending on the size of the ear and the age of the corn (older corn takes longer), corn on the cob can take anywhere from 1 to 10 minutes to cook in boiling water.
* Corn on the cob doesn't have to be husked to be cooked in boiling water. On the contrary, it's even sweeter when cooked in the husk. Gently pull back the husks, remove the silk, then replace the husks, tying them

together at the top with string. Cook as you would husked corn on the cob.

* Cover the pot when cooking corn on the cob so steam can cook the portions not submerged in water.
* Microwave method 1: Rinse off each ear (do not dry); wrap in waxed paper. Cook on high as follows: 1 medium ear—3 to 5 minutes; 2 ears—5 to 7 minutes; 4 ears—9 to 12 minutes.
* Microwave method 2: Place 4 medium unhusked ears of corn, spoke-style and stem end out, on a plate. Cook on high for about 7 minutes; let stand in the oven for 5 minutes. Put on an oven mitt and strip off the husk and silk.
* Grilling method: Remove the silk, but leave the husks; use a metal twist tie to close the husk at the top. Soak the corn in cold water for 15 minutes so the husks don't burn while grilling. Grill for 15 to 30 minutes, depending on the corn's size and age.
* Before grilling or microwaving, flavor ears of corn by rubbing or brushing with herb butter.
* Sauté shucked corn, stirring frequently, only about 3 minutes, or until crisp-tender.
* Serve corn with herb or cheese butter (see Compound Butter, page 72).

LEFTOVERS

* Remove the kernels from leftover cooked corn on the cob, refrigerate and use in soups, salads, succotash, hash, muffins, pancakes, and so on.
* Don't discard leftover cobs (either fresh or cooked)! Throw them in a pot, cover with milk or equal amounts of milk and water, and bring to a simmer. Cover and cook for 30 minutes. Remove the cobs and use the liquid as a base for soups or sauces.

GRILLED CORN OFF THE COB

In a 13 × 9-inch metal baking pan, combine ¼ cup extra virgin olive oil, 2 tablespoons balsamic vinegar, ½ teaspoon salt and ⅔ cup finely snipped herbs (such as basil, fennel and chives). Add 5 cups fresh corn kernels (6 large ears), tossing to coat. Season to taste with freshly ground pepper. Cover and refrigerate for 3 hours. At least 1 hour before grilling, soak 2 cups wood chips in water. Light a fire in the outdoor grill according to manufacturer's directions. Just before grilling, sprinkle wood chips over the heat source. Stir the corn well and place the uncovered pan of corn in the center of the grill rack. Cover the grill and cook over high heat 3 minutes; stir the corn. Cover the grill and cook 3 more minutes. Serve hot. Serves 6.

CORNBREAD *see also* BREAD, QUICK; CORNMEAL

* For crispy side and bottom crusts, put 1 to 2 tablespoons vegetable oil or bacon drippings in an 8- or 9-inch square pan, tilting the pan so the oil coats the sides and bottom. Place the pan in a preheated 400°F oven for 10 minutes. Remove the pan from the oven and immediately fill with cornbread batter (it will sizzle); bake as usual.
* Add flavor to any cornbread by adding to the batter ½ to 1 cup grated cheese; ⅓ cup chopped scallion greens; crumbled crisply cooked bacon or finely chopped ham; 1 to 3 tablespoons chopped jalapeño peppers; or 1 cup corn kernels.
* For slightly sweet cornbread, add 2 tablespoons brown sugar and ¼ teaspoon ground nutmeg to the dry ingredients.
* Nutty touch: Melt 3 tablespoons peanut butter (don't overheat it or it will turn to glue) and stir into the wet ingredients.
* Crumble leftover cornbread finely, spread it evenly over a baking sheet and bake at 300°F until completely dry and lightly browned. Use as you would any toasted bread crumbs, to sprinkle atop casseroles, veggies, and so on.

CORNISH GAME HENS *see also* CHICKEN; POULTRY, GENERAL

TIDBIT Cornish game hens (also called *Rock Cornish game hens*) are miniature, 4- to 6-week-old chickens that weigh 1¼ to 2½ pounds. They're a hybrid of Cornish and White Rock chickens.

PURCHASING

* Cornish game hens are available frozen (and sometimes fresh) in most supermarkets.
* How much per serving: Count on one small game hen or half a large hen.

STORING Refrigerate hens as soon as you get home from the market; use within 2 days. If hens are packaged tightly in cellophane and you're not going to use them within a few hours, either loosen the packaging or remove it and loosely rewrap the poultry in waxed paper; refrigerate for up to 2 days.

PREPARING

* The good news: Cornish game hens look elegant and take less time to cook than a whole chicken. The bad news: You get less cluck for your buck—they're more expensive and have less meat per pound than a regular chicken.
* To butterfly a Cornish game hen, use a sharp knife to cut it down the backbone, then flip the bird and use your palm to press down on the

breastbone until the bird lies flat. If you buy a fresh (rather than frozen) bird, have your butcher handle this for you.

* When stuffing hens, count on about ¾ cup dressing per bird.

COOKING

* Before cooking, use a pointed knife to prick the breast skin in several places so it doesn't split during cooking.
* Brush the skin with melted butter. If desired, season the butter with dried thyme or crumbled rosemary, salt and pepper.
* Place hens several inches apart on an oiled baking sheet or pan.
* Roast whole hens on the center rack of a 400°F oven for about 25 to 30 minutes for small birds, 35 to 40 minutes for larger ones. Timing depends in part on how many hens are being cooked at a time.
* Grill marinated halved or butterflied hens about 35 minutes over a medium-hot fire (*see* GRILLING).
* Cornish game hens are done when a meat THERMOMETER inserted in the thickest part of the thigh registers 170°F (the temperature will rise during standing time). The bird's juices should run clear when the flesh is pierced.
* Let the bird stand for 10 minutes to redistribute the juices throughout the flesh. Cover with foil to keep warm.

CORNMEAL   *see also* POLENTA

PURCHASING

* There are two main styles of cornmeal—steel-ground and stone- or water-ground. Most cornmeal in supermarkets is steel-ground, which means the husk and germ have been almost completely removed. Stone-ground cornmeal retains some of the corn's hull and germ, making it more nutritious. It's commonly available in natural food stores.
* Cornmeal comes in three textures—fine (often called "corn flour"), medium (the texture most commonly available commercially) and coarse (also known as "polenta"). Masa harina is a special corn flour used to make corn tortillas and tamales.

EQUIVALENTS

* 1 pound = 3 cups uncooked; 1 cup = 4 cups cooked

STORING

* Steel-ground cornmeal: Store almost indefinitely in an airtight container, in a cool, dark place.
* Stone-ground meal: Because the fat in the germ makes it more perishable, refrigerate in an airtight container, for up to 4 months.

USING

* Add a nutty nuance to polenta, cornbread and other cornmeal dishes by first toasting the cornmeal in a dry skillet, stirring occasionally, until golden brown. Cool the cornmeal to room temperature and use for cornbread or other baked goods. For polenta or mush, simply add liquid and cook as usual.
* Oven-toast cornmeal by placing a single layer of it in a shallow baking pan and roasting at 300°F for about 10 minutes.

CORNSTARCH   *see also* ARROWROOT; FLOUR; THICKENERS

TIDBIT   Cornstarch is a dense, powdery "flour" made from a corn kernel's endosperm. Sauces thickened with cornstarch are clear, whereas flour-thickened sauces are opaque.

PURCHASING   Available in a supermarket baking section.

EQUIVALENT   1 pound = 3 cups

USING

* You need half as much cornstarch to thicken mixtures as you do flour. Therefore, for each tablespoon flour called for, substitute ½ tablespoon cornstarch.
* Flour is more heat stable than cornstarch for thickening, so when cooking a high-heat mixture, use a combination of the two. If a recipe calls for 2 tablespoons cornstarch, use 1 tablespoon cornstarch and 2 tablespoons flour.
* Cornstarch clumps easily, so mix it with a small amount of cold liquid to form a thin paste before stirring it into a hot mixture.
* Stirring cornstarch together with some of the granulated sugar in a recipe will also help disperse it in liquid.
* Stir constantly as you add the cornstarch paste to a hot liquid, bringing the mixture to a boil. Cook for about 2 minutes, stirring often, for the mixture to obtain maximum thickness.
* Mixtures thickened with cornstarch will begin to thin if cooked too long, or at too high a temperature, or if stirred too vigorously.
* Some baking recipes call for using all or part cornstarch instead of flour. Such recipes produce a finer-textured, more compact product than flour alone. In British recipes, cornstarch is referred to as "corn flour."

CORN SYRUP   *see also* SYRUPS *for general information such as reliquefying, measuring, and so on.*

TIDBIT   Corn syrup is produced when starch granules from corn are processed with acids or enzymes. This thick, sweet syrup comes in light and dark forms. **Light corn syrup** has been clarified to remove all color and cloudiness. The more strongly flavored **dark corn syrup** is a mixture of corn syrup and refiners' syrup.

PURCHASING Both forms are available in a supermarket's syrup or baking section.

EQUIVALENT 16 fluid ounces = 2 cups

STORING Store in a cool, dark place almost indefinitely.

SUBSTITUTIONS (for use in cooking or baking)

* Light and dark corn syrups may be used interchangeably, however, the dark form adds color and a slightly bolder flavor.
* 1 cup light corn syrup = 1¼ cups granulated sugar plus ¼ cup water.
* 1 cup dark corn syrup = ¾ cup light corn syrup plus ¼ cup light molasses; or 1¼ cups packed brown sugar plus ¼ cup water.

USING

* Corn syrup inhibits crystallization, which makes it particularly good for making frostings, candies, jams and jellies.
* Baked goods made with corn syrup retain their moisture and stay fresh longer.
* Corn syrup gives foods a slightly dense, chewy texture.
* It can be substituted for other syrups, but it isn't as sweet as honey or maple syrup.

COTTAGE CHEESE *see* CHEESE

In Baltimore soft crabs are always fried (or broiled) in the altogether, with maybe a small jock-strap of bacon.
—H. L. Mencken, American journalist, author, critic

CRABS *see also* SHELLFISH

TIDBIT Strange but true, female blue crabs (the species most commonly eaten in its "soft-shell" state) mate only once. The event, which can take up to 48 hours, occurs during the brief period of weeks when she sheds her shell. After the deed is done, the male crab protects the female for weeks until her hard shell regenerates. Does she repay his kindness with a loving tweak? No, she attacks and eats him! And therein lies the phrase "No good deed goes unpunished."

PURCHASING

* Live crabs: They should be active, have hard shells (except for soft-shelled varieties) and be heavy for their size.

* Cooked whole crabs and crabmeat: Check for a fresh, sweet smell.
* Crab legs and claws are available cooked or frozen.
* Canned crab is available flaked and as lump or claw meat.

EQUIVALENTS
* Live: 1 pound = 1 to 1½ cups meat
* Meat: 1 pound = 3 cups
* Canned: 7½-ounce can = 1 cup

STORING
* Live crabs: Refrigerate, covered with a damp towel, until just before cooking. They can also be stored on a layer of damp newspapers in an ice-filled cooler. Cook the day they're purchased.
* Cooked crabmeat: Refrigerate, tightly covered, for no more than 2 days.
* Canned crab: Once opened, refrigerate and use within 2 days.

USING
* Before cooking, check to make sure the crab is still alive. It will be sluggish because of the cold, but should still show some leg movement.
* Taste canned crabmeat—if it has a metallic taste, let it soak in ice water for 5 minutes. Drain and blot dry before using.
* Use your fingers to pick over crabmeat—fresh or canned—to make sure there are no tiny pieces of shell.

CRANBERRIES *see also* BERRIES, GENERAL
PURCHASING
* Fresh or frozen cranberries: They're typically sold in 12-ounce plastic bags, so you can't pick through them. Look for berries that are a bright, intense color (from light to dark red). Sunken or soft spots signal decay.
* Dried cranberries: These are available packaged and in bulk in natural food stores and supermarkets.

EQUIVALENTS   12-ounce bag (fresh or frozen) = 3 cups whole berries, 2½ cups finely chopped berries, 4 cups sauce

STORING   Refrigerate cranberries in an airtight plastic bag for a month or more; freeze for up to a year. Dried cranberries can be stored airtight at room temperature for up to 6 months; frozen for up to 1 year.

PREPARING
* Discard any soft, discolored or shriveled berries. Pluck off and discard any stems on the remaining berries and wash well.
* It's not necessary to defrost frozen cranberries before using.
* Chop cranberries quickly in a food processor with quick on/off pulses.
* If you're using a meat grinder for chopping cranberries, freeze the berries first and chopping will be easier.

COOKING

* Prevent boilovers by adding 1 teaspoon vegetable oil for each 12-ounce package cranberries.
* Adding ¼ teaspoon baking soda to cranberries during cooking neutralizes some of their natural acidity, necessitating less sugar.
* Add a sophisticated touch to homemade cranberry relish by substituting red wine (a fruity Zinfandel would be perfect) for all or part of the liquid called for in the recipe. The resulting color and flavor are terrific.
* Cook cranberries only until they pop. Any longer than that and they'll turn to mush and start to get bitter.
* To rehydrate dried cranberries, cover them with water, liqueur or other soaking liquid in a medium bowl. Cover and microwave on high for 30 to 60 seconds; let stand for 3 minutes before using. Or pour a very hot liquid over the berries, cover and let stand for at least 20 minutes.

USING

* Use dried cranberries as you would raisins in baked goods or for snacks.
* Combine equal amounts of homemade cranberry sauce with your favorite chutney to create a delicious condiment for meats.
* Cranberry sauce (not the jellied type) makes a great topping for waffles and pancakes.
* Make cranberry syrup by combining cranberry sauce with a little light corn syrup, stirring over low heat until warmed through.

SPICED ZINBERRIES

Great over everything from pancakes to ice cream, and a wonderful accompaniment for ham or roasted pork, chicken or duck. Combine 1¼ cups Zinfandel, ¾ cup sugar, finely grated zest of 1 large orange, ½ teaspoon *each* ground cinnamon and allspice, ¼ teaspoon *each* ground cloves, nutmeg and salt, and half a 12-ounce package of fresh cranberries in a heavy, medium saucepan. Bring to a boil over medium-high heat. Cook, stirring occasionally, until the mixture is saucelike, about 10 minutes. Add the remaining cranberries; cook for another 5 minutes. Cool to room temperature before covering and refrigerating for up to 5 days. Makes about 3 cups.

CRANBERRY SMOOTHIE

Combine 1 cup leftover cranberry sauce (not the jellied type), ¾ cup orange juice, ½ teaspoon pure vanilla extract and 3 ice cubes in a blender. Cover and process until the mixture is smooth. Pour into a tall glass. Serves 1.

If there's life after whipped cream, it's in Thigh City.
—Erma Bombeck, American humorist, author

C

CREAM   *see also* CRÈME FRAÎCHE; MILK; SOUR CREAM

PURCHASING   Cream is categorized according to the amount of milk fat it contains. **Light cream** (also called *coffee cream* and *table cream*) can contain between 18 to 30 percent milk fat. **Light whipping cream** (also simply called *whipping cream*) contains 30 to 36 percent fat; **heavy (whipping) cream** has a fat content between 36 and 40 percent. **Half-and-half** is a mixture of equal parts whole milk and cream, and contains 10 to 18 percent milk fat. **Ultrapasteurized cream** has been briefly heated at temperatures up to 300°F to kill the microorganisms that cause milk products to sour. It has a longer shelf life than regular cream, but doesn't whip as well and has a slightly "cooked" flavor.

EQUIVALENTS   ½ pint = 1 cup heavy (whipping) cream, 2 cups whipped

STORING   Refrigerate cream in the coldest part of the refrigerator for up to a week past the date on the carton. Cream can be frozen as long as there's at least ½ inch of airspace at the top of the cardboard container. Double wrap the container in a freezer-proof plastic bag; freeze for up to 6 months. Defrost in the refrigerator overnight; shake the cream well before using.

SUBSTITUTIONS   (for use in cooking or baking)

* 1 cup half-and-half: 1½ tablespoons melted butter plus enough whole milk to equal 1 cup; or ½ cup light cream plus ½ cup whole milk
* 1 cup light cream: 3 tablespoons melted butter plus enough whole milk to equal 1 cup
* 1 cup heavy whipping cream: ⅓ cup melted butter plus ¾ cup whole milk (not to be used for whipping)

COOKING WITH CREAM

* The more fat cream contains, the more immune it is to curdling. Heavy whipping cream can be added to a sauce and cooked over high heat and usually not curdle.
* If you suspect cream has just begun to sour, whisk in ⅛ teaspoon baking soda. The soda will counteract the natural lactic acid in the cream. Taste before using to make sure the flavor is acceptable.
* If you're mixing cream with highly acidic ingredients, reduce the cream first by cooking it over medium heat until the volume is decreased by half. Then add the reduced cream to the rest of the mixture.

WHIPPING CREAM

* Use a bowl that's deep enough for the cream to double in volume.
* A small amount of cream (less than 1 cup) whips better in a deep, narrow bowl than one that's large and wide.
* Cream whips faster if you chill the beaters and bowl in the freezer for 15 minutes. The cream should also be as cold as possible. If there's no room in the freezer for the bowl, fill the bowl with ice water 15 minutes beforehand, empty and dry it thoroughly before whipping the cream.
* Does cream spatter when you whip it? Protect yourself and your kitchen by laying a sheet of plastic wrap or waxed paper (with a hole cut for the beater stems) on top of the bowl.
* Spatters will be minimal with an electric mixer if you start out at medium speed, gradually increasing the speed as the cream thickens.
* **Stages of whipped cream:** The *soft peaks* stage is determined when the cream gently folds over on the ends of the beaters. Cream whipped to *stiff peaks* will hold its shape in the bowl and on the beaters.
* You'll get more volume if you wait until the cream forms soft peaks before adding sugar or flavorings such as vanilla or liqueurs.
* Use superfine or confectioners' sugar to sweeten cream. The latter sugar not only dissolves quickly, but it also helps stabilize whipped cream because it contains cornstarch.
* Adding 1 teaspoon light corn syrup per cup of cream before whipping helps stabilize whipped cream. So does 2 tablespoons nonfat dry milk.
* **Lightened whipped cream:** Beat 1 or 2 room-temperature egg whites with ¼ teaspoon cream of tartar until stiff but not dry. Gently fold into 2 cups whipped cream (1 cup before beating).
* If you accidentally overbeat whipping cream so that it begins to turn buttery, gently whisk in additional cream, 1 tablespoon at a time. Don't "beat" the cream again or you'll be right back where you started.

USING WHIPPED CREAM

* Cream can be whipped in advance for use hours later. Simply whip it until stiff, then spoon it into a sieve lined with a double layer of cheesecloth. Set over a bowl with the bottom of the sieve 2 inches above the bottom of the bowl. Cover tightly and refrigerate for up to 48 hours. If, when you get ready to use the cream, it's a little too stiff, whisk in 1 to 2 tablespoons liquid cream.
* Softly whipped cream is very inviting with many desserts. Its silky texture gently folds over fruit, cobblers, and so on.
* Unsweetened whipped cream has its own natural sweetness and makes a striking counterpoint to very sweet desserts.

* **Savory uses for unsweetened whipped cream:** It makes a luscious garnish for dishes such as peas, mashed potatoes and hot or cold soups. If desired, you can salt the cream slightly before whipping. Or fold in 1 or 2 tablespoons minced chives or other herbs after the cream is whipped. Adding 1 to 2 tablespoons horseradish to whipped cream creates a tangy accompaniment for roast beef.

LEFTOVER WHIPPED CREAM

* Cover and refrigerate to dollop atop coffee for a luxurious way to begin or end the next day.
* Leftover whipped cream can also be frozen. Line a baking sheet with plastic wrap onto which you spoon serving-size dollops of whipped cream. Freeze, uncovered, until firm. Transfer the solid whipped-cream mounds to a plastic bag, seal airtight and return to the freezer for up to 2 weeks. Remove and use the dollops as you need them. The cream will be soft in 5 to 10 minutes, in less time for coffee and hot desserts. If the cream isn't sweetened, you can use it to enrich soups, sauces and other dishes.

CHOCOLATE WHIPPED CREAM

A decadent topping for everything from cheesecake to sundaes to coffee. Stir together 2 tablespoons unsweetened cocoa powder and 4 tablespoons confectioners' sugar in a small mixing bowl. Slowly stir in 1 cup heavy whipping cream and 1 teaspoon pure vanilla extract; cover and refrigerate for 30 minutes. Beat the cream until it forms soft mounds. Beating constantly, drizzle in 2 tablespoons Kahlúa; beat until the liquid is incorporated and the cream reaches the desired consistency. Makes 2 cups.

WHIPPED CREAM FROSTING

Adding gelatin prevents whipped cream frosting from softening and seeping into the cake. In a small bowl, stir 1 teaspoon unflavored gelatin into 3 tablespoons water or other liquid (liquids like liqueur and orange juice flavor the cream); set aside for 5 minutes to soften the gelatin. Place the small bowl in a pan of very hot water; stir until the gelatin is dissolved. Cool to room temperature. Beat 1 cup whipping cream until soft peaks form; flavor as desired. Beating constantly at medium-high speed, gradually drizzle the gelatin mixture into the whipped cream. Immediately frost the cake—the mixture sets up quickly and becomes difficult to spread.

CREAM CHEESE *see* CHEESE

CREAM OF TARTAR

TIDBIT This white powder is an acid (potassium bitartrate) that not only has several uses in the everyday kitchen but is also employed in food additives, medicines (like laxatives) and tinning metals.

PURCHASING Cream of tartar is commonly found in the supermarket spice section.

STORING Store tightly sealed in a cool, dry place for up to 1 year.

USING

* Stabilize beaten egg whites by adding ⅛ teaspoon cream of tartar per egg white before beating. For meringues (which contain sugar as an additional stabilizer) use ⅛ teaspoon cream of tartar for 2 egg whites.

* When making candy, discourage crystallization by adding ⅛ teaspoon cream of tartar for each cup of granulated sugar.

* Aluminum pan stains can be removed by filling the pan with water and adding 2 tablespoons cream of tartar per quart of water. Bring to a boil, then continue to boil gently for 15 minutes. Let water cool in pan. Scour lightly, then wash well.

* Substitute for 1 cup buttermilk (for baking): 1¾ teaspoons cream of tartar plus 1 cup milk.

* Substitute for 1 teaspoon baking powder: ⅝ teaspoon cream of tartar plus ¼ teaspoon baking soda.

CRÈME FRAÎCHE

TIDBIT Crème fraîche is a matured, thickened cream with a slightly tangy, nutty flavor and velvety-rich texture. The thickness can vary from sour cream-like to as solid as room-temperature margarine.

PURCHASING Available at specialty gourmet shops and some supermarkets. Check the date on the carton to make sure it's still fresh.

STORING Refrigerate in an airtight container for up to 10 days.

USING

* Crème fraîche can be flavored in many ways, depending on its use. If making your own (*see following recipe*), stir in the flavorings after the cream has thickened but before it's refrigerated. Flavorings can include minced fresh herbs, horseradish, crystallized ginger, honey or confectioners' sugar.

* For lighter crème fraîche, whip it until soft peaks form (it won't become stiff like whipped cream). This works only with crème fraîche made with buttermilk.

* For extra-thick crème fraîche, turn it into a sieve lined with a double layer of cheesecloth or into a paper filter–lined coffee cone. Set over a

bowl, with the bottom of the sieve or coffee cone 2 inches above the bottom of the bowl. Cover tightly and refrigerate for 24 hours.

* Crème fraîche is ideal for sauces or soups because it can be boiled without curdling.
* It's also delicious spooned over fresh fruit or warm pies, cobblers or puddings.

CRÈME FRAÎCHE

Combine 1 cup heavy whipping cream (*don't use ultrapasteurized!*) with 2 tablespoons buttermilk (or ½ cup sour cream) in a screw-top jar; shake or stir well to combine. (All ingredients should be at room temperature. If they're not, combine in a saucepan and heat just to body temperature, not over 100°F.) Cover and let stand at room temperature for 8 to 24 hours, depending on how warm the environment is. Stir well, then cover and refrigerate for at least 8 hours before using. The buttermilk-based crème fraîche is slightly tangier than that made with sour cream. Makes 1 cup.

CROCKPOTS *see* SLOW COOKERS

CROUTONS, HOMEMADE

* Croutons are a crunchy accompaniment for everything from soup to salad to vegetables.
* You can make croutons either by toasting in the oven (*see following recipe*) or by frying. They can be cut into squares or decorative designs.
* For decorative designs, use canapé cutters to cut thin slices of bread into stars or other shapes. Fry these tiny croutons in hot oil or unsalted butter until golden brown; drain on paper towels. Season with salt and paper, if desired.

TOASTED CROUTONS

Homemade croutons are fresher and better-tasting than most store-bought products, and they're easy to make. Combine your choice of seasonings, such as minced fresh (or crumbled dried) herbs, salt and pepper with extra virgin olive oil. Brush the flavored oil over both sides of bread slices (*for low-calorie croutons, use your favorite low-fat salad dressing*), then stack as many slices as you can cut at one time (it'll depend on the thickness of the slices) and cut the bread into cubes. Cut the cubes as large or as small as you wish, depending on how the croutons are to be used. Croutons used as a vegetable garnish, for example, would be much smaller than those for soups or salads. Spread the cubes in a single layer on a large baking sheet and bake at 300°F until dry and crisp; the length of time will depend on the size of the croutons. Cool croutons completely before using. Store in an airtight plastic bag at room temperature for up to a week. For longer storage, freeze for up to 6 months.

CRUMBS, GENERAL (COOKIES, CRACKERS, CEREAL) *see also* BREAD CRUMBS

* Crumbs can be used for a variety of cooking purposes. Cookie crumbs can be turned into a pie or cheesecake crust, or sprinkled atop desserts, or folded into puddings. Savory crumbs made from bread, crackers or unsweetened cereals can be used as a BREADING, as a thickener for soups and other liquid mixtures, or to garnish vegetables or casseroles.
* Use the following amounts to make 1 cup finely crushed crumbs: 14 graham cracker squares, 14 Oreos (including the middle layer); 15 gingersnaps; 16 Famous chocolate wafer cookies; 22 vanilla wafers; 24 Ritz crackers; 28 saltine squares; or 3 cups corn, wheat or bran flakes.

CUCUMBERS *see also* VEGETABLES, GENERAL

TIDBIT "Cool as a cucumber" is a phrase we've all heard. Well, it happens to be true. A cucumber's internal temperature is always several degrees cooler than its surroundings. And no wonder—cucumbers are about 96 percent water. This cool quotient translates to a slim 40 calories per medium cucumber. Filling, satisfying and low in calories and sodium . . . perfect for dieters!

PURCHASING Choose firm cucumbers with smooth, brightly colored skins. Avoid any that have shriveled or soft spots. Smaller cucumbers are younger, which means they're not as bitter, and have thinner skins and fewer seeds. Some cucumbers are coated with an edible wax to seal in moisture and extend shelf life. Although this coating is unappealing, it isn't generally harmful. **Hothouse** (or **English**) **cucumbers** are thinner and longer than regular cucumbers and virtually seedless. They're typically marketed shrink-wrapped in plastic and are comparatively more expensive than regular cucumbers.

EQUIVALENT 1 medium regular cucumber = 1½ cups chopped

STORING Refrigerate whole cucumbers, unwashed, in a plastic bag for up to 10 days. Sliced or cut-up cucumbers can be wrapped and refrigerated for up to 5 days.

PREPARING

* Wash cucumbers just before using. If the skin is thin and unwaxed, peeling usually isn't necessary. Taste the skin—if it's bitter, peel it. Remove wax by washing with soapy water (rinse well!).
* Cucumber seeds are often bitter. Seed a cucumber by cutting it in half

lengthwise, then run a teaspoon down the center of each half to scrape out the seeds.

* To give cucumber slices a scalloped look, run the tines of a dinner fork down the length of a whole unpeeled cucumber, cutting through the skin and at least ⅛ inch into the flesh. Repeat all the way around the cucumber, then slice it crosswise.
* To remove excess water from cucumbers and crisp them for use in salads or other cold dishes, toss peeled and chopped or sliced cucumbers with salt (about ½ teaspoon per cucumber); place them in a colander. Fill a zip-closure gallon plastic bag with half ice and half water; seal tightly and place atop cucumbers. Set the colander in a larger bowl and refrigerate for 2 hours. Pat the cucumbers dry with a paper towel, then cover and refrigerate until ready to use.

USING

* Cucumbers can be baked, broiled, sautéed and braised. To prepare cucumbers for use in cooked dishes, first peel and seed them, then salt them generously and let stand for 1 hour, cut side down, on paper towels. Wipe off excess salt and moisture with paper towels, then cook as desired.
* Create an edible container by cutting a cucumber in half lengthwise and using a pointed spoon to hollow it out, leaving sides ¼ to ½ inch thick. Fill with dip, sauce, salad, and so on.
* Long, ½-inch thick strips of cucumber make great swizzle sticks for drinks like Bloody Marys, Moscow Mules or a simple glass of tomato or vegetable juice.
* Cut crisp peeled cucumbers into ½-inch slices and soak them in pickle juice for 4 days for "homemade" cucumber pickles.

CUCUMBER SLAW

Up to 6 hours before serving, shred 2½ pounds cucumbers (peeling is optional). Place in a colander, pressing down with your fingers to drain as much liquid as possible. Transfer the cucumbers to a large bowl; sprinkle with 1 teaspoon salt, then toss with 8 ice cubes. Cover and refrigerate for 1 hour. Remove the ice cubes; drain the cucumbers thoroughly, squeezing dry in paper towels. Return the cucumbers to the bowl; add ½ cup low-fat sour cream or mayonnaise, 1 tablespoon balsamic vinegar, 2 teaspoons Dijon mustard, ¾ teaspoon ground coriander, ¾ teaspoon celery seeds, 2 tablespoons minced chives, and salt and pepper to taste. Toss to combine thoroughly. Cover and refrigerate until ready to serve. Serves 4 to 6.

CURRANTS   *see* RAISINS

In the beginning there was James Beard and there
was curry and that was about all.
—Nora Ephron, American author, screenwriter, producer

CURRY POWDER *For storage and purchasing information, see* SPICES
TIDBIT Authentic Indian curry powder is freshly ground each day and
can vary dramatically, depending on the region and the cook. Such curry
powder is a pulverized blend of up to twenty spices, herbs and seeds.
PURCHASING Commercial curry powders bear little resemblance to
freshly ground blends and also vary significantly, so try several to see what
you like. There are two primary styles—standard and Madras, the latter
being hotter.
USING

* To eliminate curry powder's "raw" taste, sauté it in a dab of butter or oil
  for a minute or so before using.
* A pinch of curry powder adds an exotic touch to myriad preparations,
  including baked goods, soups, vegetables, rice, dumplings and salad
  dressings. Start with a light touch—you can always add more, but too
  much can overpower a dish.
* Curry powder is one of those spices that gets hotter the longer it stands,
  so use discretion when adding it to foods that may stand before being
  eaten.

CUSTARD

TIDBIT There are two types of custard: Baked custard is firm enough to
hold its shape; stirred custard is cooked on a stovetop and is creamy and
pourable. Depending on stirred custard's texture, it can be served as a
dessert or dessert sauce.
GENERAL

* All custards require slow cooking and gentle heat in order to prevent the
  mixture from separating (curdling).
* A general rule for thickening custards is to use 2 egg yolks or 1 whole
  egg for each cup of milk.
* Although adding a vanilla bean to a custard mixture is classic, try infus-
  ing flavor with a cinnamon stick, star anise, whole allspice, citrus zest
  and so on. Strain out the flavoring at the end of the cooking time.
* All custards should be covered and refrigerated for no more than 3 days.
STIRRED CUSTARD
* Stirred custards are generally made in the top of a double boiler over hot,
  not boiling, water, so the heat is continual but gentle. High heat can

scorch the milk (which will ruin the custard's flavor) and cause the eggs to separate.

* Constant stirring is necessary in order for the protein in the eggs to coagulate evenly.
* When a recipe calls for egg yolks only, it's important to remove as much of the white as possible. That's because egg whites coagulate at a lower temperature than egg yolks, which will make the mixture look lumpy.
* If a recipe calls for whole eggs, strain the cooked custard through a fine sieve for a perfectly smooth result.
* Don't try to hurry stirred custards by raising the heat—the mixture will curdle. Most stirred custards take at least 10 minutes to cook.
* If the custard begins to curdle, pour it into a blender jar, cover and process until smooth (starting at low speed and gradually increasing to high). Return the custard to a clean pan and continue cooking.
* Or pour the curdled custard through a very fine sieve into a cold bowl.
* A stirred custard is done when it leaves a velvety coating on the back of a metal or wooden spoon. Run your finger across the custard-dipped spoon; if it leaves a definitive track, the custard's ready.
* Another test is cooking custard until it registers 170°F on a candy THERMOMETER.
* As soon as a custard tests done, remove it from the heat to stop cooking.
* If the custard's not silky smooth, pour it through a fine sieve into a bowl.
* Quickly cool a stirred custard by placing the pan in a large bowl of ice water. Stir constantly until the custard reaches the desired temperature.
* Cool cooked custard to room temperature, then immediately cover the surface with plastic wrap (put it right on the custard surface) and refrigerate. Custard thickens slightly when cold.

BAKED CUSTARD

* Baked custards are generally cooked in a water bath—the water acts as insulation and diffuses the oven heat so the mixture will set without separating.
* Don't beat a baked custard mixture until foamy or the surface of the finished custard will be crusty and pockmarked.
* If you plan on unmolding a baked custard, you'll have better luck if you bake it in metal rather than glass molds.
* To fill custard cups easily, put the custard mixture into a pitcher and pour.
* Set filled custard cups in a 13 × 9-inch baking pan, place the pan on the oven rack, then pour hot tap water into the pan almost halfway up the sides of the custard cups.

* To test a baked custard for doneness, insert a dinner knife halfway between the edge and the center. If the knife comes out clean, the custard's done. The center will still be jiggly, but will firm up as it cools.
* A custard that "weeps" (oozes liquid) has been baked too long or at too high a temperature.
* Baked custards can be served hot, warm or chilled.

CUTTING BOARDS *see also* FOOD SAFETY

* Choose a sturdy, nonabsorbent cutting board—plastic is less porous than wood.
* It's a good idea to have two cutting boards—one for foods that will be eaten raw (such as salad ingredients) and one for meats and fish.
* Bacteria can accumulate in the knife cuts made on a cutting board. If you're not going to clean the board in a dishwasher, use a scrub brush and hot soapy water after each use. Plastic boards can be washed in the dishwasher.
* To keep a cutting board from sliding around on the countertop, put a damp kitchen towel underneath it. When you're through with the chopping task, simply hang the towel up to dry. A double layer of damp paper towel can also be used. Just be sure it's a good-quality paper or you could end up with a mess of shredded paper towel.
* Wooden cutting boards may be cleaned with a paste of salt and baking soda.
* Sanitize cutting boards by scrubbing them with a mixture of 1 quart hot water and 2 tablespoons household bleach. Wash well with hot, soapy water.
* Deodorize a cutting board by rubbing with a paste of baking soda and water. Vinegar or lemon juice also works.
* Discolored boards can be improved by rubbing them with lemon juice; let stand for 5 minutes before wiping off. Or use a mixture of 1 cup water and 2 teaspoons bleach.

DANDELION GREENS *see* GREENS

DATES *see also* DRIED FRUIT
TIDBIT The word "date" comes from the Greek *daktulos*, which means "finger," for the shape of the fruit. Fresh dates are available in some specialty markets from late summer through midfall. Dried dates are available year-round packaged or in bulk, pitted or unpitted. Chopped, dried dates are also available.

PURCHASING Choose fresh dates that are plump and soft, with a smooth, shiny skin. Avoid very shriveled dates or those with mold or sugar crystals on the skin.

EQUIVALENTS
* Unpitted: 1 pound = 2½ cups pitted and chopped
* Pitted: 8-ounce package = about 1¼ cups chopped

STORING
* Fresh dates: Refrigerate in a plastic bag for up to 2 weeks.
* Dried dates: Store, wrapped airtight, at a cool, dry room temperature for up to 6 months; refrigerate for up to 1 year.

PREPARING To separate dates stuck in a solid mass, pop them into a microwave oven and heat at medium (50 percent power) for 30 to 60 seconds; let stand for 1 minute before separating. Or put the block of dates on a baking pan, cover with foil and heat in a 300°F oven for about 5 minutes.

DECANTING *see* WINE

DEEP-FRYING *see also* SAUTÉING; STIR-FRYING; THERMOMETERS (DEEP-FRYING)
PREPARING
* For a lighter batter, add ½ teaspoon baking powder per ½ cup flour.

D

* To reduce spattering, refrigerate batter-coated food uncovered for 30 minutes before frying.
* Use an oil with a high smoke point (the temperature to which it can be heated without smoking). The best oils for frying, in order of smoke points, are peanut, safflower, soybean, grapeseed and canola.
* Fill the pot no more than halfway with oil to allow for bubbling up and spattering.

FRYING

* The right oil temperature is crucial to successful deep-frying. If the oil isn't hot enough, food will absorb fat and be greasy; too hot and it will burn.
* To test an oil's temperature accurately, use a deep-fat thermometer (*see* THERMOMETERS). The thermometer tip must be completely submerged in the oil, but not touching the bottom of the pan.
* Alternatively, oil can be tested by dropping a cube of white bread into the hot oil. If it browns uniformly in 60 seconds, the temperature is 350° to 365°F; 40 seconds, the temperature is about 365° to 382°F; 20 seconds, the temperature is about 382° to 390°F.
* Or drop a piece of food into the deep fat; if it bobs up to the surface, the fat's hot enough.
* Never heat oil until it smokes, a sign that it's breaking down, which will affect the flavor of the food.
* Use tongs or a long-handled spoon to add food to the hot oil.
* Fry food in small batches. Large amounts of food lower the oil's temperature, making it more likely to soak into food.
* Keep deep-fried foods warm by placing them in a single layer on a paper towel–lined baking sheet in a 275°F oven while you finish frying.
* If the oil is overheated it can cause a flash fire. If this happens, put a lid over the pot to smother the fire. Never add water to an oil fire—it will only spread it.
* Remove food particles from used deep-frying oil by straining it through a coffee filter, or a sieve or funnel lined with a double layer of cheesecloth. Cover, tightly seal and refrigerate strained oil to use one more time.
* Refresh used oil by frying a raw potato or a handful of parsley for about 5 minutes; remove before frying "real" food.

DEEP-FRYING THERMOMETERS *see* THERMOMETERS

DESSERT *see* CAKES; CHEESECAKES; CHOCOLATE; COOKIES; CREAM; CUSTARD; FLOWERS; FROSTING; FRUIT, GENERAL; FRUITCAKE; GARNISHING; ICE CREAM; MERINGUE; PIE; SOUFFLÉS; Recipe Index, page 503

TIDBIT When deciding on what to serve for dessert, consider the other dishes of the meal. For example, if you're serving a light meal of soup and salad, a rich dessert like cheesecake or chocolate mousse would be welcome. On the other hand, a rich entrée like stroganoff might be better followed with sorbet or fresh fruit.

DEVILED EGGS *see* EGGS, COOKING METHODS (HARD-COOKED), page 184

DIETS *see* COOKING AND EATING LIGHT

DOUGHNUTS; DONUTS *see also* DEEP-FRYING

TIDBIT There are two basic styles of doughnuts: raised (leavened with yeast) and cake (leavened with baking powder). Both styles are typically fried.

STORING Raised doughnuts can be stored in a plastic bag at room temperature for up to 3 days. Cake doughnuts don't keep well and should be served the same day they are made or frozen. Freeze unglazed doughnuts in a plastic bag for up to 6 months.

MAKING THE DOUGH

* Choose recipes that have proportionately more egg yolks—such doughnuts won't absorb as much oil.
* Spice up a basic doughnut dough by adding 1 teaspoon ground cinnamon and ½ teaspoon each ground nutmeg and allspice.
* Raisins, orange or lemon zest, or dried cherries can also be added to the dough.
* The softer a doughnut dough, the more tender the doughnuts will be.
* The traditional doughnut shape is formed by using a special doughnut cutter that cuts out the center hole in the dough. It can also be made with two biscuit cutters, one large and one small (for the hole).
* Chilling the dough keeps it from absorbing too much oil during frying.
* For almost-instant doughnuts, use canned, refrigerated biscuit dough, cutting out a center hole and frying or baking as usual.

FRYING

* Fill the pot only halfway with oil to allow for bubbling up and spattering.
* The oil temperature for frying doughnuts is vital. If the fat isn't hot enough, the doughnuts will be greasy; if it's too hot, they'll burn. Use a deep-fat thermometer (*see* page 465) for accurate temperatures.
* Fry only a few doughnuts at a time. Crowding will lower the oil's temperature and produce greasy doughnuts.

D

* For less greasy doughnuts, quickly dip them in boiling water immediately after frying. Use a slotted spoon to transfer the doughnuts directly from the hot oil to the boiling water. Drain the doughnuts on paper towels.
* Cool warm doughnuts on a rack at least 10 minutes before serving.

FINISHING

* Granulated sugar coating should be applied while doughnuts are warm. Place the sugar in a paper bag, add 1 or 2 doughnuts at a time and shake gently.
* Doughnuts to be glazed or dipped in confectioners' sugar should be cooled first.
* To reheat frozen doughnuts, place them (still frozen) on an ungreased baking sheet, lightly cover with foil and heat at 350°F for 10 to 15 minutes.

BASIC SUGAR GLAZE

In a small saucepan, combine 2 cups sugar and 1½ cups water; bring to a boil. Cook 4 minutes without stirring. Cool 15 minutes before stirring in 1 teaspoon pure vanilla extract.

CONFECTIONERS' SUGAR GLAZE

In a small bowl, combine 1 cup confectioners' sugar with 1 to 2 tablespoons liquid (milk, orange juice, liqueur), adding only enough liquid to make a smooth, creamy glaze.

CHOCOLATE GLAZE

Melt 4 ounces semisweet chocolate and ⅓ cup butter together. Add 1½ cups confectioners' sugar, 2 teaspoons pure vanilla extract, and 3 to 4 tablespoons hot water, milk, or cream, stirring until glaze is smooth and creamy.

DRESSING *see* STUFFING

DRIED FRUIT *see also* CRANBERRIES; DATES; DRIED PLUMS (PRUNES); FIGS; RAISINS

STORING Wrap airtight and store at room temperature for 3 months; refrigerate or freeze for up to 1 year.

USING

* Freeze dried fruit for an hour or so and it'll be easier to chop.
* Use a food processor (with quick on/off pulses) to chop dried fruit quickly. If the fruit begins to stick together, add 1 to 2 tablespoons granulated sugar and continue chopping.
* Kitchen shears will easily snip dried fruit into uniform pieces. Keep the

fruit from sticking by dipping the shears in hot water or granulated sugar every so often.

* Whether using a food processor, kitchen shears or knife to cut dried fruit, spray the cutting edge(s) with cooking spray to minimize sticking.
* Soften hardened dried fruit by covering it with boiling water and letting it stand for 15 minutes. Drain and blot the fruit dry before using.
* Microwave softening: Speed-soak a cup of dried fruit by combining it with ½ cup water, liqueur or other soaking liquid in a medium bowl. Cover and cook on high for 30 to 60 seconds; let stand for 3 minutes before using.
* If dried fruit like raisins or dates clump together, put them in a strainer and spray hot, running water over them. Or pop them in the microwave oven and heat on high for 10 to 20 seconds.
* Before adding chopped dried fruit to a cake or muffin batter, toss it with some of the flour called for in the recipe, separating the pieces with your fingers as you do so. This will help keep the fruit from sinking to the bottom of the batter.
* Store dried fruit like apricots or peaches covered with spirits such as brandy, Cointreau or bourbon. Add the spirited fruit to baked goods, purees, sauces and so on.

DRIED PLUMS (PRUNES)   *see also* DRIED FRUIT

TIDBIT   In 2001, plum growers obtained FDA (Food and Drug Administration) permission to call prunes "dried plums." Although prunes are and always have been dried plums, consumers seem to see them as medicinal food for those in need. Plum growers are hoping the new name gives this fruit the more appealing image of being healthful and nutritional. Most package labels show both terms—"dried plums," and beneath that, "pitted prunes," or vice versa. Prune juice still goes by that name. After all, how can juice be "dried"? Oddly enough, dried plums will still be "prunes" when sold for export.

PURCHASING

* Dried plums: Choose slightly soft, flexible fruit with a blemish-free, bluish-black skin.
* Prune purée (also known as *prune butter*): This fat-free product is available in several forms, including lekvar, Wonderslim and Lighter Bake. Such products can be typically found in a supermarket's jam, baking or ethnic sections, and also in natural food stores.

EQUIVALENTS   1 pound pitted = 2½ cups, 4 to 4½ cups cooked

STORING

* Dried plums: Store unopened packages in a cool, dry place for up to 6 months. After opening, refrigerate for up to 6 months, freeze up to 1 year.

* Prune purée: Store unopened container at room temperature for up to 1 year. Once opened, refrigerate and use within 2 weeks.

USING

* Adding a couple of lemon or orange wedges to the cooking water gives dried plums a brighter flavor. Or stew them in orange juice or spiced tea for enhanced flavor. Overcooking causes the plums to become mushy.

* Soften dried plums to be stuffed by covering them with boiling water, orange juice or other liquid. Cover and let stand until cool. Blot the plums dry with paper towels before stuffing.

* Chopped dried plums make a delicious addition to all kinds of foods, including savory stuffings, breads, cakes, cookies, stews, and so on.

* Prune purée can be substituted, measure for measure, for butter or other fat in baked goods, thereby cutting fat by 75 to 90 percent. However, since fat contributes tenderness, baked goods made without it tend to have a rubbery texture. A good compromise is substituting three-quarters of the fat with prune purée.

* Prune purée has been found to make lean ground meat juicier, and to reduce that "old" flavor of cooked ground meat, particularly beef. For each pound of meat, add 1 tablespoon prune purée, an amount so small that little (if any) prune flavor is noticeable.

* For homemade prune purée, combine 8 ounces (about 1⅓ cups) pitted dried plums and ⅓ cup hot water in a blender or food processor. Process until the fruit is puréed, scraping down the sides of the container as necessary.

PORTED DRIED PLUMS

These ported plums are wonderful over everything from ice cream to pound cake, and make a flavorful garnish for chicken, duck and pork. Combine 2 cups dried plums, ½ cup packed brown sugar, 10 whole cloves, 1 cinnamon stick, a quartered orange and a 750-milliliter bottle of ruby port in a large saucepan. Bring to a boil, then cover and remove from the heat. Bring to room temperature before refrigerating for at least 1 day and up to 2 weeks. Before serving, heat just until warm.

DRY MILK (POWDERED MILK)   *see also* BUTTERMILK; MILK

PURCHASING Dry milk is marketed in three forms—whole milk, nonfat milk and buttermilk.

EQUIVALENTS

* 1 pound = 3⅔ cups, 14 cups reconstituted; 1⅓ cups = 1 quart reconstituted; ⅓ cup = 1 cup reconstituted

STORING

* Dry whole milk must be refrigerated because of its fat content. Dry non-fat milk and buttermilk can be stored, unopened, in a cool, dry place for up to 6 months. Once opened, transfer to an airtight container; refrigerating will help retain dry milk's freshness.
* Reconstituted dry milk can be covered and refrigerated for up to 3 days.

USING

* To measure dry milk powder, spoon lightly into a measuring cup, then level off with the flat edge of a knife.
* Reconstituted milk tastes better when mixed half and half with regular milk.
* Enrich everything from soups to meat loaves to breads with dry milk powder.

WHIPPED TOPPING

An easy topping for fruit and desserts. Dissolve 1 cup dry milk in ⅔ cup cold water. Place in the freezer until ice crystals form around the edges. Using a chilled bowl and beaters, whip the milk until soft peaks form; add 1 tablespoon lemon juice and beat until stiff. The entire whipping process can take up to 5 minutes. If desired, gently beat ½ to 1 teaspoon pure vanilla extract and 2 to 4 tablespoons confectioners' sugar into the whipped milk. Cover and refrigerate the whipped topping for 30 minutes before serving. Makes about 1½ cups.

DUCK

PURCHASING   Choose a fresh duck with a broad, fairly plump breast; the skin should be elastic, not saggy. The packaging on frozen birds should be tight and unbroken.

STORING

* Fresh duck: Refrigerate, loosely covered, for 2 to 3 days. Remove the giblets from the body cavity and store separately.
* Frozen duck: Defrost in the refrigerator, which can take from 24 to 36 hours, depending on the size of the bird. Never refreeze duck.

PREPARING

* Ducks are not good candidates for stuffing because the bread absorbs so much fat that it becomes inedible.
* Farm-raised duck is fattier than its wild counterpart. To diminish the fat and create a crispy skin, first rinse the bird and blot dry with paper tow-

els. Remove the excess fat in the body cavity, then prick the skin all over at ½-inch intervals, being careful not to pierce the duck's flesh. These punctures allow the fat to drain out as it melts during roasting. Generously rub the duck inside and out with salt and pepper. Place the duck, breast side down, on a baking rack set over a baking pan. Refrigerate, uncovered, overnight to let the skin dry out. Roast on the middle rack in a preheated 500°F oven for 30 minutes. Reduce the heat to 425°F and continue roasting the duck for 20 to 30 minutes until the juices run clear when a thigh is pierced (175°F on a meat THERMOMETER).

* To diminish wild duck's gamy flavor, rub it inside and out with lemon juice or a paste made with chopped fresh ginger (powdered ginger also works) and sherry before cooking. Fill the cavity with chunks of onion, celery, lemon and orange.

* Wild ducks are often so lean that the breast requires BARDING. They also do better when roasted in a moderate (350°F) oven, rather than at higher temperatures.

* Robust sauces flavored with herbs, wine, ginger, or tomato will also camouflage a duck's overt gamy flavors.

* The natural juices in a duck shift to the center as it cooks. Let the bird rest for about 15 minutes after roasting so the juices can redistribute throughout the flesh. Cover the duck lightly with foil during this rest period to keep it warm.

DUMPLINGS

* Any rich biscuit dough can be used for dumplings.

* To prevent dumplings from becoming heavy with soggy bottoms, cook them in liquid that bubbles gently but continually.

* For lighter, fluffier dumplings, cover the pan and leave it covered until the cooking time is almost complete. Drafts affect the temperature and can deflate the dumplings. If you want to watch what's happening, use a glass pie plate as a pot cover.

EGGNOG

PURCHASING Check the date code on the carton of commercial eggnog to make sure it's as fresh as possible.

STORING

* Commercial eggnog: Refrigerate for up to a week after the carton date.
* Homemade eggnog: Cover tightly and refrigerate for up to 2 days.

PREPARING

* Lighten the texture and decrease commercial eggnog's sweetness by folding in stiffly beaten egg whites.
* Reduce the calorie and cholesterol count of homemade eggnog by making it with nonfat evaporated milk and egg whites instead of whole milk (or cream) and whole eggs. Substitute 2 egg whites for each whole egg.
* For lighter homemade eggnog, separate the eggs, beat the whites until stiff, and fold them into the eggnog mixture just before serving.
* Substitute eggnog for the milk or other liquid called for in a cake or coffeecake recipe.
* Eggnog futures: Buy quarts of eggnog and freeze them right in the unopened carton (inside a large freezer bag), so you can have an eggnog "fix" whenever you want. Stand cartons upright until frozen solid, then wrap in a freezer-proof plastic bag. Freeze for up to 6 months.
* Or freeze eggnog in 1-cup portions in small freezer bags for up to 6 months. Thaw overnight in the refrigerator and use in sauces, puddings, quick breads, cakes and pies.
* Eggnog sometimes separates after defrosting. Rehomogenize by processing in a blender until smooth.

QUICK CHOCOLATE EGGNOG

In a medium glass, briskly stir 1 cup cold prepared eggnog and 2 to 3 tablespoons dark chocolate syrup. Top with whipped cream (*see* Chocolate Whipped Cream, page 159), if desired; sprinkle with nutmeg.

EGGNOG SMOOTHIE
Combine 1 cup chopped fruit and 1 cup cold eggnog in a blender; process until smooth.

EGGNOG FIZZ
Place 3 ice cubes in a tall glass. Fill it halfway with eggnog; top with cold soda water, stirring gently.

Over-the-hill eggplant betrays its age precisely in the same manner as over-the-hill debutantes: slack skin and slightly puckered posteriors.
—Dione Lucas, English cookery expert, author

EGGPLANT *see also* VEGETABLES, GENERAL

TIDBIT It's a fact of life that eggplant soaks up oil like a sponge. The good news is that when fatty foods are eaten with eggplant, some of those fats are absorbed by the eggplant before they can do any harm. So broil your eggplant and let it sponge up the bad guys in your system.

PURCHASING Look for eggplant that's firm, smooth-skinned and heavy for its size; avoid those with soft or brown spots. Male eggplants have fewer seeds (which are often bitter) than the female of the species, and have a rounder, smoother blossom end. The blossom end of a female eggplant is typically slightly indented.

EQUIVALENTS 1 pound = 3½ cups chopped, 1¾ cups cooked

STORING Store in a cool, dry place and use within 1 to 2 days of purchase. For storage up to 5 days, refrigerate in a paper bag.

PREPARING
* Young eggplants don't require peeling. Because eggplant flesh discolors rapidly, peel just before using. A vegetable peeler works well; so does an ultrasharp paring knife.
* To retard discoloring, brush exposed flesh with lemon juice or dip it in ACIDULATED WATER.
* To reduce bitterness and keep eggplant from absorbing excess oil, use the age-old salting and weighting method. Generously salt eggplant slices, then place in a single layer on several sheets of paper towels. Cover with more paper towels, then a large baking sheet. Weight the baking sheet with something heavy, such as several 16-ounce cans or a six-pack of cola. Let sit at room temperature for 30 minutes. Rinse off salt and thoroughly blot dry before cooking.

COOKING
* Eggplant absorbs oil like a sponge, so avoid frying it if you're watching calories.

* Eggplant absorbs less oil if it's breaded—dip it in beaten egg, then bread crumbs. Let the breaded eggplant dry for 30 minutes in the refrigerator before frying.
* Reduce calories by spritzing slices of eggplant with cooking spray. Salt and pepper to taste, then broil or grill, browning both sides.
* To microwave, use a fork to pierce a whole eggplant at 2-inch intervals. Cook it on high for about 8 to 10 minutes until soft, turning halfway through cooking. Cool, then halve the eggplant and scoop out the flesh to be used in soups, dips, and so on.
* To keep eggplant from turning mushy in long-cooked dishes like stews and soups, add it during the final 10 minutes of cooking time.

The egg is to cuisine what the article is to speech.
—Anonymous

EGGS *see also* EGG WHITES, page 180; EGG YOLKS, page 182
TIDBIT The majority of marketed eggs are graded under federal (USDA) supervision. In descending order, egg grades are AA, A and B, the grade determined by both exterior and interior quality. Eggs are also sorted for size based on their minimum weight per dozen: jumbo (30 ounces per dozen), extra large (27 ounces), large (24 ounces), medium (21 ounces), small (18 ounces) and peewee (15 ounces). Extra large, large and medium are the sizes most commonly found in markets. USDA-graded eggs must be carefully washed and sanitized, which removes much of nature's protective coating (called "bloom"). Producers replace this coating by lightly spraying the shell with a natural mineral oil. This thin film seals the shell's pores, thereby reducing moisture loss and preventing bacterial invasion.
PURCHASING
* Shell eggs: Buy only eggs stored in the refrigerator case—storage temperature is the major contributor to egg quality or lack of it. Those "farm-fresh" eggs sold at roadside stands may not be as "fresh" as you think. Choose grade AA or A eggs and check the carton date to be sure the eggs are fresh. Open the carton at the store to check that none of the eggs are cracked. Slightly move each one with your finger to make sure it isn't stuck to the carton (generally, due to a leak caused by a crack you can't see). **Shell color**—white or brown—is determined by the breed of hen that laid it and has nothing to do with either taste or nutritive value. **Fertile eggs** are expensive because of high production costs, and are no more nutritious than nonfertile eggs. They contain a small amount of male hormone and don't keep as well as other eggs.

* Pasteurized liquid eggs: Found in the refrigerated section of some super-markets, these are mixed whole eggs that have undergone pasteurization to eliminate potential bacteria. Pasteurized liquid eggs and egg substi-tutes (*see next tip*) are completely safe for use in raw-egg preparations such as pancakes, batters, omelets, baked goods, Caesar salads and even homemade mayonnaise. To substitute pasteurized liquid whole eggs (and egg substitutes), use ¼ cup for each large egg. For homemade may-onnaise, substitute ⅛ cup liquid eggs for each egg yolk.
* Egg substitutes: This product is comprised of about 80 percent egg white, mixed with other ingredients, including nonfat milk, tofu, veg-etable oils, emulsifiers, stabilizers, antioxidants, gums and artificial col-ors, and vitamins and minerals. Egg substitutes are cholesterol-free and can be used in cooking and baking in many (though not all) of the same ways as regular eggs.

EQUIVALENTS FOR LARGE EGGS
* 1 dozen = 2⅓ cups (yolks = about ⅞ cup, whites = 1½ cups)
* 1 cup = 5 whole, 7 whites, 14 yolks
* 1 egg = 3 tablespoons (yolk = 1 tablespoon, white = 2 tablespoons)
* ½ egg = lightly beat 1 whole egg, then measure out about 1½ tablespoons

STORING
* Shell eggs: Refrigerate eggs the minute you get home from the market. They lose more quality in one day at room temperature than in one week in the refrigerator. Eggs are highest in flavor and quality if used within a week; however the American Egg Board says that eggs refrigerated in their carton may be kept for 4 to 5 weeks beyond the carton date without significant quality loss. Storing eggs in the carton helps keep them from losing moisture and absorbing odors. Storing eggs large end up retains freshness and helps keep the yolk centered. Eggs can absorb odors right through their shells so don't put them near foods like onions.
* Egg substitutes and pasteurized liquid eggs: Refrigerate and use by the date on the carton.

GENERAL
* Unless otherwise indicated, most recipes use large eggs. Using extra-large or medium eggs in a baked-good recipe could alter the outcome.
* If eggs are stuck to a carton, fill the indentations with a little cool water and let stand about 5 minutes. The eggs should loosen easily.
* How do you tell if an egg is fresh? Place it in a bowl of salted, cool water. If it sinks, it's fresh—if it floats, throw it out.
* The thick, cordlike strands of egg white that anchor the yolk to the shell membrane so that it stays centered are called "chalazae." The more

prominent the chalazae, the fresher the egg. These strands don't inter-fere with either flavor or quality. However, because they form lumps when cooked, you may want to strain them out of mixtures that should be smooth, such as custards.

* **Egg Safety:** If you live in an area where salmonella-infected eggs are a problem (mainly in the northeastern and mid-Atlantic states), use an egg substitute, pasteurized liquid eggs or recipes that require cooking at temperatures of 160°F to kill any bacteria. Pasteurization—which kills salmonella—occurs when eggs are cooked at 140°F for 3½ minutes. Since egg whites coagulate between 144° and 149°F, and yolks between 149°F and 158°F, any method of cooking eggs in which the white is thoroughly set and the yolk has begun to thicken is sufficient to kill most salmonella.

SEPARATING EGGS

* Eggs are easier to separate when they're cold.
* Room-temperature eggs cook more evenly. To bring eggs to room temperature, let them sit on the countertop for 30 minutes.
* To quickly bring refrigerated eggs to room temperature, place them in a bowl of very warm, but not hot, water for 5 to 10 minutes. If using the eggs separated, place the yolks in one bowl, the whites in another, and then place the separate bowls in a pan of warm water. Don't fill the pan so full that the water sloshes into the eggs.
* The yolk is less likely to break if you crack an egg on a slightly rounded surface, like the edge of a bowl.
* When adding eggs to a mixture (such as a cake batter), break them one by one into a small bowl or cup before mixing into the main mixture. If you break eggs directly into a mixture, you run the risk of spoiling it all with one bad egg.
* Separating eggs by passing the yolk back and forth from one half of a shell to the other increases the risk of transferring any bacteria on the shell's surface to the egg.
* For hassle-free separation, buy an inexpensive egg separator. Or crack an egg into a funnel over a bowl—the yolk stays in the funnel while the white passes through.
* The most basic (and messiest) separation technique is to cup your hand and crack the egg into it. The white falls through your fingers while the yolk stays nestled in your palm.

USING *see also* EGGS, COOKING METHODS

* If a recipe calls for both the yolks and whites to be beaten, beat the whites first and transfer them to a plate; then immediately beat the yolks. Prop-

erly beaten whites can stand for a minute or two, and you don't have to wash the beaters, as you would if the yolks were beaten first.

* Never leave cooked-egg dishes out at room temperature for more than 2 hours, including preparation and serving time. Doing so invites bacterial growth.
* Thoroughly reheat any leftover egg dishes before serving.
* Dropping an egg on the floor can create a real mess. It'll be easier to clean up if you lightly sprinkle the egg with salt, then let it sit for 20 minutes. A damp paper towel will pick the mess right up.
* After working with raw eggs, wash your hands, utensils, countertops, and so on, with hot soapy water.
* Egg-coated dishes should be soaked in warm, not hot, water—the latter "cooks" the egg right onto the dish's surface.

EGG WHITES *see also* MERINGUE

* Tightly covered egg whites can be refrigerated for up to 4 days; frozen for up to 6 months.
* Freeze extra egg whites by placing one in each section of an ice cube tray. When solid, pop the egg-white cubes out into a freezer-weight plastic bag. Thaw what you need overnight in the refrigerator.
* Eggs separate more easily when they're cold, but you'll get more volume when beating egg whites if you wait until they're at room temperature.
* To separate eggs safely, crack one at a time, placing each white in a custard cup before transferring it to the mixing bowl. This prevents accidentally getting any broken yolk into a bowl of whites. A drop of egg yolk, which contains fat, will prevent egg whites from reaching their full volume.
* If a speck or two of yolk gets into the whites, use the corner tip of a paper towel to blot it up. A cotton-tipped swab works well, too.
* To quickly warm cold egg whites for beating, set the bowl of whites in a larger bowl of warm water. Stir occasionally until the whites have reached room temperature.
* Microwave warming: Place up to 2 to 3 egg whites in a small bowl or measuring cup. Cook, uncovered, at 30 percent power for 20 to 30 seconds; stir with a fork. If you need more egg whites, do them in batches.
* For beating egg whites, use a small, deep bowl with a rounded bottom for 4 to 5 egg whites, a large, deep bowl for more.
* The composition of the bowl you use can make a big difference. Copper bowls react chemically with egg whites to form fluffy, high-rise whites. The same result can be obtained using stainless-steel or glass bowls and adding cream of tartar to the whites. The naturally slick surface of a

glass bowl doesn't give as much traction for the egg whites to climb the sides. Never use aluminum (which can cause egg whites to turn slightly gray) or plastic or wooden bowls, which are hard to clean well enough to be fat free.

✳ Adding a small amount of acid, such as cream of tartar, lemon juice or vinegar, stabilizes egg whites and allows them to reach their full volume and stiffness. Use ⅛ teaspoon acid ingredient per egg white, except for meringues, where ⅛ teaspoon is sufficient for 2 egg whites. Add the acid to the whites just as they begin to become frothy during beating.

✳ When beating whites with an electric mixer, start at medium-low speed and gradually increase to high. For ultimate control, stop the mixer just before the whites reach the desired consistency and use a whisk to finish them. Doing this prevents accidentally overbeating the whites until they're dry.

✳ Terminology for beaten egg whites: *Frothy or foamy*—semiliquid with lots of big bubbles; *soft peaks*—when the beater is lifted, the peaks fall gently back on themselves; *stiff* or *firm peaks*—the mixture stands straight up.

✳ Egg whites beaten without sugar will not peak as firmly as those with sugar.

✳ Beat egg whites only until they're stiff, but not dry. Overbeaten whites will collapse and begin to reliquefy.

✳ If you accidentally overbeat egg whites, gently stir in another egg white that's been beaten by hand just until frothy. Once the mixture is combined and the whites are again shiny and moist, remove about ¼ cup to bring the volume back into balance.

✳ Or gently whisk 2 to 3 teaspoons ultrafine sugar into the overbeaten whites.

✳ To prevent loss of volume, use egg whites within a minute or two of beating.

✳ **Folding** stiffly beaten egg whites into another mixture must be done by hand. Using a large rubber spatula, quickly but gently cut into the middle of the mixture. Bring the bottom of the batter up and over the remaining mixture. Rotate the bowl a quarter turn with each folding motion. Fold gently to retain as much air as possible. Stop folding when no white streaks remain.

✳ When folding stiffly beaten egg whites into a very thick or heavy mixture, first fold in about a quarter of the whites. This will loosen the mixture and enable the remainder of the beaten whites to be folded in more easily.

E

EGG YOLKS

* The color of the yolk depends entirely on the hen's diet. Hens fed on alfalfa, grass and yellow corn lay eggs with darker yolks than wheat-fed hens.
* Blood spots on egg yolks are the result of a natural occurrence, such as a blood vessel rupturing on the surface of the yolk. They neither indicate that the egg is fertile nor affect the flavor or quality. If you wish, remove the blood spot with the tip of a knife, being careful not to puncture the yolk.
* When adding egg yolks to a hot mixture, temper the yolks first by stirring a small amount of the hot mixture into the yolks. Slowly stir the slightly heated yolks into the hot mixture.
* If you have leftover egg yolks, fill a small container with cold water, then slide the unbroken yolks into the water. Seal the container airtight and refrigerate for up to 2 days.
* Leftover egg yolks that won't be used within a day or two can either be cooked or frozen (see below). To cook, carefully place them in a small saucepan and cover with at least 1 inch of cold water. Bring to a boil; immediately remove from the heat, cover and let stand for 15 minutes. Remove the cooked yolks from the water with a slotted spoon. Cover and refrigerate for up to 5 days; or wrap airtight and freeze for up to 4 months.
* Freezing leftover raw yolks requires special treatment because yolks become so gelatinous when frozen alone that they're almost impossible to use. To inhibit gelation, add ⅛ teaspoon salt or 1½ teaspoons sugar or corn syrup to each ¼ cup (4 yolks) and beat to combine. Whether you add salt or sugar depends on how you'll be using the yolks later on. Label the container, indicating what you used, and freeze for up to 3 months.

Egg dishes have a kind of elegance, a freshness, an allure, which sets them quite apart from any other kind of food, so that it becomes a great pleasure to be able to cook them properly and to serve them in just the right condition.
—Elizabeth David, English food writer

EGGS, COOKING METHODS

SKILLET COOKING (Fried Eggs, Scrambled Eggs and Omelets)
* Choose heavy-gauge pans for cooking eggs on the stovetop. Heavy skillets conduct heat more efficiently and won't warp.
* Nonstick pans are a boon, particularly for omelets. The bonus is that you'll cook with less fat.

* Use vegetable oil or unsalted butter for stovetop cooking—salted butter can cause eggs to stick to the pan.
* Cooking eggs slowly over gentle heat (rather than quickly over high heat) allows for even heat penetration, which brings the yolks to a thickened (not hard) stage.
* Cooking eggs over high heat can cause the yolks to toughen and the whites to become rubbery. Overcooking at low heat produces the same results.

FRIED EGGS

* Make sure the butter or oil (1 tablespoon is plenty for a 10-inch nonstick pan) is hot before adding the eggs. Frying eggs in bacon drippings delivers a flavor bonus.
* Once the pan and fat are hot, reduce the heat to low and add the eggs. Salt toughens egg whites, so don't season until just before serving.
* To fry eggs without turning them, add 1 tablespoon water around the eggs in the skillet and cover tightly. The steam will cook the eggs' surface.

SCRAMBLED EGGS

* Lighten a scramble by adding 1 tablespoon water for every 2 eggs.
* For a rich, creamy texture, add 2 tablespoons sour cream or 3 tablespoons heavy cream for every 2 eggs.
* One teaspoon dry sherry per egg adds a great nutty flavor.
* The secret to successfully scrambling eggs is slow cooking over low to medium-low heat. Either start in a cool skillet or cook them in the top of a double boiler over hot (not boiling) water.
* A rubber spatula does a great job of moving the eggs around the pan.
* Remove the eggs from the heat a minute before you think they're done— the residual heat will continue to cook them.

OMELETS

* Before you cook an omelet, have the filling ingredients ready to go. Fillings can include crumbled cooked bacon or sausage, chopped ham or smoked salmon, grated cheese and cooked vegetables (such as spinach, mushrooms, onions, peppers or potatoes).
* Whisk the eggs and season to taste with salt, pepper and herbs. Lighten the texture by adding 1 teaspoon water per egg. Heat 1 tablespoon butter or oil in an 8-inch nonstick skillet over medium-high heat. Reduce the heat to low and pour in the egg mixture. Allow the eggs to set, without stirring, for 15 seconds. Using a pancake turner, pull a portion of the omelet edge away from the skillet, tilting the pan so the uncooked eggs fill in the space. Repeat this technique around the edge of the omelet

until most of the uncooked egg has been transferred. Sprinkle the filling mixture evenly over the surface of the omelet to within ½ inch of the edge. Cover and cook for 20 to 30 seconds. Fold the omelet in half and slide onto a plate. Or fold the omelet in thirds, as you would a letter, by folding one third over the middle, then repeating with the remaining third.

* If desired, top with a sauce that's reflective of the omelet's ingredients. For example, a marinara (tomato) sauce would be perfectly paired with an Italianate omelet filled with green peppers, Italian sausage and mozzarella.

* Omelets are classically served for breakfast or brunch, but are also great for dinner, accompanied by a salad.

HARD- AND SOFT-COOKED EGGS

TIDBIT According to the American Egg Board, the terms "hard-" and "soft-boiled" eggs are really misnomers, because boiling eggs makes them tough and rubbery. Instead, these eggs should be "hard-" or "soft-cooked" in hot (still) water.

EQUIVALENTS 1 hard-cooked egg = 6 slices, about ⅓ cup chopped

* Prevent shells from cracking during cooking by piercing the large end with an egg piercer, needle or thumbtack. Piercing the shell also makes the cooked egg easier to peel.

* If you accidentally crack the shell as you're getting ready to hard-cook an egg, wrap it in foil, then cook and cool as usual.

* To cook, place eggs in a single layer in a saucepan and top with at least 1 inch of water. Cover and bring to a boil, then remove from the heat and let stand. Timing for large eggs: Soft-cooked—3 to 4 minutes; hard-cooked—15 to 17 minutes.

* When hard-cooking eggs that will be sliced or halved, turn them over halfway through the cooking time to keep the yolks centered.

* For soft-cooked eggs: Peel and consume as soon as you can handle them.

* For hard-cooked eggs: Drain off hot water and immediately cover the eggs with cold water and a few ice cubes. Let stand until completely cool. Cooling the eggs in very cold water prevents a dark gray green surface from forming on the yolks.

* Refrigerate cooled hard-cooked eggs and use within 1 week. If possible, store in their original carton.

* An easy way to tell hard-cooked from raw eggs in your fridge: Add a few drops of food coloring to the cooking water to color the shell, or use a crayon to mark the cooled, cooked egg.

* If you haven't marked hard-cooked eggs and aren't sure if an egg is cooked or raw, give it a spin on the countertop. A cooked egg will spin easily, whereas a raw egg will wobble because the liquid is moving inside the shell.
* If hard-cooked eggs are going to be out of the refrigerator for more than 3 hours (as in the case of an Easter-egg hunt), it's safest not to eat them. Either make two batches of eggs—one for hiding, another for eating, or consider hiding plastic eggs and exchange them for the real thing later.
* Hard-cooked eggs are easier to peel if first you gently roll them between your palm and the countertop, creating dozens of hairline cracks in the shell. Starting at the large end, peel the egg under cold, running water or dip it into a bowl filled with cold water.
* If you find after peeling a hard-cooked egg that it's not done, do this: Pierce if once or twice with a fork, then microwave at medium (50 percent power) for 10 to 20 seconds. Let stand for 20 seconds before checking for doneness.
* Hard-cooked eggs are easier to slice if they're cold.
* If you use a lot of sliced hard-cooked eggs, invest in an egg slicer, available at gourmet shops, hardware stores and many supermarkets. If you don't have an egg slicer, use a wire cheese slicer or a sharp, thin-bladed knife, dipping it into cold water every few slices.
* Deviled eggs will sit flat without wobbling during stuffing and serving if you cut off a tiny piece of the bottom of each half.
* Put deviled egg–stuffing ingredients in a small, zip-closure plastic bag, seal, then squish the contents together until well mixed. Snip off a corner of the bag and pipe the mixture into the egg-white halves. Or you can simply spoon a prepared filling into the bag and pipe in the same manner.
* When packing deviled eggs for a picnic, place them in an airtight container, then pack in ice or surround with blue-ice packets.
* Make a lacy hard-cooked egg garnish by rubbing the white, then the yolk through a fine sieve onto a sheet of waxed paper. Sprinkle the egg filigree over salads, vegetables or other dishes as a garnish.

POACHED EGGS

* For a nicely shaped poached egg that won't spread excessively, add 1 tablespoon vinegar (to speed the white's coagulation) to 6 cups cooking water.
* An egg ring is a round band, usually with a handle, that holds the shape of a poached or fried egg. Butter or oil the rings well before using them for either method.

E

* Clean tuna cans (top and bottom removed) or crumpet rings can be substituted for egg rings.
* Poach eggs in part water, part broth for added flavor. Milk-poached eggs are deliciously sweet and tender (but don't add vinegar to the milk or it will curdle).
* Bring the poaching liquid to a boil, then reduce the heat until the liquid is barely simmering before adding eggs. Crack cold eggs, one at a time, into a saucer or custard cup. Holding the dish close to the liquid's surface, gently slip each egg into the simmering liquid. If you're not using egg rings, use a spoon to corral the egg white and pull it toward the yolk. Cook eggs about 3 minutes, or just until whites are set. With a slotted spoon, lift each egg from the water. Press with your fingertip—the white should be firm, the yolk soft. Don't salt and pepper until just before serving. Rest the slotted spoon holding the poached egg briefly on a paper towel to blot excess liquid.
* To make poached eggs in advance for a crowd: Have a bowl of ice water standing by; plunge the cooked eggs directly into the cold water. Transfer to a container; cover and refrigerate for up to 2 days. When ready to serve, use a slotted spoon to transfer the eggs to simmering water. Warm for 1 minute; serve immediately.
* Hard-poached eggs can be cooled, then chopped for use in egg salads or sandwiches.

BAKED (SHIRRED) EGGS

* Eggs can be baked in custard cups, small ramekins or in lidded baked-egg cups (the latter are commonly available at cookware stores).
* Long method: Place the oven shelf in the middle position; preheat the oven to 300°F. Butter one custard cup or other container for each serving. If desired, sprinkle the bottom of the container with a tablespoon or two of crumbled crisp bacon, sautéed diced onions, mushrooms or peppers, and so on. Top with 1 or 2 eggs, salt and pepper to taste, then add 1 tablespoon heavy cream and, if desired, a light sprinkling of grated cheese. Cover with foil (attach lids to baked-egg cups) and place the egg cups in a baking pan. Place the pan on the oven shelf, then pour boiling water around the cups to reach halfway up their sides. Bake 30 to 35 minutes until the white is set and the yolk is soft.
* Short method: Bake in a preheated 375°F oven without a water bath (set the cups on a baking sheet) for 8 to 10 minutes.

MICROWAVED EGGS

* Though a microwave oven can cook eggs in many ways, it isn't good for

preparations like omelets or soufflés, both of which need a dry heat to puff properly.

* Egg yolks cook faster than egg whites because they contain fat, which attracts the microwaves.
* To cook unbeaten eggs, always pierce the yolk with a toothpick or the tines of a fork to prevent steam building pressure and exploding the yolk.
* Cook unbeaten eggs at 30 to 40 percent power.
* Beaten egg mixtures cook well on high.
* Cover eggs with waxed paper, plastic wrap or a lid and they'll cook more evenly.

EGG SUBSTITUTES *see* Purchasing Eggs, page 177

EN PAPILLOTE *see* PARCHMENT PAPER

ESCARGOT *see* SNAILS

EVAPORATED MILK *see also* MILK; SWEETENED CONDENSED MILK
TIDBIT This unsweetened product is called "evaporated milk" because 60 percent of the water has been removed from fresh milk. Evaporated milk is less expensive than whole milk but because it's been heat-sterilized in the can, it has a "cooked" flavor that is off-putting to some people.
PURCHASING Evaporated milk is sold in 5- and 12-ounce cans and comes in whole (at least 7.9 percent milk fat), low-fat (about 4 percent milk fat) and nonfat (½ percent or less) versions.
EQUIVALENTS 5-ounce can = ⅔ cup; 12-ounce can = 1½ cups
STORING Store unopened cans at room temperature for up to 6 months. Once opened, transfer to an airtight container and use within 5 days.
USING

* Undiluted, evaporated milk adds richness to custards, sauces, soups, and so on.
* When mixed with an equal amount of water, evaporated milk can be substituted for fresh milk in recipes.
* Don't substitute sweetened condensed milk—which is about 40 percent sugar—for evaporated milk. The results will be drastically different.
WHIPPED TOPPING
Pour 1 cup evaporated milk into a shallow metal pan (a cake pan will do); freeze until ice crystals form around the edges. Using a chilled bowl and

E beaters, whip until fluffy. Add 1 tablespoon lemon juice (acid adds stability), 3 tablespoons confectioners' sugar and ½ teaspoon pure vanilla extract; whip just until combined. This topping will stay foamy for about 45 minutes in the refrigerator.

For a topping that holds its shape longer: Soften ½ teaspoon unflavored gelatin in ¼ cup evaporated milk for 5 minutes. Warm over low heat, stirring constantly, just until the gelatin dissolves. Stir the mixture into ¾ cup cold evaporated milk, place in the freezer and proceed as directed above, omitting the lemon juice.

FAHRENHEIT *see* TEMPERATURES—FAHRENHEIT AND CELSIUS

FATS AND OILS *see also* BUTTER; COOKING SPRAYS: DEEP-FRYING; GREASING PANS; LABEL TERMS; LARD; MARGARINE; OLIVE OIL; SHORTENING

TIDBIT   Fats and oils are used in cooking to add richness and flavor to foods, to tenderize baked goods and for frying. But not all fats are created equal healthwise, so it's important to know the facts. Most experts, including the American Heart Association, recommend that no more than 30 percent of daily calories (preferably less) come from fat. To calculate the percentage of fat calories a food contains, multiply the "fat grams per serving" on a food label by 9, which will give you the total calories from fat. Divide that number by the total calories per serving and you have the percentage of calories that come from fat. Following is a synopsis of the different kinds of fat:

* **Saturated fat** comes from tropical oils (coconut oil, palm kernel oil and cocoa butter) and animal products, like lard. It can raise total cholesterol and increases the risk of heart disease.

* **Polyunsaturated fats** are considered relatively healthy and may actually lower total cholesterol levels. They include safflower oil, sunflower oil, corn oil and soybean oil.

* **Monounsaturated fats** can help reduce the levels of LDL (the bad) cholesterol and increase HDL (the good) cholesterol. The three most widely used oils high in monounsaturates are olive oil, peanut oil and canola oil.

* **Trans fatty acids** are found in "hydrogenated" (or partially hydrogenated) fats—those that have been chemically transformed from their room-temperature liquid state into solids. The more solid the product (such as margarine), the more trans fatty acids it contains. Such fats act like saturated fat and, in fact, are thought to be more

damaging to cholesterol levels (raising LDL and lowering HDL) than regular saturated fat.

* **Omega-3 oils** are in some plants (such as flax seed) and in the tissues of all sea creatures. These special polyunsaturated oils have been found to be particularly beneficial to brain growth and development, as well as contributing to coronary health. Fish that are good sources of Omega-3 are: sardines, herring, mackerel, Atlantic bluefish, tuna, salmon, pilchard, butterfish and pompano.

PURCHASING Choose a fat according to how you'll use it. Butter, for instance, will add more flavor to baked goods like cakes and cookies; oil is a better choice for frying; OLIVE OIL or a flavored oil is great for salad dressings; COOKING SPRAYS for coating pans, and so on. Those who must reduce their cholesterol intake should avoid coconut, palm and palm kernel oil. Check prepared food labels carefully to avoid these ingredients.

STORING

* Refrigerate fats like butter and margarine, tightly wrapped, for up to 1 month, unsalted butter (which is more perishable) for 2 weeks. Or wrap airtight and freeze for up to 6 months.

* Shortening and most oils can be stored in a cool, dark place at room temperature for 3 months, but their quality will be better if they're refrigerated. Oils with a high proportion of monounsaturates—such as olive and peanut oil—are more perishable and should be refrigerated if kept longer than a month.

USING

* Economize by purchasing oil in large jugs, then fill a screw-top pint bottle with the oil, store it at room temperature and refrigerate the remainder.

* Some oil (like olive) becomes cloudy and almost solid when refrigerated. Such oils reliquefy if allowed to stand at room temperature. To reliquefy more quickly, place the sealed bottle of oil in a large bowl of very warm water. Let stand for about 10 minutes, turning the bottle every couple of minutes. Or for bottles that have no metal on them, remove the lid and microwave on high for 30 to 60 seconds. Let stand 3 minutes before pouring.

* Smell and taste an oil you haven't used in a while. Rancid oil can instantly ruin the flavor of a dish.

* Thoroughly wash and dry a dish detergent bottle and use it for cooking oil. The squirt-type spout makes quick work of measuring and pouring small amounts.

* Sprinkle bottled oil right onto salads by poking three or four holes in the foil seal that comes on many bottles.
* For the fewest calories, fill an atomizer with oil and use it to spray pans, foods to be basted, and so on.
* Use a paper towel to wipe off the sides and bottom of a bottle of oil before returning it to the cupboard.
* Homemade flavored oils are great, both for personal use and for gift-giving. But beware—combining oil with anything that contains moisture (garlic, fresh herbs, and so on) can promote the growth of botulism bacteria. If you do so, refrigerate and use the oil within 1 week to be safe. Or flavor the oil with dry ingredients (dried chiles, rosemary sprigs and so on).

COOKING

* Oil or fat used for deep-frying should have a high smoke point—the temperature to which it can be heated without smoking. Butter and margarine have low smoke points, so aren't good for frying. Shortening, lard and most oils have relatively high smoke points. The best oils for frying are peanut, safflower, soybean, grapeseed and canola.
* Caution: Heating oil or fat until it smokes can cause it to ignite. If a fire erupts, immediately turn off the heat. If the flames are in the pan, cover it with the lid. Otherwise, douse them with baking soda or salt.
* To clarify oil (or bacon or other meat drippings) for reuse after deep-fat frying: Pour into a bottle through a funnel lined with a paper coffee filter, several thicknesses of fine cheesecloth or a heavyweight paper towel. Cover the strained oil tightly and refrigerate or freeze.
* Never pour used oil or fat down the drain. Fats that become solid when cool should be poured into a plastic wrap–lined bowl and refrigerated until firm. Pull the solid fat out of the bowl and discard. Pour used oil into a screw-top bottle; seal and discard.

FENNEL   *see also* VEGETABLES, GENERAL

TIDBIT   The flavor of fresh fennel is sweeter and more delicate than that of fresh anise. When fennel is cooked, its flavor becomes even lighter and more elusive than when raw.

PURCHASING   Fresh fennel has a broad, bulbous, off-white base, pale green, celerylike stems and bright green foliage. Choose clean, crisp bulbs with no sign of browning. Any attached greenery should be soft and feathery. Note: Markets often mislabel fennel as "anise" or "sweet anise."

EQUIVALENT   1 pound = about 2 small fennel bulbs, 2½ cups sliced

STORING   Refrigerate, tightly wrapped in a plastic bag, for up to a week.
USING
* Wash, trim the base and remove the stalks and greenery.
* Fennel's fragrant, graceful greenery can be used as a garnish or snipped like dill and added to salads or other cold dishes. Stir it into hot dishes as a last-minute flavor enhancer.
* Both the base and stems of fennel can be eaten raw in salads. Its crispness adds textural contrast to tomatoes, beets, and so on.
* Fennel can be cooked by a variety of methods, including GRILLING, BRAISING, BOILING and SAUTÉING.
* PURÉE cooked fennel, season with a little butter, salt and pepper and you have a wonderful side dish. Puréed leftover cooked fennel can be used as a thickener for soups or sauces.

Shape is a good part of the fig's delight.
—Jane Grigson, British food writer

FIGS
TIDBIT   In ancient times, figs were considered sacred, and this venerable fruit was an early symbol of peace and prosperity. Figs are a good source of fiber, calcium, iron, potassium and magnesium. Among the more popular varieties are: **Mission** (or **Black Mission**)—purple black with tiny seeds; **Calimyrna** (from California) or **Smyrna** from Turkey—large, squat and green-skinned; **Brown Turkey**—pear shaped with violet to brown skin; **Kadota**—small, with a thick, yellow green skin; **Adriatic**—medium and green-skinned; and **Celeste**—pear-shaped with purple skin.
PURCHASING
* Fresh figs: Choose fruit that's plump and firm with no sign of bruising. Figs are available from June through October.
* Dried figs: These are typically sold in boxes or cellophane packages and available year-round.
* Fig concentrate: This thick, seedless purée is used as a dessert flavoring and topping. It's available in natural food stores and some supermarkets.
EQUIVALENTS
* Fresh: 1 pound = about 12 medium; 4 medium = about 2 cups chopped
* Dried: 1 pound = about 3 cups chopped, 4½ cups cooked
STORING   Fresh figs are extremely perishable. Refrigerate for up to a week; freeze for up to 6 months.
USING
* **To eat figs out of hand,** slash an X in the stem end, cutting two-thirds of

the way to the base. Gently squeeze the uncut portion, opening the fig to expose the flesh.

* Figs can be used in both sweet and savory dishes. Serve with prosciutto as a starter; use them in salads (they pair nicely with citrus) or to accompany roasted or grilled pork, in a fresh-fruit compote; or for dessert with vanilla ice cream or ricotta cheese.

OVEN-DRIED FIGS

Fresh figs are extremely perishable but this is a way to keep them if you have more on your hands than you can eat before they spoil. Cut figs into ½-inch thick slices and place 1 inch apart on a baking sheet coated with cooking spray. Bake at 225°F for 4 hours, or until they reach the desired texture. During baking, occasionally brush the fig slices with the juice they exude. Cool completely before refrigerating for up to a week or freezing for up to 3 months. Serve as a snack, or enjoy with a variety of cheeses from Cheddar to chèvre.

FILBERTS *see* HAZELNUTS

FILO *see* PHYLLO

Fish and visitors stink in three days.
—Benjamin Franklin, American statesman, scientist, writer

FISH, GENERAL *see also* ABALONE; ANCHOVIES; CLAMS; CRABS; FISH, COOKING METHODS; LOBSTERS; MUSSELS; OYSTERS; SALMON; SCALLOPS; SHELL-FISH; SHRIMP; SMOKED FISH; TUNA

TIDBIT When categorized according to fat content, fish are divided into three general groups: lean, moderate fat and high fat. **Lean fish** have a fat content less than 2½ percent (the fat is concentrated in the liver) and include black sea bass, cod, croaker, flounder, haddock, hake, halibut, perch, pollack, red snapper, rockfish, sole and tilefish. **Moderate-fat fish**, which contain generally less than 6 percent fat, include barracuda, bonito, catfish, striped bass, swordfish, trout and whiting. Salmon can range from moderate to high fat, depending on the species (*see* SALMON). **High-fat fish** can be comprised of as much as 30 percent fat (as does eel), but usually average closer to 12 percent. These include Atlantic herring, bluefish, butterfish, mackerel, sablefish, shad, smelt, sturgeon and yellowtail.

PURCHASING

* Make the fish counter your last stop before checkout, and ask for a bag of ice to keep the fish cold. Make a beeline for home and put the fish in the

fridge as soon as you get there. Choose a retailer that has a rapid turnover and a fresh, regular supply of fresh fish. Fish markets in water areas often buy directly from fishermen, and you can't get any fresher than that. Supermarkets typically purchase from wholesalers, meaning that there's already a middleman to slow the process.

* How much per serving: whole fish—¾ to 1 pound; fillets or steaks—5 to 8 ounces.

* Fresh, whole fish: Look for bright, clear full eyes, shiny, brightly colored skin; firm flesh that springs back when pressed with your finger; a fresh, mild odor and red to bright pink gills free of slime or residue. Because salt water provides more buoyancy than fresh water, fish like cod and flounder have thicker bones than freshwater fish (such as catfish and trout), which have hundreds of minuscule, filament-thin bones—a source of frustration for many diners. So, if you don't like fighting those tiny bones, choose whole saltwater species.

* Fish fillets and steaks: Select those with a fresh odor, firm texture and moist appearance. Center-cut filets will be more tender than those from the tail.

* Raw frozen fish: Flash-frozen fish can be better than fresh, depending on how both were handled during processing. Buy only fish that's solidly frozen; its wrapping should be undamaged, the fish odorless. Any white, dark, icy or dry spots signal deterioration. Avoid fish you suspect might have been thawed and refrozen.

* Dried salt cod: Choose white, thick, supple pieces.

* Fish high in Omega-3 oils: Omega-3s—polyunsaturated fats that are extremely beneficial to coronary health—are found in the tissues of all sea creatures. **Fish with over 1 gram of Omega-3 oils are:** anchovies, Atlantic bluefish, bluefin tuna, Chilean sea bass, herring, mackerel, sablefish, sardines, salmon (Atlantic, coho, king, pink, sockeye), spiny dogfish and whitefish. **Fish with between 0.5 and 0.9 grams of Omega-3:** Arctic char, oysters (Pacific), pompano, rainbow trout, salmon (chum), shark, smelt, spot, squid, striped bass, swordfish and tuna (yellowfin and others).

* Fish by flavor category: **mild fish:** Alaska pollock, cod, flounder, grouper, haddock, hake (whiting), halibut, John Dory, monkfish, opaka-paka, orange roughy, skate, sole, snapper, tilapia and whitefish (freshwater). **Moderate-flavored fish:** Arctic char, Atlantic pollock, black sea bass, catfish, drum, mahimahi, ocean perch, opah, Pacific rockfish, perch, pompano, porgy, salmon (chum and pink), shark, steelhead, striped bass, sturgeon, trout (rainbow) and walleye. **Full-flavored fish:** amberjack,

bluefish, Chilean sea bass, cobia, escolar, mackerel, sablefish, salmon (Atlantic, sockeye and king), shad, smelt, swordfish and tuna.

STORING

* Fresh fish: Immediately wrap and refrigerate; use within a day or two. If you're not going to cook it within a few hours, put the fish in a tightly sealed plastic bag (expel all the air), then into a bowl or pan filled with ice (or over blue ice packs). Never store ungutted fish, as the entrails decay much more rapidly than the flesh.

* Frozen fish: Double wrap and freeze for up to 1 month. Use a freezer THERMOMETER to make sure your freezer's at 0°F.

PREPARING

* Before handling fish, rinse your hands in cold water and they won't pick up as much fishy odor. Afterward, remove any fishy smell from hands, knife or cutting board by rubbing them all thoroughly with lemon wedges.

* Remove fish from the refrigerator 20 minutes before cooking.

* Freshen fish past its prime by soaking it in a mixture of 1½ quarts cold water, 1 tablespoon salt and 2 cups ice cubes for 20 minutes. Pat dry before cooking.

* Check a whole market fish for overlooked scales by running a serrated knife from the tail toward the head end. A grapefruit knife works well. If there are a lot of scales, loosen them by plunging the fish first into boiling hot water, then into cold water.

* To keep scales from scattering, scrape them off under cold, running water. Grasp the tail with a kitchen towel for a better grip.

* Saltwater fish requires less salt in cooking than freshwater species.

* Salt cod should be soaked for 24 hours in the refrigerator (use a glass or ceramic bowl). Change the water several times during soaking. Bone-in salt cod must be soaked a little longer. Remove bones and skin before using.

* When forming fish cakes, keep the mixture from sticking to your hands by either wetting them or spraying with cooking spray.

* Fish cakes will be easier to handle if you freeze them for 30 minutes before cooking.

* Double wrap and freeze fish bones to make a stock or soup in the future.

* To freeze a whole, cleaned fish, put it in a zip-closure plastic bag, add water to cover the fish, seal and freeze. To thaw, place the bag in a bowl in the refrigerator.

* Frozen fish fillets and steaks are better cooked from the frozen state. If thawed completely, fish loses much of its natural moisture and can

become dry during cooking. Add a few minutes to the cooking time for frozen fish.

* If thawing fish to separate individual pieces, only partially thaw it. Doing so in milk to cover will diminish any "frozen" flavor.
* One pound of frozen fish will take about 24 hours to thaw completely in the refrigerator. To quick-thaw, place the wrapped, frozen fish in cold (never warm) water, allowing about 1 hour per pound of fish.
* To thaw a pound of frozen fish in the microwave oven, place it in a covered dish and microwave at medium-low (30 percent power) for about 6 minutes, turning and separating the pieces after 4 minutes. Let stand in the microwave oven for 10 minutes.
* Pat frozen, thawed fish dry with paper towels before cooking.
* Never refreeze fish once it's been thawed.

COOKING *see* FISH, COOKING METHODS

AFTERWARD

* Leftover cooked fish makes a delicious salad. Cut it into chunks, marinate it overnight in a light salad dressing and serve the next day over greens.
* **Fish chowder:** Make a milk-based soup chock-full of diced potatoes, onions and celery; flavor with herbs and crisp bits of bacon. Stir in leftover fish chunks at the last minute so they hold their shape.
* For an easy, quick fish pâté, combine leftover fish in a blender or food processor with herbs of choice and enough moistener (stock, sour cream, mayonnaise) to make it smooth. Serve soft, or spoon into crocks, cover and chill until set.
* The odor of caramel does wonders for diminishing fishy smells. Simply put ½ cup sugar in a small, heavy saucepan (lined with heavy-duty aluminum foil to save on cleanup) and cook over medium heat until the sugar is liquid and caramelized. Let cook a few minutes (don't let it burn!) until the caramel odor permeates the air. After the caramel cools, simply lift out the foil and discard.
* If the cooking pan has a fishy odor, fill it with a half-and-half mixture of vinegar and water. Bring to a boil, cook for 5 minutes, then cool in the pan. Wash with hot, soapy water.

FISH, COOKING METHODS

GENERAL

* For moist-heat cooking methods like POACHING, STEAMING or STEWING, choose lean fish, such as cod, flounder, perch, red snapper or sole.

* You can use lean fish for dry-heat methods like BAKING as long as you baste the fish frequently to keep it from drying out.
* For dry-heat cooking methods like BAKING, BROILING and GRILLING, choose moderate-to high-fat fish, such as bluefish, butterfish, catfish, salmon, striped bass, swordfish or trout.
* For fat-based cooking methods like SAUTÉING, PAN-FRYING and DEEP-FRYING, lean to moderate-fat fish are the best choices; lean fish can also be used. High-fat fish are typically too rich to fry.
* Take the chill off and reduce cooking time by removing fish from the refrigerator 20 minutes before cooking.
* When broiling fish, preheat the unit at least 5 minutes.
* If you cook a lot of fish, invest in a wide (5 to 6 inches), slotted spatula. It makes transferring the fish from pan to plate much easier.
* If you're cooking fish ahead to serve cold, it's easier to remove any skin while the fish is warm than after it's chilled.
* Tweezers are perfect for removing fine bones from cooked fish.
* Fish cools rapidly, so have the serving plate or individual dinner plates heated and serve immediately.
* Rescue dry, overcooked fish by serving with a sauce or drizzling with melted butter.
* Toasted almonds make a flavorful garnish for almost any fish.
* Sauces flavored with sherry, brandy or ginger disguise the "fishy" flavor of some fish.
* **Quick sauce:** Add lemon juice, lemon zest and capers to a mixture of mayonnaise and sour cream; salt and pepper to taste. Serve with grilled, broiled or pan-fried fish.

TESTING FOR DONENESS

* Doneness can be tested in several ways but, whichever way you choose, remember that even after it's removed from the heat source, fish continues to cook from residual heat. Allow for this carry-over cooking when timing and testing fish. Properly cooked fish is opaque, has milky white juices and *just* begins to flake easily. Undercooked fish is still translucent and the juices are clear and watery. Overcooked fish looks dry, has little natural juice left and falls apart easily.
* Insert the tines of a table fork about halfway into the thickest point of the fish; twist the fork slightly. The top part should flake slightly, but you should feel some resistance in the midsection.
* Insert an instant-read THERMOMETER into the thickest part of the fish. It will read 145°F when done; however, remember that residual heat will

continue the cooking process, so you might want to remove it from the heat a few degrees lower.

* Canadian Department of Fisheries rule for baking (at 450°F), BROILING, FRYING, GRILLING, POACHING or STEAMING: Measure the fish at its thickest part. Cook 4 to 5 minutes per ½ inch (10 minutes per inch). For foil-wrapped fish, add 5 minutes per inch. Add 5 minutes if baking fish below 400°F.

BAKING FISH

* Baking at 450°F quickly seals in the fish's natural juices, keeping it moist and tender.

* A general rule is to cover and bake for 10 minutes for each inch of thickness. To allow for oven variances, check the fish for doneness after about 7 minutes per pound.

* Fish requires insulation to keep moist during baking. The pan can be covered, or the fish itself can be coated with butter and crumbs or topped with a sauce before being baked. Lean fish (flounder or halibut) can be covered with a layer of finely chopped vegetables, herbs, and so on.

* The French technique of enclosing fish in parchment paper or foil is the perfect way to keep baked fish moist. See the last tip under PARCHMENT PAPER for directions on cooking *en papillote*.

BROILING AND GRILLING FISH   *see also* GRILLING

* Choose fillets or steaks that are about 1 inch thick. Thicker than that and the exterior can char before the inside is done.

* Fish fillets retain their shape better if cooked with the skin on. If desired, remove the skin after cooking.

* Position the fish so that the surface is 3 to 6 inches from the heat source. The thicker the fish, the greater the distance.

* To turn broiled fish fillets or steaks, place each piece of fish along one side of a length of lightly oiled foil about 2½ times larger than the fish. When ready to turn, lift the edges of the foil on the side where the fish is, and flip the fish over so that it comes to rest on the opposite side of the foil.

* To keep fish from sticking, lightly brush the grill (or hinged fish grill) with vegetable oil, or coat it with cooking spray. Never spray the grill over the coals. Conversely, brush the fish with oil.

* Here's a trick for easy skin removal of grilled fish: Cut a piece of foil for each piece of fish—the foil should be an inch larger all around than the fish. Place the fish skin side down on the *ungreased* foil. Place the fish-on-foil pieces on the grill; cook as usual, but don't turn the fish. Transfer the fish to a cutting board, foil side up. Peel off the foil and the skin will

detach with it. Use a metal spatula to transfer the fish, right side up, onto the serving plate; discard the foil.

* Grill twice as much fish as you need for dinner, cover and refrigerate the extra to be used the next day in a cold fish salad.

FRYING FISH   *see also* DEEP-FRYING

* The surface of fish to be fried should be thoroughly dry.
* Butter and margarine have a low smoke point (*see* FATS AND OILS) so use oil or a combination of butter and oil for SAUTÉING or PAN-FRYING.
* Coatings like flour, cornmeal or CRUMBS keep fish moist and give it a crisp crust.
* Don't bread (*see* BREADING) fish too far in advance or it will become soggy.
* Batter-dip fish just before frying.
* The temperature of the fat is all-important. It can make the difference between fish that's crisp and moist or soggy and fat-laden.
* After frying, blot fish on paper towels to absorb excess grease.
* When frying in batches, keep fried fish warm in a 275°F oven until all of it is cooked. Lay the fish on a paper towel–lined baking sheet. Don't keep the fish in the warm oven for more than 20 minutes or it could become dry.

POACHING AND STEAMING FISH

* Poach fish in a wide, shallow pan (such as a skillet) or a special fish poacher.
* Many types of steamers are available in cookware or department stores. If you don't have one, improvise a steamer by setting a rack on empty tuna cans (tops and bottoms removed). The water level should not touch the fish on the rack.
* To diminish fish odor, add a couple of celery sprigs to the poaching or steaming liquid.
* Add a couple of teaspoons of lemon juice or white wine to the poaching liquid to whiten and firm up fish flesh.
* It's easier to remove whole or large pieces of poached fish from the pan if you lightly wrap the fish in cheesecloth before lowering it into the poaching liquid. Drape the ends of the cheesecloth over the top of the fish as it cooks. When it's done, simply lift out the fish by the cheesecloth ends. There are also special cheesecloth fish-poaching bags available in kitchenware shops.
* Poach fish fillets in a single layer. The poaching liquid should just reach the top of the fish.
* Once the poaching liquid comes to a boil, immediately reduce it to a simmer; letting it boil could break the fish apart.

* If you're poaching fish to be served cold, it will be moister if you let it cool in the cooking liquid.
* Save poaching liquid to use as a base for soup or sauce. If desired, freeze for future use.

MICROWAVING FISH

* Arrange fish in a single layer, the thinner portion toward the center of the plate. Cover with a lid, waxed paper or plastic wrap (vent one corner). Cook on high for a minimum of 3 minutes per pound, turning the dish once or twice during cooking. Let covered fish stand for 1 minute before testing for doneness.

CRACKED PEPPER TUNA STEAKS

Swordfish can be successfully substituted for the tuna, if you prefer. Generously sprinkle cracked black pepper over both sides of 6 tuna steaks, pressing into the surface; salt to taste. In a large skillet, over medium-high heat, heat 3 tablespoons extra virgin olive oil until hot. Sauté tuna steaks until the fish is rare to medium-rare (or done to your preference). Remove to a warm platter; cover and place in a 250°F oven. Add ¼ cup whipping cream and 2 tablespoons dry white wine to the pan drippings. Cook over medium-high heat for 3 minutes, stirring constantly. Salt to taste. Drizzle the sauce over the tuna steaks; garnish with chopped fresh chives. Serves 6.

FLAMBÉING   *see also* LIQUOR AND LIQUEURS

TIDBIT   Though it has long been thought that alcohol evaporates when heated, a USDA (U.S. Department of Agriculture) study has disproved that theory. In fact, 5 to 85 percent of the alcohol may remain in a cooked dish, depending on various factors, including how the food was heated, the cooking time, and the source of the alcohol. Even the smallest trace of alcohol may be ill-advised for alcoholics and those with alcohol-related illnesses.

* The best liquid for FLAMBÉING is brandy or an 80-proof liquor. Never use spirits that are 150 proof—they're far too volatile and could explode when lighted.
* Choose a spirit whose flavor complements the food to be flambéed.
* Heat the spirits in a small saucepan over medium heat just until bubbles begin to form around the edge of the pan. Overheating causes too much of the alcohol to evaporate and the mixture may not ignite.
* Or place up to ⅓ cup liquor in a 1-cup glass measure and microwave on high for about 20 seconds (less time for a smaller amount).
* Use a long-handled match or gas kitchen lighter to ignite a flambéed mixture.
* Always ignite the fumes, not the liquid itself.

* Never lean over the dish as you light the fumes or you could end up with singed brows.
* If the alcohol won't ignite it's probably because it isn't hot enough.
* Allow the flames to subside naturally. Blowing them out could splatter the liquid; it also doesn't let the alcohol burn off completely, which means the dish could have a raw-alcohol flavor.
* After flaming, stir the food to combine the flavors.

FLOUR *see also* BAKED GOODS, GENERAL; BREADS; CAKES; COOKIES; THICKENERS

PURCHASING Different flours are used for different purposes. Check the package label under "Nutrition Facts" to select a flour with a protein level appropriate for what you're baking. Flours with 12 to 14 grams protein per cup are best for yeast breads; those with 9 to 11 grams are better for quick breads and pie crusts. Here's a brief synopsis of the most commonly used flours:

* **All-purpose flour** is made from a blend of high-gluten hard wheat and low-gluten soft wheat. It's milled from the wheat kernel's inner portion, minus the bran (husk) and germ (sprouting section). It comes in bleached and unbleached styles, which can be used interchangeably. All-purpose flour is suitable for most kinds of baking, including quick and yeast breads, biscuits, muffins, cookies and cakes. *To substitute cake flour for all-purpose flour:* Use 1 cup plus 2 tablespoons for each cup of flour called for in the recipe. *To substitute self-rising flour for all-purpose flour in yeast breads:* Omit the salt called for in the recipe. *To substitute self-rising for all-purpose in quick breads or other baking powder–leavened baked goods:* Omit the salt and baking powder called for.
* **Bread flour** is a specially formulated high-protein product comprised of about 99.8 percent unbleached flour plus a smidgen of malted barley flour (for improved yeast activity). It's ideally suited for making yeast breads.
* **Whole-wheat flour** has a higher fiber, nutritional and fat content than all-purpose or bread flour because it's milled from the whole kernel (including bran and germ). It's pale brown in color and tastes of the grain.
* **Self-rising flour** is an all-purpose flour to which baking powder and salt have been added. *To substitute all-purpose flour for self-rising flour:* Put 1½ teaspoons baking powder and ½ teaspoon salt in a measuring cup, spoon in the all-purpose flour and level it off with a knife. Repeat for each cup of flour.

* **Cake** (or **pastry**) **flour** is a fine-textured, soft-wheat flour that's particularly suited for cakes and pastries. *To substitute all-purpose flour for cake flour:* Measure out 1 cup all-purpose flour, then remove 2 tablespoons.
* **Gluten flour** is a high-protein, hard-wheat flour treated to remove most of the starch (leaving a high gluten content). It's used for low-gluten breads like rye and to make low-calorie "gluten" breads.
* **Semolina flour** is made from durum wheat and is typically more coarsely ground than other wheat flours. Most pasta is made from semolina.
* **Instant flour** is a specially formulated granular flour used primarily to thicken sauces, soups and other cooked dishes.

EQUIVALENTS

* All-purpose, bread, self-rising or gluten flour: 1 pound = 3 cups sifted
* Whole-wheat flour: 1 pound = 3½ cups sifted
* Cake or pastry flour: 1 pound = 4½ to 5 cups sifted

STORING Store flour in airtight containers like canisters or wide-mouthed screw-top jars. All-purpose and bread flours can be kept at room temperature for up to 6 months (temperatures above 75°F invite bugs and mold). Flour containing part of the grain's germ (such as whole-wheat flour) quickly becomes rancid, so should be purchased in small quantities and refrigerated, tightly wrapped, for 6 months; freeze for up to a year.

SUBSTITUTIONS **For thickening:** Substitute 2 tablespoons flour for each tablespoon cornstarch. **For baking:** See page 201 for substitutions under all-purpose flour, self-rising flour and this page for cake (or pastry) flour.

USING

* Bring chilled flours to room temperature before using in recipes for baked goods.
* Flour absorbs less liquid during hot, humid months than in dry weather because it will have already absorbed some of the moisture from the atmosphere. Such variations are more noticeable when making yeast bread. For the best results, add only enough flour to keep the dough from being too sticky to work with. A dough that is slightly tacky to the touch will yield a much nicer loaf than one that is dry.
* Unless a recipe specifically calls for sifted flour, don't go to the trouble. Measure by stirring the flour, then gently spooning it into a measuring cup and leveling off with the flat edge of a knife. The stirring is necessary because, though most all-purpose flour is now "presifted," it settles and compacts during storage.
* Whole-wheat flour can be substituted for all-purpose or bread flour in bread recipes, but the resulting loaf will be much denser. For a lighter

consistency loaf, substitute half the all-purpose flour with whole-wheat
flour and add ⅓ cup toasted wheat germ.

* Make your own oat flour by processing rolled oats in a blender or food
  processor until powdery. Substitute the oat flour for up to a third of the
  flour called for in bread recipes.
* Flour can have a "raw" taste in cooked preparations like sauces and
  soups. To eliminate this, sprinkle the flour in an even layer on a shallow
  pan; bake at 350°F until deep golden brown.
* Put all-purpose flour in a large salt shaker and use it to dust work surfaces and pans.

FLOWERS *see also* SQUASH BLOSSOMS

TIDBIT Many flowers can be used either as a garnish for food or drink,
or as an integral part of a dish, such as a salad. Among those that are edible are chamomile, chive blossoms, chrysanthemums, daisies, geraniums,
jasmine, lavender, lilacs, marigolds, mimosa, nasturtiums, pansies, roses,
violas and violets. Not all flowers are edible. Flowers that have been
sprayed with pesticides, such as those found at a florist, should never be
eaten.

PURCHASING Edible flowers are available at specialty produce markets and some supermarkets.

STORING Refrigerate in an airtight container for up to a week.

USING

* Before using a flower from your garden that you're unsure of (assuming
  it's pesticide free), call your local poison control center to make sure it
  isn't poisonous.
* Flowers can be used whole, or you can pull off the petals and scatter
  them over a dish.
* Some of the larger flowers—like SQUASH BLOSSOMS—can be stuffed and
  deep-fried.

FOIL *see* ALUMINUM FOIL

FONDUE, CHEESE *see also* CHEESE; Instant Chocolate Fondue, page 114

TIDBIT *Fondue au fromage* (cheese fondue) is a smooth, heady amalgam
of cheese and wine—and it just doesn't get any better than that. Cheese fondue is quick and easy to make, and a fun, casual way to entertain. Not only
is fondue versatile, but there's only one pot and everyone serves themselves—what could be easier?

F

EQUIPMENT NEEDED

* **Fondue pots** are available in all shapes and sizes. They typically come with a stand in which a candle or fuel can is placed to heat the pot. If you're going to cook with it a lot, buy a good enamel-on-steel pot that can be used for both cheese and hot-oil fondues. A chafing dish can be substituted for a fondue pot.

* **Fondue forks** are long-handled, double-pronged utensils used to spear and dip food. They have distinguishing marks or colors so diners can tell which fork is theirs. Supply diners with a regular dinner forks with which to eat the food, and leave the fondue forks for dipping.

* **Fondue plates** have separate indentations in which sauces, meat and other food items can be placed. They're convenient, but certainly not necessary. Sauces, and other foods can be put in small bowls instead.

* **Fondue sets** come complete with pot, forks and, sometimes, bowls or plates.

* Fondue equipment can be found everywhere from kitchenware stores to department stores.

INGREDIENTS

* Since cheese is the primary ingredient, use one of good quality. A combination of two or more cheeses will give fondue a more complex flavor. Swiss cheese is the classic choice, Gruyère and Emmental being the most popular. Have the cheese at room temperature before adding it to the hot mixture.

* Swiss cheese isn't your only option. Cheddar, for instance, makes a particularly hearty fondue.

* Fondue won't separate if you add a thickener, such as cornstarch or flour.

* Cook fondue over low heat—cheese turns rubbery when overheated.

* Fondue can be variously flavored to suit your taste. Among the myriad additions possible are fresh herbs like tarragon, minced, sautéed shallots, a touch of mustard, roasted garlic or a tablespoon of tomato paste. The options are endless.

* Chunks or cubes of French bread may be the classic fondue dipper, but certainly not the only choice. Consider chunks of apple or pear, halved tiny roasted or boiled potatoes, cherry tomatoes or blanched veggies like broccoli or cauliflower.

* Make a complete meal by serving a salad alongside the fondue. No bread is necessary, as that's one of the items being dipped.

* Use warmed leftover fondue as a topping for potatoes or pasta; slice cold fondue for a sandwich, dice it and sprinkle over hot vegetables, or chop and add it to a scramble.

SWISS FONDUE
Combine 2 halved, peeled garlic cloves, ½ teaspoon ground white pepper, ⅛
teaspoon grated nutmeg and 1½ cups dry white wine in a fondue pot; bring
to a simmer over medium heat. Grate ½ pound each Gruyère and Emmental cheese. Put 1 tablespoon cornstarch in a small bowl; gradually stir in 2
tablespoons kirsch or Calvados. Use a slotted spoon to remove the garlic
pieces from the wine. Reduce the heat to medium-low. By handfuls, gradually add the grated cheese, stirring constantly in a zigzag pattern until the
cheese is melted before adding more. When the fondue is creamy and
smooth, remix the cornstarch mixture and gradually stir it into the fondue.
Cook over low heat until thickened, about 5 minutes. Keep warm over low
heat, and serve with dippers of choice. Serves 4 to 6.

FOOD LABELS see LABEL TERMS

FOOD PROCESSORS see also BLENDERS; IMMERSION BLENDERS
TIDBIT A food processor can be the workhorse of a busy kitchen. Having it readily available—sitting out on the countertop—is the only way
you'll get into the habit of using it for everyday cooking. An extra food processor workbowl speeds preparation time because you don't have to stop
and wash the bowl between uses. Many manufacturers sell bowl inserts that
can be lifted out after using, leaving you with a clean workbowl.
GENERAL
* There are certain tasks the food processor just can't do. Whipping potatoes is one—the machine's high speed turns potatoes into a gluey glob.
  Processors can't cut geometrical shapes like cubes or wedges, nor can
  they beat air into egg whites or cream without special attachments.
* Spraying the grating or slicing disks or the metal blade with cooking
  spray before using will make clean up easy. If you're processing a particularly sticky mixture, spray the inside of the workbowl and lid as well.
* If the lid goes on with difficulty, spritz the inside edge that touches the
  bowl with cooking spray.
* To keep the lid clean when processing a mixture that splatters, cover the
  bowl with plastic wrap, letting the excess hang over the edges. Attach the
  lid and process as usual, then whip off the clean lid and toss away the
  messy plastic.
* The small plastic blade is specifically for kneading bread.
* The tiny hole in the bottom of a processor's food pusher is for slowly
  drizzling liquid (such as oil) into the workbowl to make mayonnaise and
  other emulsions.

* To easily add dry ingredients (like sugar) while the machine is running, form a funnel out of waxed paper, place it in the feed tube and pour in the ingredient.
* Overfilling the bowl with liquid mixtures can cause them to leak out between the metal blade and the shaft as well as at the rim of the bowl. Your owner's manual will tell you how much is too much.

SLICING AND SHREDDING

* Apply a gentle but steady pressure. Soft foods like cucumbers require less pressure than dense foods like potatoes.
* For short shreds or slices, stand the food (such as carrots) upright in the feed tube, packing the tube so the food stands straight. For long pieces, lay the food horizontally in the feed tube.
* When slicing or shredding several vegetables for one dish, it's not necessary to remove them from the workbowl as they're sliced unless you plan to use them separately.
* Quickly soften butter by grating or thinly slicing it in a food processor. Let it stand for about 10 minutes.

CHOPPING AND MINCING

* When you use the metal blade technique makes all the difference in the world. **Pulsing** is a method of using quick on/off pulses to keep pieces of food from bouncing around in the workbowl and in the blade's path. It's the surest way to keep chopped onions from becoming onion purée or nuts from turning into nut butter.
* When chopping small foods like garlic or shallots with the steel blade, start the motor, then drop the garlic or shallot cloves, one or two at a time, through the feed tube. The chopped food will cling to the sides of the bowl.
* When a dish requires many foods to be cut, always start with the driest and least odoriferous food first. For instance, you might chop mushrooms, then zucchini, then bell peppers and, finally, onions. All you need is a simple paper towel wipeout between vegetables. As you chop or slice them, transfer the vegetables to individual sheets of waxed paper or paper plates to save on cleanup.
* Cut large foods into 1-inch chunks before processing.
* Don't overload the workbowl. Better to chop in batches than risk some of the food becoming pulverized while other pieces remain large.
* Foods with a similar texture, like apples and crisp pears, can be chopped together.
* Keep the motor running to PURÉE foods like fruit or pulverize foods like nuts and citrus zest. Add a little sugar from the recipe to nuts and citrus zest to facilitate chopping.

* The steel blade not only makes quick work of chopping or mincing vegetables and meat, but is great for making homemade butter (see page 72),
pie crusts and biscuits. It's also good for powdering ingredients—turning granulated sugar into superfine sugar, or tapioca into tapioca flour,
and so on.

CLEANING

* Food-processor bowls and attachments are dishwasher safe, making
cleanup easy.
* Soaking the processor bowl is sometimes necessary after working with a
particularly messy mixture, but the center hole makes filling the bowl
impossible. Here's an easy solution: Simply tear off a 4-inch wide length
of plastic wrap, fold it in half lengthwise, then neatly cover the hole with
it, pressing down the edges. Secure the plastic wrap at the top edge of the
center shaft with a rubber band (wrap it around the shaft several times to
seal tightly), then fill with soapy water.

FOOD SAFETY *see also* COOKING, GENERAL; THERMOMETERS *for information on meat and freezer/refrigerator thermometers*
TIDBIT Each year an estimated nine thousand deaths and countless millions of illnesses are linked to foodborne bacteria. Just one bacterium can
grow to over two million in seven hours. Improper food handling causes
the majority of foodborne illnesses. The people most at risk are children,
the elderly and those with weakened immune systems or chronic poor
health.

SHOPPING

* Separate raw meat, poultry and seafood from other foods. Place such
items in a plastic bag, then in the shopping cart.
* Make grocery shopping the last thing you do before going home so cold
foods will stay that way. If doing so isn't possible, put an insulated cooler
with gel-pak ice in your car to carry perishable items.
* Once you're home, immediately put the cold perishables into the refrigerator or freezer. Place raw meat, poultry and seafood on the bottom
shelf of the refrigerator so their juices won't drip onto other foods.
* Hot take-out foods should be kept hot (140°F) and eaten within 2 hours.
If purchasing food to consume later, place it in shallow containers and
refrigerate.

PREPARING FOOD

* Preventing cross-contamination (transferring bacteria from one surface
to another) is an important step to food safety. The principal way to prevent the spread of bacteria is to wash your hands before and after han-

dling food—use soap and very warm water, rubbing your hands together for 20 seconds. After preparing one food and before using them again, wash all knives, utensils and food preparation surfaces (such as cutting boards and countertops) with hot soapy water or a sanitizing solution.

* Use a nonporous cutting board, such as one made of plastic; wash it in the dishwasher.
* Have one cutting board for raw meat, and another for fruits and vegetables. Or wash a single cutting board with hot soapy water with each use.
* Wash fruits and vegetables under cool, running water. Use a vegetable brush to scrub sturdy vegetables that will be eaten with their skin on (like carrots or potatoes).
* Handle raw meat and poultry with care, never allowing their juices to come in contact with foods to be eaten raw.
* Defrost food in the refrigerator. Small amounts will thaw overnight, while larger foods, such as roasts, may take over a day. Thawing food on the countertop invites bacterial growth.

COOKING Harmful bacteria that cause foodborne illness will be killed if food is cooked long enough and at an appropriate heat. See *individual food listings for doneness criteria*.

SERVING

* **The two-hour rule:** Refrigerate or freeze food within 2 hours from the moment it comes out of the oven or refrigerator—this includes preparation and serving time. Special care should be taken with such foods as eggs, dairy products, meat, poultry and seafood.
* Never put cooked food on a plate that has held raw meat, poultry or seafood without first washing the plate with hot water and soap.
* **Buffet serving:** Keep cold foods cold (40°F or less) and hot foods hot (at least 140°F). Bacteria multiply rapidly at temperatures between 40°F and 140°F.
* **Leftovers:** Refrigerate within 2 hours of preparation. Divide large portions into smaller, shallow containers for rapid, even cooling in the fridge or freezer. Refrigerated leftovers should be used within 3 to 4 days. Reheat to a temperature of 165°F.

FREEZING FOOD *see also* individual listings for specifics on each food

* To help keep the freezer compartment clean, line the bottom with plastic wrap or foil, taking care not to cover the fan vent.
* Keep a freezer THERMOMETER in your freezer to make sure the tempera-

ture is at 0°F or slightly below. The quality of frozen food diminishes when the temperature rises 10 degrees above 0°F.

✳ Try not to open the freezer door during a power outage. It lets warm air in and can hasten defrosting.

✳ Overloading a freezer slows down the freezing process, which can affect the flavor and quality of food.

✳ When adding several containers of unfrozen food to a freezer, space them well apart to hasten the freezing process. Once they're frozen solid, stack them as desired.

✳ To retain a food's flavor and nutrients, and keep it from getting freezer burn, use wrappings specifically designed for freezing. Check labels on aluminum foil and plastic bags to make sure they're designed for freezing. Regular plastic wrap, foil and plastic bags are not vapor- or moisture-proof. If you're unsure of the wrapping or container, double wrap food by placing it inside a zip-closure plastic bag.

✳ Get more mileage from freezer space by using plastic freezer bags instead of rigid containers. Transfer the cooled food to the plastic bag, remove as much air as possible and seal tightly. Place the bag on a plate or tray until frozen solid. Then you can stand the food up on its side in the freezer, if necessary, for space. Freezer bags can be washed and reused as long as they're intact.

✳ To remove as much air as possible from plastic bags of food, zip close the bag and seal all but about ½ inch of the bag. Insert a straw into the opening and suck out as much air as possible. Remove the straw and zip up the bag in one quick move.

✳ Oxygen is food's greatest enemy, so choose solid freezer containers that are as close in size as possible to the volume of food to be frozen.

✳ Clean, dry milk or cream cartons are good storage containers and can be cut down to fit the food precisely. Double wrap the carton in a freezer-weight plastic bag.

✳ No freezer tape to label your frozen-food packages? Once the food is frozen solid, insert a small piece of paper noting the contents and the date; reseal until ready to use.

✳ Cool food completely in the fridge before freezing. Chilled food freezes faster, and therefore tastes fresher when reheated. Warm food lowers the freezer's temperature, affecting the quality of the surrounding foods.

✳ With the exception of sauced dishes, food should be as dry as possible before freezing.

✳ If a recipe calls for BLANCHING food before freezing, do so. This step is necessary for some foods to destroy natural enzymes that would affect its quality during freezing.

* Seasonings have a way of changing flavor in some frozen foods. If you're making a dish specifically to freeze, season it after it's thawed and heated.

* It's possible to freeze an entire cooked or uncooked casserole and still be able to use the dish while the food waits in the freezer. Simply line a casserole dish with heavy-duty aluminum foil. Leave enough overhang on all sides to cover and seal the food. Add the casserole ingredients and either freeze until solid or bake and cool to room temperature before freezing. Use the foil overhang to lift the frozen food from the dish; cover the food with the foil overhang and seal airtight. Double wrap in a freezer-proof plastic bag. To thaw, remove the wrapping and place the frozen food back in its original dish.

* Single-serving portions can be frozen easily in individual freezer bags, microwave-safe containers or heavy-duty foil or plastic wrap.

* Don't refreeze food that's been frozen and reheated. Not only will the flavor have deteriorated, but the chance of bacterial growth will greatly increase.

* Food that still has some ice crystallization may be refrozen, but will have a short life so should be consumed soon.

* Never refreeze frozen cooked food or seafood, both of which spoil rapidly once defrosted.

* To individually freeze cookies, cookie dough, pieces of meat (like chicken), meatballs, pastries or finger food, place them on a baking sheet and freeze uncovered until hard. Wrap airtight in a freezer-proof plastic bag or heavy-duty foil. This technique keeps food from sticking together and allows you to remove as many pieces as you need at a time. Some foods must be defrosted before heating, others can be heated frozen.

* Clues to whether or not frozen food has begun to deteriorate: (1) freezer burn—a dry-looking surface (sometimes with pale gray spots) caused by air getting into the package; (2) color change—signaling a food's been frozen too long, particularly prevalent in vegetables; (3) frost—an indicator that food either froze too slowly or that it was partially thawed and refrozen; (4) textural change—meat toughens, vegetables lose their crispness, sauces separate and turn lumpy, and so on.

* **Thawing:** The safest method to thaw food is to place it in the refrigerator overnight. The thawing time for some foods can be greatly reduced by placing them in a plastic bag (if not already frozen that way), then in a

large bowl of cold water. Most foods can also be defrosted in a micro-wave oven, following the manufacturer's directions.

FRENCH FRIES *see* POTATOES, COOKING METHODS, page 379

FRENCH TOAST
TIDBIT   In France, French toast is called *pain perdu* ("lost bread"), in reference to the fact that dipping dried-out bread in a egg-milk mixture is a way to "find" it again.

PREPARING
* Light-textured breads like challah, brioche, French or Italian are perfect for French toast. Flavored breads like raisin and cinnamon are also good choices.
* French toast can range in thickness from ½ to 1 inch thick. Buy unsliced bread and cut to desired thickness.
* Cut bread slices diagonally to create triangle shapes.
* Egg substitute can replace eggs, if desired: ¼ cup egg substitute per large egg. Or 3 egg whites can be substituted for 2 eggs.
* The average proportion of milk to egg is ¼ cup milk (or other liquid) per 2 eggs.
* When making the egg-milk dip, whisk the eggs first, then stir in the milk and other ingredients.
* Make French toast with the maple syrup built right in. Substitute pure MAPLE SYRUP, not pancake syrup, for half the milk.
* Flavor the dip for French toast to suit your taste. For instance, instead of milk use orange or other fruit juice or fruit nectar, or substitute a liqueur (almond, orange or hazelnut) for part or all of the milk, or add a table-spoon of rum or honey, or melt 2 tablespoons peanut butter and add it the mixture, or flavor the mixture with spices (ground cinnamon, all-spice or nutmeg) or orange or lemon zest.

COOKING
* **Stovetop French toast:** If you're making a large batch of French toast, preheat the oven to 350°F so you can keep the French toast warm while frying the other pieces. Spray a large nonstick skillet or griddle with cooking spray; heat for several minutes over medium-high heat. If you don't have a nonstick skillet, melt 1 to 2 tablespoons unsalted butter in a skillet over medium-high heat. Dip the bread into the egg-milk mixture. The longer the bread stands in the egg mixture, the more custardy it becomes (don't let it sit too long or the bread will fall apart). For a moist,

but not wet, end result, place the bread in the egg-milk mixture, let stand for a few seconds, then flip it with a fork and moisten the other side. Immediately transfer the egg-dipped bread to the hot skillet. Cook until nicely browned, then flip and brown the other side. Transfer the bread to a baking sheet and keep warm in the oven until you're through cooking.

* **Baked French toast:** Preheat the oven to 450°F. Put 2 tablespoons unsalted butter in a 15 × 10-inch jelly-roll pan or baking sheet(s) with raised edges (use two pans if baking more than 8 slices). (Or liberally coat the pan with cooking spray.) Place the pan in the oven for 3 minutes, or until the butter melts; tilt the pan so the butter covers the bottom. If using cooking spray, heat the pan for 3 minutes. Arrange the dipped bread slices on the hot pan. Bake for 5 minutes. Turn the slices over; bake for an additional 5 minutes, or until golden brown.

* Toppings include maple or fruit-flavored syrup (heat syrups until warm), powdered sugar, fresh fruit, toasted nuts, yogurt, whipped cream or a whipped mixture of softened cream cheese and a little milk or fruit juice.

* Cool leftover French toast, stack it (with a piece of plastic wrap between each slice) and freeze in a plastic bag. To reheat, simply pop it into the toaster.

HOT BUTTERED RUM SYRUP

Combine 1 cup sugar, ⅓ cup water and 1 cinnamon stick (broken in half) in a small saucepan. Bring to a boil over medium heat. Boil without stirring for 2 minutes; remove from the heat. Add 2 tablespoons rum and ⅓ cup butter (cut into 4 pieces), stir until the butter melts. Serve warm or at room temperature. Makes about 1¼ cups.

FRIED EGGS   see EGGS, COOKING METHODS, page 182

FROSTING; ICING   see also CAKES; PASTRY BAGS
MAKING THE FROSTING

* For frosting lovers, double the frosting recipe and split each cake layer in half crosswise (see CAKES) to double the number of surfaces to frost.

* For an easy, elegant frosting, use whipped cream—dress it up by flavoring with liqueur, sweetening with honey or maple syrup, or folding in grated chocolate or finely chopped Almond Roca. Before adding liquid (like liqueur) to whipped cream, beat the cream to the soft-peak stage. Beating constantly, gradually drizzle in the liquid, whipping until the cream is thick. Don't add more than 2 to 4 tablespoons of liquid per cup of cream or the frosting may become too soft.

* Make chocoholics happy by frosting a cake with Chocolate Whipped Cream, (*see* page 159).
* For cooked frostings, use a heavy pan that holds at least double the amount of the original ingredients to allow for expansion during cooking.
* Don't stir a boiled frosting made with sugar and water—doing so will make it grainy.
* Save a cooked frosting that's begun to sugar (turn granular) by stirring in ¼ to ½ teaspoon lemon juice or distilled white vinegar.
* Thwart lumpy frosting by sifting the confectioners' sugar. No sifter? Put the sugar in a fine sieve and push it through by stirring it with a spoon.
* Confectioners' sugar frostings can be moistened with milk, strong coffee, peanut butter (thinned with milk), fruit juice, jam or jelly (melted slightly), honey or maple syrup.
* Using warm liquids (milk, fruit juice, liqueur) helps dissolve lumps in unsifted confectioners' sugar.
* Eliminate the "raw" taste of confectioners' sugar frosting by putting it in the top of a double boiler over simmering water for about 10 minutes, stirring occasionally. Remove from the heat and cool to lukewarm before frosting the cake.
* Beat 1 to 2 tablespoons softened butter into a confectioners' sugar frosting to keep the surface supple rather than dry and crackly. If the frosting's been heated, let it cool completely before beating in the butter.
* Achieve a similarly moist frosting without the butter by adding ¼ teaspoon baking powder per cup of confectioners' sugar before stirring in the liquid.
* If a confectioners' sugar frosting has become too thick, stir in a little liquid, ½ teaspoon at a time, until the desired texture is reached.
* Fold in chopped nuts, chocolate or fruit after the frosting's finished. Doing so beforehand can thin it.
* Freeze leftover creamy or confectioners' sugar frostings for up to 6 months. Defrost in the refrigerator overnight; beat before using.

FROSTING THE CAKE

* Thoroughly cool the cake before frosting it. A cake that's even slightly warm could soften or melt the frosting.
* Use a pastry brush to remove any loose crumbs before beginning to frost.
* If a cake is extremely soft, apply a "crumb coating" by spreading a paper-thin layer of frosting over the entire cake to seal the surface, set the crumbs and fill in any imperfections. Allow this coating to dry for 5 to 10 minutes before applying the remaining frosting.

F

* Particularly delicate cake will be easier to frost if you partially freeze it first.
* Thick frosting can tear cake. Thin it by beating in a few drops of milk or other liquid.
* Uneven cake layers can be camouflaged with a thick layer of frosting.
* Frost a cake on the serving plate so you don't risk damaging it while transferring it to the serving plate. To keep the plate clean, position several strips of waxed paper around the edges of the plate, then place the cake on top of the paper. Once the cake's frosted, carefully pull out the waxed paper strips and discard.
* If you do frost a cake on the rack on which it cooled, place a sheet of waxed paper under the rack. The paper will catch any drips, which can be returned to the frosting bowl (unless it has crumbs in it).
* When a cake filling is different from the frosting, don't spread it all the way to the edges or it might run into, discolor or otherwise interfere with the frosting. Spread the filling to within ½ inch of the edges (it will probably spread a bit when the other layer is placed on top of it); the frosting will fill in any spaces. Or pipe the frosting around the edge of the bottom cake layer, then spoon the filling into the center of the circle of frosting.
* As soon as the frosting's on the cake, use a flexible metal pastry spatula to create decorative swirls and other finishing touches. When working with creamy or butter-based frostings, dip the spatula in cold water frequently to prevent the frosting from sticking to it. Confectioners' sugar or cooked frostings do better if the spreader is dipped into hot water.
* Before creating a design or writing on cake frosting, use a toothpick to draw the pattern first, then pipe the frosting over the lines.
* For cupcakes, it's often quicker to dip the tops in the frosting (which must be very soft or light), rather than spreading frosting over each one. Just be sure all crumbs have been brushed away from the cupcake's surface.
* Prevent plastic wrap from sticking to frosting by spraying it first with cooking spray.

FRUIT, DRIED *see* DRIED FRUIT

FRUIT, GENERAL *See individual fruit listings for specific and storage and usage information:* APPLES; APRICOTS; AVOCADOS; BANANAS; BERRIES, GENERAL; BLACKBERRIES; BLUEBERRIES; CHERRIES; CITRUS FRUITS; CRANBERRIES; DATES; DRIED FRUIT; GRAPEFRUIT; GRAPES; LEMONS; LIMES; MANGOES; MEL-

F

* Speed the ripening of soft fruits, such as nectarines, peaches and pears, by putting them in a paper bag with a ripe apple for 2 to 3 days. Pierce the bag in a few places with the tip of a knife, then fold the top to seal. The apple produces a natural ethylene gas that speeds ripening.
* Ripening stops when fruit is refrigerated.
* Some fruits are coated with wax before being marketed. Waxing is done to extend shelf life, seal in moisture and improve appearance. Though such waxes are safe to eat, they may contain pesticide residues. The FDA (Food and Drug Administration) requires that labels identify waxed produce as such, but this is rarely done. Some waxed fruits are obvious by their shine and feel. If you're not sure, ask the produce manager.
* There are great fiber and nutritional advantages and almost no risk of chemical residues in eating unpeeled fruit. The FDA reports that, during annual random produce testing, 99 percent of the produce is either residue free or well below EPA (Environmental Protection Agency) limits.
* Wash fruit just before using under cool, running water—use a vegetable brush, if necessary. Very dirty fruit can be washed in soapy water, then rinsed thoroughly.
* Soaking fruit in water for more than a few minutes can leach out water-soluble vitamins.
* Keep cut fruit from staining your hands during preparation by spraying your hands with cooking spray.
* Prevent fruits like apples and pears from darkening after peeling by dipping them into ACIDULATED WATER.
* Pitting fruits like peaches and nectarines is easier if you cut the fruit from stem to stem all the way to the stone. Twist the halves in opposite directions and lift out the stone.
* Pieces of fruit are less likely to sink in a cake or bread batter if you first toss them with some of the flour used in the recipe.
* Pour heavy cream over fruit about 5 minutes before serving. The fruit's natural acid will slightly coagulate the cream, making it extra thick and luscious.
* Don't throw out soft, overripe fruit! Peel it if necessary, cut off any bruised spots, then PURÉE or finely chop and use it as a topping for ice cream, shortcake, pancakes or waffles. For a more saucelike topping, add a little liquid, such as fruit juice, liqueur or cream.

FRUITSICLES

PURÉE fruit and, if desired, thin slightly with water, fruit juice, milk or yogurt. Pour into 4- to 6-ounce paper cups. When partially frozen, insert popsicle sticks in the center of each "sicle"; freeze until solid. No popsicle stick? Simply freeze the purée in paper cups until solid and either push up from the bottom to eat the frozen fruit or peel the cup downward as you eat.

FRUIT-CHEESE TORTE

For an easy last-minute dessert, PURÉE 1½ cups fruit (such as strawberries, raspberries, chopped peaches or nectarines) with 1 cup ricotta cheese; sweeten to taste. Cut a store-bought pound or sponge cake horizontally into three layers. If desired, drizzle the layers with rum, brandy or liqueur. Spread the fruit mixture between the layers and on the top. Garnish with whipped cream and whole berries or slices of fruit.

FRUITCAKE *see also* BAKED GOODS, GENERAL; CAKE; GREASING PANS

PREPARING

* To create a light fruitcake from a dark fruitcake recipe: Substitute lighter-colored spices (cardamom, mace, ginger and nutmeg) for dark spices like cinnamon and cloves; use light corn syrup instead of dark corn syrup or molasses; use only light fruits such as golden raisins, pineapple, dried apricots, apples, and so on; use pale nuts like almonds or macadamias, rather than darker ones like pecans and walnuts.
* To prevent overbrowning, line the bottom and sides of the pan with foil. It's easier to grease the foil before you line the pan with it. Leave enough overlap hanging out of the pan so you can grab the edges and pull the cake out.
* Never fill a pan more than two-thirds full with batter or it might rise over the edges.
* Create mini-fruitcakes by baking in mini-loaf pans or muffin tins (giant muffin tins are about 3 inches in diameter). Reduce the baking time by one half to two-thirds and check for doneness.

BAKING

* Fruitcakes are baked in a slow oven for a long time. To keep the outer edges from burning before the interior is baked, set the pan in a 13 × 9-inch baking pan filled half full with hot water.
* Test a fruitcake for doneness by inserting a toothpick near the center. If it comes out clean, the cake's done.
* Let fruitcake sit in the pan for 10 minutes after baking, then turn it out, right side up, onto a rack to cool completely.

* Drizzle cooled fruitcake with liquor, liqueur or wine, then wrap it in spirit-soaked cheesecloth. Seal airtight in foil or a heavyweight plastic bag and refrigerate for at least 3 weeks.
* Fruitcake will slice more easily if it's cold. Use a thin, nonserrated knife.

FRYING *see* DEEP-FRYING; SAUTÉING; STIR-FRYING

FUDGE *see* CANDY

FUNNELS
* Every kitchen should have at least two funnels, narrow-mouthed and wide-mouthed; the first for pouring liquids into a bottle, the second for transferring chunky foods to a jar or other container.
* Clip off the corner of a plastic bag to turn it into an instant, disposable funnel.
* Make a funnel by forming a cone out of heavy-duty foil or double thickness of regular foil.
* For dry ingredients, use PARCHMENT PAPER to form a funnel.

The emotional content of garlic almost equals its culinary value.
—Arthur E. Grosser, American author, actor, teacher

GARLIC   *see also* GARLIC PRESSES

TIDBIT   Down through the ages, garlic has been credited with miraculous healing powers. Modern-day research agrees, crediting this lily-family member with compounds that forestall numerous diseases, including cancer, asthma, arthritis, diabetes, cardiovascular disease and infections. Scientists say garlic is an excellent antibiotic, often more effective than penicillin and tetracycline for some bacterial infections. So enjoy the lusty pleasures of garlic and feel downright upright about being good to your body.

PURCHASING

* The primary types of garlic available are: **American garlic** (white-skinned and strongly flavored); **Mexican and Italian garlic** (both of which have mauve-colored skins and a slightly milder flavor); and the extremely mild **elephant garlic** (not a true garlic, but related to the leek), which is orange-sized with huge, 1-ounce cloves. **Green garlic** is garlic in its infant stage, before it begins to form cloves. It resembles a baby leek with its long green top and tiny white bulb. Its flavor is much softer and sweeter than that of mature garlic. Green garlic is occasionally available in specialty produce markets in the spring.

* Fresh garlic: Choose heads with firm, plump bulbs and dry skins. Avoid heads with soft or shriveled cloves, and those stored in the refrigerated section of the produce department.

* Other forms of garlic: dried and oil-packed minced garlic, garlic extract, garlic juice, garlic powder and garlic salt may be convenient to use, but they're a poor flavor substitute for the less expensive, readily available fresh garlic. All these forms are available in most supermarkets.

EQUIVALENTS
* 1 head = 12 to 16 cloves
* 1 medium clove = ½ teaspoon minced, ⅛ teaspoon garlic powder

STORING   Store in an open container (away from other foods) in a cool, dark place for up to 2 months for unbroken bulbs (they'll begin to dry out toward the end of that time). Once broken from the bulb, individual cloves will keep for 3 to 10 days.

PREPARING
* Instantly separate a head of garlic into cloves by placing it on the countertop, covering with a dishtowel and whacking it with a heavy pot.
* To quickly peel garlic cloves, position the flat side of a French knife on top of the clove and whack it with your fist (not too hard, unless you want to crush the clove). The jolt loosens the skin for easy removal.
* If you have a lot of garlic to peel, separate the bulb into cloves, drop into boiling water and blanch for 30 seconds. Turn into a colander, rinse with cold water and peel.
* Microwave method for loosening skins: Place a whole head of garlic on a paper plate; microwave on high for 1 minute, rotating the plate at 30 seconds. (You may need more or less time, depending on the garlic's size and the oven's power.) Let garlic stand in the oven for 1 minute. Peel when cool enough to handle.
* There's no need to peel garlic cloves when you're putting them through a garlic press. Simply pop the clove, skin and all, into the press and squeeze. The garlic flesh will be forced through the mesh, while the skin stays in the press, keeping it relatively unclogged and making cleanup a breeze.
* Putting a lot of papery garlic skins in the garbage disposal can clog the blades. It's better to toss them in the trash.
* Crushing, chopping, pressing or puréeing garlic releases more of its essential oils and produces a sharper, more assertive flavor than if the cloves are sliced or left whole.
* If you don't have a garlic press, crush peeled garlic by placing a clove on a piece of plastic wrap or waxed paper. Fold the wrap or paper over to cover the clove, then smash it with a meat pounder, rubber mallet, heavy, flat-bottomed glass, or the flat side of a French knife. Use your fist to give it a firm smack.
* Chop garlic with a little salt and it won't stick to the knife as much. The salt also absorbs much of the garlic juice. Turn the garlic and salt into the dish and reduce the amount of salt used accordingly.

* When chopping garlic in a food processor with the steel blade, start the motor, then drop the garlic cloves, one or two at a time, through the feed tube. The chopped garlic will cling to the sides of the bowl.
* Chop a whole head of garlic at one time (the food processor is quick), put in a screw-top glass jar and refrigerate for up to 10 days.
* For a whisper of garlic in salads, cut a clove in half (no need to peel) and rub the cut edges over the inside of the bowl.
* For sweeter, milder garlic, put unpeeled garlic cloves in a small saucepan; cover with cold water. Bring to a boil, then drain and rinse. Repeat two more times before cooling and peeling.
* Old garlic has a very harsh flavor. Diminish it by cutting halfway through a clove, then using the tip of a pointed knife to lift out and discard the center, green-colored shoot. Boiling the garlic for 3 to 5 minutes will further reduce its harshness.
* For garlic when you need it: Peel garlic cloves and put in a screw-top jar. Cover with white or red wine and refrigerate for up to a month. Actually, the garlic can be used as long as no mold grows on the wine's surface.
* Peeled garlic cloves may be stored in oil in the coldest part of the refrigerator for up to 10 days.
* Freezing garlic: The best way is to put the whole head in a freezer-weight plastic bag, expel all the air and seal tightly. Pop off the cloves as you need them. You can also separate the head into cloves and freeze them separately. Or put 2 or 3 cloves in each compartment of an ice cube tray, fill with water and freeze. Pop out the garlic cubes and place in a plastic bag. When you need some garlic, just hold the cube under cold running water, peel the cloves and go!

COOKING

* Overbrowning garlic when sautéing will turn it pungent and bitter. Over medium-high heat, minced garlic typically cooks in less than 1 minute.
* For just a little garlic flavor in sautéed foods, cook halved garlic cloves in oil over medium heat for 1 to 2 minutes, then remove with a slotted spoon.
* When sautéing both garlic and onions, cook the onions until almost done, then add the garlic and cook briefly.
* The longer and more gently garlic is cooked, the milder it becomes. In dishes like slow-cooked stews, whole garlic cloves become so soft that they can be crushed against the side of the pot and stirred into the liquid.
* Roasting garlic is arguably the best way to cook it (*see* Roasted Garlic, page 221).

* For roasted garlic purée: Place roasted garlic (loose cloves or whole head) in a potato ricer and press down firmly to extrude the garlic; discard the skins.

* For a bright, clean flavor, add garlic during the last couple of minutes of a dish's cooking time.

* Adding a little honey to a dish that's too garlicky will balance the flavor.

GETTING RID OF THE SMELL

* Love eating garlic but hate the aftertaste and odor? Alleviate the problem by: chewing on fennel seeds, a coffee bean or chlorophyll-rich greens like parsley; or drinking a tablespoon or two of lemon juice diluted with a little water and sugar; or taking some chlorophyll tablets or a product like Breath Assure, which is based on parsley oil; or, according to the people at the Gilroy's Finest Garlic Festival, eat some lime sherbet.

* Remove garlic odor from your hands by rubbing them with lemon, then with salt. Rinse, then wash with soap and warm water.

* Or rub your fingers over a stainless steel spoon under running water, then wash with soap and water.

* Deodorize a garlicky cutting board by rubbing it with a paste of baking soda and water.

GARLIC BUTTER

Mix 1 cup softened butter with 6 roasted garlic cloves, ¼ cup minced parsley, and salt and pepper to taste. Spoon the mixture onto a length of plastic wrap, enclose and form into a log. Double wrap and freeze. Cut off a disk of garlic butter to flavor vegetables, steaks, and so on.

ROASTED GARLIC

When garlic is roasted, it turns golden and buttery-soft, its flavor slightly sweet and nutty. Use roasted garlic like butter on baked or mashed potatoes, bread or grilled meats, and as an ingredient in soups, sauces and salad dressings. Gently rub off the outer layers of papery skin of a whole head of garlic. Separate into cloves and place on a square of aluminum foil large enough to enclose the garlic loosely. Drizzle the cloves with 1 teaspoon extra virgin olive oil; loosely wrap and seal. (Or drizzle a whole head of garlic with oil and wrap in foil.) Bake at 400°F until soft when pierced with a metal skewer or the tip of a pointed knife (25 to 30 minutes for loose cloves, 1 hour for the whole head). Open the foil during the final 5 minutes of cooking time. Serve warm or at room temperature. Refrigerate leftovers in an airtight jar for up to 10 days.

HOMEGROWN GARLIC "CHIVES"

Place individual garlic cloves, pointed end up and ½ inch apart, in a pot of soil so that only the tips are above the soil's surface. Water only enough to keep the soil moist (not wet) and in a few weeks you'll have garlic chives.

Snip and use them as you would regular chives to garnish salads, soups, vegetables, and so on.

GARLIC PURÉE

Put peeled cloves of 1 large head of garlic into a food processor; drizzle with about 1 tablespoon extra virgin olive oil. Process until the garlic is puréed, scraping down the sides of the workbowl and adding oil if necessary. Refrigerate in an airtight glass container for up to 10 days. For an absolutely airtight seal, level the surface of the purée and cover with about ⅛ inch oil. If any mold appears on the garlic purée, discard immediately.

GARLIC PRESSES

* Garlic presses come in all shapes and sizes and in many materials, including aluminum, stainless steel and plastic. Some have pointed "teeth" that push garlic fragments back out through the holes, making cleaning much easier.
* No need to peel garlic that will be put through a press. Simply insert the whole clove, skin and all, and squeeze. Remove and discard the skin before pressing the next clove.
* Clean a garlic press right after using it, before any residual garlic dries and clogs the holes. Or set the press in a cup of warm water until you're ready to clean it.
* Most garlic presses are difficult to clean—even those self-cleaning units with built-in prongs. Without thorough (and time-consuming) scrubbing, residual oil from the garlic can cling to the utensil. The oil, which quickly turns rancid, can easily pass its foul flavor to the next garlic clove you press. One answer is to buy a dishwasher-safe garlic press, such as one made of stainless steel. Place the press in an open position on the bottom rack, or rest it atop the silverware.
* Or clean it the old-fashioned way, with a toothbrush.

GARNISHING AND GARNISHES see also Chocolate Decorations, page 114; Frosted Grapes, page 232; JULIENNE, page 260.

TIDBIT   Few food adages are truer than "You eat with your eyes first." A simple but deft finishing touch can turn a dull-looking dish into one that's smashing. Garnishes add eye appeal to almost any dish (and drinks, too) and needn't be time-consuming. A basic rule of thumb is that any garnish should be edible and, whenever possible, an ingredient that's intrinsic to the dish. For example, if a dish has fresh basil in it, mince some extra to use as a garnish, or arrange sprigs of basil around the side of the dish. It doesn't take much effort to create a garnish while you're preparing the dish.

GENERAL

* Garnish food at the last minute. It'll look fresher than if you garnish a dish, then let it sit in the refrigerator several hours.

* Before serving food that's been standing or refrigerated, stir it lightly to return the dressing or juices up to the surface, giving it a sheen and making it look tantalizingly fresh. Likewise, turn meats over so that the top is coated with juice and looks succulent. Do this just before garnishing the dish.

* Easy, eye-catching garnishes for savory dishes include julienned vegetables, toasted nuts or bread crumbs, grated cheese, thin rings of onion or bell pepper, slices of citrus fruit, chopped pimiento, sliced or chopped olives, snipped chives or scallion greens, capers, hard-cooked egg slices, thinly sliced fresh vegetables such as zucchini or radishes, whole or halved cherry tomatoes, thinly sliced gherkins or cornichons, chopped or sieved hard-cooked eggs, cooked pearl onions, crisp celery leaves . . . the only limit to the list is your imagination!

* Give sprigs of parsley a colorful border by dipping them into cold water, shaking off the excess, then dipping the leaf edges into paprika. Let dry on a plate in the refrigerator until ready to use.

* Soup garnishes: grated cheese, toasted almond slices, a dollop of sour cream dusted with paprika or cayenne, finely snipped chives or scallion greens, minced herbs or sprigs of herbs (such as parsley or basil).

* Large strawberries and blackberries make a showy garnish for drinks. Cut a slit from the berry's tip to within ¼ inch of the stem end to make a slot for the berry to straddle the glass rim. *See also* COCKTAILS (Garnishing.)

* Desserts deserve to be garnished with something other than the ubiquitous mint leaf. A garnish doesn't have to be elaborate, but it should reflect the flavor of the dessert it adorns. It can be as simple as a perfect strawberry or as showy (but easy) as chocolate leaves, curls or scrolls (*see* pages 114–115). Or consider garnishing desserts with frosted grapes (*see* GRAPES) or candied orange or lemon zest (*see* ORANGES). Or sprinkle a few flowers (*see* FLOWERS) around a cake, or top individual servings of parfait or mousse with a single blossom. Or pull the petals off and sprinkle them over desserts.

* Toasted nuts are one of the easiest garnishes to use. Chop or grind them, then sprinkle over cakes, puddings and so on.

* Dip whole or halved nuts halfway into melted chocolate, then set on a waxed paper–lined baking sheet and refrigerate until the chocolate is set. Use to garnish cakes, cheesecakes and other desserts.

G

CHIFFONADE

French for "made of rags," this colorful garnish of green "ribbons" garnishes dishes like soup, rice and vegetables. It also can be used as a bed for foods, such as meat. Stack cleaned leaves of greens (chard, romaine, sorrel or spinach), then tightly roll them crosswise into a cigar shape. Thinly slice the "cigar" crosswise.

FLUTED MUSHROOMS

Use a citrus stripper to carve out strips at even intervals. The mushrooms must be very firm for this to work.

CUTOUTS

Use a canapé cutter or tiny cookie cutter to cut designs out of ⅛- to ¼-inch-thick slices of fruits or vegetables such as apples, carrots, citrus rind or cucumbers.

CITRUS SPIRALS

With a citrus stripper or sharp knife, cut a citrus rind horizontally around and down the fruit, forming one continuous spiral. Wind the strip around a rounded handle (such as on a wooden spoon), secure with tape, and let dry for 2 hours. Slip the spiral off and use as a garnish.

SCALLOPED FRUITS AND VEGETABLES

Use a paring knife or a citrus stripper to cut evenly spaced, lengthwise channels (at about ½-inch intervals) in an orange, lemon, zucchini, and so on. When the fruit or vegetable is sliced, the channels give the edges a scalloped effect.

TWISTS—FRUIT AND VEGETABLE

Take a thin slice of fruit or vegetable (cucumber, orange, lemon, and so on) and make one cut from the center to the edge. Twist the slice into a spiral (or S) shape.

SCALLION BRUSHES

Trim off the root end and most of the green portion of a scallion. With a sharp, pointed knife, thinly slash both ends of the scallion at ⅛-inch intervals, leaving a 1-inch uncut space in the center. Immerse the scallions in a bowl of ice water; refrigerate for 1 hour, or until the slashed portions curl.

CELERY BRUSHES

Cut celery ribs in 2- to 5-inch lengths (depending on how long you want the brush). Slit each piece lengthwise at about ¼-inch intervals to within 1 inch of the other end. Place the pieces in a large bowl of ice water; refrigerate for at least 1 hour, or until they curl.

CHILE PEPPER FLOWERS

Choose small, brightly colored chiles. Wear gloves to protect your hands from the chile's volatile oils (see chiles). Use a sharp, pointed knife to cut each pepper from the tip to the stem end at about ⅜-inch intervals. Remove the seeds and, if desired, trim the "petal" ends to form points. Place in a bowl of ice water for 1 hour, or until the chile peppers open into flower shapes.

FANS—FRUIT AND VEGETABLE

Use a sharp, pointed knife to cut the food (such as pickles, radishes or strawberries) lengthwise into thin slices to within ¼ inch of the stem end. Use your fingers to fan out the fruit or vegetable.

RADISH FLOWERS

With a sharp knife vertically cut thin petals of the red peel around the radish from the tip down almost to the stem end. Put the radishes in a bowl of ice water, cover and refrigerate for an hour or so until the petals pull away from the center portion.

CARROT CURLS

Use a vegetable peeler to cut thin, wide strips the length of a large carrot. Soak in a bowl of ice water for at least an hour; blot dry before using.

GELATIN, UNSWEETENED

TIDBIT Unsweetened gelatin is an odorless, tasteless thickener derived from the bones, cartilage and connective tissue of animals. It comes in two basic forms—granulated and leaf (or sheet).

PURCHASING

* Granulated gelatin: This most common form is sold in boxes of ¼-ounce envelopes in supermarkets. Natural food stores often sell it in bulk.
* Leaf gelatin: This form, sold in packages of paper-thin sheets, is typically available only in bakery-supply stores and some specialty shops.

EQUIVALENTS ¼-ounce envelope granulated = 1 tablespoon; 3½ (4 × 9-inch) sheets leaf gelatin

STORING All gelatin will last indefinitely if wrapped airtight and kept in a cool, dry place.

USING

* Thickening power: ¼-ounce envelope granulated gelatin gels 2 cups of liquid. Foods made with too much gelatin have a hard, rubbery texture.
* Soak gelatin in cold liquid (as directed by the recipe) for 3 to 5 minutes before dissolving it. This soaking time softens and swells the gelatin granules so they'll dissolve smoothly when heated.
* To dissolve softened gelatin: Add it to a hot mixture; set a bowl of it inside another bowl or pan of very hot water; or heat it in a microwave oven on high for about 30 seconds. Stir the heated mixture until the gelatin is completely dissolved.

* Letting a gelatin mixture boil will destroy its setting ability.

* Raw figs, guava, fresh ginger, kiwi fruit, papaya and pineapple contain an enzyme that prevents gelatin from setting properly. Such ingredients can be used if cooked or canned because heat destroys the enzyme.

* Gelatin mixtures will be easier to unmold if you rinse out the mold with cold water or coat the mold with cooking spray before pouring in the mixture to be jelled.

* Speed a mixture's setting by softening and dissolving the gelatin in a minimum of hot liquid (¼ cup is enough for 1 package). Then use ice water or other cold liquid for the balance.

* Another speed-set method is to place the bowl holding the mixture in a larger bowl of ice water. Stir constantly until the mixture reaches the desired consistency.

* Or freeze the mixture (in its mold) for 20 to 30 minutes, then transfer to the refrigerator. Set a timer so you don't freeze it solid by mistake.

* Pieces of fruit or other food won't sink in a gelatin mixture if you wait until it's partially set (the consistency of egg whites) before stirring them in.

* A gelatin mixture that has set too fast can be resoftened by placing the container in a larger bowl of warm water and stirring until it softens.

* When making layered gelatin molds, wait until the bottom layer is sticky to the touch—it should be almost set. Then carefully spoon on the second liquid gelatin layer.

* **Removing from a mold:** First release the vacuum by inserting a knife between the mold and the food in several places around the edge. Then dip the mold in hot water (up to the edge) for 5 seconds (longer and the mixture could begin to melt). Position a plate over the top of the mold and, holding both plate and mold tightly, invert so the plate is on the bottom and give the mold a firm shake. The molded food should drop onto the plate. Sometimes it takes a minute or so for gravity to work to help release the mold. If the mold won't release, dip it into hot water again for a few seconds, or drape it with a towel that was soaked in hot water and wrung out. Once the food has been unmolded, remove the mold and, if possible, return the dish to the refrigerator to refirm for 20 minutes.

* It's easier to center a gelatin-based mold perfectly if you first rinse off the plate you turn it out on with cold water.

* "Recast" a leftover gelatin-based mold by putting it in a pan and heating over low heat just until melted. Add new ingredients, if desired, then pour into a smaller mold and chill until firm.

* Gelatin dishes continue to stiffen the longer they're refrigerated.

Eat ginger and you will love and be loved as in your youth.
—Italian saying

GINGER *see also* SPICES

TIDBIT Ginger is a remarkable spice in many ways. Not only does it lend its sweet heat and exotic flavor to myriad sweet and savory dishes, but its medicinal qualities have been prized for eons. Modern-day science now confirms that ginger does, indeed, have many healing qualities—it's an antioxidant and antiinflammatory, it relieves nausea, thins the blood and destroys bacteria. Now that's ginger power!

PURCHASING

* Mature ginger: This knobby root is available year-round in most supermarket produce departments. It has a tough, tan-colored skin that must be removed. Choose firm specimens with a smooth skin and a fresh, spicy fragrance. Wrinkled or cracked ginger is dry and past its prime.

* Young ginger (also called *spring ginger*): This type has pale, tender skin that doesn't require peeling and a milder flavor than its mature form. It's available in the springtime in most Asian markets and some produce markets.

* Crystallized or candied ginger: This is ginger that's been cooked in a sugar syrup and coated with coarse sugar. Choose plump, tender-looking slices. It's readily found in most supermarkets.

* Dried ground ginger: A form commonly available in the supermarket spice section. *See* SPICES *for general storage and purchase information.*

* Ginger juice: This pasteurized juice is available in gourmet markets and some supermarkets. It can be substituted for chopped fresh ginger in equal amounts.

* Other forms of ginger (typically available in Asian markets and in many supermarkets): **Pickled ginger** (also called *sushi ginger*)—thin slices preserved in sweetened rice vinegar, which may either be dyed pink or left in its natural ivory-colored form. Pickled ginger is most often used in Japanese cooking, usually as a condiment. **Preserved stem ginger** (small knobs of ginger in heavy sugar syrup) and **red, sweet ginger** (preserved in a bright red syrup) are two sweetened forms. Both are typically used in desserts and salad dressings.

EQUIVALENT 2-inch piece mature ginger = 2 tablespoons minced

STORING

* Fresh ginger: Store unpeeled ginger at room temperature in a cool, dark place. It can be tightly sealed in a plastic bag and refrigerated for up to 3

weeks—more than that and it could get moldy. Or double wrap and freeze it for up to 6 months. Slice off what you need and return the rest of the root to the freezer.

* Young ginger: Wrap and refrigerate for up to 2 weeks.
* Crystallized ginger: Wrap airtight and store at room temperature for up to 3 months. Refrigerate for up to 6 months; freeze for up to a year.
* Pickled and preserved ginger: Refrigerate for up to 6 months.
* Ginger juice: Refrigerate for up to 3 months.

PREPARING

* When peeling ginger, be careful to remove only the thin skin—the delicate flesh just under the surface is very flavorful. An easy way to do this is by running a spoon along the ginger, scraping away the thin skin. Or use a vegetable peeler or sharp knife.
* Ginger's easier to grate if you freeze it first.
* For almost-instant minced fresh ginger, put a small, peeled chunk into a garlic press and squeeze. Freezing ginger makes it easier to crush.
* For ginger juice, freeze ½-inch chunks of unpeeled ginger in a plastic bag. When you need the juice, pop a chunk or two in a garlic press and squeeze. Freezing breaks down the ginger's fibers, making it easier to juice.
* For ginger when you need it: Cut peeled ginger into ½-inch pieces, place in a screw-top jar and cover with dry sherry or Madeira. Refrigerate for up to 3 months. The wine imparts some of its flavor to the ginger, but that's a minor quibble. The bonus is that you have ginger-flavored liquid to use in stir-fry dishes, salad dressings, sauces, and so on.
* Chop an entire jar of crystallized ginger slices at a time so you'll have minced ginger on hand when you need it. Place the slices in a food processor; use quick on/off pulses until the ginger is chopped as desired. If the ginger begins to stick together, add 1 or 2 tablespoons granulated sugar and continue to process. Store chopped ginger in an airtight jar at room temperature for up to 1 year.

USING

* Add fresh ginger to stir-fries, soups, stocks, salads, vegetables, marinades, sauces and desserts.
* Dried, ground ginger has a very different flavor than its fresh counterpart and should not be substituted for fresh ginger. It is, however, delicious in many savory dishes, such as soups, curries, meats, fruit preparations and baked goods (particularly gingersnaps and gingerbread).
* Crystallized ginger is wonderful in sweet baked goods or sprinkled over ice cream, but can also be used in savory preparations, since the amount of sweetness it adds is negligible.

* Fresh ginger contains an enzyme that prevents gelatin from setting properly. Blanch the ginger to destroy the enzyme and you're set to gel. Or use crystallized ginger, which has already been cooked.
* When flavoring milk-based dishes (such as custards or ice creams) with ginger, either BLANCH fresh ginger or use the crystallized form. Fresh ginger contains an enzyme that can curdle milk.

CHOCOLATE-DIPPED GINGER

Dip crystallized ginger slices or sticks in melted chocolate; set on a waxed paper–lined baking sheet and refrigerate until the chocolate sets. Serve with tea, or as an ice cream accompaniment, or simply for a snack.

GLASSWARE

There are dozens of different styles of glasses on the market today, many with very specific uses. Here is a basic primer:

* Beer mug: 10 to 16 ounces, made of glass, plastic or ceramic, and typically with a handle. *See also* pilsner glass (below).
* Brandy snifters: Short-stemmed with a relatively large bowl, snifters range in size from 5 to 25 ounces. They're used for brandy; the mini-snifters are sometimes used for liqueur.
* Champagne glasses: Flute or tulip champagne glasses range from 4 to 10 ounces. Their tall, graceful shape is a good showcase for a wine's bouquet, and the smaller surface area allows fewer bubbles to escape. The old-fashioned champagne saucer glass is no longer used by those in the know.
* Cocktail glass: This classic long-stemmed, flared glass (also called a *martini glass*) can range from 3 to 10 ounces, and is used for cocktails without ice.
* Collins glass: Slightly slimmer than the highball glass and named for the drink, Collins glasses range from 10 to 14 ounces. There's a tall Collins glass (also called a *chimney glass*) that holds about 16 ounces.
* Cordial glass: This is a tiny (1- to 2-ounce) stemmed glass used for brandies, liqueurs and pousse-cafés. The 1-ounce version is also called a *pony*.
* Highball glass: This straight-sided, 8- to 12-ounce glass is the most common bar glass, used for everything from Bloody Marys to, of course, highballs.
* Hurricane glass: Shaped like a hurricane lamp, and ranging from 12 to 16 ounces, this glass is used for Hurricanes and other tropical drinks.
* Irish coffee mug: Ranging from 8 to 10 ounces and typically made of tempered glass, this mug is used for Irish coffee and other hot drinks.
* Old-fashioned glass: Eponymously named for the drink, this short, squat

G

glass holds from 4 to 8 ounces. It's also called *rocks glass* and *whiskey glass*. A double old-fashioned glass is twice as large (12 to 16 ounces).

* Parfait glass: Also called a *frappé glass*, the parfait holds about 8 ounces.
* Pilsner glass: This tall, narrow, 10- to 16-ounce glass is slightly flared at the top. It's primarily used for beer.
* Sherry glass: This is a small, stemmed 3- to 4-ounce glass used for sherry, liqueurs and apéritifs.
* Wineglasses: The white wineglass ranges from 6 to 8 ounces, and has relatively straight sides. The slightly larger red wineglass (8 to 10 ounces) has a rounder, more balloonlike shape.

So far I've always kept my diet secret but now I might as well tell everyone what it is. Lots of grapefruit throughout the day and plenty of virile young men.
—Angie Dickinson, American actor

GRAPEFRUIT *For juicing, zesting and general information, see* CIRTUS FRUITS

PURCHASING Choose fruit with thin, fine-textured, brightly colored skin. It should be firm yet springy to palm pressure. The heavier the grapefruit is for its size, the juicier it will be. In general, the thinner the skin, the more juicy the fruit.

EQUIVALENTS 1 pound = 1 medium, 1½ cups segments, ¾ to 1 cup juice

STORING May be stored at room temperature for a couple of days. After that, refrigerate, wrapped in a plastic bag, for up to 2 weeks.

PREPARING

* A grapefruit knife and grapefruit spoons are inexpensive indispensable tools for working with this fruit. The knife's curved, flexible blade, serrated on both sides, is used to free the flesh from the rind and membrane. The serrated-tipped spoon allows you to cut away and scoop out the flesh as you eat it.
* For juicier grapefruit, roll it between your palm and the countertop for a few seconds just before juicing or eating.
* Or increase the juice by pricking the skin in several places with fork tines, then microwave uncovered on high for about 20 seconds. Let stand 2 minutes before cutting.
* To help grapefruit halves sit on a plate without rocking, cut a thin slice (making a flat place) off the bottoms.
* Use a stainless-steel serrated knife to slice grapefruit.

* When peeling grapefruit to use the sections in a salad, all the white pith should be removed, and that can be difficult. Make the job easier by plunking the whole fruit in a pot of boiling water; remove from the heat and let stand for 4 minutes. Remove the grapefruit from the water and cool until easy to handle. Now the pith should peel away with the skin. Pull off any remnants with a grapefruit knife.
* Another way to get pith-free segments is to cut off a small disk of peel at both ends, then stand the fruit on one flat end. Starting at the top and cutting down along the curve of the fruit, remove the peel and pith (you'll also get a little of the flesh, but that's okay). Then hold the whole skinless fruit over a bowl and use a paring knife to separate each segment from the membrane on both sides, letting the segment and any juice drop into the bowl.

USING
* Temper overly acidic grapefruit by lightly salting it.
* Use grapefruit juice instead of lemon juice or vinegar for salad dressings.
* Hollowed-out grapefruit halves make great individual serving bowls for fruit compotes or salads. Thick-skinned grapefruit make sturdier bowls than those with thin skins. After the flesh and membranes are removed, put the grapefruit shells in a large bowl of ice water in the fridge to make them as firm as possible. Drain and blot dry just before filling.
* Substitute chopped fresh grapefruit for the tomato in your favorite salsa recipe and serve with grilled fish, chicken or pork.

GRAPEFRUIT GRANITA
Serve this refresher as a light dessert on hot summer days. Grenadine is a deep red, pomegranate-flavored syrup available in liquor stores and most supermarkets. Combine 3 cups grapefruit juice, ¼ cup sugar, 2 tablespoons grenadine, ½ teaspoon rosemary leaves, 6 whole allspice berries and ¼ teaspoon salt in a medium saucepan. Bring to a boil and cook for 3 minutes, stirring once or twice. Remove from the heat, cover and let stand 10 minutes. Strain the liquid into ice cube trays; freeze until solid. Just before serving, process the juice cubes in a food processor (a single layer at a time), using quick on/off pulses, just until evenly chopped. Serve in stemmed glasses, garnished with a wedge of grapefruit or edible flower. Serves 4.

> *The word snob belongs to the sour-grape vocabulary.*
> —Logan Pearsall Smith, American essayist

GRAPES *see also* FRUIT, GENERAL
PURCHASING Choose grapes that are plump, full-colored and firmly

attached to their stems. Green (white) grapes, like Thompson seedless, are ripe when they have a slight pale yellow hue. Dark grapes should be deeply colored with no greening.

EQUIVALENT   1 pound seedless = 2½ to 3 cups

STORING   Grapes can be stored at room temperature for several days. Refrigerate, wrapped in a plastic bag, for up to 10 days.

PREPARING

* Thoroughly wash grapes just before using and blot dry with paper towels.
* The ideal serving temperature is about 60°F, where the flavor of grapes is full and sweet. To obtain this, remove the grapes from the refrigerator about 30 minutes before serving.
* Frozen grapes make a refreshing summer snack. Place small bunches of washed and dried grapes on a tray; freeze until solid. Transfer frozen grapes to a freezer-proof plastic bag; seal and freeze for up to 3 months. Pluck a cluster or two out whenever you need a sweet treat. Halve or quarter frozen grapes before feeding them to small children to prevent the possibility of their choking.
* Another way to frost grapes is to use a pastry brush to paint grape clusters with honey, maple syrup or corn syrup. Dip the coated grapes into sugar, then dry on a rack. If necessary, coat the grapes with sugar a second time.

FROSTED GRAPES

An easy, beautiful garnish for everything from fruit salads to desserts. Using coarse decorating sugar makes the grapes really sparkle. Beat 1 egg white in a small bowl until frothy. Dip small grape clusters (3 to 5 grapes) first into the egg white, then into a bowl of granulated sugar, coating either the entire grape or just the bottom half. Set the sugar-dipped grapes on a tray lined with waxed paper to air-dry completely before using.

GRATERS   *see also* NUTMEG; NUTMEG GRATERS

TIDBIT   Graters come in all shapes and sizes including flat, box and cylindrical. They're typically made of metal (stainless is the best) or strong plastic, and have cutting edges that range from tiny to large to flat.

* Spray a grater with cooking spray (or rub with a little vegetable oil) before grating foods like cheese and citrus rind and cleanup will be a snap.
* If you have several foods to grate, always start with those that won't leave much residue on the grater (like carrots); save messy foods like cheese for last.
* When grating oranges, lemons, and so on, run the fruit diagonally across

a grater, rather than up and down. Cover the grater with plastic wrap and the zest will cling to the wrap when removed.

* A toothbrush is the perfect tool for cleaning a grater.

GRAVY *see* SAUCES

GREASING PANS
* Use shortening, cooking spray or unsalted butter or margarine. Salted butter can cause baked goods to stick to pans, particularly at temperatures over 400°F.
* Too much grease on a pan can cause overbrowning.
* If you don't like getting your fingers greasy, or getting shortening under your nails, use a crumpled piece of paper towel to dip into the greasing agent and spread over the pan. Or cover your hand with a small plastic bag. Leave the bag in the shortening can for the next use.
* The term "grease and flour" refers to sprinkling a greased pan with a small amount of flour, then tapping and rotating the pan or dish until the entire surface is coated with flour. Invert the container over the sink or wastebasket and shake it gently to remove excess flour.
* Instead of "greasing and flouring" pans, use the easy, homemade Pan Magic, page 426.
* If you have trouble getting baked goods out of the pan, do this: Grease the pan, then line the bottom with PARCHMENT PAPER—don't grease the paper. Or line the bottom with waxed paper; then grease the waxed paper's surface. After the bread or cake is baked, and the baked good turned out of the pan, the parchment or waxed paper will peel right off.

GREEN BEANS *see* BEANS, FRESH GREEN

GREEN ONIONS *see* SCALLIONS

GREEN PEPPERS *see* BELL PEPPERS

GREENS *see also* SALAD GREENS; SPINACH
TIDBIT Greens have long been a Southern favorite, often flavored by bacon fat and classically accompanied by cornbread, and pot likker (the vitamin-rich liquid in which the greens were cooked). The most popular greens today include beet, chard, collard, dandelion, kale, mustard and turnip. Greens are strongly flavored and best paired with meats like ham, pork and pot roast.

PURCHASING

* For greens like chard, collards and kale, look for crisp, brightly colored leaves with no sign of browning or insect damage. Beet, mustard and turnip greens should be crisp-tender, dandelion greens should be tender.
* How much per serving: ⅓ to ½ pound of fresh greens.

EQUIVALENT   1 pound = about 3 cups cooked

STORING   Refrigerate, wrapped in a plastic bag, for up to 5 days.

PREPARING

* Discard any yellow or wilted leaves. Remove any root ends, stems and heavy ribs.
* Greens require thorough washing to remove all the grit. The easiest way to do this is to put the leaves in a sink (or large pot) of cold water, swish them around and wait a few minutes to let the grit settle. Retrieve the greens, drain the water and repeat the process.
* Tear the washed greens into bite-sized pieces.

COOKING

* Greens should be cooked until tender, the timing varying with the type of green. Rule of thumb: chard—5 to 10 minutes; mustard and turnip greens—10 to 15 minutes; kale and collard greens—15 to 20 minutes.
* Greens are typically cooked by boiling. Bring a large pot of salted water containing a ham hock or 6-ounce piece of salt pork to a boil; cook for 30 minutes. Add the greens and simmer until they're tender, or 5 to 20 minutes, depending on the greens.
* Since most greens are bitter, you might want to try this trick: Start cooking the ham hock in the water in one pot. Bring another pot of water to a boil, then add the greens and cook for 3 minutes. Pour off that bitter water, then transfer the greens to the pot with the ham hock and continue cooking.
* Greens may also be covered and braised in a smaller amount of water. More tender leaves, like beet and dandelion greens, can be steamed.
* Or cook greens partway by boiling or BRAISING, then drain, squeeze dry in a kitchen towel, and sauté with oil and garlic.
* Flavorful additions to cooking greens include chopped onion, garlic, a few tablespoons of bacon drippings or crushed red pepper.
* Never cook turnip greens in an aluminum pan. Aluminum darkens the greens and gives them a metallic flavor.
* Make a double batch of greens and freeze half for up to 3 months.
* Greens like chard can be cooked just until crisp-tender, chilled and tossed with salad dressing.

* Sprinkle cooked greens with crumbled bacon or chopped hard-cooked eggs. Serve with hot sauce, cider vinegar, pot likker and cornbread.
* For a change of pace, PURÉE cooked greens with a little butter, cream, and salt and pepper.

Grilling is like sunbathing. Everyone knows it's bad for you but no one ever stops doing it.
—Laurie Colwin, American writer

GRILLING   *see also* BARBECUE SAUCE; MARINADES; MARINATING

TIDBIT   The word "barbecue" is often used synonymously with "grill." Both terms refer to outdoor cookery, a method that can tantalize even the most jaded taste buds. Common sense should tell you never to use a charcoal grill indoors, or near dry areas that might easily ignite. And don't wear clothes with long, flowing sleeves, shirttails, fringe, and so on, that might catch fire.

THE FOOD

* If desired, marinate the food (*see* MARINADES; MARINATING) before cooking. A dry rub of herbs, spices, salt and pepper can be used at the last minute.
* Soak wooden skewers in water for 30 minutes to keep them from burning.
* Remove meat, poultry and fish from the refrigerator 20 minutes before grilling.
* Don't remove the skin from chicken until after it's grilled—the skin holds in the meat's natural moisture. Chicken grilled sans skin quickly becomes dry.
* To prevent flare-ups, trim excess fat from meat or use lean ground meat.
* Short on time? Give meats and dense vegetables (like potatoes and carrots) a jump start by cooking them partway in the microwave oven and finishing on the grill. Partially cooking vegetables like peppers or fennel means that they'll get done on the grill without charring. One caveat: *Immediately* transfer partially cooked food to the grill—letting it stand before it's fully cooked could promote bacterial growth.

BASIC GRILLING NECESSITIES

* **Wood smoke** is what gives grilled foods their characteristic flavor, but wood chips or chunks must be soaked first in water, so plan ahead. Chips require 30 to 60 minutes, chunks about 2 hours. Drain the wood thoroughly before sprinkling over hot coals. Various kinds of wood chips and

chunks are available wherever grilling equipment is sold. Mesquite lends a delicate, sweeter nuance than the more intense (but still sweet) hickory. Other grill-compatible aromatic woods include alder, apple, ash, cherry, maple, oak, pecan and walnut. Never use woods like pine or spruce, which exude noxious pitch fumes that will ruin the flavor of food.

* **What fuel should you use?** The two most popular fuels for grilling are charcoal briquettes and hardwood lump charcoal. **Charcoal briquettes** are made primarily from sawdust, wood scraps and binders. Many manufacturers add chemicals to enhance burning—such additives can definitely affect a grilled food's flavor. There are also **presoaked charcoal briquettes**, which are soaked with lighter fluid, then dried. They exude nasty-smelling fumes throughout the cooking process and are not recommended. **Hardwood charcoal** consists of natural additive-free wood chunks (mesquite, hickory and oak) that have been carbonized through burning in an oxygen-free oven. Such fuel throws off sparks when first lit, but burns cleanly, evenly and slightly hotter than briquettes.

* Storing charcoal airtight will keep it moisture-free, which means it'll ignite faster. If you don't use it often, seal the charcoal in its bag inside a large plastic trash bag.

* **Fire igniting aids** (always use a long-handled match or propane lighter). **Chimney fire starter:** a tall metal cylinder (usually with a wooden handle); the top section is loaded with charcoal, the bottom portion with crumpled newspaper. When the newspaper is lit, it creates an intense fire that's funneled into the "chimney" and heats the charcoal. The concentrated heat in such devices brings the charcoal to cooking temperature in about 15 minutes. Once the coals are ready, they're poured into the grilling unit. **Electric starters** require an extension cord and nearby electrical outlet, but are fast and efficient. Simply insert the starter's coil into the bed of charcoal, resting the handle against the grill's side. As soon as the fire is started (10 to 15 minutes), unplug and remove the starter, placing it in a safe place (away from children and pets) to cool completely. Leaving an electric starter in the fire too long can shorten its life. **Kindling** can also be used to start a fire, but the process is tedious. Start with sheets of newspaper twisted into tight tubes. Position five to seven twists as a base, topped with kindling sticks, then with a mound of coals. Light the newspaper and, as the fire builds, add more charcoal. **Lighter fluid:** a liquid, petroleum-based mixture that's squirted over a pyramid of charcoal. Allow the liquid to soak the coals for a minute before lighting. Such fuel may impart a faint chemical flavor to foods. Never add lighter fluid

to a fire that's already lit. **Paraffin-saturated starter blocks or cubes** can be placed in a mound of charcoal and lit.

READY, SET, COOK!

✳ Before starting, decide how you want to grill the food—directly or indirectly. *Direct grilling* is generally used for food that takes less than 30 minutes to cook. The food is positioned directly over the coals to cook quickly. *Indirect grilling* is for long-cooking foods. The coals are banked on either side of a drip pan, which is positioned directly under the food. This method cooks food much more slowly. Rectangular foil pans are readily available in supermarkets (line those for use in gas or electric grills with a double layer of foil so the hot fire won't burn through). Make your own drip pan by tearing off a piece of heavy-duty (18-inch wide) foil twice the length of your grill; fold it in half crosswise. Bend all the edges up 1½ inches, reinforcing the corners by folding them to the inside.

✳ Have on hand heavy-duty oven mitts and long-handled grilling implements (fork, spatulas, tongs and so on).

✳ Make sure all barbecue vents are open. Mound the briquettes or charcoal (count on about 30 briquettes to direct-grill 1 pound of meat) in a pyramid-shaped pile, add ignition fuel (*see* Fire igniting aids, page 236) and light the fire. If using the indirect-grilling method, place about 25 briquettes on each side of the drip pan—that'll cook food for about an hour with the cover on.

✳ About 10 minutes before you expect to start cooking, season the grill by using a long-handled brush to coat it with vegetable oil. Do this each time you cook and, before long, your grill will be almost nonstick.

✳ Coals are ready when they have a dull red glow and the surface is covered with a uniform layer of fine gray ash.

✳ Spread the coals out into an even layer. A thick layer of coals (or hardwood) retains heat longer than a single layer, as will keeping the cover on with the vents slightly open.

✳ **Hand test for grilling temperatures** (for charcoal and gas grills): Remove the grid and place your hand, palm down, at grid level. The number of seconds (count "one martini, two martini," etc.) you can comfortably hold your hand there will be a guide to how hot the fire is: hot (for searing)—1 to 2 seconds; medium-hot (for grilling)—3 seconds; medium (for grilling)—4 seconds; medium-low (for covered cooking)—5 seconds; low (for covered cooking)—6 seconds. Each heat stage lasts about 10 minutes with charcoal grills.

* If using the indirect-grilling method, add ½ to 1 cup liquid (wine, stock, beer) to the drip pan to help keep the food moist.

* If the coals are too hot when you're ready to begin cooking, use tongs to spread them apart, or remove a few and place them in a large can. Or if you have an adjustable grill, raise the rack so it's farther away from the heat.

* Flavor enhancements: Just before beginning to cook, sprinkle soaked wood chips (*see* "Wood smoke," page 235) or dried herbs (oregano, tarragon or rosemary) over the hot coals.

* Leave ¾ inch between pieces of food on the grill for even cooking.

* Skewered food cooks more evenly if the pieces of food are positioned about ¼ inch apart.

* Most meats should be cooked over a medium fire—high heat dries them out.

* To sear meat before smoking it, quickly brown it on both sides over an open flame. Remove the meat, add damp wood chips to the fire, then replace the grill and meat, and cover the grill.

* Fish dries quickly, so grill it at a lower temperature than you would meat or poultry.

* Forestall flare-ups by moving the coals farther apart, or by covering the grill, closing the air vents partway, or by *lightly* misting the coals with water (spritzing too vigorously could cause ashes to float onto the food).

* Basting sauce should be warm or at least at room temperature—a cold sauce will slow the cooking.

* Baste long-cooking meats during the last 30 minutes of grilling, brushing every 10 minutes for a multilayered glaze. Sauces high in sugar shouldn't be brushed on until the last 15 to 20 minutes, as sugar has a tendency to burn.

* Don't baste meat during the last 15 minutes of cooking time with a rawmeat marinade that hasn't been boiled. The cooking time may be too short to kill any bacteria that was transferred from the raw meat to the marinade.

* Remove food from the grill a minute or two before it's done—the residual heat will continue to cook it.

* As soon as you're through cooking, cover the grill and close all the vents. After dinner, while the grill's still hot, use a long-handled wire grill brush to remove all the cooked-on food particles.

* Or cover the steel grid with heavy-duty foil (shiny side down) as soon as you remove the food. Close all the vents and cover the grill. (For a gas grill, leave the heat on for 20 minutes.) When the grill is cool, scrub with

a wire brush or crumpled foil, then wipe with damp paper towels. Grills with porcelain or chrome grids should be cleaned according to the manufacturer's instructions.

GROUND MEATS *see also* BEEF; HAMBURGERS; MEAT, GENERAL; MEATBALLS; MEAT LOAF

PURCHASING Buy fresh, not frozen, ground meat—freezing and thawing causes it to lose some natural juices. Avoid any meat that smells bad, is dry and brown-looking around the edges, or that has discolored patches of brown or gray. Remember that fat supplies both flavor and moisture. The lower the fat content, the drier the cooked meat will be. Even if you're watching fat and cholesterol, high-fat ground meat might still be an option when making dishes that require that the meat be browned and the fat drained off.

STORING Refrigerate in the coldest part of the refrigerator for up to 2 days. To freeze, form ground beef into a 1-inch thick layer, then double wrap and freeze for up to 3 months. It will freeze more quickly and defrost in a fraction of the time.

USING

* Remember, the higher the percentage of fat in ground meat, the more shrinkage there is after it's cooked. Take that into consideration when making hamburger patties, meatballs or other formed, ground-meat dishes.

* To make lean ground meat juicier, add 1 tablespoon prune purée (*see* DRIED PLUMS) to each pound of meat. The amount is so small that no one will know unless you tell them.

* Thaw frozen ground meat in the refrigerator or in the microwave oven according to manufacturer's instructions just prior to cooking.

* Freezing and thawing ground meat can cause it to brown before it's cooked enough for harmful bacteria to be destroyed. Use a meat THERMOMETER to check for doneness.

* To ensure food safety and guard against bacterial infection, cook ground meats as follows: beef, veal, lamb and pork—160°F; chicken and turkey—165°F; sausage—160°F.

A definition of eternity: A ham and two people.
—Irma S. Rombauer, American cookbook author

HAM   *see also* BACON; MEAT, GENERAL; PORK; PROSCIUTTO

PURCHASING

* **Ham label terms: Cured ham** has been preserved by salt processing, either through brining or through dry-salt curing. Dry-cured hams may be aged for up to a year. Cured hams may or may not be smoked or cooked—check the label. **Sugar-cured hams** have been cured in a sugar or molasses brine. **Country-cured hams** have been dry-cured, slowly smoked and aged at least 6 months, all of which makes them firmer, saltier and darker in color than regularly cured hams. **Smoked ham** has been infused with either natural or liquid smoke; it's sold cooked and uncooked. **Fully cooked ham** is ready to eat and can be served cold or hot. **"Cook-before-eating" hams** must, as the name makes obvious, be cooked before being consumed. **Canned hams** are fully cooked, skinless, boneless sections that have been vacuum-packed. The smaller the canned ham, the more likely it's formed from bits and pieces of ham combined with gelatin and then pressed together. The words "natural juices added" or "added water" on a ham label are a signal that you're paying for these weight increasers, and getting less meat.
* Choose firm, plump hams that are rosy pink and finely grained; country hams range in color from pale pink to deep red. A slight iridescence on the ham's surface is simply a reaction some curing agents have to air and light. Larger hams are more succulent than smaller ones, the butt end meatier than the shank end. Make life easy for yourself and have the butcher remove any rind.

* How much per serving: **boneless or canned ham**—about ⅓ pound; **meaty (butt end) bone-in hams**—about ½ pound; **bony (shank end) hams**—about ⅔ pound.

EQUIVALENT   ½ pound boneless = about 1½ cups chopped

STORING

* Refrigerate a whole cured ham in its original wrapping for up to 1 week; ham slices, wrapped airtight, for 3 days. Some country hams can be stored, unrefrigerated, in a cool place for 1 to 2 months (follow label instructions).
* Store canned hams according to label directions. Some require refrigeration; others have been sterilized and don't need to be refrigerated until after they've been opened.
* Freeze leftover ham for up to 6 months, slicing off what you need to flavor soups, omelets, and so on, returning the rest to the freezer.

USING

* Removing a ham from its can is easier if you immerse the can in hot water for 1 to 2 minutes before opening.
* Many country-cured hams require special preparation before being baked, including scrubbing, soaking, simmering and skinning, the instructions for which typically accompany the ham.
* Fully cooked hams may be eaten immediately; however, their flavor is improved greatly by heating at 350°F for 8 to 10 minutes per pound to an internal temperature of 140°F.
* Hams labeled "cook before eating" must be heated to an internal temperature of 160°F.
* Before cooking or heating ham, remove any paper casing.
* Before glazing a ham, remove all but ¼ to ½ inch of fat.
* Give ham a delicious caramelized coating by sprinkling the fatty layer with sieved brown sugar before baking.
* The rind can be pulled right off a cooked ham if, before baking, it's cut lengthwise down the center. Cook it slit side down; remove the rind right after cooking.
* To prevent ham slices from curling during frying, slash the fat along the edges at 1-inch intervals. Cook slices slowly and they'll stay juicy and tender.
* Ham is easier to slice thinly if it's chilled.
* Finely chop ham to be used in stir-fries, soups, beans, and so on, and the flavor will be more evenly distributed than with a few large chunks.
* Freeze the ham bone to use later to flavor soups, stews, beans or broth.

H

A hamburger is warm and fragrant and juicy . . . soft and non-threatening . . . companionable and faintly erotic.
—Tom Robbins, American novelist

HAMBURGERS *see also* GROUND MEATS; MEAT, GENERAL

TIDBIT The name "hamburger" hails from the port city of Hamburg, Germany, where nineteenth-century Germans enjoyed pounded beefsteak in various forms. There are myriad legends of the Americanization of the hamburger—today's sandwich version. The earliest dates back to 1885, when a young Wisconsin county fair concessionaire created his butter-fried ground beef in a portable form so people could eat it while walking around the fair. In 1892, an Ohio county fair concessionaire is said to have invented the burger sandwich. And so it goes. All that matters, really, is that the hamburger is eminently down-to-earth great eating!

PURCHASING AND STORING *see* GROUND MEATS

PREPARING

* Ground sirloin makes the leanest burgers, then ground round, ground chuck and, last, regular ground beef (also simply called "hamburger"). The leaner the ground beef, the drier the cooked burger will be.
* Coarsely ground meat produces moister burgers than finely ground meat.
* Remember that the higher the percentage of fat in the meat, the more shrinkage there'll be during cooking. So if you're making burgers out of regular ground beef, form the patties so they're about ½ inch larger in diameter than the hamburger bun.
* Keep your hands clean by putting the burger ingredients in a large, zip-closure plastic bag. Seal, then squish the contents together just until well mixed. Don't overmix or the cooked patties will be heavy and dense.
* Adding 1 or 2 tablespoons vegetable oil per pound of ground sirloin replenishes the moisture (and the fat is unsaturated).
* For juicier, more flavorful burgers, add 2 to 3 tablespoons tomato or vegetable juice, beef broth or other liquid to each pound of ground meat.
* Give burgers a smoky flavor by adding ⅓ cup diced, crisply cooked smoked bacon or ham to the mixture. Reduce the salt to allow for the extra salt from the bacon or ham.
* Add nutrition and cut down meat consumption by substituting 1 cup lightly sautéed, finely grated potato or carrot (or a half cup of each) for a quarter pound of the meat.
* Or add minced leftover vegetables to a burger mixture.

- For light and juicy burgers, fold 1 stiffly beaten egg white (per pound of meat) into the seasoned meat just before forming the patties.

H

- A large ice cream scoop is perfect for portioning uniformly sized patties.
- Or, for perfectly uniform hamburgers, place the meat mixture in the center of a long sheet of plastic wrap. Use your hands to form the meat into a log the diameter you want your hamburgers (don't forget to allow for shrinkage). Wrap the log in plastic wrap, smoothing out its shape in the process. Freeze for 1 hour, or until the meat feels firm but not solid. Then cut the log into uniform slices.
- Dampen your hands with water before forming patties and the meat won't stick to your fingers.
- Use a light touch when shaping burgers so the mixture doesn't become too compacted and therefore produce a dense burger.
- Believe it or not, a little prune purée (see DRIED PLUMS) makes hamburgers juicier and prevents that "old" taste that cooked beef gets in the refrigerator. Add just 1 tablespoon per pound of meat.
- Put about 1 tablespoon grated cheese or a chunk of blue cheese or ½ tablespoon cold herb butter in the center of a hamburger patty, making sure the filling is completely sealed in with the meat. By the time the burger is done, the filling will be melted and come oozing out when the patty's cut into.
- Separate hamburger patties (raw or cooked) for freezing with squares of plastic wrap so you can easily pry them apart later.

COOKING

- To ensure food safety and guard against bacterial infection, cook burgers made from beef, lamb or pork to 160°F, ground turkey or chicken to 165°F. Use a meat THERMOMETER for testing doneness.
- For well-done burgers with lots of crusty (seared) surface, make the patties thin and large, and cook them quickly over high heat. For succulent patties, shape the meat into thick rounds and cook more slowly.
- For a nice, crispy surface for pan-fried burgers, lightly dust the patties with flour or cornstarch just before cooking.
- For "chicken-fried" hamburgers, dip the patties in beaten egg, then in finely ground bread or cracker crumbs.
- Preheat the pan or broiler so the meat's surface gets nicely seared.
- Unless your patties have a coating like flour or bread crumbs, it's usually not necessary to cook them in oil or melted fat. There's enough fat in the meat to lubricate the pan, particularly if it has a nonstick surface.

H

* Never use a metal spatula to press down on a hamburger patty while it's cooking—you'll squeeze out much of the flavorful juices.
* When cooking hamburgers for a crowd, place the patties side by side on several baking pans (with shallow sides so the grease won't drip off onto the bottom of the oven), bake at 350°F until partway done, then immediately finish cooking outdoors on the grill.
* Ketchup and mustard aren't the only garnishes for hamburgers. Next time try topping them with something different like sautéed onions and bell peppers, guacamole, chutney, barbecue sauce, salsa, crisp bacon strips or chili.

HARD-COOKED EGGS *see* EGGS, COOKING METHODS

HAZELNUTS *For general purchase, storage, toasting and usage information, see* NUTS, GENERAL
TIDBIT Depending on the region, hazelnuts are also called *filberts* and *cobnuts*.
EQUIVALENTS
* In shell: 1 pound = 1½ cups
* Shelled: 1 pound = 3½ cups whole
PREPARING
* Hazelnuts have a bitter brown skin that should be removed. To do so, soak them in cold water for 1 minute. Drain (but don't dry), then bake at 400°F for 5 to 7 minutes, until the skins begin to flake. Place a handful of the warm nuts on a kitchen towel, then fold the towel over the nuts and rub vigorously to remove most of the skins. Repeat with the remaining nuts.
* Or bring a pot of water and 1 teaspoon baking soda to a boil, stir in the nuts and cook for 45 to 60 seconds. Drain thoroughly, then turn out onto a kitchen towel. Rub vigorously with a towel to remove the skins.
* Save yourself the trouble of peeling hazelnuts and look for the packaged, chopped hazelnuts that are available in some supermarkets and specialty food stores.

HERBS *see also* BASIL; BAY LEAVES; BOUQUET GARNI; PARSLEY; SPICES
TIDBIT Healers throughout the ages have used herbs and spices for medicinal purposes. Modern science is finally confirming that basil, black pepper, cardamom, cilantro, cumin, ginger, nutmeg, oregano, rosemary, saffron, sage, tarragon, thyme and turmeric are known to have antioxidant activity that can protect cell damage from many diseases, including cancer. So now you can spice up your life and possibly live longer while you're at it!

FRESH HERBS (*see also following section on Dried Herbs*, page 246)

PURCHASING Choose fresh herbs with a clean, fresh fragrance and bright color; avoid wilting or browning herbs.

STORING Refrigerate, wrapped loosely in barely damp paper towel and sealed in a plastic bag, for up to 5 days. For bouquets of herbs (like basil, cilantro and parsley), cut off ½ inch of the stems and refrigerate the bouquet, stem ends down, in a tall glass filled halfway with cold water and a pinch of sugar. Loosely cover with a plastic bag secured to the glass with a rubber band. Change the water every 2 days.

PREPARATION: Most herbs should be washed just before using, then thoroughly blotted dry on paper towels.

USING

✻ Fresh herbs add pizzazz that dried herbs just can't match.

✻ Kitchen shears are great for snipping small amounts of fresh herbs.

✻ For food-processor and hand chopping, make sure the fresh herbs are thoroughly dry before processing.

✻ Don't automatically throw out the stems of herbs—mince and use them to flavor sauces, soups and stews.

✻ When adding chopped herbs to a cold dish (such as potato salad), cover and refrigerate for at least 2 hours so the flavors have time to mingle.

✻ The flavor of a strong herb (like oregano) can vary widely depending on the variety and season. Use restraint when adding any herb to a dish. You can always add more, but it's hard to salvage an overseasoned dish.

✻ Many fresh herbs lose flavor when heated, so add them to a long-cooking sauce or soup during the final 20 to 30 minutes of cooking time. Or add the herbs when the dish begins cooking, then stir in 2 tablespoons fresh chopped herbs just before serving to give the dish a fresh flavor.

✻ Or PURÉE fresh, cleaned herbs in a food processor and drop spoonfuls onto a plastic wrap–lined baking sheet; freeze until solid. Transfer the solid purée mounds to a plastic bag, seal airtight and return to the freezer. Use to flavor soups, stews, sauces, salad dressings and other mixtures. Defrost them before adding to cold mixtures like salad dressings; no defrosting is necessary when adding to hot mixtures.

✻ Make a BOUQUET GARNI to flavor soups or other mixtures.

✻ Make your own herb vinegar (*see* page 485). It's easy and much less expensive than store-bought vinegar.

✻ Herb butter is wonderful on meats, vegetables, fish, bread—you name it. *See* Compound Butter, page 72.

✻ Freeze fresh (washed and dried) herbs by stripping the leaves from the stems, then filling muffin cups halfway with the herb leaves. (Finely chop the stems and process them the same way.) Fill the muffin tins with cold water, making sure the herbs are submerged. Freeze until solid, then pop out the frozen herb cubes, seal tightly in a plastic bag and return to the freezer for up to 6 months. When you're ready to use the herbs, place the herb cubes in a strainer and run cold water over them until defrosted. Use immediately.

* To dry fresh herbs in a microwave oven, sprinkle about ¼ cup leaves (such as mint, oregano or tarragon) on a paper plate. Microwave on high for 1 to 3 minutes (depending on the herb and size of leaf), rotating every 30 seconds or so. Cool before storing in an airtight jar at room temperature.

* To salt-preserve fresh herbs: Choose a flat-bottomed plastic container with an airtight lid. Spread a thin layer of kosher salt over the bottom of the container, then cover with a single layer of clean, dry flat-leaf herbs (like basil, marjoram, mint, sage or tarragon). Repeat with layers of salt and herbs, topping with salt. Seal airtight and store at room temperature for at least 3 months. Remove and use the herbs (which will have darkened) as desired, making sure the remaining herbs in the container are covered with salt.

FRIED HERBS

Sprigs of fried herbs (such as parsley, tarragon and marjoram) make a crunchy, flavorful garnish. The secret is keeping the oil at a temperature that will fry the herbs but not burn them. Heat at least 2 inches vegetable or peanut oil to 285°F in a heavy 3-quart saucepan. While the oil is heating, lightly dip herb sprigs into seasoned flour, shaking off the excess. Drop the herb sprigs into the oil; fry until golden. Remove with a slotted spoon and drain on a paper towel.

DRIED HERBS

PURCHASING Commercially dried herbs have a stronger, more concentrated flavor than fresh herbs, but quickly lose their pungency. Crushed or ground dried herbs become lackluster more quickly than whole-leaf herbs.

STORING The biggest enemies of dried herbs are air, light and heat. Store them in a cool, dark place for up to 6 months. After 3 months, refrigerate them. The more airtight the container, the longer herbs will last.

SUBSTITUTIONS: 1 teaspoon dried herbs = 1 tablespoon fresh. When substituting ground herbs for dried leaf herbs, use about half the amount.

USING

* To be sure how old an herb in your cabinet is, use a felt-tip marking pen to note the purchase date on the bottom of the can or jar. Or mark the date on a strip of masking tape and stick it to the bottom.
* Alphabetize dried herbs in your cabinet to simplify finding them.
* Keep herbs on a turntable (available in the kitchen-supply section of a hardware or department store) for flick-of-the-wrist access.
* For more intense flavor, crumble dried herbs between your fingers just before adding them to a dish.
* Before adding dried herbs to an unheated mixture like salad dressing, soak them for 15 minutes in just enough hot water to moisten them.
* For a fresher flavor and color, combine dried herbs with an equal amount of minced parsley.
* If your dried herbs are over the hill and you don't have time to go to the store for more, just use a little more than you normally would to make up for their weak flavor.

HIGH-ALTITUDE ADJUSTMENTS *see also* BREADS; CAKES

* Altitudes above 3,500 feet have lower atmospheric pressure, which causes cooked or baked foods to react differently.
* Water boils at 212°F at sea level, but boils at 198°F at an altitude of 7,500 feet. That's because there's not as much air pressure at higher altitudes to slow the boiling action.
* Foods stored at high altitudes dry out more quickly than those at low altitudes. That means that an ingredient such as flour is drier and will absorb more liquid. Therefore, slightly more liquid or less flour may be required for cake batters or bread and cookie doughs to reach the proper consistency.
* High-altitude baking adjustments: Leavening must be adjusted so baked goods don't overrise, sugar reduced to prevent a porous crumb with a heavy crust, and liquid added to balance the drying effect:

Feet above sea level	Baking Powder (reduce each teaspoon by)	Sugar (reduce each cup by)	Liquid (for each cup add)
3,000	⅛ tsp.	½ to 1 Tbsp.	1 to 2 Tbsp.
5,000	⅛ to ¼ tsp.	½ to 2 Tbsp.	2 to 4 Tbsp.
7,000 and above	¼ tsp.	1 to 3 Tbsp.	3 to 4 Tbsp.

* For baking cakes and cookies at altitudes over 4,000 feet: **Egg whites** should be beaten only to the soft-peak stage; **oven temperatures** increased by 25°F; **baking time** decreased by about 5 minutes.
* No ingredient adjustment is necessary for yeast breads; however, letting the dough rise twice before the final pan rising allows it to develop a fuller flavor. Increasing the baking temperature by 25°F will help set the crust faster so bread will not overrise during the oven-spring that takes place in the first 10 to 15 minutes of baking.
* Increase the baking temperature by 25°F for cakes and cookies; slightly decrease the baking time.
* Boiled foods like dried beans and peas take longer to cook at high altitudes and may require more liquid than at sea level.
* Meat, poultry and fish usually require a longer cooking time than at sea level.
* For deep-fat frying, decrease the fat temperature by 3 degrees for each 1,000 feet above sea level; fry foods for a longer time.

HONEY   *see also* SYRUPS *for general information such as reliquefying, measuring, and so on.*
TIDBIT   Not only does this sweet elixir taste good, but it has been a honey of a deal medicinally for eons. Over two thousand years ago Hippocrates, the "father of medicine," prescribed it for sundry ailments, including fevers, coughs, sore throats, stomach pain and gout. And almost two-thirds of ancient Egypt's nine hundred-plus recorded therapeutic remedies were honey-based. Honey has long been known as an effective disinfectant, antiseptic and antibiotic, and modern medical studies have used it in preventing infections and speeding healing of topical wounds, burns and bedsores as well as in arresting gastric-ulcer bacterium. What a sweet deal!
PURCHASING
* There are hundreds of different honeys throughout the world (three hundred in the United States alone), most named for the flower from which they originated. A variety of honey is available in supermarkets, the most common being clover and orange blossom. For the broadest selection, check a gourmet or natural food store. There you'll find a panoply that could include eucalyptus, heather, lime blossom, spearmint, thyme and tupelo—each flower lending its subtle nuance to the delicately scented honey.
* Styles of honey: **liquid honey** (extracted from the comb); **whipped honey** (also called *honey fondant* and *spun, churned, sugared or creamed honey*), has a creamy-smooth consistency and spreads like softened butter;

chunk- or **cut-comb honey** (liquid honey with pieces of the honey-comb—both honey and comb are edible); and **comb honey** (a single piece of the honeycomb, with the honey inside). **Organic honey** has been pro-duced in accordance with state and federal regulations for organic farm-ing. **Raw honey** is unrefined and extracted by settling or straining and without heat. Honey can be filtered (processed to extract the extraneous solids) or not, and come from one source or be a blend of two or more sources).

EQUIVALENT   12-ounce jar = 1 cup

STORING   Store liquid honey in an airtight container in a dry place at room temperature for up to a year; cut-comb and chunk-comb honey for 6 months. Refrigerating honey crystallizes it into a grainy mass.

SUBSTITUTIONS:

* For recipes *other* than baked goods: For 1 cup of honey, substitute 1¼ cups sugar plus ¼ cup more of whatever liquid is called for in the recipe. Or you can substitute another syrupy sweetener (such as light or dark corn syrup, maple syrup or molasses), depending on the flavor you want.

* Substituting honey for sugar in baked goods is risky business, but can be done with a little experimentation. As a general rule, don't substitute honey for more than half the sugar called for in a recipe. For each ½ cup granular sugar, substitute ⅓ cup honey and reduce the liquid by 2 table-spoons; add ¼ teaspoon baking soda to the dry ingredients. Reduce the oven temperature by 25°F to prevent overbrowning.

USING

* Do not give honey to babies under a year old, as it could cause infant bot-ulism.

* Honey is sweeter than granulated sugar because of its high fructose con-tent, which means less honey is needed for the same sweetening power as sugar. But honey also has more calories: 60 per tablespoon compared to sugar's 45.

* Honey varies greatly in flavor so, when using it in cooking, it's important to know its source. For instance, buckwheat honey has far too strong a flavor for a recipe that calls for orange-flower honey, which has a light, delicate fragrance and flavor.

* Keep honey in a plastic squeeze bottle (available at supermarkets and variety stores) to easily dispense just the amount you want.

* Age-old sore throat remedy: 1 tablespoon honey mixed with 1 table-spoon lemon juice in hot tea.

HONEYDEW MELON   *see* MELONS

HORSERADISH
PURCHASING

* Fresh horseradish: Look for firm roots with no sign of withering; available in gourmet markets and some supermarkets.
* Bottled horseradish: It's available white (preserved in vinegar) and red (preserved in beet juice), and can be found either in supermarket refrigerator cases or on the shelf with other condiments.

EQUIVALENT   1 tablespoon bottled = 2 teaspoons freshly grated
STORING

* Fresh horseradish: Refrigerate, tightly wrapped in a plastic bag, for up to 3 weeks; freeze for up to 6 months.
* Bottled horseradish: Store in the refrigerator for up to 6 months.

PREPARING

* Peel fresh horseradish and cut out its fibrous core just before using.
* When grating fresh horseradish, avoid breathing the pungent fumes, which can irritate both nose and eyes.
* Within 4 weeks after opening, prepared horseradish can begin to turn bitter and lose its heat. To freeze, spoon tablespoons of it onto a plastic wrap–lined baking sheet and freeze until solid. When hard, transfer horseradish lumps to an airtight plastic bag and freeze for up to 6 months.
* Mix 2 to 3 tablespoons horseradish with 1 cup sour cream or whipped cream for a zesty accompaniment for roast beef or prime rib.
* A small amount of horseradish mixed with applesauce makes a snappy-sweet condiment for pork.

If I think I'm about to get a cold and feel achy and chilled,
I know it's time for hot apple cider. . . .
—Joyce Goldstein, American restaurateur, author

HOT DRINKS

* Serve hot drinks only in heatproof (tempered) glasses, cups or punch bowls.
* Be careful when using metal cups or mugs—metal holds heat so well it can easily burn your lips.
* Preheat nonmetal glasses, cups or bowls by filling them with very hot water and letting it stand for about 3 minutes.
* To help disseminate the drink's heat and keep the container from cracking, place a metal spoon in the cup or glass (or a metal ladle in a punch bowl) and slowly pour the hot drink onto it.

CANDIED APPLE CIDER

Those tiny red cinnamon candies give this cider its snap. Combine 1 quart (4 cups) apple cider and ½ cup cinnamon candies in a medium saucepan. Cook over medium heat, stirring occasionally, until the candies melt. Pour into warm mugs; top each serving with a dollop of unsweetened whipped cream, sprinkle with additional cinnamon candies. Serves 4

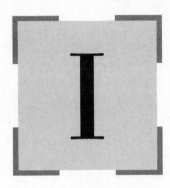

ICE

TIDBIT   Ice will taste only as good as the water from which it's made, and bad-tasting ice can ruin the flavor of whatever it chills. If your water is highly chlorinated or otherwise off-tasting, make your ice with bottled water.

EQUIVALENT   3 to 4 standard-sized ice cubes = 1 cup crushed ice

GENERAL

* Ice can easily absorb odors from other foods in the freezer. Before a party, sample the ice—if it tastes bad, buy packaged ice. Packaged ice cubes are the most versatile choice, as they can be used as is or crushed.

* When buying packaged ice cubes, figure on getting about 10 cubes per pound; a 25-pound bag will contain about 250 ice cubes.

* Inexpensive manual or electric ice crushers are widely available in department and liquor stores.

* If you don't have an ice crusher, simply place ice cubes in a heavy-duty plastic bag, seal, then wrap in a heavy towel; whack away with a mallet, rolling pin or other heavy implement until the ice is crushed as desired.

* Don't use your blender or food processor to crush ice unless the manufacturer's directions say you can.

* Crushed ice melts much faster than ice cubes and will dilute a drink more quickly.

* Speed-chill bottled drinks (including wine) by completely submerging them in a bucket or large pot filled with half ice and half water for about 20 minutes. This chilling method is much faster than using ice alone.

* Get ready for a party by starting several days in advance to make ice cubes, bagging them in tightly sealed plastic bags as each batch is finished. Separate stuck-together cubes by giving the bag a whack on the countertop.

* Discard old ice cubes—they'll give your drinks that unpleasant "freezer" taste. Sprinkle them around houseplants for slow watering. Or throw a handful into the garbage disposal to help sharpen the blades.

* **Crystal-clear ice cubes:** Boil water, then cool to room temperature before pouring into ice cube trays. Bottled spring water will also produce clear cubes.

* **Decorated ice cubes:** Place a small piece of fruit (cherry, melon ball, pineapple chunk, raspberry, lemon or orange twist, and so on) or edible FLOWER or flower petal in each section of an ice cube tray. Cover with cold water that has been boiled and cooled; freeze until firm. Tailor your cubes for their intended use—small lemon wedges or mint sprigs for iced tea, a whole raspberry or blackberry for fruit punches, a cherry tomato for Bloody Marys, and so on.

* **Flavored ice cubes** are great for icing drinks without diluting them. For instance, use lemonade cubes for lemonade, Bloody Mary mix for Bloody Marys, coffee for iced coffee—you get the idea. Forget about trying to make cubes from rum, vodka, and other liquor—alcohol freezes at a much lower temperature than water or juice and won't solidify completely.

PUNCH-BOWL ICE

* Measure your punch bowl before buying a block of ice for it. It should be small enough to allow for the punch, yet large enough to chill it.

* If you can't find a block small enough to fit your punch bowl, and don't want to take the time to whittle a large one down, make your own punch-bowl ice. Simply fill a large, appropriate-sized container (plastic or metal) with water and freeze at least 24 hours ahead of time. Ring molds, like angel-food cake or Bundt pans, make attractive punch-bowl ice. Don't use a glass mold, which can crack as the water freezes.

* **Decorated ice mold:** Fill the container half full of water and freeze until solid. Place fruit (grape clusters, pineapple rings, orange or lemon slices, and so forth) on the surface of the ice. Carefully pour cold water to cover the fruit; freeze until solid. If necessary, add more water to fill the container to the top and freeze.

* Make large or decoratively shaped ice "chunks" for punch bowls by freezing water in muffin tins, madeleine pans, mini-Bundt pans, tart tins, and so on.

* Freeze punch-bowl ice, tightly covered, for up to 2 weeks. To unmold, dip the bottom of the container in cold to lukewarm water; turn out onto a piece of heavy-duty foil. Rewrap and place in the freezer until just before serving time.

*I doubt the world holds for anyone a more soul-stirring surprise
than the first adventure with ice cream.*
—Heywood Broun, American journalist, novelist

ICE CREAM
COMMERCIAL ICE CREAM

TIDBIT All commercial ice creams have "overrun," an industry term referring to the amount of air they contain. High-quality ice creams contain 10 to 25 percent air, which gives them a dense yet creamy texture. In general, less expensive ice creams have a greater proportion of air pumped into them. Since overrun isn't listed on the carton, the only way to be sure is to weigh the carton. A pint of ice cream containing 25 percent air will weigh about 18 ounces (subtract about 1½ ounces for the container's weight); the weight is proportionately higher with a lower percentage of overrun. The bottom line is that a pint container of premium ice cream will weigh more than the same size of a store brand. This fact should be considered when you're calculating the so-called savings of low-priced ice cream, because the truth is, you're paying for a lot of cold air.

PURCHASING Sticky packaging is a signal that an ice cream, sherbet or frozen yogurt has probably thawed and leaked, then refrozen. Choose another package. Ice cream begins melting as soon as it's removed from the market's freezer section, so it should be one of the last items you put in your cart. Be sure the clerk puts it in an insulated bag.

STORING As soon as you get home, put the ice cream in the freezer. Ice cream easily absorbs food odors and forms ice crystals, so it's best consumed within 2 to 3 days. To extend its storage life a couple of days, double wrap the carton in a heavy-duty plastic bag. To keep ice crystals from forming on the surface of a partially used container, place a sheet of plastic wrap directly on the ice cream's surface, pressing down so that it forms a fairly airtight seal, before replacing the carton's lid.

USING

* Low-fat ice creams and frozen yogurts melt faster than their caloric cousins, and quickly turn to puddles of liquid when served over desserts like hot pies and cobblers.

* Slightly soften a quart of rock-hard ice cream so it'll be easier to scoop by microwaving it at medium-low (30 percent power) for 30 to 60 seconds. Test the softness by inserting a skewer or narrow knife. Hardened high-fat ice cream will soften more quickly than its less caloric cousins because microwaves are attracted to fat.

* No microwave oven to soften ice cream? Peel away the carton and cut the ice cream into slices. Use an electric knife to make quick work of it.

* Spritz a thin layer of cooking spray on scoops, spoons or whatever you use for scooping, and the ice cream will slip right off the utensil.

* Make your own premium stir-in style of ice cream by adding ½ to ¾ cup of any of the following to a softened pint of your favorite ice cream: crushed cream-filled chocolate cookies; rehydrated dried cherries, cranberries or raisins; chopped nuts; chopped fresh fruit; chocolate chunks; miniature marshmallows; chopped chocolate-covered mints; the list is endless. Return the ice cream to the freezer for at least 2 hours to refirm.

* Melted, refrozen ice cream never has the same texture as the original. But don't throw it out—use it as a creamy topping for puddings, cakes, pies . . . even hot breakfast cereal!

* Having a party? Line a baking sheet with plastic wrap, then place scoops of ice cream or frozen yogurt on it. Work quickly or the ice cream will start to melt. Cover with another sheet of plastic wrap and freeze. When you need them, the ice cream balls will lift right off and be ready to go.

* Ice cream sundae dessert buffets are a big hit for almost any occasion. Provide bowls of various-flavored ice cream and sherbet balls, chopped fruit (strawberries, bananas, peaches, and so on), sauces (hot fudge and caramel), chopped toasted nuts and whipped cream. You'll get raves!

* Top vanilla ice cream with warmed pure maple syrup and toasted pecans. Oh, my.

HOMEMADE ICE CREAM

* Before preparing any homemade ice cream, check the manufacturer's directions for your particular ice cream machine.

* For higher yield, creamier texture and faster freezing, make and chill the ice cream mixture the day before you plan to freeze it.

* Homemade ice cream won't form crystals if you add 1 envelope unflavored gelatin for each 6 cups liquid. Let the gelatin soften in ¼ cup of the liquid (*see* GELATIN), then heat until the gelatin dissolves and stir it into the rest of the liquid.

* For a lighter texture, fill the canister only two-thirds full so the ice cream has room to expand during the churning and freezing process.

* With an ice cream maker that requires rock salt and ice, use a ratio of 1 cup salt for each 6 cups of ice. As the ice melts during churning, add more salt and ice to keep the temperature cold enough.

* The faster the freezing process, the smoother the ice cream.

* Before opening a canister of ice cream, remove the ice and water to well below the level of the lid. Wipe off the lid carefully to make sure that no salt or water gets into the ice cream as you remove it.
* Homemade ice cream should be "ripened" in the freezer for at least 4 hours after making it to fully develop its flavor and texture.

FUDGED GINGER ICE CREAM

This elegant dessert never ceases to get raves. Use the best ice cream you can afford. With a rubber spatula gently fold ¼ cup minced crystallized ginger into 1 quart slightly softened premium vanilla ice cream (don't let the ice cream become so soft it liquefies around the edges). Immediately return the ice cream to the freezer; freeze at least 1 hour before serving. Serve topped with slightly warm Black Satin Sauce (recipe follows) or other chocolate sauce. Serves 4 to 6.

BLACK SATIN SAUCE

A decadent topping for everything from ice cream, to cake, to bread pudding. In a medium, heavy saucepan, stir together ½ cup unsweetened cocoa powder, 1 cup sugar and ⅛ teaspoon salt. Slowly stir in ¾ cup heavy whipping cream, blending until smooth. Add 4 tablespoons butter, cut into 4 pieces; cook over medium-low heat, stirring constantly, until the mixture comes to a boil. Reduce the heat to low; cook, stirring constantly, for 2 minutes. Remove from the heat. Cool for 15 minutes before stirring in 1 teaspoon pure vanilla extract. Serve warm or at room temperature. Cover and refrigerate for up to 2 weeks. Reheat until the sauce achieves the desired texture. Makes about 1¾ cups.

ICED TEA *see* TEA

ICING *see* FROSTING

IMMERSION BLENDERS *see also* BLENDERS

TIDBIT The immersion blender is a long, narrow, handheld appliance with rotary blades at one end. It does a good job of blending and PURÉEING both small and large amounts of food. You can put it right into a glass, pitcher, pot of soup or bowl of cooked potatoes, all of which means minimal cleanup. Some models have accessories such as a strainer, blending bowl, spatula, drink-mixing beaker and whisk (for whipping cream and beating egg whites).

* When processing hot foods, wear an oven mitt to protect your hand from spatters.
* Always remove a pan from the heat before using an immersion blender.

* If your immersion blender has variable speeds, always begin at low speed, gradually increasing to high.
* To clean the blender, unplug it, and hold the blade portion under hot, running water, using a little soap if the surface is oily. Never submerge an immersion blender.

JARS AND BOTTLES

* If a jar just won't open, turn it upside down and smack the flat top of the lid against a hard surface. Or hold the metal lid under hot, running water—the heat will cause the metal to expand. If it's a glass jar that's been refrigerated, begin with warm water, and gradually increase the temperature to hot so that you don't crack the glass.
* Get a better grip on an obstinate lid with a damp cloth or a rubber glove. Or place a wide rubber band around the lid.
* Use pliers on small bottle necks. Cover plastic lids with a kitchen towel before using pliers.
* Jar grippers—thin, pliable disks of rubber—can be purchased in many supermarkets and hardware stores.
* Keep lids from sticking to bottles filled with sticky mixtures (like maple syrup) by wiping the rim of both the lid and the container with a paper towel dampened with hot water before resealing.
* Keep your shelves clean by using a damp cloth to wipe off the sides and bottom of bottles containing ingredients like syrup or oil.
* Save screw-top, quart-sized (or smaller) soft drink or other narrow-necked bottles and use as "canisters" for cornmeal, granulated sugar and other dry, free-flowing ingredients. First of all, make sure the clean bottle is completely dry (use a hair dryer to blow hot air into it). Then position a funnel in the bottle's neck and pour in the sugar, and so on; seal tightly. Now you can pour the ingredient right into a measuring cup or other container. If lumps form (which means either the bottle wasn't thoroughly dry or the lid's not airtight), simply shake the bottle to break them up.
* Clean and save screw-top jars—they make great moisture- and odor-proof storage containers for all manner of foods.
* Glass and plastic peanut butter jars are perfect for storing food because

they're slightly wider at the top than at the bottom, which makes it easy to remove food from them.

* Never fill a glass jar or bottle with a hot mixture without warming it first with hot water—you're liable to crack the glass.
* Food freezes well in glass screw-top jars. Just be sure to leave ½ to 1 inch of headroom to allow for the natural expansion that occurs when foods or liquids are frozen. If you don't, the glass may crack.
* To quickly defrost food that's been frozen in glass jars, immerse the jar in cold water, changing the water every 10 minutes or so. Never put a frozen jar of food in hot water—it'll crack the glass and ruin the food.
* To rid jars and bottles of a lingering odor, fill them with hot water and 2 to 3 teaspoons baking soda. Let stand overnight, then rinse and dry.
* If you can't reach the bottom of a bottle with a bottle brush to clean it, fill it with warm, soapy water and let stand for 20 minutes. Then add a ½-inch layer of dried beans or pie weights and shake until the debris loosens.

JERUSALEM ARTICHOKES *see also* VEGETABLES, GENERAL

TIDBIT Jerusalem artichokes aren't really artichokes, but rather a member of the sunflower family—the reason many growers today call this vegetable "sunchoke."

PURCHASING Choose those that are firm and fresh-looking. Avoid any that are wrinkled, tinged with green or have soft spots.

EQUIVALENT 1 pound = about 2 cups chopped

STORING Refrigerate in a plastic bag for up to 1 week.

PREPARING

* Jerusalem artichokes may be peeled, but because the skin is very thin and quite nutritious, usually only need to be washed before using.
* If you do peel them, use a vegetable peeler and do it before, not after cooking, so less flesh comes off with the peel.
* This vegetable's nutty, sweet flavor and crunchy texture make it perfect to eat raw in salads.
* Cook by STEAMING, boiling or SAUTÉING, or add to soups and stews.

JICAMA *see also* VEGETABLES, GENERAL

PURCHASING This large, bulbous root vegetable has a thin brown skin and white crunchy flesh. Choose one that's heavy for its size and free of blemishes.

EQUIVALENT 1 pound = about 3 cups chopped

STORING Refrigerate in a plastic bag for up to 2 weeks. Cover peeled jicama slices in cold water to keep them crisp.

PREPARING Peel just before using. With a sharp knife, pull off the skin (and attached white fibrous layer) in sheets.

USING

* Jicama's sweet, nutty flavor is good both raw and cooked. Raw, it can be used in both fruit and vegetable salads, or sliced thinly on sandwiches.
* It can be cooked in stir-fries, boiled and mashed like a potato, sautéed on its own, or added to soups or stews (near the end of the cooking time so it retains its crisp texture).
* Can't find jicama? Substitute water chestnuts.

JULIENNE *see also* GARNISHING AND GARNISHES

* A technique whereby food is cut into thin, matchstick strips. Cut the food (such as a potato) into ⅛-inch thick slices. Then stack the slices and cut them into ⅛-inch thick strips. Those strips may then be cut into the desired length.
* Julienned food is most often used as a garnish.
* When trying to julienne something round like a beet, first cut a thin slice from the bottom so it will sit firmly and not roll on the work surface.
* If you don't want to bother with julienning food by hand, look in kitchenware shops for a julienne slicer—a special tool that cuts food into thin strips in one motion.

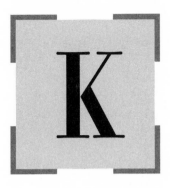

KALE *see* GREENS

KETCHUP, CATSUP

STORING   Unopened ketchup can be stored indefinitely in a cool, dark place. Once opened, ketchup can be refrigerated indefinitely.

EQUIVALENT   16-ounce bottle = 1⅔ cups

* Can't get the ketchup to pour out of the bottle? Insert a straw or knife with a long, thin blade and rotate it once or twice. Invert the bottle and give it a shake.
* To get the last bit of ketchup from the bottle, add about 1 tablespoon water or vinegar, then shake well until the bottle is clean. Depending on whether you used water or vinegar, the mixture can be added to salad dressing, spaghetti sauce, soup, or chili.

KIDNEYS

TIDBIT   Beef and veal kidneys are multilobed, while lamb and pork are single-lobed. Beef kidneys have the strongest flavor; they're also the least tender.

PURCHASING

* Choose kidneys that are firm, with a rich, even color. Avoid those with dry spots or a dull surface. In general, the younger the animal, the more tender the texture and the more delicate the flavor. Kidneys from younger animals have a paler color than those from older animals.
* How much per serving: about 4 ounces

STORING   Refrigerate, loosely wrapped, for up to 1 day. Kidneys are best used the day they're purchased. Before cooking, remove the skin and any excess fat.

PREPARING

* Soaking kidneys from more mature animals in cold salted water for 30 to 60 minutes helps reduce their strong odor. Drain and blot dry with a paper towel before cooking.
* BLANCHING kidneys in lightly salted water also helps diminish any strong flavor. Dry thoroughly before cooking them according to the recipe.

KITCHEN CLEANUP *see* CLEANUP, KITCHEN

KITCHEN PARCHMENT *see* PARCHMENT PAPER

KNEADING *see* BREAD, YEAST

KNIVES; KNIFE HOLDERS
PURCHASING

* Knives: A good knife should be sturdy and well balanced. The best knives are made of high-carbon stainless steel or forged carbon; the end of the blade (called the "tang") extends all the way to the end of the handle, where it's anchored by several rivets.
* Knife holders: Choose those made of wood, a much kinder surface to knives than the magnetic holders because wood doesn't abrade the blade. Some knife holders have acrylic dividers, which is also better than metal.

USING

* Preserve blades in a free-standing knife rack by placing the knives blade side up.
* Never keep knives in a drawer—their edges and tips get scratched and become dull. If a drawer's your only storage; make a cardboard sheath for each one (flatten a cardboard tube from foil or waxed paper). Or buy knife sheaths at a cutlery or cookware store.
* Using a sharpening steel to hone the blade before each use will give you a knife that cuts cleanly and safely every time. After sharpening, wash the blade to remove the microscopic bits of steel dust.
* Every so often, renew your knife's edge by using a whetstone, drawing the knife across it at a 20-degree angle, about 6 strokes a side.
* A wooden cutting board is easier on a blade than a hard plastic board.
* Exposing a knife to high heat can permanently damage it.

* Some foods—like onions, potatoes and artichokes—will discolor carbon knives; conversely, the knives will also discolor the food.
* Wash and dry knives right after using to keep them in top condition. Never soak knives or wash them in a dishwasher.
* Stainless-steel knives will stay shiny if you rub them with a slice of lemon peel or a rubbing alcohol–dampened rag; wash before using.

LABEL TERMS

TIDBIT Understanding food labels can be confusing, but the following term definitions ought to dispel much of the mystery. Before beginning, however, remember the basics: Most labels list ingredients in descending order by weight, not by the amount of each ingredient. Therefore, a cereal that lists sugar as the second or third ingredient might actually contain a small percentage of sugar.

FAT TERMS

* Labels must now include data on the *total amount* of fat, *saturated fat* and *unsaturated fat* (*see* FATS AND OILS), although listing the type of unsaturates is optional. The problem with this current format is that trans fatty acids (unsaturated fat altered by hydrogenation into saturated fat), which may be part of the total fat listed, will not be classified as "saturated." Verify by adding the amount of saturated and unsaturated fat grams—if the figure doesn't equal that of *total fat*, the difference is undoubtedly in trans fatty acids.
* *Reduced Fat:* At least 25 percent less fat than found in a product's regular form. Reduced *Saturated Fat:* Same as "Reduced Fat," referring to saturated fat.
* *Low-Fat:* 3 grams or less of fat per serving.
* _*% Fat Free:* May only be used for "low-fat" products. The percentage is based on the amount (by weight) of fat in 100 grams of food. Therefore, a 100-gram serving of a "98% Fat Free" food contains 2 grams of fat.
* *Low in Saturated Fat:* 1 gram or less of saturated fat per serving; no more than 15 percent of calories from saturated fat.
* *Fat Free:* Less than ½ gram of fat per serving, providing there are no added fat or oil ingredients in a product's recipe.
* *Saturated Fat Free:* Same as "Fat Free," referring to saturated fat.

CHOLESTEROL TERMS

* *Reduced Cholesterol:* At least 25 percent less cholesterol than found in a product's regular version, and 2 grams or less saturated fat per serving.
* *Low in Cholesterol:* 20 milligrams or less cholesterol per serving and 2 grams or less of saturated fat.
* *Cholesterol Free:* Less than 2 milligrams of cholesterol per serving and 2 grams or less of saturated fat.

SODIUM TERMS

* *Reduced Sodium:* at least 25 percent less sodium than found in a similar food's original form.
* *Light in Sodium:* 50 percent less sodium per serving, referring only to foods with more than 40 calories or 3 grams of fat per serving.
* *Low Sodium:* 140 milligrams or less sodium per serving.
* *Very Low Sodium:* 35 milligrams or less sodium per serving.
* *Unsalted* or *No Added Salt:* No salt was used during processing (but the product is not necessarily sodium free). If not salt free, the label will state: *"Not a Sodium-Free Food"* or *"Not for Control of Sodium in the Diet."*
* *Sodium-Free or Salt Free:* less than 5 milligrams sodium per serving.

SUGAR TERMS

* *Reduced Sugar:* at least 25 percent less sugar than found in a product's regular version.
* No Added Sugars: No sugars (including ingredients containing sugar, such as fruit juice or applesauce) were added during processing, and that processing doesn't increase the sugar content above the amount naturally present in the ingredients.
* *Sugar Free:* Less than 0.5 gram sugar per serving.

CALORIE TERMS

* *Reduced Calorie:* at least 25 percent fewer calories than the reference food in a product's regular form.
* *Low Calorie:* 40 calories or less per serving; less than 0.4 calorie per gram of food.
* *Calorie Free or No Calories:* less than 5 calories per serving.
* *Light* or *Lite:* one-third fewer calories than in the product's regular form; or less than 50 percent fat per serving. If over half the calories are from fat, the fat content must be reduced by at least 50 percent.

FIBER TERMS

* *High Fiber:* 5 grams or more per serving. Food must also meet "low fat" definition, or state the level of total fat.

* *Good Source of Fiber:* 2.5 to 4.9 grams per serving.
* *More Fiber* or *Added Fiber:* at least 2.5 grams more per serving than in the reference food.

OTHER LABEL TERMS

* *Enriched* or *Fortified:* Contains 10 percent or more of the per-serving Daily Value for protein, vitamins, minerals, dietary fiber or potassium.
* *Fresh:* raw food that has not been processed in any way, either by freezing or with heat.
* *Fresh Frozen:* Food quickly frozen from its fresh state.
* *Good Source of:* Contains 10 to 19 percent of the listed ingredient's Daily Value per serving.
* *Lean:* packaged meat, poultry or seafood with less than 10 grams total fat, less than 4 grams saturated fat and less than 95 milligrams cholesterol per 100 grams. *Extra lean:* less than 5 grams total fat, less than 2 grams saturated fat and less than 95 milligrams cholesterol per 100 grams.
* *Natural:* a general term with no legal parameters, typically meaning that the product has no artificial ingredients or intentional additives. When applied to meat or poultry, "natural" generally means the product is minimally processed and free of artificial ingredients.
* *Natural Flavorings:* flavorings whose significant function is flavoring rather than nutritional. They can be derived from a spice; fruit or fruit juice; edible yeast; herb, bark, bud, root, leaf or similar plant material; meat, seafood, poultry, egg, or dairy products. However, these broad parameters include ingredients like hydrolyzed protein and HVP, both of which contain MSG.
* *Rich in, High in* or *Excellent Source of:* Contains 20 percent of more of the Daily Value per serving.
* *RDA or Recommended Dietary Allowance:* the government-recommended daily amounts of protein, vitamins and minerals for healthy adults. Such amounts are ballpark figures and may vary slightly according to gender, conditions such as pregnancy, etc.

PRODUCT DATING This is done primarily to help stores determine the product's display life. Even if the date has expired, the product may be perfectly fine to consume. Following is a rundown of how it typically works.

* *Sell by:* A date advising the store how long to display the product. Don't buy products past the "sell-by" date, although if you have one in the fridge, it's generally perfectly safe to use.
* *Use by:* A date, determined by the product's manufacturer, after which the food is no longer at peak quality.

* *Best if used by* (or *before*): A date the manufacturer recommends for best flavor and quality.

LAMB   *see also* MEAT, GENERAL

TIDBIT   Lamb is a sheep less than 1 year old. Baby lamb is slaughtered at 6 to 8 weeks of age; spring lamb is usually 3 to 5 months old. The younger the animal, the more tender the meat is. Animals slaughtered at 12 to 24 months are called "yearlings"; over 2 years old, they are mutton.

PURCHASING

* Let color be your guide. In general, the darker the color, the older the animal. Baby lamb will be pale pink, while regular lamb is a pinkish red. Lamb should have a fine-grained flesh and creamy white fat. Domestic lamb, which is fed on grain, has a milder flavor than the grass-fed imported lamb. Domestic lamb cuts are also larger and meatier than their imported counterparts.
* Cuts: Leg of lamb—choose a plump one; the ratio of meat to bone and fat will be higher. Lamb chops—go for thick ones (1 to 1½ inches), which will be more succulent than thin chops. Bone-in cuts are always more flavorful than boneless cuts.

STORING

* Refrigerate ground lamb and small cuts like chops, loosely wrapped in waxed paper, for up to 3 days; larger cuts like roasts for up to 5 days.
* Freeze ground lamb for up to 3 months; solid cuts for 6 months.
* Cooked lamb can be refrigerated for up to 3 days.

PREPARING

* The thin, parchmentlike coating (called "fell") on a leg of lamb retains the meat's juices so don't remove it before cooking.
* If the flavor of older lamb is too strong for your palate, mix equal parts lemon juice and extra virgin olive oil, and rub all over the meat's surface. Cover and refrigerate for 2 hours, then wipe dry and cook.
* Removing most of the excess fat from lamb cuts will not only be good for the waistline, but will also reduce any "lamby" flavor many don't appreciate.
* Slash the fat at ½-inch intervals along the edges of lamb chops and they won't curl while cooking.
* Overcooking lamb makes it dry and tough. For tender, succulent lamb, cook only until medium-rare.

LARD   *see also* FATS AND OILS; LARDING

TIDBIT   Lard is rendered and clarified pork fat, the very best of which is leaf lard, which comes from the fat around the animal's kidneys. Processed lard has a mild, nutty flavor and is about the consistency of shortening.

PURCHASING Lard is typically found in a supermarket's refrigerated or freezer section.

STORING Tightly wrap and store at a cool room temperature for up to 6 months, in the refrigerator for even longer. Check the label for storage directions.

USING

* Lard is richer than many other fats and therefore makes extremely tender, flaky biscuits, pie crusts and pastries.
* When substituting lard for butter or margarine in baking, reduce the amount by 20 to 25 percent.

LARDING; LARDING NEEDLE see also BARDING; LARD

TIDBIT Many lean cuts of meat can become more succulent and juicy by larding—the technique of inserting long, thin strips of fat every inch or so throughout the flesh. The fat melts during cooking, moistening the meat.

GENERAL

* A larding needle—a special tool with a pointed tip and hollow cavity—can be found in gourmet stores.
* The fat used for larding is typically pork fat (known as "lardons"), which many butchers sell precut.
* Add flavor by soaking the lardons in wine or brandy, then rolling them in salt, pepper or herbs before insertion in the meat.
* No larding needle? Pierce the meat with a long, thin knife, then force the fat strips through the holes. When you do it this way, any seasoning on the lardon's surface will come off at the opening as you're forcing it through.
* Insert the lardons across the meat's grain.
* Slice cooked larded meat cuts on the diagonal so the fat strips look like a scattering of small white dots.

LEAVENINGS see BAKING POWDER; BAKING SODA; HIGH-ALTITUDE ADJUSTMENTS; YEAST

LEEKS

TIDBIT Leeks have been prized for centuries for everything from strength-giving qualities to magical properties. They look like a giant scallion and are related to both garlic and onion, with a flavor milder than either.

PURCHASING Choose leeks with crisp, brightly colored leaves and unblemished white sections. Avoid any with withered or yellow-spotted leaves. The smaller the leek, the more tender it will be.

STORING Refrigerate in a plastic bag for up to 5 days.

EQUIVALENTS 1 pound = 2 cups trimmed and chopped, 1 cup cooked

PREPARING Trim rootlets, then leaf ends so about 5 inches remain. Slit the leek from top to bottom and wash thoroughly under cold, running water to remove all the dirt trapped between the layers.

USING

* Leeks may be cooked whole or cut into slices. Whole leeks are best braised or steamed; sliced leeks can be sautéed.
* Chopped leeks are wonderful in a variety of foods, including salads, stir-fries and soups.
* Save the tough green leek ends you trim off, put them in a cheesecloth bag and use to flavor soups.
* *Leek "chives":* Bury a leek bulb in dirt in a pot, set it on a window ledge, keep it moist, and before long, you'll have green leek shoots that can be snipped and used like chives.

I'll be with you in the squeezing of a lemon.
—Oliver Goldsmith, British author, playwright

LEMONS *For juicing, zesting and general information, see* CITRUS FRUITS

PURCHASING Choose lemons with smooth, brightly colored skin with no tinge of green. They should be firm, plump and heavy for their size.

EQUIVALENTS

* 1 pound = 4 to 6 medium, 1 cup juice
* 1 medium lemon = 3 tablespoons juice, 2 to 3 teaspoons zest

STORING Store lemons at room temperature for a week; refrigerate for 2 to 3 weeks.

USING

* Thoroughly wash lemons before using their peel (zest) for anything.
* Buy lemons in peak season when they're most economical and enjoy their bounty throughout the year. First zest the lemons; freeze the zest for up to 6 months. Squeeze the juice and freeze it in ice cube trays. Turn the solid lemon cubes into heavyweight plastic bags, seal tightly and freeze for up to 6 months.
* After squeezing the juice, don't throw out the lemon shells. Put them in a freezer-proof plastic bag and freeze for up to 6 months. Use the shells to stuff poultry cavities, flavor stocks and sauces, add to a pot when cooking vegetables or stewing fruit, and so on.

* Room-temperature lemons yield more juice than those that are refrigerated.

* Need just a few drops of lemon juice? Pierce the skin with a toothpick and squeeze out what you need. To store, reinsert the toothpick, put the lemon in a plastic bag and refrigerate.

* To squeeze a lemon wedge over food at your plate, spear the wedge through the flesh with a fork first, then squeeze. That way, the juice won't squirt where you don't want it.

* For a restaurant-style presentation, set a lemon half, cut side down, on a small square of cheesecloth. Bring up the cheesecloth ends and tie at the top with a small ribbon or string. Place a wrapped lemon half on each guest's plate. This presentation allows diners to squeeze out the juice without worrying about seeds or chunks of flesh spurting onto their food.

* Homemade dried lemon peel is easy to make and great for flavoring everything from cakes to sauces. To make your own, simply remove the zest (the colored portion), chop finely, and dry in a single layer at room temperature overnight, or until completely dry. If you're in a hurry, place the grated zest on an ungreased baking sheet and bake at 200°F for about 20 minutes, stirring occasionally. Cool completely before storing in an airtight container at room temperature.

* Make granulated lemon zest by combining the outer peel (yellow portion only) of 1 lemon with 1 to 2 tablespoons granulated sugar in a food processor. Process until powdery and use the sugared zest in everything from tea to desserts.

* Remove berry or beet stains from fingers by rubbing them with half a lemon.

PRESERVED LEMONS

Salt transforms lemon rind, mellowing the flavor and softening the texture. There are dozens of ways to use preserved lemons—chopped in guacamole, seviche, salsa, rice, aïoli, salads, soups and stews, and sprinkled over vegetables and meat, particularly lamb. Cut 4 medium lemons lengthwise in quarters. In a large bowl, combine lemons, ⅔ cup kosher salt and 1 tablespoon black peppercorns (for added sass, add 1 teaspoon red pepper flakes); toss to combine. Layer the lemons in a 1½-quart glass or earthenware jar. As you add the lemons, use a large spoon to press down on each layer of lemon to release their juices. Add ½ cup lemon juice and just enough water to cover the lemons. Seal the jar airtight and refrigerate for 2 to 3 weeks, shaking the jar daily. To use, rinse or scrape the salt off the lemon, scrape out and discard the pulp and pith. Chop or slice the rind to use as desired.

LENTILS *see also* BEANS, DRIED; PEAS, DRIED

PURCHASING Lentils are tiny, lens-shaped, dried pulses (legume seeds); the most widely available variety is grayish brown and found in most supermarkets. There are also yellow and red varieties called *dal*.

EQUIVALENTS 1 cup dried = 2½ cups (not soaked), 3½ cups soaked

STORING

* Uncooked lentils: Store in an airtight container in a cool, dry place for up to 1 year; freeze indefinitely.
* Cooked lentils: Cover and refrigerate for up to 5 days.

PREPARING

* Before using, put lentils in a colander and rinse. Pick through them, discarding any shriveled lentils or bits of gravel.
* Unlike dried beans and whole peas, lentils don't need soaking before cooking. Soaking them overnight makes them softer (which depends on personal taste) and reduces their cooking time. Presoaked lentils cook in about 12 minutes; about 20 minutes for those that are not soaked.
* Slightly increase the cooking time when lentils are prepared with acidic ingredients, such as tomatoes or wine. Or add these ingredients when the lentils are almost done.
* Drain off the cooking liquid as soon as the lentils are done or they'll continue to cook.
* Lentils are great served alone, or added to soups and stews, or dressed with vinaigrette and served as a salad.

LETTUCE *see* SALAD GREENS

LIMA BEANS *see also* BEANS, CANNED; BEANS, DRIED

PURCHASING Lima beans are available fresh, dried and canned. Fresh limas are in season from June to September. They're typically sold in their pods, which should be plump, firm and dark green.

EQUIVALENTS

* Fresh: 1 pound unshelled = 1½ cups shelled
* Dried: 1 pound = 2⅔ cups, 6 cups cooked; 1 cup = 2½ cups cooked

STORING Refrigerate fresh limas in a plastic bag for up to 1 week.

USING

* Shell fresh limas just before cooking them. Pull on the string to open the pod. Speed the process by using kitchen shears to cut off a thin strip of the pod's inner edge.
* Cooked fresh limas are wonderful when cooled, dressed with vinaigrette and served as a salad.

L

LIMES *For juicing, zesting and general information, see* CITRUS FRUITS

TIDBIT The most common lime in the United States is the Persian lime; Florida's Key lime is not as widely available. The latter is smaller, rounder, and has a color more yellow than green.

PURCHASING Choose limes that are brightly colored, smooth skinned and heavy for their size. Small brown areas (called "scald") on the skin won't affect flavor or succulence. However, a hard or shriveled skin will.

EQUIVALENTS 1 pound = 6 to 8 medium, about ⅔ cup juice; 1 medium lime = about 1½ tablespoons juice, 1½ teaspoons zest

STORING Refrigerate uncut limes in a plastic bag for up to 10 days, cut limes for up to 5 days.

USING

* As with all citrus fruit, limes should be thoroughly washed if you plan to use the skin.
* Lime juice can be substituted for lemon juice in most recipes.

Liquor is not a necessity.
It is a means of momentarily side-stepping necessity.
—Clifton Fadiman, American author

LIQUORS AND LIQUEURS *see also* BEER; CHAMPAGNE; COCKTAILS; FLAMBÉING; ICE; WINE; WINE IN FOOD

TIDBIT Generally speaking, **liquor** is any alcoholic beverage produced by distillation (gin, vodka, bourbon, Scotch). **Liqueur** is a sweetened spirit (brandy, rum or whiskey) variously flavored with seeds, flowers, fruits, herbs, nuts, spices, and so on.

GENERAL

* The word "proof" on a liquor or liqueur bottle specifies the amount of alcohol that a potable contains. In the United States, the proof is exactly twice the percentage of alcohol. Therefore, a bottle labeled "86 Proof" contains 43 percent alcohol.
* Moderate alcohol consumption is considered to be two drinks per day. A "drink" has been standardized as ½ ounce of pure (100 percent) alcohol, meaning a moderate drinker can consume 1 ounce of pure alcohol a day. This makes a difference in the volume consumed per serving, since the percentage of alcohol in beer is much lower than that in whiskey. In general, two "drinks" a day breaks down as follows: 1 ounce of 100-proof (50 percent alcohol) liquor; 1¼ ounces of 80-proof (40 percent alcohol) liquor; 3 ounces of fortified wine (16½ percent alcohol) like sherry or port; 4 ounces of (12½ percent alcohol) table wine; or 12 ounces of (4 percent alcohol) beer.

* Rubbing the rim of a bottle with waxed paper keeps it from dripping.

* Keeping liquors such as Scotch and bourbon refrigerated means your mixed drinks won't dilute as fast when poured over ice cubes.

* For drinks to be shaken or stirred with ice (such as a Martini), don't refrigerate the liquor—some dilution with melted ice is necessary for the proper balance and texture.

* Buy miniature bottles of liquor or liqueur if you need only a little for cooking.

* Like your brandy warm on a cold winter night? Microwave it in the glass (make sure it isn't lead crystal) on high for about 10 seconds.

COOKING WITH LIQUOR AND LIQUEURS (*see also* WINE IN FOOD)

* Though it has long been thought that alcohol evaporates when heated, a USDA study has disproved that theory. In fact, from 5 to 85 percent alcohol may remain in a cooked dish, depending on various factors, including how the food was heated, the cooking time and the source of the alcohol. Even the smallest trace of alcohol may be ill-advised for alcoholics and those with alcohol-related illnesses.

* Alcohol freezes at a much lower temperature than other liquids like water and milk, which means that a frozen dessert (such as ice cream) that contains too much alcohol won't freeze properly.

* Moderation is the key when adding liquor to food. Start with a little—you can always add more.

* After adding liquor to a dish, allow enough cooking time to remove the alcohol's harsh taste. That only takes about 3 minutes in a boiling mixture, but can take up to 30 minutes in one that's simmering or baking.

* Full-bodied potables contribute more flavor than their lighter counterparts. For example, use dark or golden rum rather than light rum, gold tequila instead of white (or silver) tequila and dark beer (which, of course, isn't "liquor") over light beer.

> *The best thing about liver is how virtuous it makes*
> *you feel after you've eaten some.*
> —Bruce Jay Friedman, American author

LIVER

TIDBIT   Food for thought: Liver lovers are generally avid in their enthusiasm. Most know it's a nutritional powerhouse packed with iron and vitamins A, D and B-complex. Many know and don't care that it's also loaded with cholesterol, making it hazardous for those at coronary risk. Because the liver acts as a clearinghouse for substances that enter the body, it tends to store and absorb unwanted chemicals, medicines and hormones consumed by the animal. The older the animal, the greater the accumulation of these unwanted substances. Whether such potential contaminants are offset by liver's nutritional value is still in question.

PURCHASING Beef and calf's liver are the two most popular types of liver. Beef liver is a reddish-brown color, calf's liver a pale pinkish brown. Other animal livers used for cooking are lamb, pork, poultry and goose. Liver from a mature animal is less tender and has a stronger odor and flavor than that from a younger one. Choose liver that has a bright color and moist (but not slick) surface. It should have a fresh, clean smell.

STORING Refrigerate, loosely wrapped, for no more than 2 days.

PREPARING

* Tenderize liver by soaking it in milk to cover for 2 hours in the refrigerator. Discard the milk and cook the liver as desired.

* Tomato juice also acts as a liver tenderizer. Cover the liver with the juice and refrigerate for 3 hours. If you want to use the juice as a soup or sauce base, boil for 5 minutes before doing so.

* Liver is easier to grind if you cook it first for 5 minutes. Or cut it into strips and partially freeze before grinding. Run a piece of bread through the grinder to help clean it.

* Liver becomes very tough when overcooked. Better to slightly undercook it and allow the residual heat to finish the job.

* When making a sauce that has liver blood in it, add a teaspoon or two of lemon juice to keep it from coagulating.

> *I personally see no significant difference between a lobster and, say, a giant Madagascar hissing cockroach. . . . I do not eat lobsters, although I once had a close call.*
> —Dave Barry, American humorist

LOBSTERS *see also* SHELLFISH

TIDBIT The Latin *locusta* is thought by some to be the root for the word "lobster," as well, oddly enough, for the word "locust." The Old English *loppestre* ("spidery creature") is the predecessor of the word "lobster." All of which may explain why the lobsters are often called "insects of the sea."

PURCHASING

* Live lobsters: Choose those that are active—when picked up, the tail should curl under the body. Lobsters stored on ice may be sluggish, so the tail test is particularly important. Ask your fishmonger when the lob-

sters were caught. Some markets keep lobsters for a week or more, and these won't be as succulent as those that are fresh-caught.

* Cooked lobsters: Whole lobsters should have their tails curled, a sign that they were alive when cooked. Cooked lobster meat should be sweet-smelling and snow white.
* Frozen tails: Make sure the package is untorn, with no sign of frost. Any visible meat should be free of dry-looking spots.
* How much per serving: 8-ounce lobster tail; 1- to 1½-pound whole lobster; 5 ounces cooked lobster meat.

EQUIVALENT   Cooked meat: 1 pound = about 2 cups pieces

STORING   Refrigerate live lobsters, on a bed of ice covered by a damp cloth, for no more than a day or two. If possible, cook the lobster the day it's purchased.

PREPARING

* Be humane and kill the lobster before cooking it. Chilling it in the refrigerator (40°F) for several hours reduces nerve function and metabolic activity, which purportedly makes the lobster less sensitive. Kill it either by splitting it lengthwise along the back, which severs its nerve ganglia, or by plunging the tip of a large, sharp knife behind the head in the middle of the back.
* To keep lobster tails from curling during cooking, insert a metal or bamboo skewer lengthwise through the middle; remove the skewer from the cooked lobster.
* Lobster's done as soon as the meat turns opaque. Don't overcook it or it'll be stringy and tough.
* When broiling lobster, keep the surface moist by brushing with melted butter several times.
* Lobster that's to be served cold will be more flavorful if slightly under-cooked, and then cooled in the cooking liquid.
* A lobster's roe (called "coral") and tomalley (its liver) are prized by many lobster lovers.
* Before dismembering a cooked whole lobster, cover it with a kitchen towel so the juices won't spurt all over.
* Intimidated when a cooked whole lobster is set before you? Here's what you do: First eat the tail meat, then twist off the claws and pick out the meat. Next come the legs—break off each one and suck out the meat. Last, eat any meat in the body cavity, along with the tomalley and (if it's a female lobster) the coral.
* When making a sauce for lobster, put pieces of cracked lobster shell in the liquid to be used, bring to a boil, then reduce the heat and cook 30

minutes. After straining, this flavorful broth will add depth and richness to your sauce.

* When adding cooked lobster to a hot dish, do so at the last minute. Otherwise, the lobster will become overcooked and flavorless.

LOW-CALORIE AND LOW-FAT COOKING *see* COOKING AND EATING LIGHT

When I have eaten mangoes, I have felt like Eve.
—Rose Macaulay, British novelist

MANGO(ES)   *see also* FRUIT, GENERAL

TIDBIT   The mango tree is considered sacred in India and thought to have magical and aphrodisiacal powers. One bite of a mango's golden orange, exceedingly juicy and exotically sweet-tart flesh and you know that mangos are truly a gift of the gods.

PURCHASING

* Fresh fruit: Choose those with an unblemished, yellow skin blushed with red. The larger the mango, the higher the fruit-to-seed ratio. Ripe mangoes will yield to gentle palm pressure and have a perfumy fragrance. Avoid those with a shriveled or black-speckled skin. Green mango is the fruit in its unripe form. It's sold both fresh and dried in Asian and Indian markets.

* Other forms: **Mango purée** is available fresh or frozen in Indian, Mexican and natural food stores; **mango nectar** and **canned mangoes** can be found in supermarkets.

EQUIVALENT   1 medium (12 ounces) = about 1 cup chopped

STORING   Refrigerate ripe mangoes in a plastic bag for up to 5 days.

PREPARING

* Place underripe fruit in a paper bag (pierced with a few holes) with an apple at room temperature for 1 to 3 days. Green, rock-hard mangoes will probably never ripen.

* Peel the whole mango with a sharp paring knife before removing the fruit from the huge, flat seed to which it clings tenaciously.

* To remove the flesh from the seed, stand the fruit on its wide end. Use a sharp knife to cut the fruit vertically, sliding the knife along the seed on

one side. Repeat on the other side, which will give you 2 large pieces. Then cut away the remaining meat and cut as desired.

✴ Be careful when eating mango—the juice will stain your clothing.

MAPLE SYRUP *see also* SYRUPS *for general information on reliquefying, measuring, and so on.*

PURCHASING   There are several kinds of "maple" syrup on the market today. **Pure maple syrup** is sap that's been boiled until much of the water has evaporated. It has a more subtle flavor and isn't as sweet or viscous as artificial maple syrups. Pure maple syrup is graded according to color and flavor, the highest grade being AA or Fancy. In general, the higher the grade, the lighter the color and more delicate the flavor. Although pure maple syrup is more expensive than its imitators, its flavor is far superior. **Maple-flavored syrup** is a mixture of a low-cost syrup (such as corn syrup) and a small amount of pure maple syrup. **Pancake syrup** is nothing more than corn syrup flavored with artificial maple extract.

STORING   Refrigerate pure maple syrup for up to 1 year after opening. Artificially flavored syrups may be stored at room temperature.

SUBSTITUTION IN BAKED GOODS: For each ½ cup of granular sugar, substitute ⅓ cup maple syrup and reduce the liquid ingredient(s) by 2 tablespoons; add ¼ teaspoon baking soda to the dry ingredients. Reduce the oven temperature by 25°F.

USING

✴ Heat refrigerated syrup (or at least bring it to room temperature) before using on pancakes or waffles.

✴ To heat a glass bottle of syrup, place it in a pan of hot water over low heat. Or pour syrup into a pan and heat directly, then pour into a pitcher.

✴ Or heat syrup in the microwave on high for 30 to 60 seconds, depending on the amount and how cold it is.

✴ If mold develops on pure maple syrup, discard the syrup.

✴ For maple butter: Beat 1 stick (½ cup) softened, unsalted butter with a pinch of salt until creamy. Beating constantly, slowly drizzle in ¼ cup pure maple syrup.

✴ Maple syrup is great drizzled over ice cream, puddings, cakes, hot cereals, baked apples—you name it!

✴ Substitute pure maple syrup for honey measure for measure in baked goods like cakes, pies, breads.

✴ Use it instead of corn syrup in frostings.

✴ Maple syrup makes a delicious glaze for carrots, ham or ribs.

*Don't use margarine—the only good use for margarine
is for children's suppositories.*
—George Leonard Herter, American author

MARGARINE   *see also* BUTTER; FATS AND OILS; LABEL TERMS; LARD

PURCHASING

* **Regular margarines** are 80 percent fat. Those lowest in cholesterol are made from a high percentage of polyunsaturated liquid safflower or corn oil. Check labels for the word "hydrogenated," which refers to the process of hardening unsaturated oil into a semisolid (*see* FATS AND OILS), thereby transforming it into a saturated fat, which destroys any benefits the oil had as a polyunsaturate. **Soft margarines** are made entirely with vegetable oil and specially processed to be spreadable. **Whipped margarines** have had air (sometimes equal to half the volume) beaten into them.

* **Other forms: Cholesterol-lowering margarines** are made from a blend of polyunsaturated oils and contain no hydrogenated trans fatty acids. They can lower blood cholesterol levels by as much as 10 percent (each percentage point producing a 3 percent decrease in heart-disease risk). **Reduced-fat margarines** range from 25 to 65 percent less fat than regular margarine and contain a relatively high proportion of water. **Fat-free margarines** (yes, you heard right) contain a high proportion of water, along with gelatin, lactose and rice starch. **Liquid margarine** (sold in squeeze bottles) has been processed to be semiliquid when cold. **Butter-margarine blends** are typically proportioned 40 to 60 percent, respectively.

STORING   Refrigerate all styles for up to 2 months; freeze for up to 6 months. Margarine easily absorbs flavors, so wrap it airtight.

USING

* Regular margarine can be substituted for butter satisfactorily in most recipes, with the exception of certain preparations like Danish pastry, croissants and puff pastry, and toffee candy.

* Never substitute reduced-fat or nonfat, soft or whipped margarine in recipes calling for regular butter or margarine. Such products contain too much air and water, and the results will undoubtedly be disastrous.

* Substituting margarine for butter may affect the texture of some cookies. The dough will be slightly softer, which can affect cookies that should have a specific shape.

M MARINADES; MARINATING

TIDBIT Marinades flavor food (primarily meat, poultry and fish) but, contrary to popular belief, do little to tenderize it. Most marinades contain an acid ingredient (like lemon juice, tomato juice, vinegar or wine), which helps "relax" protein fibers. But that simply softens the surface and no more than about ¼ inch deep. Bottom line? Don't expect more from a marinade than it can deliver. If you want tender results from an inexpensive cut of meat, give it TLC with slow, long cooking.

* The easiest way to marinate is to place the food and marinade in a large plastic zip-closure bag. Squeeze out as much air as possible before sealing the bag. Turn the bag several times to coat the food with the marinade. Set the bag on a large plate and refrigerate, turning the bag occasionally to distribute the marinade. Easy, efficient and saves on cleanup.

* Any container used for marinating should be nonreactive, so use glass or ceramic dishes. The acidic ingredients in a marinade react with metal, which not only can damage the container, but can cause the food to take on an unpleasant metallic taste.

* If a marinade doesn't completely cover the food, turn the food every couple of hours so it's evenly exposed to the flavorings. Always cover the mixture to keep moisture in.

* Refrigerate marinating foods—letting them stand at room temperature invites bacteria growth.

* Large cuts of meat, such as roasts, benefit from longer marinating—at least 24 hours and up to 2 days.

* To speed the marinating process for large cuts of meat, have your butcher halve or butterfly them. This also offers more surfaces for the marinade to flavor.

* Whole chicken can take up to 12 hours to marinate; skinless pieces, a quarter of that time.

* Fish fillets and steaks require the least marinating time—30 to 60 minutes respectively.

* Cuts like skirt and flank steaks will be more tender and flavorful if you cut diagonal slashes about ⅛-inch deep against the grain on both sides in the flesh before marinating.

* A marinade often makes a delicious sauce for the finished fish, meat or poultry that's been marinating in it. Just be sure to boil the marinade for 5 minutes before serving to destroy any harmful bacteria that may have been transferred from the raw food.

* Don't baste food during the last 15 minutes of cooking time with a marinade that hasn't been boiled. The cooking time may be too short to kill

any bacteria that was transferred from the raw meat to the marinade. An option is to reserve some of the marinade before marinating the food, and use it for later basting.

* Salad dressing is an easy, instant marinade for vegetables like bell peppers, mushrooms or tomatoes.

SPICY BOURBON MARINADE

A great marinade for everything from flank steak to pork chops. Combine ½ cup bourbon, ½ cup spicy tomato juice, ¼ cup dark corn syrup, 2 medium garlic cloves, minced, 1 teaspoon coarsely ground pepper and ¼ teaspoon ground allspice in a large, shallow glass or ceramic pan. Add the meat to be marinated; cover tightly with plastic wrap. Refrigerate for 24 hours, turning meat once or twice during that time.

MARSHMALLOWS

PURCHASING Marshmallows come in regular size (about 1½ inches in diameter) and miniature (½ inch in diameter), in white or pastel colors. Marshmallow crème or fluff is a thick, whipped mixture available in jars.

EQUIVALENTS

* Regular marshmallows: 16-ounce package = about 60; 1 cup regular = about 6 to 7 whole or snipped
* Miniature marshmallows: 10½-ounce package = 400 pieces; 1 cup = about 85
* Marshmallow crème: 7 to 7½-ounce jar = 2½ cups; 16-ounce jar = 5¼ cups; 1 tablespoon = 1 regular marshmallow

STORING Marshmallows can be tightly sealed and stored at room temperature for at least 6 months. Store them in a tightly sealed plastic bag in the freezer and you won't have to worry about them drying out.

USING

* Marshmallows are easier to cut if they're frozen.
* Kitchen shears are perfect for snipping marshmallows into the right size.
* When snipping room-temperature marshmallows, dip kitchen shears in cold water whenever necessary to keep them from sticking.
* To soften hard marshmallows, tightly seal them in a plastic bag with 2 to 3 slices fresh white bread (not French or Italian) and let stand for 3 days.
* Soften them quickly in a microwave oven on high, the timing depends on how many there are. Start with 10 seconds.
* For kids' birthday parties, top home-baked cupcakes with a whole marshmallow about 3 minutes before removing them from the oven. The marshmallow will melt and form a frosting.

MARZIPAN *see* ALMOND PASTE

M

MAYONNAISE   *see also* EGGS

TIDBIT   Scottish poet and author Robert Louis Stevenson, who moved to Samoa in 1889 because he suffered from tuberculosis, was purportedly in the process of making mayonnaise when he died. Obviously he was a man of distinctive taste to the end.

PURCHASING   A wide selection of mayonnaise can be found in supermarkets today—from real to imitation, and in styles ranging from nonfat to low-fat to regular. The calorie count for 1 tablespoon ranges from 100 for the real stuff, to about 8 for the nonfat, imitation style. If your figure can afford it, there's nothing like the real thing, particularly if it's homemade.

STORING   Commercial mayonnaise can be stored, unopened, in a cool, dark place for at least 6 months. Once opened, refrigerate for up to 6 months. **Homemade mayonnaise** should be covered and refrigerated for no more than 1 week. All mayonnaise separates if frozen.

GENERAL

* If mayonnaise is too thick, gradually stir in whipping cream or milk until it reaches the desired consistency.

* Add pizzazz and flavor to store-bought mayo by stirring in 1 to 2 teaspoons of good wine vinegar, lemon juice or lime juice. You can also stir in herbs or other flavorings such as minced basil, dill, mint or watercress; or minced fresh or sautéed garlic (cooked garlic has a milder flavor); or finely grated lemon zest; or horseradish; or minced sun-dried tomatoes; or curry or chili powder; or drained pickle relish; or mustard; or crumbled blue cheese; or chopped onions or shallots.

* Instead of mayonnaise, try a mixture of half mayo, half sour cream (or plain, nonfat yogurt). The result will be a lighter, less salty flavor. To lighten the calorie count, use the low-fat versions of one or both.

* Make your own mustard mayonnaise by simply adding mustard to taste to homemade or store-bought mayo (start with about 1 teaspoon per ½ cup mayo). Use this tangy mixture in salads (like egg or tuna) and salad dressings, as a sandwich spread, or to brush over cooked baked ham or pork loin.

* Warm mayonnaise makes a wonderful sauce for chicken, fish or vegetables. Season it with minced herbs, then let stand for several hours in the refrigerator to enhance the flavors. Heat gently, just until warm, then spoon over the food just before serving.

HOMEMADE MAYONNAISE

* Once you taste homemade mayonnaise, it'll be hard to go back to the store-bought stuff—they're like completely different foods.

- If you live in an area where salmonella-infected eggs are a problem (*see* EGG SAFETY, page 179), either make homemade mayo from pasteurized liquid whole eggs or egg substitute. Use ⅛ cup for each egg yolk. For instance, if a mayo recipe calls for 2 egg yolks (or 1 whole egg), use ¼ cup of the processed eggs.

- Whole-egg homemade mayo won't be quite as rich as one made only with egg yolks.

- Extra-virgin olive oil can overpower the flavor of homemade mayonnaise. Better to use half extra virgin and half mild olive oil or vegetable oil.

- The eggs and oil should be the same temperature, so remove the eggs from the fridge at least 30 minutes before using.

- To make homemade mayo: Beat the egg yolks (or whole egg) with the salt and half the vinegar or lemon juice called for in the recipe, then begin beating in the oil—a few drops at a time—until 2 to 3 tablespoons oil have been added. At that point, you can begin adding the oil in a fine stream. When all the oil has been added, lightly beat in the remaining vinegar or lemon juice.

- The food processor makes homemade mayonnaise foolproof. The feed-tube food pusher of most machines has a tiny hole in the bottom, specifically designed with mayonnaise and other emulsions in mind. Whirl the egg yolks, salt and vinegar until combined, then fill the food pusher with oil and let the machine do the work. The oil will drip a steady drizzle into the running machine at the perfect speed for emulsification.

- If making mayo by hand (using a whisk and bowl), here's an easy way to add the oil slowly to the egg yolk-salt-vinegar mixture: Pour the oil into a paper cup with a hole punched in the bottom (hold your finger over the hole as you fill it).

- If homemade mayonnaise separates, start over with 1 beaten egg yolk; add separated mayo a drop at a time, beating continually.

- Another way to restore separated mayo is to slowly drizzle in boiling hot water, beating constantly. Start with about 1 tablespoon, adding only enough to emulsify the mixture.

JALAPEÑO AÏOLI

Aïoli is a classic garlic mayonnaise from France's Provence region. This snappy version is great with grilled meat, fish or vegetables, stirred into mashed potatoes or added to salad dressings. Turn on a food processor fitted with the metal blade. Drop in 4 peeled, medium garlic cloves, one by one; process until the garlic is chopped and clinging to the sides of the bowl. Stop the machine and scrape down the bowl. Add ½ teaspoon salt, 2½ tablespoons fresh lemon juice, 2 large egg yolks and 1½ to 2 tablespoons finely chopped jalapeño peppers; process to combine. With the machine running, gradually add 1½ cups olive oil in a very thin drizzle (or pour into the feed-tube pusher with the hole in the bottom and allow the oil to drip through on its own). Process until the oil is incorporated and the mixture is thick. For a lighter aïoli, gradually add 1 to 2 tablespoons hot water, processing until combined. Refrigerate in an airtight container for up to 1 week. Makes about 2 cups.

MEASURING; MEASUREMENTS; *see also* METRIC CONVERSIONS; METRIC MEASUREMENTS; PAN SIZES

GENERAL

* Accurate measurements are important in all cooking, but probably most crucial in baking recipes.
* A recipe's wording tells you how to measure ingredients: "1 cup flour, sifted" tells you to measure a cup of flour, then sift; "1 cup sifted flour" means to sift the flour, then measure. Likewise, "2 cups whipped cream" refers to measuring the already whipped cream, whereas "2 cups cream, whipped" tells you to measure the cream, then whip it, which would actually yield about 4 cups whipped cream.
* **Liquid measuring cups** range in size from 1 to 8 cups (the latter is really more of a measuring "bowl"). To use, set the cup on the countertop, pour in the liquid, then bend down and read the measurement at eye level.
* **Dry measuring cups** come in nested sets which typically include 2-cup, 1-cup, ½-cup, ⅓-cup, ¼-cup and ⅛-cup sizes.
* Keep a scoop (available at supermarkets or kitchenware shops) in each canister (flour, sugar, and so on) to facilitate scooping the ingredients into a measuring cup.
* A kitchen scale is great for measuring smaller amounts from a larger bag. For instance, if a recipe calls for 3 ounces of nuts, and you have a 12-ounce bag, the scale will make life easy.

MEASURING INGREDIENTS

* Never measure ingredients directly over the mixing bowl. A slip of the wrist and flour, sugar, salt, and so on, could spill over the measuring cup or spoon and into the rest of the ingredients, upsetting the recipe's balance.

* Measure ingredients like flour and confectioners' sugar by stirring, then spooning into the measuring cup and leveling off with the straight edge of a knife. Don't tap or press the ingredient into the cup before measuring.
* Put a sheet of waxed paper under the cup into which you're scooping ingredients like sugar, flour and cocoa powder so you can easily return any spills to the container.
* Measure brown sugar by packing it down firmly into the cup; level with a knife.
* For ingredients like nuts, coconut and chopped dried fruits, fill the cup and level with your fingers.
* Measure shortening or softened butter or margarine by packing it into the measuring cup or measuring spoon and leveling with the back of a knife. Keep the cup clean by lining it with plastic wrap before packing in the fat.
* Butter or margarine in stick form can be measured by simply cutting off the amount needed (the wrapping will be marked)—1 stick = ½ cup or 8 tablespoons.
* Fat can also be measured by using a liquid measuring cup. If you need ½ cup bacon fat or other type of fat, fill a 1-cup glass measure with ½ cup water. Add fat until the water reaches the 1-cup mark. Drain off the water and use the fat.
* Before measuring syrupy sweeteners, such as honey and corn syrup, lightly coat a measuring spoon or liquid measuring cup with vegetable oil. Every drop of the syrup will easily slip out. The same result can be accomplished if you measure the oil or fat called for in a recipe and then use the same (unwashed) utensil as the measure. Or dip the measuring implement in very hot water before measuring the sweetener.
* To measure ground coffee, use 2 level tablespoons (1 coffee measure, ⅛ cup) per 6 ounces (¾ cup) water.

MEASURING CONTAINERS
* To determine the size of baking pans, muffin tins, and so on, use a ruler to measure the diameter of the container's top from inside edge to inside edge. Measure the depth from the inside, bottom to the top. *See also* PAN SIZES.
* Measure the volume of a casserole or soufflé dish by filling it with water, then measuring the liquid. Such dishes are most commonly found in the following sizes: 1, 1½, 2 and 3 quarts.

COMMON MEASUREMENTS AND EQUIVALENTS *see also* MET-
RIC CONVERSIONS; METRIC MEASUREMENTS)

pinch/dash	= ¹⁄₁₆ teaspoon
dollop	= 1 rounded tablespoon
½ teaspoon	= 30 drops
1 teaspoon	= ⅓ tablespoon; 60 drops
3 teaspoons	= 1 tablespoon
½ tablespoon	= 1½ teaspoons
1 tablespoon	= 3 teaspoons; ½ fluid ounce
2 tablespoons	= ⅛ cup; 1 fluid ounce
3 tablespoons	= 1½ fluid ounces; 1 jigger
4 tablespoons	= ¼ cup; 2 fluid ounces
8 tablespoons	= ½ cup; 4 fluid ounces
16 tablespoons	= 1 cup; 8 fluid ounces; ½ pint
⅛ cup	= 2 tablespoons; 1 fluid ounce
¼ cup	= 4 tablespoons; 2 fluid ounces
⅓ cup	= 5 tablespoons plus 1 teaspoon
⅜ cup	= ¼ cup plus 2 tablespoons
½ cup	= 8 tablespoons; 4 fluid ounces
⅔ cup	= 10 tablespoons plus 2 teaspoons
⅝ cup	= ½ cup plus 2 tablespoons
¾ cup	= 12 tablespoons; 6 fluid ounces
⅞ cup	= ¾ cup plus 2 tablespoons
1 cup	= 16 tablespoons; ½ pint; 8 fluid ounces
2 cups	= 1 pint; 16 fluid ounces
3 cups	= 1½ pints; 24 fluid ounces
4 cups	= 1 quart; 32 fluid ounces
8 cups	= 2 quarts; 64 fluid ounces
1 pint	= 2 cups; 16 fluid ounces
2 pints	= 1 quart; 32 fluid ounces
1 quart	= 2 pints; 4 cups; 32 fluid ounces
4 quarts	= 1 gallon; 8 pints
1 gallon	= 4 quarts; 8 pints; 16 cups

The nearer the bone, the sweeter the meat.
—British proverb

MEAT, GENERAL *see also* BACON; BEEF; CHICKEN; CORNISH GAME HENS;
GROUND MEAT; HAM; HAMBURGERS; KIDNEYS; LAMB; LIVER; MEAT LOAF; PORK;
POULTRY; ROASTS; STEAKS; SAUSAGE; SWEETBREADS; THERMOMETERS; TURKEY; VEAL

PURCHASING

* Buy fresh meat rather than frozen. Freezing and thawing triggers the loss of some of the meat's natural juices. Cuts with a high proportion of fat and bone yield fewer servings than boneless cuts. For instance, the expected per-pound yield for spareribs is 1 to 2 servings, for chops and bone-in steaks it's 2 to 3 servings and for boneless cuts, about 4 servings. Reduce your time in the kitchen by having your butcher bone meat and chicken, cut meat for stew, or cut pockets in roasts and thick chops.
* How much per serving: boneless meat—4 to 5 ounces (3 ounces for dieters); bone-in cuts like chops and steaks—8 ounces; mostly bone cuts like shanks—10 ounces.

STORING (see individual meats for specific instructions)

* Fresh meat: Refrigerate ground meat for up to 2 days; other cuts for 3 days. All meat should be kept in the coldest part of the refrigerator. Freeze ground meats, wrapped airtight, for up to 3 months; solid cuts for up to 6 months. When freezing ground-meat patties, steaks or chops, separate them with squares of plastic wrap. That way you can pry the pieces apart and defrost as needed.
* Cooked meat: Think about how the meat will be used (for sandwiches, stir-fries and so on) and cut it to suit that purpose. Measure the quantity and label the package accordingly, including how it should be used.

PREPARING

* Defrost frozen meat overnight in the refrigerator. Or place the meat (still in its freezer-proof wrapping) in a large bowl of cool water. Change the water every half hour until the meat is defrosted.
* Whether cutting meat into slices or chunks, you'll get the most tender result if you cut against the grain.
* It's easier to thinly slice meat (like flank steak) for quick-cooking dishes like stir-fries if first you freeze the meat for 30 to 60 minutes (depending on thickness). Then use a sharp knife to cut it against the grain into ¼-inch slices.
* Freezing chunks of meat for 30 minutes will also make grinding it easier. Run a piece of bread through the grinder to help clean it.
* Avoid commercial meat tenderizers that contain MSG (monosodium glutamate) or salt, both of which extract some of the meat's natural juices.
* Papaya contains *papain*, an enzyme used chiefly in meat tenderizers. Make your own tenderizer by PURÉEING papaya and rubbing it all over the meat's surface. Or soak the meat in papaya juice, available at many supermarkets and most natural food stores. Cover and refrigerate the

meat for 3 hours. Scrape off and discard the papaya purée, pat the meat dry and cook as desired.

* Tea can also be used as a meat tenderizer, particularly for stew meat. In a Dutch oven, sear chunks of stew meat in fat or oil until very well browned. Add 2 cups strong black tea, bring to a boil, then cover and simmer for 30 minutes. Add stock or whatever liquid you wish, vegetables, herbs, and so on, and continue to cook the stew as usual.

* Other time-honored ways of tenderizing meat include pounding with a mallet, MARINATING, and long, slow, moist-heat cooking, such as BRAISING or STEWING.

* Tenderloins are covered with a thin membrane (silver skin), which contracts and warps the cut during cooking. Remove it before cooking by sliding a thin knife under the membrane and along the length of the meat; repeat until the membrane is eliminated. Or simply cut through the silver skin in 6 or 8 places along the length.

COOKING

* Don't worry if four people show up for dinner and you have only two servings of meat. Simply cut the meat in small pieces, combine it with vegetables and a sauce, and serve over rice or pasta.

* To be sure meat is cooked to a safe temperature, always use a meat THERMOMETER. According to a government survey, only 3 percent of the people who own a meat thermometer use it, particularly when cooking bacteria-susceptible meats like hamburger.

* Freezing and thawing ground meat can cause it to brown before it's cooked enough for harmful bacteria to be destroyed. Use a meat thermometer to check doneness.

* Meat will brown better and more evenly if you use paper towel to thoroughly blot the surface dry (particularly important with meat that's been marinated).

* Facilitate browning by first dusting meat lightly with flour.

* Or lightly dust all sides of a meat cut with a soupçon of sugar. The sugar will caramelize during browning, giving the meat a wonderful color and flavor with no discernible sweetness.

* Unless the cut of meat is very lean, it's often unnecessary to use much fat or oil for browning. Just lightly brush the bottom of the pan with oil. The pan should be very hot before adding the meat.

* Salt leaches some of the meat's juices, so it's best to salt toward the end of the cooking time.

* Use tongs or a pancake turner to flip meat—a fork will puncture the flesh, letting juices escape.

* **Touch test for doneness:** Press the meat lightly with your fingertip. If it's soft, the meat's rare; if it resists slightly but springs back, it's medium-rare; if the meat is quite firm, it's well-done.

* Instead of BRAISING or STEWING meat cuts in water, try more flavorful liquids like wine, beer, stock or vegetable juice.

* During cooking, a meat's juices shift to the center, causing the exterior to dry. Let cooked meat "rest" for 5 to 10 minutes to allow the juices to redistribute throughout the flesh, producing evenly moist meat that's easier to cut. Keep the meat warm during this rest period by covering it lightly with foil.

* Chop leftover cooked meat and use it in salads, soups, stir-fries, dumplings, omelet fillings, stuffed peppers or acorn squash, meat loaf, pasta sauce, tacos or burritos. Or simply slice and use it for sandwiches, or combine it with a sauce and serve over rice.

MEAT DONENESS TEMPERATURES (using a meat THERMOMETER)

* Beef and lamb: rare—120° to 130°F; medium—140° to 150°F; well-done—165° to 175°F

* Veal: medium—140°F to 150°F; well-done—160°F

* Pork: medium—145° to 155°F; well-done—165°F. Precooked ham—140°F

* Poultry: chicken and turkey—160° to 165°F for breasts, 175°F for thighs and legs; duck and goose—175°F

* Ground meats: beef, veal, lamb and pork—160°F; chicken and turkey—165°F

* Sausage: 160°F

MEATBALLS *see also* GROUND MEAT *as well as the following* MEAT LOAF *tips for general information.*

* To quickly shape meatballs that are uniform in size, spoon the mixture onto a sheet of plastic wrap or waxed paper. Pat into the thickness equal to what you want the meatball's diameter to be. In other words, if you want 2-inch meatballs, form the mixture into a square that's 2 inches thick. Cut that square into 2-inch squares, then roll the cubes into balls.

* Or, for 2-inch meatballs, form the meatball mixture into a log 2 inches in diameter, then cut the log into 2-inch lengths and roll the pieces into balls.

* Or use a small ice cream scoop to shape uniform meatballs.

* Dampen your hands with cold water before working with a meatball mixture and it won't stick.

* Use a gentle touch to form meatballs or the mixture may fall apart. Conversely, it can become too compacted and the resulting meatballs will be dense instead of tender.

* For crispy meatballs, roll them in seasoned flour or cornstarch before frying. Cornmeal adds flavor and crunch.
* Put a ½-inch chunk of cheese or cold herb butter (*see* COMPOUND BUTTER, PAGE 72) in the center of a meatball, forming the meat around it. By the time the meatballs are done, the filling will be melted and ooze out deliciously with every bite.
* Although meatballs are typically fried, they can just as easily be baked. Put them on a baking sheet with shallow sides and bake at 375°F for 20 to 25 minutes, or until done.

MEAT LOAF   *see also* GROUND MEAT
MAKING THE MIXTURE

* Plan ahead by doubling a meat loaf recipe and freeze one for later.
* Ground round is the best choice for meat loaf—it has less fat (which would be absorbed by BREAD CRUMBS) than regular ground beef and more fat than ground sirloin (which would produce a dry meat loaf).
* For a moister, more tender meat loaf, use coarsely ground meat instead of finely ground.
* Add a cup of grated cheese to the meat loaf mixture for a flavorsome treat. Top with another ½ cup grated cheese 15 minutes before the meat loaf is done.
* For a juicy, more flavorful meat loaf, add ⅓ cup of liquid (such as tomato or vegetable juice, wine or beef broth) per pound of meat.
* Enrich the flavor by substituting red wine or dark beer for any liquid called for in the recipe.
* Use soft bread crumbs instead of dried crumbs for a moister, more tender meat loaf.
* Add fiber and nutrition by substituting ⅓ cup oat bran for ⅓ cup bread crumbs. If your meat loaf recipe doesn't include bread crumbs, add ¼ cup oat bran plus 2 tablespoons liquid such as milk, water or beef broth.
* Cut back on meat and create a moist, delicious meat loaf by substituting 1 cup of finely grated potato or carrot (or a half cup of each) for a quarter pound of the meat. Or add ½ cup mashed potatoes to the mixture.
* To keep your hands clean when making a meat loaf mixture, put the ingredients in a large, zip-closure plastic bag, seal and mix the contents together. Or don a pair of latex gloves and squish away.

FORMING AND BAKING

* Make a special "meat loaf pan" so the loaf won't sit in puddles of rendered fat while it bakes. Buy an inexpensive metal loaf pan (or an alu-

minum foil pan) and use an awl or ice pick to punch holes in the bottom at 1½-inch intervals (punch from the inside out). Put the meat loaf mixture in the pierced pan and place it on a rack set inside a baking pan. The grease will drain out as the meat loaf bakes, and you'll consume fewer calories.

* Spray the meat loaf pan with cooking spray (or lightly coat with vegetable oil) to keep the meat loaf from sticking and speed cleanup.

* Make individual servings by baking meat loaf in large, greased muffin tins. Brush the tops with bottled barbecue or marinara sauce, or sprinkle with grated cheese. Small meat loaves bake faster, so watch the timing.

* Or press a meat loaf mixture into a large, greased pie plate. This thin meat "pie" will bake in half the time a loaf would.

* Once the meat loaf is in the pan, press down on it firmly with the back of a large spoon to level the surface and compress the mixture so it doesn't fall apart after baking.

* Minimize surface cracking by rubbing the top of a meat loaf mixture with cold water to smooth it.

* **Mashed potato–topped meat loaf:** About 20 minutes before the meat loaf is done, cover the top with a 1-inch thick layer of mashed potatoes. Brush lightly with extra virgin olive oil or melted butter, or sprinkle with about ¼ cup grated cheese, and return to the oven. You can also mix the cheese with the mashed potatoes before spreading them on top of the loaf. Just before serving, broil the surface until golden brown.

* For an easy hors d'oeuvre, bake meat loaf in 2 or 3 long, thin log shapes about the diameter of a baguette or loaf of cocktail rye. Refrigerate the meat loaf logs until firm, then slice thinly and serve on bread or toast slices (spread with mustard butter), and top with a thin sliver of cornichon.

* If you plan to freeze a whole meat loaf, first line the pan with foil, allowing enough overlap to cover and seal the finished loaf. Bake as usual, drain off the grease and cool in the refrigerator before sealing the foil. Double wrap in a plastic bag and freeze for up to 6 months.

* When done, meat loaf should register 170°F on a meat THERMOMETER inserted into the center.

* Use a bulb baster to remove excess grease from around a cooked meat loaf.

* After removing the baked meat loaf from the oven, run a knife around the edges, then let it stand in the pan for 10 to 15 minutes. This allows it to "set" and makes it easier to remove and cut.

* If you're tired of the proverbial meat loaf sandwich, crumble leftover meat loaf and use it in chili. Or combine it with a sauce and serve over rice or noodles.

MEAT TENDERIZERS   *see* MEAT, GENERAL

MEAT THERMOMETER   *see* THERMOMETERS

> *Success to me is having ten honeydew melons and eating only the top half of each one.*
> —Barbra Streisand, American actress and singer

MELONS   *see also* FRUIT, GENERAL; WATERMELON
TIDBIT   Melons are an ancient fruit—Egyptians are depicted with them in hieroglyphics dating back to 2400 B.C. There are two broad categories of this gourd-family fruit: WATERMELON and muskmelon. Watermelon, with its watery texture and simple flavor, is considered the less sophisticated of the two, which couldn't matter less to watermelon fans on a hot summer day. Muskmelons, with their more exotic, complex flavors, can be broken down into two types—those with netted skins (such as cantaloupe, Persian melon and Santa Claus melon) and smooth-skinned varieties (like casaba, Crenshaw and honeydew).
PURCHASING
* When ripe, muskmelons will give slightly when pressed with your finger at the blossom end; their odor will be sweet and perfumy. Choose melons that are heavy for their size; avoid those that are soft, shriveled or moldy. If you can't find a ripe melon, choose another fruit. Melons picked before maturity will never reach their full flavor potential. To confirm that a melon was picked before its time, check the perimeter of the crater at the stem end. Jagged edges signal that the melon was yanked from the vine before it was ready.
* Ripeness characteristics for the following melons: **cantaloupe**—a thick, well-raised, cream-colored netting over a golden-green rind; **casaba**—an even-colored yellow rind with a slightly wrinkled appearance; **Crenshaw**—a golden green, smooth, slightly ribbed rind; **honeydew**—an almost indistinguishable wrinkling on the creamy yellow rind's surface, often detectable only by touch; **Persian**—pale green rind with a delicate netting; **Santa Claus**—oval-shape with a splotchy green and yellow skin with stripes.

EQUIVALENTS
* Cantaloupe: 1 medium = 2 pounds, 3 cups chopped
* Crenshaw: 1 medium = 3 pounds, 4 to 5 cups chopped
* Honeydew: 1 medium = 2 pounds, 3 cups chopped

STORING Refrigerate whole, ripe melons for up to 5 days; cut melons, sealed in a plastic bag, for up to 3 days. Cut melons quickly absorb other food odors, and their own odor can ruin other foods, so make sure the wrapping's airtight. Store slightly underripe melons at room temperature. Speed softening by putting the melon in a paper bag with an apple.

PREPARING
* **Salmonella and melons:** Melons are grown on the ground, which means that their skin can become contaminated by animal or human waste, or that contamination can be transferred from the harvester's hands to the melon. In particular, a cantaloupe's netted exterior creates the perfect surface to which a pathogen called *Salmonella Poona* can cling. This means that the knife used to halve a melon can transfer any salmonella there might be on the melon's skin directly to the flesh. This is why health-safety experts recommend scrubbing a melon (particularly cantaloupes) with tepid water and a soft brush, rinsing well. Likewise, wash surfaces that have come in contact with the melon, such as cutting board and hands.
* Use a large spoon or an ice cream scoop to remove the seeds from a melon.
* Leaving the seeds in a halved melon during storage will help keep it moist.
* For the fullest flavor, serve melon at room temperature or barely chilled. Let refrigerated melon stand at room temperature for 30 minutes before serving. A sprinkling of salt brings out a melon's flavor.
* Hollow out a small cantaloupe (or other melon) half, line it with lettuce leaves and use it as a serving bowl for fruit salad.

MELON-MINT MEDLEY

Just as good for breakfast as it is for a light dessert. Combine 2 cups orange juice, ½ cup finely chopped fresh mint leaves, ½ teaspoon ground cinnamon, ¼ teaspoon *each* ground allspice and ginger, and honey or sugar to taste in a large bowl. Add 4 to 5 cups melon balls or chunks (honeydew, cantaloupe, watermelon); lightly toss to combine. Cover and refrigerate for 3 to 4 hours. Let stand for 30 minutes at room temperature before serving. Serves 4 to 6.

M

M

FROSTY MELON FRAPPÉ

An hour beforehand, put two wineglasses in the freezer to get frosty. In a blender, combine ⅔ cup plain, low-fat yogurt, 2½ cups cold melon chunks, 2 tablespoons granulated sugar, ¾ teaspoon pure vanilla extract and 4 ice cubes; process until smooth. Pour into 2 frosted glasses; garnish with mint sprigs.

MERINGUE; MERINGUES *see also* EGGS (Egg Whites, page 180); PIE

TIDBIT There are two basic styles of meringue—soft and hard. **Soft meringue,** used as a topping for pies, puddings and other desserts such as baked Alaska, is baked only until the peaks are nicely browned and the valleys golden. **Hard meringue** has a higher proportion of sugar and is formed into shapes (tiny confections or containers for fruit, ice cream, and so on), then baked at a very low temperature (200°F) until firm. Italian meringue, made by beating hot SUGAR SYRUP into stiffly beaten egg whites, can be used to create either soft or hard meringue.

GENERAL

* *See* EGG WHITES, page 180, *for general information on egg whites.*
* Making meringue on a humid day creates problems—sugar absorbs moisture, which can produce a meringue that's soft and gooey or one that beads.
* Before adding sugar to egg whites, beat the whites at high speed to the soft-peak stage. Beating constantly, add sugar 1 to 2 tablespoons at a time, beating until the sugar is dissolved and the whites are glossy and stiff.
* Meringue won't "weep" (exude moisture) if you blend 1 teaspoon cornstarch with the sugar before beating it into the egg whites.
* For high-rise meringue, blend about ½ teaspoon baking powder into the sugar before beating it into the egg whites.
* Test to make sure all the sugar is dissolved by rubbing a dab of the meringue between your thumb and index finger—it should feel smooth, not gritty.
* Additions like grated chocolate or ground nuts should be gently folded into the meringue so as not to deflate it.

SOFT MERINGUE

* If you're in an area where bacterial contamination of eggs is a problem, soft-meringue pie topping can be risky. Eliminate any threat by spreading an even layer of meringue (don't mound it in the center) over the surface of a hot pie filling. Bake at 350°F for 15 minutes.
* Beads on the surface of a baked meringue can be caused by several factors: Humid weather; the sugar didn't dissolve completely during beat-

[294]

ing (usually because it was added too fast); the meringue wasn't baked immediately; it was underbaked; it was baked at too high a temperature; or the pie cooled too quickly.

* Spread a meringue pie topping so it just touches the crust. That way, it won't shrink during or after baking and there won't be any watery edges.

* Create a delicate, crispy "crust" on a meringue's surface by sprinkling it with sifted confectioners' sugar just before baking.

* A meringue pie topping won't crack if you cool it at room temperature (away from drafts) before refrigerating.

HARD MERINGUE

* A baking sheet lined with PARCHMENT PAPER is the best surface on which to bake. Or grease the baking sheet or pie pan with shortening.

* Bake at a very low temperature (200°F) for a long period of time to dry out and crisp the meringue.

* Allow meringues to dry completely in the oven. Removing them prematurely can result in a texture that's gummy rather than crisp.

* When a hard meringue's done it'll easily peel away from the parchment paper or release from the baking sheet. If it sticks, return it to the oven for a few minutes. Cool slightly before removing from the paper or baking sheet.

* Check a meringue pie shell for doneness by flicking it with your finger. It'll sound hollow when it's done.

* Store hard meringues, wrapped airtight first in a plastic bag, then in a sealed container, for up to 2 weeks. In humid climates meringues should be frozen, and will keep for up to 3 months.

METRIC CONVERSIONS; METRIC MEASUREMENTS *see also* MEASURMENTS; MEASURING; PAN SIZES

* The metric system of weights and measures is used by most of the world's countries (the United States still predominantly uses American Standard measurements). The key in converting measurements is to remember that in each case the same number is used to either divide or multiply with. For example, when you're converting *to* metric (from cups to liters), *multiply* the number of cups by .236 for the equivalent in liters. When converting *from* metric (from liters to cups), *divide* the number of liters by .236 to get the cup equivalency. Whether converting from cups to liters or vice-versa, remember it's important to adjust all measurements. Otherwise, the proportions of the ingredients could be critically imbalanced.

* Following are some formulas to help you with metric conversion:

TO CONVERT:	DO THIS:
centimeters to inches	divide centimeters by 2.54
cups to liters	multiply cups by 0.236
cups to milliliters	multiply cups by 236.59
gallons to liters	multiply gallons by 3.785
grams to ounces	divide grams by 28.35
inches to centimeters	multiply inches by 2.54
kilograms to pounds	divide kilograms by 0.454
liters to cups	divide liters by 0.236
liters to gallons	divide liters by 3.785
liters to pints	divide liters by 0.473
liters to quarts	divide liters by 0.946
milliliters to cups	divide milliliters by 236.59
milliliters to fluid ounces	divide milliliters by 29.57
milliliters to tablespoons	divide milliliters by 14.79
milliliters to teaspoons	divide milliliters by 4.93
ounces to grams	multiply ounces by 28.35
ounces to milliliters	multiply ounces by 29.57
pints to liters	multiply pints by 0.473
pounds to kilograms	multiply pounds by 0.454
quarts to liters	multiply quarts by 0.946
tablespoons to milliliters	multiply tablespoons by 14.79
teaspoons to milliliters	multiply teaspoons by 4.93

Once we sowed wild oats, now we cook them in the microwave.
—Irena Chalmers, Anglo-American wit, author, teacher

MICROWAVE COOKING *see also* COOKING, GENERAL
TIDBIT Microwave ovens work by converting electric energy into microwave energy—short, high-frequency electromagnetic waves similar to those emitted by ordinary daylight and radio waves. This energy vibrates the water molecules in food at an incredibly fast rate, creating friction that heats and cooks the food. The reason microwaves travel so extraordinarily fast, thereby cooking food so quickly, is because they're so short. These waves are attracted to the fat, moisture and sugar in food, and cook from the outside in, penetrating only to a depth of about 1½ to 2 inches. Microwaves cook food from all directions (top, bottom and sides) at once. The center of the food is generally cooked by heat conduction.

THE OVEN

* *Note:* Timing in the following tips will depend on the wattage size, and cleanliness of your oven.
* Most microwave recipes are written for a 650- to 700-watt oven. To adjust the cooking time for an oven that's more (or less) powerful, add (or subtract) about 20 seconds per minute per 100 watts.
* Read the oven's instruction manual so you'll know exactly how your particular oven operates. It's important to know the oven's wattage: If a recipe's been tested for a 700-watt oven, and yours is only 500 watts, the timing must be adjusted.
* Determine an oven's wattage by timing how long it takes for 1 cup of room temperature water to come to a boil in a clean oven on high: 850- to 1,000-watt oven—under 2 minutes; 650- to 850-watt oven—2 to 3 minutes; 400- to 650-watt oven—3 to 4 minutes.
* Most microwave recipes are written for 650- to 700-watt ovens. To convert the cooking time to a lower-wattage oven: For a 650-watt oven, add 10 seconds (or less) for each minute stated in the recipe; for a 600-watt oven, add 20 seconds for each minute stated in the recipe; for a 500-watt oven, add 40 seconds for each minute stated in the recipe.
* All microwave ovens have areas that the waves don't cover as evenly as they do the rest of the space, which means hot spots and uneven cooking if the food isn't turned during cooking. A turntable eliminates this problem by rotating the food. Inexpensive turntables are available in the kitchenware section of most department stores and many specialty shops. Be sure to measure your oven before buying one to be sure it will fit.
* If you don't have a turntable, here's how to determine where the hot spots are: Line the oven bottom, corner to corner, with waxed paper. Spread the paper almost to the corners with a ⅛-inch layer of pancake batter. Cook on high, checking every 30 seconds, until the batter begins to cook. In most ovens, some of the batter will be cooked through, while other spots are still wet, which tells you exactly where food cooks fastest and enables you to adjust or stir as necessary.
* Lining the bottom of your oven with waxed paper keeps cleanup at a minimum.
* To clean the oven cavity: In a 4-cup measure, combine 2 cups water with 2 tablespoons each baking soda and lemon juice. Cook on high for 8 minutes; let stand 3 minutes. Remove the water and use a paper towel to wipe out the oven's interior.

M CONTAINERS AND COVERS

* Nonmetal containers are used because microwaves pass through them (unlike metal, which deflects the waves), thus the containers remain relatively cool even though the food becomes quite hot. During long cooking periods, however, the food can heat the dish, so be careful when removing it from the microwave oven.
* Metal can cause arcing (sparking) in a microwave oven, so don't use plates or cups that have a metallic design or trim, or containers (such as some insulated cups) that might have metal supports in the handles. Lead crystal should also be avoided because the lead deflects the microwaves, which not only slows the cooking process, but could damage the oven.
* If you're unsure if a dish or other container contains metal, use this test: Place 1 cup cool water in a glass measuring cup. Set it in the microwave oven next to or in the center of the dish. Microwave for 1 minute. If the dish remains cool, it's suitable for microwave cooking.
* Oddly enough, a small amount of aluminum foil can be used in microwave ovens as long as it doesn't touch the sides of the oven. If parts of a food are cooking too fast (such as the tips of chicken wings), place a tiny foil shield over them.
* Some foods can be cooked on paper plates or paper towels—just make sure they are labeled "safe for microwave cooking."
* Plastic containers not specifically made for microwave use may warp or melt during prolonged cooking.
* If possible, cook food in a round dish (like a glass cake pan). Food in the corners of square or rectangular dishes overcooks because microwaves concentrate there.
* Using a different size or shape container than a microwave recipe directs can make a noticeable difference in how long it takes a dish to cook.
* As a rule of thumb, cover any food that would be covered during conventional cooking methods.
* A paper plate makes a sturdy, disposable cover for microwaved food.
* Plastic wrap makes an excellent food cover, but don't use a bargain brand, which could melt at high temperatures, allowing the plasticizers in some brands to migrate to food in contact with the wrap. Check the plastic-wrap label to be sure it's safe for microwave cooking. And allow at least an inch of space between the plastic wrap and the food.
* When an airtight plastic-wrapped container is removed from the microwave oven, the wrap often collapses onto the food. To prevent this

from happening, before placing the food in the microwave, use a carving fork or pointed knife to pierce the tightly stretched plastic wrap in 2 places. Or vent the dish by turning back a corner of the plastic to allow steam to escape during cooking.

* Never use plastic wrap with foods high in sugar or fat, both of which attract microwaves, making them very hot.

* When removing plastic wrap from a dish of cooked food, always fold back the side away from you first to avoid the scalding hot steam.

* Waxed paper is a good food cover, particularly when you want much of the steam to escape.

* Microwave-safe paper towels are great for covering foods that spatter, such as bacon.

* Seal microwave cooking bags with unflavored dental floss in lieu of twist ties.

BASICS

* Use your microwave probe to heat liquids, such as those in which to dissolve yeast (105° to 110°F), or for scalding milk (180°F).

* Room-temperature food cooks faster than refrigerated or frozen food.

* Many characteristics affect how microwaves cook food: Shape—thin pieces cook faster than thick; fat and/or bone distribution; density; starting temperature; and the amount of moisture, sugar and fat the food contains. Foods that are low in moisture and/or high in fat or sugar cook faster.

* The volume of food also affects microwave cooking. You can't double a microwave recipe and expect it to cook in the same time. Two potatoes can take almost twice as long to cook as one.

* Cut food into uniform pieces so that it will cook evenly. Small or thin pieces will cook more quickly than large pieces.

* Because microwaves cook food at the outer edge of a plate first, always arrange the thickest or densest part at the outside of the dish. For instance, arrange the meaty part of chicken legs at the edge of a plate, with the drumsticks pointed toward the center.

* Likewise, it's important to stir foods like casseroles and puddings to distribute the food for even cooking.

* Foods that can't be stirred should be rotated a half turn halfway through the cooking time to allow for any hot spots in the oven. Of course, if the oven has a turntable, turning food manually isn't necessary.

* As a general rule, meat, poultry and vegetables will take about 6 minutes per pound in a 650-watt oven on high. Count on about 3 minutes per pound for most fish and fruit.

M

* Standing time in microwave-cooked food is particularly important—up to 25 percent of the cooking can occur during that period. That's because the vibrating water molecules are still producing heat while gradually slowing to a stop. And that's also why, if you cook food until it's "done," it will be *way* overdone by the time you serve it. Be sure to cover food during the standing time so it doesn't lose heat.

COOKING

* To allow for variances in oven wattage, always check food for doneness at the minimum cooking time given in a recipe.
* Always prick the skins of foods like eggplant, squash, chicken livers or whole potatoes or tomatoes so the steam can escape. Otherwise these foods can explode, making a mess of your microwave oven.
* Recrisp crackers and potato or corn chips that have absorbed moisture by microwaving them, uncovered, for 1 to 2 minutes on high.
* Vegetables do particularly well when microwaved, retaining both color and nutrients.
* Thaw frozen juice concentrate in a flash by turning it into a glass measuring cup and heating on high for 30 to 60 seconds, stirring halfway through.
* Almond paste, softening (*see* page 4).
* Artichokes, cooking (*see* page 12).
* Asparagus, cooking (*see* page 14).
* Avocado, softening (*see* page 16).
* Bacon: Defrosting (*see* page 19); cooking (*see* page 19); recrisping cooked bacon (*see* page 20).
* Baked goods, warming ingredients (*see* page 22).
* Blanching (*see* page 43).
* Bread, yeast: Rising (*see* page 55); thawing (*see* page 56).
* Brown sugar, softening (*see* page 454).
* Butter: Browning (*see* page 71); clarified (*see* page 72); melting (*see* page 71); softening (*see* page 71).
* Candy, making (*see* page 83).
* Caramelized sugar (*see* page 86).
* Cheese, bringing to room temperature (*see* page 96).
* Chocolate: Melting (*see* page 112); tempering (*see* page 113).
* Coconut: Opening (*see* page 127); toasting (*see* page 127).
* Corn on the cob, cooking (*see* page 149).
* Cream cheese, softening (*see* page 98).
* Dried fruit, softening and separating (*see* page 171).
* Eggs: Cooking (*see* pages 186–187); warming whites (*see* page 180).

* Fish: Cooking (*see* pages 196–200); thawing (*see* page 56).
* Garlic, loosening skins (*see* page 219).
* Gelatin, dissolving (*see* page 225).
* Herbs, drying (*see* page 246).
* Ice cream, softening (*see* page 254).
* Juicing citrus fruits (*see* page 118).
* Marshmallows, softening (*see* page 281).
* Muffins, heating (*see* page 307).
* Nuts, toasting (*see* page 315).
* Olive oil, reliquefying (*see* page 190).
* Onions, peeling (*see* page 321).
* Oysters, opening (*see* page 327).
* Pancakes, reheating (*see* page 331).
* Pasta, reheating (*see* page 339).
* Pie, freshening (*see* page 358).
* Poaching fruit (*see* page 369).
* Polenta, cooking (see page 372).
* Popcorn, recrisping (*see* page 375).
* Potatoes, cooking (*see* page 379).
* Precooking food for grilling (*see* page 235).
* Rice, cooking (*see* page 398).
* Risotto, cooking (*see* page 402).
* Sugar, caramelizing (*see* pages 85–86).
* Sweetened condensed milk, caramelizing (*see* page 457).
* Syrups, reliquefying (*see* page 459).
* Thawing food, general (*see* page 210).
* Tomato, peeling (*see* page 470).
* Winter squash, softening to cut (*see* page 444).

The cow is of the bovine ilk;
One end is moo, the other milk.
—Ogden Nash, American poet, author

MILK *see also* BUTTERMILK; CREAM; DRY MILK; EVAPORATED MILK; SWEET-
ENED CONDENSED MILK; YOGURT
PURCHASING Check the date on milk cartons and choose one with the
latest date. In other words, if you're buying on June 1, choose a carton that's
dated June 8 over one that's dated June 5. Package dates are purposely con-
servative—properly stored, most milk will be fine at least a week after the
carton's date.

M

STORING

* Refrigerate milk as soon as you get home from the market. Milk absorbs odors easily, so keep the container tightly closed. Its flavor can be altered by ordinary daylight, so if you buy milk in clear glass or plastic bottles, keep them in the dark as much as possible.
* Although freezing changes milk's consistency, you can freeze a whole quart carton of milk, double wrapped in a plastic bag, for up to 6 months. Or pour 1-cup amounts in small, zip-closure, freezer-proof bags and freeze. Defrost in the refrigerator.

SUBSTITUTIONS

* For 1 cup nonfat (skim) milk: ⅓ cup dry nonfat milk plus ¾ cup water
* For 1 cup sour milk: 1 tablespoon lemon juice or white vinegar plus milk to equal 1 cup (let stand 5 minutes)
* For 1 cup whole milk (for recipes): 1 cup nonfat milk plus 2 tablespoons melted unsalted butter or margarine; or ½ cup evaporated whole milk plus ½ cup water; or ¼ cup dry whole milk plus ⅞ cup water.

USING

* For the best flavor, serve milk icy cold.
* When milk sits at room temperature for more than 30 minutes (as when put in a pitcher for serving), its quality begins to diminish. Instead of returning the milk to the carton, cover the pitcher with plastic wrap, refrigerate and use the milk within a couple of days.
* Milk that's begun to sour isn't good to drink, but is perfectly fine to use in recipes for baked goods.
* Slightly soured milk can be substituted for buttermilk in baking recipes.
* Scalding milk was originally done to kill bacteria in milk—a process that's been rendered obsolete with pasteurization. Today, scalding most often serves to speed preparation and cooking time. For instance, warm milk melts fat and dissolves sugar more quickly.
* Before heating milk, rinse the pan with cold water to keep it from scorching and sticking. Rub the top edge of the pan with butter to prevent boilovers.
* Milk scorches easily because the whey proteins sink and stick to the pan's bottom. Cooking over medium heat or in a double boiler diminishes the problem.
* Keep skin from forming on heated milk either by covering the pan or by beating the milk so that a froth forms on the surface.
* There's no cure for the flavor of scorched milk. Throw it out and start anew.
* Milk products curdle easily, especially when combined with acid-containing foods, such as tomatoes and wine.

WHIPPED TOPPING
Put ⅓ cup instant dry nonfat milk in a small mixing bowl; gradually stir in ⅓ cup nonfat milk. Place in the freezer for 20 to 30 minutes until ice crystals begin to form around the edges. Use a hand-held mixer to beat the mixture on high until soft peaks form, about 2 minutes. Add ¼ teaspoon pure vanilla extract and 1 tablespoon sugar or honey; beat 2 more minutes, or until firm peaks form. Use immediately—the topping will only hold its shape for about 15 minutes.

> *Mint is an aggressive herb—no doubt about it. [It's] also hell on a garden—and the gardener!*
> —Bert Greene, American author, journalist, wit

MINT

TIDBIT   The two most widely available varieties of mint today are peppermint and spearmint. There are several ways to distinguish them from each other. Peppermint has bright green leaves and purple-tinged stems. It has a slightly peppery flavor and is the more pungent of the two. Spearmint leaves can be either gray green or true green; they have a milder flavor and fragrance.
PURCHASING   Choose mint with evenly colored leaves that show no sign of wilting.
STORING   Refrigerate a mint bouquet, stems down in a glass of water with a plastic bag over the leaves, for up to a week. Change the water every 2 days.
USING
* Don't think of mint only for sweet dishes. It's wonderful in all manner of savory dishes and has long been used in many Asian cuisines.
* Mint has a particular affinity for tomatoes. The next time you make a tomato salad, add a little minced mint to the dressing. Or toss chopped mint with tomatoes, then dress the salad. Fresh tomatoes, mint and lemon zest make a wonderful pasta sauce.
* Mint makes an attractive garnish for fruit compotes or salads, some meats (like lamb) and drinks (the classics being iced tea and mint juleps).
GINGER-MINT JULEP
The perfect refresher for a hot summer day. Put 8 large fresh mint leaves and 1 teaspoon *each* superfine sugar and water in a tall glass. Use a long-handled spoon to muddle the ingredients until the leaves are crushed and the sugar dissolved. Add 1 cup crushed ice; top with about ¾ cup chilled ginger ale, stirring gently but well. Garnish with a mint sprig; serve with a straw.

MIXED DRINKS   *see* COCKTAILS; LIQUORS AND LIQUEURS

MOLASSES   *see also* SYRUPS *for general information such as reliquefying, measuring, and so on*

PURCHASING   Molasses, a by-product of sugarcane, comes in three basic forms: **light molasses** comes from the first boiling of the sugar syrup extracted from the cane; **dark molasses**, from the second boiling, is darker, thicker and not as sweet as the first boiling; **blackstrap molasses**, from the third boiling, is extremely thick, dark and slightly bitter. **Unsulfured molasses** describes the purest form, made from the juice of sun-ripened sugarcane, giving it a lighter, cleaner sugarcane flavor. **Sulphured molasses** is derived from green sugarcane, which has been treated with sulfur fumes to extract the juice.

EQUIVALENT   12 fluid ounces = 1½ cups

STORING   Store, tightly sealed, in a cool, dark place at room temperature for up to 2 years.

USING

* The robust flavor of dark molasses makes it perfect for classics like gingerbread, shoofly pie, Indian pudding and Boston baked beans. The milder-flavored light molasses is often used as a pancake and waffle syrup. Blackstrap, most often found in natural food stores, is rarely used in cooking; in the United States, it's more commonly used as cattle food.
* Light and dark molasses are interchangeable in recipes, the latter having a slightly more robust flavor.
* In baked goods, balance the natural acidity of molasses by adding 1 teaspoon baking soda to the dry ingredients for each cup of molasses used.
* Baked goods with a high percentage of molasses tend to overbrown, so reduce the oven heat by 25°F.

MOLASSES BUTTER

Great on muffins, pancakes, waffles, and so on. Beat 1 stick softened butter, 1 tablespoon brown sugar, ½ teaspoon pure vanilla extract and a pinch of salt together until creamy. Slowly drizzle in 1 tablespoon light or dark molasses, beating constantly until thoroughly incorporated. Cover and refrigerate for up to 5 days. Remove from the refrigerator 30 minutes before serving. Makes about ⅔ cup.

MONOSODIUM GLUTAMATE   *see* MSG

MORTAR AND PESTLE

TIDBIT   Mortars and pestles come in a wide variety of materials, including wood, stone (from lava to marble), clay, ceramic and brass. The mortars can range in size from a few inches in diameter to a foot or more. The function of the mortar is to provide an unyielding surface on which ingredients are crushed with the pestle.

PURCHASING Buy the biggest one you have room for—large mortars can handle small jobs, but it doesn't work in reverse. Some mortars are sold in a nested set of three, which may be just what you want. Deep mortars keep ingredients like spices in the bowl, instead of bouncing out. Choose a mortar and pestle by how it will be used: a wooden surface for pounding delicate ingredients (like basil leaves), a stone surface for crushing spices. If you want only one mortar, stone is the most versatile. Just use a lighter touch to crush delicate ingredients.

USING

* Use a simple up-and-down motion to pound the ingredients, adding a little at a time.
* Don't overwork your muscles—gravity and the pestle's weight will do the job.
* Ceramic or marble mortars and pestles don't absorb food odors and are easier to clean. Wash by hand.
* Pesto and brandade are two of the most popular dishes made in a mortar.

MSG (Monosodium Glutamate)

* MSG is derived from glutamic acid, one of the twenty-two natural amino acids. Though it has no pronounced flavor of its own, MSG has the ability to intensify the flavor of savory foods. However, some people have negative reactions to MSG, including headache, dizziness, flushing and burning sensations.
* If you're MSG-sensitive, you should know that MSG is hidden in many foods under other names. The Food and Drug Administration (FDA) doesn't require a separate MSG listing when any of the following (MSG-laden) ingredients are present: hydrolyzed vegetable protein, hydrolyzed plant protein, Kombu extract, and natural flavoring or seasoning.

When I am in trouble, eating is the only thing that consoles me. . . .
At the present moment I am eating muffins because I am unhappy.
Besides, I am particularly fond of muffins.
—Oscar Wilde, Anglo-Irish playwright, critic

MUFFINS *see also* BAKED GOODS, GENERAL; BAKING POWDER; BAKING SODA; BISCUITS; BREAD, GENERAL; BREAD, QUICK; GREASING PANS; HIGH-ALTITUDE ADJUSTMENTS; POPOVERS

M STORING Store muffins in a tightly sealed plastic bag at room temperature for up to 3 days. Freeze in a single layer in heavy-duty foil or freezer-weight plastic bags for up to 3 months.

MUFFIN PANS

* There are several muffin pan sizes: Standard muffin pans have cups that measure about 2½ inches in diameter; giant muffin pans have 3¼-inch cups; miniature muffin pans have cups that can range from 1¼ to 2 inches in diameter; muffin top pans have indentations 4 inches in diameter but only ½ inch deep.
* Cooking spray is the quickest way to grease muffin cups.
* Keep your fingers clean by using a crumpled piece of paper towel dipped into shortening to grease muffin cups.
* Don't grease muffin cups that won't be used—the grease will burn and make a mess of your pan.
* Put 2 or 3 tablespoons water in unused muffin cups to keep the pan from warping during baking.
* For perfectly rounded muffin tops, grease only the bottoms and halfway up the sides of the muffin cup.
* Save on cleanup by using paper or foil baking cups.

PREPARING THE BATTER

* Turn the oven on before you begin to make the batter so it can preheat for at least 10 minutes.
* For light, tender muffins, substitute buttermilk or yogurt for milk in a recipe. Add ½ teaspoon baking soda for each cup of buttermilk or yogurt used.
* Any muffin can be made lighter by separating the eggs. Mix the yolks with the other moist ingredients; beat the whites until stiff and fold them into the batter just before baking.
* Vigorously beating the batter creates tough muffins with pointed, peaked tops. Stir the batter only until all the dry ingredients are moistened. Don't worry about small lumps—they'll disappear during baking.
* For uniformly shaped muffins, use a dry measuring cup or an ice cream scoop to distribute the batter.
* If you fill muffin cups more than three-quarters full, you're liable to get "flying saucer" tops.

BAKING

* If your oven runs hot, place a small pan with a cup of hot water on the bottom shelf during baking. The steam produced helps prevent the muffin edges from overbrowning.

* Check muffins for doneness by inserting a toothpick in the center. If it comes out clean, the muffins are done.
* To remove muffins from their cups, run a dinner knife around the edges, then under the muffin to tilt it out of the pan. Tilting the muffins in their cups keeps the bottoms from getting soggy with steam.
* If muffins are stuck to the bottom, set the hot muffin tin on a wet towel for 2 minutes. The muffins should be easier to remove.
* To cool muffins completely, transfer them to a rack.
* Keep just-baked muffins warm for a few minutes by slightly tilting each one in the pan and returning to the turned-off oven with the door ajar.
* To reheat leftover muffins: Loosely wrap in foil and warm in a 325°F oven for about 10 minutes; or microwave on high for 15 to 30 seconds, until warmed through. Overheating in the microwave oven can turn the muffins into stones.
* Muffin crisps: Thinly slice leftover muffins, place the slices on a baking sheet, and toast both sides under the oven broiler or in a toaster oven until golden brown. If desired, brush one side lightly with melted butter before toasting.
* Split leftover savory muffins, toast under the broiler, and top with a creamed mixture for lunch or dinner.

CINNAMON SURPRISE MUFFINS

Make a batch of your favorite muffin batter. Stir together ½ cup packed brown sugar, ⅓ cup finely chopped walnuts or pecans and 1 teaspoon ground cinnamon. Fill each muffin cup halfway with batter, put a teaspoon of the sugar-nut mixture in the center, then top with the remaining batter. Sprinkle any leftover sugar-nut mixture over the top of the batter before baking.

Life is too short to stuff a mushroom.
—Shirley Conran, British writer

MUSHROOMS *see also* VEGETABLES, GENERAL

TIDBIT Early Greeks and Romans were among the first to cultivate mushrooms and enjoy them in a wide array of dishes. In fact, according to Maggie Waldron, in *Cold Spaghetti at Midnight*, "Fungi were so highly prized in early Roman times that no mere servant was allowed to cook them. Aristocrats prepared their own mushroom dishes in special silver vessels called boleteria. Guests could tell where they stood in their host's esteem by the number and variety of mushroom dishes served them." The word "boleteria," by the

M

way, is undoubtedly a derivative of *Boletus*, a genus of fungus, the most well known of which is the porcini mushroom, which is also known as *cèpe*.

PURCHASING

* Common cultivated mushrooms: This favorite is commonly found in supermarkets and ranges in color from white to brown. You'll have more control if you hand-select mushrooms, rather than buying them prepackaged. Choose firm, evenly colored mushrooms with tightly closed caps. If all the gills underneath are showing, the mushrooms are past their prime, but certainly still usable. Avoid mushrooms that are broken, damaged or have soft spots. If mushrooms are to be cooked whole, select those of equal size so they'll cook evenly.

* Wild mushrooms: **Chanterelle mushrooms** are trumpet-shaped with a bright yellow to orange color—choose whole, plump, spongy specimens; **enoki mushrooms** come in clumps of long, spaghetti-like stems topped with tiny, snowy white caps—select those that are firm and white; **morels** have a cone-shaped, beige to dark brown cap that's spongy, honeycombed and golden brown—choose firm, slightly spongy mushrooms; **oyster mushrooms** have a fan-shaped cap that varies in color from pale gray to dark brownish gray—they should be firm, and the young, small (1½ inches in diameter) ones are considered best; **shiitake mushrooms** have a dark brown, floppy cap that can be as large as 8 to 10 inches in diameter—choose plump mushrooms with edges that curl under.

* How much per serving: ⅓ pound

EQUIVALENTS

* Fresh: 1 pound = 5 cups sliced, 6 cups chopped, 3 ounces dried, reconstituted; 4 ounces = ⅔ cup sliced

* Dried: 3 ounces, reconstituted = 1 pound fresh

STORING

* Fresh mushrooms: Refrigerate, unwashed, for up to 3 days. Place them in a single layer on a tray; cover with a damp paper towel. Mushrooms will stay firmer if there's air circulating around them so they can "breathe." Storing them in a plastic bag speeds deterioration. If you don't have room to store mushrooms on a tray, refrigerate them in a paper bag. Mushrooms stored over 3 days will certainly still be usable, but they begin to dry out.

* Dried mushrooms can be stored in a cool, dark place for up to 9 months.

PREPARING

* Clean mushrooms just before using. Never immerse mushrooms in water—they're highly absorbent and become soggy if soaked in water. Simply rinse under cold running water and blot dry with paper towels.

Or you can simply wipe off mushrooms with a damp paper towel, or use a mushroom brush. Trim about ¼ inch off the stem ends, except for enokis, which should be separated from the base at the stem end. Shiitakes have very tough stems that should be removed completely (save them to flavor stocks or soups).

* Cover and refrigerate mushroom stems for up to 3 days for use in soups, sautés or sauces. The stems can also be frozen for up to 6 months.
* Peeling mushrooms eliminates much of their flavor.
* White mushrooms will stay that way if you wipe them with a paper towel dipped in lemon water.
* Air will quickly darken a mushroom's flesh. So, if you're cutting mushrooms to be used raw in a salad or as crudités, do so at the last minute. Or you can take a more labor-intensive approach and cut them ahead of time, wiping the cut surfaces with a paper towel dipped in lemon juice.
* Slice mushrooms evenly and in one step by using an egg slicer. Stand trimmed mushroom upright and slice one at a time. For mushroom wedges, use an egg wedger.
* Marinate small, cleaned button mushrooms in your favorite vinaigrette for 2 days in an airtight container in the refrigerator. They're great in salads, as a garnish or as a snack with apéritifs.
* **Rehydrate dried mushrooms** by covering them with warm water and soaking for about 30 minutes. Use a slotted spoon to retrieve the mushrooms from the water to avoid any grit the mushrooms may have released. Rinse the mushrooms and blot thoroughly with a paper towel; cut off tough stems. Strain the soaking liquid through a sieve lined with a paper towel. Use the liquid to flavor soups, stews and sauces. Label and freeze it until you're ready to use it.
* Make your own mushroom powder by putting dried mushrooms in a blender and processing until powdery. Store the powder in a tightly sealed jar at room temperature. Use it to enrich sauces, stews and soups.
* For a showy garnish, use a citrus stripper to flute mushrooms by carving out strips at even intervals.

COOKING

* Cooking mushrooms in an aluminum pan will cause them to darken.
* SAUTÉING mushrooms brings out and concentrates their flavor. Make sure the pan and oil are hot and don't overcrowd the pan—mushrooms exude a lot of moisture during cooking and there should be enough room to stir them. Crowding will cause them to steam, rather than sauté.
* PURÉE leftover raw or cooked mushrooms (add a little vegetable or chicken broth, if necessary) and freeze in ice cube trays. Turn mushroom

cubes into a plastic bag and freeze until ready to use. Great for flavoring sauces, soups, casseroles, and so on.

MUSKMELONS *see* MELONS

> *Mussels have a bad reputation: something mysterious has to be done to them before they can be eaten with safety and no-one seems able to tell one exactly what it is.*
> —James Laver, British art critic, author

MUSSELS *see also* SHELLFISH
PURCHASING
* Live mussels: Look for tightly closed shells or slightly open shells that snap shut when tapped—otherwise, they're not alive and should be discarded. Avoid mussels with broken shells, that feel heavy (meaning they're full of sand), or that feel light and loose (signaling the mussel is dead). In general, smaller mussels will be more tender than larger ones.
* Shucked mussels: They should be plump, their liquor (liquid) clear.
* How much per serving: Shell on—2 to 3 pounds.

EQUIVALENTS 1 quart = 25 mussels, 1 cup meat

STORING
* Live mussels: Refrigerate in a single layer on a tray, covered only with a damp cloth, for up to 2 days. Discard dead mussels before cooking.
* Shucked mussels: Refrigerate, completely covered with their liquor, for up to 3 days. If there's not enough liquid, cover the mussels with a mixture of 1 cup water and ½ teaspoon salt. Freeze shucked mussels in their liquor for up to 3 months.

PREPARING
* Rid mussels of sand by soaking for 1 hour in cold, salted water (⅓ cup salt per gallon of water).
* Before cooking, use a stiff brush to scrub mussels under cold, running water. Pull out the dark threads (beard) that protrude from the shell by grasping them between your thumb and a small knife. Mussels die when debearded, so don't do this until just before cooking.
* Like all shellfish, mussels should be cooked gently to prevent toughening.
* Mussels cooked in their shells are done when their shells open. Discard any with unopened shells.

Eat safely—use condiments.
—Vinnie Tonelli, American artist

M

MUSTARD, PREPARED   *see also*; MUSTARD SEED, POWDERED MUSTARD, MUSTARD OIL

TIDBIT   In general, prepared mustard is made from powdered mustard, a liquid such as water, vinegar, wine or beer, and various seasonings. Grainy mustards get their texture from the addition of crushed or whole mustard seeds. Among the more popular mustards are: **American-style mustard** ("ballpark" or hot dog mustard)—made from mild white (also called yellow) mustard seeds, sugar, vinegar and turmeric (which produces its characteristic bright yellow color). It has a smooth texture and mild flavor. **Dijon mustard**—a smooth-textured, pale grayish yellow mixture from Dijon, France, is known for its clean, sharp flavor, which can range from mild to hot. It's made from brown mustard seeds, white wine, unfermented grape juice and a blend of seasonings. Dijon mustards are usually spicier and more pungent than their American counterparts. Mustards labeled "Dijon-style" are made in the same way, but are not from Dijon. **English mustard** is made from both white and brown or black mustard seeds, flour and turmeric. It's bright yellow and extremely hot. **German mustard** can range in color from pale yellow to brown and in texture from smooth to coarse. Its spicy, slightly sweet flavor ranges from mild to hot. **Creole mustard** is a hot, spicy mixture of vinegar-marinated brown mustard seeds and horseradish.

STORING   Prepared mustard can be stored for at least 2 years; refrigerate after opening.

USING

* It's important to use the type of mustard a recipe calls for. Otherwise, you could end up with a completely different flavor than was intended.
* Mustard adds a mysterious piquancy to all manner of dishes, including seafood salads, soups and stews, potato or bean salads, savory soufflés, quiches, bread doughs, quick bread batters, baked beans, and so on. Err on the side of caution when adding mustard—powdered or prepared— to a dish. You can always add more, but there's no way to remove it.
* Personalize store-bought mustard by flavoring a good Dijon mustard with finely chopped herbs (basil, dill or tarragon), garlic, shallots, onions, olives, fennel seeds, capers, green peppercorns, grated lemon zest, and so on.
* **Horseradish mustard** makes a great spread for meat sandwiches. Mix 1 part horseradish to 3 parts mustard. For a Bloody Mary with a twist, stir in ½ teaspoon of this fragrant blend.
* **Mustard mayonnaise:** Combine 2 to 3 teaspoons mustard with ½ cup

mayo. Use as a sandwich spread, in salads (like egg or tuna), salad dressings, or to brush over meat, such as baked ham or pork loin.

* **Mustard butter:** Blend 2 to 3 teaspoons of your favorite prepared mustard with ½ cup softened butter (and ¼ cup minced fresh herbs, if desired). Great for basting meats, poultry and fish, for cooking with scrambled eggs, spread on sandwiches, melted over cooked vegetables, and so on.
* Make a delectable glaze for ham by combining your favorite mustard with maple syrup, honey or melted orange marmalade.

MUSTARD GREENS   *see* GREENS

MUSTARD SEED; POWDERED MUSTARD; MUSTARD OIL   *see also*
GREENS; MUSTARD, PREPARED
PURCHASING

* Mustard seed: There are three main types—white (also called yellow), brown and black. White or yellow mustard seeds are larger than the darker varieties, but also less pungent. Brown seeds have a strong flavor; the slightly milder black seeds are most often used by Indian cooks. Whole white mustard seeds are commonly available in supermarkets. Black seeds can be found in Indian markets; the brown seeds are occasionally available in specialty gourmet markets.
* Powdered mustard: a powder made of finely ground mustard seeds. It's available in supermarkets.
* Mustard oil: a pale golden, aromatic oil that's pressed directly from mustard seeds. It's extremely hot and pungent. Mustard oil is available in ethnic markets, specialty gourmet shops and many supermarkets.

STORING

* Mustard seed: Store in a cool, dark place for up to 1 year.
* Powdered mustard: Store at room temperature for up to 6 months.
* Mustard oil: Refrigerate for up to 9 months.

PREPARING

* Homemade mustard: Combine about 2 parts powdered mustard with 1 part liquid (such as water, wine or vinegar); stir until the mixture is the consistency of a smooth paste. If desired, add fresh herbs, garlic or other seasonings. Let stand about 15 minutes before using for the flavor to develop. Taste the mustard—if it's too hot, stir in 1 teaspoon each cream and granulated or brown sugar. This type of mustard quickly loses its potency and should be made fresh before each use.
* Add intrigue to your next stir-fry by using a *touch* of mustard oil (it's very hot and pungent), fresh ginger and garlic.
* A soupçon of mustard oil in salad dressing adds both flavor and piquancy.

Talking of pleasure, this moment I was writing with one hand, and with the other holding to my mouth a nectarine. . . . It went down all pulpy, slushy, oozy—all its delicious embonpoint melted down my throat like a large, beatified Strawberry.
—John Keats, British poet

NECTARINES *see also* FRUIT, GENERAL

PURCHASING Choose fragrant, brightly colored nectarines that give slightly to palm pressure. Avoid those with bruises or other blemishes as well as any that are hard or overly green.

EQUIVALENTS 1 pound = 3 to 4 medium, 2 cups chopped, 1½ cups puréed

STORING Refrigerate ripe nectarines for up to 5 days. Ripen underripe fruit at room temperature. Speed ripening by placing nectarines in a paper bag with an apple.

USING

* Wash nectarines just before using; no peeling required.
* Once cut, a nectarine's flesh will begin to discolor. If the nectarine won't be combined with an ingredient containing acid (such as a salad dressing), dip the nectarine pieces quickly in and out of ACIDULATED WATER.
* At the height of their season, make nectarine (rather than strawberry) shortcake. Flavor the whipped cream with a little nutmeg and amaretto and you'll get raves.

Nature was indeed at her artistic best when she created the nutmeg, a delight to the eye in all its avatars, from the completely garbed to nudity.
—Waverly Root, American writer

NUTMEG; NUTMEG GRATERS *For storage and purchasing information, see* SPICES

PURCHASING Nutmeg can be found ground or whole in a market's spice section.

GENERAL

* Freshly grated nutmeg is much more pungent than its canned, ground counterpart. Use in vegetables, soups, stews, breads and desserts.
* There are several styles of nutmeg graters and grinders, which are commonly found in kitchenware shops. Most graters have a fine-rasp, slightly curved surface over which a whole nutmeg is rubbed. Many graters store the whole nutmegs in containers attached to the bottom or back of the unit. Nutmeg grinders use a spring-mounted post to hold a whole nutmeg against a sharp blade that, when a crank is rotated, grates the nutmeg.
* A toothbrush is the perfect tool for cleaning nutmeg graters and grinders.
* Mace is the dried, ground outer membrane that covers the nutmeg seed, which is why mace tastes and smells like a pungent version of nutmeg.

NUTS, GENERAL *see also* ALMONDS; ALMOND PASTE; BRAZIL NUTS; CHESTNUTS; HAZELNUTS; PEANUTS; PECANS; PISTACHIOS; WALNUTS

PURCHASING

* Unshelled nuts: Choose those that are heavy for their size, the shells solid, sans cracks or holes. Buy nuts in small amounts from a supplier with rapid turnover.
* Shelled nuts: They should be plump, crisp, and uniform in color and size, not shriveled or discolored. Packaged shelled nuts are harder to test for freshness. If they're in a cellophane bag, snap a couple through the wrapping. If they bend, rather than break crisply, the nuts are past their prime.

EQUIVALENT As a general rule, 4 ounces of most nuts = 1 cup chopped nuts. See *individual listings for specific yields*.

STORING As with any high-fat food, nuts must be stored properly to forestall rancidity. Store them airtight in a cool place. Place cellophane-packaged nuts in a plastic bag to keep as fresh as possible. Shelled nuts can be refrigerated for up to 4 months, frozen for up to 8 months. As a general rule (and depending on their freshness at the time of storage), unshelled nuts will keep twice as long as shelled.

PREPARING

* Always taste nuts before using them—rancid nuts will ruin a dish.
* Place hard-to-crack nuts in a large saucepan and cover with water. Bring to a boil, then remove from the heat, cover and set aside for at least 15

minutes, or until cool. Blot the nuts dry, then crack them with a nut-cracker.

* Freeze nuts to make shelling easier.
* To shell nuts so that the nutmeats are relatively intact, gently press on the middle of the shell with a nutcracker, rotating the nut three or four times as you do.
* To eliminate bits of shell in freshly hulled nuts, turn the nuts into a large bowl of cool water. The shells should float and can be poured or skimmed off. Drain and dry the nuts thoroughly before using.
* Nuts are easier to chop when they're warm. Either heat in a microwave oven on high for 2 to 3 minutes or in a conventional oven at 325°F for 5 minutes.
* Toasting nuts intensifies their flavor and adds crunch. Another bonus—toasted nuts aren't as likely to sink in cakes, breads and other batter-based foods. **Skillet toasting:** Cook in an ungreased skillet over medium heat, stirring frequently, until golden brown. **Oven toasting:** Spread in a single layer on a baking sheet. Bake at 350°F, stirring occasionally, for 10 to 15 minutes. **Microwave toasting:** Place 1 cup chopped nuts on a paper plate. Cook on high, uncovered, for 3 to 4 minutes, rotating the plate a half turn after 2 minutes, or until the nuts smell toasted. Microwave-toasted nuts barely change color, but they taste toasted (wait until they're cool to taste them).
* **Chopping nuts in a food processor:** Place about 1 cup whole nuts or large nut pieces in a food-processor bowl and use quick on/off pulses until nuts are chopped as desired. Don't overprocess or you'll wind up with nut butter. If this happens, see how to make nut butter, below.
* **Chopping nuts in a blender:** Because of the shape of the jarlike container, it's hard to chop nuts in a standard blender without turning at least part of them into paste. First rule—never chop more than 1 cup of nuts at a time, and process with short on/off bursts of power. Adding 1 tablespoon flour, cornstarch or sugar will help keep the nuts separate. Some blenders come with 1-cup containers, which work well for chopping nuts. Fill them only half full, and use quick on/off pulses until the nuts reach the desired texture.

USING
* Add flavor to baked goods like breads, cakes and cookies by substituting ⅓ cup finely ground nuts for ⅓ cup of the flour.
* Ground, toasted nuts are great in meatballs, meat loaf and burgers.
* Sprinkle chopped, toasted nuts over salads (fruit or green), vegetables and pasta.

* To make any pastry pie crust nutty: Once the dough is in the pan and fluted, sprinkle the bottom and sides with about ¼ cup ground or finely chopped, toasted nuts. Use the back of a spoon to gently press the nuts into the pie crust; bake or fill as usual.
* Make your own nut butter by grinding nuts in a food processor or blender. When the nuts are pastelike, add enough vegetable oil to create the texture you desire. Honey and maple syrup add sweetness to nut butters, and salt will enliven the flavor.
* When using chopped nuts for a garnish, put them in a strainer first and toss them a few times to remove bits of nuts and skin that would mar the look of whatever you're decorating.

SKILLET COCKTAIL NUTS

Sauté 2 cups nuts in 2 tablespoons oil or melted butter in a skillet over medium-high heat, stirring often, until they begin to brown. Season to taste with salt, pepper, cayenne, curry powder, and so on, tossing the nuts with a wooden spoon. Turn out onto paper towels to cool. Store in an airtight container.

SASSY-SWEET NUTS

These crowd-pleasers are great with cocktails and apéritifs. Chinese five-spice powder, available in most supermarkets, is a pungent mixture that commonly includes equal parts of cinnamon, cloves, fennel seed, star anise and black pepper. Combine 1 tablespoon Chinese five-spice powder, ¼ to ½ teaspoon cayenne pepper, ½ teaspoon salt and the finely grated zest from 1 large orange in a large bowl. Beat 1 egg white in a separate bowl until frothy. Slowly beat in ¼ cup sugar; beat until the egg white forms soft mounds. Fold into the spice mixture. Add 3 cups mixed nuts, folding to coat with spice mixture. Turn the nuts out onto a baking sheet that's been sprayed with cooking spray; use two forks to separate the nuts into a single layer. Bake on the center rack of a 275°F oven for about 1 hour, using a metal spatula to turn halfway through; separate any nuts that are stuck together. Cool to room temperature. Store airtight for up to 2 weeks.

OATS; OATMEAL
PURCHASING

* Oatmeals: **Old-fashioned (rolled) oats** have been steamed, then flattened into flakes. They take about 15 minutes to cook and have a firmer texture than quick-cooking oats. **Steel-cut oats** (also called *Irish oatmeal or Scotch oats*) have been cut, but not rolled. They take a longer time to cook (about 20 to 30 minutes) and have a decidedly chewy texture. **Quick-cooking oats** have been cut into several pieces before being steamed and flattened. They cook in about 5 minutes. **Instant oats** have been cut into very small pieces, precooked and dried so they need no real cooking. All these products are typically available in supermarkets.

* Other oat products (found more commonly in natural food stores): **Oat groats** are cleaned oats that have been toasted and hulled. Cooked groats are typically served as cereal or as a side dish, like rice. **Oat flour** is the finely ground grain. It doesn't contain gluten, and must be combined with a flour that does contain gluten when used for baked goods that need to rise (like yeast breads). **Oat bran** is the ground outer casing of the grain and is particularly high in soluble fiber.

STORING   Store oats in an airtight container in a cool, dry place for up to 6 months. Oat bran should be stored no longer than 3 months. Oat products may be double wrapped and frozen for up to 1 year.

EQUIVALENTS   Rolled oats: 1 pound = 5 cups uncooked, 1 cup = 1¾ cups cooked

USING

* Old-fashioned oats and quick-cooking oats can usually be interchanged in recipes.

* Instant oats are unsuitable as a substitution in recipes for old-fashioned (rolled) or quick-cooking oats. Using them can turn baked goods like muffins or cookies into gooey lumps.

* For a toasty flavor, roast oats either in a dry skillet or in a little melted butter over medium-high heat until golden. Cool before cooking for oatmeal or adding to cookie and muffin recipes.
* Give cookies, muffins, and so on a nutritional boost by adding ¼ cup oat bran to the ingredients.

OKRA *see also* VEGETABLES, GENERAL

TIDBIT According to Bert Greene's *Greene on Greens,* "Ancient Arab physicians called okra pods 'sun vessels.' They believed the ripening seeds contained therapeutic properties that, once consumed, floated through a man's body forever."

PURCHASING Choose firm, brightly colored pods under 4 inches long; larger pods may be tough and fibrous. Avoid dull, limp or blemished pods.

EQUIVALENT 1 pound = 2¼ cups chopped

STORING Refrigerate in a plastic bag for up to 3 days.

PREPARING

Just before cooking, wash okra pods and trim stem ends.

COOKING

* Okra can be cooked whole or cut crosswise into slices. Cut okra gives off a viscous substance that thickens any liquid in which it's cooked.
* It's typically boiled (either alone or in soups or stews), sautéed or cooked in a microwave oven, but it's particularly delicious when grilled (*see following recipe*).
* Okra is also delicious paired with tomatoes, onions or corn.
* Marinate cooked okra slices overnight in your favorite vinaigrette and add to a salad the next day.

GARLIC GRILLED OKRA

For a spicy treat, dip these garlicky, smoky pods in Jalapeño Aïoli (page 283). In a 13 × 9-inch baking pan, combine ⅓ cup vegetable or olive oil, 2 tablespoons red wine vinegar, 3 medium garlic cloves, minced, ½ teaspoon salt and ¼ teaspoon cayenne. Add 1 pound cleaned, trimmed okra (or one 16-ounce bag whole, frozen okra, thawed), tossing to thoroughly coat okra. Cover and refrigerate at least 3 hours, preferably overnight. At least 1 hour before grilling, soak 2 cups of wood chips in water to cover. Just before grilling, sprinkle the wood chips over the heat source. Use tongs to arrange the okra pods crosswise over the grill grids. Cover and cook over medium-high heat for about 3 minutes, or until lightly browned. Turn the okra; grill an additional 2 to 3 minutes, until lightly browned. Serve hot or at room temperature. Serves 4 to 6.

OILS *see* FATS AND OILS

O

OLIVE OIL *see also* FATS AND OILS *(for general information on storing, using, and so on)*; OLIVES
TIDBIT Prized olive oils hail from around the world, with Spain, Italy, Greece and Portugal among the world's top producers. The most desirable olive oils are those that are **cold-pressed**, a natural, chemical-free process that simply employs pressure.
STYLES OF OLIVE OIL
* **Extra-virgin olive oil**, the first pressing of the olives, is considered the finest and fruitiest of the olive oils; it's also the most expensive.
* Virgin olive oil (superfine, fine and virgin in order of descending quality) is next in quality and flavor.
* Products labeled simply "**olive oil**" are a combination of refined and virgin oils, and are less flavorful and expensive.
* **Light** (or **extra light**) olive oil (an American marketing term) has a lighter flavor, but contains the same number of calories and beneficial monounsaturated fat.

> *. . . black olives between the teeth. A taste older than meat,*
> *older than wine. A taste as old as cold water.*
> —Lawrence Durrell, British novelist

OLIVES *see also* OLIVE OIL
TIDBIT The silvery-leaved olive tree has long been considered sacred, the olive branch a symbol of peace. There are hundreds of different olive varieties, the final flavor of each depending on the ripeness when picked and the processing the olives undergo.
STORING Unopened olives in a jar or can, can be stored in a cool, dark place for 1 year. Once opened, refrigerate olives for up to 1 month.
USING
* If olives are in a can, transfer them and their brine to an airtight glass jar before refrigerating.
* Extend olive storage life by floating a thin layer of vegetable oil on the brine's surface.
* Bulk olives can be put in a jar and covered with oil. Sealed airtight, they'll keep in the refrigerator for up to 2 months.
* If a white film develops on an olive brine's surface, simply skim it off and rinse off any film on the olives.

* If olives are too salty for your taste, cover them with water and simmer for 10 minutes; drain well.
* Discard olives once they begin to turn soft.
* Hate the tedious job of pitting olives? Do it the easy way by placing several olives in a row on a work surface, holding the flat side of a French knife on top of them and giving the knife a gentle but firm whack with your other fist. The jolt will split the olive and free the pit. Or roll over the olives with a rolling pin. Either way, the pits should slip right out.

OMEGA-3 OILS *see* FATS AND OILS

OMELETS *see* EGGS, COOKING METHODS

> *Life is like an onion. You peel it off one layer at a time;*
> *and sometimes you weep.*
> —Carl Sandburg, American poet

ONIONS *see also* CHIVES; LEEKS; SCALLIONS; SHALLOTS; VEGETABLES, GENERAL

PURCHASING There are two main onion classifications—SCALLIONS and dry onions, the subject of this listing. Choose those that are heavy for their size with dry, papery skins. Avoid onions with soft areas, moist or spotted skins, or that have begun to sprout. **Pearl onions** should be about the same size so they'll cook evenly. Among the more mild-flavored onions are the yellow- or white-skinned **Bermuda** and **Spanish,** and the **red** or **Italian.** Three particularly sweet and juicy onions (often available only by mail order outside their area) are **Maui** (Hawaii), **Vidalia** (Georgia) and **Walla Walla** (Washington).

EQUIVALENTS
* Fresh: 1 pound = 4 medium, 3½ to 4 cups chopped; 1 medium = ¾ to 1 cup chopped, 1 tablespoon onion powder
* Frozen: 12 ounces = 3 cups chopped

STORING
* Whole onions: Store in a cool, dry place with good air circulation for up to 2 months, depending on their condition when purchased. Spring and summer onions have a milder flavor and shorter storage life than fall and winter onions. Humidity breeds spoilage. To extend an onion's life, wrap it in newspaper. Or cut off the top of a clean, used pair of pantyhose. Drop an onion into one leg, tie a knot in the hose, and add other onions

the same way. Hang in a cool, dry place. Such storage allows air to circulate, which helps keep the onions longer.

* Cut onions: The best storage container is an airtight screw-top glass jar. Or seal in plastic wrap, and double wrap in a plastic bag. Refrigerate for up to 1 week. Raw or sautéed chopped onions can be frozen in an airtight container for up to 3 months. Add cooked onions directly to dishes like soups and stews without thawing; thaw raw onions and blot dry before sautéing.

PREPARING

* Peeling: Onions will be easier to peel and have a milder flavor if you microwave them on high for 1 to 2 minutes (depending on the onion's size). To peel pearl onions, put them and about ¼ cup water in a 1-quart covered casserole and microwave on high for about 2 minutes, stirring halfway through cooking time. Drain the onions and turn into a bowl of ice water until cool enough to handle.

* To peel a large onion, cut a small slice off the top and root ends. Then hold the onion under warm running water, pulling the skins off as you do. Or you can use the same boiling water–ice water technique in the previous pearl-onion tip. Or halve the onion from top to root and peel off the skin.

* To peel pearl onions, drop them into boiling water; cook 1 to 2 minutes, depending on their size. Drain and turn the onions into a bowl of ice water. Pinch the onion at the root end and it will pop out of its skin.

* Putting papery onion skins in the garbage disposal can clog the works.

* Chopping: It's the sulfuric compounds in onions that turn them pungent and make us weep. Tricks for winning the crying game while cutting onions include the following: Freeze onions for 20 minutes before chopping; hold a wooden kitchen spoon between your teeth; bite down on two kitchen matches, sulfur tips positioned under your nose; brush the cutting board with distilled white vinegar before chopping onions; hold a piece of bread in your mouth; turn on the stovetop exhaust fan and chop on a cutting board on the stove; light a candle and put it within a foot of where you're chopping; wear a pair of safety goggles from the hardware store.

* The sharper your knife and the quicker you chop, the fewer tears you'll suffer.

* Chopping by hand: Cut the onion in half from the top to the root. Place the halves cut side down, then cut into parallel vertical slices. Holding the slices together, slice crosswise to your original cuts.

* Leaving the stem end intact while slicing an onion holds it together.
* Food-processor chopping: Cut the onion into eighths, then process with quick on/off bursts until desired texture is achieved.
* Onions chopped more than 2 hours in advance can lose flavor due to oxidation. However, chopped onions can be stored for up to 6 hours if covered with ice water and refrigerated in an airtight glass container.
* To reduce the harshness of strong onions: Slice or chop the onions, then soak in ice water for 30 to 60 minutes, changing the water two or three times during that time. Drain and thoroughly blot onions dry with a paper towel before using. This is particularly effective for onions that are to be served raw in salads, dips or spreads.
* If you need only part of an onion, leave the skin on the unused portion, cover tightly and refrigerate.
* For almost-instant onion juice, coarsely chop a peeled onion, PURÉE in a food processor or blender, then strain off the juice.
* Home-dried onions: Cut the onion into paper-thin slices, separate slices into rings. Arrange the rings in a single layer on a baking sheet; bake at 275°F until dry and golden brown, 30 to 60 minutes (depending on the onion's natural moisture content). Refrigerate in an airtight container for up to 1 month, adding to dishes as desired.

COOKING

* Before adding onions to dishes like casseroles, soups and stews, briefly sauté them in extra virgin olive oil or butter. This 5-minute process will greatly improve their flavor in the finished dish. Stir 1 teaspoon sugar into the oil or butter before adding the onions for a delicious caramelized flavor.
* Whole onions will stay intact during boiling if you first cut an X about ¼ inch deep in the stem end.
* "Boiled" onions keep their shape better when simmered, rather than cooked at a rapid boil.
* When cooking particularly sharp, pungent onions, boil them for 2 minutes and drain off the water. Repeat this process twice, letting the onions complete their cooking time in the third change of water. The result will be mild, sweet cooked onions.
* Onion rings: One of the most important secrets for supercrisp onion rings is to keep the oil right around 375°F. After BREADING the onion rings, let them air-dry for 30 minutes in the refrigerator before frying. Crowding the onion rings in the pan will bring the oil temperature down and produce greasy rings. Transfer fried onion rings to a paper towel–lined baking sheet and keep warm in a 300°F oven until all the rings are fried (see DEEP-FRYING).

* To grill onions: Cut them into ½-inch thick slices. Run a metal skewer through each slice from side to side. If the skewers are long enough, put 2 or 3 slices on each one. Brush the skewered slices with oil, then sprinkle with salt and pepper. Grill one side of the onions, then use tongs to flip each skewer and grill the second side. Count on 3 to 5 minutes per side, depending on how hot the fire is.

AFTERWARD

* Diminish a lingering onion smell in your kitchen by combining 4 cups water, 1 cup vinegar and 1 teaspoon ground cloves in a large pot. Bring to a boil, then reduce heat and simmer for 15 minutes.
* To help remove onion odor from your hands, rub them with lemon wedges, parsley, salt or vinegar. Wash with soap and hot water.
* Diminish "onion breath" by eating several sprigs of vinegar- or salt-dipped parsley. Or chew on fennel seeds, coffee beans or chlorophyll tablets.

CARAMELIZED ONIONS

These classics add a deep, rich flavor to everything from sandwiches to roasted meats. The trick is slow, lengthy cooking, so patience is required. Place 2 to 3 tablespoons extra virgin olive oil (or half oil, half unsalted butter) in a heavy 10-inch skillet or pot over very low heat. Add 1½ to 2 pounds sliced onions (1 pound of raw onions yields about 1 cup caramelized). The onions will be 2 to 3 inches deep; stir to coat with oil. Cover tightly and cook over very low heat, stirring occasionally, for 45 to 60 minutes, until completely softened and beginning to brown. Increase the heat to medium; remove the lid and add 1 cup liquid (water, wine, broth), scraping the pan to loosen any browned bits on the pan's bottom. Cook until the liquid evaporates and the onions are a deep caramel brown color.

QUICK CARAMELIZED ONIONS

Cook sliced onions as in the preceding recipe, only increase the heat to medium or medium-high. Cover and stir often until the onions are softened and beginning to brown. Remove the lid; sprinkle the onions with 1 to 2 tablespoons granulated sugar, stirring to combine. Continue to cook until the onions are caramelized as desired.

CARAMELIZED ONIONS BALSAMICO

Stir 1 to 2 tablespoons good quality balsamic vinegar into the caramelized onions; cook until liquid evaporates.

OPENING JARS AND BOTTLES *see* JARS AND BOTTLES

O

*. . . there is nothing more delicious than an orange. The very sound of
the word, the dazzling exotic color that shimmers inside the word,
is a poem of surpassing beauty, complete in this line:*
Orange
—Joyce Carol Oates, American writer

ORANGES *For juicing, zesting and general information, see* CITRUS FRUITS
TIDBIT The three primary types of oranges are sweet oranges, loose-
skinned oranges and bitter oranges. **Sweet oranges,** prized both for eating
and for their juice, are generally large; their skin is usually more difficult to
remove than that of their loose-skinned relatives. Among the more popular
sweet oranges are the seedless *navel*, the juicy, coarse-grained *Valencia* and
the red-fleshed *blood orange*. **Loose-skinned oranges** have skin that readily
slips off the fruit; their segments are also loose and divide easily. Members
of the *mandarin orange* family are all loose-skinned and include the thick-
skinned *tangerine*, the multiseeded *Dancy*, the almost seedless *satsuma* and
the tiny *clementine*. **Bitter oranges** (such as *bergamot* and *Seville*) are typically used for preparations such as marmalade and liqueur, since they're too
sour and astringent to be consumed raw.
PURCHASING Choose oranges that are firm and heavy for their size.
Avoid any with mold or spongy spots. A rough, brownish area (called "rus-
seting") on the skin doesn't affect flavor or quality; neither does a slight
greening, which sometimes occurs in fully ripe oranges. Because oranges
are occasionally dyed with food coloring, a bright color isn't necessarily an
indicator of quality. Before you buy that economical bag of oranges, think
about it. You can't see the surface areas of each orange, and a moldy orange
or two in the bag can speed deterioration of the whole lot.
EQUIVALENTS
* Fresh: 1 pound = 3 medium, about 1 cup juice; 1 medium = about ⅓ cup
  juice, 1½ tablespoons zest
* Canned: 11-ounce can = 1¼ cups segments
STORING Oranges can be stored at a cool room temperature for several
days, but they'll last up to 2 weeks when refrigerated.
PREPARING
* Before squeezing the juice, use a citrus zester to remove the outer col-
  ored portion of the peel. Freeze this zest for up to 6 months to use later to
  flavor both sweet and savory dishes.
* Did you know that all forms of orange juice—frozen concentrate, fresh-
  squeezed or pasteurized—contain the same proportion of vitamin C?

And orange juice retains up to 90 percent of its vitamin C for up to 1 week if you store it in the refrigerator.

* Frozen orange juice concentrate will retain its vitamin C for up to a year if stored at 0°F or lower.

CANDIED ORANGE ZEST

These delicate, shimmering strands add intrigue to dishes like sweet potatoes and roasted pork, and instant elegance to almost any dessert. The syrup that's left over after cooking the zest makes a flavorful topping for pancakes, waffles and even ice cream. Remove the zest from 2 medium oranges with a citrus zester (make long, thin strands). Or remove the colored part of the peel with a paring knife and finely JULIENNE lengthwise. Combine ¾ cup sugar, ½ cup water and orange zest in a small saucepan. Cook over high heat until mixture comes to a full rolling boil. Reduce the heat to a simmer; cover and cook without stirring for 15 minutes. Strain off and refrigerate the syrup. Place the orange zest on a large lightly greased plate and separate into individual strands with two forks. Cool for 10 minutes. Sprinkle the zest with ¼ cup sugar; toss as you would pasta to coat the zest thoroughly with sugar. Turn the zest and sugar onto a sheet of waxed paper, making sure the strands are separate; let dry, uncovered, overnight. Transfer the candied zest to an airtight container; store at room temperature for up to 2 weeks. May be refrigerated for up to 3 months; frozen for 6 months. Makes about 1 cup.

The accepted way to test the heat of an oven was to thrust in the hand and count seconds till one had to pull it out with a faint scream.
—J. C. Furnas, American author

OVENS, CONVENTIONAL *see also* BAKING; BROILING; CONVECTION OVENS; MICROWAVE COOKING; TEMPERATURES—FAHRENHEIT AND CELSIUS

Oven Level	Fahrenheit	Celsius
Warming Foods	200° to 250°	93° to 121°
Very Low (or Slow)	250° to 275°	121° to 133°
Low (or Slow)	300° to 325°	149° to 163°
Moderate	350° to 375°	177° to 190°
Hot	400° to 425°	204° to 218°
Very Hot	450° to 475°	232° to 246°
Extremely Hot	500° to 525°	260° to 274°

* Oven temperatures can be off as much as 50° to 100°F, a discomfiting thought, since baked goods can be seriously affected by oven variances. That's why a good oven thermometer is an excellent investment (*see* THERMOMETERS).

* To check oven accuracy, place the thermometer on the center rack and preheat the oven for 15 minutes. If the thermometer reading doesn't agree with the oven setting (for example, if it reads 400°F when the oven is set at 350°F), you know that your oven runs 50°F too hot. Therefore, when a recipe requires a 350°F temperature, set your oven to 300°F.

* Sans oven thermometer, the age-old method for testing an oven temperature is to sprinkle 1 tablespoon flour over the bottom of a metal pan and place it in a preheated oven for 5 minutes. If the flour turns tan, the temperature is 250° to 325°F; golden brown, 325° to 400°F; dark brown, 400° to 450°F; darkest brown, 450° to 525°F.

* In a hurry? Turn on the oven the second you walk through the door so it can be preheating while you begin meal preparations.

* Preheat an oven for 10 to 15 minutes before baking foods such as breads, pastries, soufflés and cakes. Foods requiring 1 hour or more of baking can usually be started in a cold oven. If you start baking in a cold oven, be sure to factor that into the recipe's baking time.

* Most ovens have hot spots. To ensure even baking, rotate baking dishes and pans from top to bottom, and from front to back.

* Line the oven floor with heavy-duty aluminum foil. When the foil gets dirty, throw it out. Make sure you don't cover the pilot or any vents with the foil or you could throw the temperature off.

* Oven spills can be cleaned more easily if you immediately pour salt on them. Wait until the oven cools before wiping up the spill.

* Ovens without automatic- or self-cleaning units are less of a chore to clean if you heat the oven to 200°F, then turn it off and set a shallow glass bowl containing ½ cup ammonia on the middle shelf. Close the oven and let stand overnight. The next day, open the oven and let it air out before you wipe it clean with damp paper towels.

* Clean the inside of your oven window by dampening a cloth, then dipping it into a small bowl of baking soda and scrubbing in a circular motion. Rinse well.

* To get rid of unpleasant cooking (or even oven cleaner) odors in your oven, peel an orange and lay the strips of peel on the oven racks. Heat the oven to 350°F, and leave the peels in the oven for 30 minutes. Turn off the oven and leave the peels until cool.

O

What a flavor [oysters] have—mellow, coppery, with almost a creaminess when you chew and analyze. I drank some good beer with them and floated on a gastronomically sensual cloud. Good food is so sexy in its way.
—James Beard, American cookery expert, author

OYSTERS *see also* SHELLFISH

TIDBIT A popular food fable is that it's dangerous to eat oysters during months that don't have an R in their name. In fact, since refrigeration became the norm, oysters can be safely eaten throughout the year. What is true is that oysters are at their best (particularly for serving raw) during fall and winter—during the summer months, when they spawn, oysters become soft and fatty.

PURCHASING

* Live oysters: Buy from a store with good turnover for maximum freshness. Reject oysters with broken shells, or that don't have tightly closed shells, or have shells that don't snap shut when tapped with your fingernail. The smaller an oyster is for its species, the younger and more tender it will be.
* Shucked oysters: They should be plump, uniform in size, have a good color and smell of the sea; their liquor (liquid) should be clear.

EQUIVALENTS

* Shucked: 1 cup = 13 to 19 medium; 1 quart = about 50
* Canned, smoked: 3.66-ounce can = 14 to 16 oysters

STORING

* Live oysters: Refrigerate (larger shell down), covered with a damp towel, for up to 3 days. The sooner they're eaten, the better they'll taste. If any shells open during storage, tap them—if they don't close, throw them out.
* Shucked oysters: Refrigerate, covered by their liquor, for up to 2 days; freeze for up to 3 months. If there's not enough liquor to cover the shucked oysters, make your own by dissolving ½ teaspoon salt in 1 cup water.

PREPARING

* Scrub live oysters under cold, running water before opening.
* Oyster and clam shells will open more easily if placed in the freezer for 10 to 20 minutes beforehand.
* Or ready oysters for opening by placing them, hinge facing out, around the rim of a 10-inch plate and microwaving on high for about 30 seconds—just until the shells open slightly.

* Wear a heavy glove to protect your hand when opening oysters. Or hold the oyster in a heavy kitchen towel folded in quarters.
* Tools for opening oysters: Prying the shells apart is difficult, so use a strong tool like a short, squat screwdriver or the pointed end of a can or bottle opener.
* Firmly and forcefully insert the oyster-shucking tool between the shells, right into the hinge segment. Twist sharply to lever the shells, popping the top one off.
* Use an oyster/clam knife to slide along the inside of the top of the shell to release the oyster. If necessary, use a paring knife to cut the muscle holding the oyster.

COOKING

* Poached oysters should be cooked only until their edges curl; their bodies should be plump and opaque.
* Try poaching oysters in beer or wine—add a little garlic to the mix.
* Oysters become tough when they're overcooked, so watch carefully.

PANCAKES *see also* FRENCH TOAST; MAPLE SYRUP; WAFFLES
THE BATTER

* Instead of using milk in pancake batter, try substituting an equal amount of fruit juice. Orange juice plus 1 tablespoon orange zest is particularly flavorful. Or try peach nectar, with ½ cup minced fresh peaches.

* Batters containing fruit juice should also contain baking soda to counteract the fruit's natural acidity. If baking soda isn't called for in the recipe, reduce the baking powder by ½ teaspoon and add ½ teaspoon baking soda.

* Create maple-flavored pancakes by substituting ¼ cup pure maple syrup for ¼ cup of the milk or other liquid in the recipe.

* Make spiced pancakes by adding ½ teaspoon each ground cinnamon, nutmeg and vanilla to any batter.

* Sweeten any batter by adding 2 tablespoons granulated or brown sugar and 1 teaspoon pure vanilla extract to the batter.

* For gingerbread pancakes, substitute 2 tablespoons molasses for an equal amount of milk, and add ½ teaspoon ground ginger and ¼ teaspoon each ground cinnamon and allspice to the dry ingredients.

* For ultralight pancakes, substitute room-temperature club soda for the milk. Mix the wet and dry ingredients just before using the batter.

* Pancakes will also be fluffier if you separate the eggs and mix the yolks in with the rest of the liquid. Combine the wet and dry ingredients as usual, then beat the egg whites until stiff and fold into the batter at the last minute.

* Mix the batter only until the dry ingredients are moistened, which means there still may be some lumps. Beating the batter until smooth will produce tough pancakes.

* For easy pancakes in the A.M., get things ready the night before. Combine the dry ingredients in one bowl; cover and leave at room temperature. Mix the wet ingredients together; cover and refrigerate. The next morning, mix the two together and start cooking.

* Most pancake batters can be covered and refrigerated overnight. If the batter thickens too much, gently stir in 1 to 2 tablespoons milk.
* A batter stored for more than a day will need a leavener boost—mix in ¼ teaspoon baking powder blended with 1 teaspoon cold milk.
* Leftover (unsweetened) pancake batter can be used to thicken a sauce or soup. Simply whisk it into a hot mixture and stir until thickened.

COOKING

* Nonstick griddles and skillets make cooking pancakes a breeze. Use a paper towel to lightly rub the pan's surface with only about ½ tablespoon oil. Excess oil causes pancakes to brown unevenly and makes the edges crisp. Oiling a nonstick griddle between pancake batches is usually unnecessary.
* A pancake griddle should be very hot. To test it, flick a few drops of cold water on the griddle—if the water dances on the surface, the griddle is ready.
* Use a ¼-cup dry measure to pour the batter onto the griddle. Depending on the batter's thickness, ¼ cup will make the pancakes 3 to 4 inches in diameter.
* Or use a wide-mouthed pitcher to mix and pour pancake batter.
* For maximum pancake panache, make them right at the table on an electric griddle or skillet.
* Make kids of all ages happy by forming fun shapes with pancake batter. Spoon or pour the batter onto the griddle in the form of a teddy bear, a child's initial, a heart, you name it.
* Cook pancakes until bubbles break all over the surface. Flip the cakes, cooking the second side only until golden brown.
* Never press down on a pancake to speed cooking. Doing so will compress the cake and make it heavy.
* Turning a pancake more than once also toughens it.
* If you're not cooking pancakes on an electric griddle at the table to be served as you make them, place the cooked cakes in a single layer on a large baking sheet lined with a kitchen towel. Keep them warm in a 200°F oven until ready to serve. Don't cover the pancakes unless you want them to steam.

SERVING AND REHEATING

* Warm the syrup to be served with pancakes—½ cup will heat in a few minutes on the stovetop, in 30 to 60 seconds in the microwave on high.
* There are dozens of pancake toppings other than maple or fruit-flavored syrup. Try finely chopped fresh strawberries or other fruit; your favorite jam or jelly thinned with a little fruit juice or melted until liquefied; sour cream or crème fraîche sweetened with a little brown sugar; or honey or a simple dusting of powdered sugar, just to name a few.

* Cool leftover pancakes, then place them in a freezer-proof container separated by waxed-paper squares. Seal and freeze for up to 3 months.
* Reheat frozen pancakes in a single layer on a baking sheet at 325°F for about 8 minutes, or until warmed through. A toaster oven works as well, and sturdy pancakes can be heated in a toaster.
* Or cover frozen pancakes lightly with waxed paper and microwave on high for 10 to 30 seconds. Don't overmicrowave pancakes or you'll turn them into Frisbees.

PANCAKE SYRUP *see* MAPLE SYRUP; SYRUPS

PANS *see* COOKWARE AND BAKEWARE; PAN SIZES; SEASONING PANS

PAN SIZES *see also* MEASUREMENTS; MEASURING; METRIC CONVERSIONS; METRIC MEASUREMENTS

* There are times when you just don't have the size pan a recipe calls for. Pan substitutions can be made, but be sure to choose a pan as close to the size and volume as the original.
* To measure a pan's volume: Fill it with water, then measure the liquid.
* To measure a pan's dimensions: Measure from inside edge to inside edge. Measure the depth by standing the ruler in the pan and checking the distance to the rim (don't slant the ruler, as with a pie pan).
* Once you know the volume or dimensions, mark the measurements right on the outside bottom of the pan. Scratch the information into metal pans; use a waterproof marking pen on glass or ceramic pans.
* The following table will help determine substitutions of pans of similar sizes. For example, if a recipe calls for an 8-inch square baking pan (which has a 6-cup volume), you can see by this table that a 9-inch round cake pan holds approximately the same volume.

PAN SIZE	VOLUME
1¾" × ¾" mini-muffin cup	⅛ cup (2 tablespoons)
2¾" × 1⅛" muffin cup	¼ cup
2¾" × 1⅜" muffin cup	scant ½ cup
5½" × 3" × 2½" loaf pan	2 cups
7" × 1¼" pie pan	2 cups
5" × 2" round cake pan	2⅔ cups
6" × 4½" × 3" loaf pan	3 cups
8" × 1¼" pie pan	3 cups
6¼" × 2½" ring mold	3½ cups

PAN SIZE	VOLUME
6" × 2" round cake pan	3¾ cups
1-quart soufflé dish	4 cups
8" × 4" × 2½" loaf pan	4 cups
8" × 1½" pie pan	4 cups
8" × 1½" round cake pan	4 cups
9" × 1¼" pie pan	4 cups
11¾" × 7½" × ¾" jelly roll pan	4 cups
8½" × 2½" ring mold	4½ cups
8½" × 4¼" × 3" loaf pan	5 cups
9" × 1½" pie pan	5 cups
7" × 2" round cake pan	5¼ cups
7½" × 3" Bundt (tube) pan	6 cups
8" × 2" round cake pan	6 cups
8" × 8" × 1½" square pan	6 cups
9" × 1½" round cake pan	6 cups
10" × 2" deep-dish pie pan	6 cups
11" × 7" × 2" rectangular pan	6 cups
8" × 8" × 2" square pan	8 cups
9" × 5" × 3" loaf pan	8 cups
9" × 2" deep-dish pie pan	8 cups
9" × 2" round cake pan	8 cups
9" × 9" × 1½" square pan	8 cups
9½" brioche pan	8 cups
11" × 7" × 2" rectangular pan	8 cups
9" × 3" Bundt (tube) pan	9 cups
8" × 3" tube pan	9 cups
9" × 9" × 2" square pan	10 cups
9½" × 2½" springform pan	10 cups
9" × 3" tube pan	10 cups
15½" × 10½" × 1" jelly roll pan	10 cups
9" × 4" Kugelhopf (tube) pan	11 cups
10" × 2" round cake pan	11 cups
9" × 3" tube pan	12 cups
10" × 2½" springform pan	12 cups
10" × 3½" Bundt (tube) pan	12 cups
17¼" × 11½" × 1" jelly roll pan	13 cups
13" × 9" × 2" rectangular pan	15 cups
12" × 2" round cake pan	15½ cups
10" × 4" tube pan	16 cups

PANS, CLEANING   *see* CLEANUP, KITCHEN

PAPAYAS   *see also* FRUIT, GENERAL

TIDBIT   The wondrous papaya tree takes only 18 months to grow from seed to a towering fruit-bearing 20-footer. The pear-shaped papaya (also called *pawpaw*) can range in size from 1 to 20 pounds.

PURCHASING   Choose richly colored papayas that give slightly to palm pressure. Green fruit will ripen quickly at home.

EQUIVALENTS   1 medium = 10 to 12 ounces, 1½ to 2 cups chopped

STORING   Refrigerate ripe papayas in a plastic bag for up to 1 week.

USING

* Ripen papayas quickly by placing them in a paper bag with an apple at room temperature. Pierce the bag in a couple of places with the tip of a knife, then seal.
* Ripe papaya is best eaten raw; slightly underripe fruit can be cooked as a vegetable.
* Peel a papaya, then cut it in half and use a spoon to scoop out the seeds.
* The shiny, grayish black seeds are usually discarded; however, they have a nice peppery taste and make a delicious salad dressing. Combine some of the seeds with your favorite vinaigrette in a blender and process until the mixture is puréed (*see* PURÉEING).
* Papaya contains *papain*, an enzyme that prevents gelatin from setting properly. Heat destroys the enzyme, so cooked papaya can be added to a gelatin mixture.
* This same enzyme is used in meat tenderizers. Make your own tenderizer by puréeing papaya and rubbing it all over the meat's surface. Or soak the meat in papaya juice, available at many supermarkets and most natural food stores. Cover and refrigerate the meat for 3 hours. Scrape off the papaya purée, pat the meat dry and cook as desired.
* Scoop out most of the flesh from a papaya and use the shell as a serving container for salads or fruit compotes.

PAPRIKA   *see also* SPICES *for purchase and storage information*

TIDBIT   Paprika is a powder made by grinding dried, aromatic sweet red peppers. Its flavor can range from mild to hot, the color from bright orange red to blood red. Most commercial paprika comes from Spain, South America, California and Hungary. The full-flavored Hungarian variety is considered superior, and comes in both mild and hot forms. Hot Hungarian paprika packs a punch similar to cayenne.

* Increase paprika's flavor by roasting it in a dry skillet for a few minutes. Cool before using.

PARBOILING   see BLANCHING; see also COOKING, GENERAL

PARCHMENT PAPER; KITCHEN PARCHMENT   see also ALUMINUM FOIL; PLASTIC WRAP; WAXED PAPER

TIDBIT The heavyweight parchment paper used culinarily is both grease and moisture resistant and doesn't scorch or discolor at high temperatures.

PURCHASING It's available in rolls, sheets and the precut 8- or 9-inch rounds at supermarkets, cake-supply stores and kitchenware shops.

USING

* Parchment paper is good for everything from stovetop to microwave to conventional oven cooking. It can be used to cover foods that are steamed or poached, and formed into packets around food to be baked.

* It requires no greasing, making it ideal for lining pans for cakes, cookies and candies, as well as for making collars for soufflé dishes. It makes a quick and disposable PASTRY BAG.

* To cut parchment paper into rounds: Set the pan to be traced upright on the paper and draw around it with a pencil; cut just inside the line you've drawn. For multiple rounds, simply fold or stack the parchment into layers and cut from one stencil.

* Before positioning parchment, grease the bottom of the pan so the paper will stay put.

* Lining cookie sheets with parchment paper has many benefits. You don't have to grease the cookie sheet, the cookie bottoms won't burn, you can slip the baked cookies on the parchment right off the baking sheet onto a rack to cool, and then slide on another sheet of parchment loaded with cookie dough.

* *En papillote* is a technique whereby food (fish, chicken, vegetables, fruit) is cooked inside a sealed parchment-paper packet. Delicate or quick-cooking foods are the best choices for this method. Fold a square or round (classically a heart shape) of parchment paper in half—the paper should be about twice the size of the food to be cooked in it. Position the food on one half of the paper, about an inch from the fold. Season or sauce the food as desired, dot with butter or sprinkle with wine or other liquid. Fold the parchment to enclose the food, crimping the edges with a series of small folds. Brush the parchment with melted butter and bake

at about 375°F for 10 to 20 minutes, depending on the food. During baking, the packet puffs and browns. Such food is served in the packet, with each diner opening his or her own portion, releasing a fragrantly flavorful puff of steam and revealing the delicately cooked food.

PARSLEY see also HERBS

TIDBIT The two most popular varieties of this herb are curly-leaf parsley and the more strongly flavored Italian or flat-leaf parsley.

PURCHASING Choose parsley with bright green leaves with no sign of wilting.

STORING Wash fresh parsley, then thoroughly blot off excess moisture with paper towels (or spin the parsley dry in a lettuce spinner). Wrap loosely in dry paper towels, then in a plastic bag and refrigerate for up to 1 week. Or cut off ½ inch of the stems and refrigerate a parsley bouquet, stem ends down, in a tall glass filled halfway with cold water and a pinch of sugar. Loosely cover with a plastic bag secured to the glass with a rubber band. Change the water every 2 days.

USING

* Revive wilted parsley by cutting off ½ inch of the stems, then standing the parsley in a glass of ice water. Refrigerate for at least 1 hour.
* No need to tear parsley leaves meticulously from their stems before chopping. Simply cut off the stems of an entire bunch as close to the leaves as possible. Parsley stems are relatively tender, so a few won't be noticeable in a batch of minced parsley.
* Thoroughly dry parsley leaves are much easier to chop than those that are damp.
* Instead of chopping them, hold parsley sprigs together and snip with kitchen shears.
* Finely chopped parsley will stay fluffy and light if you squeeze it in a double thickness of paper towels to remove all excess moisture. Loosely wrap in more paper towels, then in a plastic bag; refrigerate for up to 5 days.

GREMOLATA

Add a fresh lively flavor by sprinkling this classic blend over grilled meats, fish or poultry, soups, vegetables, almost anything. In a small bowl, combine ¼ cup finely chopped parsley, the finely minced zest of 1 medium lemon, and 3 garlic cloves, finely chopped. Can be made in advance, covered and refrigerated for up to 6 hours.

PARSNIPS see also VEGETABLES, GENERAL

PURCHASING Choose firm, small to medium, well-shaped parsnips. Avoid those that are limp, shriveled or spotted.

EQUIVALENTS 1 pound = 4 medium, 2 cups peeled and chopped

STORING Refrigerate in a plastic bag for up to 2 weeks.

USING

* Peel parsnips and trim the ends just before using.
* Parsnips have a naturally sweet flavor and can be used as you would carrots.
* Though one of the most popular ways to prepare parsnips is to cook and mash or PURÉE them, they're wonderful chopped and quickly sautéed. Pair them with chopped, tart apples as an adjunct to grilled or roasted meats.
* Add chopped parsnips to soups, stews and stir-fries. Or blanch (see BLANCHING), cool and use in salads.
* Parsnips quickly turn mushy when overcooked, so add them to soups, stews and sautés toward the end of the cooking time.

Everything you see I owe to spaghetti.
—Sophia Loren, Italian actor

PASTA *see also* CELLOPHANE NOODLES; PASTA SHAPES

TIDBIT It has long been reputed that the great Venetian traveler Marco Polo brought the concept of noodles back with him when he returned to Italy from China. Archaeological studies have since proved otherwise, with evidence that noodles most likely originated in Central Asia, possibly dating back to at least 1000 B.C. We now know that, in fact, this food form existed independently in both Asia and Europe well before Polo's expeditions.

PURCHASING

* Look for pasta made with durum wheat (also called *semolina*), which absorbs less water, has a mellow flavor and retains a pleasant "bite" when cooked.
* Dried pasta: Always check the package to make sure the pieces are unbroken. If it looks crumbly or dusty, air has gotten to it—choose another package.
* Fresh pasta: Check the date on the package to be sure the pasta is as fresh as possible. Inspect the package, checking to make sure the pasta looks fresh, not dry, and has no signs of mold.
* How much per serving: dried pasta—2 ounces per side-dish serving, 4 ounces per main-dish serving; fresh pasta—about 3 ounces per side-dish serving, 5 ounces per main-dish serving.

EQUIVALENTS

* Macaroni-style (1-inch shells, elbows, and so on): 1 pound dry = about 9 cups cooked; 1 cup = 1¼ cups cooked
* Spaghetti-style pasta (12 inches long): 1 pound dry = 7 to 8 cups cooked

STORING

* Dried pasta can be stored almost indefinitely in an airtight glass or plastic container in a cool, dark place. Dried whole-wheat pasta is the exception, as it may turn rancid if stored for more than 1 month.
* Fresh pasta can be wrapped airtight in a plastic bag and refrigerated for up to 5 days, or double wrapped and frozen for up to 4 months. Frozen fresh pasta should go directly from freezer to boiling water.

COOKING

* If you don't have a pasta pot with a removable, perforated inner basket, use a colander, large strainer or French-fry basket inside a pot of boiling water in which to cook pasta. That way, you can simply lift out the basket and shake it to drain off excess water.
* Use 3 to 4 quarts of water per pound of pasta. Unsalted water will reach a boil faster than salted water, so add salt to rapidly boiling water just before adding the pasta. Use about 1 teaspoon salt for each quart of water.
* Adding 1 tablespoon vegetable oil to the cooking water keeps pasta from sticking together while cooking. Although some cooks say adding oil to the water will cause sauce to slide off the pasta, I haven't found that to be true. Oil in the water also keeps the water from boiling over.
* Rubbing vegetable oil around the top of the pot will prevent boilovers.
* Have the water boiling rapidly before adding the pasta.
* No need to break long pasta like spaghetti and fettuccine into shorter pieces to fit in the pot. Simply put the pasta in the boiling water and, as it softens (in just a few seconds), use a long-handled spoon to ease it around and down into the pot.
* After you add pasta to boiling water, cover the pot to speed the water returning to a boil. Stir the pasta once or twice to keep it moving so it doesn't stick together.
* Once the water returns to a rolling boil, take the cover off. Stirring isn't necessary because the churning water moves the pasta.
* **When's it done?** The key is not to overcook pasta. Most commercial dried pasta needs less time to cook than the package recommends, while fresh pastas typically take about 2 minutes. The best way to test pasta for doneness is to bite into a piece. Perfectly cooked pasta should

be *al dente*—tender but still firm to the bite. If there's a noticeable "line" running through the thickest part of the pasta, it's not done. When you're testing for doneness, remember that residual heat continues to cook the pasta for a few seconds after it's removed from the water.

* When cooking pasta to be used in a dish requiring further cooking—such as a casserole or soup—reduce the cooking time by a third. The pasta will continue to cook and absorb liquid in the final dish.

* Cooking twice as much pasta at one time gives you a head start on the next night's meal. Thoroughly drain the portion you're not using, then put it in a bowl of ice water to stop the cooking. Drain thoroughly, then toss with 1 to 2 teaspoons oil. Cover and refrigerate for up to 4 days. You can use it in a salad or casserole, add it to soup (at the last minute) or toss it with your favorite sauce.

* Be sure to drain cooked pasta thoroughly. Cooking water clinging to the pasta will dilute the sauce.

* No need to rinse pasta with hot water unless you've let it stand and it sticks together. Then spritz it gently with hot running water for just a few seconds. Drain thoroughly before saucing.

* If the pasta will be used for salad, rinse it under cold running water to remove excess starch and keep the pieces from sticking together. Toss the pasta with a tablespoon of oil to ensure separation.

SAUCING THE PASTA

* Count on about 2 cups sauce per pound of pasta. Remember, the pasta should be coated with sauce, not submerged in it.

* Don't hesitate to use canned tomatoes for cooked pasta sauce. Their flavor is often superior to that of some fresh tomatoes.

* When making a long-cooking sauce, prepare it before putting the pasta on to boil, so the pasta won't have to wait around and become soggy.

* When saucing pasta, a general rule is: Thin or smooth noodles require a light, smooth sauce that won't overpower or weigh down the pasta; sturdy shapes like rotini can handle chunkier sauces.

* The next time you make pasta sauce, try doing so in a 12- or 14-inch skillet. That way you can turn the drained pasta right into the skillet and have plenty of room to toss it.

* Or return the drained pasta to the warm pot in which you cooked it, add the sauce and toss. This keeps the pasta warm and avoids dirtying another container.

SERVING AND EATING

* Pasta cools quickly, so always heat the serving bowl or plates before you dish it up. Dishes can be heated in a 250°F oven until warm, about 10 minutes. Or fill a serving bowl with very hot water, then pour it out and dry the bowl just before serving.

* The trick to eating long strands of pasta is to start with just a few strings near the edge of the plate, positioning your fork vertically to the plate's surface. Then begin twisting your fork, winding the long strands into a tight, bite-sized bundle. All that's left is to eat it!

* Try serving the pasta and sauce separately, letting diners sauce their servings according to taste.

* Reheating: There are several ways to reheat unsauced pasta. You can microwave it right in the storage container (if it's a plastic bag or freezer container, open one corner; if it's a lidded glass casserole, leave the cover on) on high for 2 to 4 minutes, stirring halfway through. The timing depends on the amount and temperature of the pasta. Room-temperature pasta can also be reheated simply by tossing it with hot sauce. Sauced pasta can be reheated in a covered saucepan over low heat or in the microwave, as previously suggested.

* Make a gratin out of leftover pasta by placing it in a shallow baking dish and layering it with sautéed mushrooms or green peppers or other vegetables. Moisten with a sauce of your choice and top with bread crumbs and grated cheese. Bake at 350°F until warmed through and the top is golden brown, about 25 minutes.

TOMATO-MINT PASTA SAUCE

Make this sauce in the summertime when fresh tomatoes and mint are rife. This sauce is just as good cold or at room temperature as it is hot. Heat ¼ cup olive oil in a medium saucepan over medium-high heat. Add 1 medium garlic clove, minced; cook 1 minute. Reduce the heat to medium; add 1½ pounds (6 to 7 medium) tomatoes that have been cored, seeded and coarsely chopped, and the finely grated zest of 1 medium lemon (about 2½ teaspoons). Cook, stirring often, for 2 minutes. Stir in ⅓ cup chopped fresh mint leaves; cook for 1 more minute. Salt and pepper to taste. Overcooking the sauce will cause it to lose its fresh flavor. Serve immediately over hot pasta. Serves 4.

PASTA SHAPES The hundreds of different shapes and sizes of pasta can be confusing, and the fact that manufacturers often use different names for the same shape (fusilli and rotini, for example) simply complicates matters.

P The following pasta-shape glossary should help you with those pastas most commonly available in supermarkets and Italian markets.

* *acini di pepe* ("peppercorns") Tiny peppercorn-shaped pasta
* *agnolotti* ("priests' caps") Small, crescent-shaped stuffed pasta
* *anellini* Tiny pasta rings
* *angel hair see capelli d'angelo*
* *bavettine* Narrow linguine
* *bucatini* Hollow, spaghettilike strands
* *cannaroni* Wide tubes; also called *zitoni*
* *cannelloni* ("large reeds") Large, round tubes generally used for stuffing
* *capelli d'angelo; capellini* ("angel hair") Long, extremely fine strands
* *capelvenere* Very thin noodles
* *cappelletti* ("little hats") Hat-shaped stuffed pasta
* *cavatappi* Short, thin, spiral macaroni
* *cavatelli* Short, narrow, ripple-edged shells
* *conchiglie* ("conch shells") Shell-shaped pasta, sometimes called *maruzze*
* *coralli* Tiny tubes, generally used in soup
* *ditali* ("thimbles") Small macaroni about ½ inch long; *ditalini*—smaller ditali
* *elbow macaroni* From small to medium tubes
* *farfalle* ("butterflies") Bow- or butterfly-shaped pasta
* *farfallini* Small *farfalle; farfallone* are large *farfalle*
* *fedelini* ("little faithful ones") Very fine spaghetti
* *fettuccine* ("little ribbons") Thin, flat egg noodles about ¼ inch wide; *fettucce* (about ½ inch wide) are the widest of the fettuccines; *fettuccelle* (about ⅛ inch wide), the thinnest
* *fideo* Thin, coiled strands that resemble *vermicelli* when cooked.
* *fusilli* ("little springs") Traditional *fusilli* comes in spaghetti-length spiral-shaped noodles; cut *fusilli* is about 1½ inches long
* *gemelli* ("twins") Short, 1½-inch twists that resemble two strands of spaghetti twisted together
* *gnocchi* Small, ripple-edged shells
* *lasagne* Long, very broad noodles (2 to 3 inches wide); straight or ripple-edged
* *linguine* ("little tongues") Very narrow (⅛ inch wide or less) ribbons
* *lumache* ("snails") Large shells intended for stuffing
* *macaroni* Tube-shaped pasta of various lengths
* *maccheroni* The Italian word for all types of macaroni, from hollow tubes, to shells, to twists

* *mafalde* Broad, flat, ripple-edged noodles
* *magliette* ("links") Short, curved tubes of pasta
* *manicotti* ("little muffs") Very large tubes, used for stuffing
* *margherite* ("daisies") Narrow, flat noodles, with one rippled side
* *maruzze see* CONCHIGLIE
* *melone see* SEMI DE MELONE
* *mezzani* Very short, curved tubes
* *mostaccioli* ("little mustaches") Pasta tubes about 2 inches long
* *orecchiette* ("little ears") Tiny disk shapes
* *orzo* Pasta grains, the size and shape of rice
* *pappardelle* Wide noodles (about ⅜ inch) with rippled sides
* *pastina* ("tiny dough") Any of various tiny pasta shapes (such as *acini di pepe*), generally used in soups
* *penne* ("pens" or "quills") Diagonally cut tubes with either smooth or ridged sides
* *perciatelli* Thin, hollow pasta about twice as thick as spaghetti; similar to *bucatini*
* *pizzoccheri* Thick buckwheat noodles
* *quadrettini* Small, flat squares of pasta
* *radiatore* ("little radiators") Short, chunky shapes (about 1 inch long and ½ inch in diameter) that resemble tiny ripple-edge radiators
* *ravioli* Square-shaped stuffed pasta
* *rigatoni* Large grooved macaroni about 1½ inches wide
* *riso* Rice-shaped pasta, similar to *orzo*
* *rotelle* ("little wheels") Small, spoked-wheel shapes
* *rotini* Short (1 to 2 inches long) spirals
* *ruote; ruote de carro* ("cartwheels") Small, spoked-wheel shapes
* *semi de melone* ("melon seeds") Tiny, flat melon-seed shapes
* *spaghetti* Long, thin, round strands; *spaghettini* is very thin spaghetti
* *tagliarini* Long, paper-thin ribbons, usually less than ⅛ inch wide (also called *tagliolini*)
* *tagliatelle* Long, thin, flat egg noodles about ¼ inch wide
* *tagliolini see* TAGLIARINI
* *tortellini* ("little twists") Small stuffed pasta, similar to *cappelletti; Tortelloni* is a larger version
* *trenette* A narrower, thicker version of *tagliatelle*
* *tripolini* Small bow ties with rounded edges
* *tubetti* ("little tubes") Tiny, hollow pasta tubes
* *vermicelli* ("little worms") Very thin strands of spaghetti

* *ziti* ("bridegrooms") Slightly curved tubes, ranging in length from 2 to 12 inches
* *zitoni see* CANNARONI

PASTRY BAGS

TIDBIT   Pastry bags are used for decorating cakes, forming cookies and pastries, and so on. They come in a variety of sizes and are cone-shaped with two open ends. The small, pointed end can be fitted with decorative tips; the large end receives the mixture to be piped. The most popular pastry-bag materials are nylon and plastic-lined cotton or canvas, polyester and clear plastic (which are disposable). Pastry bags can be found in gourmet shops, some supermarkets and department stores.

* Use a small, zip-closure plastic bag for a quick, disposable pastry bag in one of several ways. Spoon the frosting into the bag, squeeze out the air and seal, then snip off one of the corners and pipe your design. Or snip ¼ to ½ inch from a corner of a plastic bag and insert a piping tip into the opening. Fill the bag with frosting and seal.
* Make an instant, disposable pastry bag by folding a square of PARCHMENT PAPER or waxed paper in half diagonally to form a triangle. Shape the triangle into a cone, securing the top edge with Scotch tape or a paper clip. Fill two-thirds full with frosting, melted and cooled chocolate or filling of your choice. Fold down the top of the bag a couple of times to seal, then snip off the pointed end so the hole is the desired diameter.
* Filling a pastry bag is much easier if you can use two hands. Twist about 2 inches of the tip end so the filling won't come out. Set the bag, twisted end down, in a wide-mouthed jar or 4-cup measuring cup; fold the cuff of the bag over the jar's rim. Fill the bag about two-thirds full, then twist the top closed and lift the bag out of its holder.
* After you fill a pastry bag, put your finger over the opening and give it a shake to compact the filling and eliminate air pockets.
* Melt chocolate right in the bag: Put finely chopped chocolate or chocolate chips in a small, heavy-duty plastic bag (a regular-weight bag could melt). Set the unsealed bag upright in a small bowl and microwave at medium (50 percent power) until the chocolate is almost melted; let stand for 5 minutes until completely melted. Squeeze out the air, seal the bag, snip a tiny hole in a corner of the bag and pipe directly onto the dessert. Or seal the bag of chopped chocolate and set in a bowl of very hot water until the chocolate melts (make sure no water gets into the chocolate). Thoroughly dry the bag with a paper towel, and proceed as above.

* Pipe a mixture from a pastry bag by applying pressure from the top, continually twisting it tight against the filling as the bag empties.

PASTRY BRUSHES Small brushes that are used for applying liquids like glazes and marinades to foods. Pastry brushes can be made of natural (sterilized) bristles, nylon bristles or goose feathers. Natural bristles are preferred because they're soft and hold more liquid than nylon bristles and are more durable than feathers. Nylon bristles can melt when subjected to high heat.
* A good all-purpose pastry brush is 1½ inches wide.
* Smell a used pastry brush to make sure no rancid odor remains from its last use. Off odors can transfer easily to food.
* Make quick work out of greasing pans, baking sheets and muffin tins by using a pastry brush dipped in oil or melted shortening.
* Wash pastry brushes in hot, soapy water (or put in the dishwasher) to rid them of any oil or other ingredient that might turn rancid. Be sure to rinse brushes thoroughly after washing.

PASTRY, PIE *see* PIE CRUST

PEA *see* PEAS

Rather one bite of peach than a basketful of apricots.
—Chinese proverb

PEACHES *see also* FRUIT, GENERAL
TIDBIT Although the phrase "Georgia peach" suggests that state is the land of peaches, California is by far the largest grower in the United States. Peaches fall into two classifications—**freestone**, in which the stone or pit easily comes away from the flesh, and **clingstone** (or **cling**), where the fruit adheres stubbornly to the pit. Freestone peaches are more commonly available in markets, while clings are widely used for commercial purposes.
PURCHASING Choose intensely fragrant fruit that gives slightly to palm pressure. Avoid peaches that are hard, show signs of greening or have soft spots (bruises).
EQUIVALENTS 1 pound = 4 medium, 2¾ cups sliced, 1 cup purée
STORING Refrigerate ripe peaches in a plastic bag for up to 5 days. Store unripe fruit at room temperature.

USING

* Ripen underripe peaches at room temperature by placing in a paper bag with an apple; pierce the bag in several places with the tip of a knife.
* The flavor of a peach is intensified at room temperature, so take it out of the fridge at least 30 minutes before eating.
* Washing a peach will remove much of the fuzz—something to consider when eating a peach out of hand.
* Peel peaches to be cooked—the skin becomes tough during cooking and could ruin the texture of a pie, preserves and so on.
* To peel a peach, dip it in boiling water for 30 to 45 seconds, then use a slotted spoon to transfer it immediately from the hot water to a bowl of ice water. Use a paring knife to pull off the skin. If the skin's resistant, repeat the process or simply use the knife to peel off any obstinate skin. Return the peeled peaches to the ice water.
* Or loosen the peel by microwaving at 100 percent about 15 seconds; let stand for 2 minutes.
* When cutting peaches, do so over a bowl so none of the perfumy juice is lost.
* A peach's flesh will discolor rapidly after being cut or peeled. If not combining peaches with an ingredient containing acid (such as a salad dressing), quickly dip the fruit in ACIDULATED WATER; drain well.
* Pit peaches by cutting from stem to stem all the way to the stone. Twist the peach halves in opposite directions to separate them, and pull out the pit.
* Few fruit desserts are better than the classic peach Melba—poached peach halves and vanilla ice cream topped with raspberry sauce.

PEACH MELBA SHORTCAKE

Beat whipping cream to soft-peak stage. Add 2 tablespoons seedless raspberry jam; beat the cream until stiff. Spoon the cream over layers of shortcake (or biscuits, sponge or angel-food cake) and sliced peaches that have been tossed with a little Chambord (raspberry-flavored liqueur).

GINGER-BOURBON PEACHES

Southern-style peaches that can be served plain, or drizzled with cream, or topped with a dollop of whipped cream or served over ice cream. In a large bowl, combine 2 teaspoons minced crystallized ginger and ¼ cup packed brown sugar. Use the back of a kitchen tablespoon to crush the sugar into the ginger to release its essence. Add ½ teaspoon ground allspice, 1 tablespoon lemon juice, 2 teaspoons pure vanilla extract and ½ cup bourbon. Add 4 large, ripe (but firm) peaches, peeled and cut into about ½-inch chunks, folding to coat with the bourbon mixture. Cover tightly and refrigerate for at least 3 hours. Let the peaches stand at room temperature for 30 minutes before serving. Serves 4 to 6.

Man cannot live by bread alone. He must have peanut butter.
—Bill Cosby, American comedian, actor, author

PEANUT BUTTER *see also* PEANUTS

TIDBIT Peanut butter was developed in 1890 and touted as "health food" at the 1904 St. Louis World's Fair. Today about half of the peanuts grown in the United States are used to make peanut butter—about 822 peanuts go into making an 18-ounce jar. Most of the fat in peanut butter is unsaturated. Hydrogenated oils (*see* FATS AND OILS) are added to regular peanut butter to keep the natural oils from separating, but the resulting trans fatty acids in 2 tablespoons are typically no more than 0.1 grams.

PURCHASING There are three primary styles of peanut butter, all commonly available in supermarkets. **Regular peanut butter** is typically a blend of ground peanuts, vegetable oil, salt, sugar and stabilizers. It comes in smooth and chunky styles; some are flavored variously with chocolate, fruit or honey. **Reduced-fat peanut butter** contains 12 grams of fat per serving instead of 16, but it has the same amount of calories because it contains more sugar. **Natural peanut butter** simply contains peanuts and, sometimes, a soupçon of salt.

EQUIVALENT 18-ounce jar = 1¾ cups

STORING

* Regular and reduced-fat peanut butter can be stored, unopened, in a cool, dry place for at least 1 year. Once opened, regular peanut butter can be stored at room temperature for about 3 months. Refrigerate after that to keep the oil from turning rancid.

* Natural peanut butter must be refrigerated after opening, and will keep for about 6 months.

USING

* Because natural peanut butter doesn't contain stabilizers, the oil typically separates and rises to the top. Some people pour off the oil to save calories, which results in a dry spread. For peanut butter the way it was intended, simply stir the oil back into the mixture. Do this slowly so as not to make a mess. If you think of it ahead of time, turn the jar on its head and allow the oil to rise up through the peanut butter and soften it.

* Homemade peanut butter: Chop peanuts (plain or dry roasted) in a food processor or blender. When the nuts are very finely ground, add a little

vegetable or peanut oil and salt, if desired; process until the peanut butter reaches the consistency desired.

* Peanut butter in soup is an old Southern favorite. Stir a tablespoon or two into your next batch of chicken soup and taste the magic.
* Add an exotic touch to sauces and marinades for poultry and meat by adding 1 to 2 tablespoons peanut butter.
* Morning toast spread with peanut butter and drizzled with a little honey or maple syrup is delicious and much more nutritious than butter or margarine.
* Make a special bread pudding by spreading the bread slices with peanut butter before layering them with the custard mixture.
* Tired of peanut butter and jelly sandwiches? Next time, mix a little chutney or mashed banana with the peanut butter, or put a layer of potato chips, dill-pickle slices or rashers of crispy bacon on top of the peanut butter.
* Don't throw out used peanut butter jars—their wide-mouth openings make them great for storing food.

PEANUT-GINGER SAUCE

Just as yummy over hot noodles as it is with chicken or pork. Combine 1 cup very hot chicken broth, ¾ cup peanut butter (creamy or chunky), 3 tablespoons light-sodium soy sauce, 3 tablespoons fresh lime juice, 2 garlic cloves, 1 tablespoon minced fresh ginger and ¼ to ½ teaspoon cayenne pepper in a blender. Cover and process at high speed until the mixture is smooth. Turn into a small saucepan; heat gently just until hot. Cooking it too long will overthicken peanut butter—if this sauce becomes too thick, simply thin with hot water. Makes about 2 cups.

> *I hate television. I hate it as much as peanuts.*
> *But I can't stop eating peanuts.*
> —Orson Welles, American actor, filmmaker

PEANUTS *For general purchase, storage, toasting and usage information, see* NUTS, GENERAL. *See also* PEANUT BUTTER

TIDBIT Peanuts don't grow on trees like other nuts—in fact, they aren't really nuts at all. Peanuts are actually legumes (like beans) and, at one stage of its growth, the peanut plant looks very much like the common garden pea plant. The plant's seeds have a papery brown skin and are contained in a thin, netted, tan-colored pod. After flowering, the plant bends down to the earth and buries its pods in the ground, which is why peanuts are also called *groundnuts, earth nuts*, and, in the South, *goobers* or *goober peas*.

PURCHASING Although there are several peanut varieties, the two most popular are the small, round **Spanish peanut** and the larger, more oval **Virginia peanut.**

✳ Unshelled peanuts should have clean, unbroken, unblemished shells and shouldn't rattle when shaken.

✳ Shelled peanuts, often available in vacuum-sealed jars or cans, are usually roasted and sometimes salted.

EQUIVALENTS

✳ In shell: 1 pound = 3 cups shelled

✳ Shelled: 2 cups = 1 cup peanut butter

STORING

✳ Refrigerate unshelled peanuts, tightly wrapped, for up to 6 months.

✳ Unopened, vacuum-packed peanuts can be stored at room temperature for up to 1 year. Once opened, refrigerate airtight and used within 3 months.

USING Don't think of eating peanuts just for snacks. They're great in main dishes (everything from meat loaf to soups), tossed in salads, in fillings for acorn squash or bell peppers, in muffins or as a garnish for vegetables like carrots.

> *Two of life's mysteries—how does the ship get into the bottle, and how does the pear get into the bottle of pear eau de vie.*
> —Jane Grigson, British food writer

PEARS *see also* FRUIT, GENERAL

TIDBIT To answer one of the mysteries Jane Grigson mentioned, the pear inside the bottle of pear *eau de vie* (known also as *Poire Williams*) is grown there. The bottle is placed over the budding fruit, the fruit grows inside, then the bottle is removed from the branch and is filled with Williams-pear brandy.

PURCHASING Choose pears that are fragrant, blemish free and firm, but not hard. Pears for out-of-hand eating should be just slightly soft at the stem end; those for cooking, somewhat firmer.

EQUIVALENTS 1 pound = 3 medium, 2 cups sliced

STORING

✳ Ripe fruit should be refrigerated in a plastic bag for up to 5 days.

✳ Unripe fruit can be ripened at room temperature by placing them in a

P

paper bag with an apple. Pierce the bag in several places with the tip of a knife. Unlike most fruit, pears are still fairly firm when ripe.

USING

* No need to peel a pear for eating out of hand. Simply wash it well and enjoy.
* Peel pears for cooking—the skin darkens and toughens when heated. A vegetable peeler or sharp knife will easily remove the thin skin.
* Core with a paring knife or melon baller, making sure to get all the surrounding gritty flesh.
* The flesh of a pear quickly browns when exposed to air. To preserve the pale color, dip cut pears in ACIDULATED WATER. This isn't necessary when using pears with an acidic ingredient, such as a salad dressing.

PEPPERED PEAR SOUP

Make this supereasy soup the day before so the flavors can mingle and mellow. In a blender, combine 2 cups defatted chicken broth, 6 peeled, cored ripe pears, cut into chunks, 2 tablespoons lemon juice, 1½ tablespoons finely chopped crystallized ginger and ¼ teaspoon freshly ground pepper. Cover and process, starting on low and gradually increasing to high, until the soup is smooth. Salt to taste; refrigerate overnight. Garnish each serving with a dollop of crème fraîche or sour cream, dusted with ground pepper. Serves 4 to 6.

PEAS, DRIED (SPLIT PEAS, FIELD PEAS) *see also* BEANS, DRIED; LENTILS; PEAS, FRESH GREEN

TIDBIT Field peas are a variety of yellow or green pea grown specifically for drying. Such peas usually split along a natural seam, in which case they're called *split peas*.

PURCHASING Dried peas are available, whole and split, in supermarkets and natural food stores.

EQUIVALENTS 1 pound = 2¼ cups, 5 cups cooked

STORING

* Store dried peas in an airtight container in a cool, dry place for up to 1 year; freeze indefinitely.
* Refrigerate leftover cooked whole or split peas for up to 5 days.

PREPARING

* Before using, pick through dried peas, discarding any that are discolored or shriveled. Tiny holes signal bugs.
* Split peas don't require soaking before being cooked.
* Dried whole peas must be soaked before being cooked. **Soaking**

overnight: Put the whole peas in a large bowl or pot and cover with at least 3 inches of cold water; soak overnight. (If flatulence is a problem, change the water at least twice during the soaking process.) **Quick-soak:** Put the peas in a large pan, cover with water and bring to a boil. Remove from the heat, cover and let stand for 1 to 2 hours. Drain the water and cook.

✻ Salt peas after they're cooked. Adding salt to the cooking liquid slows down the cooking and toughens the peas.

✻ For a great flavor, add smoked sausage, ham or bacon to cooked split peas and split-pea soup.

✻ After cooking, immediately drain off the hot cooking liquid or the peas will continue to cook. Unless, of course, you're cooking split peas for soup, in which case it doesn't matter if they're soft.

In the vegetable world, there is nothing so innocent, so confiding in its expression, as the small green face of the freshly shelled spring pea.
—William Wallace Irwin, American politician

PEAS, FRESH GREEN see also PEAS, DRIED; PEAS, POD

TIDBIT Fresh green peas, long a sign that spring has sprung, are also known as *English peas, shell peas* and *garden peas*. Overindulgence in green peas can be dangerous, however—it's said that England's King John so loved peas that he died after consuming seven bowls of them.

PURCHASING Choose those that have firm, plump, unblemished, bright green pods; avoid pale or shriveled specimens. The peas inside should be glossy, crunchy and sweet, not starchy. The tiny, young *petits pois* are generally available only in specialty produce markets. Peas begin the sugar-to-starch conversion process the moment they're picked, so buy them as fresh as possible.

EQUIVALENT 1 pound peas in pod = about 1 cup shelled

STORING Refrigerate, unwashed, in a plastic bag for no more than 2 days.

PREPARING

✻ Shell peas just before using. To do so, snap off the stem end and use it to "unzip" the pod by pulling on the string. Press on the seam to pop it open, then run your thumb or finger under the peas to free them.

✻ Don't discard the pods. Either freeze them (for up to 3 months), or add them to a pot of chicken or vegetable stock, simmer for 1 hour, then remove with a slotted spoon. The flavored broth can be frozen and used for your next soup.

COOKING

* Cook peas only until crisp-tender. Overdone peas lose both color and flavor.
* Adding baking soda to the cooking water may keep peas green, but it'll leach out valuable nutrients in the process and affect their flavor detrimentally.
* Peas lose their bright green color when cooked with acidic ingredients, like lemon juice, wine or tomatoes, in a covered pot.
* Young green peas are perfectly wonderful raw in salads.
* Frozen green peas—especially the tiny, sweet *petits pois*—don't need defrosting before being added to a cooked dish. Simply add them 2 to 3 minutes before the cooking time is finished. The heat of the dish will cook them just enough, and they'll be crisp and fresh-tasting rather than mushy.
* To use frozen peas in salads, simply pour cold water over the frozen peas and let stand for about 5 minutes, or until the peas are defrosted. Drain well before adding to the salad.

PEAS, POD see also PEAS, FRESH GREEN

TIDBIT Pod peas are completely edible—pod and all. The two main varieties of pod peas are snow peas and sugar snap peas. **Snow peas** (also known as **Chinese pea pods**) are thin, crisp and have almost translucent, bright green pods. The **sugar snap pea** is a cross between the snow pea and the English pea (common green pea). It has a plump, crisp, bright green pod in which the peas are more prominent.

PURCHASING Choose snow and sugar snap peas that fit the descriptions in PEAS, FRESH GREEN. Avoid pods that are limp or broken.

STORING Refrigerate unwashed snow and sugar snap peas in a plastic bag for up to 3 days.

PREPARING

* Before using, wash pod peas, then snap off the stem ends, using them to pull off the string, if necessary.
* Pod peas should either be served raw or cooked only briefly. When using in dishes like stir-fries, add them during the last minute or so of cooking time.

Pecan pie, with loads of cream, will be part of the American-built heaven.
—Tom Stobart, British author, TV producer

PECANS *For general purchase, storage, toasting and usage information, see* NUTS, GENERAL

TIDBIT   Pecans have a fat content of over 70 percent.

PURCHASING   Choose unshelled nuts with crack-free shells. The nut shouldn't rattle when shaken.

EQUIVALENTS

* In shell: 1 pound = 3 cups shelled
* Shelled: 1 pound = 4 cups halves, 3¾ cups chopped

PREPARING   Pecans will be easier to crack if you cover them with water, then bring to a boil. Remove from the heat, cover and set aside for at least 15 minutes, or until cool. Blot the nuts dry, then crack end to end.

> *Don't be too daring in the kitchen. For example, don't suddenly*
> *get involved with shallots. . . . Even with coriander you're*
> *on thin ice. . . . Stay with safe things, like pepper.*
> —Bruce Jay Friedman, American author

PEPPER; PEPPERCORNS   *see also* SPICES

TIDBIT   Pepper was once so extremely rare and valuable that it was used as currency. Indeed, it was covetousness of the precious peppercorn that launched myriad fifteenth-century sailing expeditions in search of alternate trade routes to this spice's primary source, the Far East.

PURCHASING   All the following types of pepper are usually available in supermarkets.

* **Black peppercorns** are the strongest flavored of the three primary types. They're picked when the berry's not quite ripe, then dried until it shrivels and darkens. Black peppercorns are slightly hot with a hint of sweetness. Among the world's best black peppers are the Tellicherry and the Lampong.
* **White peppercorns** are the fully ripe berries from which the skin has been removed; they have a milder, less pungent flavor.
* **Green peppercorns,** the soft, underripe berries, are usually preserved in brine and have a fresh, "green" flavor. They're also sold dried.
* **Cayenne pepper** (also called *red pepper*) is ground from a variety of chile peppers, therefore its hot, spicy flavor.
* **Szechuan pepper** berries come from the prickly ash tree and resemble black peppercorns but with a tiny seed; they're mildly hot and have a distinctive flavor and fragrance.
* **Pink peppercorns** are actually the dried berries from the Baies rose plant; they're pungent and slightly sweet.

STORING

* Dried peppercorns: Store in a cool, dark place for at least 1 year.
* Green peppercorns: Brine-packed peppercorns should be refrigerated

P

once opened and can be kept for 1 month; water-packed peppercorns for 1 week. Freeze-dried forms can be stored in a cool, dark place for about 6 months.

* Ground pepper: Store in a cool, dark place for no more than 3 months— it quickly loses its flavor.

USING

* Nothing compares to the flavor of freshly cracked, crushed or ground pepper. If you don't have a pepper mill, use a mortar and pestle to crush the peppercorns to the texture you like. Or put peppercorns in a heavy-weight plastic bag and whack firmly with a rolling pin, mallet or the bottom of a heavy saucepan.
* Use white pepper if you don't want to mar the appearance of light-colored sauces and other preparations.
* Adding ½ teaspoon peppercorns to a shaker full of ground pepper will freshen the flavor and keep it shaking freely.
* Set a pepper mill in a small glass dish to keep the counter- or tabletop clean.

PEPPERS, BELL *see* BELL PEPPERS

PERSIMMONS *see also* FRUIT, GENERAL

TIDBIT The two most widely available persimmon varieties in the United States are the Hachiya (also called *Japanese persimmon*) and the Fuyu. The **Hachiya** is large and round, with a slightly elongated, pointed base; the **Fuyu** is smaller and more tomato-shaped.

PURCHASING Choose plump persimmons with a glossy, brilliant red orange skin; their caps should be green. The Hachiya should be quite soft (but not mushy) when ripe, whereas a fully ripe Fuyu will be firm, yet give to gentle palm pressure.

STORING Refrigerate ripe persimmons in a plastic bag for up to 3 days.

PREPARING

* Ripen persimmons by putting them in a pierced paper bag with an apple at room temperature. Overripe persimmons turn mushy, so watch them carefully.
* Cold temperatures have an amazing effect on persimmons—it makes them sweeter. If you want to PURÉE persimmons for use in a recipe but the fruit's a little underripe, speed up the process by putting the persimmons in a freezer-weight plastic bag and freezing until solid. Thaw at room temperature and the persimmons will be sweet and ready to go.

* For persimmons to be eaten out of hand, simply wash thoroughly. For cooking, peel the fruit first.
* Some Hachiyas contain a few black seeds, which should be removed before using the flesh in baked goods and other dishes.
* If a Hachiya persimmon is eaten even slightly underripe, it will pucker your mouth with an incredible astringency. The Fuyu, on the other hand, is not at all astringent.
* For persimmon "sherbet," cut the fruit in half, wrap each half in plastic wrap, and freeze for about 4 hours, then eat right out of the skin. Or peel (and seed, if necessary), cut into chunks and freeze. When the persimmon chunks are solid, PURÉE in a food processor.
* Persimmons are usually puréed before being used in cooking or for baked goods. To keep the fruit from darkening, add 1 teaspoon lemon juice for each persimmon.

PHYLLO; FILO

TIDBIT Phyllo is the Greek word for "leaf," and describes a tissue-thin pastry dough used in sweet and savory dishes of Greek and Near Eastern origin.

PURCHASING Phyllo is typically sold in 1-pound boxes, and can be found fresh in many Middle Eastern markets and frozen in most supermarkets.

STORING Refrigerate, tightly wrapped, for up to a month. Once opened, use phyllo within a few days. Freeze for up to 1 year.

USING

* Thaw frozen phyllo overnight in the refrigerator. It becomes brittle if refrozen.
* Phyllo sheets quickly become dry and brittle, so have everything ready to go before removing them from their wrapping.
* Keep phyllo sheets you're not working with from drying out by covering them with waxed paper topped by a slightly damp cloth. Don't let the cloth touch the phyllo—it'll make it soggy and unmanageable.

Everything tastes better outdoors.
—Claudia Roden, food writer

PICNICS *see also* FOOD SAFETY

TIDBIT Each year thousands of deaths and millions of illnesses are linked to food poisoning. One bacterium can grow to over two million in seven hours. Make your picnic safe by following a few simple guidelines.

P

PACKING THE FOOD

* All perishable food should be well chilled before being packed in a cooler.
* Double wrap raw poultry, meat or fish so juices won't leak and contaminate other foods.
* If the trip will be long, freeze raw chicken and meat, and put it frozen into the cooler. It will thaw during the journey.
* Never partially cook food (like meat or poultry) to be finished at the picnic site. Partially cooked food is the perfect breeding ground for harmful bacteria.
* Contrary to popular belief, foods containing commercial mayonnaise are not destined to cause food poisoning. On the contrary—store-bought mayo has enough acid (lemon juice or vinegar) to prevent bacterial growth, and the eggs used to make it are pasteurized.
* Keep cold foods cold (40°F or less) and hot foods hot (at least 140°F). Bacteria multiply rapidly at temperatures between 40°F and 140°F.
* Pack perishable food in a well-insulated cooler, surrounded by sufficient gel packs or ice to maintain a temperature of 40°F.
* No cooler? Line a picnic basket or cardboard box with a thermal blanket and then a large plastic bag. Fill with blue-ice packs and the items that need chilling.
* If you don't have ice packs, soak sponges in water, then put them in plastic bags, seal and freeze until solid. In an insulated cooler, they should last for up to 3 hours, depending on the size of the sponge.
* Homemade ice packs: Fill clean milk cartons with water and freeze. Or line large, shallow plastic storage containers with foil or plastic wrap, fill with water and freeze until solid. Transfer the chunk of ice to a zip-closure plastic bag. Large chunks of ice melt more slowly than ice cubes.
* A full cooler will stay cold longer than one that's only partially filled.
* Keep beverages in one cooler and food in another for easy access.
* If possible, put the cooler and other containers of food inside the car during the trip to the picnic site. The trunk gets too hot.
* Keep hot foods hot by insulating the containers with a layer of heavy-duty foil, then several layers of newspaper. Don't forget the two-hour rule (*see* page 355).
* Use a small muffin tin as a condiment server, each section holding something different—ketchup, mustard, chopped onions, sliced pickles, relish, and so on.
* An egg carton makes a handy container for small, bruisable items that

need protection, such as apricots, plums, tomatoes and deviled eggs (individually wrap the latter in plastic wrap).

* Make portable, disposable salt and pepper shakers by filling separate paper straws with the seasoning, then tightly twisting the ends to close.

PACKING OTHER THINGS

* Pack plenty of serving plates and utensils—never put food on a plate that has held raw meat, poultry or seafood. Likewise, never eat with a fork that has touched raw meat or poultry.
* Take along a large plastic bag in case there are no trash barrels.
* If you think the ground might be damp, take a plastic tarp or several large plastic bags to spread out underneath the tablecloth or blanket.
* Wrap a napkin around each place setting (fork, spoon and knife) and tie with a 6-inch piece of colorful yarn.
* Take plenty of towelettes for cleaning hands and soapy sponges or cloths for cleaning surfaces.

AT THE PICNIC

* Put the cooler in the shade and cover it with a blanket.
* The more you open the cooler lid, the faster the internal temperature will rise.
* If you're grilling at a picnic site, leave the meat in the cooler until just before cooking, and remove only the amount of meat that'll fit on the grill.
* After handling raw meat, clean your hands well with a hand-sanitizer product or the soapy sponges or cloths you brought.
* **The two-hour rule:** Food must be consumed within 2 hours from the time it's taken out of the cooler or off the grill. Special care should be taken with foods such as eggs, dairy products, meat, poultry and seafood.
* Several clove-studded lemon halves set on the table will help diminish flies.
* Keep bugs from getting into drinks by covering the glass with foil, then poking a straw through the foil.
* Bacteria grow rapidly at warm temperatures, so at the picnic's end, throw out perishables like lunch meats, potato or pasta salad, and cooked or raw meat or poultry.

For generations, it has been as American as apple pie to want a piece of the pie, even though getting it might not be as easy as pie. . . .
—Jay Jacobs, American author, food critic

PIE see also GREASING PANS; MERINGUE; PIE CRUSTS; PIE PANS

THE CRUST *see* PIE CRUSTS

THE FILLING

* Taste the fruit to be used for a filling. If it isn't sweet enough, slice it very thinly so there'll be more surfaces to absorb the sugar.

* When making a pie with superjuicy fruit, stir 1 tablespoon quick-cooking tapioca into the filling. During baking, the tapioca will absorb and thicken some of the excess juice and keep the filling from bubbling over.

* Fruit-pie boilovers can also be avoided by sticking 3 or 4 pieces of raw tubular macaroni through the top crust in a circle about 1 inch from the center. The macaroni tubes allow the steam to vent, thereby releasing the pressure that would force out the juices. Short pieces of paper drinking straws will also do the trick. Needless to say, remove the macaroni or straws from the pie after baking.

* To prevent a fruit pie's juices from spreading when you dish it up, just before baking fold into the filling 1 egg white, beaten until stiff with 2 tablespoons of the sugar in the recipe.

* Have your fruit-and-cheese course in a pie. Sprinkle ½ to 1 cup grated Cheddar over the top of an apple or pear pie before positioning the top crust. The cheese will melt down over the fruit during baking and add a delicious flavor.

* Instead of "dotting the surface with butter" (as for apple pie), you'll get better coverage if you rub a stick of cold butter over the coarse side of a grater, evenly sprinkling the grated butter over the surface.

* Wait until just before baking before filling the pie shell. Doing so in advance and letting the unbaked pie stand can cause a soggy bottom crust. If you want to prepare things in advance, refrigerate the crust and filling separately, and complete the pie right before baking.

* Freeze a pie filling during the summer when fruit is plentiful and enjoy fruit pie during the winter. Simply line a pie pan with heavy-duty foil, leaving plenty of overlap to cover and seal the top. Fill the foil-lined pan with the fruit filling of your choice, seal and freeze. When solid, remove the foil-wrapped filling from the pie pan, label the contents and return to the freezer for up to 6 months. When ready to bake, unwrap and place frozen filling in the pie crust, then position and flute the top crust, cover-

ing the edges with foil. Bake at 425°F for 30 minutes; remove the foil and bake 25 to 30 minutes longer until the crust is golden brown.

* Add a new dimension to pumpkin pie by adding ¼ cup pure maple syrup; decrease the sugar and liquid by 2 tablespoons each.
* When making any kind of custard pie (including pumpkin), stir the mixture only until it is well combined. Beating it until frothy will cause unsightly bubbles to form on the surface of the baked pie.
* To prevent a custard filling from spilling as you put the pie in the oven, pull out the oven rack a few inches, place the unfilled pie shell on the oven rack, then pour in the filling. Very gently return the rack to its original position.
* For cream pies, where the pie shell and filling are cooked separately, be sure both are cooled completely before turning the filling into the shell. This prevents the crust from becoming soggy.

BAKING AND COOLING

* Before beginning to bake, position the oven rack in the middle of the oven; preheat the oven for 10 to 15 minutes. Use an oven THERMOMETER for accurate temperature.
* Grease and flour pie pans for fruit pies where bubbling juices might cause the crust to stick to the pan.
* Save on messy oven cleanup by baking pies prone to boilovers—such as fruit pies and those with liquid sweeteners like molasses—on a baking sheet coated lightly with cooking spray.
* It's important that oven heat circulate freely and evenly. If baking two pies on one shelf, position the pans so there's at least 2 inches between each pie and the sides of the oven. If baking on two shelves, position the pans so that one doesn't sit directly beneath the other.
* If a crust's fluted edges begin to brown too fast, the quickest remedy is to cut the bottom out of a disposable aluminum pie plate (the same size as the pie you're baking) and invert it over the pie, covering the fluted edges and leaving the center open to the oven heat. Or you can make a crust shield by cutting a 12-inch wide piece of foil 3 inches longer than the pan's diameter (for example, an 11-inch length of foil for an 8-inch pie pan). Cut out a center circle that's 2 inches smaller than the pan's diameter. When the crust begins to brown, place the foil over the pie, gently curving the excess to cover the fluted edge.
* There are two ways to test a custard pie for doneness. The first is to insert a dinner knife into the pie about an inch from the center. If the knife comes out clean, the pie's done. The second, "jiggle" method is done by holding the edge of the pie pan with a potholder and gently

shaking the pie. If you can't get a grip on the pan, shake the oven shelf. If the center inch of the pie shows a gentle (rather than sharp) wave, remove it from the oven. Residual heat will continue to cook the filling as the pie stands.

* Cool pies on a rack so circulating air can speed the process.
* To speed-cool pies: Fill a 9 × 13-inch pan with ice cubes, then set the pie plate atop the cubes. Watch to make sure that, as the ice melts, the water doesn't reach the top of the pie plate.

FINISHING

* Glaze single-crust fruit pies or tarts by lightly brushing the surface with warm, light corn syrup 10 minutes after removing the pie from the oven. Or, depending on the fruit's flavor and color, you can brush the surface with melted currant or apple jelly. Apple or pear pies are wonderful when glazed with warm maple syrup.
* When decorating the top of a pie, always place the garnishes (strawberries, chocolate leaves, and so on) between where the cuts will be so you won't have to cut through or remove a garnish in order to serve the pie.
* See MERINGUE *for information on meringue-topped pies*.

STORING AND SERVING

* Always refrigerate custard pies (including pumpkin pie) after cooling to room temperature. Consume within 3 days.
* Refrigerate leftover meringue pie by covering it with plastic wrap that's been rubbed with vegetable oil so it won't stick to the surface.
* Cover fruit pies with foil or plastic wrap and store at room temperature for up to 3 days.
* Cream pies cut more cleanly if you wipe the blade often with a dampened paper towel.
* Keep meringue from sticking to the knife by dipping the knife in very hot water between cuts. Rubbing the knife with vegetable oil or butter also works.
* Add that just-baked touch by reheating fruit pies in a 300°F oven for 10 to 15 minutes before serving. Or freshen day-old pie by heating it in the microwave on high for 10 to 15 seconds.

ICE CREAM SUNDAE PIE

Fast and delicious and easy as pie. Bake and cool a homemade or commercial pie crust (or use a graham-cracker crust) and fill with slightly softened ice cream or sherbet, mounding high in the center. If desired, fold mix-ins (such as chocolate, or chopped crystallized ginger, or crumbled cookies) into the ice cream before filling the shell. Freeze the pie until solid, then wrap and store for up to 1 week. Remove the pie from the freezer, and let stand at room temperature for 10 minutes to facilitate cutting. During that time, spoon on a topping, such as fresh fruit, caramel or fudge sauce, chopped nuts, crumbled cookies or M&M candies. Or serve the pie plain, and pass bowls of different toppings for diners to add their own.

PIE CRUSTS *see also* CRUMBS, GENERAL; PIE; PIE PANS
INGREDIENTS FOR PIE PASTRY (*see also* Crumb Crusts, page 363)

* For the best results, have all pie crust ingredients (even the flour) cold.
* The best flour for pie pastry is all-purpose or pastry flour. Bread flour has too much gluten to make a tender crust; cake flour is too soft and won't produce the proper body.
* Lard and shortening produce a shorter (more tender) crust than butter or margarine. Of course, a butter crust tastes better. For the best of both worlds, use half lard or shortening and half butter.
* Frozen, unsalted butter (cut into 1-inch chunks) produces the flakiest pie crust.
* A crust made with vegetable oil won't be as flaky as one made with solid fat.
* Sugar both tenderizes and sweetens dough.
* Personalize pastry dough by adding flavor enhancers such as ground cinnamon, allspice, nutmeg or ginger. For savory pies, add chili or curry powder, or crushed dried basil or tarragon leaves, and so on. Stir flavorings into the flour before cutting in the fat.
* Water (or any liquid) added to pie dough must be ice cold.
* Substitute ice-cold sour cream or whipping cream for water for an extra-flaky crust.

MAKING PIE PASTRY

* The balance of ingredients is important, so measure carefully. Too much flour creates a heavy, tough crust; too much fat makes it crumbly and greasy; too much liquid makes it shrink.
* It's the tiny pockets of fat encased in flour that make a pie crust crisp and flaky. After combining the dry ingredients in a bowl, use chopping motions with a pastry blender or two knives to cut the fat into the flour mixture. Process only until the mixture resembles coarse crumbs. For the flakiest crust, cut the fat in half until the coarse-crumb stage, then add the remaining fat and cut to pea-sized pieces. Since body heat melts the fat and toughens the crust, touch the dough with your hands as little as possible.

* Add ice water or other liquid to the dough gradually, sprinkling it over the other ingredients a tablespoon at a time. For ultimate control, fill a small plastic bottle with ice water and spritz it over the flour mixture. Toss the mixture gently, blending only until it holds together when pinched. Overworking dough will make it tough.
* Turn the crumbly mixture onto a large piece of plastic wrap; fold the edges over and lightly press the dough into a ½-inch disk. Refrigerate for 30 minutes.
* If you've added too much liquid and the dough's wet, wrap it in plastic wrap and freeze until firm (but not rock hard) before rolling it out. Note that too much water causes pastry to shrink, so make allowances.
* Pie dough can be made ahead, wrapped and refrigerated for up to 4 days. Let it stand at room temperature until pliable enough to roll.
* **Food-processor method:** The key here is not to overprocess. Put the dry ingredients in the bowl with the steel blade; use a couple of on/off pulses to combine. Add chunks of ice-cold fat, processing with quick on/off pulses until the pieces are the size of large peas. With the machine off, sprinkle in the ice liquid, a tablespoon at a time; process with quick on/off pulses *just* until the dough begins to gather on the blades. Mixing the dough until it forms a ball will produce a tough crust. Turn the crumbly mixture out onto a piece of plastic wrap, folding the edges over, and lightly form the dough into a disk. Refrigerate for 30 minutes.

ROLLING OUT PIE PASTRY

* Use a large pastry board and heavy rolling pin. Marble and textured acrylic boards are the easiest to work with. Both pin and board should be lightly floured.
* Or roll the dough out on a lightly floured pastry cloth. Or cover the rolling pin with a stockinette cover (available at kitchenware shops).
* Cornstarch can be substituted for flour on both the work surface and rolling pin. It works great, doesn't give a starchy aftertaste and is easier to clean up than flour.
* Rolling out dough on a waxed paper–covered countertop makes cleanup a breeze. To keep the waxed paper from slipping, sprinkle a few drops of water on the countertop before arranging the paper.
* Most doughs can be rolled out on a smooth countertop without sticking if you spray the surface beforehand with cooking spray. Use a soapy sponge or cloth for easy cleanup.
* To make chilled dough easier to roll, whack it a couple of times with your rolling pin, making ridges in the disk of dough. Press down with

the pin and start rolling from one of the ridges, rotating the dough a quarter turn after each roll.

* To roll out a disk of softened dough, position the rolling pin in the center, then roll firmly and evenly out to the edge. Continue rolling from the center outward until the dough circle is 3 inches larger than the pie pan's inside diameter.
* Lattice strips are easy to cut with a pizza cutter.
* Use a pastry scraper or a large metal spatula to loosen stuck dough from a pastry board.

FORMING THE PIE CRUST

* To transfer the dough from pastry board to pan, fold the dough circle in half, gently lift and position it so the fold is across the pan's center. Unfold the dough, easing it into the pan. Or you can drape the dough over a flour-dusted rolling pin, position it over the pie pan and remove the pin.
* Don't stretch the dough as you place it in the pan—stretched dough shrinks.
* Use kitchen shears to trim the dough overhang.
* Once the dough's in the pan, patch any thin spots or holes with bits of leftover dough, pressing down gently with your fingertips.
* Add flavor to the bottom crust by sprinkling it with toasted ground nuts. Use the back of a dinner tablespoon to press the nuts lightly into the dough. The nuts also help keep the crust from becoming soggy.
* Forestall a soggy crust by refrigerating the unbaked bottom crust for 20 minutes. Or brush it with slightly beaten egg white, which serves as a sealant, then refrigerate for 10 minutes.
* Don't pour a filling into an unbaked pie shell until just before baking—otherwise, it could become soggy.
* Lightly brush the edge of the bottom crust with water before positioning the top crust and pressing the edges together. Doing so helps the two crusts stick together.
* To crimp the crust, start by using a knife to trim the edge of the top crust, creating a ¾- to 1-inch overhang. Fold the overhang under, then form a raised edge by pressing the dough gently between your thumb and index finger. Decoratively crimp or flute the edge as desired.
* To make pie crusts in advance: Line a pie pan with pastry, then put it in a plastic bag or other airtight wrapping and refrigerate for up to 4 days, freeze for up to 6 months. Defrost frozen pie shells completely before filling and baking. Glass pie pans should be close to room temperature to prevent cracking with the oven heat.

P

* Many cookie doughs make fine pie crust—and you don't have to roll them out. Simply buy a log of chocolate chip or sugar cookie dough, cut into ¼-inch slices and press the dough into the pan. Make a raised and fluted edge, if desired. Work quickly and use a light touch so as not to overwork the dough and create a tough crust. Prick the dough and refrigerate it for at least 30 minutes before baking as a blind crust (*see below*).

* The upper crust: Add sheen or flavor to the top crust of your pie by brushing it with a glaze (don't glaze crimped edges until the last 10 to 15 minutes of baking time to prevent overbrowning). Glazes include: Lightly beaten egg white or cold milk (for sheen); whipping cream or an egg yolk beaten with 1 teaspoon water (for a glossy, dark golden brown finish); 2 tablespoons water mixed with 1 tablespoon granulated sugar (for a crisp, sweet crust); or plain water to make it crisp. Make sure no puddles of sugar or egg glaze remain on the crust—they tend to overbrown.

* Spice up the top crust by sprinkling with sugar and ground cinnamon, nutmeg or allspice. Sprinkle savory pies with caraway, poppy or sesame seeds.

BAKING A PASTRY CRUST

* Setting the pie pan on a baking sheet helps keep bottom crusts crisp.

* Custard pies are notorious for their soggy crusts. One remedy is to prebake the unpricked crust for 5 minutes, then let it cool for 15 minutes before filling. Using a heavyweight, freezer-to-oven glass pie pan also helps, because glass absorbs heat better than metal and produces a well-baked crust.

* For prebaked (or *blind-baked*) pie shells (to which a filling's added later): Put the crust in the pan and crimp as desired; place in the freezer for 10 minutes. Use a fork to prick the bottom and sides of the unbaked shell at ½-inch intervals. Freeze for 20 more minutes before baking. The dough should be extremely cold before being baked so the crust sets before the fat melts and causes it to lose its shape.

* Dress up blind-baked crusts by sprinkling the bottom with fine cookie crumbs. Press the crumbs into the dough with the back of a spoon, then chill and bake the crust as usual.

* No time to refrigerate a crust to be prebaked? Line the unbaked crust with a double thickness of heavy-duty foil. Pour about 1½ cups pie weights (available at gourmet kitchen shops), dried beans or rice onto the foil (save the beans or rice and use again for the same purpose). Bake the shell at 400°F for 15 minutes; remove the foil and weights. If the pie shell is for a filling that requires baking, continue baking it for 10 minutes.

For a completely baked crust that will be filled later, continue baking about 35 minutes, or until a deep golden brown.

* Seal a prebaked pastry or cookie-crumb crust to be used for a refrigerated filling by using the back of a dinner teaspoon to spread 2 to 3 ounces melted semisweet chocolate over the bottom of the baked crust and halfway up the sides. Pop the coated crust in the refrigerator for about 10 minutes to set the chocolate before filling.

* Leftover pie crust makes great comfort food. Roll out the dough until ⅛- to ¼-inch thick; sprinkle generously with ground cinnamon and granulated sugar. Cut into strips or irregular shapes, and bake in a 350°F oven until golden brown. Instead of sugar and cinnamon, you can brush the dough with maple syrup, honey or melted, cooled jelly.

* Or roll out the dough, cut into rounds or triangles, top as desired and bake. Use to top cooked fruit or serve as a "cookie" with ice cream.

* Or freeze leftover pie dough for up to 6 months to be thawed and used to top cobblers, mini-potpies, and so on. If you have just a few scraps of leftover dough, use canapé cutters or small cookie cutters to cut out decorative garnishes for soups and stews. Remember, however, that rerolling the dough will reduce the pastry's tenderness.

CRUMB CRUSTS

* Pie pans for graham cracker and cookie-crumb crusts need to be well greased.

* If you like the ease of graham cracker or cookie crusts, but think they're too sweet, substitute ½ cup of the crumbs with Ritz or saltine cracker crumbs; omit salt from the crust recipe.

* You can use Oreo or other cream-filled cookies—including the filling—to make a great pie crust that doesn't require extra sugar. Just combine 1½ cups Oreo cookie crumbs (about 22 cookies) with 3 tablespoons melted butter and press into the pan as usual.

* Crumbs must be firmly packed into a pie pan for the crust to hold together. Use the back of a dinner tablespoon or a rubber spatula to do this. Or wrap your hand in a piece of plastic wrap or in a small plastic bag and press the crumbs into place. Or spread the crumbs in place, then press them down with another pie plate (but then you have to wash the second pie plate).

* Prebaking a crumb crust for 10 minutes at 350°F will help keep it crisp. Completely cool a prebaked crumb crust before filling.

* A pie crust made with cookie or graham cracker crumbs will sometimes stick to the pan when the pie is chilled. A quick remedy is to soak a dish-

towel in very hot water, wring it out and wrap it around the base of the pie plate for 5 minutes. The heat will soften the butter in the crust, thereby loosening it for easy removal.

PIE PANS   *see also* PAN SIZES; PIE; PIE CRUSTS

* Not sure of the size of your pie pan? Measure the diameter from the inside edge of the rim. Pie-pan measurements may vary up to ½ inch—a 9-inch pan is often only 8½ inches in diameter.
* Glass, dark-metal and dull-metal pans absorb heat and produce a crisp, golden brown crust; shiny aluminum pans reflect heat and produce paler crusts.
* When using glass pie pans, reduce the oven heat by 25°F.
* Lightweight foil pans are usually smaller than regular pie pans. Extra filling may be poured into individual muffin tins.
* Unless otherwise indicated in a recipe, pie pans do not need to be greased.

PINEAPPLES   *see also* FRUIT, GENERAL

PURCHASING   Choose pineapples that are heavy for their size, slightly soft to the touch, with a full, strong color and no signs of greening. The stem end should smell sweet and aromatic; the leaves should be crisp and green with no yellow or brown tips. Avoid pineapples with soft or dark areas on the skin. Pineapples that aren't picked ripe will never ripen, which means they won't be as sweet because the starch hasn't completely converted to sugar.

STORING   Refrigerate whole, ripe pineapples, tightly wrapped, for up to 5 days. Slightly underripe pineapples should be kept at room temperature for several days to decrease their acidity (tartness), though their sweetness won't increase. Once cut, refrigerate pineapple, tightly wrapped, for up to 3 more days.

EQUIVALENT   1 medium, peeled and cored = about 5 cups chunks

USING

* To peel and cut a pineapple, use a very sharp knife to cut off both the base and the leaves, then stand the pineapple on one end and cut off strips of the skin from top to bottom. The easiest way to remove the eyes is to cut wedge-shaped grooves on either side of the eyes, following their pattern, which spirals diagonally. Cut away as little of the pineapple's flesh as possible.
* Or you can slice the pineapple, then cut away the peel.

* Or you can buy a relatively inexpensive gadget available in kitchenware shops that cores and peels the pineapple at the same time.
* To core a pineapple, cut the peeled fruit in quarters, then stand the quarters on one end and cut downward to remove the core.
* Don't throw out a fresh pineapple core. It's tough, but can be used as swizzle sticks for fruit drinks. Cut it lengthwise into quarters unless it's a very thin core.
* If a pineapple's simply too acidic to eat, make a SUGAR SYRUP of 2 parts water to 1 part sugar; bring the mixture to a boil. Be sure and make enough syrup to cover the pineapple. Cut the pineapple into chunks or slices; put in a flat-bottomed bowl. Pour the hot sugar syrup over the pineapple, cool to room temperature, then cover and refrigerate overnight. Drain the pineapple before using in salads, compotes, and so on.
* Pineapple contains an enzyme, *bromelain*, that prevents gelatin from setting properly. Heat destroys the enzyme, so cooked pineapple can be used in a gelatin mixture.
* That same enzyme is a natural meat tenderizer. Add pineapple juice to marinades, or simply marinate meat in the juice alone. The pineapple flavor is particularly compatible with pork or chicken.
* Give the edges of pineapple chunks a beautiful blush by cutting a pineapple into spears, then laying them in a shallow ceramic or glass dish. Pour raspberry or cranberry juice over the spears; cover and refrigerate for 24 hours. Drain the spears, then cut into chunks and use in salads, compotes or as a garnish.

PISTACHIOS *For general purchase, storage, toasting and usage information, see* NUTS, GENERAL

TIDBIT   The shells of pistachios are either red or naturally tan. The first pistachios marketed in the United States were from the Middle East, and were always red. Today, some American-grown pistachios (98 percent of which are from California) are still dyed red primarily because some people are more familiar with them.

PURCHASING   Choose pistachios with partially open shells that are free of defects.

EQUIVALENTS

* In shell: 1 pound = 2 cups nutmeats
* Shelled: 1 pound = 3½ to 4 cups

USING

* Pistachio shells split and expand as the nut kernel grows. Unsplit pistachios are immature and flavorless—discard them.

* To open pistachios: Wedge half of the shell from an opened pistachio into the split of an unopened nut and twist to pry the shells apart.

PITA BREAD   *see also* BREAD, GENERAL

PURCHASING   This Middle Eastern flat bread can be found in super-markets and ethnic markets in both white flour and whole-wheat forms.
STORING   Store, tightly wrapped, at room temperature for up to 5 days; freeze for up to 3 months.

GREEK PIZZA

Split a pita bread horizontally, sprinkle the inside of each half with cheese (half grated mozzarella, half crumbled feta), capers, sliced olives and crumbled oregano. Broil for about 3 minutes, or just until cheese melts. Cut into wedges.

PITA CHIPS

Split pita rounds horizontally and lightly brush the insides with olive oil; salt and pepper to taste. Stack the rounds, then cut the stack into 12 wedges. Arrange the wedges in a single layer on a lightly oiled baking sheet and bake at 350°F for 8 to 10 minutes until golden brown. Cool on paper towels and store airtight for up to 5 days.

> *You better cut the pizza in four pieces because*
> *I'm not hungry enough to eat six.*
> —Yogi Berra, American baseball player, manager

PIZZA

* Does your favorite commercial pizza arrive with a limp crust? Try sautéing the slices in a large, lightly oiled skillet until the crust is crisp and browned. Or place the pizza on a rack set on a baking sheet and bake at 400°F for 5 minutes. The skillet method produces a crisper crust without overcooking the topping. Use two skillets for a large pizza, and put a second round of slices on to crisp over low heat while you're eating the first round.
* Make it easy on yourself and buy a 10-ounce tube of Pillsbury Pizza Crust.
* To prevent a homemade pizza crust from getting soggy, lightly sauté vegetables like mushrooms, bell peppers, onions and spinach (all of which have a high water content) before using them as toppings.
* For the crispest crust, try putting a thin layer of cheese under the sauce and toppings; top with more cheese, if desired. The bottom cheese layer provides a buffer between the crust and moist toppings.

✳ No pizza cutter? Use kitchen shears to cut pizza.

FOCACCIA PRONTO

Focaccia isn't really pizza, but a simple Italian bread based on pizzalike dough and topped simply with oil and herbs. This superquick rendition is great with apéritifs, soups or salads. Unroll a 10-ounce tube of Pillsbury Pizza Crust; place it on a greased baking sheet. It'll measure about 8½ × 10 inches—don't stretch it. Brush the dough lightly with extra virgin olive oil; sprinkle with salt, pepper and 1 to 2 tablespoons finely chopped fresh herbs of your choice (basil, tarragon, oregano), or 2 teaspoons fennel seeds. Use the back of a spoon to press herbs or seeds lightly into the dough. If desired, sprinkle with 2 to 3 tablespoons grated Asiago or Parmesan cheese. Bake at 400°F for 10 to 13 minutes until golden brown. Immediately cut 6 strips lengthwise and 3 crosswise (I use kitchen shears). Makes 18 strips. Serve warm.

PLASTIC WRAP *see also* ALUMINUM FOIL; PARCHMENT PAPER; WAXED PAPER

✳ Storing plastic wrap in the freezer will keep it from sticking to itself.

✳ If plastic wrap won't adhere to ceramic, glass or metal containers, dip your finger in water and moisten the dish's rim, then cover with the wrap.

✳ Plastic wrap doesn't stick well to plastic or acrylic surfaces. Instead, cover such containers with a plastic bag, twisting and sealing the top with a wire fastener.

✳ Protect yourself and your kitchen from spatters when whipping cream by laying a sheet of plastic wrap (with a hole cut for the beater stems) on top of the bowl.

✳ Place a sheet of plastic wrap between layers of stored candy.

✳ Separate layers of decorated, moist or sticky cookies with plastic wrap to prevent their sticking together.

✳ Use sheets of plastic wrap to separate layers of cookies before freezing.

✳ Shape a ground-meat mixture into burgers or meatballs by spooning a portion between 2 sheets of plastic wrap, then forming the desired shape. Your fingers won't get messy and neither will the countertop.

PLUMS *see also* DRIED PLUMS; FRUIT, GENERAL

PURCHASING Choose firm plums that give slightly to palm pressure; the color should be good for its variety. Avoid plums with skin blemishes such as cracks, soft spots or brown discolorations. A pale gray film on the skin is natural and certainly doesn't affect quality.

EQUIVALENTS 1 pound = 6 to 8 two-inch whole plums, 2½ cups sliced, 2 cups cooked

STORING

* Refrigerate ripe plums in a plastic bag for up to 5 days.
* Ripen plums by placing in a paper bag with an apple at room temperature for a day or two. Pierce the bag in several places with the tip of a knife.

USING

* Plums don't need peeling, but wash them thoroughly just before using.
* Plums are great quartered, sautéed in a little butter (sprinkled with ¼ to ⅓ cup sugar) just until they begin to soften, then spooned over vanilla-bean ice cream.

PLUMS, DRIED   see DRIED PLUMS

POACHED EGGS   see EGGS, COOKING METHODS

POACHING   see also EGGS, COOKING METHODS (POACHED)

TIDBIT   A method whereby food is cooked in a barely simmering liquid. Among foods most commonly poached are eggs (see page 185), fruit, fish and chicken. Poaching gives food a particularly delicate flavor.

GENERAL

* During poaching, the food is flavored by the liquid, and vice versa. For that reason, chicken is typically poached in chicken stock (sometimes with wine), fruit in a SUGAR SYRUP, fish in fish stock, and so on.
* White wine adds flavor to poaching liquids, whether for sweet or savory foods. Add liqueur or sweet wine to fruit-poaching liquids.
* Poaching liquids can be flavored variously with additions (depending on the food being cooked) such as allspice berries, bay leaves, cinnamon sticks, cloves, fennel seeds, lemon or orange zest, mint leaves, peppercorns, rosemary and vanilla beans.
* Salting poaching liquids adds flavor. A soupçon of salt will intensify the flavor of sweet poaching liquids.
* Use a pan just large enough to accommodate the food and poaching liquid. Use only enough poaching liquid to submerge the food.
* Combine all the poaching-liquid ingredients (including herbs or spices) in a pan. Bring to a boil, then reduce to a simmer and cook for 5 minutes before adding the food to be cooked.
* **Poaching method 1:** Add the food to the *barely* simmering poaching liq-

uid (the surface should just "shimmer") and cook until done. With this approach, PARCHMENT PAPER is typically placed directly atop the ingredients to hold in the heat (covering the pan with a lid would raise the temperature too high). If the food floats, weight it with a heavy plate to keep it beneath the liquid's surface.

* **Poaching method 2:** Bring the poaching liquid to a boil. Add the food and remove from the heat. Cover and let the food stand in the poaching liquid until cooked as desired (*see* the following tips on timing suggestions for fish, chicken and fruit).

* **Poaching method 3 (for fish and poultry):** Combine the flavorings, fish or chicken, and poaching liquid to cover in a pan. Bring to a boil, then cover and remove from the heat. Let stand 20 to 30 minutes until done as desired.

* Don't throw out the flavorful poaching liquid. It can be used either to make a sauce for the poached food or as a soup base.

* Use a reserved poaching liquid within a couple of days or label and freeze it for up to 6 months.

POACHING FRUIT

* Choose ripe but firm fruit. Overly ripe fruit will become too soft during poaching, underripe fruit won't have much flavor. Prepare the fruit as desired by washing, peeling, quartering, and so on.

* For the best flavor, which is not too sweet, use a light syrup (5 parts water to 1 part sugar). Bring the syrup and flavorings to a boil; reduce the heat and simmer for 5 minutes to flavor the syrup.

* Fruit can be poached in all manner of liquids, such as spiced tea or apple cider for pears and apples.

* Poach fruit by either Method 1 or 2 (*see* preceding "General" tips). Cook until the fruit is done as desired—the timing could take from a few minutes to 30 minutes or more, depending on the fruit. Test by piercing the fruit with a skewer or a knife tip.

* Let firm fruit like pears cool in the poaching liquid to absorb more flavor; remove softer fruit with a slotted spoon and cool at room temperature.

* Microwave "poaching": In a flat-bottomed, 2-quart microwave-safe baking dish, combine ¼ cup fruit juice, liqueur or sugar syrup with 2 teaspoons lemon juice and 1 teaspoon pure vanilla extract. Halve, then core or pit 4 pears or peaches; peeling is optional, as the skin can be easily removed after cooking. Place the fruit, cut side down, in the dish; cover and cook on high for 4 minutes. Let stand, covered, for 4 minutes.

POACHING FISH AND CHICKEN

* High-fat fish like butterfish or sablefish are inclined to fall apart with moist-heat methods like poaching. Choose instead lean fish such as cod, flounder, perch, red snapper or sole.

* A whole fish and large fish pieces retain their shape better during poaching if wrapped in cheesecloth. Drape the cheesecloth ends over the top of the fish as it cooks and use those ends to lift the cooked fish out of the pan. There are also special cheesecloth fish-poaching bags available in kitchenware shops.

* Poached fish is extremely delicate, so handle it gently when removing it from the pan. Use two slotted metal spatulas for large pieces, a slotted spoon for small ones.

* Bones contribute flavor to both meat and poaching liquid, so you may want to cook chicken with the bone in.

* When poaching bone-in chicken to use in salads or other dishes, save the chicken bones, put them back in the poaching liquid and cook for 30 minutes to extract as much flavor as possible. Strain, cool and use the liquid for soups, sauces, and so on.

POLENTA   see also CORNMEAL

TIDBIT   Very simply, polenta is cornmeal and liquid, stirred together and cooked until it becomes what many think of as the quintessential comfort food. It's no longer necessary to stand over the stove, constantly stirring the pot for an hour or more. Today's polenta can just as easily be made with occasional stirring and can even be made in the oven. Polenta can be served soft or firm, graced simply by grated cheese and butter, or embellished exotically with wild mushrooms and game reductions. However you serve it, polenta is sure to please.

PURCHASING   Polenta (essentially medium- or coarse-ground cornmeal) is available in supermarkets, natural food stores and gourmet shops. There are also instant polenta and cooked polenta packaged in tubes.

STORING   Polenta can be stored airtight in a cool, dark place for up to 6 months. Stone-ground polenta can quickly turn rancid, so tightly seal and refrigerate it for up to 3 months. Refrigerate polenta in tubes for up to 1 month.

GENERAL

* Since water is the most common liquid used in making polenta, make sure it tastes good. A water that tastes of chlorine or minerals can ruin the flavor of polenta.

* Likewise, the flavor of the cornmeal makes a big difference. The fresher it is, the better the taste.
* Count on 1 cup uncooked polenta making 4 to 6 servings.
* In general, salt the cooking water just before stirring in the polenta; add other seasonings (such as pepper, butter and cheese) 5 minutes before it's done.
* Flavorings: Although purists feel that salt, pepper, butter and cheese are the only embellishments needed, there are many other ways to flavor polenta. Ingredients including chopped sun-dried tomatoes, lemon zest or sautéed leeks or shallots can be added at the start of cooking, while fresh herbs and toasted nuts should be stirred in 5 minutes before serving.
* Polenta can take 15 to 60 minutes to cook, depending on the age and type used. Even though the mixture can thicken in 10 to 15 minutes, most polenta requires more time to develop the classic soft and creamy texture.
* Let polenta stand for 5 minutes after it finishes cooking; give it a stir before serving.
* Cooked polenta can be kept warm in the top of a double boiler over simmering water for at least 30 minutes.

COOKING METHODS

* **Traditional method:** Bring 3 cups water to a boil in a heavy, medium saucepan (have another 2 cups water simmering in a second pan). Add 1 tablespoon kosher salt and, stirring rapidly with a whisk to create a whirlpool, *slowly* add 1 cup polenta. Keep stirring briskly until all the grain is added to prevent lumps. Reduce the heat to low and cook, whisking continually, until the mixture begins to thicken. If you see any lumps, break them up by mashing against the side of the pan. Stir in 1 more cup hot water. Continue stirring the polenta until it begins to pull away from the pan. Stir in 2 tablespoons butter, ½ cup grated Parmesan or aged Asiago, and freshly ground pepper to taste.
* **Cold-water method:** Simply whisk 1 cup cornmeal into cold water before heating and cooking as in the traditional method.
* **Double-boiler method:** Put enough water in the bottom portion of a double boiler to *almost* touch the upper half; bring to a boil. On a second burner, bring 3 cups water to a boil in the top half of the double boiler. Combine 1 cup cornmeal with 1 cup cold water; rapidly stir the polenta mixture and 1 tablespoon kosher salt into the water in the top portion of the double boiler. Set that pan on the bottom pan and bring the polenta back to a boil. Cover tightly, reduce heat to medium-low and cook until the polenta is tender, stirring every 15 minutes or so. Stir in 2 tablespoons

butter, ½ cup grated Parmesan or aged Asiago and freshly ground pepper to taste.

* **Oven method:** Preheat the oven to 350°F. In a 1½-quart casserole, stir together 4 cups water, 1 cup polenta, 1 tablespoon kosher salt, and pepper to taste. Bake, uncovered, in the top third of the oven for about 40 minutes. Stir in 2 tablespoons butter, ½ cup grated Parmesan or aged Asiago and freshly ground pepper to taste; return to the oven to bake an additional 10 minutes.

* **Microwave method:** In a large bowl (I use an 8-cup measuring cup), stir together 4 cups water, 1 cup polenta and 2 teaspoons kosher salt; let stand for 10 minutes. Cover with a lid or plastic wrap. If using the latter, either poke a hole in the top or fold back a small corner for venting. Cook on high for 5 minutes. Remove from the oven and stir well. Re-cover and cook for 5 more minutes. Remove from the oven and stir well. Return to the oven *uncovered*; cook for 3 more minutes. Remove from the oven; let stand for 5 minutes. Stir in 2 tablespoons butter, ½ cup grated Parmesan or aged Asiago and freshly ground pepper to taste.

* **Firm polenta** (*for grilling, broiling or sautéing*): Cook polenta by the method you prefer, adding flavorings as desired. Remove the polenta from the heat and let stand for 15 minutes. Line a shallow pan with plastic wrap. Turn the polenta into the pan, smoothing the surface with a rubber spatula dipped in cold water. Place another sheet of plastic wrap over the polenta's surface; cool at room temperature for 30 minutes. Refrigerate for at least 1½ hours before cutting and cooking as desired.

* After serving soft polenta, turn the leftovers into a plastic wrap–lined flat-bottomed pan, smoothing the surface. Cover and refrigerate; cut into shapes and sauté.

POMEGRANATES   see also FRUIT, GENERAL

TIDBIT Pomegranates—nature's most labor-intensive fruit—can be eaten as fruit, puréed for the juice, or used as a garnish for salads, meats, fruit compotes, drinks or desserts. Pomegranate molasses is a syrupy, slightly astringent, sour-sweet juice reduction. The sweetness comes from the intense concentration of the fruit's natural sugars, not from added sugar.

PURCHASING

* Fresh pomegranates: They should be heavy for their size, have a bright, fresh color and blemish-free skin.
* Pomegranate molasses (also called *juice*): This is available in bottles in Middle Eastern markets, as well as some gourmet and specialty shops.

EQUIVALENTS   1 medium = about ¾ cup seeds *or* ⅓ to ½ cup juice

STORING

* Fruit: Store whole pomegranates in a cool, dark place for up to 1 month, refrigerate for up to 2 months. **Pomegranate seeds** can be frozen for up to 1 year. Refrigerate **pomegranate juice** in glass containers—plastic ones may stain.
* Pomegranate molasses: Refrigerate almost indefinitely.

USING

* The vivid red juice of a pomegranate makes nasty stains. Protect your clothes with an apron. And you might want to wear rubber or latex gloves, unless you don't mind red-tinged fingers and nails.
* The easiest way to seed a pomegranate is to do it under water. Fill a sink or a large bowl or pot with cold water. Hold the pomegranate submerged with one hand and with your other hand use a sharp knife to cut the fruit in half. Use your fingers to pull apart the pomegranate, removing the papery membranes and gently separating the seeds. The seeds sink and the membranes float up to the water's surface. Now you can scoop off the membranes, drain the water and retrieve the seeds. The bonus with this method is that your fingers won't get stained!
* Another seeding method is to cut off the fruit's crown and carefully remove some of the core. Use a sharp, pointed paring knife to score the rind vertically in quarters, then pull the sections apart. Gently pull out and discard the papery skin covering the seeds, then bend back the rind and the seeds will pop out.
* If you're not worried about keeping all the seeds intact, simply cut the pomegranate in half, then into quarters. Use your fingers to pry out the pulp-encased seeds, removing any of the papery membrane that adheres.
* The seeds can be simply eaten out of hand. Many people chew on the seeds to release the juice from the surrounding sacs, then spit out the seeds. Others release the juice in the mouth, then swallow the seeds, which are a good source of roughage.
* If you don't want to bother with the seeds, energetically roll the pomegranate on a countertop until the fruit softens. Cut a small hole in the end, insert a straw and enjoy the juice.
* There are several ways to juice a pomegranate. Cut it in half and juice it like an orange. Or remove the seeds and process in a blender, using quick on/off pulses. Or use a food mill to separate the juice from the seeds. With any method, strain the juice before using, pressing down on the pulp to extract as much liquid as possible.
* Refrigerate freshly squeezed juice and use within 2 to 3 days.
* Pomegranate juice and the store-bought pomegranate molasses can be

used to lend a sweet-tart nuance to salad dressings, savory sauces, marinades and dessert sauces.

POPCORN

TIDBIT   Popcorn is a special variety of dried corn that pops when heated because of the natural moisture trapped inside the hull. In simple terms, when the corn's heated, the moisture vaporizes, which causes immense pressure. When the pressure becomes too great, the hull bursts open and the kernel's starchy contents explode outward, expanding in volume while turning the kernel inside out. *Food for thought:* 1 cup plain popcorn = about 30 calories; 1 cup buttered popcorn = 90 to 120 calories, depending on the amount of butter.

EQUIVALENT   3 tablespoons kernels = about 6 cups popped corn

STORING

* Unpopped loose popcorn can be stored at room temperature for about a year. Refrigerating or freezing it will help popcorn retain its natural moisture, which means it'll produce larger popped kernels.
* Packaged popcorn (with oil) should be stored no longer than about 3 months at room temperature. Longer than that and the oil could turn rancid.
* Store leftover unbuttered popcorn in an airtight plastic bag at room temperature for up to 2 weeks. Refrigerate buttered popcorn.

PREPARING

* Unpopped kernels (lovingly called "old maids") occur because corn has lost its natural moisture—dried-out kernels won't pop. To restore some of that moisture, combine 3 cups popcorn with 1 tablespoon cool water in a screw-top jar. Shake the contents every 15 minutes until the water is absorbed. Refrigerate for a couple of days before popping. Shortcut rehydration: Cover the kernels with very warm water; let stand for 5 minutes before draining, blotting dry with a paper towel and popping.
* As popcorn pops, it produces steam, which is absorbed by the popcorn. Keep it as crisp as possible by leaving the pan lid ajar about ¼ inch—just enough for the steam (but not the corn) to escape. Remove the pan lid the second the popping stops to prevent further steaming.
* Personalize popcorn by adding seasonings (anything from grated Parmesan cheese to dried oregano leaves to chili or curry powder) to the oil, then stirring in the corn kernels to coat well with the flavorings.
* Garlic-butter popcorn: Add a quartered garlic clove to the butter as it melts; cook over low heat for 1 minute before removing the garlic and

pouring the butter over the popcorn. Add ½ teaspoon chili powder to the blend for Southwestern popcorn.

* Lightly spritz air-popped popcorn with cooking spray before adding salt or other flavorings and tossing. The seasonings will stick to the popcorn instead of falling to the bottom of the bowl.

* To recrisp popcorn, place it in a single layer in a baking pan with shallow sides (like a jelly-roll pan) and heat at 325°F for 5 to 10 minutes. Or recrisp in a microwave oven on high for about 3 minutes.

POPOVERS *see also* BAKED GOODS, GENERAL; BREAD, GENERAL; GREASING PANS; HIGH-ALTITUDE ADJUSTMENTS

TIDBIT Popovers are puffy muffin-sized breads with a moist interior and brown, crispy crust. They're extremely easy to mix and bake. Unlike most other breads, popovers are leavened by eggs and steam, the latter produced by the high proportion of liquid in the batter.

MAKING THE BATTER

* Bring the milk and eggs to room temperature before mixing the batter. If the ingredients are cold, heat the milk just until barely lukewarm; put the eggs in a bowl of very warm water for 10 minutes.

* Measurements must be precise—don't use extra-large or small eggs if the recipe calls for large. (Most recipes that don't specify egg size use large eggs.)

* Popover batter can be made ahead, covered tightly and refrigerated overnight. Before using, let the batter stand at room temperature for 30 to 60 minutes; stir well before pouring into baking cups.

BAKING

* Special popover cups and pans are available at department and kitchenware stores. Or you can use custard cups or a muffin tin. If using separate popover or custard cups, place them on a heavy baking sheet before filling.

* Generously grease (about ½ teaspoon grease per popover) the containers in which popovers are baked, or they'll stick tenaciously to the pan.

* Always preheat the containers for popover batter.

* Popovers rise extremely high—don't fill the baking cups more than half with batter.

* Position the oven rack to the center position and preheat the oven to 400° to 450°F. If using glass baking cups, reduce the heat by 25°F.

* Remove the preheated popover pans from the oven and quickly pour in the batter (have it in a pitcher for quick pouring)—you don't want the pans to cool down too much.

* Leave the oven door shut during the first 20 minutes of baking! Drafts can easily collapse popovers.
* Bake the popovers until they're nicely browned and firm to the touch. Underbaking can cause popovers to collapse after they're removed from the oven.
* Remove the popovers from the oven as soon as they're done, and use a fork to prick each one in several places to let the steam escape so the insides won't become too soggy.
* Popover interiors are naturally moist. For drier, crisper popovers, return the pricked popovers to the turned-off (but still warm) oven for about 10 minutes. Leave the oven door ajar 1 to 3 inches so the popovers won't continue cooking.
* Loosen the popovers from their baking cups by running a knife around the edge. Remove all popovers from the pan so the bottoms won't get soggy.
* Leftover popovers can be frozen in an airtight plastic bag for up to 3 months. Reheat by placing frozen popovers on a baking sheet and heating in a preheated 400°F oven for 10 to 15 minutes.
* Split popovers (leftover or fresh-baked) and fill the cavities with poached or scrambled eggs, fruit salad, or creamed chicken or tuna.

POPPY SEED   see SEEDS

PORK   see also BACON; HAM; MEAT, GENERAL; ROASTS

TIDBIT   Thanks to modern technology, trichinosis in pork is now rarely an issue. Take normal precautions, however, such as thoroughly washing in hot, soapy water anything (hands, knives, cutting boards) that comes in contact with raw pork. Never taste uncooked pork.

PURCHASING   Choose meat that's pale pink with a small amount of marbling and white (not yellow) fat. The darker the flesh, the older the animal. For succulent chops, select those that are about 1 inch thick. Thin chops tend to dry out quickly, no matter how careful the cook.

STORING

* Fresh pork: Refrigerate to be used within 6 hours of purchase in its store packaging. Otherwise, remove the packaging and loosely wrap it with waxed paper. Store meat cuts in the coldest part of the refrigerator for up to 3 days, ground pork and pork sausage for up to 2 days. Freeze for 3 to 6 months; larger cuts have longer storage capabilities than chops or ground meat.

* Cooked pork: Refrigerate within 2 hours of cooking and consume within 2 days.

COOKING

* Cooking pork to an internal temperature of 137°F will kill any trichinae. However, to allow for a safety margin for thermometer inaccuracy, most experts recommend an internal temperature of 145° to 160°F. This range produces pork that's juicy and tender, whereas the 170° to 185°F range recommended in many cookbooks produces dry, overcooked meat.

* The best way to test pork's doneness is with a meat THERMOMETER. Cutting it to see if it's still pink lets too many good juices run out.

* To cut a pocket in pork chops for stuffing, choose loin or rib chops that are about 1½ inches thick (have your butcher cut some if those on display aren't thick enough). Cutting from the fat side, use a sharp, pointed knife to make a horizontal slit about 3 inches wide almost to the bone. Make the inside pocket larger than the actual slit. Fill the pocket with stuffing and secure the opening with toothpicks.

Throughout my life, friends and fortune have come and gone, but I've always been able to count on a baked potato to see me through.
—Maggie Waldron, American author, editor

POTATOES *see also* POTATOES, COOKING METHODS; POTATO SALAD; SWEET POTATOES; VEGETABLES, GENERAL

TIDBIT The humble potato is easily digestible, fat and cholesterol free, and a powerhouse of nutrition (low in sodium, high in potassium, and a storehouse of minerals, complex carbohydrates and vitamins C and B-6). Furthermore, one 6-ounce potato contains only about 120 calories. Naturally, some preparation methods deliver more of its nutritional dividends than others. For example, a potato's skin (and the flesh just beneath it) is particularly nutrient-rich, so cooking potatoes unpeeled is smart. The only really bad news is that a potato's calorie count can triple with frying.

PURCHASING

* Choose potatoes that are firm, well shaped for their type and blemish free. Avoid wrinkled, sprouted or cracked specimens. A slight green tinge indicates the presence of solanine (caused by prolonged light exposure), an alkaloid that can be toxic if eaten in quantity. Cut away or scrape off this bitter green portion and use the potato as desired.

* The varieties of potatoes most commonly available are: **russet potato** (also called *Idaho* and *baking potato*) is long with slightly rounded ends

and a rough, brown skin with numerous eyes—it's low in moisture and high in starch; **long white potatoes** are similarly shaped (though slightly flatter) and have a thin, pale brown skin with almost imperceptible eyes and a firm, slightly waxy flesh; **round red potatoes** and **round white potatoes** (often marketed as *boiling potatoes*) have thin red or tan skins, a high moisture content, waxy flesh, and range in size from small to medium; **new potatoes**—the youngsters of any variety—are small, have a crisp, waxy texture and thin, undeveloped wispy skins; **Yukon Gold potatoes** are typically round, small to medium sized, with a thin, pale tan to light brown skin and a pale to deep yellow, waxy flesh.

* Select potatoes by how they'll be used. **For baking**—russets; **for boiling** (as for salads)—long whites, round reds and whites, new potatoes, Yukon Golds; **for frying**—russets, long whites, Yukon Golds; **for gratins and scalloped dishes**—long whites, round reds and whites, Yukon Golds; **for mashing**—russets and Yukon Golds; **for roasting**—long whites, round reds and whites, small Yukon Golds; **for steaming**—long whites, round reds and whites.

EQUIVALENTS 1 pound = 3 medium russets or long whites, 4 to 5 red or white rounds or 8 to 14 new potatoes; about 3½ cups chopped; 2 to 3 cups mashed (depending on type of potato and amount of liquid added)

STORING

* Store potatoes in a cool, dark, well-ventilated place for up to 2 weeks. When stored at around 50°F, potatoes will keep for up to 3 months. New potatoes should be used within a week of purchase.

* Refrigerating potatoes causes them to become overly sweet and to turn dark when cooked. Warm temperatures encourage sprouting and shriveling.

* Cut off the leg of an old (clean) pair of pantyhose, drop potatoes into it and hang it in a cool, dark, dry place. The hose lets air circulate, which helps keep the potatoes longer.

* Storing potatoes near onions can cause the potatoes to rot more quickly as a result of the interaction of their natural gases.

COOKING, GENERAL *see also* POTATOES, COOKING METHODS, *page 379*

* Whether baked, boiled, steamed or microwaved, whole potatoes will cook more evenly and get done at the same time if they're relatively the same size.

* A potato's peel has lots of flavor and nutrients, so don't remove it if you don't have to.

* Use a vegetable brush to scrub potatoes to be cooked with the skin on.

* Get a jump on the next night's meal by cooking twice as many potatoes

as you need for one meal. The leftovers can be mashed or added to salad, soup or other vegetables.

* A potato's flesh darkens when exposed to air. To cut ahead of time, dip the cut potatoes in a mixture of 1 quart cool water and 3 tablespoons lemon juice. Drain, cover and refrigerate until ready to use. If using a cooking method where potatoes should start out dry, wrap the cut potatoes in a damp paper towel to absorb excess moisture.

* If potatoes cut ahead of time have darkened, cook them in milk to whiten them (don't let the milk boil). After cooling, the milk can be refrigerated for up to 3 days for use in sauces, soups, and so on.

* A teaspoon or two of lemon juice in the cooking water will also keep potatoes white.

* Potato skins are easier to remove while the potatoes are still hot.

* Potatoes cooked in water lose much of their vitamins to the liquid, which is a mighty good reason to save and use the cooking water.

POTATOES, COOKING METHODS
BAKED POTATOES

* Russets are best for baking. Choose potatoes about the same size (6 to 8 ounces) so they'll be done at the same time.

* Scrub potatoes well, blot dry with paper towels, and use the tines of a fork to prick about 1 inch deep in several places to let the steam out during baking.

* Cut a potato's baking time by almost a third by skewering it with an aluminum potato nail (but not in a microwave oven).

* For a crispy, brown skin, rub a little butter, bacon fat, or vegetable or olive oil on the skin before baking. Oiled potatoes also bake slightly faster.

* Wrapping potatoes in foil doesn't allow the steam to escape, so the skin will be soft, not crisp.

* Place potatoes to be baked right on the oven rack.

* If you have a lot of potatoes to bake at one time, stand them on end in a 12-cup muffin tin.

* Potatoes can be baked at temperatures from 350°F to 450°F, and will take anywhere from 45 minutes to 1½ hours to cook, depending on the size and number of potatoes being baked and the oven's temperature. The higher the temperature, the crisper the skins.

* Another method for baking potatoes with a crispy skin: Drop whole potatoes into a pot of boiling water; boil for 15 minutes. Place wet potatoes in a preheated 450°F oven; bake for 30 minutes, or until done.

* In a hurry? Pierce potatoes in several places with a fork and cook in a microwave oven on high as follows: 1 potato—3 minutes, 2 potatoes—4 minutes; 3 potatoes—5 minutes; and so on. Remove from the microwave and transfer to a preheated 425°F oven; bake for 20 to 25 minutes until done.

* In a *huge* hurry? Put fork-pierced potatoes in a microwave oven and cook on high for: 1 potato—4 to 6 minutes; 2 potatoes—6 to 8 minutes; 3 potatoes—8 to 10 minutes; 4 potatoes—10 to 12 minutes, and so on (these are approximate cooking times and will depend on the size of the potatoes and the wattage of the oven). Let the potatoes stand for 5 minutes in the microwave oven before serving. Microwave baked potatoes won't have the same flesh or skin texture as those baked in a conventional oven.

* Doneness test: Insert the tines of a fork deep into the center of the potato; there should be no resistance.

* Bake more potatoes than you need and dice the leftovers (with skins on) for hash browns the next day.

* Use a sharp knife to slit a baked potato down the center as soon as it's done. Just before serving, squeeze both ends together to open the potato and expose the flesh.

* Watching calories? Use low-fat instead of regular sour cream. Or mix ¼ cup salsa with 1 cup sour cream for a zesty topping. Or use a couple of tablespoons of low-fat cream cheese for a decadent flavor and creamy texture.

* Or put some cottage cheese and a dash of milk in the blender and process until smooth; season with salt and pepper.

* For a low-calorie sour cream substitute, try QUARK—a soft, unripened cheese with the texture and flavor of sour cream. It comes in two versions—low fat and nonfat. Quark isn't as tart as yogurt, and its texture is richer than either low-fat sour cream or yogurt.

* Personalize your potato topping by combining sour cream, Quark, or whatever topping you desire with any of a dozen additions, including chopped basil, chives, dill, scallions or watercress; crumbled bacon; grated Cheddar, Monterey Jack, Parmesan or Swiss cheese; crumbled feta or blue cheese; toasted caraway, celery, fennel, poppy or sesame seed; curry; cayenne or chili powder; freshly ground pepper; or diced, seeded tomatoes.

* For real comfort food, top a baked potato with chili.

* Leftover whole baked potatoes can be cooled, then wrapped and refrigerated for up to 3 days. To reheat, soak the potato in very hot water for 2 minutes, then bake at 350°F for about 20 minutes.

* Freeze whole (cooled) baked potatoes for up to 3 months by wrapping in

heavy-duty foil, then in a plastic bag. Thaw overnight in the fridge, then unwrap and bake at 375°F for 30 minutes. Or bake frozen, foil-wrapped potatoes at 375°F for about 45 minutes; remove the foil during the final 10 minutes.

CRACKLE-BAKED POTATOES

This recipe is the inspiration of James Beard, that inimitable bard of pushing the envelope. The skin becomes crunchy and toasty-tasting, the insides soft and creamy. Scrub and bake medium to large potatoes at 450°F for 1½ to 2 hours (*this isn't a typo!*).

CRISPY POTATO SKINS

These crispy strips are great for snacks and appetizers. Or crumble and use as a garnish for soups and salads. Scrape all but ⅛ inch of flesh out of leftover baked potatoes. Brush the skins with extra virgin olive oil. Use kitchen shears to cut the skins into ½-inch wide strips. Season to taste with salt and freshly ground pepper; or use other seasonings such as chili powder, cayenne or minced fresh herbs. Bake at 400°F until crispy (about 10 minutes).

Show me a person who doesn't like French fries and we'll swap lies.
—Joan Lunden, American TV personality

FRENCH FRIES *see also* DEEP-FRYING

* Food for thought: Ounce for ounce, French fries contain twelve times the fat and almost three times the calories of a baked potato.
* Russets are the best potatoes for frying, although long whites and Yukon Golds also work well. Count on 1 medium potato per person.
* Scrub potatoes well and peel or not—French fries with peels have more flavor.
* Cut potatoes into ¼- to ½-inch thick lengthwise strips, then soak the strips in a bowl of cold water for 30 minutes to remove excess starch.
* Thoroughly dry potatoes with paper towels. Any trace of moisture will cause the fat to spatter and boil up.
* Line a couple of baking sheets with a double layer of paper towels to use for draining fried potatoes.
* Use a large pot filled no more than halfway with oil (canola, corn, peanut or safflower). Heat the oil to 375°F.
* **Regular method:** Drop about one-third of the potatoes at a time into oil. Adding too many potatoes at once will lower the oil's temperature and the potatoes will get greasy. Use a deep-fat THERMOMETER to check the oil's temperature. Fry potatoes until golden brown.

* **French method:** This technique is more labor intensive but produces crispier fries. Fry potatoes in 325°F oil 3 to 5 minutes, or until golden. Drain on paper towels; cover and let stand at room temperature for up to 4 hours. Just before serving, fry potatoes in 375°F oil until golden brown.
* Transfer French fries to paper towel–lined sheets and place in a 275°F oven to keep warm while you fry the rest.
* Season fries with salt (and pepper, if desired) as soon as you put them on the baking sheet to drain.
* Always reheat the oil between batches.

FEISTY OVEN FRIES

Preheat the oven to 450°F; generously coat two large baking sheets with cooking spray (make three passes). In a small bowl, combine ¼ cup cornstarch and 2 tablespoons hot pepper sauce. Gradually stir in 2 tablespoons chicken broth and salt to taste. Turn into a large, flat-bottomed dish, spreading the mixture over the surface. Cut about 2 pounds of russet potatoes into strips about ½ inch wide. Add the potatoes, a few at a time, to the cornstarch mixture, turning to coat all sides. Place ½ inch apart on the prepared baking sheets. Bake for 20 minutes. Flip the potatoes and switch the baking sheets so the top one is on the bottom rack and vice versa. Bake 15 to 20 minutes more until golden brown. Serves 4.

MASHED POTATOES

* Almost any potato can be used for mashing—russets produce light, fluffy results, while waxy potatoes like Yukon Golds become creamy smooth.
* Leaving the skin on adds flavor and nutrition, but be sure to cut the potatoes into small cubes before you cook them so large pieces of skin won't clog a potato ricer.
* Cook potatoes for mashing with the skins on. Remove the skins and return them to the water. When cool, PURÉE the potato skins and water, then freeze for future use. The skins add flavor and nutrition.
* For extra-rich mashed potatoes, simmer them in milk (boiling will cause milk to separate), then add some of the milk when mashing.
* Add a ham hock, piece of raw bacon or smoky sausage link to the cooking water for potatoes, bring the water to a boil and cook for 5 minutes before adding the potatoes. The cooked potatoes will have a delicious smoky nuance.
* Cook the potatoes only until they're fork-tender; drain immediately so they don't absorb excess moisture.

* After draining the potatoes, return them to the pan and cook over low heat for about 1 minute, shaking the pan often, to evaporate excess moisture.
* Baked potatoes can be used for mashing as well.
* The amount of liquid added to mashed potatoes depends on the type of potato—drier potatoes like russets require more liquid than higher-moisture types.
* The moistener added to mashed potatoes affects both flavor and texture. Cream, butter, olive oil and sour cream add richness and body, while non- or low-fat milk creates light, fluffy potatoes. Nonfat sour cream creates rich, fluffy potatoes, as does buttermilk. Adding some of the water in which the potatoes cooked delivers a flavor bonus and is fat free. White wine also delivers flavor without a lot of calories.
* It's preferable to add a hot or warm liquid to potatoes but not absolutely necessary. If using a cold liquid, add it slowly, blending constantly.
* The preferred tools for mashing potatoes include a potato masher, a potato ricer or a large fork. An electric mixer can be used, but go slowly and don't overbeat or the potatoes will get sticky. Don't even think about using a food processor, which will turn potatoes to glue.
* Mash potatoes only until they're light; overworking makes them turn sticky and starchy.
* For complete decadence, whip ½ cup heavy cream and fold into mashed potatoes just before serving.
* Add sass with a tablespoon of freshly grated horseradish.
* **Mashed potato mix-ins** add color and flavor, and the endless options include: minced herbs (like basil, parsley or watercress), minced cooked vegetables (such as fennel, scallions or red or green bell peppers), crumbled crisp bacon, grated Cheddar or Gruyère or crumbled blue cheese, and so on. Add the mix-ins just before serving—they'll "cook" with the heat of the hot potatoes, and the flavor will be wonderfully fresh.
* Stirring in 1 cup shredded Cheddar at the last minute adds flavor as well as beautiful streaks of color.
* Mashed potatoes are best served immediately, but you can make them 15 to 20 minutes ahead and reheat in a microwave oven. Cover the potatoes and cook on high for 1 to 2 minutes, depending on the amount of potatoes. Stir the potatoes before serving.
* Or put mashed potatoes in an ovenproof dish, brush with melted butter, cover and place in a 250°F oven for 30 minutes.

* If you're going to hold mashed potatoes, as in the previous tips, don't stir in any mix-ins until just before serving.
* Leftover mashed potatoes make a great thickener for soups and sauces.

MASHED POTATO CAKES

Form leftover mashed potatoes into patties about ½ inch thick. Dip the patties in beaten egg, then bread crumbs (I use panko, Japanese bread crumbs). Refrigerate, uncovered, for 1 hour to let dry. Melt 2 tablespoons unsalted butter in a large skillet. Sauté the pancakes until golden brown and crispy on both sides, and enjoy the raves.

ROASTED POTATOES

* Any potato can be roasted, although long whites, round reds and whites, and new potatoes are considered preferable.
* Pan drippings or lard add great flavor to roasted potatoes.
* Halve small potatoes; cut larger ones into quarters, sixths or eighths. Pour ¼ to ⅓ cup olive oil, a melted butter and oil combination, pan drippings or other fat into a shallow baking dish or pan. Add the potatoes, tossing to coat liberally with fat; salt and pepper to taste. Roast in a preheated 375°F oven for 1 to 1½ hours until crisp and brown on the outside and fork-tender.
* One secret for perfectly roasted potatoes is to turn them often—about every 15 minutes—so they get evenly crisp and brown.
* Serve roasted potatoes hot from the oven. Once they cool, they never regain that crispy texture.
* Leftover roasted potatoes make excellent potato salad.

POTATO SALAD   see SALADS

POTS AND PANS   see COOKWARE AND BAKEWARE; PAN SIZES; SEASONING PANS

POT ROASTING   see BRAISING

Poultry is for the cook what canvas is for the painter.
—Jean-Anthelme Brillat-Savarin, French gastronome, writer

POULTRY, GENERAL   see also CHICKEN; CORNISH GAME HENS; DUCK; TURKEY

PURCHASING

* "Poultry" is a generic term for any domesticated bird used for food, the

most common being chicken, Cornish game hen, duck and turkey. Choose meaty, full-breasted poultry—a scrawny bird means you're paying proportionally for too much bone. The skin should be smooth and soft, not bruised or torn. Generally, the younger the bird, the more tender the meat and the milder the flavor; the pinker the bone ends, the fresher the bird. Avoid poultry with an off odor. If buying prepackaged poultry, make sure the cellophane isn't torn and that the package isn't leaking. Check the date on the label to be sure the bird isn't past its prime.

* Also check for the USDA (U.S. Department of Agriculture) inspection stamp on the package label, an indication that the bird is wholesome and accurately labeled. The USDA also has three grades for poultry—A, B and C. Grade A, most often found in markets, is the highest quality—an indicator that the bird is essentially defect free.

* Add an extra ounce per serving of boneless poultry to allow for shrinkage. Add another 2 ounces per serving to allow for bone. Therefore, if you plan on 4-ounce, bone-in portions, buy enough for 7-ounce servings.

STORING

* Raw poultry: Store in the coldest part of the refrigerator (40°F or below) as soon as you get it home from the market. If it's packaged tightly in cellophane and you're not going to use it within a few hours, either loosen the packaging or remove it and loosely rewrap the poultry in waxed paper. It can be refrigerated for up to 2 days. Freezing causes a loss of natural juices and can reduce tenderness. If you must freeze it, seal it airtight in a freezer-proof plastic bag or foil. If using foil, press it closely to the meat. If you opt for a plastic bag, use one with a zip closure and squeeze out as much air as possible. Freeze for up to 6 months.

* Cooked poultry: Refrigerate for up to 3 days; freeze for up to 3 months.

PREPARING

* Thaw frozen poultry in the refrigerator, allowing about 5 hours per pound. Thawing at room temperature increases the risk of bacteria formation.

* Thawing can also be done by submerging frozen poultry (still in its freezer wrapping) in a large container of cold water. Allow 30 minutes per pound and change the water every 30 minutes.

* If poultry takes on an unpleasant "refrigerator" smell, refresh it by squeezing lemon juice inside the cavity.

* Let refrigerated poultry sit at room temperature for 15 to 30 minutes to take some of the chill off before cooking.

* Bacteria flourish in poultry at temperatures between 40° and 140°F, so don't let it sit out at room temperature too long before cooking.

* Poultry shears are often easier to use than a knife when cutting up chicken or duck.

* To pull the skin off chicken parts, hold the skin with a paper towel, pulling it back to remove.

* Toss all the poultry parts you're not planning to use (giblets, tail, backbone, skin, bones, and so on) into a saucepan along with a handful of parsley and a chopped carrot, cover with water, and bring to a boil. Reduce to a simmer, cover and cook for 30 to 60 minutes until the liquid has reduced by half. Strain the stock and refrigerate to solidify the fat. After removing the fat, freeze, if desired, and use the stock when you want to enrich soups or sauces.

* Freeze chicken livers until you accumulate enough to make a pâté or other dish. Simply put the livers in a freezer-proof, airtight container, cover with milk and freeze. Add more livers as you get them (covering with more milk) until you're ready to use them. Defrost overnight in the refrigerator.

* Out of string and want to truss a bird? Try using unflavored dental floss.

* Or don't truss at all—simply tuck the wing tips under the bird's back.

* Commercial salad dressing makes an easy, instant marinade for all kinds of poultry.

* To prevent bacteria growth, don't stuff poultry until just before cooking. You can make the dressing and prepare the bird separately, combining them at the last minute. *See also* STUFFING.

* Stuff a bird only three-quarters full to allow for the stuffing to expand during cooking.

* Bacteria on raw poultry can contaminate other food it comes in contact with. Always wash anything used with raw poultry (your hands, cutting board and utensils) with hot, soapy water. Never allow juices from raw poultry to come in contact with cooked poultry.

COOKING

* A bird will baste itself if you cover it with a double layer of cheesecloth soaked with canola or olive oil (use melted, unsalted butter if not watching cholesterol); baste as necessary. At the end of the roasting time when the cheesecloth is removed, the bird will be moist and golden brown. Removing the cheesecloth 30 minutes before the bird is done will produce a crisp, brown skin.

* White meat cooks slightly faster than dark meat so, when cooking separate parts, add white-meat pieces about 5 minutes after the dark meat.

* Boneless poultry will cook in a third to half the time of that needed for bone-in birds. For instance, boneless chicken breasts will cook in 20 to 30 minutes in a 350°F oven, while bone-in breasts need 30 to 40 minutes.

* When grilling or broiling poultry, leave the skin on during cooking. It keeps the juices in and creates a more tender result. If desired, remove the skin after the dish is cooked.

* As a general rule, poultry is done when the juices run clear and the meat near the bone at the thickest part is no longer pink. Legs should twist easily in their sockets. Large birds can be tested with a meat THERMOME-TER, which should register 175°F when inserted in the thigh's thickest part, the breast should register 160° to 165°F. Be sure not to touch the bone when inserting the thermometer or it will throw the reading off.

* Let poultry "rest" for a few minutes after cooking to allow the juices to redistribute throughout the flesh and set. This produces an evenly moist result and makes the bird easier to carve. Allow about 10 minutes for small birds, 20 minutes for larger ones. Keep poultry warm during this rest period by covering it lightly with foil.

* In cooked poultry, bones that have dark splotches indicate that the bird's been frozen. When poultry is frozen, the blood cells in the bone marrow rupture. Upon thawing, the ruptured cells leak, which causes the discoloration. Cooking turns the red splotches dark brown.

* Don't let cooked poultry sit out at room temperature for more than 2 hours. To prevent bacterial growth, it should be kept either hot (145° to 165°F) or refrigerated at 40°F.

* Remove cooked poultry from the bones before refrigerating to keep the flavor fresher longer.

* Put all the bones in a large pot, cover with water and bring to a boil. Reduce the heat, cover and simmer for 1 hour. Cool to room temperature, strain, then refrigerate or freeze for use in soups, stews, sauces, and so on.

* Thoroughly heat leftover poultry (to about 175°F) and gravy (bring it to a boil and cook for 5 minutes).

* Dice leftover cooked poultry and sauté with diced potatoes, onions and green peppers. This makes a great hash for breakfast or dinner.

POWDERED MILK *see* DRY MILK

POWDERED SUGAR *see* SUGAR (CONFECTIONERS' SUGAR, page 454)

PRESSURE COOKERS; PRESSURE COOKING *see also* COOKING, GENERAL
TIDBIT Pressure cookers have a locking, airtight lid and a valve system to regulate internal pressure. They operate on a principle whereby the pres-

surized steam (produced by boiling liquid) inside the sealed pot cooks food at a very high temperature. The more pounds of pressure, the higher the internal temperature and the quicker the food cooks. Pressure cooking reduces cooking time by as much as two-thirds while retaining the food's nutritional value.

PURCHASING   Buy a pressure cooker with at least a 6-quart (or 5-liter) capacity. Anything smaller will limit the cooked yield of foods like beans, which can fill a cooker only halfway. For large families, select an 8-quart (7-liter) cooker. Choose a stainless-steel cooker (over one made of aluminum); the bottom should have a core of copper or aluminum for even heat conductivity. A cooker with two handles is convenient for moving the pot from stove to sink. Whereas first-generation (jiggle-top) cookers are equipped with detachable pressure regulators, the new, improved models feature built-in valves and indicator rods that eliminate guesswork by precisely indicating the pressure. They're also much quieter than older styles. Accessories that come with some cookers include a rack and steamer basket.

GENERAL

* Thoroughly read the owner's manual before you even think about using your pressure cooker. Details vary from brand to brand on such things as how much food can be placed in a cooker for it to operate properly and how to tell when pressure is reached.

* Pressure cookers quickly tenderize inexpensive, tough cuts of meat and older poultry like stewing hens. They make quick work of soups, stews and rice dishes like risottos and pilafs. Beans and whole grains cook (without presoaking) in about 30 minutes.

* About the only downside to pressure cooking is that foods cannot be checked during cooking, nor can they be added without first reducing the pressure.

* Accurate timing is essential when pressure cooking—don't guesstimate, use a timer.

* Rule of thumb: Fill the cooker only two-thirds full, especially with high-liquid foods like soups. Beans and grains shouldn't fill more than half the cooker, whereas other foods can fill it three-quarters. Again—read your cooker's instructions.

* The more food there is in a cooker, the longer it typically takes to reach full pressure. However, once high pressure is reached, a large quantity of the same type of food cooks just as quickly as a small quantity.

* Generally, you can use slightly more liquid than called for; however,

using less can promote scorching. Don't forget, liquid is necessary to build steam.

* When ingredients are cooked together under pressure, the flavors become intense, which means many recipes require less salt.

* More seasonings are required because the high heat of pressure cooking diminishes the flavor of herbs, garlic, and so on. Taste the finished dish and stir in additional seasonings if necessary.

* Cut up ingredients in accordance with how fast they'll cook. Otherwise, you may want to cut dense ingredients like carrots into small pieces so they'll be done at the same time as quicker-cooking ingredients.

* When cooking soups and stews, begin heating the liquid while you're chopping the other ingredients. This will reduce the time it takes for the pressure to reach the proper level once the lid is locked in place.

* No matter what you're cooking, having the ingredients hot will reduce the time it takes for pressure to build once the lid is locked in place.

* Pressure cooking turns greens like spinach an olive-drab color. If you want such ingredients to stay green, add and cook them after the pressure's been reduced.

* Wine can take on an acrid taste under pressure. Forestall this by bringing the wine to a boil and cooking for a few minutes to burn off the alcohol before beginning the pressure process.

* Pressure can be released naturally at the end of the cooking time by letting the pot sit off the heat. This can take 3 to 20 minutes (the longest time for a full pot of soup and such), and the food continues to cook during this time. This method works well for foods like beef, which remain more tender with a gradual release of pressure.

* Pressure may be quickly released by running cold water over the cooker. Tilt the cooker, so the water doesn't run over the pressure vents or regulator. The new generation of pressure cookers have a "quick-release" lever or button (check the owner's manual). This quick release can be hastened by also running cold water over the cooker.

* Thoroughly wash your cooker after each use, removing and cleaning the gasket and scrubbing the vent/valve area if necessary. Let the gasket air-dry completely before seating it back in the lid.

* To store a pressure cooker, turn the lid upside down and set it on top of the pan. Or store the lid completely separately. Locking the lid into place seals in air and odors.

PROSCIUTTO

TIDBIT Prosciutto is the Italian word for "ham." This special, Italian-style ham has been seasoned, salt-cured (but not smoked) and air-dried. It's available in gourmet and Italian markets and some supermarkets. Italian prosciuttos are designated *prosciutto cotto*, which is cooked, and *prosciutto crudo*, which is raw but ready to eat because of its curing.

PURCHASING Look for golden pink, moist-looking prosciutto with pure white fat. Buy sliced prosciutto only as needed, as the thin slices quickly dry out.

STORING Refrigerate sliced prosciutto, tightly wrapped, for up to 3 weeks.

USING

* Prosciutto is classically served with figs or melon as a first course.
* It's also a wonderful last-minute addition to pasta dishes.
* If using prosciutto in cooked dishes, have it sliced slightly thicker than usual, then cut it into strips or chunks. Stir it in at the very last minute; prolonged cooking toughens it.
* Prosciutto's easier to chop or slice if partially frozen.
* Mince prosciutto and mix it with mascarpone cheese or pesto to use as a spread for crostini.

PROSCIUTTO-WRAPPED ASPARAGUS

A classic Italian preparation is to wrap a thin slice of prosciutto around three cooked thin asparagus spears, their tips exposed. Count on two bundles per serving. Lay wrapped asparagus side by side in a buttered baking dish. Drizzle with about 2 tablespoons melted butter; sprinkle liberally with freshly grated Parmesan cheese. Bake at 350°F for about 5 minutes, or until the cheese is melted and the asparagus is warmed through.

PRUNES *see* DRIED PLUMS

PUMPKINS *see also* SQUASH, WINTER; VEGETABLES, GENERAL

PURCHASING Choose pumpkins that are brightly colored and heavy for their size; their rinds should be free of blemishes. In general, the flesh of smaller pumpkins will be sweeter and more tender and succulent than that of the larger of the species. If you plan to use pumpkin for cooking, choose a variety specifically grown for its eating quality, such as the sugar pumpkin, which typically weighs 1½ to 3 pounds.

EQUIVALENTS

* Fresh: 5-pound pumpkin = about 4½ cups cooked and mashed
* Canned: 15-ounce can = 1¾ cups mashed; 29-ounce can = 3½ cups mashed

STORING Store whole pumpkins at room temperature for up to 1 month; refrigerate for up to 3 months.

USING

* Pumpkin can be prepared in almost any way suitable for winter squash (*see* SQUASH, WINTER), such as for soup, as a vegetable, and so on. Likewise, winter squash (such as acorn or hubbard) can be substituted for pumpkin in recipes.

* Preparing a whole sugar pumpkin: Wash the exterior, then cut off and reserve the top. Scrape out the seeds and pulp, then use a damp paper towel to wipe out the inside of both the top and bottom. Brush the surface of the flesh with melted butter that's been seasoned with salt and pepper. Replace the lid; bake at 350°F for 30 minutes. Brush the inside with seasoned butter; bake 15 to 20 more minutes, until the flesh is fork-tender.

* To cook cut pumpkin: Halve or quarter the pumpkin, scrape out the seeds, wipe and brush with butter as in preceding tip. Place, flesh side down, in a baking pan with just enough water to barely cover the bottom. Bake at 350°F for 40 to 60 minutes (depending on the size of the pieces) until fork tender.

* Mashed pumpkin contributes flavor and moistness to many baked goods such as muffins and cakes.

* Use an electric mixer to beat cooked pumpkin—any strings will wind around the beaters and can easily be rinsed right off.

* Halloween pumpkins will keep longer if you coat them inside and out with spray antiseptic.

* Store pumpkin pie in the refrigerator and consume within 3 days.

PUMPKIN-SEED TARTAR SAUCE

Perfectly wonderful on grilled, baked and fried fish, and makes a great crudités dip. Combine ½ cup plain, low-fat yogurt, ½ cup mayonnaise, 1 cup ground, toasted, hulled pumpkin seeds, 2 tablespoons minced shallots, 1 tablespoon sweet pickle relish, and 1 teaspoon lemon juice in a medium bowl. Cover and refrigerate for at least 2 hours. Remove from the refrigerator 30 minutes before serving. Makes 1½ cups.

ROASTED PUMPKIN SEEDS

Rinse pumpkin seeds clean of all pulp and strings, then spread in a single layer on a double layer of paper towel. Let air-dry for about 4 hours. Toss the seeds with 2 tablespoons vegetable oil, spread in a single layer on a baking sheet, and bake at 350°F for about 30 minutes, or until golden brown. Stir seeds every 5 to 10 minutes during roasting time. Salt to taste and cool to room temperature before using.

P PURÉEING; PURÉE

TIDBIT Puréeing food simply means to pulverize it until it is smooth. Such food is called a "purée." This technique may be done by hand by using a food mill or by pressing the food through a fine sieve. The food processor or blender can handle the task more quickly.

QUARK *see also* CHEESE

TIDBIT   Quark is a soft, unripened cheese with the texture and flavor of sour cream. It has a milder flavor and much richer texture than yogurt.

PURCHASING   Quark comes in low-fat and nonfat versions, and can be found in a supermarket's refrigerated section.

STORING   Refrigerate and use within a week of the date on the carton.

GENERAL

* The numbers for 1 ounce of low-fat Quark versus 1 ounce regular and low-fat sour cream (the sour cream figures are in parenthesis) are: calories—35 (61/35), fat grams—2 (6/3), cholesterol milligrams—3.4 (13/8). One ounce of nonfat Quark has 18 calories and 1 gram cholesterol.

* Besides being a low-calorie topping for baked potatoes, Quark is a great sour cream substitute in a variety of dishes, including cheesecakes, dips, sauces, salads and salad dressings.

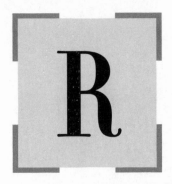

RADISHES *see also* VEGETABLES, GENERAL

PURCHASING Choose radishes that feel firm when gently squeezed. If a radish gives to pressure, the interior will likely be pithy instead of crisp. Any attached leaves should be green and crisp.

EQUIVALENTS ½ pound = 10 to 14 radishes, about 1⅔ cups sliced

STORING Refrigerate radishes in a plastic bag for up to 1 week. Remove and discard the leaves before storing.

USING

* Wash radishes and trim both ends just before using.
* For added crispness, cover radishes with ice water and refrigerate for 2 hours.
* Most of a radish's heat is in the skin—peel for a milder flavor.
* Radish flowers make a showy garnish (*see* page 225).
* Radish sprouts can be found in some supermarkets and specialty produce stores. They add a peppery accent to salads and other cold dishes.
* Don't think of radishes only as raw vegetables. They're wonderful thinly sliced, sautéed quickly (just until crisp-tender) in butter or olive oil, and seasoned simply with a dusting of sugar, freshly ground pepper and salt.

RAISINS *see also* DRIED FRUIT

TIDBIT The most common grapes used for raisins are Thompson seedless. The tiny Zante grape is used primarily for dried currants. Dark raisins are sun-dried for several weeks, thereby gaining their dark color and shriveled appearance. Golden raisins have been treated with sulfur dioxide (to prevent darkening) and dried with artificial heat, which leaves them plumper and moister than dark raisins.

EQUIVALENT 15-ounce package = about 2½ cups

STORING Store raisins in a tightly sealed plastic bag at room temperature for several months; refrigerate or freeze for up to 1 year.

USING

* Frozen raisins are easier to chop.

* Freezing also helps separate wads of stuck raisins. Place raisins in a plastic bag, freeze, then whack the bag against the countertop and the raisins will break up.

* If raisins clump together, put them in a strainer and spray hot, running water over them. Or pop them in the microwave and heat on high for 10 to 20 seconds.

* Rather than taking the time to chop raisins, substitute currants. Their small size and similar flavor will produce the same results.

* To plump raisins or currants, combine them with liquid (water, orange juice, liqueur, and so on) to cover; bring to a boil. Cover, remove from heat and let stand 10 minutes.

* Or plump by combining raisins or currants with the soaking liquid in a medium bowl. Then cover and microwave on high for 30 seconds; let stand for 5 minutes before using.

* If you use raisins or currants in baked goods often, put them in a large, screw-top jar and cover with brandy, rum or liqueur. Store at room temperature or in the refrigerator; blot well before using.

* Before adding raisins or currants to a cake, bread or cookie batter, toss with some of the flour called for in the recipe, separating the pieces with your fingers as you do so. This will help keep the fruit from sinking to the bottom of the batter.

RASPBERRIES *For storage and cleaning information, see* BERRIES, GENERAL

TIDBIT According to Greek mythology, raspberries were once all white until one day when a nymph picking raspberries to soothe the crying baby Zeus pricked her finger on a thorn. The nymph's blood stained the berries, and they've been a brilliant red ever since. Myths aside, today not all raspberries are red, but come in a variety of hues, from almost black to golden.

PURCHASING Choose brightly colored, fragrant, plump berries sans hull. Attached hulls are a sign that the berries were picked too early and will undoubtedly be tart. Avoid soft, shriveled or moldy berries. Black and golden raspberries are usually available only in specialty produce markets.

EQUIVALENTS

* Fresh: ½ pint = 1⅓ cups
* Frozen: 10-ounce package = 1¾ cups

USING

* Raspberries are commonly thought of for dessert, but make an excellent addition to chicken salads or in sauces for pork or poultry such as game hens.
* About the only adornment necessary for raspberries is a kiss of cream.
* For a spectacular dessert, combine golden, black and red raspberries in a compote, and top simply with a dollop of softly whipped cream.

PEPPERED RASPBERRY VINEGAR

Use this lively vinegar for dressings, sauces and gifts. Put 3 cups raspberries, 3 tablespoons black peppercorns and 1 tablespoon allspice berries in a very clean 1-quart glass jar. Use a long-handled wooden spoon to crush the berries. Add 2 cups rice vinegar, stirring to combine. Cover tightly and let stand in a cool, dark place for at least 1 week and up to 2 weeks, depending on desired flavor intensity. Pour the vinegar through a fine sieve lined with cheesecloth into a 3-cup glass jar with a tight-sealing lid. Refrigerate for up to 6 months. Makes about 2½ cups.

REDUCING; REDUCTION

* "Reducing" refers to the process of boiling a liquid until the volume is reduced through moisture evaporation. The consistency of the resulting liquid (often called a *reduction*) is thicker, the flavor more intense.
* Don't season such a liquid until it's completely reduced or the resulting flavor could be overpowering.

RHUBARB

TIDBIT   Rhubarb is nicknamed *pieplant* because of its popularity in pies. However, although rhubarb is most often served as dessert, it isn't—as many assume—a fruit, but rather a member of the buckwheat family.

PURCHASING   There are two kinds of rhubarb on the market: **Hot-house rhubarb** has pink to pale red stalks and yellow green leaves; **field-grown rhubarb** has cherry red stalks, bright green leaves and a more pronounced flavor. Choose rhubarb with crisp, brightly hued stalks. The leaves should be fresh-looking and blemish free.

EQUIVALENTS

* Fresh: 1 pound = 3 cups chopped, 2 cups cooked
* Frozen: 12-ounce package = 1½ cups

STORING

* Refrigerate, tightly wrapped in a plastic bag, for up to a week.
* Cut in chunks and freeze in a freezer-proof plastic bag for up to 9 months.

PREPARING

* Wash, trim ends and remove the leaves just before using. The leaves and roots of rhubarb contain oxalic acid and therefore can be toxic.
* Field-grown rhubarb has a fibrous, stringy skin that must be removed. Start at one end and cut under a small section of skin, then pull that section down the length of the stalk and discard. Repeat until all skin is removed.
* Cooking rhubarb in orange juice not only adds flavor but diminishes acidity.
* Strawberries are classically paired with rhubarb, but blackberries and raspberries are also good mates.
* For a change of pace, top your next cheesecake with stewed *(see following recipe)* or baked rhubarb.
* Try orange-scented baked rhubarb *(see following recipe)* as an accompaniment to ham.

STEWED RHUBARB

Cut 2 pounds peeled rhubarb into 1-inch chunks. Combine 1 cup *each* water and sugar in a large saucepan; bring to a boil, stirring until the sugar dissolves. If desired, finely grated orange or lemon zest and ½ teaspoon ground cinnamon can be added to the sugar mixture. Add the rhubarb; simmer, uncovered, for about 15 minutes, or until the rhubarb is crisp-tender. Cool and serve in syrup.

BAKED RHUBARB

Place 2 pounds peeled rhubarb (cut into 1-inch chunks) in a 9 × 13-inch pan. Sprinkle with 1½ cups superfine sugar, and about ¼ teaspoon *each* ground ginger and nutmeg. Drizzle with ½ cup orange juice. Cover with foil and bake at 350°F for 30 minutes. Stir to combine; bake, uncovered, for 10 more minutes, or until rhubarb is crisp-tender.

> *Brown rice is ponderous, overly chewy, and possessed of unpleasant religious overtones.*
> —Fran Lebowitz, American writer

RICE *see also* RISOTTO; WILD RICE

TIDBIT Rice is classified by its size: long-, medium- or short-grain. **Long-grain rice** has a length four to five times that of its width; when cooked, it produces light, dry grains that separate easily. **Short-grain rice** has fat, roundish grains with a high starch content; when cooked, the grains are moist and tend to stick together. **Medium-grain rice** has a size and character between the other two—shorter and moister than long-grain, not as starchy as short-grain.

R

PURCHASING   All the following rices are available in supermarkets.

* **Brown rice** is the entire grain with only the inedible outer husk removed. The nutritious, high-fiber bran coating gives brown rice a light tan color, nutlike flavor and chewy texture. Brown rice takes at least twice as long to cook than regular white long-grain rice. There's a quick brown rice that cooks in about 15 minutes.
* **White rice** has had the hull and bran layers completely removed. *Converted or parboiled* white rice has undergone a steam-pressure process that makes a fluffy, separated cooked grain; it takes slightly longer to cook than regular white rice.
* **Instant or quick-cooking rice** has been fully or partially cooked, then dehydrated; it takes only a few minutes to cook, but its flavor and texture don't match those of regular rice.
* **Aromatic rice** is a collective term for rice varieties that naturally have a fragrant, nutlike flavor. Such rices, commonly marketed, include Basmati, Jasmine, Texmati, Wehani and Wild Pecan Rice.

EQUIVALENTS
* Regular rice: 1 cup = 3 cups cooked
* Converted rice: 1 cup = about 3¼ cups cooked
* Instant rice: 1 cup = 2 cups cooked
* Brown rice: 1 cup = 3½ to 4 cups cooked

STORING
* Store white rice in an airtight container in a cool, dark place for up to 1 year. Brown rice, which is susceptible to rancidity because of the oil in the bran layer, can be stored the same way for up to 6 months. In warm climates, or for longer storage, refrigerate or freeze rice in airtight packaging.
* Refrigerate leftover cooked rice for up to 4 days. Freeze in 1-cup portions for up to 3 months.

COOKING
* No need to wash rice before cooking—you'll only remove nutrients.
* Rice that has been stored for a long time at low humidity can lose some natural moisture and therefore may require more liquid and a longer cooking time.
* Proportions of water (or other liquid) per cup of rice: For short-, medium- and long-grain rice—1½ cups liquid; long-grain brown rice and converted rice—2 cups; short-grain brown rice—3 cups; wild rice—4 cups.
* Basic stovetop cooking method: Bring water to a boil. Stir in rice and salt; cover and simmer for 15 minutes to 20 minutes for white rice, about

40 minutes for brown rice. Remove from the heat; let stand, covered, for 10 minutes.

* Modified stovetop method: Combine rice, salt and twice as much cold water as rice in a wide-bottomed pot. Bring to a mild boil; cook, uncovered, for 5 minutes. Reduce the heat; cover and cook for 15 or 20 minutes until rice is done as desired.

* Boiling method: Prepare as you would pasta, adding the rice to plenty of boiling, salted water and cooking, uncovered, to the desired texture. Drain in a strainer.

* Pilaf-style rice: Sauté rice in oil or butter (1 tablespoon per cup of rice) over medium heat for 3 to 5 minutes. For a nuttier flavor, sauté rice until golden brown. Then add boiling liquid, cover the pan and cook as usual.

* Baked rice: Combine rice (sautéed, if desired; see pilaf-style, above) and boiling liquid in an ovenproof casserole, cover tightly and bake at 375°F until the liquid is absorbed, about 25 minutes.

* Microwaved rice: This takes as much time as cooking it on the stovetop. Combine rice and liquid in a microwave-safe dish. Cover and cook on high for 5 minutes. Stir, then re-cover and cook at medium (50 percent power) for 15 minutes. Let stand, covered, for 5 minutes.

* Electric rice-cooker method: If you eat a lot of rice, an electric rice cooker is efficient and convenient. Cookers vary, so follow the manufacturer's directions.

* No matter how you cook rice, sautéing it in a little butter or oil for 2 to 3 minutes before adding liquid will improve its flavor.

* Make a double batch of rice and use leftovers in a subsequent meal in a stir-fry, meat loaf, soup or bell-pepper stuffing.

* Or freeze cooked rice in individual serving portions and reheat in the microwave oven.

* Stirring rice during cooking will bring out the starch and make it stickier.

* Rice cooked with highly acidic ingredients such as tomatoes often requires extra liquid and cooking time.

* A teaspoon or two of lemon juice in the cooking water will make cooked rice whiter.

* Cooking rice in chicken, beef or vegetable broth adds flavor and nutrition. Wine, sherry or beer may also be substituted for part of the cooking water.

* One or 2 teaspoons vegetable oil added to the cooking water will keep rice from boiling over and keep the grains separate.

* Give rice a smoky nuance by adding a ham hock, one or two pieces of

raw bacon or a smoky sausage link to the cooking water; bring the water to a boil and cook for 10 minutes. Remove the meat, add ½ cup more water and bring to a boil again before adding the rice.

* The lid for the pan in which you cook rice should fit tightly. Remedy a loose lid by covering the pan with two layers of waxed paper, punch a hole in the center, then put the pan cover on, pressing down to seat it firmly.

* Lifting the lid to peek while rice is cooking lets out valuable steam and slows the cooking process.

* If rice scorches, the best thing to do is start over, as the flavor can permeate and spoil the lot. But if there's no time, gently spoon the rice into a clean, ovenproof casserole or pan, being careful not to scrape up any of the scorched portion. Immediately cover the rice with a single layer of either fresh white-bread slices or onion skins. Cover the bread or onions with a piece of paper towel; put a lid on the casserole or pan. Place in a 250°F oven for about 10 minutes; remove and discard the towel and bread or onions, and serve.

* Test rice for doneness by biting into it. It should be firm but tender.

* If the cooked rice is too firm, add about ¼ cup hot liquid, cover and cook until absorbed. Repeat if necessary.

* If the rice is done but there's still some liquid left, remove the cover and cook over low heat, fluffing the rice with a fork, until the liquid evaporates.

* Enrich cooked rice at the last minute by adding a tablespoon of butter or oil, tossing until the grains are coated.

* Don't rinse cooked rice unless a recipe directs you to do so—you'll lose nutrients by doing so.

* Toss the finished rice with a fork before serving to let steam escape and separate the grains.

* Hold cooked rice for up to 30 minutes by removing it from the heat and tossing with a fork. Cover the pot first with a kitchen towel, then with the pan lid. The towel prevents condensation from falling into the rice and making it sticky. Or cover the pan with a towel and the lid and place in a 250°F oven until ready to serve.

LEFTOVERS

* Add leftover rice to soups or stews at the last minute so it doesn't get soft and mushy.

* PURÉE leftover rice with a little liquid and use as a soup or sauce thickener.

* Reheat leftover rice with 1 to 2 tablespoons liquid (such as water or chicken broth) to restore its fluffy tenderness. The heating can be done in a covered saucepan, or in a covered casserole in a microwave oven.

* Or put leftover rice in a sieve; set it in a pan over simmering water, being careful not to let the rice touch the water. Cover and let steam for 5 to 10 minutes; fluff with a fork.

* When heating frozen leftover rice in a microwave oven, defrosting isn't necessary. Microwave on high for about 2 minutes per cup, tossing the rice halfway through the cooking time.

* Leftovers make great fried rice. Bring the rice to room temperature, then sauté in a little oil with other minced ingredients like scallions, mushrooms, maybe a little smoked sausage, some minced fresh ginger, and so on.

* Give leftover rice salad a different look by packing it firmly into a well-oiled mold (large or individual size). Cover with foil or plastic wrap, and weight down with full cans. Refrigerate for at least 1 hour before unmolding onto a serving plate.

* Short-grain rice makes great rice pudding because it has a higher proportion of starch, which results in a creamier texture.

* For fluffy, cold rice pudding, fold softly whipped cream into chilled rice pudding.

GINGER RICE

Wonderful in cold rice salads, stir-fries or simply as a side dish, particularly for pork, chicken or seafood. Preheat the oven to 400°F. Cut a 3-inch length of peeled fresh ginger lengthwise in ¼-inch wide strips. Combine 2¾ cups chicken stock broth and 2 tablespoons light soy sauce with the ginger strips in a medium saucepan; bring to a boil. Meanwhile, heat 2 tablespoons vegetable oil in a heavy, ovenproof skillet or sauté pan with a lid, over medium-high heat. Add 1½ cups Jasmine or Basmati rice; cook, stirring often, just until it begins to brown, about 5 minutes. Add 2 large garlic cloves, minced; cook for 1 more minute and remove from the heat. Pour the boiling broth (with the ginger) into the rice, stirring to combine. Immediately cover tightly. Bake until the rice is tender and the liquid is absorbed, about 20 minutes. Remove the ginger strips. Salt to taste; stir the rice to fluff. Serves 4 to 6.

Risotto is the ultimate comfort food.
—Joyce Goldstein, American restaurateur, author

RISOTTO   *see also* RICE

TIDBIT   This creamy, classic northern Italian dish is made with short-grain, high-starch rice, typically Arborio. Pass freshly grated Parmesan or aged Asiago at the table so diners can add their own.

* Never rinse rice before making risotto or you'll wash off some of the grain's starch, which is so valuable in this creamy dish.

* Before beginning to cook risotto, sauté the rice (and any shallots or garlic) in a couple of tablespoons of oil for 2 minutes, or just until the rice is opaque.

* Heat the liquid for the risotto and keep it hot and ready to use over a second burner. If using part wine, make it the first liquid you stir into the rice so its full flavor will be absorbed.

* **Classic method:** Add ½ cup of the hot liquid (keep it hot over another burner) to the rice; stir constantly, cooking until the rice absorbs the liquid. Add the next ½ cup hot liquid, stirring continually until the rice absorbs it. Repeat until all the liquid has been added and absorbed by the rice. Typically, liquid is absorbed more rapidly at the beginning of the process than at the end. Keep the heat level relatively low—the mixture should just bubble slightly.

* Sauté ingredients to be added—like mushrooms or bell peppers—just until barely done (blanch [see BLANCHING] vegetables like peas), then stir them into the risotto a few minutes before serving.

* Add richness without a lot of fat by stirring in 1 tablespoon unsalted butter at the last minute.

* **Microwave method:** This technique is less labor intensive, but doesn't produce the same creamy texture. In short, it's passable if you're in a hurry. In a microwave-safe bowl, cook rice in oil (*see second tip*) on high for 2 minutes (in a 650- to 700-watt oven). Add chopped shallots and garlic, if desired; cook for 1 minute. Stir in two-thirds of the liquid; cook on high, uncovered, for about 12 minutes (for 1 cup uncooked rice), stirring vigorously halfway through. Add the remaining liquid, stirring well; cook on high for about another 6 minutes. Stir in butter, cheese and cream, if desired; let stand, covered, for 5 minutes.

* Leftover risotto makes a wonderful stuffing for mushrooms.

RISOTTO CAKES

Use leftover risotto to make cakes 3 inches wide and ½ inch thick. Sauté in melted butter over medium-high heat until golden on both sides. Lighten

the cakes by mixing the risotto with stiffly beaten eggs whites before forming. Use 1 egg white for each cup of risotto.

ROASTING   *see also* BAKING; TURKEY

TIDBIT   Although spit-roasting over a fire was the original form of this
art, today the term "roasting" typically refers to the oven method. In a nutshell, roasting is a specific, dry-heat baking technique whereby food is
oven-cooked in a shallow pan without liquid and typically uncovered. The
oven heat completely surrounds the food, turning it brown and crispy. Fat
is often used to facilitate roasting, as in roasted potatoes. In some cases, the
food is covered during the first part of cooking, then uncovered to roast and
brown.

PREPARING

* For most roasting purposes, the oven rack should be in the center of the
  oven so air can circulate freely. Position the rack before turning on the
  oven; thoroughly preheat the oven.
* Choose a pan large enough to hold the food in a single layer.
* Remove meat from the refrigerator 2 to 3 hours before cooking.
* Cut vegetables like carrots, potatoes and turnips into 1½-inch chunks.
  Toss them with a little oil or melted unsalted butter before seasoning to
  taste with salt and pepper. If desired, add some finely chopped fresh
  herbs.
* If a roast doesn't already have a layer of fat on it, cover the top with
  something like fatback or lightly salted bacon. Fat not only keeps the
  meat from drying out, but flavors it as well.
* Add flavor to both meat and drippings by cutting tiny pockets in any
  external fat and inserting slivers of fresh garlic.
* Searing a roast until nicely browned before beginning to cook contributes both flavor and color. Sprinkle a soupçon of sugar over the meat
  before roasting—the sugar will caramelize, enhancing both browning
  and flavor.
* Whenever possible, elevate the meat so the heat and air can circulate
  underneath. If you don't have a roasting rack to set inside the roasting
  pan, use a small cooking rack or several canning jar rings.

COOKING

* Always preheat the oven. Preheating the roasting pan gives browning a
  head start.
* Vegetables can be roasted alone or alongside meat. Occasionally turn
  vegetables to ensure even browning.

* Vegetables roasted at high heat will have a better flavor and texture if they're covered during the first half of the cooking time, then uncovered and roasted until done.
* Cook meat fat side up so the melting fat naturally bastes it during roasting.
* Slow roasting at temperatures of 250° to 300°F is particularly good for large pieces of tough meat, such as a bottom round roast. Slow-roasted meats should be browned well on the stovetop before being placed in the oven. In general, slow-cooked roasts shrink less than those cooked at higher temperatures.
* High-temperature roasting is best for tender cuts like tenderloins, which won't become tough or dry with high heat. There are two high-heat roasting methods. My favorite comes from Christopher Kimball, author of *The Cook's Bible:* Preheat the oven and pan at 400°F. Place the tenderloin (generously seasoned with salt and pepper) into the hot pan and roast, uncovered, for 10 minutes. Turn the meat, then continue roasting for a total time of 10 minutes per pound for medium-rare.
* The more common high-heat roasting method is to preheat the oven to 500°F, roast the meat for 15 minutes, then reduce the heat to 350°F and cook until the meat is done to your preference (*see* MEAT, GENERAL, *for doneness temperatures*).
* Turning a roast at least twice during cooking helps it to brown evenly. Baste it often with the pan juices.
* Basting too often with too much liquid (stock, wine, and so on) produces excessive moisture in the oven—the meat could end up steamed rather than roasted.
* Checking for doneness: Allow for the fact that residual heat will continue to cook the meat after it's removed from the oven. Count on the internal temperature increasing by 5° to 10°F or more.
* Because meat juices shift to the center of a roast while it cooks, the exterior becomes dry. Letting the roast rest for 10 to 15 minutes after it's finished cooking allows the juices to redistribute throughout the flesh. This also makes the roast easier to carve. Keep it warm during this rest period by covering it lightly with foil.

ROASTS   *see also* MEAT, GENERAL; ROASTING
* The most popular beef, lamb or pork cut for roasting is the rib roast, also called a *rack*. Loin (pork and veal) and leg (lamb, pork and veal) roasts are also favorites. The next time you buy a boneless roast, remember that bones deliver a lot of flavor to the meat. What you gain in carving conve-

nience, you lose in flavor. A bone-in roast won't take as long to cook as one that's boneless—the bone acts as a heat conductor to the meat's center.

* *see* BRAISING (for pot roasts); ROASTING

ROCK CORNISH GAME HENS   *see* CORNISH GAME HENS

ROUX   *see also* SAUCES AND GRAVIES; THICKENERS

TIDBIT   Roux is a simple mixture of equal parts flour and fat, cooked to improve the flour's flavor. It's typically used to thicken liquid mixtures such as sauces, gravies, soups and stews. The color and flavor of a roux are determined by the length of time the mixture's cooked.

GENERAL

* **White roux** and **blond roux** are both made with butter or oil—the former is cooked just until it begins to turn beige, the latter until pale golden. Light roux take 5 to 15 minutes to cook.
* **Brown roux** can be based on butter, pork or beef fat, lard or drippings. After being cooked, its color can range from deep golden brown to mahogany brown. The darkest roux, which develops a nutty flavor, sometimes takes up to 1 hour to cook—it's most often used for specialties like Cajun gumbo.
* **Dry roux:** A shortcut to a dark roux is to cook the flour, stirring often, in a dry skillet or saucepan over medium heat until well browned. Cool, then store in an airtight container at room temperature or in the fridge until ready to use. Simply put the dry roux in a pan, add the fat (oil, drippings, and so on) and cook for 3 to 4 minutes.

A man who is stingy with the saffron is capable
of seducing his own grandmother.
—Norman Douglas, British writer

SAFFRON *For information on storing see* SPICES

TIDBIT Saffron—the yellow orange stigmas from a small purple crocus—is the world's most expensive spice. That's because each flower provides only 3 stigmas (which must be painstakingly handpicked and dried), and it takes 14,000 of these tiny threads for each ounce of saffron!

PURCHASING Saffron comes either powdered or in threads (the whole stigmas). Powdered saffron loses its flavor more readily and can easily be adulterated with less expensive powders like turmeric. Buying cheaper saffron won't save money in the long run, since more will be needed for the same flavor impact. Many markets keep this precious spice in the manager's office because it's so expensive and packaged in such small containers (making it easy to shoplift). Ask a clerk to get you some.

USING

* Just before using saffron threads, crush them between your fingers to crumble and help dissolve in liquids.
* Heat releases saffron's flavor essence, so increase its impact by mixing it with 1 tablespoon very hot water; let stand for about 10 minutes before using.
* A pinch of saffron adds a beautiful golden hue to rice or mashed potatoes.

SALAD DRESSINGS *see also* FATS AND OILS; SALAD GREENS; SALADS; VINEGARS

* **Vinaigrette:** The classic ratio is 3 parts oil to 1 part vinegar, lemon juice, and so on. Make a triple batch and store in the refrigerator indefinitely.
* Red- or white-wine vinegar are common standbys for dressings, but

there's a dazzling array of other vinegars available. Look for those made with fruit (blueberries, cranberries or raspberries) or herbs (basil, dill, rosemary or tarragon). The mild Asian rice vinegars also complement many salads. Experiment to see what you like best.

* Wine is acidic and can be substituted for all or part of the vinegar or lemon juice.

* The next time a dressing recipe calls for lemon juice or vinegar, try using lime juice—it adds a lively touch to greens and goes particularly well with avocado and seafood salads.

* When substituting yogurt for sour cream, use a little less vinegar to compensate for the yogurt's natural acidity.

* Fruit juices—such as pineapple, orange or mango—make great salad dressings. Simply combine the juice with a dash of oil, a sprinkle of nutmeg and maybe a little honey. Great for fruit salads, as well as mixed greens or seafood.

* For an extra-smooth vinaigrette, combine the ingredients and an ice cube in a screw-top jar and shake vigorously. Discard the ice cube once the dressing is mixed.

* Processing in a blender makes almost any salad dressing creamier.

* Cut down on oil in dressing by substituting wine, vegetable or defatted chicken broth, or vegetable or tomato juice for up to a third of the oil. Whisk into the dressing after the other ingredients are combined.

* Salad dressings with less oil typically have a thinner texture. Compensate for this by adding ¼ to ½ cup overcooked rice or 1 or 2 chunks cooked potato and processing in the blender until smooth.

* PURÉE roasted peeled red peppers (available in jars) to thicken and flavor dressings *see* ROASTED PEPPERS, page 37.

* No need to mix a dressing separately. Simply toss the greens with enough oil to coat the leaves lightly, then sprinkle lightly with vinegar, lemon juice, and so on, and season with salt and pepper to taste.

* Give dressing an exotic flavor by adding 1 or 2 teaspoons minced fresh ginger.

* Quick avocado dressing: Combine half an avocado with ¾ cup vinaigrette dressing in a blender; process until smooth.

* When using a salad-dressing mix, combine it with 2 to 4 tablespoons boiling water, stirring until combined. Cool to room temperature before adding the remaining liquid. This technique releases the flavors almost instantly.

* Give a commercial dressing a homemade touch by mixing in some minced fresh herbs, garlic or shallots.

LIME CREAM DRESSING

A spicy-hot dressing that's great on everything from slaws to mixed greens to potato salads. Drop 1 large garlic clove into a running food processor with the steel blade; process until the garlic is chopped and clinging to the sides of the bowl. Scrape down the sides of the bowl. Add ⅔ cup olive oil, ⅓ cup sour cream, ¼ cup fresh lime juice, 2 teaspoons Dijon mustard, ¾ teaspoon chili powder, ½ to ¾ teaspoon cayenne and ½ teaspoon salt; process 20 seconds, or until creamy. Cover and refrigerate until ready to use. Stir before using. Makes about 1¼ cups.

SALAD GREENS   *see also* SALAD DRESSINGS; SALADS

TIDBIT   There are literally hundreds of lettuces and salad greens grown throughout the world and, because their seasons peak at different times of year, there's always a wide variety available. Besides the many lettuces (like butterhead, iceberg, romaine and red-tip), there's a plentitude of greens that can be used in salads, including arugula, Belgian endive, curly endive, frisée, escarole, dandelion greens, mâche, mustard greens, radicchio, spinach and watercress.

PURCHASING   The general rule when buying lettuce or other greens is to look for those that are crisp and free of blemishes. They should smell fresh, never sour.

EQUIVALENT   1 pound = about 6 cups pieces

STORING   Refrigerate clean greens, wrapped loosely in dry paper towels, then in a tightly sealed plastic bag (remove as much air as possible from the bag before sealing), for up to 1 week. Put a couple of sheets of paper towel in with the greens to absorb any excess moisture.

PREPARING

* Salad greens will last longer if they're washed as soon as you get them home.
* The easiest way to clean greens is to cut off the bottom to separate the leaves, then put them in a sink or large container full of cold water. Swish the greens around with your hands, then let them stand for a few minutes for any dirt to sink to the bottom.
* Clean iceberg lettuce differently. First remove the core by firmly smacking it against the countertop. Then grab the core with your fingers, twist and lift out. Run cold water into the resulting cavity, flushing thoroughly. Invert the head to let the water drain out.
* All greens must be thoroughly dried before using or storing. The easiest way to dry greens is in a salad spinner, which is one of the best $15 invest-

ments you can make. Rather than overload the spinner (which won't get the greens as dry as you want), do the greens in batches.

* You can also dry salad greens by shaking off excess moisture, laying them out on a double layer of paper towels (or a kitchen towel), then blotting the surface dry.

* To renew greens that have begun to wilt, place them in ice water to which you've added 2 tablespoons lemon juice; cover and refrigerate for 1 hour. If you have time, wrap the dried greens in dry paper towels and refrigerate for about 4 hours.

* Many kitchen pundits have long insisted that lettuce leaves must be torn by hand or their leaf edges will turn brown. Not true, if you do it right. Using a sharp stainless-steel knife to cut lettuce won't cause it to brown any faster than if you tear it. The main difference is in appearance—many feel that torn leaves have more eye appeal than those that are cut.

* Add color to large lettuce leaves (for lining a plate) by dipping the edges in water (shake off well), then into a saucer of paprika. Just a little paprika—the effect should be subtle, not blatant.

* Don't think of greens as just for salads. They're wonderful sautéed, stir-fried or braised, and served as a side dish.

You can put everything, and the more things the better, into a salad, as into a conversation; but everything depends on the skill of mixing.
—Charles Dudley Warner, American editor, writer

SALADS *see also* COOKING AND EATING LIGHT; FLOWERS; SALAD DRESSINGS; SALAD GREENS; VEGETABLES, GENERAL
TIDBIT Today it's not uncommon for salad to take center stage as the main dish, in myriad guises and in all shapes and sizes. Salads are friendly and versatile; they can just as easily feature meat and potatoes as Asian noodles and peanuts. They can be light and fruity or hearty and earthy; hot, cold or in between. The best salad is a study in contrast and balance of textures, colors and flavors. Mix crunchy ingredients with those that are soft, tangy flavors with mild or slightly sweet ones, and bright colors with those that are more muted. The result will be eye-pleasing, palate-teasing and downright delicious.
PREPARING

* Salads don't have to consist of greens. There are dozens of fresh vegetables that you can make a delicious salad with, including broccoli, cauli-

flower, celeriac, corn, cucumbers, fennel, green beans, jicama and turnips. Simply peel if necessary, and dice, chop or shred.

* Chilling the salad plates or serving bowl will keep your salads crisp longer. Use hollowed-out large tomato or bell-pepper halves as edible containers for bean, pasta, rice, tuna or other salads.

* The presentation of a salad is almost as important as its flavor. An easy way to add color is with edible FLOWERS. The flowers can be used whole, or the petals can be scattered over the top of the salad. The key is being subtle, not cutesy.

* After cleaning wooden salad bowls, rub them with a crumbled piece of waxed paper to seal the surface.

DRESSING GREEN SALADS (*see also* SALAD DRESSINGS)

* Dress salad greens just before serving so they won't become soggy.

* Or try this trick. Put the dressing in the bottom of the bowl, add any veggies like chopped bell peppers and cucumbers. Put the tossing spoon and fork in the bowl, topped by the greens. The tossers will keep most of the greens raised above the dressing. Cover tightly with plastic wrap and refrigerate until 30 minutes before serving.

* Don't overdress salad—too much dressing weighs down the ingredients and masks their flavor. The dressing should highlight, not overpower, the ingredients.

* Save on cleanup by refrigerating cleaned salad greens in a large plastic bag; then, just before serving, pour the dressing over the greens, seal the bag and toss. Arrange the dressed salad on individual plates; throw out the bag.

* Another work saver is to mix the dressing right in the salad bowl, then add the salad ingredients and toss.

PASTA AND POTATO SALADS *See also* PASTA; POTATOES

* Pasta salad should always be made with very *al dente* pasta to allow it to absorb some of the dressing and still be firm, not mushy. Hot pasta can be combined with vinaigrette dressing, but let it cool to room temperature before adding other ingredients (fresh herbs, vegetables, and so on) to keep them crisp.

* When using long noodles for salad, rinse them under cold, running water after cooking to remove excess starch so they won't stick together.

* For potato salad, choose varieties that will hold their shape, such as new potatoes (*see* POTATOES).

* Keep potatoes for salad snowy white by adding a teaspoon or two of lemon juice to the cooking water.

* Potatoes absorb more dressing if dressed while they're hot.

* Add fresh herbs and ingredients like tomatoes to potato salad just before serving to retain their texture.
* Personalize deli-bought potato salad by adding finely chopped red or green bell peppers, cucumbers, dill or sweet pickles, hard-cooked eggs, grated Cheddar cheese, or herbs such as basil, cilantro, dill or parsley.

LEFTOVERS

* Leftover meat, fish or poultry can form the base for a main-course salad the next day. Add salad greens or chopped fresh vegetables, croutons and your favorite dressing, and voilà!
* Use leftover bean, pasta, rice, meat, fish or vegetable salads to stuff pita pockets for an instant sandwich the next day.
* Don't throw out leftover tossed salad because it's limp and soggy. Recycle it into soup by puréeing (*see* PURÉE), then adding broth and chopped vegetables.

> *Salmon are like men: too soft a life is not good for them.*
> —James de Coquet, French food writer

SALMON *For buying, storing and cooking information, see* FISH, GENERAL; FISH, COOKING METHODS. *See also* SMOKED FISH

TIDBIT Most North American salmon are found off the Pacific coast and about 90 percent come from Alaskan waters. **Chinook** or **king salmon** is considered the finest and is the most expensive; its soft-textured, high-fat flesh ranges in color from off-white to bright red. The **coho** or **silver salmon** has a high-fat (but lower than chinook), firm-textured, pink to red orange flesh. The moderate-fat **sockeye** or **red salmon** has a firm, deep red flesh that's highly prized for canning. Among the low-fat varieties are pink-fleshed **pink** or **humpback salmon**—the most delicately flavored of the Pacific varieties— and **chum** or **dog salmon**, which has the lightest color and lowest fat content.

USING

* Check salmon fillets for pinbones (tiny needle-sized bones) before cooking by running your fingers over the surface—bumps typically signal bones. Use tweezers to find and extract the rascals.
* Salmon can be cooked by almost any method, including BAKING, GRILLING, MICROWAVING, POACHING, SAUTÉING or STEAMING.
* Whenever you grill or poach salmon, cook twice the amount you need for dinner. Chill half the salmon and use the next day, cut into strips or chunks and served over greens for a cold salmon salad.
* Or toss leftover cooked salmon pieces with a chunky pasta, like radiatore or rotini, and salad dressing for a pasta salad.

* Toss leftover salmon chunks with hot pasta, fresh dill and a little extra virgin olive oil for a delicious entrée.

SALSA

TIDBIT In most cases, salsa is a highly seasoned, cooked or uncooked sauce, used either for dipping or as a garnish. Though the original mixtures were made with a base of chopped tomatoes, today cookbooks and menus abound with "salsas" made with almost everything, including fruit.

PURCHASING A wide variety of salsas are available in most supermarkets. They may be fresh or cooked, and they range in spiciness from mild to hot. **Salsa cruda** on a label or menu indicates an uncooked mixture. **Salsa verde** means "green sauce," and refers to mixtures made with tomatillos, green chiles, cilantro and various seasonings.

STORING Refrigerate fresh salsas, tightly covered, in the refrigerator for no more than 5 days. Canned salsas may be stored unopened at room temperature for up to 6 months. Once opened, refrigerate for up to 1 month.

USING

* Make fresh salsa in a snap by combining the ingredients in a food processor and processing in on/off pulses until the desired texture is reached.
* Soften the harshness of raw garlic and onions by sautéing lightly before adding them to salsa. Or chop them and microwave, covered, until softened.
* Add pizzazz to cooked vegetables (corn, green beans, summer squash) by tossing them with a little salsa.
* Spoon salsa atop baked potatoes or toss with hash browns. Stir a couple of spoonfuls of salsa into mashed potatoes to update an old-fashioned favorite.
* Bring salsa to room temperature and use as a garnish for sautéed, grilled or broiled meat, chicken or fish.
* Stir several teaspoons of salsa into sour cream or yogurt for an almost-instant dip for crudités or chips.
* Toss your favorite salsa with greens for a snappy, low-fat salad dressing.
* Salsa makes a great sandwich spread—just make sure it's not too liquid or your bread will get soggy.

MANGO SALSA

This sassy salsa is great with grilled pork or chicken, on sandwiches or even mixed into a salad dressing. In a medium bowl, combine 1 medium peeled, seeded and diced mango, 1 seeded and diced large, ripe tomato, 1 minced, seeded jalapeño chile, 2 tablespoons minced fresh or pale pink seasoned ginger, 2 tablespoons finely chopped mint and 1 tablespoon fresh lime juice. Cover and refrigerate at least 1 hour for flavors to blend. Taste and salt if necessary. Let stand at room temperature for 30 minutes before serving. Makes about 2 cups.

> *Without salt, food is bland. Bread is dry. Life has no flavor.*
> —Marlena Spieler, American food writer, columnist

SALT   *see also* COOKING AND EATING LIGHT

TIDBIT   Salt helps balance and brighten the flavors of a dish. Not putting salt and pepper on the table for guests to season their food as they wish is the height of culinary arrogance. At the very least, it indicates a thoughtless host. That goes for restaurants, too. Chefs who are imperious enough to think their palate is superior to anyone else's aren't worth their salt.

PURCHASING

* **Table salt** is a fine-grained, refined salt with additives that make it free-flowing; **iodized salt** is table salt with added iodine.
* **Kosher salt** is a coarse-grained salt that's usually additive free; many chefs and gourmet cooks prefer its texture and flavor.
* **Sea salt** does, as its name indicates, come from the sea; many culinary experts like its fresh, distinct flavor. It's available fine- or coarse-grained, and most of that available in the United States is imported.
* **Rock salt** has a grayish cast because it's not highly refined; its chunky crystals are used predominately as a bed for oysters and clams and in combination with ice to make ice cream in crank-style makers.
* **Pickling salt** is additive free and fine-grained and used to make brines for pickles, sauerkraut, and so on.

STORING   Salt will last indefinitely if stored in an airtight container. Although it may clump with lengthy exposure to humidity, it separates easily when smashed with a spoon or rubbed between your fingers.

USING

* Keep salt out on the countertop in a container just large enough for you to grab a pinch or dip in a measuring spoon. There are a variety of containers available under the various names of "salt pig," "salt cellar" and "salt box." Salt pigs are open shapes designed to keep out humidity—I've had one on my countertop practically since I started cooking. Salt cellars and boxes typically have lids. Look for them in cookware and antique stores, as well as on the Internet.
* Never salt a sauce or other preparation that will be reduced (*see* REDUCING), a process that concentrates flavors, until the end of the cooking time.

* Cold foods usually require more salt than hot dishes because chilling mutes flavor.
* The best way to prevent oversalting is to season dishes at the end of the cooking or preparation time. Many foods contain a high level of natural sodium, or taste saltier when combined with other ingredients.
* If you've ruined a dish by oversalting it, try stirring in 1 teaspoon each sugar and vinegar; cook for a few minutes and taste.
* For an oversalted liquid preparation such as a soup or stew, add a sliced, peeled raw potato and simmer for 10 to 15 minutes. Use a slotted spoon to remove the potato before serving the soup.
* Oversalted soups can also be helped by adding a salt-free liquid like cream or puréed (see PURÉEING) vegetables. Or quickly cook some rice or potato in water, purée with a little liquid, then stir it into the soup.
* Always retaste foods you've made ahead of time—flavors have a way of shifting and changing during refrigeration or standing time.
* If you're on a low-salt diet, season foods by adding more herbs, garlic and/or lemon juice.
* A few rice grains (about 10 for an average shaker) in your salt shaker will keep salt from clumping in humid climates.
* One tablespoon of cornstarch combined with a box of salt will also keep it pouring freely.
* If a salt shaker pours too freely, plug up several holes by cleaning the lid, then painting over the excess holes (on the inside) with clear nail polish. Let the polish air-dry at least 1 day so there won't be any residual odor.
* Salt-free cooks should always include salt and pepper on the table for guests. Unsalted food tastes flat and bland to those who aren't used to it.

I like the philosophy of the sandwich, as it were. It typifies my attitude to life, really. It's all there, it's fun, it looks good, and you don't have to wash up afterwards.
—Molly Parkin, American author

SANDWICHES
THE BREAD
* For the calorie-conscious, frozen bread is easier to cut into very thin slices.
* Create a "two-faced" sandwich by using 1 slice white bread and 1 slice rye or wheat bread.
* Always cut off the crusts before rolling bread flat for canapés.
* There are options other than "regular" bread. Wrap your sandwich

ingredients in a softened flour tortilla or egg-roll wrapper, or in lettuce leaves. Or spoon a sandwich filling into a split pita bread, or atop a bagel. Toasted, split croissants or brioches make elegant sandwich breads.

THE SPREAD

* Cut calories by blending together half butter or margarine and half non-fat imitation mayonnaise for a sandwich spread. Even better, use half nonfat mayo and half low- or nonfat cream cheese.

* "Seal" bread to keep it from getting soggy with moist fillings by spreading the slices all the way to the edges with butter, margarine or cream cheese.

* Stir chopped chutney into cream cheese to use on ham or turkey sand-wiches.

* Snap up the flavor of grilled sandwiches by spreading the side of the bread to be grilled with mayo (or a mustard-mayo blend) instead of butter.

* Finely chop leftover meat or fish from last night's dinner and combine with mayo, celery and pickle relish for a quick spread.

MAKING SANDWICHES

* To make messy sandwiches like Sloppy Joes less messy, buy unsliced buns and cut off the top quarter of each bun. Hollow out the bottom por-tion, then spoon the filling into it and replace the bun's top.

* Use leftover bean, pasta, rice, meat, fish or vegetable salads to stuff pita pockets for an instant sandwich the next day.

* Keep bread from becoming soggy on made-ahead sandwiches by spread-ing mustard, pickle relish or ketchup between cheese or meat slices, instead of directly on the bread.

* When making sandwiches to be eaten later (as for a lunchbox or picnic), keep them from becoming soggy by packing additions like tomato and pickle slices in separate plastic bags. Add the extras to the sandwiches just before eating.

* Wrap sandwiches made in advance airtight and refrigerate—they'll keep for at least a day.

* Meat sandwiches can be made in advance and frozen in sandwich bags, then in a larger, freezer-weight plastic bag for up to 1 month. Mayon-naise, cream cheese and hard-cooked eggs are unsuitable for freezing, but butter, margarine and mustard are fine. Cheese can be used, but many become crumbly after defrosting. Your best bet is processed cheese which, though fairly flavorless, is pretty indestructible. Take the frozen sandwich out in the morning and it'll be thawed by lunchtime. Pack additions like lettuce and pickle and tomato slices separately.

* Making crustless sandwiches ahead for a party? The edges will stay

fresher if you wait until just before serving to cut off the crusts. Stack 2 or 3 sandwiches at a time and cut the crusts off all at once.

SAUCES AND GRAVIES *see also* ARROWROOT; BARBECUE SAUCE; CORN-STARCH; FLOUR; ROUX; THICKENERS

* **Thickeners:** The most commonly used thickeners for sauces and gravies are ROUX—a flour-fat mixture—and CORNSTARCH, the latter quicker to make and less caloric than roux. Raw eggs are also classic thickeners (as for hollandaise sauce), so is reduced cream. But less conventional thickeners like mashed potatoes, cooked rice and bread work great and don't carry a payload of fat. *See* THICKENERS for a variety of ways to densify everything from sauces to stews.

* Of the many roux-based sauces, white sauce (*béchamel*) is one of the most common. It's made by stirring milk into a butter-flour roux. The sauce's thickness depends on the proportion of flour and butter to milk. For 1 cup milk, use 1 tablespoon each butter and flour for a thin sauce; 2 tablespoons each butter and flour for a medium sauce; and 3 tablespoons each for a thick sauce.

* Give almost any sauce a satiny texture by whisking in 1 or 2 tablespoons cold butter (cut into small pieces) just before serving. The same amount of heavy whipping cream works in a similar manner. Small amounts return large dividends in flavor and consistency.

* Use the cooking liquid from vegetables or meats, or leftover pan juices as a sauce base. The liquid can be frozen until you need it.

* Delicate sauces (like *béarnaise* or *beurre blanc*) can separate if kept waiting over even the lowest heat. Keep such sauces warm and silky smooth by pouring them into a warmed thermos bottle.

* The technique of REDUCING a liquid (such as wine or stock) intensifies and enriches its flavor dramatically. Reductions can be used as a sauce base or as the sauce itself. To reduce a liquid, simply boil it until the volume is at least halved. Additions such as minced shallots or herbs are often cooked in the liquid for added flavoring.

* Deglazing a pan creates an almost-instant sauce. Here's what you do: After food has been sautéed, remove it and any excess fat from the pan. Deglaze (*see* DEGLAZING) the pan by heating a small amount of liquid (wine, stock, and so on) in the pan and stirring to loosen browned bits of food on the bottom. Cook for a few minutes to reduce and thicken, then drizzle the liquid over the cooked food.

* Leftover soups, stews, meats or vegetables can be puréed (*see* PURÉEING) and used as a base for sauce or gravy.

* For more flavor, the next time you make a giblet gravy, finely chop the gizzard, heart, neck, and so on, then sauté in a little oil before adding the liquid and remaining ingredients.
* If a sauce containing meat blood begins to separate, stir in 1 to 2 teaspoons lemon juice.
* A separated sauce can be saved by processing the mixture at low speed in a blender just until smooth. Return the sauce to a clean pan and continue cooking over very low heat.
* Save a separated hollandaise sauce by adding a tablespoon or two of boiling water and vigorously whisking until once again smooth.
* Add color to a pale sauce or gravy by stirring in a few drops of Kitchen Bouquet, which is readily available in supermarkets.
* One or 2 teaspoons instant coffee powder or unsweetened cocoa powder adds both color and a rich flavor to a sauce or gravy.
* After stirring sour cream or yogurt into a hot sauce, heat it gently and only until the mixture is warmed through. Boiling will cause it to curdle. Such milk products won't separate as easily in flour-based sauces.
* For an "almost-instant" pasta sauce that tastes homemade, sauté 1 pound Italian sausage or ground chuck with 1 medium chopped onion until browned, drain off fat, stir in 16 to 24 ounces commercial pasta sauce, and cook until hot. Stirring in ¼ cup fresh chopped herbs at the last minutes gives it a fresh flavor.
* To allow for the normal moisture evaporation that occurs while a sauce is cooking (which intensifies flavor), wait until the end of cooking to season with salt and pepper.
* Correct an oversalted sauce in one of several ways: (1) Add a peeled raw potato, cut into eighths, stir and cook for 5 to 10 minutes, then remove the potatoes; (2) Stir in ½ teaspoon sugar, then taste and add more sugar—a little at a time—if necessary; (3) a teaspoon of vinegar added with the sugar helps balance oversaltiness.
* Don't salt a sauce or gravy until just before serving. Not only can many ingredients contribute sodium but the mixture otherwise will intensify in flavor as it cooks and reduces.

SAUERKRAUT

PURCHASING **Precooked sauerkraut** is available in jars and cans on supermarket shelves. **Fresh sauerkraut** is sold in delicatessens and in Cryovac packages in a supermarket's refrigerated section. It generally has a milder flavor than its canned counterpart.

STORING

* Precooked, canned sauerkraut: Store in a cool, dark place for up to 6 months. Refrigerate, covered, after opening and consume within 5 days.
* Fresh sauerkraut: Refrigerate and use within 1 week.

PREPARING

* To reduce sauerkraut's briny flavor, put it in a sieve and rinse it well under cold, running water. Drain well before using.
* Taste fresh sauerkraut—if it's too salty for your palate, soak it for 15 to 30 minutes in cold water; drain well before using.

COOKING

* Put fresh sauerkraut in a large saucepan with just enough liquid (broth, wine, beer, water, and so on) to cover. Simmer, covered, for about 30 minutes, or until tender.
* To heat precooked sauerkraut, place in a saucepan with its liquid and cook over medium heat until hot, 5 to 10 minutes. If the sauerkraut liquid is too salty, drain it off and cover sauerkraut with water, wine or beer.
* Sauerkraut pairs nicely with roast pork, spareribs, smoked sausages and corned beef.
* Caraway seeds are a perfect complement to sauerkraut, as is crumbled, crisp bacon.
* Apples also pair well. Cook fresh sauerkraut for about 15 minutes, then add apple chunks and continue cooking until done.
* Or add chopped apples and scallions to cooked, cooled sauerkraut and serve cold as a salad.

Laws are like sausages. It's better not to see them being made.
—Prince Otto von Bismarck, chancellor of the German Empire

SAUSAGE *see also* MEAT, GENERAL

TIDBIT Sausages come in all shapes, sizes and flavors, in links, patties and in bulk, and in or out of casings. They can be fresh or cured; the latter extends storage life. Some sausages are also dried; the longer a sausage is dried, the firmer it becomes.

PURCHASING Sausage comes in several forms—**fully cooked** (ready to eat), **partially cooked** (enough to kill any trichinae) and **uncooked,** which may or may not require cooking depending on how or whether it's been cured. Some sausages use fillers, such as cereal, soybean flour and dried-milk solids, to stretch the meat. Read the label to make sure of what you're buying.

STORING   As a general rule, refrigerate all sausage—how long it can be stored depends on the type of sausage. **Uncooked, fresh sausage** (like pork sausage) is very perishable and should be refrigerated, well wrapped, for no more than 2 days; **uncooked, smoked sausage** (like mettwurst) for up to 1 week; **cooked sausage** (such as braunschweiger) for 4 to 6 days; cooked, **smoked sausage** (like knockwurst) in unopened vacuum-sealed package for 2 weeks, 1 week after opening; **dry** and **semidry sausage** (like pepperoni) for up to 3 weeks. Sausage can be frozen for about 2 months.

USING

* Hard sausages like pepperoni will last longer if you cut off only what you need at one time.
* Sausage should be cooked to a temperature of 160°F on a meat THER-MOMETER; when pierced with a knife, the juices should run clear.
* For extra-crispy sausage patties, dip them into flour before frying. Cook them over medium-low heat to reduce shrinkage; turn once during the cooking time.
* Keep link sausages from bursting by puncturing the casing in several places with fork tines. Sauté over medium-low heat; the punctures give both steam and rendered fat an exit.
* Uncooked link sausages won't burst if you put them in a skillet with about ½ inch of water. Bring to a boil, then cover and reduce heat to a simmer. Drain thoroughly before browning over medium-high heat.
* To reduce shrinkage in link sausages, boil them for 5 minutes, drain well, then fry.
* Broil or grill link sausages by placing several links crosswise on one skewer. Now you can flip them all with one turn.
* Roasted sausages are deliciously crisp. Preheat the oven to 400°F and place a rack on a shallow pan (no more than 1-inch high sides). Pierce each sausage in 3 to 4 places, then put them an inch or two apart on the rack. Roast 20 to 35 minutes (depending on the size) until well browned. Turn several times during roasting to brown all sides.
* To taste homemade sausage for seasoning, fry a little of it until well done, cool, then taste. Never taste uncooked sausage.
* Most sausages are calorie-laden, but you don't have to eat a plateful. Use sausage, finely chopped, to flavor everything from scrambles and hash to soups and stir-fries.
* Before adding sausage to such dishes, sauté it to render some of the fat—to get the flavor without so many calories.

SOUSED SAUSAGES

Use skinless links (not brown-and-serve!) so that the sausage can absorb maxi-

mum sauce. Make and refrigerate these saucy bites a day ahead so any fat can congeal and be removed before serving. Cut 24 skinless pork link sausages into thirds. Cook the sausage in a very large skillet until nicely browned. Pour off the grease throughout cooking and at the end; remove from the heat. Blot up excess fat in the skillet and on the sausages with a paper towel. Combine 1½ cups dark rum, ½ cup dark brown sugar and ¼ teaspoon *each* ground cloves and cayenne in a 2-cup glass measure; pour over the sausages. Bring the mixture to a bubbling simmer over medium-low heat. *Caution: Heat slowly—if the mixture gets too hot before the alcohol burns off, it can flame.* Cover and cook for 30 minutes, stirring every 10 minutes to coat the sausages with sauce. Refrigerate, covered, for up to 2 days. Scoop off the congealed fat; serve at room temperature or slightly warm, accompanied by toothpicks for spearing. If the sauce becomes too thick, thin it slightly with a little water. Serves about 10.

SAUTÉING   *see also* COOKING, GENERAL; DEEP-FRYING; STIR-FRYING
TIDBIT Sautéing is a technique of cooking tender foods quickly in a very small amount of oil or other fat. The result is a crisp surface and juicy interior.
GETTING READY
* Use a heavy skillet or sauté pan with a handle and low, straight or sloping sides. It should be large enough for the food to be cooked in a single layer. Pans with high sides can steam rather than sauté food. A pan with sloping sides is used for tossing pieces of food during cooking; pans with straight sides allow larger items to be turned manually.
* Room-temperature food browns more quickly and evenly, and absorbs less fat than cold food; the latter also sticks to the pan more.
* The food should be dry; blot with a paper towel if necessary. Dredge moist meats (like chicken cutlets) in seasoned flour.
* Parboil (*see* BLANCHING) dense foods like carrots or potatoes so they can be combined with quick-cooking ingredients like celery. This ensures that all the ingredients will complete cooking at the same time, to the same degree of doneness.
* Salt impedes browning—season after sautéing.
* Sprinkle meat with a little sugar before sautéing—the sugar caramelizes, creating a dark color and rich flavor with negligible sweetness.
COOKING
* For the crispest results, thoroughly heat the oil before adding the ingredients. You don't need much oil for sautéing—a tablespoon or so will do for most foods.

* Add a flavor bonus by using flavorful oils, such as sesame or hazelnut.
* How do you know when the oil is hot enough to begin cooking? Drop a chunk of vegetable (onion or bell pepper) into the pan. If it sizzles, the oil's ready.
* Use a nonstick pan, and all you'll need for sautéing is a spritz of cooking spray.
* Rather than overcrowding one pan, sauté food in two pans—it will cook more evenly, brown better and won't have a tendency to steam, as it will if crowded.
* Or save on cleanup by sautéing veggies until almost done, then transferring them to the serving dish and keeping them warm in a 250°F oven. Then use the same pan to sauté meat.
* While the food is sautéing, grab the handle and shake the pan often so the food moves around and gets evenly browned.
* Use a bulb baster to remove any rendered fat from the pan.
* Don't cover the pan during cooking. Doing so will steam the food.
* Transfer sautéed food to a plate or other container and remove any excess fat from the pan. Deglaze (*see* DEGLAZING) the pan—a technique of heating a small amount of liquid (wine, stock, and so on) in the pan and stirring to loosen browned bits of food on the bottom. This flavorful liquid may either be used as a sauce base or reduced (*see* REDUCING) until slightly thick and simply spooned over the food.

SCALLIONS (GREEN ONIONS) *see also* CHIVES; ONIONS; VEGETABLES, GENERAL

TIDBIT   Scallions are a distinct variety of the onion family, though some markets sell immature (green) onions as scallions. True scallions have a milder flavor than young onions. They can also be identified by the fact that the sides of the base are straight, whereas the others are usually slightly curved, showing the beginnings of a bulb. The bottom line is that scallions and young onions can be used interchangeably. The entire scallion—white and green parts—is edible. The white portion of a scallion has a slightly stronger flavor than the green stems.

PURCHASING   Choose scallions with crisp, bright green tops and a firm white base. Those no larger than ½ inch in diameter are best.

EQUIVALENTS

* With tops: 5 medium = 1¾ cups chopped
* Bulbs only: 5 medium = ½ cup chopped

STORING   Refrigerate, unwashed, in a plastic bag for up to 5 days.

PREPARING

* Trim roots; discard the outer white layer.
* The white end is best cut with a knife, but kitchen shears are better for the green portion, particularly if you want to keep the round shape.
* Cutting a green onion in half lengthwise before chopping will give you smaller pieces with which to season foods.
* Snipped scallion greens make a colorful garnish and a flavorful addition to tossed green salads.
* Freezing a scallion's green portion turns it dark and limp, but the white base can be chopped and frozen (raw or sautéed) in an airtight container for up to 3 months. Add the frozen scallion directly to dishes like soups and stews; thaw and blot dry for sautéed dishes.
* For cooked dishes, add the green portion during the final few minutes of cooking time to retain its bright color.
* Whole scallions make a delicious side dish: Trim the green portion to a length of 3 to 4 inches, then sauté briefly in olive oil and season with salt and pepper.
* For an easy, showy garnish, make scallion brushes (*see* page 224).

SCALLOPS *see also* SHELLFISH

TIDBIT Though there are many species, scallops are classified in two broad groups: **Bay scallops**—with meat about ½ inch in diameter, are sweeter, more succulent and more expensive than the larger, more widely available (but less tender) **sea scallops,** which average 1½ inches in diameter. The small **calico scallops**—though they're deep-sea creatures—are often sold as bay scallops on the West Coast.

PURCHASING Because scallops perish quickly out of water, they're usually sold shucked. Look for those with a sweet smell and a fresh, moist sheen. Avoid any with a strong sulfur odor. Scallops can range in color from pale beige to creamy pink to orangey. Avoid those that are stark white—it's a sign that they've been soaked in water, a marketing ploy to increase the weight.

EQUIVALENTS

* Bay scallops: 1 pound shucked = 100
* Sea scallops: 1 pound shucked = 30

STORING Cover and refrigerate immediately; use within 1 to 2 days.

USING

* Scallops can be cooked by almost any method, from GRILLING to SAUTÉING to BAKING. They're wonderful in myriad dishes, including salad, séviche, croquettes, chowders, curries and with pasta.

* One caveat: Cook briefly—1 to 3 minutes, depending on the size. Like all shellfish, scallops become tough when overcooked.
* Before sautéing, pat scallops dry with paper towels.

SCRAMBLED EGGS *see* EGGS, COOKING METHODS

SEASONING PANS
TIDBIT Seasoning is a technique for sealing the porous surface of cast-iron cookware, thereby creating a nonstick coating.
* Method 1: Generously coat the pan's interior with vegetable oil. Place in a preheated 350°F oven and bake for 1 hour. Cool completely, then burnish the surface with a paper towel.
* Method 2: Generously coat the pan's interior with vegetable oil. Place over medium heat and cook until the pan begins to smoke, about 10 minutes. Remove from the heat and cool completely. Wipe out excess oil with a paper towel, pressing down hard and buffing the surface. Repeat the process three times.
* Seasoned pans should be gently cleaned. Use a paper towel to wipe out food as soon as you're through cooking. Loosen stubborn bits with a nylon pad. Rinse well, then wipe with a paper towel and dry thoroughly over a low burner for a minute or two. Let the pan sit on the turned-off burner until cool before storing.
* Keep cast-iron pans in a dry place so they remain rust free. If used infrequently, wrap the pan in plastic.
* Reseason pans whenever food begins to stick to the surface.

SEEDS *see also* MUSTARD SEED
PURCHASING There are myriad seeds on the market today, but the three most popular are poppy, sesame and sunflower.
* Poppy seed: The bluish charcoal gray–colored poppy seed is most commonly available in supermarkets. Asian and Middle Eastern markets also often carry brown and beige varieties. It takes about 900,000 tiny poppy seeds to comprise a pound.
* Sesame seed: America was introduced to sesame seed by African slaves, who called it *benne seed*. The most usual color for this seed is grayish ivory, although there are also brown, red and black varieties. The former can be found in supermarkets, the latter in ethnic markets.
* Sunflower seeds: These seeds, shelled and unshelled, roasted and raw, salted and unsalted; are commonly available in supermarkets.

STORING All seeds have a relatively high fat content and therefore should ideally be refrigerated in an airtight container for up to 6 months.

USING

* The flavor of any seed will be augmented by toasting. Cook them in an ungreased skillet over medium heat, stirring frequently, for about 5 minutes, or until golden brown.
* Seeds used as a topping for baked goods don't require toasting because the oven does the job.
* When sunflower seeds are combined with baking soda in baked goods, a chemical reaction occurs that causes the baked product to take on a blue-green tinge that, though not aesthetically appealing, has no toxic threat.
* Chopping seeds can cause them to fly all over the kitchen. To keep this from happening slightly moisten the seeds with a little oil, then chop away.

SERVING AND PASSING FOOD *see also* TABLE SETTINGS

* When serving food to seated guests, serve from the left; remove plates from the right.
* Since glasses are on the right side of a table setting, it's appropriate to pour beverages while standing to the right of your guest.
* When passing food around the table, pass it in a clockwise direction (from your right to your left).
* When passing salt and pepper, etiquette prescribes that you put the shakers or mills down on the table, rather than hand them directly to the guest requesting the seasoning.

SESAME SEED *see* SEEDS

SHALLOTS

TIDBIT Shallots taste like a combination of onion and garlic, but are milder than either. They're formed more like garlic than onions, with a head composed of multiple cloves, each covered with a thin, papery skin.

PURCHASING Choose shallots that are plump and firm with dry skins. Avoid those that are wrinkled or sprouting.

EQUIVALENT 4 ounces = ½ cup chopped

STORING Store shallots in a cool, dry, well-ventilated place for up to 1 month.

USING

* A recipe calling for 1 shallot typically means 1 clove, not the whole head.
* If you have a lot of shallot cloves to peel, drop them in boiling water and

let stand 1 minute. Turn them into a colander and rinse with cold water before peeling.

* Cook shallots over low heat just until soft; too much heat will scorch them.

SHELLFISH *see* ABALONE; CLAMS; CRABS; FISH, GENERAL; LOBSTERS; MUSSELS; OYSTERS; SCALLOPS; SHRIMP

TIDBIT The shellfish family is divided into two basic categories—crustaceans and mollusks. **Crustaceans** have elongated bodies and jointed crust-like shells (crabs, lobsters and shrimp). **Mollusks** are classified in three groups: *Gastropods* (or univalves), such as abalone, have a single shell and single muscle; *bivalves*, like the clam and oyster, have two shells hinged together by a strong muscle; and *cephalopods*, such as squid, have tentacles and ink sacs.

SHORTENING, SOLID *see also* FATS AND OILS; GREASING PANS; MEASURING

TIDBIT Shortening (also called "vegetable shortening") is a solid fat made from hydrogenated vegetable oil. The classic form is white and flavorless; however, some brands offer a "butter" version, flavored artificially. Shortening is used in baking, both as an ingredient and for greasing pans .

PURCHASING Shortening can generally be found in the supermarket oil section in 16-ounce and 3-pound cans. Some brands also package premeasured shortening "sticks."

EQUIVALENT 1 pound = 2⅓ cups

STORING Store at a cool room temperature for 6 months, or refrigerate up to 1 year.

SUBSTITUTION: ⅞ cup shortening = 1 cup butter

USING

* To measure shortening, pack it into a measuring cup or spoon and level it with a knife. Keep the cup clean by lining it with plastic wrap before filling.
* Shortening can also be measured by water displacement. If you need ½ cup shortening, fill a 1-cup glass measure with ½ cup water. Add shortening until the water reaches the 1-cup mark; drain off the water.
* Shortening is good for frying and produces tender baked goods.
* Keep your fingers clean when greasing pans by using a crumpled piece of paper towel to dip into the shortening and spread over the pan. Or

cover your hand with a small plastic bag; leave the bag in the shortening can for the next use.

* To get every last bit of shortening out of the can, pour in 1 to 2 cups boiling water and slosh around until all the shortening clinging to the sides melts. Cool, then refrigerate overnight. The next day, skim off the fat that's solidified on the surface.

PAN MAGIC

Use this easy homemade blend instead of "greasing and flouring" pans. Beat until smooth ½ cup *each* room-temperature shortening, vegetable oil and all-purpose flour. Refrigerate in an airtight container for up to 6 months. Use to coat muffin tins, cake and bread pans, and so on.

> *The sort of shrimp hidden under a pound and a half of batter on what Midwestern menus call "French-fried butterfly shrimp" could as easily be turnips.*
> —Calvin Trillin, American writer, satirist

SHRIMP   *see also* SHELLFISH

PURCHASING

* Raw, shelled shrimp: Choose firm, moist and translucent specimens. Unshelled shrimp should have shiny, firm shells; avoid those with black spots. Shrimp should smell of the sea with no hint of ammonia. Note: In the United States, colossal and jumbo shrimp are sometimes referred to as "prawns," although prawns are a separate species.
* Cooked, shelled shrimp: They should look plump and succulent.
* How much per serving: ¾ pound unshelled shrimp; ⅓ pound shelled shrimp. Rule of thumb: On average, 3 pounds of shrimp will weigh only half as much after peeling and cooking.

EQUIVALENTS   The average number of shrimp per pound depends on the size, and this can vary from market to market. As a rule, the larger the shrimp, the larger the price. Figure amounts per pound as follows: **Colossal shrimp** = 10 or fewer; **jumbo shrimp** = 11 to 15; **extra-large shrimp** = 16 to 20; **large shrimp** = 21 to 30; **medium shrimp** = 31 to 35; **small** = 36 to 45; **miniature** = about 100.

STORING

* Fresh, uncooked shrimp should be rinsed well under cold, running water and drained thoroughly before refrigerating, tightly covered, for up to 2 days. To freeze, cover completely with cold water; defrost under cold, running water.

* Cooked shrimp can be refrigerated airtight for up to 3 days.
* Freeze shrimp for up to 3 months. Thaw overnight in the refrigerator, or place a sealed package of frozen shrimp in a bowl of cold water and change the water every 10 minutes until the shrimp is defrosted.

PREPARING

* Though there are slight differences in texture and flavor, the various sizes of shrimp (except the miniatures) can usually be substituted for each other.
* Raw shrimp are easier to peel and devein than cooked shrimp.
* Whether or not to devein shrimp is a matter of personal preference. In general, small and medium shrimp don't need deveining except for cosmetic purposes (unless the vein is particularly thick). However, because the intestinal vein of larger shrimp contains noticeable grit, it should be removed.
* To devein peeled shrimp, use a sharp, pointed knife to cut a shallow slit down the middle of the outside curve. Pull out the dark vein, then rinse the slit under cold, running water.
* To devein shrimp in the shell, use small, pointed scissors to snip down the center back of the shell. Expose the vein and lift out the vein with a scissor tip and discard.
* To shell shrimp (either before or after cooking), start at the large end and peel away the shell. The tail fin may or may not be left on the shrimp.
* The tail can be left on shrimp to be fried or sautéed.
* Don't throw out the shrimp shells. Wash them well, put them in a skillet with at least ½ cup melted butter or oil, and cook for about 10 minutes. Strain the butter or oil and discard the shells; use the shrimp-flavored fat for sautéing or flavoring seafood dishes, pasta, and so on.
* Or place washed shrimp shells, a couple of stalks of chopped celery and a small, quartered onion in a saucepan. Cover with water or clam juice (or half of each) and bring to a boil. Reduce to a simmer, cover and cook for 30 minutes. Let the shells cool in the liquid, then strain the broth and use as a base for fish soups or stews. Freeze for up to 6 months.
* Or cook shrimp shells in water for 10 minutes, strain and discard the shells, then use the water to cook the shrimp in.
* Shrimp spirals are perfect for dishes like salads and pasta, where you want smaller bites. Cut peeled, raw shrimp (large, medium or small) in half lengthwise down the back. After cooking, the halves will coil into bite-sized pieces.

COOKING

* As with all shellfish, shrimp should be cooked briefly or it becomes tough and rubbery. Cook only until the flesh turns opaque; whole shrimp should just begin to curl. If the shells are on, they should turn pink.
* Shrimp cooked in its shell is more flavorful than shrimp shelled before cooking. For easier peeling, snip the shell lengthwise along the back before cooking.
* Simmering unshelled shrimp in beer gives it a wonderful, slightly sweet flavor.
* For frying, dust shrimp with cornstarch or flour (seasoned with salt, pepper and whatever else you wish), then dip it in lightly beaten egg white. Fry until golden.
* For grilling, thread shrimp lengthwise on a skewer (first through the tail, then bend around to spear the front section).
* An iodine flavor tells you that the shrimp has fed on dead plants.

SIEVES; STRAINERS

PURCHASING Choose a sieve with strong handles and frame; it should have a hook or other extension for resting the sieve on top of bowls or pans. Buy one that's dishwasher-safe to save time on cleanup.

USING

* Some foods need help to pass through a sieve. Use a wooden spoon (better for the sieve than a metal one) to push the food through.
* The container into which you're straining food or liquid should be deep enough so that the bottom of the sieve won't touch the strained food.
* Don't have a fine sieve or strainer? Just line a colander or coarse sieve with several layers of dampened cheesecloth. Or dampen and use the leg section of an old, clean pair of pantyhose.
* No flour sifter? Simply spoon the flour into a fine sieve, then shake or tap it over a measuring cup set on a piece of waxed paper. This also works with confectioners' sugar. If necessary, use the back of a wooden spoon to stir the flour or sugar so it goes through with ease.
* Make your own colander or sieve by using an ice pick or pointed knife to poke holes in an aluminum pie plate from the inside out. This substitute is appropriate only for liquid mixtures.
* Wash a sieve as soon as you're through using it. Otherwise, dried food will clog the tiny holes and make cleaning difficult. A clogged sieve can be cleaned by soaking it in hot, soapy water, then scrubbing with a vegetable brush. Put dishwasher-safe strainers on the dishwasher's bottom shelf.

SIMMERING *see also* COOKING, GENERAL; POACHING

TIDBIT Simmering is a technique whereby food is cooked over heat so low that tiny bubbles periodically break the liquid's surface.

GENERAL

* The temperature of a simmering liquid is about 185°F.
* Among the foods that are commonly simmered are soups, stews, stocks, dried beans and rice.
* Stewing hens and tough cuts of meat like pot roast benefit from lengthy moist, low-heat simmering (*see* BRAISING), during which time their connective tissue melts into a rich sauce.
* Covering a pot simmering on the stovetop will increase the temperature, causing the mixture to boil. If necessary, its better to partially cover the pan so that steam can escape, which should keep the temperature low.

SIMPLE SYRUPS *see* SUGAR SYRUPS

SLOW COOKERS (CROCKPOTS) *see also* COOKING, GENERAL

TIDBIT Two great advantages of the slow cooker is that it doesn't heat up the kitchen, and the dish can cook all day while you're at work. It uses steady, moist wraparound heat (the low setting is about 200°F) to cook food over a period of 8 to 12 hours. Slow cookers have tight covers, which keeps food moist during lengthy cooking. Most have adjustable heat levels so, if necessary, the heat can be increased to quickly finish the dish.

PURCHASING Slow cookers range in size from 1 to 6 quarts, the average being 3½ quarts. The 1-quart cooker is good for cooking for 1 to 2 people, or for keeping party foods like dips and meatballs warm. Large families will most probably need the 6-quart cooker. For easy cleanup, choose a cooker with a removable liner.

USING

* Thoroughly read the manufacturer's instructions, particularly those for converting conventional recipes to slow cooking.
* Slow cooking at elevations over 3,500 feet typically takes longer than at lower altitudes.
* If you'll be away longer than the cooking time, plug your slow cooker into an automatic timer (available at any hardware store). Set the timer to start the cooker while you're gone. For a delayed starting time, the food should be thoroughly chilled before placing it into the cooker. Never let the food stand for more than 2 hours before the cooking starts.

* Coat the inside of the cooker with cooking spray for easy cleanup.
* Because liquid doesn't evaporate in the tightly sealed cooker, don't add more liquid than the recipe calls for.
* Dense vegetables like potatoes and carrots should be cut into pieces no larger than 1 inch thick so they'll cook through. When cooking meat with such vegetables, put the veggies on the bottom, place the meat on top, then place any remaining veggies along the sides of the cooker. Since the heat comes from the bottom and sides of the cooker, this ensures that the vegetables get thoroughly cooked.
* Some vegetables (such as celery, zucchini and tomatoes) may become mushy by the time the other ingredients are done. Add them during the last 30 minutes of cooking.
* Leaving the peel on slow-cooked vegetables not only retains their nutrients, but also helps them keep their shape.
* Fish and seafood aren't particularly good candidates for lengthy cooking—delicate fish will almost disintegrate; seafood (shrimp or scallops) will toughen and become inedible. Add such foods no more than 45 minutes before the dish is done.
* Because of the long cooking and moist heat, less expensive cuts of meat can be used.
* To prevent bacterial growth, ground meat should be cooked thoroughly before being added to a dish that will be slow-cooked.
* Ingredients like milk or cheese shouldn't be added until about 30 minutes before the dish is done to prevent the milk from curdling and the cheese from toughening.
* For a fresher flavor, stir in fresh herbs 15 minutes before serving.
* Adding cold ingredients to a hot cooker can crack a crockery insert.
* Don't remove the lid during the minimum cook time—doing so can set cooking back by as much as 30 minutes.
* Let a crockery insert cool completely at room temperature before removing and washing. Trying to speed cooling with water can crack it.
* Never immerse the outside electric unit in water. Simply wipe clean with a damp paper towel or sponge.

SMOKED FISH   see also FISH, GENERAL; SHELLFISH
TIDBIT Though smoked salmon is probably the most popular smoked fish in the United States, others include mackerel, trout and whitefish.
PURCHASING Buy smoked fish that looks fresh, not dry around the edges. Plan on 2 slices of smoked fish per serving.
STORING Refrigerate, tightly wrapped, for up to 3 days.

USING

* Thin slices of smoked fish are easier to separate when cold.

* Smoked whole fish is easier to skin and bone while it's cold.

* Arrange slices of smoked fish on a serving plate, cover with plastic wrap, and let stand at room temperature for 30 minutes to bring out the natural, rich flavors of the fish.

* Accompaniments for smoked fish include: Capers, caviar, lemon wedges, sour cream, melon slices, or finely chopped chives, cucumbers, dill, red onion or tomatoes.

SMOOTHIES

TIDBIT Smoothies are essentially fruit- or vegetable-based drinks whirled together with juice, milk, yogurt or other liquids (see below).

PREPARING

* An electric blender is the machine of choice. Food processors often don't blend the ingredients as thoroughly or quickly, and often leak in the process.

* For the best blending results, start at low speed and gradually increase to high.

* Start with chilled ingredients and you won't have to dilute the blend with ice.

* In wintertime, when something chilly isn't appealing, use room-temperature ingredients.

* Smoothie proportions per serving are typically 1 cup fruit, ½ to 1 cup liquid (depending on the thickness), plus various flavorings and nutritional enhancements.

* Cut fruit like bananas, mangoes, melon and papayas into chunks; berries and small fruit like apricots and grapes go into the mix whole.

* Use frozen fruit for a milkshake consistency.

* Liquids for smoothies can include fruit juices and nectars, milk, flavored yogurt, coffee, tea, low-fat coconut milk, and even tomato or vegetable juice. For more nutrition and fewer calories, choose soymilk, buttermilk, silken tofu and unflavored yogurt.

* Nutritional boosts include protein powder, vitamin C powder and acidophilus. Add fiber with enhancements like cooked brown rice or toasted nuts.

* Ground spices, extracts and liquid sweeteners like maple syrup or honey can all be used as flavorings.

* It's hard to go wrong with a smoothie. If it's too thick, add liquid and blend again; too thin, add more fruit.

TROPICAL TWISTER

Combine 1 small diced, seeded, peeled papaya, 1 medium quartered ripe banana, ¾ cup cold low-fat coconut milk, 1 tablespoon fresh lime juice and 4 ice cubes in a blender. Cover and process until smooth. Pour into tall glasses; garnish with toasted coconut or papaya chunks. Serves 2.

SNAILS

TIDBIT   Fresh *escargots* (snails), cultivated in Europe and the United States, are available year-round in specialty markets. They must be soaked, trimmed and cooked before they can be substituted for canned snails in recipes.

PURCHASING

* Canned snails: They're sold with an attached bag of shells and may be found in gourmet markets and some supermarkets.
* Fresh snails: Buy the day you plan to use them from a purveyor with a rapid turnover.
* How much per serving: 6 to 8 snails

EQUIVALENT   Fresh American snails: 1 pound = about 48 canned

STORING

* Fresh snails: Refrigerate for no more than a day or two.
* Canned snails: Store unopened at room temperature for up to a year; refrigerate after opening and use within 3 days.

PREPARING

* Soak live snails in a shallow pan of lukewarm water to cover for about 10 minutes. Discard any snails that haven't begun to emerge from their shells after that time. Drain the remaining snails, cover with cold water mixed with 1 teaspoon salt and let stand at room temperature for 1 hour. Prevent the snails from escaping by dampening the rim of the bowl and coating it with salt.
* Canned snails will taste better if you rinse them with cold water, then put them in a bowl of salted water with a little fresh garlic. Cover tightly and refrigerate overnight; blot dry with paper towels before using.
* Clean empty snail shells by covering them with 1 quart water mixed with 2 tablespoons baking soda and 1 tablespoon salt. Bring to a boil; cover and simmer for 30 minutes. Drain, rinse well and dry thoroughly before using. Snail shells can be used repeatedly if they're carefully washed and dried after each use.

COOKING

* Place fresh snails in boiling water, then reduce the heat to simmer and cook for 5 minutes. Drain, then use a snail fork or skewer to remove the

snails from their shells. Snip off the heads, black tails and any bit of green gall; thoroughly rinse.

* Poach fresh snails in water to cover (or use half wine or beef broth) for 1½ to 2 hours until tender. Add a bay leaf, 1 chopped small carrot and 1 chopped celery stalk to the liquid, if desired. Cool the snails in the broth to room temperature. Now the snails are ready to be used in recipes calling for canned snails.

SNOW PEAS   *see* PEAS, POD

SOFT-COOKED EGGS   *see* EGGS, COOKING METHODS

SOUFFLÉS
TIDBIT   A **cold soufflé**, which is based on gelatin and stiffly beaten egg whites, is really more of a mousse. Such soufflés can be chilled in the refrigerator or frozen. Cold soufflés are usually served as dessert. A **baked soufflé** is composed of stiffly beaten egg whites, which give it the traditional light texture, and a base mixture, which provides flavor.

PREPARING

* Position the oven rack in the middle of the oven. If it's a particularly high-rising soufflé, position the rack in the lower third of the oven. Preheat the oven for 15 minutes (375°F is typical for soufflés), using an oven THERMOMETER for accuracy.

* Always use a classic soufflé dish—the straight sides force the expanding soufflé upward. It's important to use the size dish called for in the recipe.

* Butter a soufflé dish unless otherwise indicated. You may choose to make individual soufflés rather than one large soufflé.

* To prepare a soufflé-dish collar, cut a piece of foil or PARCHMENT PAPER (foil is easier to handle) 2 inches longer than the circumference of the dish. Fold the foil lengthwise in thirds; lightly butter one side. Wrap the foil tightly, buttered side in, around the buttered soufflé dish. Press the foil so that it conforms to the shape of the dish. The collar should rise 2 to 3 inches above the rim of the dish. Securely fasten the foil base with tape or string. If using string, tie it about ½ inch below the rim of the dish; use a paper clip to secure the top edge of the foil.

* For dessert soufflés, sprinkle about 2 tablespoons granulated sugar into the buttered soufflé dish. Rotate and tilt the dish until the sugar coats the inside of the dish and collar.

* For savory soufflés, sprinkle the dish and collar with dried bread crumbs or finely grated cheese.

* The components of a soufflé may be prepared in advance for easy last-minute assembly. Butter and sugar the soufflé dish; set aside the unbeaten egg whites in a covered container. Prepare and cover the base mixture. Allow both the egg whites and base mixture to stand at room temperature for at least 30 minutes before using. At the last minute, simply beat the egg whites, fold them into the base mixture and pop the soufflé into a preheated oven.
* Recipes calling for more egg whites than egg yolks ensure lighter soufflés.
* When doubling a soufflé recipe, add an extra egg white to ensure proper rising. For example, if the original recipe calls for 3 egg whites, use 7 egg whites in the doubled recipe.
* Beating egg whites properly is crucial to a successful soufflé. They must be beaten to firm but glossy peaks to incorporate as much air as possible, but not overbeaten so that they become dry or collapse (*see* Egg Whites, page 180).
* Immediately after beating the egg whites, fold them into the base mixture. Whites that are allowed to stand will begin to deflate, and your soufflé won't be as light as it could have been.
* Fold a small amount of the beaten egg whites into the soufflé base to lighten the mixture and make it easier to fold in the remaining egg whites.
* Don't overblend the mixture once the egg whites have been folded in.
* To create a soufflé with a "crown," once the mixture has been turned into the soufflé dish, run a knife vertically all through the mixture (almost all the way to the bottom) about 1 to 1½ inches from the edge of the dish.
* If necessary, a soufflé can be refrigerated for up to 2 hours before being baked.

BAKING

* Never open the oven door to check a soufflé's progress. If there's no window in the oven door, don't open it before three-quarters of the baking time has passed.
* If the top of your soufflé is browning too quickly, butter a piece of foil slightly wider than the soufflé dish. Open the oven and quickly place the foil, buttered side down, over the soufflé.
* Soufflés may be baked in the European manner—slightly underdone, with a custardy center, or cooked until the center is well done and dry.
* To check a soufflé for doneness, insert a long skewer or a sharp knife into the center. It will be moist if the soufflé is slightly underdone; dry if it is well done.

SERVING

* A soufflé must be taken to the table as soon as it's taken out of the oven. The collar may be removed in the kitchen, but the soufflé will begin to deflate. For this reason, you may choose to take the soufflé to the table with the collar still attached to the dish. Have a plate ready on which to place the foil and string, and remove the collar at the table with ceremony and flair.
* To serve a soufflé, use two forks, back to back, to separate it gently into serving portions, then scoop out each portion with a large spoon.
* If your soufflé collapses before you get it to the table, just pretend that's the way it's supposed to be. If it's a hot dessert soufflé, drizzle it with sauce or top with whipped cream and call it a "baked pudding." If it's a cheese soufflé, sprinkle it with grated cheese, broil the top until bubbly, and call it a "cheese pudding" or "torte."

Do you have a kinder, more adaptable friend in the food world than soup?
Who soothes you when you are ill? . . .
Who warms you in the winter and cools you in the summer? . . .
Soup does its loyal best. . . . You don't catch steak hanging around
when you're poor and sick, do you?
—Judith Martin (Miss Manners), American etiquette expert

SOUPS AND STEWS *see also* THICKENERS
GENERAL

* Soup makes an elegant first course for any special meal. Choose one that will complement the flavors of the other dishes in the meal. For example, a creamy bisque is the perfect prelude for simple grilled meat and sautéed vegetables, but would be too much with a rich entrée like stroganoff.
* If you can, make soups a day ahead and refrigerate overnight to let the flavors meld and heighten. Refrigeration also allows any fat to solidify, making it easy to remove.
* The food processor is a great timesaver when making soups. It chops and slices vegetables in a fraction of the time it would take most of us by hand. If different vegetables go into the pot at different times, chop or slice them separately, transferring each one to a dish, paper plate or sheet of waxed paper as it's cut. Start with the least messy vegetable. Mushrooms, for example, should be cut and set aside before chopping something moist like bell peppers or onions. Wiping out the workbowl between vegetables is optional. If it's all going into the same pot anyway, why bother?

THE LIQUID BASE

* Save and freeze leftover poultry and meat bones to make stock (see any general cookbook for stock recipes).
* Add a husky richness to chicken broth by using the bones and skin from a smoked chicken (which must often be specially ordered through your meat market or supermarket).
* When using canned broth, be aware of the style you purchase: *ready-to-serve* (which is already diluted) and *condensed* (which requires adding water or milk). An undiluted condensed broth will produce an unpalatably salty soup.
* Keep canned broth in the refrigerator so the fat congeals and can be easily removed before using. There are also several fat-free broths available.
* For a flavor dividend, add full-flavored beers, or wines like sherry and Madeira.
* Substitute vegetable juice for a third to half of the water in the recipe.
* Roasted soup bones (baked at 400°F until brown) will enrich any soup or stew.
* Maximize flavor by starting items like soup bones and ham hocks in cold liquid (water, stock, broth), then begin heating the soup.
* Use the cooking liquid from vegetables or meats as a nutritious base for soups or stews. The liquid can be frozen until you need it.
* Save and freeze leftover pan juices to enrich soups or stews.

OTHER INGREDIENTS

* Finely chopped vegetables and meat will cook much faster than large chunks.
* Use leftover vegetables from dinner in soup the following night. Add cooked vegetables to the mix 5 or 10 minutes before serving—just long enough for them to get hot but not overcook.
* Browning meats and vegetables enriches the flavor of soups and stews. Try adding 1 teaspoon sugar to the fat, then heat, stirring often, until the fat is hot. The sugar caramelizes and gives everything a beautiful color and flavor with negligible sweetness.
* For no-fat browning, put the meat on a rack and broil until brown.
* Vegetables will retain their texture if you add them toward the end of the cooking time. Cook dense vegetable like carrots for 20 to 30 minutes (depending on their size), add quick-cooking veggies like celery during the last 10 minutes.
* Compact pasta shapes like ditali (tiny macaroni), orzo (rice-shaped), radiatore (chunky, radiator-shaped), and rotini (small spirals) do better than noodle-style pastas in soups and stews.

* Pasta can easily become soggy in long-cooking mixtures. Either cook it separately and add at the last minute, or add it to the mixture and allow 5 to 10 minutes longer cooking time than the package directs. The cooking time depends on the composition of the soup or stew base. If it's thick, the pasta will take longer; thin mixtures will cook the pasta in about the usual time.

* Add minced clams to soups and stews at the last minute so they won't toughen.

* Gingersnap cookies (no, I'm not kidding) add an intriguing nuance to hearty meat soups and stews and also thicken them slightly. Use only ½ to 1 cup crumbs for a soup that serves 4 to 6, adding the crumbs 30 to 60 minutes before the dish is done.

COOKING SOUPS AND STEWS

* Instead of cooking stew on the stovetop, cover and bake it in a 350°F oven. There's not as much pot-watching and stirring because the heat surrounds and cooks the stew evenly.

* After stirring sour cream or yogurt into a hot soup or stew, reduce the heat to low and cook only until the mixture is warmed through. Letting the mixture boil will cause curdling. Milk products won't separate as easily in flour-thickened mixtures.

* To help prevent curdling when working with milk-based mixtures, add acidic ingredients (tomatoes, lemon juice or wine) to the blend, rather than adding the milk product to the acidic ingredients. A touch of whipping cream also helps prevent curdling.

* Another way to keep milk-based soups from curdling is to make a thin, syrupy paste of flour and water and whisk it into the milk before adding acidic foods.

* If a soup mixture curdles, simply strain the liquid into a blender jar and process until smooth. Don't fill the blender more than two-thirds full with a hot liquid. Securely seat the lid on the blender jar, put on an oven mitt and hold the lid down as you begin blending at low speed and gradually increase to high.

* Evaporated non- or low-fat milk (undiluted) lends richness without excess calories.

* Too much garlic? Place a handful of parsley in a tea infuser or a cheesecloth bag tied with string and simmer the mixture in the stew for 10 minutes. Or stir in 1 to 3 teaspoons honey.

* Burned stew? Pour the stew into another pan. Don't scrape up any that sticks—it'll be singed. Taste the stew in the clean pot to see if it tastes burned. If so, try adding a little wine, cream or sour cream. Don't let the

stew return to a boil if you've added sour cream. Chili powder can also mask a singed flavor—of course, then you'd have chili stew, which is exactly what you should call it and no one will know the difference.

FINISHING SOUPS AND STEWS

* Remove as much fat as possible before thickening soups.
* Siphon fat off the surface with a baster, or soak it up with a fat "mop" (available in kitchenware shops) or sheets of paper towel.
* Or remove fat by putting ice cubes in a plastic bag and dragging the bag over the soup's surface. As the ice melts, the fat will congeal around the bag.
* Lettuce leaves also act like a sponge for fat. Add 2 or 3 leaves to the finished soup and let stand for a few minutes before removing.
* Or spoon off as much fat as possible, then blot the remaining fat with crumpled wads of paper towel.
* Thicken soups and stews just before serving (see THICKENERS). Of course a foolproof, flavorful thickener is to simply PURÉE some of the vegetables in the soup or stew and stir back into the mixture.
* Add acidic ingredients like wine, lemon juice or tomatoes to a flour- or cornstarch-thickened soup after the mixture's been thickened.
* Some herbs—like basil—lose much of their flavor and aroma when cooked for more than about 15 minutes. Taste the soup or stew at the end of the cooking time and, if necessary, stir in chopped fresh herbs.
* Does your finished dish taste flat and flavorless? Heighten the flavor by adding extract or bouillon (chicken, beef, mushroom, and so on). Minced herbs will also brighten the taste.
* For a rich taste and texture without too many calories, stir 1 tablespoon butter or 2 tablespoons heavy cream into soup just before serving.
* Rescue oversalted soups by adding a peeled, thinly sliced raw potato and simmering for 10 to 15 minutes. Remove the potato before serving the soup. Of course, the best way to prevent oversalting is to season after the soup is done.
* Balance the flavor of an oversalted mixture by stirring in 1 teaspoon each vinegar and brown sugar for each quart of liquid.
* Darken pale-colored soups and stews by stirring in 1 to 3 teaspoons caramelized sugar or instant coffee powder, or a few drops of Kitchen Bouquet, available in supermarkets.
* Keep a cream- or milk-based soup warm (or reheat) in the top of a double boiler over hot water. Such soups can scorch over direct heat.
* Cold soups: Remember that chilling food mutes its flavor, so taste just

before serving and adjust the seasoning if necessary. Keep in mind that most cold soups will be thicker than when they were hot.

GARNISHING AND SERVING

* Garnishing not only adds eye appeal, but flavor and textural contrast as well. Easy, last-minute garnishes include finely snipped chives or scallion greens, a dollop of sour cream dusted with paprika for color, minced herbs like parsley or basil, toasted, sliced almonds, and even popcorn.

* Another easy garnish is to float croutons or a crostini (a thin, toasted baguette slice) atop soup. Or sprinkle the soup with butter-toasted bread crumbs.

* A dusting of freshly grated Parmesan or other cheese makes a simple, delicious garnish. Or pass small cubes of cheese for diners to drop into their soup. In minutes the cheese will melt into flavorful blobs.

* For real comfort food, make a mashed-potato nest in a soup bowl, and spoon a hearty stew into the indentation.

* Stretch a thick stew by serving it over rice.

* Add panache by serving soup in edible hollowed-out containers, such as a large tomato (for cold soups), or a toasted French roll, or an acorn-squash half.

LEFTOVERS

* Enliven the flavor of leftover soup by stirring in 1 to 2 tablespoons chopped, fresh herbs just before serving.

* Or stir in a tablespoon or two of wine, sherry or Madeira. Heat for at least 10 minutes to dispel any raw liquor taste.

* Transform leftover vegetable soup by puréeing it in the blender with grated Cheddar cheese, then heating and serving it as "country Cheddar soup." Convert potato soup to vichyssoise by adding sautéed minced leeks, puréeing and thinning with milk, then refrigerating until cold. Or create a "stew" by thickening a soup and adding chunks of sautéed beef or pork and a splash of wine.

* The microwave oven makes quick work of reheating soup in individual soup bowls. Stir it after about a minute to distribute the heat; continue cooking until hot. Thick soups like split pea can have little explosive bursts, so it's better to cover the bowl with waxed paper to prevent spattering the oven interior.

* To freeze soup or stew, place a freezer-weight plastic bag inside a bowl, pour in the mixture, then freeze. When solid, lift the plastic bag out of the bowl, seal and return to the freezer for up to 3 months.

* Freeze leftover soups and stews in individual portions to be heated in minutes in the microwave.
* Even if you don't have enough soup left over for a couple of servings, freeze it and add other soups as you make them. Defrost and purée the lot to use as a soup base.
* Make instant soup by combining leftover vegetables with chicken, beef or vegetable broth in a blender and processing until smooth.
* For soup in minutes, add chicken or beef broth to leftover rice, risotto or beans, and stir in some lightly sautéed vegetables. Heat just until hot.

SOUR CREAM *see also* CREAM
PURCHASING Regular commercial sour cream contains 18 to 20 percent fat. There are also light (30 to 50 percent less fat than regular) and nonfat versions.
STORING Refrigerate sour cream in its carton for up to 1 week after the date on the package.
SUBSTITUTIONS (for 1 cup sour cream)
* For a topping: Combine ½ cup cottage cheese, ¼ cup milk, and 2 teaspoons lemon juice in a blender; process until smooth. Or substitute 1 cup unflavored yogurt.
* For use in cooking or baking recipes: 1 cup plain whole-milk yogurt; ¾ cup sour milk, buttermilk or low-fat plain yogurt plus ¼ cup butter, melted; 1 tablespoon lemon juice plus evaporated whole milk to equal 1 cup.
USING
* Bring sour cream to room temperature before adding to a hot mixture.
* Stir sour cream into a hot soup or sauce just before serving, heating gently and only until the mixture is warmed through. Letting the mixture boil will cause curdling. Nonfat sour cream enriches mixtures and no one will miss the calories.
* Sour cream won't separate as easily when heated in mixtures that are flour-based.
* For a low-calorie sour cream substitute, try QUARK.

SOYBEAN CURD *see* TOFU

SPICES *see also* CINNAMON; CLOVES; CURRY POWDER; GINGER; HERBS; NUTMEG; PAPRIKA; PEPPER; SAFFRON
PURCHASING Ground spices quickly lose their aroma and flavor so,

unless you use them fast, buy in small quantities. Some spices, such as allspice, cloves and nutmeg, can be purchased whole and used as is or ground as needed. To ensure that spices are as fresh as possible, buy them from a store with rapid turnover.

STORING Store spices in airtight containers in a cool, dark place for no more than 6 months. Never store them over the stovetop or in any other hot location. For longer storage, refrigerate spices as soon as you buy them. Refrigeration is particularly important for spice blends like chili and curry powders.

USING

* Keep track of how old a spice is by marking the date it was opened on the bottom of the can or jar with a felt-tip marking pen. Or note the date on a strip of masking tape and stick it to the container's bottom.
* Whole spices that are ground fresh have more punch than preground spices.
* Simplify finding your spices by arranging them alphabetically in your cabinet.
* Buy a turntable in the kitchen-supply section of a hardware or department store, and keep your spices on it for flick-of-the-wrist convenience.
* Enhance and intensify the flavor of whole spices like allspice berries or peppercorns by roasting them in a 350°F oven for about 10 minutes. Alternatively, you can pan-roast them over medium-high heat for about 5 minutes, stirring often. Cool completely before using.
* Sautéing ground spices in oil for a few seconds before adding other ingredients also brings out their flavor.

On the subject of spinach: divide into little piles. Rearrange again into new piles. After five or six maneuvers, sit back and say you are full.
—Delia Ephron, American author

SPINACH *see also* SALAD GREENS; VEGETABLES, GENERAL
TIDBIT It's true that spinach is packed with iron (as well as vitamins A and C, calcium, potassium, folic acid and other nutrients), but it also contains oxalic acid, which inhibits the body's absorption of both iron and calcium (don't worry—spinach doesn't affect calcium absorption from other foods). That's not to say spinach isn't good for you. It is, in fact, one of the healthiest greens we can eat, and it is known to be a preventative for everything from cancer to cataracts. Bottom line—enjoy your spinach, but get your calcium from other sources.

S PURCHASING Spinach leaves may either be curled or smooth, depending on the variety. The smaller New Zealand spinach has flat, spade-shaped leaves that are often covered with a fine fuzz. Choose spinach with crisp, dark green leaves that have a nice fresh fragrance. Avoid leaves that are limp, damaged or that have yellow spots.

EQUIVALENTS

* Fresh: 1 pound = about 10 cups torn pieces, about 1½ cups cooked
* Frozen: 10-ounce package = about 1½ cups

STORING Refrigerate spinach, wrapped loosely in paper towels and tightly sealed in a plastic bag, for up to 3 days.

USING

* Stem spinach by simply cutting off the stems. You can pull the leaves off the stems if you like, but that's generally unnecessary unless the stems are particularly tough.
* Wash spinach by placing the leaves in a sink or large container full of cold water. Swish the leaves around with your hands, then let them stand for a few minutes for any dirt to sink to the bottom. Lift the leaves out of the water. If the spinach is very gritty, repeat the process.
* To use spinach for salad, thoroughly dry the leaves, either in a salad spinner or by shaking off excess moisture, laying them out on a double layer of paper towels (or a kitchen towel), then blotting the surface dry.

COOKING

* Spinach discolors if cooked in an aluminum pan or served in silver. Turnabout's fair play—the spinach also discolors those metals.
* For the fullest flavor, cook spinach only until it begins to go limp.
* To steam spinach, place the washed leaves (don't shake off or dry) in a hot pan, then cover and steam for 2 to 3 minutes.
* If using steamed spinach in another preparation, wrap it in a kitchen towel (or a double layer of sturdy paper towel), hold it over the sink and twist to wring out moisture. Then use or chop as desired.
* Expel excess moisture in thawed, frozen spinach the same way. If you want the liquid for soups and so on, squeeze the spinach over a bowl.
* Spinach is great when sautéed briefly in bacon fat, salt and peppered to taste, and garnished with crumbled, crisp bacon.
* Freshly grated nutmeg makes magic with spinach. Add it at the beginning of the cooking time.
* Thoroughly drain cooked spinach so excess moisture doesn't transfer to other foods on the plate.
* A tasty garnish for cooked or raw spinach is sieved, hard-cooked eggs.

SPLIT PEAS *see* PEAS, DRIED

SPROUTS

TIDBIT Edible sprouts are produced from a variety of seeds and beans, and can be found in produce markets, natural food stores and many supermarkets. The most popular sprouts are alfalfa, lentil, mung bean, pea, radish and wheat.

PURCHASING Choose crisp-looking sprouts with the buds attached. Avoid musty-smelling, dark or slimy-looking sprouts.

STORING Refrigerate sturdy sprouts—like mung-bean sprouts—in a plastic bag for no more than 4 days. More delicate varieties—such as alfalfa sprouts—should be refrigerated for no more than 2 to 3 days in the ventilated plastic container in which they're usually sold.

USING

* Wash sprouts just before using; thoroughly blot dry on paper towels.
* Cut off any roots; the seed or bean end of a sprout need not be removed.
* For optimum crispness, sprouts should be eaten raw. They add both flavor and texture to salads and sandwiches.
* The only sprouts that are firm enough to cook without immediately wilting are mung-bean sprouts. Even so, add them last to stir-fries and such, and cook for less than a minute.

SQUASH, SUMMER *see also* SQUASH, WINTER; SQUASH BLOSSOMS; VEGETABLES, GENERAL

TIDBIT Squash are divided into two categories—summer squash and winter squash. Summer squash have thin, edible skins and soft seeds. The most widely available varieties are crookneck, pattypan and zucchini.

PURCHASING Choose firm summer squash with bright-colored skin free of spots and bruises. In general, the smaller the squash, the more tender it will be.

EQUIVALENTS 1 pound = about 3 medium, 3 cups chopped

STORING Refrigerate summer squash in a plastic bag for up to 5 days.

PREPARING Just before using, wash squash and trim both ends; peeling isn't required (except for the chayote, also called *mirliton*). Blot dry with paper towels if sautéing or using in salads. Squash that's to be cooked with a moist-heat method like steaming doesn't require drying.

COOKING

* The tender flesh of summer squash has a high water content and doesn't require long cooking. It can be steamed, baked, sautéed or deep-fried.

* To grill, cut zucchini lengthwise into ½-inch thick slices. Brush with olive oil, season with salt and pepper. Grill for about 2 minutes over a hot fire. Use tongs to turn the slices; grill the second side for 1 to 2 minutes.

STUFFED ZUCCHINI

Cut zucchini in half lengthwise, scoop the flesh out of the center, leaving a ½-inch shell. Chop the zucchini flesh and combine with sautéed onions, garlic, bell peppers, tomatoes and bread crumbs; season to taste. Fill the zucchini cavities and sprinkle with grated cheese. Bake at 400°F for about 30 minutes. You can also stuff zucchini halves with a meat and rice filling, or just cheese and chopped zucchini.

SQUASH, WINTER   *see also* PUMPKINS; SQUASH, SUMMER; SQUASH BLOSSOMS; VEGETABLES, GENERAL

TIDBIT   Winter squash have hard, thick skins and seeds. Their deep yellow to orange flesh is firmer than that of summer squash and therefore requires longer cooking. The most popular varieties are acorn, buttercup, butternut, hubbard, spaghetti and turban.

PURCHASING   Choose those that are heavy for their size. Their rinds should be hard, deep colored, dull (not shiny), and free of moldy or soft spots.

EQUIVALENTS: 1 pound = about 2 cups cooked pieces; 1 cup mashed squash

STORING   Store in a cool, dark, well-ventilated place for up to 1 month.

USING

* The skin of winter squash is extremely hard and requires a heavy knife to cut through it. First slice off the stem, then cut down through the stem to halve the squash.
* Winter squash are easier to cut if microwaved on high for 1 to 2 minutes (depending on the size); let stand for 3 minutes before cutting. Pierce the rind in a couple of places before microwaving so the squash doesn't explode.
* Use an ice cream scoop or a large spoon to scoop out and discard the seeds and membranes from the cavity.
* Peeling winter squash is much easier after they're cooked.
* Very large squash, such as hubbard, can be cut into smaller pieces before cooking.
* Winter squash can be baked, boiled, steamed or simmered.
* Pierce the rind of acorn squash with a fork in several places before baking it whole. This technique, which allows steam to escape, is particularly important when microwaving squash to prevent it from exploding.

* Or halve a squash, scrape out the seeds, wipe out the cavity and brush with melted butter. Place, flesh side down, in a baking pan with just enough water to barely cover the pan's bottom. Bake at 350°F for 40 to 60 minutes (depending on the size) until fork-tender.
* Pumpkin can be used in most recipes calling for winter squash.
* Fresh ginger and ground ginger have a natural affinity for winter squash. So does nutmeg.

SQUASH BLOSSOMS   *see also* FLOWERS

TIDBIT The flowers from both summer and winter squash are edible and delicious. They come in varying shades of yellow and orange, with flavors that hint of the squash itself.

PURCHASING Squash blossoms can be found from late spring through early fall in specialty produce markets and some ethnic markets. Choose those that look fresh (they're naturally soft and limp) with closed buds.

STORING Refrigerate the blossoms in a sealed container (not a plastic bag) for no more than 1 or 2 days.

USING
* Squash blossoms may be used as a garnish (whole or slivered) for everything from salads to soups to main dishes.
* When cooked, they're most often stuffed with a soft cheese, dipped into a light batter and fried or deep-fried.
* Cooked squash blossoms can be served as a side dish for dinner, or with honey for breakfast.

STEAKS   *see also* BEEF; MEAT, GENERAL
PREPARING
* Remove steak from the refrigerator 30 to 60 minutes before cooking. Room-temperature meat not only browns better, but cooks faster and more evenly.
* Prevent steak from curling during cooking by slashing the edging fat almost all the way to the meat at 1-inch intervals.
* Fat greatly contributes to a steak's flavor, so don't trim it all off.
* For well-browned steak, make sure the surface is thoroughly dry, particularly if it's been marinated. Use a paper towel to blot up excess moisture.
COOKING
* Salt steak toward the end of the cooking time or the salt will leach some of the juices from the meat.
* With dry-heat methods like BROILING or GRILLING, the longer the meat cooks, the tougher it gets.

* When broiling thick steaks, position the broiler rack farther from the heating unit so they'll cook through before burning on the outside.

* When panbroiling steak, it's not necessary to add fat or oil, unless the cut is very lean. Use a heavy skillet and simply brush the pan with oil. The pan should be very hot before adding the meat. A light dusting of flour on the meat will facilitate browning.

* When cooking T-bone and porterhouse steaks, position them so the tenderloin portion, which cooks faster than the strip portion, is on the outer perimeter of the heat source, whether panbroiling, broiling or grilling. That way, the tenderloin won't be overdone by the time the strip is perfect.

* Cutting into a steak to determine its doneness releases some of its juices. Though it takes practice, you can tell whether a steak's done to your liking by using the touch technique. Press the meat lightly with your finger: if it's soft, the meat's rare; if it resists slightly but springs back, it's medium-rare; if the meat is quite firm, it's well done.

* Another way to check steaks is to insert a meat THERMOMETER at least 1 inch into the side (not top) of the meat. This technique is particularly effective for thin cuts where the probe would go completely through the meat if inserted from the top.

* Cooked flank steak requires careful slicing in order to get the most tender, attractive cut. Slice across the grain for tenderness; position the knife at a 45-degree angle for slices that look ample rather than meager.

STEAMING *see also* COOKING, GENERAL

TIDBIT Steaming is probably the most nutritious method of cooking because, unlike boiling, it doesn't wash away water-soluble nutrients. It also retains the purity of a food's flavor, which can be a disadvantage with bland foods.

GENERAL

* Steamers are commonly available in kitchenware and hardware stores, and even supermarkets. The least expensive style is the collapsible basket, which typically costs under $10. There are also tiered steamers and stackable bamboo steamers, in which two or more types of food can be steamed. Electric steamers are like electric rice cookers—available, but not really necessary.

* If you don't have a steamer, improvise by using a footed colander or large, flat-bottomed sieve.

* The foods most often steamed are vegetables and fish.

S

* The pan in which food is steamed must be large enough to allow steam to circulate freely or the food won't cook evenly.
* The cover for the pan in which food is steamed must fit tightly. Otherwise, some of the steam will escape and impede cooking. If the cover doesn't fit tightly, cover the pot with a sheet of foil, then position the lid on top of the foil, seating it firmly.
* Add flavor to foods to be steamed by marinating (see MARINADES, MARINATING) them overnight before cooking.
* Or add herbs or spices to the boiling water; cook for 5 minutes before beginning to steam.
* Or put food in a shallow pan, season with aromatics such as herbs, garlic or ginger, then put the pan on a rack or atop a basket steamer.

COOKING

* Water should never directly touch the food. Place the food on a rack at least 1 inch above the hot liquid.
* During the steaming time, shake or stir the ingredients once or twice to make sure they cook evenly.
* Watch the liquid to make sure it doesn't boil away, leaving a dry pan. Keep a separate pot of boiling liquid to replenish that in the steamer, if necessary.
* Food can also be "steamed" by sealing it with 1 or 2 tablespoons liquid in a moisture-proof wrapping like foil or PARCHMENT PAPER, then baking. The heat produces steam from the food's natural moisture, thereby producing a moist, succulent end result.

STEWING *see* BRAISING
TIDBIT   In general, stewing and braising are almost identical moist-heat cooking methods whereby food is simmered in a liquid in a covered pot, either on a stovetop, in an oven or in a SLOW COOKER. With both methods, food is generally browned before liquid is added. Braised food typically uses a small amount of liquid and is always covered tightly, whereas stewed food is normally covered with liquid and often cooked in a partly closed pot. Additionally, in general, stewing involves small pieces of food, whereas braising is usually done for a single large item like a roast.

STEWS *see* SOUPS AND STEWS

STIR-FRYING *see also* DEEP-FRYING; SAUTÉING
TIDBIT   Stir-frying quickly cooks small pieces of food in a modicum of oil over very high heat. The food is constantly and briskly stirred through-

out cooking. A wok is the classic pan for stir-frying; however, any large, deep skillet will do. The important thing is to have enough room for the ingredients to be tossed around in during cooking.

GENERAL

* Buying a wok: For an electric range, a flat-bottom wok is best for even heat distribution. Gas ranges can accommodate either flat- or round-bottom woks. When using a round-bottom wok, place the ring stand, narrow side up, over a large burner. Electric woks are free-standing.

* Seasoning a steel wok: Thoroughly scrub the wok and lid inside and out to remove the rust-resistant coating. Rinse and dry well, then pour in 2 tablespoons vegetable oil, rotating the pan to coat it thoroughly and evenly. Heat over high heat until the oil is very hot. Let cool, then use a crumpled paper towel to rub in the oil. Season the lid (removing any nonmetal handles) in the same manner, placing it directly on the burner. After each use, clean and thoroughly dry the wok (heat-dry it on the range). Then reseason by rubbing in about 1 teaspoon oil.

* Fish for stir-frying should be firm-textured—monkfish, sea bass, shark, swordfish or tuna would all be good choices.

* Vegetables should be harmonious in color, texture and flavor. Cooking time depends on how the vegetables are cut. Matchstick pieces will take less time to cook than chunks. Start with the vegetable that will take the longest to cook, like carrots; add delicate ingredients (like bean sprouts) at the last minute.

* For stir-fries with lots of components, before cooking arrange the chopped ingredients on paper plates (several to a plate, if possible). Add the foods in the order desired, then discard the plates.

* Speed the cooking process by getting everything ready the day before, chopping and refrigerating the ingredients in separate plastic bags. When ready to stir-fry, you'll have a meal in minutes.

* Partially cooking (*see* BLANCHING) particularly dense vegetables before stir-frying them will help get everything done at the same time.

COOKING

* Before starting to cook, heat the oil until a piece of vegetable sizzles when tossed into the pan.

* Reduce calories by spraying the room-temperature pan with cooking spray first. After heating the pan, stir-fry the vegetables, then add a small amount of oil to cook any meat.

* If you have a large amount of meat to cook, it's better to cook it in two batches. Otherwise, the pan can become too cool, and the meat will end

up braising, rather than frying. Cook one batch until almost done to your liking, then transfer it to a plate and cook the second batch.

* Make magic with leftovers by turning stir-fries into soups (add broth), salads (toss with your favorite dressing and salad greens), or main dishes (combine with a sauce and serve over noodles or rice).

STRAINERS *see* SIEVES

Doubtless God could have made a berry, but doubtless God never did.
—William Butler (on the strawberry), British writer

STRAWBERRIES *For storage and cleaning information, see* BERRIES, GENERAL
PURCHASING Choose brightly colored, plump strawberries that still have their green caps attached. They should have a potent strawberry fragrance; those without it aren't fully ripe and won't ripen after being picked. Avoid soft, shriveled or moldy berries.
EQUIVALENTS

* Fresh: 1 pint = 1½ to 2 cups sliced
* Frozen: 10-ounce package = 1½ cups

PREPARING

* Wash strawberries before hulling.
* My savvy editor, Harriet Bell, shared this unconventional way to store strawberries for up to a week. Wash and air-dry the berries, leaving the stems intact. When the berries are completely dry, put them in a large, screw-top jar. Place a paper towel on top of the berries (to absorb excess natural moisture), seal the jar tightly and refrigerate. Unwashed berries can also be stored in this manner. If you wash them first, however, the berries will be ready and waiting for hungry snackers.
* When making strawberry pie, always wash, then hull the berries, letting them drain upside down on paper towels for 30 minutes. That way, you'll remove as much excess moisture as possible and not end up with a soggy pie.

STRING BEANS *see* BEANS, FRESH GREEN

STUFFED (DEVILED) EGGS *see* EGGS, COOKING METHODS (HARD-COOKED), page 184

S

STUFFING *see also* BREAD CRUMBS; TURKEY

TIDBIT Whether you call this American favorite "dressing" or "stuffing" depends on the part of the country you're from.

STORING Refrigerate leftover stuffing and use within 3 days; freeze up to 4 months. Individual portions can be frozen to reheat quickly in a microwave oven.

GENERAL

* How much per serving: Count on about ¾ to 1 cup stuffing—this should give you leftovers.

* Things to stuff: Many foods besides poultry are naturals for stuffing—acorn squash, bell peppers, tomatoes, and baked apples (*see* Sausage-Stuffed Baked Apples, page 9), to name a few. *See also* Stuffing a Turkey, page 451.

* Stuffing can be made the day before and refrigerated. The best bet is to prepare the stuffing ingredients ahead of time, then combine the dry ingredients and any vegetables with the liquid (such as broth and melted butter) with the bread crumbs just before making it.

* Make a double batch of stuffing and freeze half of it to be baked at a later date. Put the stuffing in an even layer in a plastic, freezer-weight bag, then place the bag on a tray. Freeze until solid, then remove the tray. Next time you want stuffing, defrost the stuffing in the refrigerator and bake as usual.

* Stuffing baked inside a bird will be much moister than stuffing that's baked separately. On the other hand, stuffing baked separately will have a much crisper top.

* To bake stuffing separately: Stuffing baked in a pan will require a little extra moisture—add ½ to ¾ cup chicken, turkey or vegetable broth, or half stock and half sherry or other wine. The resulting mix should be moist, but not soggy. Place the stuffing in a well-oiled pan and dot the surface with bits of butter. Cover and bake at 350°F for 30 to 45 minutes until the temperature in the center reaches 165°F and the top is crispy. Baste the stuffing halfway through the baking time with the turkey drippings. If the top isn't crisp enough when the stuffing's done, broil it for a minute or two.

* Stuffing must be cooked to a temperature of 165°F in order to be free of harmful bacteria. Insert a cooking THERMOMETER into the middle of the mixture to get an accurate reading.

* Puffed Wild Rice, page 491, is a wonderful addition to stuffing. To make a little go a long way, sprinkle it atop the finished stuffing.

* Leftover stuffing doesn't have to be eaten plain. Make a hash by sautéing chopped turkey, crumbled stuffing, onions and garlic together. Or make

soup based on chicken or turkey broth (add a little turkey gravy, if you like) and vegetables; stir in crumbled stuffing about 5 minutes before serving.

STUFFING A TURKEY

* Stuffed turkeys take longer to cook than those that are not stuffed.
* Be sure and remove the giblet bag from the turkey cavity before spooning in the stuffing.
* Don't stuff a turkey until just before you're ready to cook it. Doing so invites the growth of harmful bacteria, which can result in food poisoning.
* For easy stuffing retrieval, place a cheesecloth bag (available at specialty gourmet shops and some supermarkets) inside the turkey body cavity, then fill with stuffing. When the turkey's done, simply pull out the bag. If it won't come out readily, spoon out some of the stuffing, then pull the bag out to retrieve the rest.
* Always cool a stuffing before spooning it loosely (to allow for expansion from absorbed juices) into a turkey. Begin by filling the neck cavity, then loosely fill the body cavity. Stuffing that's packed tightly will come out compact and dense.
* Alternatively, the stuffing can be spooned between the skin and the meat. The bird will look puffy, but the result is crisp, brown skin and moist breast meat.
* If there's extra stuffing after filling the bird, cook it separately in a dish (see preceding tip).
* Close the stuffing openings either by sewing with kitchen twine and a poultry needle or, more easily, by using poultry skewers, available at most supermarkets. Pull the loose skin from one side of the cavity to the other. Poke the skewer through the loose skin and into the skin and meat on the other side. Repeat with other skewers until the openings are closed. Skewers are easy to pull out of the cooked bird.
* If you don't have a THERMOMETER to make sure that the stuffing is cooked to 165°F, cook the stuffing separately.
* As soon as you remove the turkey from the oven, scoop out the stuffing and transfer it to a large, oiled baking dish. Place it in a 450°F oven and bake for 10 to 15 minutes. For a crispy topping, brown under the broiler for a minute or two. Meanwhile, cover the bird with foil and let stand for 20 minutes to let the turkey's natural juices redistribute throughout the meat.
* Never store the turkey with the stuffing still in it. Doing so invites bacterial growth.

*Once in a young lifetime one should be allowed to have as much
sweetness as one can possibly want and hold.*
—Judith Olney, American food writer

SUGAR *see also* CARAMELIZING SUGAR; CORN SYRUP; HONEY; MAPLE SYRUP;
MOLASSES; SUGAR SUBSTITUTES

TIDBIT Sugar was once so rare and expensive that only the exceedingly
wealthy could afford it, which is why it was called "white gold." However,
the first sugar wasn't white at all, but light brown to cream-colored. Today,
sugar is easy to come by, which is sweet news to those with a sweet tooth.
And sugar comes in myriad shapes and forms, the most common being
granulated (or white) sugar, brown sugar and confectioners' (or powdered)
sugar. *See following sections on individual types.*

GENERAL

* Besides its sweetening value, sugar adds tenderness and color to baked
  goods, volume and stability to mixtures like beaten egg whites, color and
  flavor to caramelized foods and—in sufficient quantity—acts as a preservative for some foods.
* If you're avoiding sugar, check food labels carefully. Just because the
  word "sugar" isn't used doesn't mean it's not there. Look for *dextrose,
  fructose, lactose, maltose and sucrose*—all of which are sugars. Of
  course, corn syrup, honey, maple syrup and molasses are also forms of
  sugar.

GRANULATED (WHITE) SUGAR

PURCHASING This dry, free-flowing sugar comes in several forms, the
most commonly available in supermarkets being **fine** and **superfine** or
ultrafine. The latter (known as *castor sugar* in Britain) is so finely pulverized
that it dissolves in cold mixtures and drinks. **Coarse (decorating) sugar** has
large crystals and is more commonly found in gourmet and cake-
decorating supply shops. White sugar is also available in cubes of various
sizes.

EQUIVALENT 1 pound = 2¼ cups

STORING   All types of white sugar can be stored airtight indefinitely.

SUBSTITUTIONS 1 cup regular granulated sugar = 1 cup superfine
sugar, 1 cup firmly packed brown sugar, or 1¾ cups confectioners' sugar

USING

* Superfine sugar dissolves almost instantly, making it perfect for use in
  meringues and for sweetening cold liquids.
* Make your own superfine sugar by processing regular granulated sugar
  in a food processor until powdery.

VANILLA SUGAR

Deliciously fragrant vanilla sugar can be used as a recipe ingredient, for decorating cookies and cakes, or for sweetening coffee, fruit or even cereal. Bury 2 whole vanilla beans in a pound of granulated or confectioners' sugar. Store at room temperature in an airtight container for 2 weeks, stirring once or twice. Remove the beans and reuse in this fashion for up to 6 months.

CITRUS-FLAVORED SUGAR

Combine sugar with long strips of zest (from 1 large orange, 2 medium lemons or 4 medium limes). Stir well, then let stand for at least 1 week before using.

COLORED SUGAR

Use colored sugar to decorate myriad desserts, from cookies to fruit. Making your own allows you more control over the color. Put 1 cup regular (or coarse) sugar in a bowl and dot with 8 to 12 drops of food color (or a combination of colors). Toss with two forks or mix with a whisk until the color's evenly distributed. Turn the sugar onto a baking sheet in an even layer; let stand several hours, or until dry.

BROWN SUGAR

TIDBIT   This soft, moist sugar is the result of sugar crystals being coated with molasses. Some manufacturers actually boil a special molasses syrup until crystals form, then dry the crystals.

PURCHASING   Brown sugar comes in light and dark granulated forms. **Light brown sugar** has a delicate molasses flavor; **dark** (or "old-fashioned") **brown sugar** has a richer, more pronounced molasses essence. There is also a drier, **free-flowing brown sugar** that has a medium molasses flavor and the texture of granulated sugar. Because it contains less moisture, this style doesn't clump or harden.

EQUIVALENT   1 pound = 2¼ cups firmly packed

STORING   Store in a thick, plastic, airtight bag or an airtight canister in a cool, dry place. Boxed brown sugar should be transferred to a plastic bag. To ensure the sugar stays moist, place an apple wedge or two inside the sugar bag.

SUBSTITUTIONS

❋ 1 cup firmly packed brown sugar = 1 cup granulated sugar

❋ 1 cup light brown sugar = ½ cup dark brown sugar plus ½ cup granulated sugar

❋ 1 cup packed regular brown sugar = 1 cup free-flowing brown sugar

USING

❋ Unless a recipe states otherwise, always measure brown sugar by packing it firmly into a measuring cup.

* Brown sugar hardens when the sugar's moisture evaporates. There are several ways to restore that moisture. (1) Add an apple wedge to the bag. Seal and let stand for 1 to 2 days until the sugar softens; remove the apple. (2) Place brown sugar in a dish covered by two damp paper towels, then a lid (plastic wrap will do). Microwave on high for 30 to 60 seconds (depending on the amount of sugar). Use a fork to break up sugar (be careful, it's hot); repeat if necessary. Watch carefully so that it doesn't start to melt. (3) Put hardened brown sugar in an ovenproof dish, cover with a damp cloth (don't let it touch the sugar) and heat in a preheated 250°F oven for 10 minutes. (4) Put the sugar in a bowl, cover with a damp cloth, then foil; let stand overnight at room temperature.

* Use a food processor to break up lumps in brown sugar. A blender also works, though you'll have to either process the sugar in small batches, or keep stopping the blender to move the sugar at the top down toward the blades.

* Substituting brown sugar for granulated sugar will produce a slightly moister baked good with a slight butterscotch flavor.

CONFECTIONERS' (POWDERED) SUGAR

TIDBIT   This is granulated sugar that's been crushed into a fine powder. It contains a small amount (about 3 percent) of cornstarch, added to prevent clumping. Confectioners' sugar is called *icing sugar* in Britain and *sucre glace* in France.

PURCHASING   Confectioners' sugar labels have an "X" designation, which refers to the fineness of the sugar particles. The range goes from 4X (larger particles) to 10X (the finest); the latter is what's commonly found in supermarkets. They can be used interchangeably.

EQUIVALENTS   1 pound = 4 cups unsifted, 4½ cups sifted

STORING   Store airtight at room temperature indefinitely.

SUBSTITUTION   1¾ cups confectioners' sugar = 1 cup granulated sugar

USING

* Some recipes call for sifting confectioners' sugar before using. If you don't have a sifter, spoon the sugar into a fine sieve, then shake or tap it over a measuring cup set on a piece of waxed paper. If necessary, use the back of a wooden spoon to stir the sugar so it "sifts" more easily.

* Quick-sift confectioners' sugar by tossing it into a food processor and whirling until light. Gently spoon the "sifted" sugar into the measuring cup.

* Put confectioners' sugar in a large salt shaker to use when all you need is a dusting to garnish or flavor a dish. Or buy a special sugar

dredger—a perforated screw-top container (metal or glass) found in kitchenware stores. Or put it in a fine sieve and gently shake to sprinkle the sugar.

* Never sprinkle confectioners' sugar over a moist cake, pudding or other dessert until just before serving. The moisture will liquefy the sugar and turn it an unappealing pale gray color.
* Vanilla-flavored confectioners' sugar: See recipe for Vanilla Sugar, page 453.

SUGAR SNAP PEAS   *see* PEAS, POD

SUGAR SUBSTITUTES *See also* SUGAR

PURCHASING The most commonly available sugar substitutes (also called *artificial sweeteners*) today are **aspartame** (180 to 200 times sweeter than sugar), **Acesulfame-K** or **Ace-K** (200 times sweeter) and **saccharin** (300 times sweeter than sugar).

STORING Store airtight at room temperature indefinitely.

SUBSTITUTIONS Each sweetener is different—check the label for amounts to determine its equivalent to sugar for the purpose of sweetening.

USING

* Aspartame breaks down and loses its sweetness when heated. It is, however, good for sweetening cold dishes, and can be added to cooked foods (like pudding) after they're cooked and have slightly cooled.
* Granular aspartame looks and measures like sugar. Spoonful for spoonful, it provides the same sweetness as sugar with about one-eighth the calories.
* Acesulfame-K can be used in cooked foods because it retains its sweetness when heated. It can, however, become bitter when used in large amounts.
* Saccharin comes in both liquid and powdered forms. It has a slightly bitter aftertaste that becomes more pronounced when food is heated.
* Be careful when adding sugar substitute to food. A little goes a lot further than you might expect, and a dish can be ruined by adding too much.
* Never replace sugar with a sugar substitute in baked goods like cakes and breads, which require sugar for structure and volume.

SUGAR SYRUP   *see also* CANDY; SYRUPS *(for general information on reliquefying, measuring and so on)*

TIDBIT Sugar syrups (also called *simple syrups*) can be variously flavored and have many uses, including soaking cakes, glazing baked goods, poaching or preserving fruit, and so on. They're also the foundation for most candies.

* Sugar syrups are made in various densities: Light (5 parts water to 1 part sugar), thin (3 parts water to 1 part sugar), medium (2 parts water to 1 part sugar), and heavy (equal parts water and sugar).
* To make a sugar syrup, cook sugar and water together over low heat until the sugar dissolves. Bring the syrup to a boil and cook for 1 minute.
* A variety of flavorings can be added before the cooking begins. For spiced syrup, add cinnamon sticks, whole cloves and whole allspice. For a citrus-flavored syrup, add lemon, orange or lime zest. For coffee-flavored sugar syrup, substitute strong coffee for the water (or add 1 rounded teaspoon instant espresso powder for each cup of water). Let the flavorings cool in the syrup, then strain them out and discard.

SUNCHOKE *see* JERUSALEM ARTICHOKES

SUN-DRIED TOMATOES *see* TOMATOES

SUNFLOWER SEEDS *see* SEEDS

SWEETBREADS
TIDBIT Sweetbreads are the thymus glands of veal, beef, lamb and pork. Those from milk-fed veal or young calves are considered the best. Those from young lamb are quite good, but beef sweetbreads are tougher, and pork sweetbreads (unless from a piglet) have a rather strong flavor.
PURCHASING Choose sweetbreads that are white (they become redder as the animal ages), plump and firm. In general, sweetbreads from younger animals are the most tender.
STORING Sweetbreads are highly perishable and should be refrigerated, tightly sealed, for no more than 1 day.
PREPARING
* Sweetbreads must undergo several steps before being cooked. First soak them in cold, ACIDULATED WATER for at least 1 hour to draw out any blood. Then blanch (*see* BLANCHING) the sweetbreads for 3 to 5 minutes, and plunge into cold water to firm them. Drain the cooled sweetbreads; trim away and remove the outer membrane and any connective tissue.
* Sweetbreads will retain their shape better during cooking if you put them on a plate, cover with something flat like a small cutting board, and weigh it down with a couple of 1-pound cans. Refrigerate weighted

sweetbreads for about 2 hours. Very large sweetbreads should be sliced before being weighted.

* Sweetbreads can be braised, grilled, poached and sautéed. They're also sometimes used in pâtés and soufflés.

Condensed milk is wonderful. I don't see how they can get a cow to sit down on those little cans.
—Fred Allen, American humorist

SWEETENED CONDENSED MILK see also EVAPORATED MILK; MILK

TIDBIT Sweetened condensed milk is whole milk from which about 60 percent of the water has been removed. This condensed milk is then mixed with sugar, which makes up about 40 percent of its volume. This product is typically used in candies, custards, puddings, pies and some baked goods.

EQUIVALENTS 14-ounce can = 1¾ cups

STORING Store unopened cans of condensed milk at room temperature for up to 6 months. Once opened, transfer unused milk to an airtight container, such as a screw-top jar; refrigerate and use within 5 days.

USING

* Drizzle sweetened condensed milk over baked apples 15 minutes before they're done for a sweet, shiny glaze.

* **To carmelize sweetened condensed milk:** When heated (by microwave, oven or stovetop), sweetened condensed milk becomes thick, turns a rich golden color and takes on the flavor of caramel.

* Microwave oven method: Pour milk into a 2-quart glass or ceramic container. Cook at medium (50 percent power) for 4 minutes, stirring halfway through. Reduce power to medium-low (30 percent power); cook for 12 to 18 minutes, stirring briskly every 2 minutes until smooth, thick and caramel-colored. The cooking time will depend on the wattage of your oven.

* Oven method: Pour sweetened condensed milk into a 9-inch pie plate and cover with foil. Place the pie plate in a larger pan; fill the pan with hot water that reaches halfway up the side of the pie plate. Bake at 425°F for 1½ hours, or until thick and caramel-colored.

* Stovetop method: Pour milk into the top of a double boiler and cook over simmering water for 1½ hours. At the end of the cooking time (whichever method you use), beat the caramel until smooth.

* Heating an unopened can of sweetened condensed milk can cause it to explode.

* Don't substitute sweetened condensed milk for evaporated milk or vice

versa. The sugar in the former would ruin the flavor of dishes calling for evaporated milk.

SWEET POTATOES   *see also* POTATOES; VEGETABLES, GENERAL; YAMS

TIDBIT   The two most widely grown sweet potatoes in the United States are a pale variety and a darker-skinned species that many Americans erroneously call "yam." **Pale sweet potatoes** have a thin, light yellow skin and pale yellow flesh. Their cooked texture is dry and crumbly, much like a white baking potato, and their flavor isn't sweet. The **dark sweet potato** variety has a thicker, dark orange skin and vivid orange, sweet flesh that, when cooked, is much moister.

PURCHASING   Choose firm, small to medium specimens with smooth, unblemished skins free of soft spots.

STORING   Store in a cool, dry, well-ventilated place for up to a week. Under perfect temperature conditions (dry and around 55°F), they can be kept for up to 4 weeks. Do not refrigerate.

USING

* The pale variety of sweet potato can be substituted for regular potatoes in most recipes.
* Keep peeled, raw sweet potatoes from turning dark by soaking them in cold ACIDULATED WATER for a few minutes. Drain well before using. If the potatoes are to be fried, thoroughly blot them dry with paper towels.
* Sweet potatoes are more nutritious if cooked in their skins.
* Peeling boiled sweet potatoes is easy—just drain off the hot water, then immediately plunge the potatoes into cold water. The skins will slip right off.
* Large sweet potatoes are often very fibrous. If you use an electric mixer to beat cooked sweet potatoes, the stringy fibers will wind around the beaters, thereby leaving the potatoes smooth.
* Sweet potatoes have a natural affinity for maple syrup and freshly grated nutmeg.

BOURBON-SMASHED SWEETS

If you're not a bourbon fan, dark rum makes a tasty substitute. Those who are liquor-sensitive can use orange or apple juice with equally delicious (though decidedly different) results. Cook 2 pounds sweet potatoes until tender. Combine cooked, peeled sweet potatoes with ½ teaspoon ground cardamom, ¼ teaspoon ground nutmeg, ⅓ cup whipping cream and 2 tablespoons bourbon in a medium saucepan. Mash with a potato masher until smooth. Cook over low heat until warmed through. Salt and pepper to taste. Serves 4.

SYRUPS; SYRUPY SWEETENERS *see also* CORN SYRUP; HONEY; MAPLE SYRUP; MOLASSES; SUGAR SYRUPS

* To measure syrups, use clear measuring cups; bend down and read the measurement at eye level.

* Before measuring syrupy sweeteners such as honey and corn syrup, lightly coat the measuring cup or spoon with vegetable oil. Every drop of the syrup will easily slip out instead of clinging to the sides of the cup. The same thing can be accomplished if you measure the shortening called for in a recipe and then use the same (unwashed) utensil to measure a syrup. Or dip the measuring implement in very hot water before measuring the sweetener.

* Lightly oil a pitcher before pouring in the honey. Afterward, every speck of what's left will slip out easily and back into the honey jar.

* Reliquefy syrups that have crystallized (like honey or maple syrup) by setting the container in a pan or bowl of very hot water that comes halfway up the container. Stir after 5 minutes, then every minute or so until the honey or maple syrup is once again smooth. *To reliquefy in the microwave oven*, remove the metal lid, if there is one, and cook on high for 15 to 60 seconds, depending on how full the container is.

* Use hot water to rinse the caps of honey, maple syrup or corn syrup bottles and they'll be easier to remove the next time. Wipe off the jar or bottle rim with a paper towel soaked in warm water as well.

* Keep a syrup pitcher from dripping by dabbing some oil or butter on the inside of the pouring spout.

* Use a damp cloth to wipe off the sides and bottom of syrup bottles before returning them to the cupboard or refrigerator.

TABLE SETTINGS   *see also* SERVING AND PASSING FOOD

* Silverware setting: Forks go on the left, knives and spoons on the right; the knives should be positioned with the cutting side toward the plate. No more than 3 pieces of silverware should be placed on each side of the plate. Arrange the silver in the order it will be used, from the outside working in. Dessert utensils should be positioned at the top of the plate—the spoon should be closest to the plate, the handle on the right; the fork above the spoon, facing in the opposite direction.

* Napkins can be placed in one of several positions including under the forks, to the left of the forks, on the plate or above the plate. They may be folded in squares, rectangles or in myriad decorative shapes (*see* a napkin-folding book).

* Glassware setting: Glasses go on the right, with the water glass directly above the knife, and wine or other glasses to the right (angled, if space allows) of the water glass.

* Plate positions: The bread plate goes opposite the glasses, above the forks, with a butter knife sitting across the top of the plate. If a salad plate is used, place it to the left of the forks.

* When serving messy-to-eat foods like artichokes, corn on the cob, ribs and fried chicken, provide guests with finger bowls—a small bowl (such as a custard cup) of water with a lemon slice floating on top. Or buy inexpensive washcloths, soak them in lemon water, squeeze out excess water and fold into quarters. Place the dampened cloths in a plastic bag and set aside. Before offering them to guests, microwave for a minute or so, just until warm, not hot.

* The water should be poured and candles lit when the guests sit down. Pour the wine after they're seated.

TANGERINES   *see* ORANGES

TAPIOCA

PURCHASING Tapioca, a starch extracted from cassava roots, is commonly available in three forms. **Pearl tapioca** (which comes in both small and large sizes) and **quick-cooking tapioca** are available in most supermarkets. **Tapioca flour** or **starch** (also called *cassava flour*) is more commonly found in natural food stores and Asian and Latin American markets.

STORING Stored airtight in a cool, dry place, tapioca will keep indefinitely.

USING

* Pearl tapioca is typically used to make puddings; it must be soaked for several hours to soften it before cooking.
* Quick-cooking tapioca, a granular form, is most often used as a THICK-ENER and doesn't require presoaking.
* Both pearl and quick-cooking tapioca are cooked through when they're absolutely clear.
* Tapioca flour and quick-cooking tapioca are excellent thickeners for sauces, fruit fillings, soups, glazes, and so on. Tapioca-thickened mixtures don't require stirring during cooking, can withstand long cooking times, and don't get cloudy. Unlike cornstarch- and flour-thickened preparations, tapioca-based mixtures don't break down when frozen, then reheated. However, quick-cooking tapioca leaves tiny pieces of tapioca suspended in whatever it thickens, whereas tapioca flour produces a smooth mixture.
* If you can't find tapioca flour, and don't like the small, cooked bits that quick-cooking tapioca leaves in soups, sauces, and so on, process quick-cooking tapioca in a blender or food processor until powdery.
* To thicken mixtures with tapioca flour, first make a thin paste by combining it with water, then stir it into a hot liquid.
* Once tapioca is added to a liquid, don't let the mixture boil or the tapioca may get stringy.
* Overstirring a tapioca mixture while cooling produces a sticky, gelatinous texture.

Love and scandal are the best sweeteners of tea.
—Henry Fielding, English novelist

TEA

TIDBIT It might surprise you to know that tea wasn't always a British predilection. In fact, Britons much preferred coffee until about 1850. The gradual conversion to tea came about because it was simply more affordable—a pound of tea produced many more servings than the same amount

T of coffee. By the end of the nineteenth century, U.K. residents were consuming an average of 10 pounds per capita and never looked back.

PURCHASING Teas are available today in a variety of forms: tea bags, loose-leaf tea, regular or decaffeinated tea, instant tea, flavored tea and so-called "herbal tea." The latter isn't biologically a tea, but rather a *tisane*—a tealike drink made by steeping any of various herbs, flowers, spices, and so on, in boiling water.

STORING Store tea, tightly sealed, in a dark, cool place for up to 1 year. Add a personal touch to tea bags by storing them in an airtight jar with vanilla beans, cinnamon sticks or other spices.

ICED TEA

* Use about twice as much tea when making iced tea as you would for hot tea.
* For clear iced tea, combine tea leaves or bags with cold water; cover and refrigerate for at least 24 hours. Strain as you pour the tea into glasses.
* "Sun tea" is another way to get clear tea. Combine tea and cold water in a clear pitcher or jar; cover and let stand in the sun for about 4 hours.
* Keep brewed tea from becoming cloudy when iced by simply letting it cool to room temperature before refrigerating. Tea will become cloudy if made with boiling water and refrigerated while hot. It will clear if you stir in a little boiling water.

HOT TEA

* Use a china, glass or ceramic teapot—metal can affect the tea's flavor.
* Warm a teapot by pouring in boiling water and letting it sit for a few minutes. Drain the water just before beginning to steep the tea.
* Begin the tea-making process by filling a kettle with fresh, cold water; bring to a boil. Count on 6 ounces of water per cup of tea. If your tap water has a mineral or other off taste, use bottled water.
* Count on 1 teabag per cup; use 1 heaping teaspoon loose tea per cup, plus 1 teaspoon for the pot. Put loose leaves in a tea caddy (also called an *infuser*) to avoid straining.
* Put the tea infuser or tea bags in the warmed teapot, add boiling water and give it a quick stir. Replace the teapot lid, cover with a tea cozy, and let steep 4 to 6 minutes, depending on the tea and your palate.
* While the tea is steeping, warm the cups with hot tap water.
* Remove the tea infuser or tea bags, give the tea a gentle stir, then pour into warm cups. (Pour through a strainer if using loose tea without a caddy.)
* Whole milk has the perfect textural balance for tea. Nonfat milk makes it too thin, cream is too heavy for it.
* Sweeten tea with maple syrup for a nice change of pace.

* Forestall staining the teapot by pouring out the tea as soon as you're through; wash the pot with hot soapy water.

GENERAL

* Remedy a stale-smelling teapot by filling it with a mixture of boiling water and 2 teaspoons baking soda. Cover and let stand until cool. Wash as usual with soap and water.
* Remove teapot stains by rubbing the inside with a paste of baking soda and water; wash well with soap and hot water.
* Remove lime deposits from a tea kettle by filling it with equal amounts of white vinegar and water. Bring the mixture to a boil, then remove it from the heat and let it stand overnight. The next day, wash and use as usual.
* Drill a hole in the bottom of an old teapot and turn it into a planter. Or put ¾-inch aquarium gravel in the bottom of an undrilled tea pot and cover with soil.

TEMPERATURES—FAHRENHEIT AND CELSIUS (or CENTI-GRADE) *see also* OVENS; THERMOMETERS

* To convert Celsius (centigrade) temperatures to Fahrenheit, multiply the Celsius number by 9, divide by 5 and add 32.
* To convert Fahrenheit temperatures to Celsius (centigrade), subtract 32 from the Fahrenheit reading, multiply by 5 and divide by 9.

GENERAL TEMPERATURE EQUIVALENTS

	Fahrenheit	Celsius
Freezer	0°	−18°
Water freezes	32°	0°
Refrigerator	40°	4°
Wine storage	55°	13°
Room temperature	68°	20°
Dough-rising temp.	80°–95°	27°–35°
Lukewarm	98.5°	37°
Water simmers	180°	82°
Water boils	212°	100°

OVEN TEMPERATURES—FAHRENHEIT, CELSIUS, BRITISH, FRENCH

Oven Level	Fahrenheit	Celsius	British (Regulo) Gas Mark	French Gas Setting
Warming foods	200°–250°	93°–121°	0–¼	2–3
Very low (slow)	250°–275°	121°–133°	½–1	3
Low (or slow)	300°–325°	149°–163°	2–3	4
Moderate	350°–375°	177°–190°	4–5	4–5
Hot	400°–425°	204°–218°	6–7	5–6
Very hot	450°–475°	232°–246°	8–9	6
Extremely hot	500°–525°	260°–274°	10	

TEMPERING see CHOCOLATE (Tempering, page 112)

THAWING see FREEZING FOOD

THERMOMETERS

TIDBIT   There are many thermometers on the market, and specific types for particular uses. Cooking thermometers can range from $10 to $100, and are available in department and hardware stores, supermarkets and kitchen stores. As important as choosing the right thermometer for the right cooking method is correctly inserting the thermometer into the food.

* **Meat/all-purpose thermometers** can be used to read temperatures of everything from baked bread to fish to meat. There are many styles of food thermometers, the most popular of which follow.

* **Dial bimetal thermometers** and **liquid-filled thermometers** are oven-safe, which means they can be left in the food while it's cooking. They must be inserted about 2 inches (making them unsuitable for thin foods); the reading takes 1 to 2 minutes.

* **Dial instant-read bimetal thermometers** can be used to check temperatures toward the end of the cooking time. Insert 2 to 2½ inches and the reading will be ready in 15 to 20 seconds.

* **Digital instant-read thermometers** (also called *thermistors*) are used for readings at the end of cooking, which take only 10 seconds when inserted ½ inch deep.

* **Thermocouple thermometers,** the fastest of all, take 2 to 5 seconds to read and need only to be inserted into the food ¼ inch. They have a needlelike probe, which makes them good for meats. Look for these special thermometers in kitchenware and restaurant supply stores.

* Whichever type of thermometer you buy—regular or instant-read—look for one with a clear readout.
* Thermometers with thin probes make smaller holes in the meat from which fewer juices can escape.
* Insert a thermometer in the thickest section of the meat. If you hit a bone, gristle or fat pocket, the reading will be distorted.
* When testing the temperature of shallow liquids, tilt the pan slightly so the thermometer can go deep enough for an accurate reading.

CANDY/DEEP-FAT THERMOMETERS

* Indispensable for candymaking and deep-fat frying, most of these thermometers are in the shape of a long glass tube with a small bulb at the end. Others are a metal probe with a dial readout. Choose a clearly marked, easy-to-read thermometer with an adjustable clip to secure it to the pan.
* To use, stand the thermometer upright in the candy syrup or fat so the end is completely immersed. Don't let it touch the bottom of the pan or the temperature readout could be affected. Stoop down to read glass-tube thermometers at eye level. Watch the thermometer carefully—it can look like it's not moving for several minutes, then surprise you by shooting up above the necessary temperature.
* Check a thermometer's accuracy every so often by placing it in boiling water for 3 minutes. If it doesn't measure 212°F, calculate the difference and adjust your temperature accordingly. For example, if your thermometer reads 202°F in boiling water, it's recording temperatures 10 degrees lower than they actually are. So if a recipe specifies a candy temperature of 250°F, cook the mixture until your thermometer reads 240°F. (Note: The boiling temperature of water at high altitudes will be about 2 degrees lower per 1,000 feet above sea level.)

OVEN THERMOMETERS

* There are two styles of oven thermometer—the spring-operated dial type and the mercury-style glass tube. Glass-tube thermometers are usually much more expensive, but then they're also consistently more accurate.
* Place the thermometer on the center rack and preheat the oven for 15 minutes. If the thermometer reading doesn't agree with the oven setting, you'll need to make an adjustment. For example, if it reads 400°F when the oven is set at 350°F, you know that your oven runs 50°F hot. Therefore, when a recipe requires a 350°F temperature, set your oven to 300°F.
* It's a good idea to leave an oven thermometer in the oven, but be sure and remove it before using any automatic cleaning cycle.

T

FREEZER/REFRIGERATOR THERMOMETERS

* This type of thermometer reads temperatures from about −20° to 80°F. It's an important tool because, unless food is frozen at a temperature of 0°F or below, it will begin to deteriorate, losing both quality and nutrients.
* Position the thermometer near the top and front of the freezer. Leave it there for at least 6 hours without opening the door before checking the readout.
* If the thermometer's temperature doesn't read 0°F or below, adjust the temperature regulator as necessary; check the reading in another 6 hours.
* Refrigerator temperature may be checked in the same way, and should register at 40°F.

THICKENERS   *see also* ARROWROOT; CORNSTARCH; FLOUR

GENERAL   There are many ways to thicken sauces, soups, stews and other foods. The following are among the more popular thickeners.

* **Roux,** a mixture of flour and fat, is typically used to thicken sauces, gravies, soups and stews. The color and flavor of a roux are determined by the length of time the mixture's cooked. The roux's flavor, of course, becomes incorporated into that of the food. See ROUX for details.
* ***Beurre manié*** is a mixture of equal parts flour and softened butter, blended together to form a smooth paste. Bits of *beurre manié* are stirred into a boiling mixture until it thickens.
* **Slurry** is a simple mixture of equal amounts of flour and cold water used for thickening. No precooking is required; however, after the slurry is stirred into a hot mixture, it should be cooked for at least 5 minutes to diminish the flour's raw taste.
* **Cornstarch** and **arrowroot** both have a stronger thickening power than that of flour. When using these thickeners, combine them first with a little liquid (broth, wine, water), stirring to make a paste. Always stir the liquid into the starch, rather than vice versa. Adding dry cornstarch or arrowroot directly to a mixture will create lumps. *See* ARROWROOT and CORNSTARCH for individual preparation details.
* Use a whisk when adding a flour-, cornstarch- or other starch-based paste to a hot liquid. Whisk the liquid rapidly while drizzling in the starch mixture to thoroughly disperse it.
* **Eggs** are typically used to thicken custards, sauces and soups. You can use either whole eggs, yolks only or a combination of the two. When thickening with eggs, care must be taken not to heat them too quickly.

[466]

The best way to handle this is to lightly beat the eggs, then rapidly stir in some of the hot mixture. Over low heat, slowly stir in the warmed egg fusion and keep stirring until the mixture is thickened as desired.

* **Potatoes** are one of my favorite thickeners. Combine cooked potatoes with a little liquid, PURÉE, then stir into the mixture being thickened. Cook a potato quickly by quartering it and putting it in a microwave-safe bowl with a tablespoon of water. Cover and cook on high for 5 minutes, or until the potato is done. Mash the potato with a fork, then scoop it out of the skin directly into the mixture being thickened. You can also freeze leftover mashed potatoes in ½-cup blobs and stir into a sauce or gravy. Or save the flesh of leftover baked potatoes, mash with a little liquid and use the same way. And, though I don't recommend them for general consumption, instant mashed potatoes also work. Add a tablespoon or two, then wait a minute to check the thickening action before adding more.

* **Cooked rice** works the same way. Purée it with enough liquid (wine, broth or some of the mixture you'll be thickening) to create a thick but pourable mixture.

* **Bread** also makes a good thickener. Cut off the crusts, then crumble the bread, a little at a time, directly into the liquid to be thickened. Start with about ¼ cup crumbs and add more if necessary. White bread isn't your only option—rye or wheat can add a hearty flavor to soups and stews.

* **Quick-cooking oatmeal** can be used in the same way as bread, as can leftover cooked oatmeal.

* **Tapioca flour** and **quick-cooking tapioca** are good for thickening mixtures such as sauces, fruit fillings, soups and glazes. Tapioca-thickened mixtures don't require stirring during cooking, can withstand long cooking times and don't get cloudy. Tapioca flour produces a smooth texture; quick-cooking tapioca leaves tiny pieces of tapioca suspended in whatever it thickens. For details, *see* TAPIOCA.

* **Vegetable purée** can thicken and flavor soups and sauces. If you're making a soup, simply cook more vegetables than you'll need, remove them from the soup with a slotted spoon, and purée them in a blender with a little liquid. Stir the purée back into the soup. It's a low-calorie, high-nutrition way to thicken soup. Save leftover cooked vegetables to purée and stir into sauces.

TOFU

TIDBIT   Also known as bean *curd* and *soybean curd*, tofu is made from curdled soymilk, an iron-rich liquid extracted from ground, cooked soybeans. It has a bland, slightly nutty taste that has the chameleonlike capability of taking on the flavor of whatever food with which it's cooked.

PURCHASING Tofu is available in natural food stores, Asian markets and supermarkets. It's sold packaged in water, vacuum-packed and in bulk in large crocks. Unrefrigerated tofu sitting out in water invites unfriendly bacteria, so it's safest to buy it in sealed, refrigerated packages. **Regular tofu** is sold in blocks or cakes in three styles—soft, firm and extra-firm. It comes in regular, low-fat and nonfat varieties. **Silken tofu** is named for its smooth texture and comes in soft, regular and firm styles. Various producers make flavored or smoked tofu.

EQUIVALENTS 1 pound = 2¾ cups cubes, 2 cups crumbled, 1⅔ cups puréed

STORING Because it's highly perishable, tofu should be refrigerated for no more than a week. If it's packed in water, drain and cover with fresh water. All tofu should be covered with water, which should be changed daily. Tofu can be frozen (sans water) for up to 3 months, but will have a slightly chewier texture when thawed.

USING

* Tofu can be baked, broiled, sautéed, fried, deep-fried and grilled. It can be used in myriad preparations, including salads, salad dressings, spreads, dips, egg dishes, soups, sandwiches, sauces and even desserts.
* Add flavor by marinating tofu in your favorite marinade or salad dressing. Cut it in cubes so there will be more sides to absorb the marinade.
* When stir-frying, add cubes of tofu to the dish during the last few minutes to keep them from breaking up.
* Marinate and skewer tofu cubes, brush with oil and grill.
* Freezing helps tofu keep its shape in long-cooking dishes like soups. Cut the tofu into bite-sized cubes, then double wrap in freezer-weight bags and freeze overnight or for up to a week. Pop the frozen cubes right into the soup, and cook as desired. Freezing will darken the color of tofu and alter its texture, but won't affect its flavor.
* Silken tofu is so light that it can be whipped and stirred or folded into puddings, scrambled eggs, soups, and so on.

TOMATILLOS

TIDBIT Tomatillos resemble small green tomatoes in size, shape and appearance except for their thin parchment-like husks. They have a crisp texture and a flavor that hints of a lemon-apple-herb combination. They're also called *Mexican green tomatoes* (*tomate verde* in Mexico).

PURCHASING Choose firm, evenly colored tomatillos with dry, tight-fitting husks. The smaller the fruit, the sweeter it will be. Tomatillos can ripen to yellow, but are more generally available (and used) green. They can be found in Latin-American markets, produce stores and some supermarkets. Tomatillos are also available canned.

EQUIVALENTS   1 pound = about 2 cups sliced, one 11-ounce can

STORING   Refrigerate tomatillos in a paper bag for up to 1 month. They may also be frozen whole or sliced.

PREPARING   Remove husks and wash tomatillos (they're sticky).

USING

* Though tomatillos are often used raw in salads and salsas, cooking enhances their flavor and softens their skin.

* They can be halved or sliced and briefly sautéed, grilled or broiled. As with tomatoes, tomatillos will soften and collapse if cooked too long.

* Halve and simmer tomatillos in a small amount of water, covered, until they become saucelike (about 5 minutes). Add this "sauce" to everything from sauces to dressings to soups as a flavoring.

> *I grow my own tomatoes every summer for the same*
> *reason I diet: it makes me feel righteous!*
> —Bert Greene, American author, journalist, wit

TOMATOES   *see also* TOMATO PASTE; TOMATO PURÉE; TOMATO SAUCE

TIDBIT   Although typically thought of as a vegetable, the tomato is really a fruit and a member of the nightshade family, along with potatoes, red peppers and eggplant. Tomatoes are low in sodium and pack a nutritional bonus of vitamins A, B and C, potassium, magnesium, phosphorus and fiber. They also contain lycopene, an antioxidant that may help prevent heart disease and that retains its value throughout cooking or freezing. Tomatoes are culinary changlings, assuming an entirely different character when raw than with slow, lengthy cooking.

PURCHASING

* Fresh tomatoes: There are thousands of tomato varieties ranging in size from ½ inch to 5 inches in diameter and in colors from red to orange to purple. Buy those that are firm, well shaped, richly colored (for their variety) and noticeably fragrant. They should be free of blemishes, heavy for their size and give slightly to palm pressure. Vine-ripened tomatoes are very perishable and therefore have a short shelf life. That's why most supermarkets carry tomatoes that have been picked green and ripened with ethylene gas. And there's no way that gassed tomatoes will ever have the texture, aroma and taste of vine-ripened fruit.

* Sun-dried tomatoes: These can be dried either in the sun or by artificial methods. The resulting dark red tomato is chewy, intensely flavored and sweet. Sun-dried tomatoes are typically packed in oil or dry-packed in cellophane.
* Canned tomatoes: Surprisingly, this form is often a more flavorful choice for cooked dishes and can even be used in salads. The flavor of canned Italian plum tomatoes is better by far than that of underripe or out-of-season fresh tomatoes.

EQUIVALENTS

* Fresh: 1 pound = about 3 medium globe tomatoes, 8 small plum tomatoes, 25 to 30 cherry tomatoes, 2 cups chopped
* Canned: 14½-ounce can = 1¾ cups, including juice

STORING

* Fresh tomatoes: Store ripe tomatoes, stem side down, at room temperature away from direct sunlight and use within a few days. Never refrigerate tomatoes! Cold temperatures make the flesh pulpy and destroy the flavor.
* Sun-dried tomatoes: Unopened dry- and oil-packed forms can be stored at room temperature for up to a year. Once opened, store dry-packed tomatoes in a zip-closure bag in a cool, dark place for 6 months. Oil-packed tomatoes should be covered with olive oil and refrigerated for up to 3 months.

PREPARING FRESH TOMATOES

* Ripen tomatoes by putting them with an apple in a paper bag pierced with a few holes. Let stand at room temperature for 2 to 3 days.
* Wash the tomatoes thoroughly before you stem, core and cut them.
* A good tomato knife with a sturdy, 4- to 5-inch serrated blade is relatively inexpensive and easily cuts tomatoes into neat slices. The next best bet is to pierce the skin with the tip of a sharp knife then cut into the pierced place.
* Tomato slices will hold their shape better and exude less juice if you slice vertically, from stem end to blossom end.
* Tomato peel contains fiber and nutrients, so don't peel tomatoes to be used raw for salads, salsas and sandwiches, or for quickly cooked dishes.
* In long-cooking dishes, tomato skins shrivel and toughen, adding an unappetizing texture. Peeling is optional for tomatoes that are to be finely chopped, as the tiny bits of skin aren't typically objectionable, particularly in chunky mixtures.
* **Tomato peeling method 1:** Skewer a cored tomato with a large, two-pronged fork and hold it over a gas flame, turning continually, just until

the skin begins to split, from 30 to 60 seconds, depending on the size and variety of tomato. Pull off the shreds of puckered skin.

* **Tomato peeling method 2:** Use a sharp knife to cut a shallow X-shaped slash on the tomato's base. Drop the tomatoes into a pot of boiling water for about 15 seconds for very ripe tomatoes, up to 30 seconds for firmer tomatoes. Remove the tomatoes from the hot water with a slotted spoon and place in a bowl of ice water to stop the cooking process. Use a paring knife to peel the skin away from the cooled tomatoes.

* **Tomato peeling method 3:** Pierce the top of a tomato with the tines of a fork. Microwave on high for 15 seconds; let stand for 2 minutes before peeling.

* **To core:** Insert the tip of a paring knife at an angle at the edge of the core. Cut about 1 inch into the flesh all the way around the core.

* **To seed:** Cut round tomatoes in half horizontally, plum tomatoes in half vertically. Set a strainer over a bowl and either scoop out the seeds with a spoon or gently squeeze the seeds out into it. The strainer will trap the seeds while any juice goes into the bowl to use as you like. *Seed a whole tomato* by cutting off the top ½ inch. Use a grapefruit spoon or dinner teaspoon to scoop out seeds and core. *Seed cherry tomatoes* by cutting them in half, then sticking your thumb or finger into the halves and flicking out the seeds.

* Crush seeded tomatoes by rubbing the cut side over the large holes of a box grater.

* **Freezing tomatoes:** Save the summer tomato bounty by making sauce out of them and then freezing the sauce. Or freeze the tomatoes whole with a method my friend Lee Janvrin taught me: Place fresh-picked, ripe but firm tomatoes in a freezer-weight plastic bag and freeze until solid. If you want the tomatoes cored, do so before freezing, but *don't wash them*. When ready to use, briefly run the frozen tomato under luke-warm (not hot!) water, which not only washes the tomato, but loosens the skin. Use your fingers or a paring knife to pull off the skin, then core and add the frozen tomato to a sauce, soup or any other dish where you would normally use puréed tomatoes (freezing breaks down the tomato's cells so that they don't hold their shape). One caveat: Thawing the tomatoes before using them allows much of their juice to escape.

* Whole canned tomatoes can be cut right in the can by snipping them with kitchen shears.

PREPARING SUN-DRIED TOMATOES

* The flavor of sun-dried tomatoes is quite intense—a little goes a long way.

T

* Dry-packed tomatoes can be rehydrated by soaking them in hot water to cover for 30 minutes. Drain before using; save the flavorful water to use in other dishes.

* Moisten dry-packed tomatoes by covering them with a good olive oil and letting them stand at room temperature for at least 24 hours. Use the flavorful oil for sautés or salad dressings, or simply to drizzle over French bread.

* When cutting one or two sun-dried tomato halves, use kitchen shears to snip as desired.

* PURÉE oil-packed or softened dry-packed tomatoes, mix with a little olive oil, tarragon, salt and pepper, and spread on crostini. Add to salad dressings or soups, or rub on chicken to be baked, or combine with sour cream to make a dip.

USING TOMATOES

* Add tomatoes to a tossed green salad just before serving so the natural juices don't make the greens soggy or dilute the dressing.

* Improve the flavor of raw or cooked tomatoes by adding a pinch of sugar and a dash of salt. Both bring out a tomato's natural flavors. A small amount of sugar will temper overtly acidic tomatoes.

* Cooking tomato-based dishes in an aluminum pan gives them a bitter undertaste and darkens the bright red color.

* For stuffed tomatoes, either cut the tomato in half or cut a slice off the top, then scoop out the seeds and pulp with a spoon. Turn the hollowed-out tomatoes upside down on paper towels to drain for at least 15 minutes before stuffing.

* Support stuffed tomatoes while baking by placing them in lightly greased muffin tins.

* To prevent tomato-based foods such as pasta sauce from staining plastic utensils and storage containers, liberally spray the containers with cooking spray.

ICED TOMATO SOUP

So easy, so delicious! Save on calories by using a good low- or nonfat sour cream (I like the Naturally Yours brand). This recipe doubles easily (make it in batches) and can be refrigerated for up to 2 days. Combine 2 large, ripe tomatoes (cored and quartered), 2 cups V-8 juice, 1 cup sour cream, 2 tablespoons chopped fresh tarragon or mint leaves, 1 small garlic clove and 1 teaspoon sugar in a blender. Cover and process (starting at low speed and gradually increasing to high) until smooth. If a perfectly smooth texture is desired, pour through a fine strainer into a large bowl. Salt and pepper to taste. Cover and refrigerate for 2 hours, or until cold. If the soup is too thick, add V-8 juice to thin. Serve cold, garnished with tarragon sprigs, if desired. Serves 6.

ROASTED TOMATOES

Roasting tomatoes intensifies their flavor, making even lackluster specimens taste better. Chop and toss with pasta, use to top crostini, add to polenta, salads, rice— the list is endless. Preheat the oven to 200°F. Cut the tomatoes in half (crosswise for regular tomatoes, lengthwise for plum tomatoes). Place tomatoes, cut sides up, in a baking pan large enough for them to be in a single layer. Drizzle with a little extra virgin olive oil (combined with minced garlic, if you like); salt and pepper to taste. Roast for 6 to 8 hours—the longer they cook, the more intense their flavor. Cool, then refrigerate in an airtight container for up to 2 weeks. Bring to room temperature before using.

TOMATO PASTE; TOMATO PURÉE; TOMATO SAUCE *see also*

TOMATOES

PURCHASING

* Tomato paste: A deep red, richly flavored concentrate that's made of tomatoes that have been cooked for several hours, strained and reduced. It's available in cans or tubes.
* Tomato purée: A thick, rich mixture made of tomatoes that have been cooked briefly and strained. It's available in cans.
* Tomato sauce: This is a slightly thinner tomato purée. Some styles are seasoned so that the sauce is ready to add to soups, sauces and other preparations.

EQUIVALENTS

* Tomato paste: 4½-ounce tube = 5 tablespoons
* Tomato purée: 1 cup=½ cup tomato paste plus water to equal 1 cup
* Tomato sauce: 1 cup=⅜ cup tomato paste plus water to equal 1 cup

USING

* When a recipe calls for tomato paste and all you have is tomato sauce, for each tablespoon of tomato paste, add ½ cup tomato sauce and reduce the liquid in the recipe by ¼ cup.
* The next time you need a small amount of tomato paste, buy it in a tube instead of a can. Because so little of the tubed paste is exposed to the air, it can be tightly sealed and refrigerated for up to 1 year.
* To freeze leftover tomato paste: Line a pie pan with plastic wrap. Place level tablespoons of paste at 1-inch intervals on the plastic wrap. Freeze, uncovered, until solid. Fold over the edges of the plastic wrap to cover the tomato paste, place the contents in a plastic bag and freeze until ready to use. The tablespoons of frozen paste can be dropped right into hot mixtures like soups and sauces.
* Use a dab of tomato paste to enliven flat-flavored soups or sauces.

TORTILLAS

PURCHASING Tortillas are available in supermarkets, either on the shelf or in the refrigerated section. Corn tortillas are made from corn flour (masa), flour tortillas are made with all-purpose or whole-wheat flour. There are also low-cholesterol tortillas, which are made without lard.

STORING Refrigerate in a plastic bag for up to 1 week. Freeze for up to 3 months; place a sheet of waxed paper between tortillas so they'll separate easily.

USING

* Tortillas can be eaten plain, as bread with chili or other dishes, or wrapped around various fillings, as for a sandwich.
* To warm tortillas, stack them on top of each other, wrap in foil and heat at 350°F for 10 to 15 minutes.
* Or wrap them loosely in waxed paper or place in a plastic bag and microwave on high—15 seconds for 2 tortillas, 25 seconds for 4, 40 seconds for 8.

TORTILLA CHIPS

Lightly brush flour or corn tortillas with olive or vegetable oil, season to taste with salt and pepper or chili powder. Stack the tortillas; cut the stack into 12 wedges. Arrange the wedges in a single layer on a lightly oiled baking sheet; bake at 350°F for 5 to 10 minutes (flour tortillas don't take as long as corn) until crisp. Cool on paper towels and store airtight at room temperature for up to 5 days.

TRANS FATTY ACIDS *see* FATS AND OILS

TUNA *For buying, storing and cooking information, see* FISH, GENERAL; FISH, COOKING METHODS

PURCHASING

* Fresh tuna: **Albacore tuna** has a pale pink, high-fat, mild-flavored flesh; **yellowfin tuna** is ruby red and full-flavored; **bluefin tuna** is a deep ruby color, high in fat and moderately flavored; and **bonito** has a dark red, moderate- to high-fat, strongly flavored flesh.
* Canned tuna: This popular favorite is cooked before being packed in oil or water. Albacore tuna is the only one that can be labeled "white meat," although the color may range from tan to pink. Canned tuna comes in three grades, the best being solid or fancy (large pieces), followed by chunk (smaller pieces) and flaked (bits and pieces).

EQUIVALENT 6-ounce can = about ⅔ cup drained

STORING

* Fresh tuna: *See* FISH for storage information.
* Canned tuna can be stored, unopened, in a cool place for several years, providing the cans are intact. Once opened, refrigerate and use within 2 days. Canned tuna can be frozen if transferred to a container suitable for freezing.

USING

* Fresh tuna has a tender, rich-flavored flesh that's so firm it feels like meat in the mouth. It can be cooked by almost any cooking method, but is particularly good grilled or sautéed. This fish becomes exceedingly firm when cooked, so watch it carefully. *See* FISH, GENERAL, for cooking suggestions.
* Water-packed canned tuna (which also contains vegetable broth) not only has many fewer calories than oil-packed tuna, but it also has a fresher flavor.
* Keep a can or two in the refrigerator to speed making tuna salad or sandwiches.
* Be sure to wash the blades of a can opener after opening tuna or other cans.
* Canned tuna is good for myriad preparations, including tuna casseroles, sandwiches, salads, dips, soups and spreads.
* For tuna sandwiches, don't waste money on solid- or chunk-style tuna, since the mixture will be broken up anyway.
* Avoid "wet" sandwiches and salads by draining tuna well—put it in a strainer and press down with the back of a spoon.

TURKEY *see also* CHICKEN; GROUND MEAT; POULTRY, GENERAL; STUFFING; THERMOMETERS

TIDBIT Wild turkeys populated the United States, Mexico and Central America long before colonists arrived in the New World. The conquistadors returned to Spain with crates of domesticated turkeys, which soon became quite popular. Most turkeys raised in the United States today are of the White Holland variety and are bred to produce a maximum of white meat (America's favorite). As a matter of fact, today turkeys have breasts that are so massive they can't get close enough to mate and have to rely on artificial insemination.

PURCHASING

* Choose a turkey that's plump and white with a well-rounded breastbone. Hens and toms are about equally tender, although hens are com-

T

monly more expensive. You'll get more meat per pound with a large turkey. Buying two small turkeys instead of one large one offers a double bonus: more drumsticks, thighs, wings and giblets, and a shorter cooking time.

✳ Turkey-label terms: **Fresh**—chilled to at least 40°F but not lower than 26°F; **frozen**—rapidly frozen to below 32°F, then stored at 0°F or lower; **natural**—contains nothing artificial or synthetic (such as coloring or chemical preservatives) and is minimally processed; **kosher**—prepared under rabbinical direction; **basted/self-basting**—injected or marinated with a liquid (typically a combination of broth, stock or water, butter or other fat, flavorings and preservatives) that can add up to 12 percent of the net weight.

✳ How much per serving (add extra if you want leftovers): **Whole turkeys**—6 to 12 pounds, about ¾ to 1 pound; over 12 pounds, ½ to ¾ pound. **Bone-in cuts**—breast, ⅓ to ½ pound; thigh or drumstick—½ pound. **Boneless cuts**—⅓ pound.

EQUIVALENT   12-pound turkey = about 16 cups cooked meat
STORING

✳ Whole raw turkeys and breasts: Refrigerate in the original wrapping for up to 2 days. Double wrap and freeze whole turkeys for up to 1 year, turkey breasts for up to 3 months.

✳ Frozen whole turkeys and breasts: Keep frozen until ready to defrost.

✳ Cooked turkey: Refrigerate for up to 4 days. Freeze sliced turkey in a freezer-proof container or wrapping for up to 4 months; turkey covered with gravy for up to 6 months.

THAWING TURKEY

✳ Whole turkeys must be thawed at a safe temperature (40°F or below) to prevent harmful bacteria present before freezing to begin growing again.

✳ **Refrigerator thawing:** This is the best, safest method but advance planning's required. Allow 24 hours per 5 pounds—an 8-pound turkey can take 1½ days, whereas a 20-pound turkey can take at least 4 days.

✳ **Cold-water thawing:** Place the turkey in sealed, leakproof packaging; submerge in cold water. Change the water every 30 minutes until the turkey is thawed. Count on a minimum of 30 minutes per pound: 8 to 12 pounds—4 to 6 hours; 12 to 16 pounds—6 to 8 hours; 16 to 20 pounds—8 to 19 hours; 20 to 24 pounds—10 to 12 hours. Since this type of thawing isn't temperature controlled, the turkey should be cooked immediately.

✳ **Microwave thawing:** Follow your microwave oven instruction booklet for thawing a whole turkey. Immediately cook the turkey once it's thawed to prevent bacterial problems.

STUFFING TURKEY *see* STUFFING

PREPARING TURKEY FOR COOKING

* Remove a whole fresh or thawed turkey from the refrigerator about 1 hour before cooking.
* Remove the giblets, neck and liver from the body or neck cavity. Wrap and refrigerate until ready to use in gravy and/or stuffing. Rinse off the turkey and use paper towels to pat it dry inside and out.
* Season the cavity of an unstuffed turkey with salt, pepper and poultry seasoning; place a couple of quartered onions in it.
* Pull the skin over the neck and fasten with a skewer. Tie the legs and tail together; twist the wings under the back.
* Brush the exterior with melted butter or oil and season with salt and pepper.
* Or add a delicious smoky flavor by covering the turkey with strips of bacon secured with toothpicks.
* Turkey will almost baste itself if you cover it with a double layer of cheesecloth that's been soaked in butter or canola or olive oil. When the cheesecloth's removed at the end of the roasting time, the bird will be moist and golden brown. For a crisp, brown skin, take off the cheesecloth 30 minutes before the bird is done.
* Place turkey breast side up or down (turkeys started breast side down will be flipped halfway through cooking), on a rack in a roasting pan. A turkey will cook faster in dark pans. The depth and size of the pan also affect heat flow around the bird. The larger the pan, the more freely the heat circulates.
* An oven-cooking bag can reduce a turkey's cooking time by up to 1 hour and give you a beautifully browned bird.
* Don't let the raw turkey juices touch any ready-to-eat food.
* Thoroughly wash your hands and any utensils, dishes or surfaces that came in contact with the raw turkey with hot, soapy water.

ROASTING TURKEY

* The recommended temperature for roasting turkey is 325°F. To crisp and brown the skin, increase the temperature to 400°F during the last 10 minutes of cooking time.
* If you start the turkey breast side down, flip it breast side up halfway through the cooking time.
* **Timing** depends on the temperature of the turkey when it goes into the oven. The following approximate cooking times are based on thawed turkeys just out of the refrigerator (40°F). For frozen or partially thawed turkeys, count on the cooking time taking at least 50 percent longer.

* **Unstuffed turkey:** 8 to 12 pounds—2¾ to 3 hours; 12 to 14 pounds—3 to 3¾ hours; 14 to 18 pounds—3¾ to 4¼ hours; 18 to 20 pounds—4¼ to 4½ hours; 20 to 24 pounds—4½ to 5 hours.
* **Turkey breasts:** 4 to 6 pounds—1½ to 2¼ hours; 6 to 8 pounds—2¼ to 3¼ hours.
* **Stuffed turkey:** 8 to 12 pounds—3 to 3½ hours; 12 to 14 pounds—3½ to 4 hours; 14 to 18 pounds—4 to 4¼ hours; 18 to 20 pounds—4¼ to 4¾ hours; 20 to 24 pounds—4¾ to 5¼ hours.
* Never partially cook a turkey, to be finished later—that invites food poisoning.
* To speed the cooking, put a lid on the pan.
* If the breast is cooking faster than the thigh, cover it lightly with foil and continue roasting.
* Basting turkey toughens the skin slightly and it won't be as crispy. But if you do baste it, don't do so more than once an hour. Each time the oven door's opened, heat is lost and the cooking time is lengthened.
* Pop-up timers found in many turkeys can often be broken or otherwise unreliable. Use a meat THERMOMETER to test a whole turkey for doneness.
* **Doneness test:** Check for doneness about ½ hour before the turkey's due to be finished. Insert a thermometer into the thickest (innermost) part of the thigh. The thigh should read 175°F, the breast (at the thickest part) should be 160° to 165°F. If the bird is stuffed, the center of the stuffing should read 165°F.
* When the thermometer registers about three degrees below the desired temperature, remove the turkey from the oven. Residual heat will continue to cook it.
* No thermometer? Pierce the turkey with a fork—the juices should run clear, not pink. The meat should be fork-tender, the leg move easily in the joint.
* Cover the roasted turkey lightly with foil and let it stand at room temperature for 20 minutes to allow the natural juices to redistribute throughout the flesh. This produces an evenly moist bird that's easier to carve.
* Remove stuffing from the turkey before storing leftovers.

TURNIPS   see also GREENS; VEGETABLES, GENERAL
TIDBIT   The true turnip has a white skin with a purple-tinged top. The so-called yellow turnip, though a turnip relative, is actually a rutabaga.

PURCHASING Small, young turnips have a delicate, slightly sweet taste. Look for those that are about 2 inches in diameter and heavy for their size. They should be firm and have unblemished skins; any attached greens should be brightly colored.

EQUIVALENT 1 pound = about 2½ cups chopped

STORING

* Refrigerate turnips in a plastic bag for up to 2 weeks. Turnips do best, however, if stored in a cool (55°F), dark, well-ventilated place.

* Turnip greens should be removed before the turnips are stored. Remove the leaves from the midrib; wash the greens and pat dry with paper towels. Wrap loosely in dry paper towels, then put in a tightly sealed plastic bag and refrigerate for up to 3 days.

PREPARING Before using, trim turnip stem and root ends. Baby turnips can simply be scrubbed and cooked whole; larger turnips should be peeled and quartered or chopped before cooking.

COOKING

* Turnips may be boiled or steamed, then mashed or puréed (see PURÉE-ING). They're also delicious cubed and sautéed, either alone or with other vegetables. Chopped turnips add texture and flavor to soups and stews.

* Add crunch to salads with cubed or julienned raw turnips.

* For information on cooking turnip greens, see GREENS.

* A salad of tossed greens (including turnip greens) and julienned turnips packs a double flavor whammy.

T

The truth about vanilla is that it's as much a smell as a taste.
—Diane Ackerman, American author, poet

VANILLA

TIDBIT The term "plain vanilla" has nothing to do with reality. Indeed, the sweet promise of vanilla's seductive aroma and complex flavor is at once comforting and intensely sensual. And no wonder vanilla has such an exotic appeal—it's derived from a luminous celadon-colored orchid—the only one of over 20,000 orchid varieties that bears anything edible. The labor-intensive pollination process must be done either by the Melipone bee and the hummingbird or by human hands. So let's not hear any more "plain vanilla" talk, for nothing about this tropical orchid fruit is ordinary.

PURCHASING Always buy **pure vanilla extract**, which is clear, dark brown and richly fragrant. It's more expensive than its imitator, but you only have to use half as much. **Imitation vanilla** is made entirely of artificial flavorings and often has a harsh, bitter aftertaste. Both pure and imitation vanillas are available in supermarkets. **Pure vanilla essence** is a distilled product so concentrated that only a few drops are typically necessary to flavor food. **Vanilla powder** has an advantage in that the flavor doesn't dissipate as rapidly when heated. The vanilla essence and powder are available in gourmet shops, cake-decorating supply shops and through mail order. **Vanilla beans** should be plump and moist, not dry and shriveled.

EQUIVALENTS 1 whole vanilla bean = about 1 tablespoon pure vanilla extract; 1 (2-inch) length = about 1 teaspoon pure vanilla extract

STORING

* Extract: Store, sealed airtight, in a cool, dark place indefinitely.
* Vanilla beans: Wrap tightly in plastic wrap, place in an airtight jar and refrigerate for up to 6 months.

USING

* Vanilla descriptions on labels can be confusing. *Natural vanillin* is a substance intrinsic to the vanilla bean, whereas *artificial vanillin* is made from wood-pulp by-products. Foods like ice cream or pudding that carry the label "natural vanilla flavoring" contain only pure vanilla extract. The words "vanilla flavoring" mean that a blend of pure and imitation vanillas was used, whereas "artificially flavored" tells you it's entirely imitation.

* To use a vanilla bean in foods like ice cream mixtures, custards and cake batters, use a pointed knife to slit it lengthwise down the center. Scrape out the minuscule seeds with the tip of a pointed spoon or knife and add directly to the mixture.

* Removing the seeds is easier if the pods are soft. Soften by steaming 1 to 2 minutes in a steamer or sieve over boiling water. Cool slightly before slitting the pod.

* Or you can split the vanilla bean (leaving the seeds intact) and drop it into a cooked mixture such as custard. Remove the bean before serving.

* Don't throw out a whole vanilla bean that you've used whole to flavor a sauce or custard. Simply rinse it well, dry thoroughly and store for use in recipes or for sprinkling over baked goods.

* Reuse a dried vanilla bean by processing it in a food processor with ½ to 1 cup granulated or confectioners' sugar until the bean's finely ground. Strain through a fine sieve and store to use as desired. *See also* Vanilla Sugar recipe, page 453.

* The flavor of vanilla extract diminishes greatly with heat, so always add it to a cooked mixture after it's cooled slightly.

* Sweeten your refrigerator by putting a few drops of vanilla extract on a cotton ball. Set it in a custard cup and put it at the back of a shelf.

VANILLA EXTRACT

Place a split vanilla bean and ¾ cup vodka in a screw-top jar. Seal tightly and let stand in a cool, dark place for 4 to 6 months; shake the jar occasionally during that time.

VEAL *see also* BEEF; MEAT, GENERAL

PURCHASING Though there are no precise age standards for veal, the term is generally used to describe a young calf 1 to 3 months old. However, many markets sell meat from animals up to 9 months old when slaughtered as veal. Milk-fed veal is considered premium, and comes from calves that have been raised on milk. Their delicate flesh is firm and creamy white with a pale grayish pink tinge. Other calves are fed grain or grass, which results in a slightly coarser texture and stronger flavor—the flesh is a pale pink color. In general, the darker the meat, the older the calf. Choose fine-textured veal that's ivory-colored with a pink to creamy pink tinge; the fat should be very white.

STORING If it will be cooked within 8 hours of purchase, leave veal in its store wrapping. Otherwise, remove the packaging and wrap loosely with waxed paper. Store in the coldest part of the refrigerator for no more than 2 days. The object is to let the air circulate and keep the meat's surface somewhat dry, thereby inhibiting rapid bacterial growth.

PREPARING
* Pound veal scallops before cooking to make them as thin as possible.
* Breading cutlets and chops helps seal in veal's precious moisture.
* Veal is delicate and should be cooked gently, more like poultry than beef. Moist-cooking methods like braising and low-temperature roasting or brief sautéing work well.
* Because it's so lean, veal roast requires barding to keep it moist. Or you can simply lay strips of salt pork over the roast's surface.
* Let a cooked veal roast rest at room temperature for about 15 minutes to set the juices. Remove the roast from the oven when it reaches an internal temperature of 155°F. Residual heat will continue to cook the roast during the resting time, raising the temperature 5° to 10°F.
* Overcooking any cut of veal will toughen and ruin its texture.
* Ground veal needs added fat or it becomes too dry during cooking.
* Strongly flavored sauces or side dishes will overpower veal's delicate flavor.

No vegetable exists which is not better slightly undercooked.
—James Beard, American cookbook author

VEGETABLES, GENERAL *see also* ARTICHOKES; ASPARAGUS; BEANS, FRESH GREEN OR WAX; BEETS; BELL PEPPERS; BOK CHOY; BROCCOFLOWER; BROCCOLI; BROCCOLINI; BRUSSELS SPROUTS; CABBAGE; CARROTS; CAULIFLOWER; CELERY; CELERY ROOT; CORN; CUCUMBERS; EGGPLANT; FENNEL; GREENS; JERUSALEM ARTICHOKES; JICAMA; MUSHROOMS; OKRA; ONIONS; PARSNIPS; POTATOES; PUMPKINS; RADISHES; RUTABAGA; SCALLIONS; SPINACH; SQUASH, SUMMER; SQUASH, WINTER; SWEET POTATOES; TURNIPS; YAMS

TIDBIT Research indicates that the family of cruciferous vegetables may provide protection against certain cancers. Those vegetables—all high in fiber, vitamins and minerals—include broccoli, Brussels sprouts, cabbage, cauliflower, chard, kale, mustard greens, rutabagas and turnips.

GENERAL

* The "baby vegetables" available in many markets can be one of two things—they're either the early-harvested youngsters of the species, or specially developed miniature yet mature vegetables.
* In general, the smaller the vegetable, the younger it is and the more tender it will be.
* Some vegetables—such as bell peppers and cucumbers—are coated with wax to extend shelf life, seal in moisture and improve appearance. Though the waxes are safe to eat, they may contain pesticide residues. The FDA (Food and Drug Administration) requires waxed produce to be identified with signs, but this is rarely done. Some waxed vegetables are obvious by their shine and feel. If you're not sure, ask the produce manager.
* Buying vegetables in prepackaged bags is risky because you can't check for signs of spoilage.
* Remove the leaves from root vegetables like beets and carrots as soon as you get home. The greens leach moisture from the vegetable.
* Leaving the peel on vegetables and fruits gives you a bonus of fiber and nutrition. Don't worry about any chemical residues on vegetable peels. The FDA reports that, during annual random produce testing, 99 percent of the produce is either residue free or well below EPA (Environmental Protection Agency) limits. Scrub the vegetables with tap water and a vegetable brush to reduce or remove any chemical residue.
* Recrisp limp vegetables like carrots, celery and cucumbers by soaking them in ice water for at least 1 hour.
* Chop enough vegetables or herbs (bell peppers, carrots, onions or parsley) for two meals. Cover and refrigerate part of the vegetables to use the next day.

COOKING

* It's not necessary to thaw frozen vegetables (such as corn and peas) before adding them to dishes like soups and casseroles. Add them frozen to stir-fries and sautés, and cook for about 3 minutes.
* Don't add baking soda to the cooking water for green vegetables like green beans and peas. It may help keep them green, but it will leach out valuable nutrients in the process. The best way to keep veggies green is not to overcook them.
* Retain the color of vegetables like broccoli and green beans by cooking them uncovered, and never with acidic ingredients like lemon juice, vinegar or wine. The condensation that forms on the pan lid and drips back onto the vegetables and acid ingredients causes a chemical reaction that turns the vegetable's color drab.

* On the other hand, the natural acid in lemon juice preserves and improves the naturally white color of vegetables like cauliflower, celeriac and potatoes.
* Keep blanched (*see* BLANCHING) vegetables bright and crisp by draining off the hot water, then immediately turning them into a bowl of ice water. Remove from the water as soon as the veggies are cool to prevent waterlogging.
* Parboil (*see* BLANCHING) dense vegetables like carrots that will be sautéed with other vegetables. The parboiling partially cooks the vegetables so they'll get done at the same time as other, less dense vegetables like mushrooms.
* Salting the cooking water for vegetables can draw out some of their vitamins—salt after cooking.
* Adding ½ to 1 teaspoon sugar to cooked vegetables like carrots, corn, and peas reduces starchy flavors and highlights natural sweetness.
* Vegetables overcooked? Purée them in the food processor with a little butter or cream, salt and pepper. Pretend that's how you intended to serve them in the first place.
* Don't throw out the fibrous ends of vegetables like asparagus. Cook them until tender, then purée, strain and use for soups or sauces.
* Save any liquid in which vegetables have been cooked to use in soups, stews or sauces. Freeze it for up to 6 months.
* Make your own pickled vegetables by marinating cauliflower florets, carrot or cucumber sticks, strips of green pepper, and so on, in leftover pickle juice for 3 days.

VEGETABLE SHORTENING   *see* SHORTENING

VINEGARS

PURCHASING There are myriad vinegars on the market today. Among the more commonly available are the fruity **apple cider vinegar**, made from fermented apple cider; the harsh-tasting **distilled white vinegar**, made from a grain-alcohol mixture; and the pleasantly pungent **wine vinegar**, which can be made from either red or white wine. Then there's **malt vinegar**, obtained from malted barley, the mild, slightly sweet **rice vinegar**, made from fermented rice; and a dazzling array of fruit- and herb-flavored vinegars, many of which can be made at home. Last, but certainly not least, is the superb **balsamic vinegar**, a barrel-aged reduction of white Trebbiano grape juice. Those who are sulfite-sensitive should know that some balsamics contain sulfites (typically added to prevent unfavorable bacteria from affecting the flavor).

STORING Store vinegar in a cool, dark place. Unopened, it will keep almost indefinitely; once opened, store at room temperature for up to 6 months.

GENERAL

* Because of vinegar's volatility, it loses much of its pungency when heated. If that's what you want, then add vinegar at the beginning of the cooking time. However, if you want that jolt of acidity, stir vinegar into a mixture after the dish is removed from the heat.

* If a dish lacks pizzazz and tastes "flat," try stirring in 1 or 2 teaspoons of full-flavored vinegar such as balsamic.

* Or add a dash of good aged balsamic vinegar to cooked vegetables, tomato or potato salads, cole slaw or soups.

* Good vinegar can be used as a salt substitute on everything from salads to vegetables to meats, fish and poultry.

* Enrich the flavor of a red wine or balsamic vinegar by adding a tablespoon of brown sugar to a 12-ounce bottle.

* Some aged balsamic vinegars are syrupy and somewhat sweet. For a wonderful treat, add a few drops to fresh strawberries or melon.

* If you somehow oversweeten a savory dish (sauces, salad dressings, and so on), stir in ½ to 1 teaspoon vinegar to balance the sweetness.

FLAVORED VINEGAR

Homemade vinegars are easy to make and much less expensive than store-bought brands. Bring a quart (4 cups) of white or red wine vinegar to a boil. Remove from the heat and stir in one or more flavoring ingredients such as: 8 peeled, smashed garlic cloves; 1½ cups chopped fresh herbs; 5 medium jalapeño peppers, seeded and coarsely chopped; 3 tablespoons crushed peppercorns; 2 cups fresh or loose-packed frozen raspberries, blueberries or cranberries (crushed); the grated zest from 2 large oranges or 4 medium lemons. If desired, add whole spices like cloves or allspice berries and, for a sweet-tart vinegar, stir in a little honey. Cover and let stand until cooled to room temperature. Refrigerate for a week before straining through a fine sieve lined with cheesecloth. Pour flavored vinegar into a scrupulously clean bottle—one with a screw top that can be tightly sealed. Refrigerate for up to 6 months.

BALSAMIC NECTAR

Drizzle this sweet-and-sour amalgam over greens, tomatoes, rice, grilled meat or fish, or add it to salad dressings, stir-fries or sautés for a touch of pizzazz. Combine 1 cup balsamic vinegar and ½ cup sugar in a small saucepan; bring to a boil over high heat. Cook until reduced by half. Cool to room temperature. Pour into a screw-top jar and refrigerate indefinitely. Makes about ½ cup.

He gave her a look you could have poured on a waffle.
—Ring Lardner, American writer,
sports reporter

WAFFLES; WAFFLE IRONS   *see also* FRENCH TOAST; MAPLE SYRUP; PANCAKES

WAFFLE IRONS

* Seasoning a waffle iron: Follow the manufacturer's instructions pertaining to your particular appliance. If you have an iron that hasn't been used in a long time, reseason it by heating the iron, then brushing the grids with vegetable oil. Turn off the iron and cool completely. Lightly wipe off excess oil from the iron, then reheat before unplugging and cooling. Once cooled, thoroughly wipe off excess oil. The first time you use it after seasoning, throw the first waffle away.
* Nonstick waffle irons typically don't need to be oiled.
* Don't wash a well-seasoned waffle iron; simply brush off any residue with a toothbrush.
* After baking waffles and brushing off the grid, unplug the iron, cover the bottom grid with a sheet of waxed paper, close the iron and let it cool.

WAFFLES

* **For lighter waffles,** separate the eggs, mix the yolks in with the rest of the liquid, then combine the wet and dry ingredients as usual. Beat the egg whites until stiff and fold into the batter at the last minute.
* Adding 1 to 2 tablespoons sugar to the batter will produce tender, crisp waffles.
* For extra-crisp waffles, add 1 to 2 tablespoons additional vegetable oil to the batter. The oil will also help keep waffles from sticking.

* Substituting buttermilk for regular milk produces delicate, tender waffles. Add ¼ teaspoon baking soda to the dry ingredients.
* For a regular, four-square waffle iron, use about 1 cup batter. Using less batter produces a thinner, crisper waffle.
* Never open a waffle iron during the first minute of baking or the waffle is likely to break apart.
* Waffles are done when the waffle-iron lid rises slightly, steaming has completely stopped and the sides are golden brown. If the top resists when you try to lift it, the waffle's not done.
* Use a fork to lift the waffle from the iron.
* To keep waffles warm until serving time, place them on a rack set on a baking sheet in a 350°F oven.
* Stacking warm waffles makes them sweat and turn soggy.
* Make a double batch of waffles and freeze the leftovers for an instant waffle breakfast. Cool waffles completely before freezing for up to 6 months.
* Slightly underbake waffles you plan to reheat so they won't dry out when warmed.
* The best way to reheat waffles is in a toaster or toaster oven. They can also be heated in a 350°F oven for about 5 minutes. You can reheat them in a microwave oven on high for about 7 seconds, but they usually won't be as crisp.

WALNUTS *For general purchase, storage, toasting and usage information, see* NUTS, GENERAL

EQUIVALENTS
* In shell: 1 pound = 2 cups nuts
* Shelled: 1 pound = 3¾ cups halves, 3½ cups chopped

GENERAL
* The two most popular varieties of walnut are the **English walnut** and the **black walnut**. The so-called **white walnut** is more commonly known as the *butternut*.
* Walnuts will be easier to crack if you cover them with water, then bring to a boil. Remove from the heat, cover and set aside for at least 15 minutes, or until cool. Blot the nuts dry, then crack end to end.

When one has tasted watermelons one knows what angels eat. It was not a Southern watermelon that Eve took; we know it because she repented.
—Mark Twain, American author, humorist

WATERMELONS   *see also* MELONS

PURCHASING Watermelon varieties range from giant 35-pounders to cantaloupe size. Their flesh can be red, pink, yellow or creamy white; the speckled or solid-colored seeds can be black, brown, green, red or white.

* Whole watermelons: Choose symmetrically shaped melons without any flat sides. Depending on the variety, the shape can be round or oblong-oval. Slap the side of a watermelon—if it resounds with a hollow thump, that's a good indicator that it's probably ripe. But also check the rind, which should be evenly colored, dull (not shiny) and just barely yield to pressure. Avoid watermelons with soft spots, gashes or other blemishes on the rind. **Seedless watermelons** actually do more often than not have a few scattered seeds, though they're generally small, soft and edible—much like the seeds in a cucumber.

* Cut melon: The melon should be tightly wrapped, the flesh should appear firm, juicy and brightly colored. Avoid any with grainy or dry-looking flesh. With the exception of "seedless" watermelons, an abundance of small, white seeds indicates an immature melon, which means it won't be as sweet.

EQUIVALENT   10-pound melon = 20 cups cubes

STORING

* Whole melons: If you have room, refrigerate a whole watermelon for up to 1 week. If it's too large for the fridge, keep the melon in a cool, dark place for up to 4 days.

* Cut melon: Tightly wrap and refrigerate for up to 3 days.

USING

* Unlike most melons, watermelon should be served cold.

* Add watermelon balls or chunks to a fruit salad at the last minute or their exceedingly juicy flesh will make the mixture watery.

* If you don't want to pick up a watermelon wedge and bury your face in it, make a horizontal cut from end to end about 1 inch down from the surface of the flesh. Then make lengthwise cuts about 1 inch apart, followed by crosswise cuts. This will give you 1-inch chunks, which you can spear with a fork. When that layer's gone, repeat the process until you almost reach the rind.

SPIRITED WATERMELON

Cut a plug out of a whole melon, insert a funnel and slowly pour in rum until the melon won't accept any more. Reinsert the plug in the opening and refrigerate for 24 hours. The rum will disperse throughout the melon, producing a sweet, exotically flavored flesh that tastes delicious, but not particularly like rum.

WAX BEANS *see* BEANS, FRESH

WAXED PAPER *see also* ALUMINUM FOIL; PARCHMENT PAPER; PLASTIC WRAP

* Keep bottles and jars (such as those for maple syrup and honey) from dripping by rubbing the rim with a crumpled piece of waxed paper.
* Solution for a loose pan lid: Place a double layer of waxed paper between the pan and the lid; press the lid down firmly.
* After cleaning a wooden salad bowl, rub it with a crumbled piece of waxed paper to seal the surface.
* Keep your waffle iron relatively nonstick by doing this: As soon as you finish the last waffle, unplug the iron, brush off the grids and place a sheet of waxed paper on the bottom grid before closing the iron. When the iron is cool, remove the paper.
* Whenever measuring cocoa powder or confectioners' sugar, set the measuring cup on a sheet of waxed paper and spoon the ingredient into it. Afterward, transfer any cocoa or sugar spills on the waxed paper back into the container.
* Grating foods like chocolate and lemon zest over a sheet of waxed paper saves on cleanup.
* Roll out pastry or cookie dough on a waxed paper–covered countertop. Anchor the waxed paper by sprinkling a few drops of water on the countertop before arranging the paper.
* Separate layers of decorated, moist or sticky cookies with waxed paper to prevent them from sticking together. The same goes for homemade candy like fudge.
* Put layers of waxed paper between layers of cookies before freezing.
* Cakes and breads won't stick to the pan if you grease the pan, line the bottom with waxed paper, then grease the waxed paper. Turn the baked cake or bread out of the pan and peel off the waxed paper while it's still warm. If a cake or loaf of bread has cooled so long that the waxed paper sticks, lightly brush the paper with warm water, let stand 1 minute, then remove the paper.
* To keep the plate clean while frosting a cake, place several strips of waxed paper around the edges of the plate before positioning the cake on top. Once the cake's frosted, carefully pull out the waxed paper strips and discard.

* When frosting a cake on a cooling rack, place a sheet of waxed paper under the rack to catch any drips. The frosting on the paper can either be returned to the frosting bowl (providing it's crumb free) or given to your favorite frosting licker. In either case, the countertop's clean.

* Make an instant, disposable PASTRY BAG by folding a square of waxed paper in half diagonally to form a triangle. Shape the triangle into a cone, securing the top edge with Scotch tape or a paper clip. Fill two-thirds full with frosting, melted chocolate, and so on, fold down the top of the bag, then snip off the pointed end so the hole is the desired diameter.

* When piping a decorative design with melted chocolate, do so on a waxed paper–lined baking sheet. Refrigerate until the chocolate is set, then peel off the waxed paper and transfer the chocolate decoration to the dessert.

* Protect yourself and your kitchen from spatters when whipping cream by laying a sheet of waxed paper (with a hole cut for the beater stems) on top of the bowl.

* Lining the bottom of your microwave oven with waxed paper will keep things clean.

* Waxed paper is a good cover for microwaved food when you want much of the steam to escape.

* When melting butter or cooking or reheating thick mixtures like oatmeal or pea soup in a microwave oven, cover the container with waxed paper to protect oven walls against spatters.

* Heat tortillas quickly in the microwave oven by wrapping them loosely in waxed paper.

* Waxed paper is the perfect wrap for microwaved corn on the cob. Start by rinsing each ear off with water, then immediately wrap in waxed paper, twisting the ends to seal.

* After cooking soup that contains fat-rendering ingredients like meat, lay a double sheet of waxed paper on the surface, then refrigerate until cold. When you remove the waxed paper, the solidified fat will lift right off with it.

WHIPPED CREAM *see* CREAM

WHITE CHOCOLATE *see* CHOCOLATE

WILD RICE

TIDBIT Wild rice isn't really a rice at all, but a long-grain marsh grass. This grass was such an important Native American crop that in 1750, the Ojibway warred with the Sioux in the Battle of Kathio for possession of the northern Minnesota lakes' wild-rice stands. Wild rice has a luxurious, nutty flavor and chewy texture. Nutritionally, it's high in dietary fiber and rich in iron, protein and niacin.

PURCHASING Wild rice can be found in supermarkets either packaged alone or with other, less expensive rices. Natural food stores also sell it in bulk.

EQUIVALENT 1 cup = 3½ cups cooked

STORING Store in an airtight container in a cool, dark place. Stored properly, it can be kept almost indefinitely.

PREPARING

* Wild rice requires thorough cleaning before being cooked. The best method is to place the rice in a medium bowl and fill it with cold water. Give it a couple of stirs and set it aside for a few minutes. Any debris will float to the surface and the water can then be poured off.

* Wild rice can be cooked by either boiling or baking. Its distinctive flavor and texture make it an ideal accompaniment for duck and other game birds and meats.

* Make the relatively expensive wild rice go farther by combining it with brown or white rice or bulghur wheat. Because different grains have slightly different cooking times, cook them separately, then combine.

* Grind wild rice to a powder in a blender and use it in baked goods like breads, muffins and pancakes. Substitute up to a quarter of all-purpose flour with wild-rice "flour."

* Wild rice can be used in all kinds of soups and stews. Or make a wild-rice soup by PURÉEING cooked brown rice with enough broth to make a nice soup base, then stir in cooked wild rice and some sautéed garlic and onions.

* Cooked wild rice is great in salads, and as stuffings for poultry or acorn squash and pilafs. Combine it with other ingredients—a little of this flavorful food goes a long way.

PUFFED WILD RICE

These crunchy, nutty niblets make a great garnish for everything from soup to salad to vegetables, or mix them into a holiday stuffing, or simply snack on them. In a large skillet over medium heat, sauté about ⅔ cup cleaned (rinsed and blotted dry) wild rice in 1 tablespoon extra virgin olive oil. Cook, stirring often, until most of the grains have cracked open and puffed slightly. Turn out onto paper towels; salt and pepper to taste. Makes about 1 cup.

> *No, Agnes, a Bordeaux is not a house of ill-repute.*
> —George Bain, Canadian author

WINE; WINE BOTTLES *see also* BEER; CHAMPAGNE; COCKTAILS; LIQUORS AND LIQUEURS; WINE IN FOOD

TIDBIT Don't take offense if someone calls you an "enophile." It simply describes someone who enjoys wine, and is often used to refer to a connoisseur.

PURCHASING

* Here are a few basic wine terms to help you through the maze at the store. **Vintage wine** is made from grapes harvested in a specific year (1997, for example), which is indicated on the wine label. **Nonvintage wine** is made from the juice of grapes harvested from several years, in which case no year is noted on the label. **Blush wines** are generally made with red grapes (some producers mix red and white grapes), but the juice has had a very brief contact with the grape skins, which produces wines that can range in color from shell pink to barely red. Blush wines can range from dry to sweet and may be light- to medium-bodied. They should be served chilled, but not icy. **Fortified wine** is one to which brandy or other spirit has been added in order to increase the alcohol content. Such wines include Madeira, Marsala, port and sherry.
* **Wine bottle sizes:** The **standard wine bottle** is 750 ml (milliliters), which is almost exactly equivalent to an American fifth (four-fifths of a quart, or 25.4 ounces). In answer to the stricter driving/alcohol limits in many states, the wine industry is introducing a new **500-ml bottle** size. This new size—midway between a standard bottle and a **half-bottle** (12.8 ounces)—is about 17 ounces, or two-thirds of a standard bottle. Other wine bottle sizes are: **split** (one-quarter of a standard wine bottle); **magnum** (equivalent to 2 standard bottles in 1); **Jeroboam** (4 in 1); **gallon** (5 in 1); **Rehoboam** (6 in 1); **Methuselah** (8 in 1); **Salmanazar** (12 in 1); **Balthazar** (16 in 1); and **Nebuchadnezzar** (20 in 1).

EQUIVALENTS

* 375 ml (half-bottle) = 12.7 ounces; ample 1½ cups
* 750 ml (whole bottle) = 25.4 ounces; scant 3¼ cups
* 1 liter = 33.8 ounces; 4¼ cups
* magnum = 1.5 liters, 50.7 ounces; 6⅓ cups

STORING The three basic parameters for a wine-storage location are that it be dark, vibration free and kept at an even temperature. The ideal temperature for wine storage is 55°F. However, wine can be kept anywhere from 45° to 70°F, provided the temperature is consistent. The higher the temperature, the faster a wine will age; white wines are more susceptible to heat than are reds. Store wine bottles on their sides so the cork stays moist. Dry corks shrink, allowing in air, which negatively affects a wine's flavor.

GENERAL

* When serving several wines at a meal remember these guidelines: Serve a young wine before an older one; a white wine before a red one; a light-bodied wine before a robust wine; and a dry wine before a sweet one.

* White wine should be served at temperatures somewhere between 50° and 55°F. Since cold mutes flavors, the cheaper the wine, the colder you want it. Refrigerate white wine for only about 2 hours before serving. Longer than that can dull a wine's flavor and aroma.

* Speed-chill white wine at the last minute by completely submerging the bottle for about 20 minutes in a large container filled with equal amounts of ice and water. This chills the wine much faster than ice alone. If the container is shallow, invert the bottle for the last 5 minutes to make sure all the wine is chilled.

* Red wine should be served at around 65°F. The term "room temperature" is now outdated—it's based on the chillier room temperatures of days gone by, not the 72°F average of today's home.

* **Opening wine:** Cut through the foil all the way around, about ¼ inch below the lip of the bottle. There are special foil-cutter tools available in wine shops, or you can simply use a sharp knife. Remove the foil at the point you cut it. Use a damp cloth or heavy-duty paper towel to wipe any mold or other residue off the cork; also wipe the rim of the bottle. Position the corkscrew in the cork's center, turn the screw as far as it will go, then gently ease the cork out of the bottle. Wipe the rim of the bottle again, making sure to remove any bits of cork. During the entire uncorking process, handle the bottle gently so as not to disturb the wine unnecessarily.

* Red wines more than 8 years old often have a natural, harmless sediment in the bottle. Hold the bottle up to a strong light to check it. If you see sediment, decant the wine so no one gets the gritty residue in his or her mouth.

* **Decanting** a wine is done either to separate the wine from any sediment deposited during the aging process, or to allow a wine to "breathe" in order to enhance its flavor. When decanting an older wine, care should

be taken not to disturb the sediment. A wine basket (also called a *cradle* or *Burgundy basket*) can be used to move the bottle in a horizontal position from where it was stored to where it will be decanted. This keeps the sediment from being disturbed and disseminating through the wine. If you don't have a basket, stand the bottle upright for an hour so the sediment can settle to the bottom of the bottle. Once the foil and cork are removed, gently wipe the mouth of the bottle. Then begin slowly pouring the wine into the decanter, placing a strong light (a candle is charming, but a flashlight is more practical) behind or below the neck of the bottle. The light lets you see the first signs of sediment, at which point you stop pouring.

* If tiny pieces of cork break off and fall into the wine, strain the wine through a fine sieve or a double thickness of cheesecloth into a decanter.

* When pouring wine, forestall drips by giving the bottle a slight twist just as you finish pouring.

* Use wineglasses made of clear glass, with a rim that curves in slightly (the exception being the champagne flute). The clear glass allows you to see the true color of the wine, and the inwardly curving rim makes it possible to swirl the wine in order to release its bouquet.

* Wineglasses should be filled only half to two-thirds full so the wine has room to be swirled, thereby releasing more of its aroma.

* **Corkage:** In some states (California, for example) it's not uncommon for people to bring a special bottle of wine to a restaurant. A quick call to the establishment will confirm if this is possible, as well as determining the amount of the corkage fee—a charge for opening and serving a patron's bottle of wine.

* Contact with air over a prolonged period can ruin the flavor of most wines. Transfer leftover wine to a smaller bottle to minimize airspace, seal tightly and drink the next day. It's a good idea to keep a clean, empty half-bottle (*see* WINE BOTTLES) on hand for just this purpose.

* Another way to dispel air from an opened bottle of wine is to "gas" it. A harmless combination of nitrogen (N_2) and carbon dioxide (CO_2) can be found in wine stores and specialty markets. It's squirted into a partially full wine bottle, and the gas blankets the wine's surface, blocking the flavor-destructive oxygen. Don't worry if the can feels empty—remember, gases are weightless.

* Cut down on calories and wine consumption by making wine spritzers. Pour about 4 ounces wine into a wineglass filled with ice cubes, fill the glass with seltzer or other carbonated water, and stir gently. Garnish with a thin slice of lemon or lime, if desired.

W

* Never cook with any wine or spirit you wouldn't drink. Cooking—and the process of REDUCING a sauce—will bring out the worst in an inferior potable.
* If you're serving an expensive bottle of Cabernet or Bordeaux with dinner, there's no need to cook with the same wine (unless you're wealthy). Instead, choose a less expensive wine with comparable qualities.
* The "cooking wine" found in supermarkets is generally an inferior product that would not be drunk on its own or, in some opinions, even cooked with. It not only lacks distinction and flavor, but some of these potables are adulterated with salt.
* If you don't need a full bottle of wine, buy a half-bottle.
* If you have a little wine left after dinner, recork and refrigerate it and use it the next day as part of a marinade for meat, chicken or fish (depending on the wine). Or add it to soups, stews or sauces.
* The flavor of wine in a dish should be subtle and never overpower the central essence. Start by adding 1 to 2 tablespoons, cook the dish for a few minutes, then taste for flavor. You can always add more.
* In general, use dry, white wines for seafood and poultry dishes; full-bodied wines are better partnered with hearty meat dishes, stews and dark sauces. Of course, there are always exceptions to the rule, such as red wine in the classic coq au vin.
* Fortified wines like Madeira, port and sherry have very strong flavors, so caution is the byword when adding them to food.
* If you want a nice, rich wine flavor without a lot of liquid, boil 1 cup wine until it's reduced by half or two-thirds.
* When preparing slow-cooking dishes like stew, add a splash of wine 20 minutes before the cooking time is finished. The flavor of wine dissipates during long cooking, and the final addition will give it more balance.
* Poaching fish in white wine (or part broth and part wine) bestows a rich flavor.
* Use wine mixed with a little oil or melted butter to baste meat and poultry.
* Wine is excellent for deglazing a pan. After food (usually meat) has been sautéed and removed from the pan, add a little wine to the pan and stir to loosen the browned bits of food on the bottom. Cook for a few minutes, then spoon the rich liquid over the cooked food.
* Add leftover wine (up to 1 cup per quart) to vinegar for instant wine vinegar.

* When eating a soft-ripened cheese like Brie or Camembert, remove the edible downy-white rind—its salt concentration and slight ammonia compound will kill the flavor of most wines.

WOKS *see* STIR-FRYING

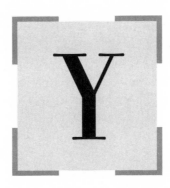

YAMS *see also* SWEET POTATOES

TIDBIT Yams and sweet potatoes are often confused with one another, though they're from different plant species. In the southern United States, sweet potatoes are often called "yams"; to add to the confusion, canned sweet potatoes are frequently labeled "yams." True yams are seldom grown in the United States.

PURCHASING Yams are similar in size and shape to sweet potatoes, but have a higher moisture and sugar content. They can be found in most Latin-American markets. Look for specimens with tight, unwrinkled skins free of blemishes.

STORING Store yams in a cool, dry, well-ventilated place for up to 1 week. Under perfect temperature conditions (dry and around 55°F), they can be kept for up to 4 weeks. Do not refrigerate.

USING Yams may be substituted for and cooked as SWEET POTATOES in most recipes.

YEAST *see also* BREAD, GENERAL; BREAD, YEAST

TIDBIT Yeast is a living organism that thrives on the natural sugar in starch. When combined with moisture and warmth, yeast begins to ferment, converting the flour's starchy nutrients into alcohol and carbon dioxide gas. Gas bubbles trapped in the elastic gluten mesh of a dough or batter make it rise.

PURCHASING

* Active dry yeast: Available in ¼-ounce envelopes, jars and sometimes in bulk. Dry yeast comes in two forms—regular and quick-rising, which may be used interchangeably. All active dry yeast has been dehydrated; its cells are alive, but dormant. Quick-rising yeast leavens breads in a third to half the time of regular dry yeast. It can be substituted for regular active dry yeast in most bread recipes, measure for measure.

* Compressed fresh yeast: This moist, very perishable form is sold in 0.6-ounce and 2-ounce cakes.

EQUIVALENTS ¼-ounce package dry yeast = 1 scant tablespoon dry yeast, one 0.6-ounce cake compressed, fresh yeast

STORING

* Dry yeast: Store in a cool, dry place; it can also be refrigerated or frozen. Properly stored, dry yeast is reliable when used by the expiration date stamped on the envelope or jar. Bulk dry yeast can be risky because you don't know how old it is or under what conditions it's been stored.

* Compressed fresh yeast: Store in a plastic bag in the refrigerator for 2 to 4 weeks. It can also be frozen for up to 6 months; defrost it at room temperature. Use it by the expiration date on the package.

USING

* Bring compressed fresh yeast to room temperature before using.

* Generally, one package or cake of yeast will leaven 4 to 5 cups flour.

* Extra yeast may be used to speed leavening, but too much produces a porous texture and yeasty flavor.

* Too little yeast creates heavy, dense baked goods.

* Today's yeast is very reliable, but if you're unsure of yours (either because it's past the expiration date or because it's bulk yeast), proof it by combining the yeast and 1 teaspoon sugar with the warm liquid called for in the recipe; let stand for about 3 to 5 minutes. The yeast's alive and active if the mixture begins to swell and bubble. If there's no activity, start over with new yeast—you can't revive dead yeast.

* The temperature of the liquid in which yeast is dissolved is very important. Too much heat will kill the yeast, too little will slow its growth. Dissolve dry yeast in liquids at 105° to 115°F; compressed yeast at 95°F. Unless you're an experienced baker, use a thermometer for accurate temperature readings.

* Quick-mix method: Dry yeast doesn't have to be dissolved before it's used, but can be combined with part of the flour, then mixed with very warm water with a temperature range of 120° to 130°F. The flour buffers the yeast from the higher water temperature.

* Doughs rich in butter, eggs, sweeteners, fruits or nuts often require double the amount of yeast.

YOGURT

TIDBIT The benefits of yogurt have been touted for eons. It's a good source of B vitamins, protein and calcium, and is much more digestible than fresh milk. It's said to keep the intestinal system populated with good bacteria and, therefore, healthy. Most of this last benefit, however, is lost when yogurt is frozen.

PURCHASING   Check the date on the carton to be sure you're buying the freshest possible. In other words, if the present date is May 12, choose yogurt that's dated May 20 over one dated May 15.

STORING   Refrigerate for up to 10 days after the carton date.

USING

* Stirring yogurt vigorously can cause it to become thin and runny.
* For extra-thick yogurt to use in sauces and desserts, turn it into a sieve lined with a double layer of dampened cheesecloth; set over a bowl. Cover with plastic wrap and refrigerate for 1 hour. Use a rubber spatula to gently stir the yogurt. Cover and refrigerate for 4 to 6 hours until yogurt reaches the desired thickness. Discard the liquid in the bowl, or save and use in baked goods. Cover and refrigerate thickened yogurt for up to 1 week.
* Bringing yogurt to room temperature before adding it to a hot mixture will prevent the mixture from separating.
* When cooking with yogurt, heat it gently and only until the mixture is warmed through. Allowing the mixture to boil will cause it to separate.
* Yogurt won't separate as easily in hot preparations that are flour-based.
* Or stir a teaspoon of cornstarch into a couple of tablespoons of yogurt, then stir the cornstarch mixture into the remaining yogurt, mixing well. Slowly stir the mixture into hot liquid over low heat. Count on about 1 teaspoon cornstarch per cup of yogurt.
* Heating yogurt to temperatures higher than 120°F destroys the beneficial bacteria, though nutrients like protein and calcium remain. To retain the friendly bacteria in mixtures such as soups and sauces, stir the yogurt into the hot mixture toward the end of the cooking time and heat only until warmed through.
* To reconstitute a cooked yogurt mixture that has separated, try this: For each cup yogurt, mix 1 teaspoon cornstarch or 2 teaspoons all-purpose flour with ½ tablespoon cold water and stir into the separated mixture. Heat slowly, stirring constantly, until the mixture recombines and thickens.
* Make your own fruit-flavored yogurt by buying plain yogurt and adding crushed or chopped fruit, honey, vanilla extract, spices, and so on. That way you know exactly what you're getting and get exactly what you want.
* Reduce calories in salad dressing and dips by substituting plain yogurt for mayonnaise or sour cream.
* Yogurt can also be substituted for sour cream in baked goods.

Frozen Yogurt Slices

Mix plain yogurt with chopped or crushed fruit, flavor with vanilla and spices, if desired, and sweeten to taste. Turn the mixture into a plastic wrap–lined loaf pan, freeze until solid, then wrap airtight. Cut off slices of this frozen fruit yogurt as you want them. Let the slices stand at room temperature for about 10 minutes before serving.

ZEST, CITRUS *see* CITRUS FRUITS

ZESTER *see* CITRUS ZESTER

ZUCCHINI *see* SQUASH, SUMMER

RECITE INDEX

ABOUT THE AUTHOR

Sharon Tyler Herbst, dubbed the foremost writer of user-friendly food and drink reference works, is an award-winning author of six books. She gained her reputation as an accomplished culinary powerhouse with *The New Food Lover's Companion,* broadly hailed as "a must for every cook's library." This book, as well as *The Wine Lover's Companion* (co-authored with her husband, Ron), are the online dictionaries on several major food-and-drink Internet sites. Julia Child praised Sharon's *Food Lover's Tiptionary* as "an invaluable help for all." TV's popular quiz show *Jeopardy!* often cites Sharon's books as references. She is also a food and travel journalist and a media personality with myriad appearances on national radio and television shows, including *Good Morning America* and the *Today* show. She's a consultant and spokesperson for national food and beverage companies, and a past president of the International Association of Culinary Professionals (IACP). Her Internet site is Food and Drink INK® (www.sharon tylerherbst.com).